Assembly Language Tutor
for the IBM PC and Compatibles

Assembly Language Tutor
for the IBM PC and Compatibles

Richard E. Haskell

Oakland University, Rochester, Michigan

REGENTS/ PRENTICE HALL, Englewood Cliffs, New Jersey 07632

Library of Congress Cataloging-in-Publication Data

HASKELL, RICHARD E.
   Assembly language tutor for the IBM PC and compatibles / Richard E. Haskell.
      p.   cm.
   Includes bibliographical references and index.
   ISBN 0-13-454349-1
   1. Assembler language (Computer program language).   2. IBM Personal
Computer--Programming. 3. IBM compatible computers--Programming.
I. Title.
QA76.73.A8H37   1993
005.265—dc20

92-22015
CIP

Editorial/production supervision: *Cathy Frank*
Cover Design: *20/20 Services, Inc.*
Prepress buyer: *Ilene Levy*
Manufacturing buyer: *Ed O'Dougherty*
Acquisitions editor: *Holly Hodder*
Editorial assistant: *Melissa Steffens*

Cover Photograph: *Stephen Marks/The Image Bank*

© 1993 by REGENTS/PRENTICE HALL
A Division of Simon & Schuster
Englewood Cliffs, New Jersey 07632

Printed in the United States of America

10 9 8 7 6 5 4 3 2 1

ISBN 0-13-454349-1

PRENTICE-HALL INTERNATIONAL (UK) LIMITED, *London*
PRENTICE-HALL OF AUSTRALIA PTY. LIMITED, *Sydney*
PRENTICE-HALL CANADA INC., *Toronto*
PRENTICE-HALL HISPANOAMERICANA, S.A., *Mexico*
PRENTICE-HALL OF INDIA PRIVATE LIMITED, *New Delhi*
PRENTICE-HALL OF JAPAN, INC., *Tokyo*
SIMON & SCHUSTER ASIA PTE. LTD., *Singapore*
EDITORA PRENTICE-HALL DO BRASIL, LTDA., *Rio de Janeiro*

Contents

Chapter 7   Screen Display   144

Chapter 8   Computer Arithmetic   181

Chapter 9   Floating Point Arithmetic   217

Chapter 10   Disk Input/Output   240

Chapter 11   PC Hardware   263

Chapter 12   Graphics   284

Chapter 13   Serial Communication   308

Preface

This book is a major revision of an earlier book by the author entitled *IBM PC – 8088 Assembly Language Programming*. The TUTOR monitor used with the earlier book remains (with a few enhancements) as a central learning aid in the book. The major difference between this book and its predecessor is the inclusion on the TUTOR disk of the files *screen.asm*, *number.asm*, *dos.asm* and *graph.asm*. These files contain dozens of useful subroutines that can be linked with a user's program, for performing numerous screen I/O operations, number conversions, disk file I/O, and graphics. These subroutines are described in detail in the book. A second major change is the development (in Chapters 8, 9 and 14) of a complete subroutine threaded Forth-like language capable of serving as an integer and floating point calculator and of running turtle graphics programs. Much of the material in Chapters 7 – 10 and Chapters 12 – 14 is completely new.

The IBM PC and numerous PC compatibles have become the most popular microcomputers used today for business and professional applications. To get the maximum performance from these computers, it is sometimes necessary to write programs and/or certain routines in assembly language. This book will teach you how to write assembly language programs for the IBM PC and compatibles. You will also learn a lot about computer organization and the inner workings of the PC. The book can be used as a text for an introductory course in computer organization and assembly language programming. It can also serve as an introduction to microprocessors using the 8086 of the IBM PC or PC compatibles as the example. PCs containing an 80286 or 80386 can just as easily be used with this book since when these computers are turned on they come up in the real mode, which means they look like a fast 8086.

The book describes the use of a powerful software monitor program called TUTOR that comes with the book. This monitor enhances the understanding of the 8086 microprocessor by allowing the student to easily see what is going on inside the computer. The TUTOR monitor displays the contents of all registers and any region of memory within both the code segment and the data segment simultaneously. It allows the student to single step through programs, set breakpoints, disassemble any program code, load and inspect any disk file, and much more. It can be used as a powerful debugging tool for .EXE files created with a macro assembler. Such .EXE files can be loaded directly into TUTOR to be inspected, debugged, and executed. The resulting debugged program can then be executed from DOS without change. This disk containing TUTOR also contains most of the examples discussed in the book. This means that the student can load these examples into TUTOR and execute them and/or single step through the program to see exactly what the program does in detail.

A brief history of computers and microprocessors is given in Chapter 1 and number systems are covered in Chapter 2, where you will learn how hexadecimal and binary numbers are related to decimal numbers. In Chapter 3, you will take a look inside the 8086 with the help of the TUTOR monitor and learn how the 8086 address space is made up of a segment address and an offset address. You will see how to examine and change the contents of any memory location and you will observe how a simple program is actually executed instruction by instruction. You will also see how ASCII codes are used to represent characters in the computer.

The 8086 instructions are studied in Chapter 4. Using the TUTOR monitor as your guide you will be able to observe the operation of move and exchange instructions, shift and rotate instructions, and basic arithmetic and logical instructions. In Chapter 5, you will learn how to write complete 8086 programs that include branching instructions, subroutines and software interrupts. You will learn how to use the macro assembler and linker in this chapter. A more detailed discussion of addressing modes is given in Chapter 6. All 8086 addressing modes are described with simple examples to illustrate their use.

The way in which the PC displays characters on the screen is described in Chapter 7. This chapter describes the operation of numerous screen display subroutines (which are available on the TUTOR disk) that can be used for character and string output, cursor control, attribute control and keyboard input. Techniques for allocating and deallocating memory are also covered in this chapter.

Computer arithmetic, including the design of a Reverse Polish Notation (RPN) calculator and multiple-byte BCD arithmetic, is covered in Chapter 8, where subroutines to convert number ASCII strings to binary numbers, and vice versa, are developed. Floating point arithmetic, including the operation of the 8087 floating point coprocessor, is discussed in Chapter 9.

Chapter 10 describes a collection of subroutines (also available on the disk) that can be used to access files on disk. Several hardware topics including interrupts, sound, and the printer interface are covered in Chapter 11. Graphics is discussed in Chapter 12, where a subroutine to plot a line is developed. A basic understanding of how graphics work is achieved by developing a number of Hercules graphics subroutines. An interrupt driven terminal program is developed in Chapter 13 as an example of asynchronous serial communication.

The final chapter shows how to write your own subroutine threaded Forth-like language. This language will allow you to write your own high-level turtle graphics programs, load them into memory and run them.

Many colleagues and students have influenced the development of this book. Their stimulating discussions, probing questions, and critical comments are greatly appreciated. Special thanks are extended to those who reviewed the manuscript and contributed to its improvement:

Robert W. Campbell, Los Angeles Trade-Technical College,
    Los Angeles, CA
Shirish K. Shah, New Community College of Baltimore,
    Baltimore, MD
Yusuf M. Motiwala, Prairie View A&M University, Prairie
    View, TX
Tae-Sang Chung, University of Kentucky, Lexington, KY
Charles Meuser, Albuquerque Technical-Vocational
    Institute, Albuquerque, NM

Richard E. Haskell
Computer Science and Engineering Department
Oakland University
Rochester, Michigan 48309

CHAPTER 1

Computers and Microprocessors

1.1 HISTORY OF COMPUTERS

The computer as we know it today dates only from the time of the second world war. In fact the impetus for building the ENIAC in 1944 at the Moore School of Electrical Engineering at the University of Pennsylvania was the need to compute ballistic firing tables for artillery shells. However, the history of computers goes back a long way as can be seen from the summary in Table 1.1.

Although the abacus has been used for thousands of years as an aid to calculation, it is really that, an aid in which the person doing the calculating has to actually move the beads on the wires in the appropriate way. The idea of having a machine actually *do* the calculation originated in the early 1600s. The most famous of these was the Pascaline, designed by Blaise Pascal at the age of 19 to help his father, who was tax commissioner for upper Normandy, figure tax levies. Pascal built 5- to 8-digit versions of the Pascaline in which a dial, axle and gears were associated with each digit. The calculator could add, subtract by forming the 9's complement of the subtrahend and adding, and multiply and divide by repeated addition and subtraction. The Pascaline tended to malfunction due to mechanical failures, had limited computing capability and was a commercial failure.

Charles Babbage (1792 - 1871) is considered to be the father of computing. In an effort to produce a machine that could compute mathematical tables (such as logarithms) he built a working model of his *Difference Engine* in 1822. This model could compute 6-digit numbers in a table by a *method of differences*. Babbage made detailed plans for a full-scale Difference Engine that could calculate numbers to 20 places and produce a metal plate for printing the tables. The machine was to be run with steam and would be ten feet high, ten feet wide and five feet deep. With funds from the British government, Babbage and his chief mechanical engineer, Joseph Clement, worked for the next dozen years in an attempt to build the Difference Engine.

Table 1.1

Some Important Events in the History of Computers

DATE	EVENT
3000 BC	The abacus is developed in Babylonia. This device, which uses columns of beads on wires or rods to represent digits, is still used in some places in the Far East today to perform calculations.
1614-1617	John Napier, a Scottish mathematician, invents logarithms which allow one to multiply by adding and to divide by subtracting. He invented rods, or numbered sticks, which allowed one to multiply or divide large numbers by moving the rods in a particular way.
1623	Wilhelm Schickard, German professor, invents the first mechanical calculator called the Calculating Clock.
1630	William Oughtred, English mathematician and clergy-man, invents the slide rule.
1642-1644	Blaise Pascal, French mathematician, physicist and religious philosopher invents the Pascaline, the first mechanical calculator that became widely known.
1672-1674	Gottfried Wilhelm von Leibniz, German mathematician, diplomat, historian, jurist and inventor of differential calculus, invents a mechanical calculator called the Stepped Reckoner. The calculator had a unique gear, the *Leibniz wheel*, that served as a mechanical multiplier. Although the calculator never worked, its design had a major influence on future mechanical calculators.
1823-1839	Charles Babbage, English mathematician and inventor, begins work on his *Difference Engine*, which was designed to automate the process of calculating logarithms. With much work and funding from the government the Difference Engine was never finished. In 1834 Babbage starts work on a more powerful machine, called the *Analytical Engine*, which is recognized as the first general purpose computer. It was about 100 years ahead of its time, required precision mechanical gears that could not be accurately produced at the time and never worked. Babbage is considered to be the father of computing.
1854	George Boole, English logician and mathematician, publishes *Investigation of the Laws of Thought* which gave a mathematical basis for logic.
1890	Herman Hollerith, American inventor, uses his punched cards for tabulating the 1890 census. He founded the Tabulating Machine Company in 1896 which eventually became IBM in 1924.
1906	Lee De Forest, American physicist, invents the triode, a three electrode vacuum tube. These tubes would not be used in computers until the 1940's.
1936	Alan M. Turing, English logician, publishes a paper, *On Computable Numbers*, which demonstrates that arbitrary computations can be made with a finite state machine (an automaton). Turing plays a significant role in the development of the early computers in England after World War II.
1937	George Stibitz, a Physicist at Bell Telephone Laboratories, builds binary circuits using relays that can add, subtract, multiply and divide.
1938	Konrad Zuse, German engineer, constructs the Z1, the first binary calculating machine. In 1941 he completed the Z3, a general purpose electromechanical calculating machine.

Table 1.1 (continued)

1938	Claude Shannon, based on his master's thesis at MIT, publishes *A Symbolic Analysis of Relay and Switching Circuits* in which he showed how symbolic logic and binary mathematics could be applied to relay circuits.
1942	John V. Atanasoff, Iowa State University professor, completes a simple electronic computing machine.
1943	The IBM-Harvard Mark I, a large electromechanical calculator, is operational.
1944-1945	J. Presper Eckert and John W. Mauchly design and build the ENIAC at the Moore School of Electrical Engineering at the University of Pennsylvania. This was the first fully functional electronic calculator.
1946	John von Neumann, who had been a consultant on the ENIAC project and had written an influential report on the follow-on EDVAC project, begins his own computer project at the Institute for Advanced Study at Princeton.
1947	Walter Brattain, John Bardeen and William Schockley invent the transistor at Bell Laboratories.
1948	The first stored program is run on the Manchester Mark I electronic computer in England.
1951	The first commercially manufactured computers, the Ferranti Mark I and the UNIVAC, are delivered.
1953	IBM's first electronic computer, the 701, is delivered.
1957	FORTRAN, the first high-level computer language, is introduced by IBM.
1958	Jack Kilby, an engineer at Texas Instruments, builds a phase-shift oscillator as the first integrated circuit (IC).
1959	Robert Noyce, co-founder of Fairchild Semiconductor in 1958, produces the first planar process integrated circuit. This would lead to the practical mass-production of reliable integrated circuits. In 1968 Noyce will establish Intel.
1963	The first minicomputer is introduced by the Digital Equipment Corporation (DEC).
1964	IBM introduces the System/360 family of mainframe computers
1969	IBM researchers develop the first on-chip programmable logic array (PLA).
1971	Marcian E. Hoff, Jr., an engineer at Intel, invents the first microprocessor.
1975	William Gates and Paul Allen write a BASIC interpreter for the Altair home computer. They established Microsoft Corporation and released MS-DOS, the operating system for the IBM PC in 1981.
1977	Stephen Wozniak and Steven Jobs introduce the Apple II personal computer.
1981	The IBM PC is introduced.

There were many technical (current machine tools could not meet the precision required by Babbage) and personal (Babbage's wife died and he had serious disagreements with Clement) problems that kept the Difference Engine from being completed. In 1834 Babbage conceived of a more powerful *Analytical Engine* that could solve any mathematical problem, not just those based on the method of differences. This new engine would make his Difference Engine obsolete so he turned his attention to the Analytical Engine. The government eventually got fed up and cancelled the project in 1842. Babbage continued to work on the design of his Analytical

Engine for the rest of his life, even though he knew that it could not be built at that time. He produced thousands of pages of notes on the Analytical Engine which would contain hundreds of axles and thousands of gears and wheels of all kinds. It had many of the components of present day computers including a store (memory) and a mill (CPU). Punched cards were used for external programming of the machine.

The use of punched cards for programming was inspired by the automatic loom, invented by Joseph-Marie Jacquard in 1801, that was controlled by punched cards. In 1880 Herman Hollerith was working as a special agent for the U.S. Census. The data from the 1880 census would take years to tabulate. In the meantime Hollerith, who became an instructor in mechanical engineering at MIT in 1882, invented an electromechanical system that could count and sort punched cards containing statistical data. Hollerith's tabulating machine was used to tabulate the 1890 census data in six weeks. In 1896 Hollerith formed the Tabulating Machine Company which was later to become IBM.

The next major thrust in the development of computers came during World War II with the development of the ENIAC (Electronic Numerical Integrator and Computer) at the Moore School of Electrical Engineering at the University of Pennsylvania. J. Presper Eckert and John W. Mauchly were the chief designers of this large electronic calculator. In 1944 under a contract from the Ordnance Department they began work on a follow-on computer, EDVAC (Electronic Discrete Variable Calculator), that was to be the first stored program computer. However, disagreements over patent rights caused Eckert and Mauchly to resign from the Moore School in 1946 and to start their own company, the Electronic Control Company with the goal of producing a Universal Automatic Computer, the UNIVAC. Financial problems caused them to reorganize as the Eckert-Mauchly Computer Corporation in 1948 and to finally sell out to Remington Rand in 1950. The first UNIVAC was delivered to the Census in 1951.

IBM quickly got into the act and delivered their first electronic computer in 1953 — and as they say — the rest is history! Six years earlier the invention of the transistor at Bell Laboratories was to have a major impact on the development of computers. The idea that electrons inside a *semiconductor* could control electric currents and voltages the way that large power-hungry vacuum tubes did was to transform the electronics industry in a fundamental and far-reaching way. The advances in solid state technology led to the development of the integrated circuit in the 1960s and the microprocessor in the 1970s. The last entry in Table 1.1 is the introduction of the IBM PC in 1981. This event had a major impact on the development of small personal computers. In the past decade many other companies have produced *PC compatible* computers which will run MS-DOS (produced by Microsoft Corporation) and all programs that run under MS-DOS on an IBM PC.

1.2 IBM PC AND COMPATIBLES

The IBM Personal Computer (PC) and PC compatibles have become an industry standard for a small, desktop computer used in the office and the lab. The first IBM PC introduced in 1981 used the Intel 8088 microprocessor. Newer versions of the PC introduced since that time have used newer Intel microprocessors including the 8086, the 80286, the 80386 and the 80486. The assembly language for the 8086 is identical to that of the 8088. The main difference between these two chips is the fact that the 8088 uses only 8 data lines to address memory while the 8086 uses 16 data lines. While the newer 80x86 microprocessors have introduced some new instructions they are upward compatible with the 8086. The assembly language studied in this book forms the basis for programming with any of these chips. PCs based on the 80386 are popular today. When they are turned on they come up in the *real* mode which means that they look like a fast 8086. These 80x86 microprocessors can also be programmed in the *protected* mode. Programs written in the protected mode cannot be run on the older 8086. All of the programs written in this book will run on PCs that contain any of these microprocessors running in the real mode. Throughout this book we will refer to 8086 assembly language programming with the understanding that these programs will also run on an 8088 machine and an 80x86 machine running in the real mode.

What is the 8086 microprocessor and how does it work? That is what this book is about. This book is unique in that it uses a special monitor program called TUTOR that runs on any IBM PC or PC compatible to help you learn about microprocessors. The TUTOR monitor shows you what is going on inside the computer at any instant of time. It has been specially designed to be easy to use and to make it easier for you to learn about microprocessors.

When writing assembly language programs you will need to use an assembler that automatically converts instruction mnemonics to machine language code. We describe the operation of the IBM PC Macro Assembler (MASM) and related macro assemblers in Chapter 5. However, you will gain considerable insight into the operation of microprocessors if you initially use the TUTOR monitor to load some short programs we have already written in Chapters 3 and 4. The TUTOR monitor will make it easy for you to enter these programs into the computer, run them, and watch them execute by single stepping through each instruction. The TUTOR monitor can also be used as a powerful debugging aid for programs that you later write using an assembler.

A summary of the TUTOR monitor and a description of how to run it are given in Appendix B. You should take a quick look at this appendix now. It will be a helpful guide to you until you become familiar with its use. Most of the commands will be introduced in the book, with examples, as the need arises. You will find the TUTOR monitor very easy to use. We will start using the TUTOR monitor in Chapter 3.

Before studying number systems in Chapter 2 we will take a brief look at the history of microprocessors and the factors that have led to the development of different families of 8-bit, 16-bit and 32-bit micro-processors.

1.3 MICROPROCESSORS

A major revolution in the computer industry has taken place in the past twenty years. A few of the major milestones during this period are shown in Table 1.1. The making of the first microprocessor was made possible by the remarkable development of integrated circuits during the 1960s. This technology allowed hundreds and then thousands of transistors to be etched onto a single piece of silicon. This led to the design of integrated circuits in which more and more logic elements were incorporated into a single chip. In 1969 Intel undertook a contract to develop a set of integrated circuits that could be used to make a programmable electronic calculator. Instead of developing yet another special purpose integrated circuit with only a limited function, Intel chose to produce a more general purpose device, the 4004 microprocessor, that could be programmed to perform many different functions. This first microprocessor had only four data lines over which both address information and data had to be sent to memory devices. Intel put this chip on the market in 1971 as part of a four chip set that formed a micro-programmable computer. The 4004 had many limitations and the following year Intel introduced the 8008 and two years later the 8080 which became widely used in a host of different applications.

Table 1.2		
History of Microprocessors		
DATE	MICROPROCESSOR	COMMENT
1971	Intel 4004	1st microprocessor – 4 bits
1972	Intel 8008	1st 8-bit microprocessor
1974	Intel 8080	
1975	Motorola 6800	5 volts only — 1 MHz
1976	MOS Technology 6502	Used in Apple II, PET, Atari
1977	Motorola 6802	128 bytes internal RAM
1978	Motorola 6801	Single chip microcomputer
1978	Intel 8086/8088	40,000 transistors – 16-bit data
1979	Motorola 68000	68,000 transistors
1979	Motorola 68701	MCU_EPROM–I/O
1979	Motorola 6805	Low-cost microcontroller
1979	Motorola 6809	Used in TRS-80 color computer
1981	**IBM PC** – uses Intel 8088	
1982	Motorola 68010	
1982	Motorola 68008	
1984	Intel 80286	10 MHz – 130,000 transistors
1984	Motorola 68020	32-bit address & data busses
1985	Motorola 68020 -- 20 MHz	
1986	Motorola 68020 -- 25 MHz	
1986	Intel 80386	16 MHz 275,000 transistors
1987	Motorola 68030	
1988	Motorola 68030 -- 33 MHz	
1989	Intel 80486	25 MHz – 1,000,000 transistors
1990	Intel 80486	50 MHz
1992	Intel 80586	4,000,000 transistors
1995	Intel 80686	22,000,000 transistors
2000	Intel 80786	100,000,000 transistors – 250 MHz

The Intel 8080 was an 8-bit microprocessor which means that it had eight data lines going to memory. It also had 16 address lines which meant that it could address a total of $2^{16} = 65,536$ different memory locations. The Motorola 6800, 6802, 6801, 68701, 6805 and 6809 as well as the MOS Technology 6502 all have this basic 8-bit structure as shown in Figure 1.1.

In Figure 1.1 eight separate lines form the 8-bit bidirectional *data bus*. All data move between the microprocessor chip and the memory chips over this data bus in groups of 8 bits called *bytes*. A high voltage (5 volts) is considered to be a binary digit (bit) 1 and a low voltage (0 volts) is considered to be a binary digit 0. Thus, at some instant of time the data bus might contain the 8 bits, or byte, 01101010. The right-most bit is bit 0, the least significant bit (LSB) and the left-most bit is bit 7, the most significant bit (MSB) (see Figure 1.2). In Chapter 2 we will see how this 8-bit byte can represent a binary number in a base 2 number system.

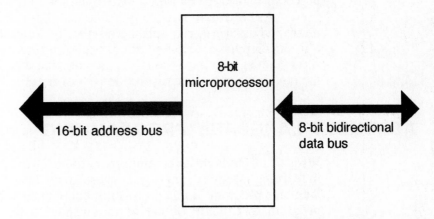

Figure 1.1   An 8-bit microprocessor has an 8-bit data bus
and a 16-bit address bus

Intel introduced the 8086/8088 microprocessors in 1978. The 8088 still had an 8-bit data bus while the 8086 provided a 16-bit data bus so that two bytes of data could be moved to and from memory at the same time. The 8086/8088 also increased the number of address lines to 20. This means that these microprocessors can address $2^{20} = 1,048,576$ possible memory locations. This number is equal to 1,024K where 1K = 1,024. It is also called 1 Mbyte (megabyte) of memory. We will look in detail at how to address all of these memory locations in Chapter 3.

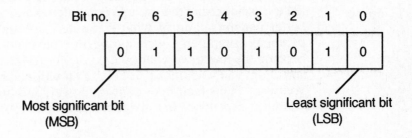

Figure 1.2 A byte (8 bits) of data on the data bus

In 1979 Motorola introduced its first 16-bit microprocessor — the 68000. This is the microprocessor that Apple chose to use in its Macintosh computers. The 68000 has a 16-bit data bus and a 24-bit address bus. This means that a 68000 can address a total of $2^{24} = 16$ Mbytes of memory. The Motorola 68020, introduced in 1984, increases the size of both the data bus and the address bus to 32 bits. This means that four bytes at a time can be moved to and from memory and the microprocessor can, in principle, address directly $2^{32} = 4$ Gbytes (gigabytes) of memory, where a Gbyte is equal to 1,024 Mbytes.

Intel's 80386, introduced in 1986, also provides complete 32-bit operation. However, as we will see in Chapter 3 the register structure of the 8086 does not lend itself to an easy extension to 32-bit addresses. This is not the case with the Motorola 68000 family of microprocessors in which all registers are 32-bits wide. This made their migration from 8-bit to 32-bit processors an easier transition than in the Intel family of microprocessors.

As you can see from Table 1.1 both the speed at which the microprocessor can run and the number of transistors that can be packed into the chip have increased dramatically in recent years. The predictions, shown at the bottom of the table, indicate that this trend will continue over the next few years. The revolution isn't over yet!

1.4 ASSEMBLY LANGUAGE PROGRAMMING

With all of the high-level languages around, why should you be interested in learning assembly language? There are several reasons. First, assembly language programs are fast. It is not uncommon for an assembly language program to execute orders of magnitude faster than a corresponding program written in BASIC. This can be important if you want to fill the screen instantaneously with information or if you need to control some time critical process.

Second, assembly language programming lets you access the lowest levels of the computer hardware. This is essential when interfacing the computer to external devices or when trying to get the most performance from the computer hardware. Third, most applications of microprocessors are in dedicated systems in which a single program is always executed. This program is normally stored as machine code in a read-only memory (ROM) or in a programmable read-only memory (PROM). Most such programs are written in assembly language.

Finally, learning assembly language will give you a much better understanding of how a computer works. There has traditionally been considerable mystery surrounding computers. Such mystery has inevitably led to suspicion and fear. Large computer facilities have not contributed to a better understanding of what computers are and how they work. Small personal computers, such as the PC, have made it possible for you to become the master of your own computer. This book will open up the PC and show you what makes it tick. You will be able to make it do anything you want. This feeling of control, power, and understanding is something you must experience to fully appreciate. Therefore, let's begin.

CHAPTER 2

Number Systems

Data inside a computer are represented by *binary digits* or *bits*. The logical values of these binary digits are denoted by 0 and 1 while the corresponding physical values can be any two state property such as a high (5 volts) or low (0 volts) voltage or two different directions of magnetization. It is therefore convenient to represent numbers inside the computer in a binary number system. Hexadecimal and octal numbers are often used as a shorthand for representing binary numbers. In this chapter you will learn:

- How to count in binary and hexadecimal
- How integers and fractional numbers are represented in any base
- How to convert numbers from one base to another
- How negative numbers are represented in the computer

By the end of this chapter you should be able to:

- Convert any binary, hexadecimal or octal number to the corresponding decimal number
- Convert any decimal number to the corresponding binary, hexadecimal or octal number
- Take the two's complement of any binary or hexadecimal integer

2.1 COUNTING IN BINARY AND HEXADECIMAL

Consider a box containing one marble. If the marble is in the box, we will say that the box is *full* and associate the digit 1 with the box. If we take the marble out of the box, the box will be empty, and we will then associate the digit 0 with the box. The two binary digits 0 and 1 are called *bits* and with one bit we can count from zero (box empty) to one (box full) as shown in Figure 2.1.

Consider now a second box that can also be full (1) or empty (0). However, when this box is full it will contain *two* marbles as shown in Figure 2.2. With these two boxes (two bits) we can count from zero to three as shown in Figure 2.3. Note that the value of each 2-bit binary number shown in Figure 2.3 is equal to the total number of marbles in the two boxes.

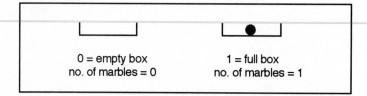

Figure 2.1   You can count from 0 to 1 with one bit

Figure 2.2   This box can contain either two marbles (full) or no marbles

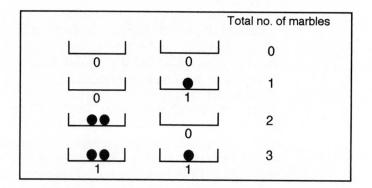

Figure 2.3   You can count from 0 to 3 with two bits

We can add a third bit to the binary number by adding a third box that is full (bit=1) when it contains 4 marbles and is empty (bit=0) when it contains no marbles. It must be either full (bit=1) or empty (bit=0). With this third box (3 bits) we can count from 0 to 7 as shown in Figure 2.4.

If you want to count beyond 7 you must add another box. How many marbles should this fourth box contain when it is full (bit=1)? It should be clear that this box must contain 8 marbles. The binary number 8 would then be written as 1000. Remember that a 1 in a binary number means that the corresponding box is full of marbles and the number of marbles that constitutes a full box varies as 1, 2, 4, 8 starting at the right. This means that with 4 bits we can count from 0 to 15 as shown in Fig 2.5.

It is convenient to represent the total number of marbles in the four boxes represented by the 4-bit binary numbers shown in Figure 2.5 by a single digit. We call this a *hexadecimal* digit and the sixteen hexadecimal digits are shown in the right-hand column in Figure 2.5. The hexadecimal digits 0-9 are the same as the decimal digits 0-9. However, the decimal numbers 10-15 are represented by the hexadecimal digits A-F. Thus, for example, the hexadecimal digit D is equivalent to the decimal number 13.

In order to count beyond 15 in binary you must add more boxes.

Each full box you add must contain twice as many marbles as the previous full box. With eight bits you can count from 0 to 255. A few examples are shown in Figure 2.6. The decimal number that corresponds to a given binary number is equal to the total number of marbles in all of the boxes. To find this number just add up all of the marbles in the full boxes (the ones with binary digits equal to 1).

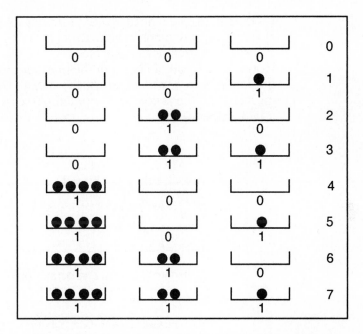

Figure 2.4 You can count from 0 to 7 with three bits

Number of marbles in each full box (bit = 1)				Total number of marbles	Hex digit
8	4	2	1		
0	0	0	0	0	0
0	0	0	1	1	1
0	0	1	0	2	2
0	0	1	1	3	3
0	1	0	0	4	4
0	1	0	1	5	5
0	1	1	0	6	6
0	1	1	1	7	7
1	0	0	0	8	8
1	0	0	1	9	9
1	0	1	0	10	A
1	0	1	1	11	B
1	1	0	0	12	C
1	1	0	1	13	D
1	1	1	0	14	E
1	1	1	1	15	F

Figure 2.5 You can count from 0 to 15 with four bits

As the length of a binary number increases, it becomes more cumbersome to work with. We then use the corresponding *hexadecimal number* as a shorthand method of representing the binary number. This is very easy to do. You just divide the binary number into groups of 4 bits starting at the right and then represent each 4-bit group by its corresponding hexadecimal digit given in Figure 2.5. For example, the binary number

is equivalent to the hexadecimal number 9AH. We will often use the letter H following a number to indicate a hexadecimal number. You should verify that the total number of marbles represented by this binary number is 154. However, instead of counting the marbles in the *binary boxes* you can count the marbles in *hexadecimal boxes* where the first box contains A x 1=10 marbles and the second box contains 9 x 16=144 marbles. Therefore, the total number of marbles is equal to 144 + 10 = 154.

Number of marbles in each full box (bit = 1)								Total number of marbles
128	64	32	16	8	4	2	1	
0	0	1	1	0	1	0	0	52
1	0	1	0	0	0	1	1	163
1	1	1	1	1	1	1	1	255

Figure 2.6 You can count from 0 to 255 with 8 bits

A third hexadecimal box would contain a multiple of $16^2 = 256$ marbles and a fourth hexadecimal number would contain a multiple of $16^3 = 4,096$ marbles. As an example, the 16-bit binary number

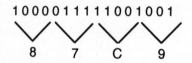

is equivalent to the decimal number 34,761 (that is, it represents 34,761 marbles). This can be seen by expanding the hexadecimal number as follows:

$$
\begin{array}{lcll}
8 \times 16^3 & = & 8 \times 4,096 = & 32,768 \\
7 \times 16^2 & = & 7 \times\ \ \ 256 = & 1,792 \\
C \times 16^1 & = & 12 \times\ \ \ \ 16 = & 192 \\
9 \times 16^0 & = & 9 \times\ \ \ \ \ \ 1 = & \underline{\ \ \ \ \ \ 9} \\
& & & 34,761
\end{array}
$$

You can see that by working with hexadecimal numbers you can reduce by a factor of 4 the number of digits that you have to work with.

Table 2.1 will allow you to conveniently convert hexadecimal numbers of up to four digits to their decimal equivalent. Note, for example, how the four terms in the conversion of 87C9H can be read directly from the table.

2.2   POSITIONAL NOTATION

Binary numbers are numbers to the base 2 and hexadecimal numbers are numbers to the base 16. An integer number N can be written in any base b using the following positional notation:

$$N = P_4P_3P_2P_1P_0 = P_4b^4 + P_3b^3 + P_2b^2 + P_1b^1 + P_0b^0$$

where the number always starts with the least significant digit on the right.

Table 2.1							
Hexadecimal and Decimal Conversion							
15	BYTE		8	7	BYTE		0
15 CHAR 12		11 CHAR 8		7 CHAR 4		3 CHAR 0	
HEX	DEC	HEX	DEC	HEX	DEC	HEX	DEC
0	0	0	0	0	0	0	0
1	4,096	1	256	1	16	1	1
2	8,192	2	512	2	32	2	2
3	12,288	3	768	3	48	3	3
4	16,384	4	1,024	4	64	4	4
5	20,480	5	1,280	5	80	5	5
6	24,576	6	1,536	6	96	6	6
7	28,672	7	1,792	7	112	7	7
8	32,768	8	2,048	8	128	8	8
9	36,864	9	2,304	9	144	9	9
A	40,960	A	2,560	A	160	A	10
B	45,056	B	2,816	B	176	B	11
C	49,152	C	3,072	C	192	C	12
D	53,248	D	3,328	D	208	D	13
E	57,344	E	3,584	E	224	E	14
F	61,440	F	3,840	F	240	F	15

For example, the decimal number 584 is a base 10 number, and can be expressed as

$$584_{10} = 5 \times 10^2 + 8 \times 10^1 + 4 \times 10^0$$
$$= 500 + 80 + 4$$
$$= 584_{10}$$

A number to the base b must have b different digits. Thus, decimal numbers (base 10) use the 10 digits 0-9.

A binary number is a base 2 number and therefore uses only the two digits 0 and 1. For example, the binary number 110100 is the base 2 number

$$110100_2 = 1 \times 2^5 + 1 \times 2^4 + 0 \times 2^3 + 1 \times 2^2 + 0 \times 2^1 + 0 \times 2^0$$
$$= 32 + 16 + 0 + 4 + 0 + 0$$
$$= 52_{10}$$

This the same as the first example in Figure 2.6 where the total number of marbles is 52 (32 + 16 + 4).

A hexadecimal number is a base 16 number and therefore needs 16 different digits to represent the number. We use the ten digits 0-9 plus the six letters A-F as shown in Figure 2.5. For example, the hexadecimal number 3AF can be written as the base 16 number

$$
\begin{aligned}
3AF_{16} &= 3 \times 16^2 + A \times 16^1 + F \times 16^0 \\
&= 3 \times 256 + 10 \times 16 + 15 \times 1 \\
&= 768 + 160 + 15 \\
&= 943_{10}
\end{aligned}
$$

Microcomputers move data around in groups of 8-bit binary bytes. Therefore, it is natural to describe the data in the computer as binary, or base 2, numbers. As we have seen, this is simplified by using hexadecimal numbers where each hex digit represents four binary digits. Some larger computers represent binary numbers in groups of three bits rather than four. The resulting number is an *octal*, or base 8, number. Octal numbers use only the 8 digits 0-7. For example, the octal number 457 can be written as the base 8 number

$$
\begin{aligned}
457_8 &= 4 \times 8^2 + 5 \times 8^1 + 8^0 \\
&= 256 + 40 + 7 \\
&= 303_{10}
\end{aligned}
$$

Fractional Numbers

The positional notation given above for integer numbers can be generalized for numbers involving fractions as follows:

$$
\begin{aligned}
N &= \ldots P_2 P_1 P_0 . P_{-1} P_{-2} P_{-3} \ldots \\
&= \ldots + P_2 b^2 + P_1 b^1 + P_0 b^0 \\
&\quad + P_{-1} b^{-1} + P_{-2} b^{-2} + P_{-3} b^{-3} + \ldots
\end{aligned}
$$

As an example, consider the base 10 number 375.17. Using the above definition this is equal to

$$
\begin{aligned}
N &= 3 \times 10^2 + 7 \times 10^1 + 5 \times 10^0 + 1 \times 10^{-1} + 7 \times 10^{-2} \\
&= 300 + 70 + 5 + 0.1 + 0.07 \\
&= 375.17
\end{aligned}
$$

In this case the *radix*, or base, is 10 and the *radix point* (decimal point) separates the integer part of the number from the fractional part.

Consider now the binary number 1101.11. This is equivalent to what decimal number? Using the above definition we can write

$$
\begin{aligned}
1101.11_2 &= 1 \times 2^3 + 1 \times 2^2 + 0 \times 2^1 + 1 \times 2^0 + 1 \times 2^{-1} + 1 \times 2^{-2} \\
&= 8 + 4 + 0 + 1 + \frac{1}{2} + \frac{1}{4} \\
&= 13.75_{10}
\end{aligned}
$$

Following the same technique we can write the hexadecimal number 1AB.6 as

$$
\begin{aligned}
1AB.6_{16} &= 1 \times 16^2 + 10 \times 16^1 + 11 \times 16^0 + 6 \times 16^{-1} \\
&= 256 + 160 + 11 + \frac{6}{16} \\
&= 427.375_{10}
\end{aligned}
$$

As a final example consider the octal number 173.25. We can find the equivalent decimal number by expanding the octal number as follows.

$$173.25_8 = 1 \times 8^2 + 7 \times 8^1 + 3 \times 8^0 + 2 \times 8^{-1} + 5 \times 8^{-2}$$
$$= 64 + 56 + 3 + \frac{2}{8} + \frac{5}{64}$$
$$= 123.328125_{10}$$

The examples in this section show how you can convert a number in any base to a decimal number. In the following section we will look at how to convert a decimal number to any other base and how to convert between binary, hexadecimal and octal.

2.3 NUMBER SYSTEM CONVERSIONS

In the previous section you saw how you can convert a number in any base to its decimal equivalent by expanding the number using the definition of the positional notation of the number. For a hexadecimal number containing a maximum of four hex digits it is easy to use Table 2.1 to find the conversion by simply adding the corresponding decimal value from each of the four columns. Note that the entries in the four columns of Table 2.1 are simply the hex digits multiplied by 16^3, 16^2, 16^1 and 16^0 respectively.

If you don't have Table 2.1 (or a calculator that converts hex numbers to decimal) you can use the following shortcut to convert a hex integer to decimal. To convert the hexadecimal number $A7_{16}$ to decimal, multiply A x 16 and add 7. For longer hexadecimal numbers, start with the left-most digit (the most significant), multiply it by 16, and add the next hex digit. Multiply this result by 16 and add the next hex digit. Continue this process until you have added the right-most digit. For example, to convert $87C9_{16}$ to decimal, you can do this:

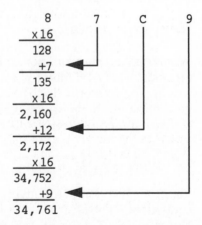

Therefore, $87C9_{16} = 34,761_{10}$. This technique will work for any base. You just multiply by the current base, rather than 16, in each step of the process.

Binary <--> Hex

Converting a binary number to hex is trivial. You simply partition the binary number in groups of four bits, starting at the radix point, and read the hex digits by inspection using the hex digit definitions in Figure 2.5. For example, the binary number 11010101000.1111010111 can be partitioned as follows:

$$0110 | 1010 | 1000 | . | 1111 | 0101 | 1100$$
$$6 \quad | \quad A \quad | \quad 8 \quad | . | \quad F \quad | \quad 5 \quad | \quad C$$

Therefore, $11010101000.1111010111_2 = 6A8.F5C_{16}$. Note that leading zeros can be added to the integer part of the binary number and trailing zeros can be added to the fractional part to produce a 4-bit hex digit.

Going from hex to binary is just as easy. You just write down the four binary digits corresponding to each hex digit by inspection (using the table in Figure 2.5).

Binary <--> Octal

Converting a binary number to octal is just as easy as converting it to hex. In this case you just partition the binary number in groups of three bits rather than four and read the octal digits (0 - 7) by inspection. Again the grouping is done starting at the radix point. Using as an example the same binary number 11010101000.1111010111 that we just converted to hex we would convert it to octal as follows:

$$011 | 010 | 101 | 000 | . | 111 | 101 | 011 | 100$$
$$3 \quad | \quad 2 \quad | \quad 5 \quad | \quad 0 \quad | . | \quad 7 \quad | \quad 5 \quad | \quad 3 \quad | \quad 4$$

Therefore, $11010101000.1111010111_2 = 3250.7534_8$. Note again that leading zeros must be added to the integer part of the binary number and trailing zeros must be added to the fractional part to produce 3-bit octal digits.

You reverse the process to go from octal to binary. Just write down the three binary digits corresponding to each octal digit by inspection.

Hex <--> Octal

When converting from hex to octal or from octal to hex it is easiest to go through binary. Thus, for example, to convert $6A8.F5C_{16}$ to octal you would first convert it to the binary number 11010101000.1111010111_2 by inspection as shown in the example above. Then you would convert this binary number to 3250.7534_8 as we just did in the previous example.

Decimal to Hex

Suppose you want to convert a decimal integer 167 to its hexadecimal equivalent. The easiest way to figure this out is to look at Table 2.1. The closest decimal value in this table that does not exceed 167 is 160 in the second column from the right. This corresponds to the hexadecimal digit A as the second digit from the right ($A \times 16^1 = 10 \times 16 = 160$). To find the hexadecimal digit to use in the right-most position just subtract 160 from 167. Thus the decimal number 167_{10} is equivalent to the hexadecimal number $A7_{16}$. What binary number is this?

How can you convert a decimal integer to hexadecimal if you don't have Table 2.1 around? Here's a shortcut. Divide the decimal number by 16 and keep track of the remainder. Keep dividing the results by 16 and writing down the remainders at each step until the result is zero. The equivalent hexadecimal number is just all of the remainders read backward. For example, this is how to convert the decimal number 167_{10} to hexadecimal:

```
167/16 = 10   with remainder   7
 10/16 =  0   with remainder  10 = A
```

read backward ⟶

$\therefore$ $167_{10} = A7_{16}$

Here's the example we gave at the beginning of this section.

$$34,761_{10} = ?_{16}$$

```
34,761/16 = 2,172   with remainder   9
 2,172/16 =   135   with remainder  12 = C
   135/16 =     8   with remainder   7
     8/16 =     0   with remainder   8
```

read up ⟶

Therefore, $34,761_{10} = 87C9_{16}$. Again this technique will work for converting a decimal integer to any base. You just divide by the base, keep track of the remainders and read up.

When converting a decimal number containing a fractional part you divide the problem into two parts. First convert the integer part using the technique just described. Then you can use the following rule to convert the fractional part: Multiply the fractional part by the base, keep track of the integer part and read down. As an example, suppose you want to convert the decimal number 3901.78125_{10} to its hexadecimal equivalent. You would first convert the integer part by dividing by the base, keeping track of the remainder and reading up.

```
3901/16 = 243   with remainder 13 = D
 243/16 =  15   with remainder      3
  15/16 =   0   with remainder 15 = F
```

read up ⟶

Therefore, $3901_{10} = F3D_{16}$. Now to convert the fractional part multiply by the base, keep track of the integer part and read down.

read down ⟶

```
0.78125 x 16 = 12.5   integer part = 12 = C
    0.5 x 16 =  8.0   integer part =  8
```

Therefore, $0.78125_{10} = 0.C8_{16}$. Combining the integer and fractional parts we have found that $3901.78125_{10} = F3D.C8_{16}$.

This rule for converting the fractional part of a decimal number will work for any base. Sometimes the remainder may never become zero and you will have a continuing fraction. This means that there is no exact conversion of the decimal fraction. For example, suppose you want to represent the decimal value 0.1_{10} as a binary number. Following our rule we would write

read down ⟶

```
0.1 x 2 = 0.2     integer part = 0
0.2 x 2 = 0.4     integer part = 0
0.4 x 2 = 0.8     integer part = 0
0.8 x 2 = 1.6     integer part = 1
0.6 x 2 = 1.2     integer part = 1
0.2 x 2 = 0.4     integer part = 0
0.4 x 2 = 0.8     integer part = 0
0.8 x 2 = 1.6     integer part = 1
0.6 x 2 = 1.2     integer part = 1
```

It is clear that the remainder will never go to zero and that the pattern 0011 will go on forever. Thus, 0.1_{10} can only be approximated as

$$0.1_{10} \approx 0.000110011..._2$$

This means that 0.1_{10} cannot be represented exactly in a computer as a binary number of any size!

2.4 NEGATIVE NUMBERS

An eight-bit binary number can represent one of 256 (2^8) possible values between 0 and 255. However we also need to represent negative numbers. The left-most bit in a binary number is the *sign bit*. If this bit is zero the number is positive; if this bit is one, the number is negative. In the 8086, however, (and in most computers today) when the most significant bit is one, the magnitude of the negative number is *not* given by the binary value of the remaining bits in the number. Rather a *two's complement* representation of negative numbers is used. The reason for this is that the same circuitry, namely an adder, can be used for both addition and subtraction.

The idea of being able to subtract by adding can be seen by an example using decimal (base 10) numbers. Suppose you want to subtract 35 from 73. The answer is 38. You can obtain this result by taking the 10's complement of 35 (this is what you have to add to 35 to get 100; that is, 65) and adding it to 73. The result is 138 as shown in Figure 2.7. If you ignore the leading 1 (the carry) then the remaining value, 38, is the correct answer.

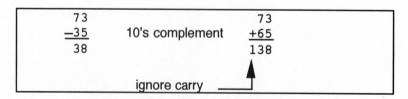

Figure 2.7   Decimal subtraction can be done by taking the 10's complement of the subtrahend and adding

In binary arithmetic, negative numbers are stored in their *two's complement* form. You can find the two's complement of a binary number in several ways. Note that the 10's complement of 35 can be found by subtracting 35 from 99 (this gives the 9's complement) and then adding 1. That is,

$$
\begin{array}{r}
99 \\
- \ 35 \\
\hline
64 \\
+ \ \ 1 \\
\hline
65
\end{array}
$$

The two's complement of the eight-bit binary number 01001101 is the eight-bit binary number you must add to this number to obtain 100000000. You can find it by subtracting the number from 11111111 and adding 1. Note that subtracting an eight-bit binary number from 11111111 (called the one's complement) is equivalent to complementing each bit in the byte; that is, each 1 is changed to a 0, and each 0 is changed to a 1. Therefore, the one's complement of 01001101 is 10110010 and the two's complement of 01001101 is:

$$
\begin{array}{rl}
& 01001101 \\
\text{one's complement} \ = & 10110010 \\
\text{add} & \underline{\hspace{4em} 1} \\
\text{two's complement} \ = & 10110011
\end{array}
$$

There is an easier way to take the two's complement of a binary number. You just start at the right-most bit and copy down all bits until you have copied down the first 1. Then complement (that is, change from 1 to 0, or 0 to 1) all of the remaining bits. For example,

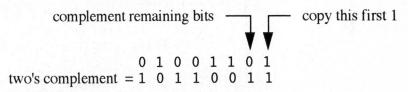

As a second example,

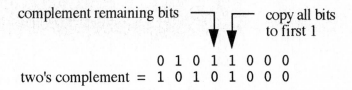

Verify that if you add the 8-bit binary numbers given in the examples above to their two's complement value, you obtain 100000000.

An 8-bit byte can contain positive values between 00000000 and 01111111; that is, between 00H and 7FH. This corresponds to decimal values between 0 and 127. A byte in which bit 7 is a 1 is interpreted as a negative number, whose magnitude can be found by taking the two's complement. For example, how is -75_{10} stored in the computer? First write down the binary or hex value of the number, 4BH, as shown in Figure 2.8. Then take its two's complement. The value -75_{10} is therefore stored in the computer as B5H. Note that if you take the two's complement of a positive number between 0 and 7FH, the result will always have bit 7 (the most significant bit) set to 1.

Given a negative number (with bit 7 set) you can always find the magnitude of this number by taking the two's complement. For example, the two's complement of B5H (-75_{10}) is 4BH ($+75_{10}$) as shown in Figure 2.8.

```
                          75₁₀  =  4BH  =  01001011
   two's complement  =   -75₁₀  =  B5H  =  10110101
   two's complement of     B5H  =  4BH  =  01001011
```

Figure 2.8   The negative of a binary number is found
by taking the two's complement

Note that the two's complement of 01H is FFH and the two's complement of 80H is 80H, as shown in Figure 2.9. This last example shows that signed 8-bit binary numbers "wrap around" at 80H. That is, the largest positive number is 7FH = 127_{10} and the smallest negative number (largest magnitude) is 80H = -128_{10}. This is shown in Table 2.2.

```
                          1₁₀  =  01H  =  00000001
   two's complement  =   -1₁₀  =  FFH  =  11111111
                        128₁₀  =  80H  =  10000000
   two's complement  = -128₁₀  =  80H  =  10000000
```

Figure 2.9   Negative 8-bit numbers can range
between FFH (-1) and 80H (-128)

Table 2.2			
Positive and Negative Binary Numbers			
Signed Decimal	Hex	Binary	Unsigned Decimal
-128	80	10000000	128
-127	81	10000001	129
-126	82	10000010	130
...	...	...	...
...	...	...	...
...	...	...	...
-3	FD	11111101	253
-2	FE	11111110	254
-1	FF	11111111	255
0	00	00000000	0
1	01	00000001	1
2	02	00000010	2
3	03	00000011	3
...	...	...	...
...	...	...	...
...	...	...	...
125	7D	01111101	125
126	7E	01111110	126
127	7F	01111111	127

Table 2.2 also shows that the hex values between 80H and FFH can be interpreted *either* as negative numbers between -128 and -1 *or* as positive numbers between 128 and 255. Sometimes you will treat them as negative numbers and sometimes you will treat them as positive values. It is up to you as the programmer to make sure you know whether a particular byte is being treated as a signed number or as an unsigned number.

Whereas bit 7 is the sign bit in an 8-bit byte bit 15 is the sign bit in a 16-bit word. A 16-bit signed word can have values ranging from 8000H = $-32,768_{10}$ to 7FFFH = $+32,767_{10}$. Similarly, bit 31 is the sign bit in a 32-bit double word. Such a double word can have values ranging from 80000000H = $-2,147,483,648_{10}$ to 7FFFFFFFH = $+2,147,483,647_{10}$.

EXERCISES

Exercise 2.1
Convert the following decimal numbers to their hexadecimal equivalent.

a) 42
b) 31729
c) 2173
d) 249
e) 125
f) 62433

Exercise 2.2
Convert the following hexadecimal numbers to their decimal equivalent.

a) EF
b) 7134
c) 5AC
d) AA
e) 5C
f) F21C

Exercise 2.3
Convert the follow numbers:

a) $110101001011_2 = ?_{16}$
b) $10101101010_2 = ?_8$
c) $533.25_{10} = ?_2$
d) $1010.101_2 = ?_{10}$
e) $42.36_8 = ?_{10}$

Exercise 2.4
Convert the follow numbers:

a) $3B4.C_{16} = ?_{10}$
b) $8000_{16} = ?_{10}$
c) $241.1_{10} = ?_8$
d) $241.1_{10} = ?_{16}$
e) $1AE7.B_{16} = ?_{10}$

Exercise 2.5
Find the hex values for the following decimal numbers.

a) -7
b) -101
c) -68
d) -25
e) -120
f) -5

Exercise 2.6
The following hex values correspond to what negative decimal numbers?

a) CDH
b) F3H
c) E2H
d) 85H
e) 99H
f) ABH

CHAPTER 3

A Look Inside the 8086

In this chapter we will begin our look at the 8086 microprocessor by using the TUTOR monitor to see what goes on inside the 8086 and how it executes programs. You will learn:

- The basic components of a computer system
- The internal register structure of the 8086
- How the 8086 microprocessor addresses different memory locations
- How to load and execute simple programs using the TUTOR monitor
- How ASCII data can be entered from the keyboard and displayed on the screen

3.1 THE BASIC STRUCTURE OF A COMPUTER

The basic structure of a computer system is shown in Figure 3.1. Although computers may seem complicated, at the basic level they really do only three different things. A computer can:

- Store data
- Move data from one place to another
- Perform some basic arithmetic and logical operations

By combining these basic operations in sophisticated ways, it is the software, or computer program, that gives a computer its apparent power.

In Figure 3.1 data can be stored in external devices such as floppy disks or hard disks. Data can also be stored temporarily in the internal registers of the *central processing unit* (CPU). In the next section we will look at the internal registers of the 8086 microprocessor. Data can also be stored in *read-only memory* (ROM) and in *read-write memory* (RAM). Read-only memory is permanent memory in which data are retained when the power to the computer is turned off. The typical PC will contain a BIOS (Basic Input-Output System) ROM that contains basic Input/Output (I/O) routines for accessing the computer hardware such as the keyboard and video screen. RAM (which stands for random-access memory) is really read-write memory, which means that the program can change the contents of RAM while it cannot change the contents of ROM. In most cases the contents of RAM are lost when you turn off the power to the computer. However, it is possible to have battery backed-up RAM whose data is preserved with a battery when the main power to the computer is turned off.

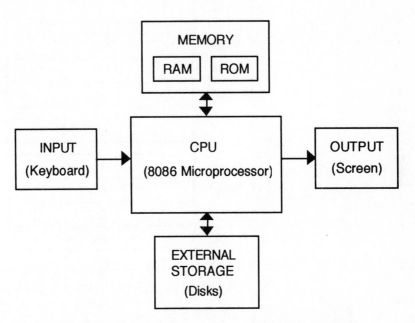

Figure 3.1 Basic structure of a computer system

The INPUT and OUTPUT boxes in Figure 3.1 show how data get into and out of the computer. For the PC, this is usually a keyboard for input (and possibly a mouse for pointing on the screen) and a video screen for output. You will also generally have some type of printer as an output device. These I/O devices will have some type of RAM associated with them for storing data. For example, when you type keys on the keyboard, the data associated with each key pressed are stored in a section of RAM called the keyboard buffer. Similarly, when you display characters on the screen, the data associated with each character are stored in a section of RAM called the video buffer. Thus, we can think of data as being stored in all of the boxes in Figure 3.1.

The arrows in Figure 3.1 show how the computer moves data from one place to another. A large part of all computer programs consists of moving data from the CPU registers to memory, from memory to the CPU registers, from the input to the output and to and from external disk drives. Once data has been moved into the internal registers the CPU can perform some simple arithmetic and logical operations on this data. We will look at some examples of these operations later in this chapter. First, we will take a look at the internal registers of the 8086 microprocessor.

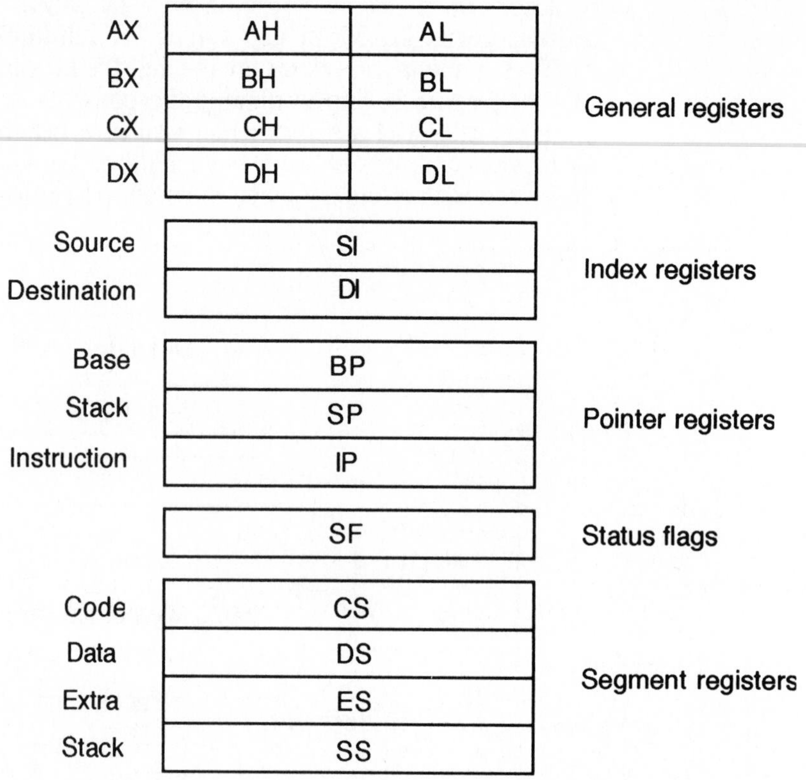

AX	AH	AL
BX	BH	BL
CX	CH	CL
DX	DH	DL

General registers

Source	SI
Destination	DI

Index registers

Base	BP
Stack	SP
Instruction	IP

Pointer registers

	SF

Status flags

Code	CS
Data	DS
Extra	ES
Stack	SS

Segment registers

Figure 3.2 The internal registers in the 8086 microprocessor

3.2   INTERNAL 8086 REGISTERS

The 8086 microprocessor has several internal registers that can store binary data.   These are shown in Figure 3.2.   All of the registers are 16-bit registers.   The general registers *AX*, *BX*, *CX* and *DX* can each be divided into an 8-bit high-order byte and an 8-bit low-order byte.   For example, *AX* is made up of the high-order byte *AH* and the low-order byte *AL*.   We will look at these registers in more detail in Chapter 4.

If you run the TUTOR monitor program, you will obtain the screen display shown in Figure 3.3.   The contents of the general registers *AX*, *BX*, *CX* and *DX* are displayed in the upper-left-hand part of the screen.

The white horizontal line across the bottom of the screen is called the command line.   When you press the key containing the slash (/), the following message will appear on the command line:

COMMAND: ABDEFGIJLMPRSTUQXZ

The computer is now waiting for you to press a key containing one of the letters following the word COMMAND.   You will learn what all of these letters do as we progress through the book.   For now press the key *R*. This will produce the message

REGISTER CHANGE: G P I S F

on the command line.   Pressing one of the letters *G*, *P*, *I*, *S*, or *F* will allow you to change a register within one of the following groups:

G - General Registers: $A\ B\ C\ D$ (AX,BX,CX,DX)
P - Pointer Registers: $S\ B\ I$ (SP,BP,IP)
I - Index Registers: $S\ D$ (SI,DI)
S - Segment Registers: $S\ D\ C\ E$ (SS,DS,CS,ES)
F - Status Flags

```
        8086 Microprocessor TUTOR          Press F7 for Help

      AH AL    BH BL     CH CL     DH DL     DATA SEG    08 19 2A 3B 4C 5D 6E 7F
  AX 00 00   BX 13 A3   CX 00 C5   DX 3A B3   174F:0000   A1 76 57 FF 06 76 57 3D
                                              174F:0008   00 04 72 0E B8 97 00 50
     SP 0FFF      SI 0000      IP 0000        174F:0010   B8 84 09 50 E8 86 1A 83
     BP 0000      DI 0000                     174F:0018   C4 04 E8 66 3B 88 86 78
     SS 174F      DS 174F      CS 174F        174F:0020   FF 2A E4 50 8D 86 79 FF
  SP+SS 184EF  SI+DS 174F0     ES 174F        174F:0028   50 E8 4C 23 83 C4 04 B8
  BP+SS 174F0  DI+DS 174F0  IP+CS 174F0       174F:0030   FF 7F 50 2B C0 50 E8 B7
  STATUS FLAGS 7202 0111001000000010          174F:0038   23 83 C4 04 2B C0 50 B8
                        ODITSZ A P C          174F:0040   03 00 50 8D 86 78 FF 50
  174F:0000 A17657       MOV   AX,[5776]      174F:0048   E8 17 FC 83 C4 06 8B F0

  SEG 174F:  08 19 2A 3B 4C 5D 6E 7F                        174F: STACK
     FFE8    05 55 4E 41 53 34 20 00     . U N A S 4  .       0FFF
     FFF0    F0 5E 00 00 C0 5E FF FF     . ^ . . . ^ . .
     FFF8    01 00 78 09 96 1D 27 00     . . x . . . ' .
     0000   >A1 76 57 FF 06 76 57 3D     . v W . . v W =
     0008    00 04 72 0E B8 97 00 50     . . r . . . . P
     0010    B8 84 09 50 E8 86 1A 83     . . . P . . . .
     0018    C4 04 E8 66 3B 88 86 78     . . . f ; . . x

                                         / : Command     > : Go To Memory
                                         Use Cursor Keys to Scroll thru Memory
```

Figure 3.3 Initial screen display of the TUTOR monitor

For example, to change the contents of general register *AX*, press key *G*. This will produce the message

CHANGE GENERAL REG: A B C D

Press key *A*. This will produce the entry *AX=* followed by a blinking cursor on the bottom line of the screen (this is called the entry line). Type in any four-digit hexadecimal number. When you press the *Enter* key this new number will be stored in the general register *AX*. Try it. If you enter more than four digits, the last four will be used. If you enter a digit other than *0-9* or *A-F*, the computer will ignore your request, sound a beep, and clear the command and entry lines. You can then type */R* again to change a register value. If you make a mistake while entering a hexadecimal value on the entry line, you can back the cursor up (and thereby erase the most recently entered value) by pressing the *backspace* key.

3.3 COMPUTER MEMORY

In this section we will look at how the 8086 addresses the RAM and ROM in Figure 3.1. In Chapter 1 we saw that the 8086 has a 20-bit *address bus* which produces a 20-bit address. This means that the 8086 can address one of 2^{20} = 1,048,576 possible memory locations. Each memory location contains one 8-bit byte of data. Thus, the 8086 can address 1 Mbyte of memory.

The 20-bit address can be represented by a 5-digit hexadecimal number in the range 00000-FFFFF. The internal registers of the 8086, however, are only 16 bits or 4 hex digits long. Some of these registers are used to point to various memory locations. How can a 16-bit register be used to point to an address in a 20-bit address range? The answer is that the 20-bit address is broken up into two parts; a 16-bit *segment address* and a 16-bit *offset address*, which are offset from each other by 4 bits as shown in Figure 3.4.

The 1 Mbyte address range can be thought of as broken up into 64 Kbyte segments as shown in Figure 3.5. The starting address of a segment is given by the segment address *XXXX0*. Note that this address must be a multiple of 16 in the actual address space. We call this a paragraph boundary. The offset address *0YYYY* is the 16-bit address (64K) within a given segment. The actual address is found by adding the segment address to the offset address.

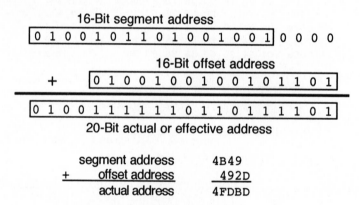

Figure 3.4 An actual 20-bit address is formed by adding a 16-bit segment address to a 16-bit offset address that is shifted 4 bits to the right

On the TUTOR display five actual addresses are displayed: *SP+SS, BP+SS, SI+DS, DI+DS,* and *IP+CS.* These actual addresses are formed by adding the segment addresses in *SS, DS,* or *CS* to the offset addresses in *SP, BP, SI, DI,* or *IP.* Note that on the screen the segment addresses are shifted 4 bits (one hex digit) to the left of the offset addresses.

The 8086 has four segment registers (*CS, DS, SS,* and *ES*) that define four different segments within the 1 Mbyte address range. These four segments may partially or completely overlap. The uses of the four segment registers will be described in Chapter 4. For now let us see how we can use the TUTOR monitor to examine the contents of any memory location.

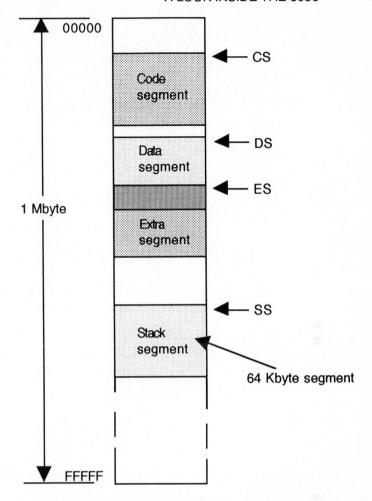

Figure 3.5 The actual 1 Mbyte address range is divided into 64 Kbyte segments

TUTOR's Memory Display

When you run the TUTOR monitor program the screen display is as shown in Figure 3.3. Along the left lower side of the screen are seven rows of reverse video four-digit hexadecimal addresses.[1] Note that the addresses of adjacent rows differ by eight. These are *offset addresses* relative to the *segment address* labeled *SEG* just above the offset addresses. In Figure 3.3 the value of this segment address is 174FH. Your segment address value may be different from this. When TUTOR is executed it displays the first available free memory in the memory display. This means that you should be able to change these memory values without crashing the system. The fourth row of offset addresses contains the address 0000H. The eight bytes following this address (remember that each byte is represented by a two-digit hexadecimal number) are the contents of offset addresses 0000H-0007H. The eight bytes in the next row (following the address 0008H) are the contents of offset addresses 0008H-000FH.

The white bar at the top of the memory display contains the digits

```
08 19 2A 3B 4C 5D 6E 7F
```

[1]The memory display in the upper-right section of the screen is part of the data segment. We will look at this data segment display in Chapter 5.

This is a guide that gives the last digit of a memory address. Note that the starting address on each line ends with either a 0 or an 8. If it ends with a 0, then the addresses of the eight bytes on that line end with the *first* digit in each pair (0–7) of the guide line shown above. If the starting address ends with an 8, then the addresses of the eight bytes on that line end with the *second* digit in each pair (8–F) of the guide line shown above.

A position cursor, > , points to the contents of offset address 0000H. Note that the preceding line begins with address FFF8H and ends with FFFFH. Thus, this display shows the contents of the beginning of a segment from offset addresses 0000H-00018H and the top of the segment from offset addresses FFE8H-FFFFH. It is possible to look at the contents of any offset address in between by scrolling the display.

The cursor keys can be used to scroll through memory. Table 3.1 gives the function of each cursor key.

Table 3.1	
Cursor Keys to Scroll through Memory	
Key	Function
Right Cursor	Advance 1 byte
Left Cursor	Back up 1 byte
Down Cursor	Advance 1 row
Up Cursor	Back up 1 row
PgDn	Advance 7 rows
PgUp	Back up 7 rows
Home	Go to offset address 0000H

Press the right cursor key containing the right arrow --> (located on key 6 of the numeric key pad at the right of the keyboard or in a separate group of cursor keys) and watch the position cursor >. Note that it moves to offset address 0001H. Press the right cursor key several more times. Note that when you get to the end of the line (offset address 0007H) and advance to offset address 0008H all of the memory locations scroll up one line, and a new line containing addresses 0020H-0027H appears at the bottom of the display.

Press all of the cursor keys given in Table 3.1 until you become familiar with how they work. Note that if you hold down one of the cursor keys the function will repeat continuously (until the keyboard buffer becomes full and the computer beeps at you).

Scrolling through memory is not a convenient way to get to a memory location that is a long way off. You can use the > symbol to go to any memory location within a segment, or to go to the beginning of another segment. Press the key containing the symbol >. It is not necessary to hold down the *shift* key. Pressing this key with or without the *shift* key will cause the following message to appear on the command line:

```
goto: Offset or Seg address
```

You now go to any offset address within the current segment by pressing key *O* ("oh", *not* "zero"), or you can go to the beginning of a new segment by pressing key *S*. Press key *O*. The message

ENTER OFFSET ADDRESS

will appear on the command line and a blinking cursor will appear on the entry line. Enter any address and press the *Enter* key. The position cursor will immediately move to the memory address that you entered. You do not have to type leading zeros when entering the address. For example, if you enter *B* the position cursor will move to offset address 000BH.

If you make a mistake while entering an address, pressing the backspace key will move the blinking cursor back one space and erase the most recently entered digit. Try this. If you back up the blinking cursor beyond the starting position, the command line will clear and you will return to the TUTOR monitor. Note that you may enter the hex digits *A-F* with or without pressing the shift key. They will always be displayed in upper case.

If you type an invalid address (any digits other than *0-F*), the command line will clear, a beep will sound, and you will return to the TUTOR monitor.

To go to the beginning of a new segment type *>S*. The message

ENTER SEGMENT ADDRESS

will appear on the command line and a blinking cursor will appear on the entry line. Enter the address 2100 and press the *Enter* key. Note that the value of the *SEG* address displayed near the left center of the screen has changed to 2100 and the offset address has returned to 0000 as shown in Figure 3.6. The position cursor > is really pointing to the actual address 21000 formed by adding the segment address 2100 and the offset address 0000 as follows:

```
2100        segment address
0000        offset address
21000       actual address
```

We sometimes indicate the actual address by writing it in the form

segment_address:offset_address

Thus the address 2100:0000 is the actual address 21000 shown in Figure 3.6.

Note that there are many different ways that an actual address can be divided between a segment address and an offset address. For example, memory location 21000 shown in Figure 3.6 can be expressed as

2000:1000

That is, the segment address could be 2000 and the offset address could be 1000. To verify this change the *SEG* address to 2000 by typing *>S* and entering 2000. Then go to the offset address 1000 by typing *>O* and entering 1000. Note that the same value, 2B, is in location 21000 as shown in Figure 3.7.

```
        8086 Microprocessor TUTOR          Press F7 for Help

    AH AL    BH BL    CH CL     DH DL     DATA SEG    08 19 2A 3B 4C 5D 6E 7F
 AX 00 00  BX 11 C5  CX 00 C5  DX 3A EE   1574:0000   FF 7F 50 2B C0 50 E8 B7
                                          1574:0008   23 83 C4 04 2B C0 50 B8
    SP 0FFF     SI 0000      IP 0000       1574:0010   03 00 50 8D 86 78 FF 50
    BP 0000     DI 0000                    1574:0018   E8 17 FC 83 C4 06 8B F0
    SS 1574     DS 1574      CS 2100        1574:0020   0B F6 74 03 E9 CE 00 E8
 SP+SS 1673F  SI+DS 15740    ES 1574        1574:0028   29 3B 89 86 76 FF 3D 61
 BP+SS 15740  DI+DS 15740  IP+CS 21000      1574:0030   00 74 5D 3D 62 00 74 05
 STATUS FLAGS 7206 0111001000000110         1574:0038   E8 FB 22 EB 11 E8 DD FD
                        ODITSZ A P C        1574:0040   89 46 F8 89 56 FA 2B C0
 2100:0000 2B4353       SUB   AX,[BP+DI+5   1574:0048   89 46 FE 89 46 FC B8 FF
 3H]
 SEG 2100:   08 19 2A 3B 4C 5D 6E 7F                    1574: STACK
    FFE8    66 6C 61 67 00 00 00 00        f l a g . . . .      0FFF
    FFF0    00 00 00 00 09 00 01 31        . . . . . . . 1
    FFF8    61 62 63 64 65 66 67 68        a b c d e f g h
    0000   >2B 43 53 53 54 41 54 55        + C S S T A T U
    0008    53 20 46 4C 41 47 53 00        S   F L A G S .
    0010    4F 44 49 54 53 5A 20 41        O D I T S Z   A
    0018    20 50 20 43 00 30 38 20        P   C . 0 8

                                          / : Command      > : Go To Memory
                                          Use Cursor Keys to Scroll thru Memory
```

Figure 3.6 The address 2100:0000 contains the value 2B

```
        8086 Microprocessor TUTOR          Press F7 for Help

    AH AL    BH BL    CH CL     DH DL     DATA SEG    08 19 2A 3B 4C 5D 6E 7F
 AX 00 00  BX 11 C5  CX 00 C5  DX 3A EE   1574:0000   FF 7F 50 2B C0 50 E8 B7
                                          1574:0008   23 83 C4 04 2B C0 50 B8
    SP 0FFF     SI 0000      IP 0000       1574:0010   03 00 50 8D 86 78 FF 50
    BP 0000     DI 0000                    1574:0018   E8 17 FC 83 C4 06 8B F0
    SS 1574     DS 1574      CS 2000        1574:0020   0B F6 74 03 E9 CE 00 E8
 SP+SS 1673F  SI+DS 15740    ES 1574        1574:0028   29 3B 89 86 76 FF 3D 61
 BP+SS 15740  DI+DS 15740  IP+CS 20000      1574:0030   00 74 5D 3D 62 00 74 05
 STATUS FLAGS 7206 0111001000000110         1574:0038   E8 FB 22 EB 11 E8 DD FD
                        ODITSZ A P C        1574:0040   89 46 F8 89 56 FA 2B C0
 2000:1000 2B4353       SUB   AX,[BP+DI+5   1574:0048   89 46 FE 89 46 FC B8 FF
 3H]
 SEG 2000:   08 19 2A 3B 4C 5D 6E 7F                    1574: STACK
    0FE8    45 47 53 50 2B 53 53 53        E G S P + S S S      0FFF
    0FF0    49 2B 44 53 42 50 2B 53        I + D S B P + S
    0FF8    53 44 49 2B 44 53 49 50        S D I + D S I P
    1000   >2B 43 53 53 54 41 54 55        + C S S T A T U
    1008    53 20 46 4C 41 47 53 00        S   F L A G S .
    1010    4F 44 49 54 53 5A 20 41        O D I T S Z   A
    1018    20 50 20 43 00 30 38 20        P   C . 0 8

                                          / : Command      > : Go To Memory
                                          Use Cursor Keys to Scroll thru Memory
```

Figure 3.7 The address 2000:1000 contains the same value 2B as address
2100:0000 in Figure 3.6

Notice that the offset addresses between FFE8H and FFFFH in Figure 3.6 are *not* the same as the corresponding offset addresses in Figure 3.7. This is because the offset addresses 0000H-FFFFH wrap around within a given segment. Thus, for example, the address 2100:FFF8 is the actual address 30FF8:

$$
\begin{array}{r}
2100 \\
\underline{FFF8} \\
30FF8
\end{array}
$$

```
        8086 Microprocessor TUTOR           Press F7 for Help

    AH AL    BH BL    CH CL    DH DL     DATA SEG   08 19 2A 3B 4C 5D 6E 7F
  AX 00 00  BX 11 C5  CX 00 C5  DX 3A EE   1574:0000  FF 7F 50 2B C0 50 E8 B7
                                           1574:0008  23 83 C4 04 2B C0 50 B8
    SP 0FFF     SI 0000     IP 0000        1574:0010  03 00 50 8D 86 78 FF 50
    BP 0000     DI 0000                    1574:0018  E8 17 FC 83 C4 06 8B F0
    SS 1574     DS 1574     CS 30FF        1574:0020  0B F6 74 03 E9 CE 00 E8
  SP+SS 1673F  SI+DS 15740  ES 1574        1574:0028  29 3B 89 86 76 FF 3D 61
  BP+SS 15740  DI+DS 15740  IP+CS 30FF0    1574:0030  00 74 5D 3D 62 00 74 05
  STATUS FLAGS 7206 0111001000000110       1574:0038  E8 FB 22 EB 11 E8 DD FD
                      ODITSZ A P C         1574:0040  89 46 F8 89 56 FA 2B C0
  30FF:0008 61          ???                1574:0048  89 46 FE 89 46 FC B8 FF

  SEG 30FF:  08 19 2A 3B 4C 5D 6E 7F                      1574: STACK
      FFF0  00 00 00 00 00 00 00 00     . . . . . . . .      0FFF
      FFF8  00 00 00 00 00 00 00 00     . . . . . . . .
      0000  00 00 00 00 09 00 01 31     . . . . . . . 1
      0008 >61 62 63 64 65 66 67 68     a b c d e f g h
      0010  10 00 10 00 69 6E 69 31     . . . . i n i 1
      0018  3A 09 63 61 6C 6C 09 69     : . c a l l . i
      0020  6E 69 74 32 00 00 00 00     n i t 2 . . . .

                                        / : Command    > : Go To Memory
                                        Use Cursor Keys to Scroll thru Memory
```

Figure 3.8   The address 30FF:0008 contains the same value 61 as address 2100:FFF8 in Figure 3.6

On the other hand, the address 2000:0FF8 is the actual address 20FF8:

$$
\begin{array}{r}
2000 \\
\underline{0FF8} \\
20FF8
\end{array}
$$

Verify that the value 61 (or whatever value is in your computer) shown stored at 2100:FFF8 in Figure 3.6 is really stored at address 30FF8. Note that this address is outside the segment starting at 2000 shown in Figure 3.7. Go to a segment starting at 30FF and note that address 30FF:0008 is the same as address 2100:FFF8 as shown in Figures 3.6 and 3.8.

3.4 YOUR FIRST COMPUTER PROGRAM

We have seen how data are stored in the 8086 registers and in memory. As we saw in Section 3.1 the other two basic functions of a computer are to move data from one place to another and to perform certain arithmetic and logical operations. We will illustrate these functions by executing the simple program shown in Figure 3.9, which is a sample of a typical assembly language program listing.

```
0000   B8 34 12          mov  ax,1234h
0003   8B D8             mov  bx,ax
0005   F7 D8             neg  ax
0007   03 C3             add  ax,bx
0009   F7 D3             not  bx
000B   CC                int  3
```

Figure 3.9 Your first sample program

The numbers on the left side of Figure 3.9 are the offset addresses at which the first byte of each instruction in the program is stored. This address is followed by the bytes that make up each instruction. The assembly language instructions themselves are given on the right-hand side of Figure 3.9. For example, the instruction *mov ax,1234h* is stored in memory starting at offset address 0000 as the three bytes *B8 34 12*. The first byte is the opcode for the instruction "move into *ax* the two following bytes." Note that the 16-bit value 1234H is stored in memory low-byte first; that is, the low-byte 34 is stored at address 0001 and the high-byte 12 is stored at address 0002. This is the way that Intel always stores 16-bit values in memory — low-byte first. (Incidentally, the Motorola microprocessors do just the opposite — storing the high-byte first.)

It is easy to enter this program into memory using the TUTOR monitor. This can be done by using the command /M. Go to offset address 0000 within the current segment. Then type /M. This will produce the following message on the command line:

```
MEMORY CHANGE:   H A
```

You have two choices at this point. You can enter *hex* data by pressing key *H*, or you can enter ASCII data by pressing key *A*. We will consider ASCII data in the next section. For now, press key *H*. The message *ENTER HEX VALUES* will appear on the command line. Type the bytes making up the program in Figure 3.9, namely

```
B8 34 12 8B D8 F7 D8 03 C3 F7 D3 CC
```

Note that you do not have to type a space between each byte. Each time you type a byte it appears on the entry line and is stored in the memory location pointed to by the position cursor. The position cursor is then automatically advanced to the next memory location and a space is added on the entry line. You can enter as many hex bytes as you want. When you come to the end of the entry line, it will automatically clear and start again at the beginning of the line. When you finish entering hex values just press *Enter*. Pressing any non-hex key while entering hex values will clear the command line, sound a beep, and return to the TUTOR monitor.

After you have entered these program bytes into memory move the position cursor back to offset address 0000 by pressing the *Home* key. Then type */UP*. This will disassemble the code you just typed in and display the program in the upper-right part of the screen as shown in Figure 3.10. This will verify that you typed in all the bytes correctly. Note also that the first instruction pointed to by the position cursor is disassembled directly above the memory display near the center of the screen.

You can execute this instruction by pressing function key *F1*. Do it. Note that the 16-bit value 1234H is moved from the two bytes following the opcode into register *AX* and the position cursor moves to the next instruction at offset address 0003 as shown in Figure 3.11. The code for this next instruction is disassembled and the instruction *MOV BX,AX* is displayed directly above the memory guide near the center of the screen.

```
8086 Microprocessor TUTOR            Press F7 for Help


     AH AL      BH BL      CH CL      DH DL
  AX 00 00  BX 11 C5   CX 00 C5   DX 3A EE    1574:0000 B83412        MOV    AX,1234H
                                              1574:0003 8BD8          MOV    BX,AX
     SP 0FFF      SI 0000      IP 0003        1574:0005 F7D8          NEG    AX
     BP 0000      DI 0000                     1574:0007 03C3          ADD    AX,BX
     SS 1574      DS 1574      CS 1574        1574:0009 F7D3          NOT    BX
  SP+SS 1673F  SI+DS 15740     ES 1574        1574:000B CC            INT3
  BP+SS 15740  DI+DS 15740  IP+CS 15743       1574:000C 2BC0          SUB    AX,AX
  STATUS FLAGS 7246 0111001001000110          1574:000E 50            PUSH   AX
                     ODITSZ A P C             1574:000F B80300        MOV    AX,0003H
  1574:0000 B83412          MOV   AX,1234H    1574:0012 50            PUSH   AX

  SEG 1574:    08 19 2A 3B 4C 5D 6E 7F                                1574: STACK
        FFE8   00 00 00 00 00 00 00 00     . . . . . . . .            0FFF
        FFF0   00 00 00 00 00 00 00 00     . . . . . . . .
        FFF8   00 00 00 00 00 00 00        . . . . . . .
        0000  >B8 34 12 8B D8 F7 D8 03     . 4 . . . . . .
        0008   C3 F7 D3 CC 2B C0 50 B8     . . . . + . P .
        0010   03 00 50 8D 86 78 FF 50     . . P . . x . P
        0018   E8 17 FC 83 C4 06 8B F0     . . . . . . . .

                                           / : Command      > : Go To Memory
  _____     Use Cursor Keys to Scroll thru Memory
```

Figure 3.10 /UP will disassemble the code at the position cursor

This second instruction *MOV BX,AX* moves the contents of the register *AX* to the register *BX*. To execute this instruction, press function key *F1* again. Note that *BX* now contains the value 1234H. The next instruction *NEG AX* will take the two's complement of *AX* and leave the result in *AX*. The value in *AX* is 1234H. What will its two's complement be? Press function key *F1* and see if you predicted the correct value. Remember from Chapter 2 that if you add the two's complement of a 16-bit hex number to the number itself you should get 10000H. The instruction *ADD AX,BX* will add the original number in *BX* to the two's complement of that number in *AX* and leave the sum in *AX*. Press function key *F1* to execute this next instruction. Note that the value in *AX* is now 0000H and the 1 is in the carry bit (the right-most bit in the status flags near the center of the screen). The next instruction is *NOT BX*. This will take the one's complement of the value 1234H that is in *BX*. Execute this instruction by pressing *F1*. What value do you get in *BX*? How is this value related to the two's complement?

```
┌─────────────────────────────────────────────────────────────────────────┐
│        8086 Microprocessor TUTOR           Press F7 for Help              │
│                                                                           │
│      AH AL     BH BL     CH CL     DH DL                                  │
│   AX 12 34  BX 11 C5  CX 00 C5  DX 3A EE    1574:0000 B83412    MOV  AX,1234H │
│                                             1574:0003 8BD8      MOV  BX,AX    │
│       SP 0FFF      SI 0000      IP 0003     1574:0005 F7D8      NEG  AX       │
│       BP 0000      DI 0000                  1574:0007 03C3      ADD  AX,BX    │
│       SS 1574      DS 1574      CS 1574     1574:0009 F7D3      NOT  BX       │
│   SP+SS 1673F   SI+DS 15740     ES 1574     1574:000B CC        INT3         │
│   BP+SS 15740   DI+DS 15740  IP+CS 15743    1574:000C 2BC0      SUB  AX,AX    │
│   STATUS FLAGS 7246 0111001001000110        1574:000E 50        PUSH AX       │
│                      ODITSZ A P C           1574:000F B80300    MOV  AX,0003H │
│   1574:0003 8BD8          MOV   BX,AX       1574:0012 50        PUSH AX       │
│                                                                           │
│   SEG 1574:  08 19 2A 3B 4C 5D 6E 7F                     1574: STACK       │
│       FFE8   00 00 00 00 00 00 00 00    . . . . . . . .   0FFF             │
│       FFF0   00 00 00 00 00 00 00 00    . . . . . . . .                   │
│       FFF8   00 00 00 00 00 00 00 00    . . . . . . . .                   │
│       0000   B8 34 12>8B D8 F7 D8 03    . 4 . . . . . .                   │
│       0008   C3 F7 D3 CC 2B C0 50 B8    . . . . + . P .                   │
│       0010   03 00 50 8D 86 78 FF 50    . . P . . x . P                   │
│       0018   E8 17 FC 83 C4 06 8B F0    . . . . . . . .                   │
│   ─────────────────────────────────────  / : Command      > : Go To Memory │
│                                           Use Cursor Keys to Scroll thru Memory │
└─────────────────────────────────────────────────────────────────────────┘
```

Figure 3.11 Press function key F1 to single step an instruction

The last instruction in the program in Figure 3.9 is the software interrupt instruction *INT 3*. This instruction has the opcode *CCH* and produces a breakpoint instruction in TUTOR that will prevent us from single stepping beyond this instruction. We will discuss software interrupts and breakpoints in detail in later chapters.

This simple example has shown us how data can be moved around within a computer and how simple operations such as *ADD*, *NEG* and *NOT* can change the values in a register. In Chapter 4 we will look at some additional instructions and begin to write some simple programs. Before doing that, however, let's look a little closer at our INPUT and OUTPUT blocks in Figure 3.1 and see how we can get characters from the keyboard and display them on the screen.

3.5 KEYBOARD INPUT AND SCREEN OUTPUT

I/O in the PC can be carried out at three different levels. At the lowest level the program controls the hardware directly. This often involves programming certain peripheral chips that are part of the hardware system. We will look at some examples of this type of programming in later chapters. At the next higher level we can use the built-in BIOS ROM routines for accessing the hardware. These are written in the form of software interrupts that are easy to access. The highest level of I/O processing is to use the various DOS commands that are part of the disk operating system. Each of these levels of processing has its advantages and disadvantages. The lowest level is the most difficult to program but gives you the most control over the hardware and the most potential speed of execution of your program. It is, however, very dependent on the particular type of hardware you are using and therefore the programs are the least portable from one type of computer to another. At the other end of the spectrum the idea of an operating system such as DOS is to hide all these grubby details from the user and to provide a consistent I/O interface that a programmer can use on potentially different types of hardware. The problem with some of the DOS I/O routines is that they hide too much from the user and you often can't do exactly what you want to do. Also many of the DOS routines do a lot of error checking (good) which makes their execution somewhat slow and sluggish (bad).

In the middle level are the BIOS ROM routines which are relatively fast and generally give you access to what you need. While different PCs and PC compatibles may use different BIOS ROMs they all perform the same basic I/O functions by calling the same software interrupts. Thus, programs that call the BIOS ROM routines are generally just as portable (from one PC compatible to another) as those that call the DOS routines. We will show you how to call both types of I/O routines. We will use the DOS routines to do all of our disk I/O. However, we will generally use the BIOS routines for keyboard and screen I/O because it will give us better control over exactly what we want to do. Before looking at how to get data from the keyboard or to the screen let us first look at the form that these data usually take.

ASCII Data

The name ASCII stands for *American Standard Code for Information Interchange*. In this standard code a certain 7-bit binary number is associated with each character (letter, digit, or special character). This code is used extensively throughout the industry for sending information from one computer to another or for sending data from a terminal to a computer. The hex values for the ASCII codes of all characters are shown in Table 3.2. To use this chart read the first hex digit across the top and the second hex digit along the left side of the chart. For example, the ASCII code for A is 41H.

Note that only the hex digits 0 – 7 are listed across the top of the chart. This means that bit 7 is assumed to be zero. This is because the standard ASCII code uses only seven bits (0 – 6). The eighth bit (bit 7) is often used as an error checking parity bit when sending data from a terminal to a computer.

The IBM PC uses an enhanced ASCII code that is slightly different from the standard. The ASCII codes for the characters that are displayed on the IBM PC are shown in Table 3.3.

The characters corresponding to the ASCII codes stored in the 56 memory bytes on the TUTOR screen are displayed to the right of the memory section at the bottom of the screen. Typing */A* will toggle these ASCII characters on and off off. You can enter ASCII codes directly into memory by typing */MA*. The message

```
PRESS ASCII KEY
```

will be displayed on the command line. Press keys *A*, *B*, *C*, *D*, and *E*. Note that the normal ASCII codes for the lowercase letters *a–d* (61H-65H) are stored in consecutive memory locations and the ASCII characters *a–d* are displayed to the right of the memory display. They are also displayed on the entry line (the bottom line of the screen).

Table 3.2								
Standard ASCII codes								
Dec	→	0	16	32	48	64	80	96	112
↓	Hex	0	1	2	3	4	5	6	7
0	0	NUL	DLE	blank	0	@	P		p
1	1	SOH	DC1	!	1	A	Q	a	q
2	2	STX	DC2	"	2	B	R	b	r
3	3	ETX	DC3	#	3	C	S	c	s
4	4	EOT	DC4	$	4	D	T	d	t
5	5	ENQ	NAK	%	5	E	U	e	u
6	6	ACK	SYN	&	6	F	V	f	v
7	7	BEL	ETB	'	7	G	W	g	w
8	8	BS	CAN	(	8	H	X	h	x
9	9	HT	EM	)	9	I	Y	i	y
10	A	LF	SUB	*	:	J	Z	j	z
11	B	VT	ESC	+	;	K	[	k	{
12	C	FF	FS	,	<	L	\	l	l
13	D	CR	GS	-	=	M	]	m	}
14	E	SO	RS	.	>	N	^	n	~
15	F	SI	US	/	?	O	_	o	DEL

You can enter IBM PC ASCII codes into particular memory locations associated with the video screen. As an example, if you're using the monochrome display, go to memory location B000:0000 by typing >*SB000*. If you're using a graphics monitor (such as VGA), go to memory location B800:0000 by typing >*SB800*. Memory location B0000 is the first memory location of the *video RAM* for the monochrome display and memory location B8000 is the first memory location of the video RAM for a graphics monitor display. Every two bytes in the video RAM correspond to a particular location on the video screen. The first byte of each pair contains the ASCII code for the character that is currently being displayed at that location on the screen. The second byte of each pair contains the attribute of the displayed character. The attribute byte determines if the character is underlined, blinking, or displayed in reverse video or increased intensity. These details will be described in Chapter 7.

Memory location B000:0000 for the monochrome display or B800:0000 for the graphics monitor display corresponds to the upper left-hand corner of the video screen. Note that it contains the hex value 20. From Table 3.3 you see that this is the ASCII code for a blank (black), which is what is being displayed at the upper left-hand corner of the screen. You can change this value by typing /*MA*. The message *PRESS ASCII KEY* is displayed on the command line. Press key *A*. Note that the normal ASCII codes for a lowercase *a*, 61H, is stored in memory location B000:0000 (or B800:0000) which causes the *a* to be displayed in the upper left-hand corner of the screen. Note that it is displayed in normal video which is controlled by the byte at address B000:0001.

Table 3.3

IBM PC ASCII Codes

DECIMAL VALUE →		0	16	32	48	64	80	96	112	128	144	160	176	192	208	224	240
HEXADECIMAL VALUE →		0	1	2	3	4	5	6	7	8	9	A	B	C	D	E	F
0	0	BLANK (NULL)	►	BLANK (SPACE)	0	@	P	`	p	Ç	É	á	▓	└	╨	∞	≡
1	1	☺	◄	!	1	A	Q	a	q	ü	æ	í	▒			β	±
2	2	☻	↕	"	2	B	R	b	r	é	Æ	ó	█			Γ	≥
3	3	♥	‼	#	3	C	S	c	s	â	ô	ú				π	≤
4	4	♦	¶	$	4	D	T	d	t	ä	ö	ñ				Σ	∫
5	5	♣	§	%	5	E	U	e	u	à	ò	Ñ				σ	
6	6	♠	▬	&	6	F	V	f	v	å	û	ª				µ	÷
7	7	•	↨	'	7	G	W	g	w	ç	ù	º				τ	≈
8	8	◘	↑	(	8	H	X	h	x	ê	ÿ	¿				Φ	°
9	9	○	↓	)	9	I	Y	i	y	ë	Ö	⌐				Θ	•
10	A	◙	→	*	:	J	Z	j	z	è	Ü	¬				Ω	·
11	B	♂	←	+	;	K	[	k	{	ï	¢	½				δ	√
12	C	♀	∟	,	<	L	\	l	|	î	£	¼				∞	ⁿ
13	D	♪	↔	–	=	M	]	m	}	ì	¥	¡				φ	²
14	E	♫	▲	.	>	N	^	n	~	Ä	₧	«				∈	■
15	F	☼	▼	/	?	O	_	o	△	Å	ƒ	»				∩	BLANK

(Reprinted by permission from IBM PC Technical Reference Manual, c 1981 by International Business Machines Corporation)

The *a* is also displayed on the entry line and the position cursor advances to memory location B000:0001 which is the attribute byte 07H for the *a* displayed in the upper left-hand corner of the screen. You can continue to enter ASCII values. For example, type the letter *P* which will change the attribute value to 70H. Note that this causes the displayed *a* in the upper left-hand corner of the screen to be displayed in reverse video. Continue to type *b p c p*. Note that the letters *abc* appear in reverse video on the top line of the screen as the ASCII codes and attribute value for each letter are stored in memory locations B000:0000-B000:0005 (or B800:0000-B800:0005). We will take a closer look at how characters are displayed on the screen in Chapter 7.

Keyboard Input

A built-in BIOS software interrupt routine can be used to read the keyboard. The following two instructions will wait for a key to be pressed and then return the ASCII code of the key in AL and the scan code of the key in AH.

```
B4 00  MOV  AH,0
CD 16  INT  16H
```

The scan codes and ASCII codes associated with each key are given in Table 3.4. The program shown in Figure 3.12 can be used to verify all of the scan and ASCII codes in Table 3.4. Enter this program at offset address 0000 using /MH. This time single step through this program using function key *F2* instead of *F1*. When you single step the instruction *INT 16H* using function key *F2* the program will go and execute the entire BIOS routine and then return to offset address 0004. However, when executing the BIOS routine the program will be waiting for you to press a key. Therefore, after you press *F2* when the position cursor is at offset address 0002 press any other key on the keyboard. The value of the scan code for that key will be stored in *AH* and the value of the ASCII code will be stored in *AL*. The position cursor will move to the *JMP KEYIN* instruction which will just jump back to offset address 0000 when you press *F2* again. Keep single stepping through this program checking the codes for a number of keys. We will look at keyboard input routines in more detail in Chapter 7.

```
0000   B4 00      KEYIN:   MOV   AH,0
0002   CD 16               INT   16H
0004   EB FA               JMP   KEYIN
```

Figure 3.12 Program to find scan and ASCII codes of any key pressed

Table 3.4			
Keyboard Scan/ASCII Hex Codes			
Function Keys			
	Unshifted	Shifted	Ctrl	Alt
F1	3B/00	54/00	5E/00	68/00
F2	3C/00	55/00	5F/00	69/00
F3	3D/00	56/00	60/00	6A/00
F4	3E/00	57/00	61/00	6B/00
F5	3F/00	58/00	62/00	6C/00
F6	40/00	59/00	63/00	6D/00
F7	41/00	5A/00	64/00	6E/00
F8	42/00	5B/00	65/00	6F/00
F9	43/00	5C/00	66/00	70/00
F10	44/00	5D/00	67/00	71/00
Numeric Keypad	Unshifted	Shifted	Ctrl	Alt
Ins 0	52/00	52/30		
End 1	4F/00	4F/31	75/00	00/01
↓ 2	50/00	50/32		00/02
PgDn 3	51/00	51/33	76/00	00/03
← 4	4B/00	4B/34	73/00	00/04
5		4C/35		00/05
→ 6	4D/00	4D/36	74/00	00/06
Home 7	47/00	47/37	77/00	00/07
↑ 8	48/00	48/38		00/08
PgUp 9	49/00	49/39	84/00	00/09
–	4A/2D	4A/2D		
+	4E/2B	4E/2B		
Del .	53/00	53/2E		

Table 3.4 (continued)

Keyboard Scan/ASCII Hex Codes

Key	Unshifted	Shifted	Ctrl	Alt
A	1E/61	1E/41	1E/01	1E/00
B	30/62	30/42	30/02	30/00
C	2E/63	2E/43	2E/03	2E/00
D	20/64	20/44	20/04	20/00
E	12/65	12/45	12/05	12/00
F	21/66	21/46	21/06	21/00
G	22/67	22/47	22/07	22/00
H	23/68	23/48	23/08	23/00
I	17/69	17/49	17/09	17/00
J	24/6A	24/4A	24/0A	24/00
K	25/6B	25/4B	25/0B	25/00
L	26/6C	26/4C	26/0C	26/00
M	32/6D	32/4D	32/0D	32/00
N	31/6E	31/4E	31/0E	31/00
O	18/6F	18/4F	18/0F	18/00
P	19/70	19/50	19/10	19/00
Q	10/71	10/51	10/11	10/00
R	13/72	13/52	13/12	13/00
S	1F/73	1F/53	1F/13	1F/00
T	14/74	14/54	14/14	14/00
U	16/75	16/55	16/15	16/00
V	2F/76	2F/56	2F/16	2F/00
W	11/77	11/57	11/17	11/00
X	2D/78	2D/58	2D/18	2D/00
Y	15/79	15/59	15/19	15/00
Z	2C/7A	2C/5A	2C/1A	2C/00
Space	39/20	39/20	39/20	39/20
ESC	01/1B	01/1B	01/1B	
1 !	02/31	02/21		78/00
2 @	03/32	03/40	03/00	79/00
3 #	04/33	04/23		7A/00
4 $	05/34	05/24		7B/00
5 %	06/35	06/25		7C/00
6 ^	07/36	07/5E	07/1E	7D/00
7 &	08/37	08/26		7E/00
8 *	09/38	09/2A		7F/00
9 (	0A/39	0A/38		80/00
0)	0B/30	0B/29		81/00
- _	0C/2D	0C/5F	0C/1F	82/00
= +	0D/3D	0D/2B		83/00
[{	1A/5B	1A/7B	1A/1B	
] }	1B/5D	1B/7D	1B/1D	
backspace	0E/08	0E/08	0E/7F	
; :	27/3B	27/3A		
' "	28/27	28/22		
` ~	29/60	29/7E		
, <	33/2C	33/3C		
. >	34/2E	34/3E		
/ ?	35/2F	35/3F		
Enter	1C/0D	1C/0D	1C/0A	
Tab	0F/09	0F/00		
\ |	2B/5C	2B/7C	2B/1C	

Screen Output

We have already seen that data is stored on the screen by writing an ASCII code and an attribute byte to a particular location in the video RAM. This is an example of low-level I/O. We can also write to the screen by using BIOS or DOS calls. We will look in more detail at doing screen I/O in Chapter 7 where we will write a series of very useful subroutines that will allow you to do whatever you want on the screen. For now we will give you two DOS calls and one BIOS call that will allow you to get characters stored on the screen.

To print a character on the screen you can use the following DOS routine:

DOS Character Output	
DL = ASCII code of character	
B4 02	MOV AH,2
CD 21	INT 21H

This DOS routine will print the character in *DL* at the current cursor position on the screen and increment the cursor position. The only question is: where is the cursor to begin with? If you want to display characters at a particular location on the screen you must first set the cursor to that location. You can do this by calling the following BIOS routine:

Set Cursor	
DH = row	DL = column
B7 00	MOV BH,0
B4 02	MOV AH,2
CD 10	INT 10H

Finally, to print a string of characters on the screen the ASCII codes of the character string are stored in memory starting at *DS:DX* and the string must be terminated with a *$* character (ASCII code 24H). Then you execute the following code:

String Output	
$ terminated string at DS:DX	
B4 09	MOV AH,9
CD 21	INT 21H

As an example of using these routines, go to offset address 0000 and enter the word *Hello$* by typing */MA* followed by *Hello$*. Note that the data segment *DS* is the same as *CS* and your current segment, *SEG*. Then enter the program shown in Figure 3.13 starting at offset address 0008h. Verify that you typed it in correctly by pressing */UP* to disassemble the code. This program should set the cursor at the beginning of the bottom line on the screen and then print the word *Hello* there. To execute this entire program move the position cursor to offset address 0008h and type */EG*. This will execute the program and display the word *Hello* as shown in Figure 3.14.

```
0008   B7 00           mov bh,2        set the cursor
000A   B2 00           mov dl,0        at column 0
000C   B6 18           mov dh,24       row 24 = 18h
000E   B4 02           mov ah,2
0010   CD 10           int 10h
0012   BA 00 00        mov dx,0        set string address to 0000h
0015   B4 09           mov ah,9        DOS string output function
0017   CD 21           int 21h
0019   CC              int 3           stop program with breakpoint
```

Figure 3.13 Program to print string at DS:0000 on bottom line of screen

```
        8086 Microprocessor TUTOR        Press F7 for Help

    AH AL    BH BL     CH CL     DH DL
 AX 09 24  BX 00 C5  CX 00 C5  DX 00 00   1574:0008 B700      MOV   BH,00H
                                          1574:000A B200      MOV   DL,00H
    SP 0FFF     SI 0000     IP 0019       1574:000C B618      MOV   DH,18H
    BP 0000     DI 0000                   1574:000E B402      MOV   AH,02H
    SS 1574     DS 1574     CS 1574       1574:0010 CD10      INT   10H
 SP+SS 1673F SI+DS 15740     ES 1574      1574:0012 BA0000    MOV   DX,0000H
 BP+SS 15740 DI+DS 15740  IP+CS 15759     1574:0015 B409      MOV   AH,09H
 STATUS FLAGS 7246 0111001001000110       1574:0017 CD21      INT   21H
                   ODITSZ A P C           1574:0019 CC        INT3
 1574:0019 CC          INT3               1574:001A 42        INC   DX

 SEG 1574:   08 19 2A 3B 4C 5D 6E 7F                1574: STACK
     0000   48 65 6C 6C 6F 24 D8 03    Hello$..      0FFF
     0008   B7 00 B2 00 B6 18 B4 02    ........
     0010   CD 10 BA 00 00 B4 09 CD    ........
     0018   21>CC 42 B4 02 CD 21 CC    !.B...!.
     0020   0B F6 74 03 E9 CE 00 E8    ..t.....
     0028   29 3B 89 86 76 FF 3D 61    );..v.=a
     0030   00 74 5D 3D 62 00 74 05    .t]=b.t.

                                     / : Command    > : Go To Memory
 Hello                               Use Cursor Keys to Scroll thru Memory
```

Figure 3.14 TUTOR display after executing the program in Figure 3.13

PROGRAMMING PROBLEMS

Problem 3.1 – 8086 Registers and Memory

a. Run the TUTOR monitor by typing *tutor*. Use the */R* command described in Section 3.2 to set the 8086 registers to the following hex values:

```
AX = 1234   BX = 5678   CX = 89AB   DX = CDEF
SI = 1111   DI = 2222
```

b. Go to offset address 1000 within the current segment by typing *>O1000*. Enter eight bytes into memory by typing */MH* followed by

```
11 22 33 44 55 66 77 88 <Enter>
```

c. Enter the ASCII codes for letters *A – H* in the next eight memory locations (offset addresses 1008 – 100F) by typing */MA* followed by

```
A B C D E F G H <Enter>
```

Print the TUTOR screen on the printer by pressing *Shift-Print Screen*.

d. Go to a new segment (by typing *>S....*) in which the data you have just typed in starting at offset address 1000 will be stored at offset address 0000. Print the TUTOR screen on the printer. Go to the segment in which you can find your data at offset address 100. Print the TUTOR screen on the printer.

e. Enter the bytes of the program shown in Figure 3.9 starting at offset address 0000. Move the cursor to the beginning of the program (by pressing the *Home* key), disassemble the code by typing */UP*, and then single step each instruction by pressing function key *F1*. Observe the registers after you execute each instruction. After executing all of the instructions print the TUTOR screen on the printer.

f. Go to the segment address of the video RAM in your computer (either B000 or B800) and write the inverse video letters *abc* in the upper-right corner of the screen by typing */MA* followed by

```
a p b p c p <Enter>
```

Print the TUTOR screen on the printer.

g. Type in the program shown in Figure 3.12 starting at offset address 0000. Single step through the program using function key *F2*. When you execute the instruction at offset address 0002 you will need to press any key to continue. The scan code and ASCII code for this key will be stored in *AH* and *AL*. Check several of the scan codes and ASCII codes given in Table 3.4.

h. Modify the program in Figure 3.13 so as to display your first name on the bottom row of the screen starting in column 10. Print the TUTOR screen on the printer.

Problem 3.2 – TUTOR Commands

a. Go to memory location 2000:0000 and enter the eight hex values

```
11  22  33  44  55  66  77  88
```

Transfer these eight bytes to locations 2C00:0FF8 – 2C00:0FFF using the TUTOR command /T described in Appendix B. Transfer the same bytes to locations 2D00:1010 - 2D00:1017.

b. Go to memory location 2E00:0003 and insert the three bytes *AA BB CC* between 33 and 44 using the TUTOR command /I (see Appendix B).

c. Delete the three bytes you inserted in step 2) using the TUTOR command /D (see Appendix B).

d. Save the eight bytes from locations 2E00:0000 - 2E00:0007 on a disk using the TUTOR command /SS described in Appendix B. Type /QD to exit to DOS and list the directory (*dir*) to see the file you saved. Run TUTOR again and load the eight bytes you saved at memory location 2E00:0100 using the /SL command (see Appendix B).

e. When you first run TUTOR observe the value stored in *BX* and *CX*. The value in *BX* is the segment address that contains the TUTOR program. The value in *CX* is the starting offset address of TUTOR. Go to this starting address and press /UP. The beginning of the tutor program will be disassembled on the right side of the screen. Now press /LP. This will disassemble a page of code on the entire screen. To print disassembled code on the printer type /P. Press P and a page of disassembled code will be printed. You can use the command /PB to print a specified block of code.

EXERCISES

Exercise 3.1

To change the value in the index register *SI*, type */R I S*. Then enter a 4-digit hexadecimal value. To change the value in the base pointer register *BP*, type */R P B*, and enter a 4-digit hexadecimal value.

Change the contents of the following registers to the indicated hex values:

```
AX = 003F        SI = 4444        SS = 0F13
BX = 142C        DI = 5555        DS = 0413
CX = 7777        SP = 0FFF        ES = 0F11
DX = 000F        BP = ABCD        IP = 1000
```

Exercise 3.2

To change the value in the status register *SF*, type */R F*. Then enter a 4-digit *hexadecimal value*. Note that this hex value will be displayed on the screen as both a 4-digit hexadecimal number and as the corresponding 16-bit *binary value*.

What 4-digit hexadecimal number must you enter on the entry line in order for each of the following 16 bits to be displayed in the status register *SF*? Verify your answers by changing the contents of *SF* on the screen to each of the following values:

```
a) 01110010 11000011
b) 11101000 10101010
c) 00011111 00001111
d) 10110100 11101100
e) 11001101 11001100
f) 10100101 10101110
g) 00111001 01010101
h) 00000110 00000011
```

Exercise 3.3

What 16-bit binary number is equivalent to each of the following hexadecimal numbers? Verify your answers by changing the contents of the status register to each of these values and noting its binary value on the screen.

```
a) 65AB        e) 9DA4
b) 0A0B        f) C3E2
c) 4872        g) F2AC
d) BE17        h) 1703
```

Exercise 3.4

Fill in the missing offset addresses.

```
a. 152F:29D2 = 1000: _____
b. 0300:155A = 0000: _____
c. 1380:FFFF = 2000: _____
```

Exercise 3.5

Fill in the missing segment addresses.

```
a. 117F:49C3 = _____ :3333
b. 1728:3821 = _____ :4321
c. 0E10:0300 = _____ :0000
```

CHAPTER 4

8086 Instructions

In the last chapter we took a look inside the 8086 and saw how basic instructions are executed. In this chapter we will take a closer look at some of the 8086 instructions that we will need to understand before we can begin to write our own programs. All 8086 instructions are related in one way or another to the register structure that we looked at in the last chapter. Therefore, we will begin this chapter with a closer look at functions of these 8086 registers. In this chapter you will learn:

- The function of each of the 8086 registers including the meaning of the bits in the status register
- How the instructions *MOV* and *XCHG* can transfer and exchange data between two registers
- How the 8086 shifting and rotate instructions work
- To use the immediate and register addressing modes
- The basic arithmetic instructions
- The basic logical instructions

4.1 A CLOSER LOOK AT THE 8086 REGISTERS

In the last chapter we saw that the 8086 microprocessor contains the set of registers shown in Figure 4.1. We will take a closer look at each of these register groups in this section.

The General Registers

The registers *AX*, *BX*, *CX*, and *DX* are general purpose 16-bit registers. The upper halves of each of these registers are called *AH*, *BH*, *CH*, and *DH*. These are 8-bit registers that can be accessed directly. Similarly, the lower halves of these registers are called *AL*, *BL*, *CL*, *DL*. These registers are shown in Figure 4.1. Although all of the general registers can be used interchangeably for many operations, each of the registers are used for certain specific purposes. This is what gives rise to the names *accumulator, base, count,* and *data* for the registers *A X , B X ,*

CX, and DX shown in Figure 4.1. All general registers are used for storing intermediate results. When you want to move a byte (8 bits) or word (16 bits) from one memory location to another you must first load the byte or word into one of the registers such as *AX* (with a *MOV* instruction) and then store the byte in the other memory location (with a second *MOV* instruction). The details of how to address various memory locations will be described in Chapter 6.

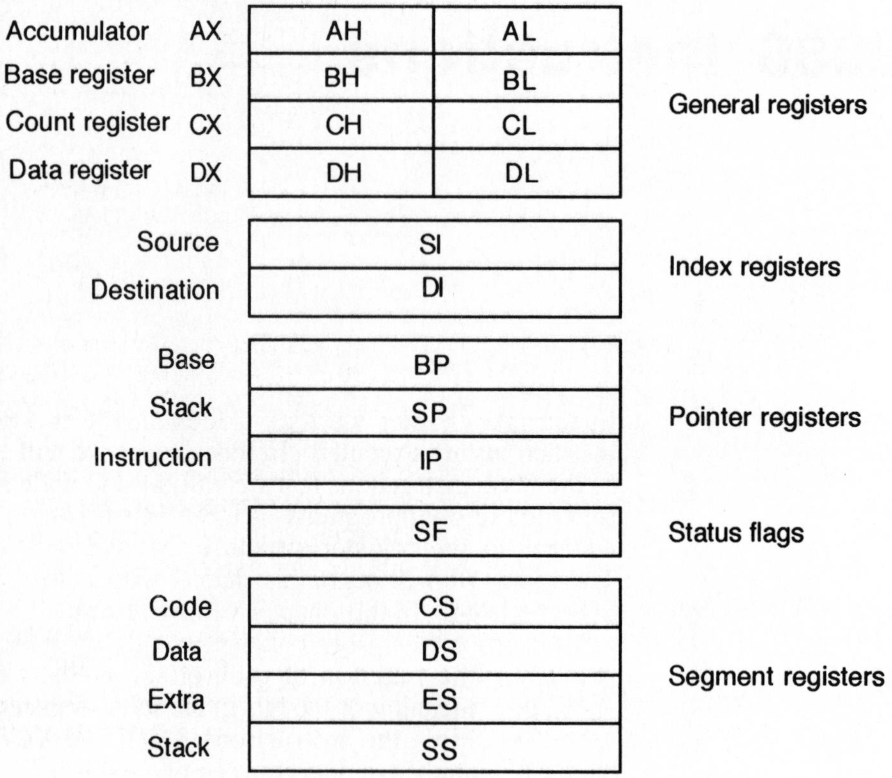

Accumulator	AX	AH	AL
Base register	BX	BH	BL
Count register	CX	CH	CL
Data register	DX	DH	DL

General registers

Source	SI
Destination	DI

Index registers

Base	BP
Stack	SP
Instruction	IP

Pointer registers

SF

Status flags

Code	CS
Data	DS
Extra	ES
Stack	SS

Segment registers

Figure 4.1 The 8086 registers

Index Registers, SI and DI

The index registers *SI* and *DI* are 16-bit registers that are used for several different purposes. They can be used in a manner similar to the general registers for temporary storage when moving 16-bit data to and from memory using the *MOV* instruction.

The main use of the index registers *SI* and *DI* is in conjunction with various modes of addressing. An addressing mode is what specifies where a particular data item is to be found. For example, the instruction *MOV AX,1234H* that we used in the last chapter is an example of the *immediate addressing mode*. This means that the data 1234H immediately follows the opcode in memory. The instruction *NEG AX* that we also used in the last chapter is an example of the *register addressing mode*. This means that the data of interest is in the register *AX*. One of the most important addressing modes associated with the index registers *SI* and *DI* is register indirect addressing. For example, the instruction

MOV AL,[SI]

means move into *AL* the byte in the data segment at the offset address that is in *SI*. We say that *SI* is pointing to a byte in the data segment. We will look in detail at this and related addressing modes in Chapter 6.

Pointer Registers

Stack Pointer, SP and Base Pointer, BP

The stack is a region of memory that is set aside for storing temporary data. The stack pointer *SP* is a 16-bit register that contains the offset address of the top of the stack. The actual address is found by adding the segment address stored in the stack segment register, *SS*. The stack is used by the 8086 to save the return address when a subroutine is called. It is also used to save register values when an interrupt is called. Subroutines will be discussed in Chapter 5 and interrupts will be described in Chapters 5 and 11.

The stack can be used to save the contents of any register using the *PUSH* instruction. Data are removed from the stack using the *POP* instruction. Examples of using these instructions together with a discussion of subroutines will be given in Chapter 5 where the operation of the stack will be described in detail.

The base pointer, *BP*, is a 16-bit register that is used to access data in the stack segment. The stack segment register, *SS*, is used to find the actual address associated with an offset address in *BP*. Addressing modes involving *BP*, including the method of passing subroutine parameters on the stack, will be discussed in Chapter 6.

The Instruction Pointer, IP

The instruction pointer, *IP*, is a 16-bit register that contains the offset address of the next instruction to be executed. When an instruction is executed the instruction pointer is automatically incremented the number of times needed to point to the next instruction. Instructions may be from one to six bytes long. Therefore, the program counter may be incremented by 1 to 6 depending upon the instruction being executed.

You can change the value stored in the instruction pointer by pressing */RPI* and then entering a new four-digit hex value. Normally, however, the instruction pointer will automatically change itself as a program is executed.

For example, go back to the last chapter and reenter the program given in Figure 3.9. As you single step through this program by pressing function key *F1* note how the instruction pointer, *IP*, is automatically incremented to the offset address of the next instruction to be executed.

The *NOP* instruction (opcode 90) does nothing except advance the instruction pointer by one. The *NOP* instruction takes three clock cycles to execute and it is sometimes used when short delays of a few microseconds are required.

The Status Register

The 8086 has a status register that contains six status flags and three control flags. The six status flags are the carry flag (C) , the zero flag (Z), the sign flag (S), the overflow flag (O), the auxiliary flag (A) and the parity flag (P). The three control flags are the interrupt enable flag (I), the direction flag (D), and the trap flag (T). Each flag is one bit in the status register. The location of each flag is shown in Figure 4.2 and the value of each flag is displayed in the status register shown near the center of the TUTOR screen.

You can change the contents of the status register by typing */RF* and then entering a *hexadecimal* value. For example, if you enter 9C1 then the bit pattern 0000100111000001 will be displayed in the status register. We will now look at the meaning of each flag.

Carry (C)

The carry flag is bit 0 of the status register. It can be considered to be an extension of a register, or memory location operated on by an instruction. The carry bit is changed by three different types of instructions. The first are arithmetic instructions such as addition and subtraction. These include *ADD* and *ADC* (add with carry) or *SUB* and *SBB* (subtract with borrow) described in Section 4.4 and compare instructions (*CMP*) described in Chapter 5.

The second group of instructions that can change the carry bit are the shifting and rotating instructions (such as *SAL*, *SHL*, *RCL*, *RCR*) that will be described in Section 4.3.

Finally, the carry bit can be set to 1 with the instruction *STC* (set carry, opcode = F9), cleared to zero with the instruction *CLC* (clear carry, opcode = F8), and complemented with the instruction *CMC* (complement carry, opcode = F5).

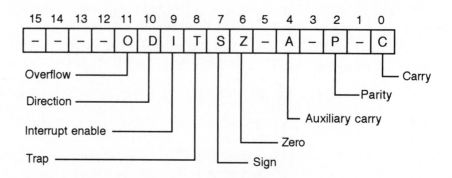

Figure 4.2 The status register

Zero Flag (Z)

The zero flag is bit 6 of the status register. This flag is set to 1 when the result of an instruction is zero. If the result of an instruction is not zero, the *Z* flag is cleared to zero. This *Z* flag is tested by the branching instruction *JE* (jump if equal to zero, $Z = 1$) and *JNE* (jump if not equal to zero, $Z = 0$). We will describe how these branching instructions work in Chapter 5.

Sign Flag (S)

The sign flag is bit 7 of the status register. Negative numbers are stored in 8086 computers using the two's complement representation. In this representation a negative number is indicated when bit 7 (the left-most bit) of a byte is set to 1. When the result of an instruction leaves the sign bit set (bit 7 of a byte or bit 15 of a word), the *S* flag is set to 1. If the result of an instruction is positive, (the sign bit is 0), the *S* flag is cleared to 0. The *S* flag is tested by the branching instruction *JS* (jump on sign, $S = 1$) and *JNS* (jump on not sign, $S = 0$). We will discuss branching instructions in Chapter 5.

Overflow Flag (O)

The overflow flag is bit 11 of the status register. It is set any time the result of a signed (two's complement) operation is out of range. Its relationship to the carry flag will be described in Section 4.4. The *O* flag is tested by the branching instructions *JO* (jump overflow, $O = 1$) and *JNO* (jump on not overflow, $O = 0$). We will discuss branching instructions in Chapter 5.

Interrupt Enable Flag (I)

The interrupt enable flag is bit 9 of the status register. When it is cleared to 0, hardware interrupts entering the *INTR* pin of the microprocessor (pin 18) are masked and the 8086 will not respond to an interrupt. When the *I* flag is set to 1, interrupts are enabled and the 8086 will service hardware interrupts.

The *I* flag is set to 1 with the instruction *STI* (set interrupt enable flag, opcode = FB) and is cleared to zero with the instruction *CLI* (clear interrupt enable flag, opcode = FA). A detailed discussion of interrupts will be given in Chapter 11.

Auxiliary Carry (A)

The auxiliary carry flag is bit 4 of the status register. It contains the carry from bit 3 to bit 4 resulting from an 8-bit addition or subtraction operation. The auxiliary carry flag is used by the microprocessor when performing binary-coded decimal (BCD) addition.

Parity Flag (P)

The parity flag is bit 2 of the status register. It is set to 1 if the low-order 8 bits of the result of an instruction contains an even number of 1 bits. The parity flag will be 0 if an instruction produces an 8-bit result with an odd number of 1 bits.

Direction Flag (D)

The direction flag is bit 10 of the status register. This bit determines whether the index registers *SI* and *DI* are automatically incremented or decremented in certain string manipulation instructions. If $D = 0$, then *SI* and *DI* are incremented. If $D = 1$, then *SI* and *DI* are decremented. These string manipulation instructions will be described in Chapter 6. The *D* flag is cleared to 0 with the instruction *CLD* (clear direction flag, opcode = FC) and is set to 1 with the instruction *STD* (set direction flag, opcode = FD).

Trap Flag (T)

The trap flag is bit 8 of the status register. When set to 1 it will produce an interrupt after a single instruction is executed. This is how the TUTOR monitor executes a single instruction when you press the *F1* key. A description of how this works will be given in Chapter 11.

Segment Registers, CS, DS, SS, ES

In Chapter 3 you saw how an 8086 memory address is made up of two parts: a segment address and an offset address. The TUTOR monitor displays an offset address relative to the segment address displayed on the screen as *SEG*.

The 8086 microprocessor has four registers that contain segment addresses. These are called the code segment register, *CS*, the data segment register, *DS*, the stack segment register, *SS*, and the extra segment register, *ES*. This means that at any instant four different 64 Kbyte segments are defined. These were shown in Figure 3.5 in the last chapter. Note that these four segments may partially, or completely, overlap. For example, if *CS*, *DS*, *ES*, and *SS* all contain the same value, then a single 64 Kbyte segment is defined.

The code segment defined by *CS* contains the program that is being executed. The instruction pointer, *IP*, that points to the next instruction uses the code segment register *CS* to form the actual address of the next instruction.

The data segment defined by *DS* contains data used by the program. Most of the data addressing modes to be described in Chapter 6 use the data segment register to form the effective address of the data.

The segment defined by *SS* contains the stack. The pointer registers, *SP* and *BP*, described above use the stack segment register to form the actual address of the data. A complete discussion of the stack will be given in Chapter 5.

The extra segment defined by *ES* is used for a variety of useful purposes. Sometimes you need to access data that are not properly defined relative to the current data segment. The extra segment register is also used by certain string manipulation instructions to be described in Chapter 6.

4.2 MOVE AND EXCHANGE INSTRUCTIONS

We saw in Chapter 3 that the instructions

```
B8 34 12      MOV AX,1234H
B6 18         MOV DH,24
```

will move the hex value 1234H into *AX* and the decimal value 24 (18H) into *DH*. These are examples of *immediate addressing*. The opcodes B8 and B6 are always used to move 16-bit immediate data into *AX* and 8-bit immediate data into *DH* respectively. The opcodes to move immediate data into the other general registers are given in Table 4.1.

The opcodes in Table 4.1 can be found from the instruction opcode map shown in Table A.2a in Appendix A. The opcodes are read from this table by reading the first hex digit from the left column and the second hex digit from the top row. Note that the row labeled *B* includes all of the instructions shown in Table 4.1. It also includes four additional instructions (opcodes BC – BF) for moving immediate data into the pointer and index registers.

Figure 4.3 defines the *MOV* instruction that can be used to transfer data between any two 8-bit registers or between any two 16-bit registers. The *MOV* instructions in Figure 4.3 are two-byte instructions in which the first byte is the opcode (88 or 8A for 8-bit byte registers and 89 or 8B for 16-bit word registers) and the second byte is a postbyte that defines the two registers involved in the transfer according to Figure 4.3.

Table 4.1
MOV Immediate Data Instructions for General Registers.

Opcode	Instruction	Operation
B0	MOV AL,imm8	imm8-->AL
B1	MOV CL,imm8	imm8-->CL
B2	MOV DL,imm8	imm8-->DL
B3	MOV BL,imm8	imm8-->BL
B4	MOV AH,imm8	imm8-->AH
B5	MOV CH,imm8	imm8-->CH
B6	MOV DH,imm8	imm8-->DH
B7	MOV BH,imm8	imm8-->BH
B8	MOV AX,imm16	imm16-->AX
B9	MOV CX,imm16	imm16-->CX
BA	MOV DX,imm16	imm16-->DX
BB	MOV BX,imm16	imm16-->BX

imm8 = 8-bit data byte
imm16 = 16-bit immediate data (low byte,high byte)

For example, suppose you want to transfer the value in accumulator *AL* to register *CH*. The postbyte (for the 88 opcode) would be

1	1	0	0	0	1	0	1	= C5H

AL   CH

Therefore, the instruction to transfer *AL* to *CH* is

```
88 C5    MOV  CH,AL
```

Note from Figure 4.3 that this instruction can also use the opcode 8A together with the postbyte

1	1	1	0	1	0	0	0	= E8H

CH   AL

and be written as

```
8A E8    MOV  CH,AL
```

The reason that there are two ways to do apparently the same thing is that the postbyte really has the following more general form:

mod	reg	r/m

If the first two bits (*mod*) in the postbyte are 11 as in Figure 4.3 then the last three bits in the postbyte (*r/m*) represent a register. If the value of *mod* is not 11 then the last three bits in the postbyte will define some memory location rather than a register. In this case the opcode 88 will move a byte from a memory location to a register while the opcode 8A will move a byte from a register to a memory location. We will look at these *MOV* instructions in Chapter 6.

Machine Code	Assembly Language Instruction	Operation
88 PB	MOV RB1,RB2	move RB2 to RB1
89 PB	MOV RW1,RW2	move RW2 to RW1
8A PB	MOV RB2,RB1	move RB1 to RB2
8B PB	MOV RW2,RW1	move RW1 to RW2

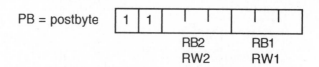

PB = postbyte

	1	1						

RB2   RB1
RW2   RW1

RB1,2	RW1,2
000 = AL	000 = AX
001 = CL	001 = CX
010 = DL	010 = DX
011 = BL	011 = BX
100 = AH	100 = SP
101 = CH	101 = BP
110 = DH	110 = SI
111 = BH	111 = DI

Figure 4.3 Form of MOV instructions to transfer register contents

Figure 4.4 defines the exchange instruction, *XCHG*. There are two forms of the *XCHG* instruction shown in Figure 4.4. The first will exchange the 16-bit contents of *AX* with any of the 16-bit registers given in Figure 4.4. This is a one-byte instruction with an opcode 9*X*, where *X* depends on the register involved according to Figure 4.4. For example, the instruction

              93   XCHG BX

will exchange the contents of *AX* and *BX*.

The second form of the *XCHG* instruction involves the same postbyte as in Figure 4.3. For example, the instruction

              87 FE   XCHG SI,DI

will exchange the contents of *SI* and *DI*.

4.3 SHIFT AND ROTATE INSTRUCTIONS

There are 14 instructions that allow you to move bits around in registers or in any memory location. We will study these instructions by using the general registers. Similar results can be obtained on registers *SP*, *BP*, *SI*, and *DI* or any memory location by using some of the addressing modes described in Chapter 6.

Machine Code	Assembly Language Instruction	Operation
9X	XCHG reg	Exchange AX and reg
86 PB	XCHG RB1,RB2	Exchange RB1 and RB2
87 PB	XCHG RW1,RW2	Exchange RW1 and RW2

X	reg	X	reg
000	AX	100	SP
001	CX	101	BP
010	DX	110	SI
011	BX	111	DI

PB, RB1,2 and RW1,2 same as in Figure 4.3

Figure 4.4 XCHG instruction

Shift Left, SHL or SAL

The *SHL AL,1* instruction with an opcode of *D0 E0* will cause the eight bits in accumulator *AL* to be shifted one bit to the left. The left-most bit (bit 7) will be shifted into the carry bit. A zero will be shifted into the right-most bit (bit 0).

To see how this instruction works, store the hex value *AAH* in accumulator *AL* by typing */RGA AA*, and store the instruction *D0 E0* at offset addresses 0000 – 000F by typing

/MH   D0 E0 D0 E0 D0 E0 D0 E0 D0 E0 D0 E0 D0 E0 D0 E0

Now move the position cursor back to offset address 0000H by pressing the *Home* key and single step (*F1*) eight times. You should observe the shifting of the bits in accumulator *AL* as shown in Figure 4.5. Note how the carry bit in the status register is changed each time you execute *SHL AL,1*.

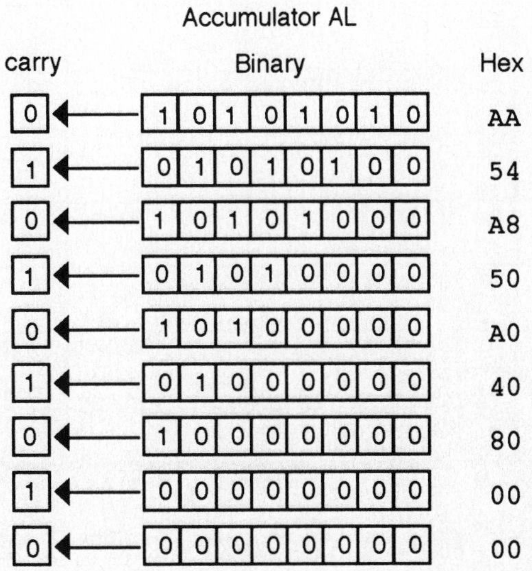

Figure 4.5 Result of executing SHL AL,1 instruction eight times

The opcodes for shifting the 8-bit general registers are given in Table 4.2.

Shift Right, SHR

The *SHR AL,1* instruction with an opcode of *D0 E8* will cause the eight bits in accumulator *AL* to be shifted one bit to the right. The right-most bit (bit 0) will be shifted into the carry bit. A zero will be shifted into the left-most bit (bit 7). A picture of what this instruction does is shown in Figure 4.6.

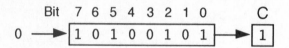

Figure 4.6 The shift right, SHR, instruction

Table 4.2								
8-bit Register Shifting and Rotate Instructions								
	AL	CL	DL	BL	AH	CH	DH	BH	
ROL	D0 C0	D0 C1	D0 C2	D0 C3	D0 C4	D0 C5	D0 C6	D0 C7	Rotate Left
ROR	D0 C8	D0 C9	D0 CA	D0 CB	D0 CC	D0 CD	D0 CE	D0 CF	Rotate Right
RCL	D0 D0	D0 D1	D0 D2	D0 D3	D0 D4	D0 D5	D0 D6	D0 D7	Rotate thru Carry Left
RCR	D0 D8	D0 D9	D0 DA	D0 DB	D0 DC	D0 DD	D0 DE	D0 DF	Rotate thru Carry Right
SHL/ SAL	D0 E0	D0 E1	D0 E2	D0 E3	D0 E4	D0 E5	D0 E6	D0 E7	Shift Left
SHR	D0 E8	D0 E9	D0 EA	D0 EB	D0 EC	D0 ED	D0 EE	D0 EF	Shift Right
SAR	D0 F8	D0 F9	D0 FA	D0 FB	D0 FC	D0 FD	D0 FE	D0 FF	Shift Arith. Right
ROL reg,CL	D2 C0	D2 C1	D2 C2	D2 C3	D2 C4	D2 C5	D2 C6	D2 C7	Rotate Left CL bits
ROR reg,CL	D2 C8	D2 C9	D2 CA	D2 CB	D2 CC	D2 CD	D2 CE	D2 CF	Rotate Right CL bits
RCL reg,CL	D2 D0	D2 D1	D2 D2	D2 D3	D2 D4	D2 D5	D2 D6	D2 D7	Rotate thru Carry Left CL bits
RCR reg,CL	D2 D8	D2 D9	D2 DA	D2 DB	D2 DC	D2 DD	D2 DE	D2 DF	Rotate thru Carry Right CL bits
SHL reg,CL	D2 E0	D2 E1	D2 E2	D2 E3	D2 E4	D2 E5	D2 E6	D2 E7	Shift Left CL bits
SHR reg,CL	D2 E8	D2 E9	D2 EA	D2 EB	D2 EC	D2 ED	D2 EE	D2 EF	Shift Right CL bits
SAR reg,CL	D2 F8	D2 F9	D2 FA	D2 FB	D2 FC	D2 FD	D2 FE	D2 FF	Shift Arith. Right CL bits

Rotate through Carry Left, RCL

The rotate through carry left instruction *RCL* differs from the shift left instruction in that the carry bit is shifted into the right-most bit rather than a zero as shown in Figure 4.7. Each time that the instruction is executed, all bits are shifted one bit to the left. Bit 7 is shifted into the carry and the carry bit is shifted into bit 0.

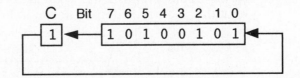

Figure 4.7 The rotate through carry left, RCL, instruction

Rotate through Carry Right, RCR

The rotate through carry right instruction *RCR* is just the opposite of rotate left. As shown in Figure 4.8 each bit is shifted one bit to the right. Bit 0 is shifted into the carry and the carry bit is shifted into bit 7.

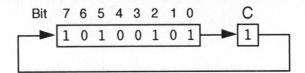

Figure 4.8 The rotate through carry right, RCR, instruction

Rotate Left and Rotate Right, ROL, ROR

In addition to the two rotate instructions *RCL* and *RCR* that rotate the bits through the carry bit, the 8086 has two rotate instructions that do *not* rotate through the carry. These two instructions are shown in Figure 4.9. The rotate left instruction, *ROL*, shifts the left-most bit into the carry *and* into the right-most bit position. Similarly, the rotate right instruction, *ROR*, shifts the right-most bit into the carry *and* into the left-most bit position. Note carefully the difference between the instructions *RCL* and *RCR* in Figs. 4.5 and 4.6 and the instructions *ROL* and *ROR* in Figure 4.9.

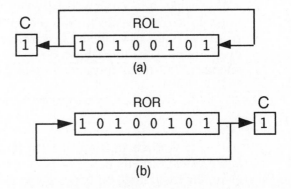

Figure 4.9 The rotate left, ROL, and rotate right, ROR, instructions
do not rotate the bits through the carry

Shift Arithmetic Right, SAR

The shift arithmetic right instruction, *SAR*, differs from the shift right instruction, *SHR*, shown in Figure 4.6 in that the sign bit (the left-most bit) remains the same. This means that if the sign bit is a 1 (corresponding to a negative number) this 1 will continually be shifted to the right. A picture of what this instruction does is shown in Figure 4.10.

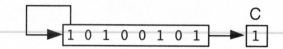

Figure 4.10 Shift Arithmetic Right, SAR, instruction

Shift and Rotate with Count Instructions

The shifting and rotate instructions described above shift all bits in a register one bit. These instructions are shown in the top half of Table 4.2. The instructions shown in the bottom half of Table 4.2 allow you to shift or rotate the bits in a register a given number of bits. The number of bits to shift is stored in register *CL*.
For example, the two instructions

```
0000   B1 03      MOV   CL,3
0002   D2 E0      SHL   AL,CL
```

will shift the contents of *AL* left 3 bits. This is equivalent to multiplying the contents of *AL* by $2^3 = 8$.
As a second example, the two instructions

```
0000   B1 0A      MOV   CL,10
0002   D3 EA      SHR   DX,CL
```

will shift the contents of *DX* right 10 bits. This is equivalent to dividing the contents of *DX* by $2^{10} = 1024$.
Note that all of the shifting and rotate instructions in Table 4.2 contain two bytes and that the first byte is *D0* in the first seven rows of the table and the first byte is D2 for all the instructions in the last seven rows. If you look up the opcodes *D0* and *D2* in Table A.2a in Appendix A you will see that there is an asterisk (*) for that opcode. This means that you must go to Table A.2b to find the form of a postbyte for this instruction. Note that in the row labeled *D0* there are seven different shifting and rotate instructions. The three-bit code at the top of each column is the postbyte opcode (*PBOC*) that must be put into the following postbyte:

mod	PBOC	r/m

If you are shifting or rotating the contents of a register, then the value of *mod* in this postbyte is 11 and the *r/m* value is the register value using the same three bit codes given in Figure 4.5 for the *MOV* instruction. For example, the postbyte opcode (PBOC) for the instruction *RCR CH,1* (4th column in Table A.2b) is 011. Therefore, the complete postbyte is

mod		PBOC			r/m		
1	1	0	1	1	1	0	1	= DD
reg		RCR			CH		

and the instruction code

DO DD   RCR CH,1

agrees with the entry in Table 4.2. In fact, this is how Table 4.2 was generated. You should be able to verify any of the entries in Table 4.2.

4.4 BASIC ARITHMETIC INSTRUCTIONS

In this section we will take a look at the basic addition, subtraction, multiplication and division instructions that are available in the 8086.

Binary Addition

The addition of binary numbers is carried out bit by bit starting with the least-significant bit (the right-most bit) according to Table 4.3. The 8086 addition instructions are shown in Table 4.4.

Table 4.3				
Binary Addition				
Carry(in)	A	B	A + B + Carry	Carry(out)
0	0	0	0	0
0	0	1	1	0
0	1	0	1	0
0	1	1	0	1
1	0	0	1	0
1	0	1	0	1
1	1	0	0	1
1	1	1	1	1

Table 4.4	
Addition Instructions	
Mnemonic	Meaning
ADD ac,data	Add immediate data to AX or AL register
ADD mem/reg, data	Add immediate data to register or memory location
ADD mem/reg1,mem/reg2	Add register to register, register to memory, or memory to register
ADC ac,data	Add with carry immediate data to AX or AL register
ADC mem/reg,data	Add with carry immediate data to register or memory location
ADC mem/reg1,mem/reg2	Add with carry register to register, register to memory, or memory to register

Consider the following binary addition:

```
                  Binary    Hex Decimal
        Carry 0 01100010
          A       00110101   35    53
          B     +00011001   +19   +25
                  01001110   4E    78
```

Note that the initial carry bit is zero and the final carry bit (0) is shown in the box. This is the carry bit that is displayed in the status register after an instruction such as *ADD ac,data* is executed. The intermediate carry bits are determined according to Table 4.3.

The binary values of *A* and *B* shown above are equivalent to the hexadecimal numbers 35H and 19H. These can be added directly (in hexadecimal) as shown above. The equivalent decimal addition (53 + 25 = 78) is also shown.

Carry and Overflow

The program shown in Figure 4.11 adds the hexadecimal numbers 35H and 19H. Enter this program at offset address 0000 using the TUTOR monitor. The result of this addition is shown in Figure 4.12. Single step through this program. Note that when the addition instruction at address 0002 is executed, the carry flag C and the overflow flag O are both cleared to zero.

```
0000   B0 35    MOV   AL,35H    ;AL = 35H
0002   04 19    ADD   AL,19H    ;AL = AL + 19H
```

Figure 4.11 Program to add 35H and 19H.

```
Decimal   Hex         Binary

     53    35        00110101
    +25   +19        00011001
     78    4E       001001110

              carry = 0
              overflow = 0
```

Figure 4.12 There is no carry from bit 6 to bit 7 and no carry from bit 7 to the carry flag

Now modify this program by changing the 19 at offset address 0003 to 5BH. This is equivalent to adding the decimal numbers 53 and 91 as shown in Figure 4.13. Single step through this new program and note that when the addition instruction at address 0002 is executed, the carry flag *C* is cleared to zero but the overflow flag *O* is set to one. There is an overflow because the answer 90H is really the *negative* (two's complement) value -112_{10}. (Verify this.) Although 90H is equivalent to the positive value 144_{10} when thinking about the result as an eight-bit unsigned number, the overflow flag, *O*, in the status register always thinks of the result as a signed number between -128 and +127. If the correct result is outside this range (144 in Figure 4.13) then the overflow flag O is set to 1.

Now modify the program again by changing the 5BH offset address 0003 to D3H. The hex value D3H represents the negative decimal number -45 as can be seen by taking the two's complement of D3H.

```
        D3H = 11010011
two's complement = 00101101 = 2DH = 45₁₀
```

two's complement = 00101101 = 2DH = 45_{10}

```
Decimal   Hex        Binary

   53      35        00110101
  +91     +5B        01011011
  144      90        010010000
                       ==

              carry = 0
              overflow = 1
```

Figure 4.13 An overflow occurs when there is a carry from bit 6 to bit 7 and no carry from bit 7 to the carry flag

Therefore, adding D3H to 35H is the same as subtracting 45_{10} from 53_{10}, as shown is Figure 4.14. Single step through this program and note that when the addition instruction at address 0002 is executed, the carry flag C is set to 1 but the overflow flag O is cleared to zero. There is no overflow because the binary addition result (08H) is correct. The result will always be correct (and therefore O will be cleared to zero) if there is a carry from bit 7 to C *and* a carry from bit 6 to bit 7.

```
Decimal   Hex        Binary

   53      35        00110101
  -45     +D3        11010011
    8     108        100001000
                       ==

              carry = 1
              overflow = 0
```

Figure 4.14 The overflow flag is cleared to zero when there is a carry from bit 6 to bit 7 *and* a carry from bit 7 to the carry flag

Finally, change the value at address 0001 from 35H to 9EH. The hex value 9EH is equivalent to the negative decimal value -98:

```
        9EH = 10011110
two's complement = 01100010 = 62H = 98₁₀
```

two's complement = 01100010 = 62H = 98_{10}

Figure 4.15 shows that adding -98 and -45 produces the decimal value -143 and the hex value 71H, which is incorrect. The O flag and the carry are both set to one. Verify this by single stepping through the program.

The results illustrated in Figures 4.12 through 4.15 show that the overflow flag, O, is set to one if there is a carry from bit 6 to bit 7 with no carry from bit 7 to C (Figure 4.13) *or* if there is a carry from bit 7 to C with no carry from bit 6 to bit 7 (Figure 4.15). If there is no carry from bit 6 to bit 7 *and* no carry from bit 7 to C (Figure 4.12), *or* if there is a carry from bit 6 to bit 7 *and* a carry from bit 7 to C (Figure 4.14), then there is no overflow and $O = 0$. This can be summarized by saying that the overflow flag, O, is the *exclusive or* of a carry from bit 6 to bit 7 and a carry from bit 7 to C. That is,

$$O = (\text{carry from bit 6 to bit 7}) \oplus (\text{carry from bit 7 to } C)$$

where the *exclusive-or* operation $A \oplus B$ is given in Table 4.5.

```
Decimal    Hex           Binary

  -98      9E           10011110
  -45     +D3           11010011
 -143      171         101110001

                    carry = 1
                 overflow = 1
```

Figure 4.15 The overflow flag is set to 1 when there is a carry from bit 7 to the carry flag but no carry from bit 6 to bit 7

Table 4.5		
Exclusive OR Operation $\oplus$		
A	B	$A \oplus B$
0	0	0
0	1	1
1	0	1
1	1	0

Binary Subtraction

The subtraction of binary numbers can be carried out bit by bit starting with the least-significant bit according to Table 4.6. The first four rows have no borrow in. The results in rows 1, 3 and 4 are obvious and result in no borrow out. In row 2 we are subtracting a 1 from a zero. This means that we need to borrow from the bit to our left in a binary number. Because we are in base 2 this means that we are really borrowing a 2 and therefore the result in row 2 of the table is $2 - 1 = 1$ plus a borrow. In a similar way you should convince yourself that the last four rows in the table make sense.

An example is shown is Figure 4.16. Note how a borrow may be required when subtracting bits. The 8086 uses the carry flag as a borrow flag.

Table 4.6				
Binary Subtraction				
Borrow (in)	A	B	A - B - Borrow	Borrow(out)
0	0	0	0	0
0	0	1	1	1
0	1	0	1	0
0	1	1	0	0
1	0	0	1	1
1	0	1	0	1
1	1	0	0	0
1	1	1	1	1

```
Decimal   Hex          Binary

Borrow   0 1         1 1   111
   181    B5          10110101
  -111   -6F         -01101111
    70    46          01000110
```

Figure 4.16 Example of binary subtraction

The subtraction shown in Figure 4.16 is equivalent to taking the two's complement of the subtrahend and adding, as shown in Figure 4.17. Note that this addition causes the carry flag C to be set. However, there is no borrow. The 8086 complements the carry bit after a subtraction and uses the carry flag as the borrow flag. Therefore, the carry bit in the status register will not be set following this subtraction.

```
   B5        B5          10110101
  -6F       +91         +10010001
   46      1 46        1 01000110

           Borrow = 0
```

Figure 4.17 Binary subtraction is equivalent to taking the two's complement of the subtrahend and adding

The 8086 subtraction instructions are given in Table 4.7. The subtraction illustrated in Figures 4.16 and 4.17 can be performed by executing the instructions shown in Figure 4.18. Type in this program using TUTOR and observe the contents of accumulator *AL* and the status register as you single step through the program. Note that after the subtraction the carry bit is zero, indicating *no borrow*. The carry will always be zero if the magnitude (0 through 255) of the minuend (B5H in Figure 4.18) is larger or equal to the magnitude of the subtrahend (6FH in Figure 4.18). If the magnitude (0 through 255) of the minuend is *less than* the magnitude of the subtrahend, the carry flag will be set to 1 (corresponding to a borrow).

```
0000   B0 B5        MOV AL,B5H      ;AL = B5H
0002   2C 6F        SUB AL,6FH      ;AL = AL - 6FH - C
```

Figure 4.18 Program to subtract 6FH from B5H

The overflow flag *O* only has meaning when you are subtracting signed (two's complement) numbers. As in addition the overflow flag *O* is set to one when the result is outside the range -128 through +127 for an 8-bit subtraction.

Table 4.7	
Subtraction Instructions	
Mnemonic	Meaning
SUB ac,data	Subtract immediate data from AL or AX register
SUB mem/reg, data	Subtract immediate data from register or memory location
SUB mem/reg1,mem/reg2	Subtract register from register, register from memory, or memory from register
SBB ac,data	Subtract with borrow immediate data from AL or AX register
SBB mem/reg,data	Subtract with borrow immediate data from register or memory location
SBB mem/reg1,mem/reg2	Subtract with borrow reg. from reg., reg. from memory, or memory from reg.

16-bit Addition and Subtraction

The instructions *ADD* and *SUB* can be used to add and subtract 16-bit data using the 16-bit registers. For example, suppose you want to add the two hex values 37FAH and 82C4H. The result is BABEH as shown by the following hexadecimal addition.

```
37FAH
+82C4H
BABEH
```

The program shown in Figure 4.19 will add these two 16-bit numbers. Note that the instruction *MOV AX,37FAH* loads a 16-bit value into register *AX* and the instruction *ADD AX,82C4H* adds a 16-bit value to *AX* with the result in *AX*. Enter this program and single step the two instructions.

The carry flag is set if there is a carry from bit 15 of *AX* (bit 7 of AH). Bit 15 (the left-most bit) of *AX* is the sign bit of *AX*. Negative numbers are represented as two's complement 16-bit numbers. Signed 16-bit numbers can have values ranging from 8000H (-32,768) to 7FFFH (+32,767).

```
0000   B8 FA 37     MOV   AX,37FAH   ;AX = 37FAH
0002   05 C4 82     ADD   AX,82C4H   ;AX = AX + 82C4H
```

Figure 4.19 Program to add 37FAH and 82C4H

Suppose you want to add the negative number FBH (-5) to the positive number 123AH. You can load the value FBH into accumulator *AL* (the low byte of *AX*) but what should be in accumulator *AH* (the high byte of *AX*)? Bit 7 of *AL* is the sign bit of the 8-bit number in *AL*. This bit must be extended through *AH* to give the proper 16-bit signed value in *AX*. If bit 7 of *AL* is 0 then *AH* should contain 00H; if bit 7 of *AL* is 1 then *AH* should contain FFH. The 8086 instruction *CBW* (convert byte to word) will extend the sign bit of *AL* into *AH*. For example, the program shown in Figure 4.20 will add FBH to 123AH. Note that the answer, 1235H, is in register *AX*. Enter this program and single step the three instructions.

```
0000   B0 FB        MOV   AL,0FBH     ;AL = -5
0002   98           CBW               ;AX = -5
0003   05 3A 12     ADD   AX,123AH    ;AX = AX + 123AH
```

Figure 4.20 Program to add FBH to 123AH

Suppose you want to *subtract* the 16-bit value 8315H from A1C9H. The result is 1EB4H as shown by the following hexadecimal subtraction:

$$\begin{array}{r} \text{A1C9H} \\ -\text{8315H} \\ \hline \text{1EB4H} \end{array}$$

The program shown in Figure 4.21 will subtract these two 16-bit numbers. Type in this program and single step the two instructions.

```
0000   B8 C9 A1     MOV   AX,A1C9H    ;AX = A1C9H
0003   2D 15 83     SUB   AX,8315H    ;AX = AX - 8315H
```

Figure 4.21 Program to subtract 8315H from A1C9H

After executing the *SUB* instruction with a 16-bit register the carry bit will be set to 1 if the magnitude of the 16-bit minuend is *less than* the magnitude of the 16-bit subtrahend.

In addition to *ADD* and *SUB* the instructions *INC* and *DEC* can be used to increment by 1 or decrement by 1 the contents of an 8-bit or 16-bit register or memory.

Binary Multiplication

Binary multiplication can be carried out bit-by-bit, in a manner similar to decimal multiplication, using Table 4.8.

Table 4.8 Binary Multiplication Table		
	0	1
0	0	0
1	0	1

Consider the multiplication example shown in Figure 4.22. Note that as 1101 is multiplied by each binary digit in 1100, the partial product is shifted one bit to the left before adding the result. This is the same as in decimal multiplication. The binary multiplication example just given is equivalent to the hexadecimal multiplication

$$
\begin{array}{r}
D \\
\underline{\times\ C} \\
9C
\end{array}
$$

where the result can be read from the hexadecimal multiplication table given in Table 4.9.

```
Decimal                    Binary

    13                      1101
  x 12                      1100
    26                      0000
    13                      0000
   156                      1101
                           1101
                         100011100
                         9      C 16
                           = 156 10
```

Figure 4.22 Example of binary multiplication

Multiplying two 8-bit binary numbers is equivalent to multiplying two 2-digit hex numbers. The example in Figure 4.23 shows how to do this using Table 4.9.

The 8086 instruction *MUL* (opcode = F6) will multiply the contents of accumulator *AL* by the contents of an 8-bit register or memory location specified by a postbyte, and store the result in register *AX*. To try this instruction, type in the program shown in Figure 4.24 and single step through it. This program loads the value 3DH into *AL* and the value 5AH into *BL* and then multiplies them. The result, 1572H, should be displayed in register *AX*.

```
Decimal    Hex

    61      3D
  x 90     x 5A        A x D = 82
    00      262        A x 3 = 1E + 8 = 26
   549      131        5 x D = 41
  5490     1572        5 x 3 = F + 4 = 13

       Note: 1572 16 = 5490 10
```

Figure 4.23 Performing binary multiplication using Table 4.9

Table 4.9

Hexadecimal Multiplication Table

	0	1	2	3	4	5	6	7	8	9	A	B	C	D	E	F
0	0	0	0	0	0	0	0	0	0	0	0	0	0	0	0	0
1		1	2	3	4	5	6	7	8	9	A	B	C	D	E	F
2			4	6	8	A	C	E	10	12	14	16	18	1A	1C	1E
3				9	C	F	12	15	18	1B	1E	21	24	27	2A	2D
4					10	14	18	1C	20	24	28	2C	30	34	38	3C
5						19	1E	23	28	2D	32	37	3C	41	46	4B
6							24	2A	30	36	3C	42	48	4E	54	5A
7								31	38	3F	46	4D	54	5B	62	69
8									40	48	50	58	60	68	70	78
9										51	5A	63	6C	75	7E	87
A											64	6E	78	82	8C	96
B												79	84	8F	9A	A5
C													90	9C	A8	B4
D														A9	B6	C3
E															C4	D2
F																E1

```
0000   B0 3D      MOV   AL,3DH      ;AL = 3DH
0002   B3 5A      MOV   BL,5AH      ;BL = 5AH
0004   F6 E3      MUL   BL          ;AX = AL x BL
```

Figure 4.24 Program to multiply 3DH by 5AH

The postbyte E3 given in Figure 4.24 can be determined from the description of the *MUL* instruction given in Figure 4.25. The form of the postbyte shown in Figure 4.25 can be used to multiply the contents of *AL* or *AX* by an 8-bit or 16-bit register respectively. The more general form of the postbyte

mod	PBOC	r/m

can be used to multiply the contents of *AL* or *AX* by a value in memory. In Chapter 6 we will show how different values of *mod* and *r/m* in this postbyte correspond to different addressing modes. Also note from Table A.2b in Appendix A that the value of *PBOC* in the postbyte for the *MUL* instruction is 100. This is the value used in Figure 4.25.

When performing 8-bit multiplication using the form *MUL reg8* the 16-bit product is stored in *AX* with the most significant 8 bits in *AH* and the least significant 8 bits in *AL*. When performing 16-bit multiplication using the form *MUL reg16* the 32-bit product is stored in registers *DX* and *AX* with the most significant 16 bits in *DX* and the least significant 16 bits in *AX*. As an example consider the following hex multiplication:

```
        31A4
     X  1B2C
       253B0
        6348
      2220C
      31A4
     544D430
```

Machine Code	Assembly Language Instruction	Operation
F6 PB	MUL reg8	AX = AL x reg8
F7 PB	MUL reg16	DX:AX = AX x reg16

PB = postbyte:

1	1	1	0	0			

reg8,16

reg8	reg16
000 = AL	000 = AX
001 = CL	001 = CX
010 = DL	010 = DX
011 = BL	011 = BX
100 = AH	100 = SP
101 = CH	101 = BP
110 = DH	110 = SI
111 = BH	111 = DI

Figure 4.25 The instruction MUL performs unsigned multiplication

The program shown in Figure 4.26 will perform this multiplication. Type in the program and single step through it. Note that the result is stored in registers *DX* and *AX*.

```
0000   B8 A4 31      MOV   AX,31A4H    ;AX = 31A4H
0003   BB 2C 1B      MOV   BX,1B2CH    ;BX = 1B2CH
0006   F7 E3         MUL   BX          ;DX:AX = AX x BX
```

Figure 4.26 Program to multiply 31A4H by 1B2CH

Signed Multiplication

Consider the following multiplication

```
   Decimal              Hex
     165                 A5
   x  36               x  24
   ──────              ──────
     990                294
    495                 14A
   ──────              ──────
    5940               1734
```

Note that $5940_{10} = 1734_{16}$.

This is an example of *unsigned* multiplication. The *MUL* instruction given in Figure 4.25 applies only to unsigned multiplication. To check this, multiply the values A5H and 24H using the program in Figure 4.26. The result should be 1734H stored in *AX*.

Now the value A5H could be interpreted as a two's complement value:

```
          A5H = 10100101
two's complement =    01011011 = 5BH = 91₁₀
```

In this case A5H represents -91_{10}. The multiplication given above should then be as follows:

```
Decimal
 -91
x 36                      3276₁₀ = 0CCC₁₆
 546                            = 0000 1100 1100 1100
 273    two's complement        = 1111 0011 0011 0100
-3276                           = F334H
```

Therefore, considered as *signed* multiplication the result of multiplying A5H by 24H should be F334H.

The program shown in Figure 4.27 will multiply A5H (-91_{10}) by 24H (36_{10}) using the *signed* multiplication instruction, *IMUL*, given in Figure 4.28. The (signed) result is F334H (-3276_{10}) and is stored in *AX*. Note that the machine code difference between *MUL* and *IMUL* occurs in the postbyte. Type in this program and single step through it.

```
0000  B0 A5      MOV  AL,A5H      ;AL = A5H
0002  B3 24      MOV  BL,24H      ;BL = 24H
0004  F6 EB      IMUL BL          ;AX = AL x BL
```

Figure 4.27 Program to multiply (signed) A5H by 24H

Binary Division

The 8086 has two instructions for performing binary division: *DIV* performs *unsigned* binary division and *IDIV* performs *signed* binary division. These instructions, involving 8- or 16-bit registers, are shown in Figure 4.29. The more general form of the postbyte described earlier for the multiply instruction can be used to replace *reg8* and *reg16* with memory locations. Note that the first byte of the opcode is the same as the corresponding *MUL* (or *IMUL*) instruction. Only the postbyte distinguishes these different instructions as is clear from Table A.2b in Appendix A.

Machine Code	Assembly Language Instruction	Operation
F6 PB	IMUL reg8	AX = AL x reg8
F7 PB	IMUL reg16	DX:AX = AX x reg16

PB = postbyte: `1 1 1 0 1 _ _ _`
reg8,16

reg8	reg16
000 = AL	000 = AX
001 = CL	001 = CX
010 = DL	010 = DX
011 = BL	011 = BX
100 = AH	100 = SP
101 = CH	101 = BP
110 = DH	110 = SI
111 = BH	111 = DI

Figure 4.28 The instruction *IMUL* performs signed multiplication

Machine Code	Assembly Language Instruction	Operation
F6 PB	DIV reg8	AL = AX/reg8 (unsigned) AH = remainder
F7 PB	DIV reg16	AX = DX:AX/reg16 (unsigned) DX = remainder
F6 PBI	IDIV reg8	AL = AX/reg8 (signed) AH = remainder
F7 PBI	IDIV reg16	AX = DX:AX/reg16 (signed) DX = remainder

PB = postbyte (DIV) | 1 | 1 | 1 | 1 | 1 | 0 | | | |
                                                   reg8,16

PBI = postbyte (IDIV) | 1 | 1 | 1 | 1 | 1 | 1 | | | |
                                                   reg8,16

reg8	reg16
000 = AL	000 = AX
001 = CL	001 = CX
010 = DL	010 = DX
011 = BL	011 = BX
100 = AH	100 = SP
101 = CH	101 = BP
110 = DH	110 = SI
111 = BH	111 = DI

Figure 4.29 The 8086 binary division instructions

As an example of using the *DIV* instruction consider the following hexadecimal long division where you can use Table 4.9 to help "guess" the next hex digit in the quotient and to perform hex multiplication of the divisor by the quotient digits.

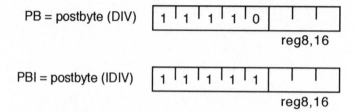

The program shown in Figure 4.30 will perform this division. After executing this program the quotient (CAH) should be stored in *AL* and the remainder (63H) should be stored in *AH*.

```
0000   B8 2F BC      MOV   AX,OBC2FH      ;AX = BC2FH
0003   B3 EE         MOV   BL,OEEH        ;BL = EEH
0005   F6 F3         DIV   BL             ;AL = AX/BL
```

Figure 4.30 Program to divide (unsigned) BC2FH by EEH

Note that the instruction *DIV* involves dividing a 16-bit number by an 8-bit number (or a 32-bit number by a 16-bit number) with the quotient being an 8-bit number (or a 16-bit number). If the divisor is too small, the quotient may be larger than FFH (or FFFFH for a 16-bit number). If this happens a "divide by zero" interrupt occurs. We will discuss interrupts in Chapters 5 and 11.

Packed BCD Arithmetic

Whereas computers add and subtract binary numbers, the people using the computers are more familiar with dealing with decimal numbers. For this reason decimal numbers are normally entered through the keyboard and displayed on the screen. This means that the computer must convert a decimal number entered from the keyboard to a binary number, perform a calculation, and then convert the binary result to a decimal number before displaying it on the screen.

An alternative is to do the calculation in *decimal*, thus avoiding the conversion to binary. The 8086 microprocessor uses the decimal adjust instructions, *DAA* (after addition) and *DAS* (after subtraction), to convert the result of a binary addition or subtraction to a packed *binary coded decimal (BCD)* result. A BCD digit is one of the decimal digits 0-9. These digits are coded using the 4-bit binary equivalent representations 0000-1001. The 4-bit combinations corresponding to the hex digits A–F are not allowed. An 8-bit byte can contain two BCD digits. Thus, the decimal number 35 is stored in packed BCD format as 35H = 00110101. Note that as a BCD number this is interpreted as 35_{10} and *not* as $35_{16} = 53_{10}$.

BCD Addition

An example of the difference between binary and decimal addition is shown in Figure 4.31. Note that the *hex values* 35H and 47H are used in both cases. The 8086 instruction *ADD AL,data* will always perform the binary addition shown on the left in Figure 4.31. However, if this addition instruction is followed by the decimal adjust instruction, *DAA* (opcode = 27H), the binary result (7CH) will be changed to the corresponding decimal result (82H).

	Binary			Decimal	
	35H	00110101		35H	00110101
+	47H	01000111	+	47H	01000111
	7CH	01111100		82H	10000010

Figure 4.31 Binary and decimal addition

To see this, enter the program shown in Figure 4.32 and single step through the three instructions. Following the *DAA* instruction, the carry will be set when the result of the decimal addition exceeds 99.

Note that packed BCD numbers use all eight bits in a byte (four bits for each of two digits). Therefore, no sign bit is associated with BCD numbers. You must keep track of the sign of BCD numbers separately. The decimal adjust instruction, *DAA*, can only be used after an *addition to accumulator AL.*

```
0000   B0 35        MOV   AL,35H      ;AL = 35H
0002   04 47        ADD   AL,47H      ;AL = AL + 47H
0004   27           DAA               ;Decimal adjust
```

Figure 4.32 Program to add BCD numbers

BCD Subtraction

The statement *DAS* (opcode = 2FH), *decimal adjust accumulator after subtraction*, can be used following a binary subtraction from *AL* to convert the binary result to a BCD result. As an example, the program shown in Figure 4.33 will subtract the BCD number 25 from 52. Type in this program and single step through it. Note particularly the effect of the *DAS* instruction.

```
0000   B0 52        MOV   AL,52H      ;AL = 52H
0002   2C 25        SUB   AL,25H      ;AL = AL - 25H
0004   2F           DAS               ;Decimal adjust
```

Figure 4.33 Program to subtract BCD numbers

Unpacked BCD Arithmetic

The decimal adjust instructions *DAA* and *DAS* described above assume that the data is stored in packed BCD format; that is, two BCD digits per byte. When data is entered from the keyboard, for example, the data is initially stored as an ASCII code. That is, the BCD digits 0 through 9 are stored, one digit per byte, as the hex ASCII values 30H through 39H. Note that the low-order four bits in these ASCII codes are the correct BCD digits for the corresponding decimal value. If multiple-digit BCD numbers are stored one digit per byte (in the low-order four bits) we call this an *unpacked BCD format*.

The 8086 has four instructions that can be used in conjunction with unpacked BCD arithmetic. These are given in Figure 4.34. The first two instructions (*AAA* and *AAS*) are used in a similar manner to *DAA* and *DAS* except that they assume unpacked BCD data. The instruction *AAM* is used following a binary multiply instruction when the original data is in unpacked BCD form. The instruction *AAD* is used *before* a binary division instruction to convert a BCD number in *AX* to a corresponding binary value. We will look at examples that use each of these instructions.

Machine Code	Assemble Language Instruction	Operation
37	AAA	Adjust result of ASCII addition
3F	AAS	Adjust result of ASCII subtraction
D4 0A	AAM	Adjust result of BCD multiplication
D5 0A	AAD	Adjust AX for BCD division

Figure 4.34 ASCII adjust instructions for unpacked BCD arithmetic

ASCII Addition

Consider the following decimal and ASCII addition:

```
        Decimal              ASCII

            9                    39
         +  6                 +  36
           15                 01 05
                              AH AL
```

If the ASCII code for 9 (39H) is stored in *AL* (unpacked BCD) and the ASCII code for 6 (36H) is added to *AL* using the instruction *ADD AL,36H*, the result (6FH) will be stored in *AL*. If the instruction *AAA* is then executed, the correct unpacked BCD result (15) will be stored in *AH* (01) and *AL* (05). (This assumes that the initial value of *AH* is 00). To test this, type in the program in Figure 4.35 and single step through it. Note that the result following the *AAA* instruction is stored in unpacked BCD form in *AH* and *AL*. If *AH* contained an initial value other than 00 then this initial value would simply have the 01 added to it. Following the execution of the *AAA* instruction the carry flag, *C*, will be set to 1 if the BCD sum is greater than 9. Note that this is the case in Figure 4.35.

```
0000   B8 39 00      MOV   AX,0039H      ;AL = 39H
0003   04 36         ADD   AL,36H        ;AL = AL + 36H
0005   37            AAA                 ;ASCII adjust
```

Figure 4.35 Example of unpacked BCD addition using
ASCII adjust for addition, AAA

ASCII Subtraction

Consider the following decimal and ASCII subtraction:

```
             Decimal              ASCII

                 6                    36
              -  9                 -  39
 Borrow = 1      7                 FF 07  Carry flag = 1
                                   AH AL
```

The program in Figure 4.36 will perform this subtraction. Following the *AAS* instruction the contents of *AL* will contain the unpacked BCD result of the subtraction. If a borrow is required the carry flag will be set and 1 will be subtracted from the *AH* register. Type in this program and single step through it.

```
0000   B8 36 00      MOV   AX,0036H      ;AL = 36H
0003   2C 39         SUB   AL,39H        ;AL = AL - 39H
0005   3F            AAS                 ;ASCII adjust
```

Figure 4.36 Example of unpacked BCD subtraction using
ASCII adjust for subtraction, AAS

BCD Multiplication

Consider the following decimal, binary (hex), and BCD multiplication:

```
     Decimal      Binary (HEX)      BCD

        8             08              08
      x 7           x 07           x  07
      ────          ─────         ────────
       56             38           05   06
                                   AH   AL
```

The *AAM* instruction can be used following an unsigned multiplication of two unpacked BCD numbers (with the high order 4 bits equal to 0) to produce a BCD result with the high-order unpacked BCD digit in *AH* and the low-order unpacked BCD digit in *AL*.

The program in Figure 4.37 will multiply 08 (in *AL*) by 07 (in *BL*) using the instruction *MUL BL* at offset address 0004. The result of this binary multiplication will be 38H, which is the binary representation of the decimal value 56. The instruction *AAM* divides this result by 10 (this is the value 0A in the machine code D4 0A) and stores the quotient (05) in *AH* and the remainder (06) in *AL*. These are the unpacked BCD digits of the decimal product. Type in this program and single step through it. Note that the final result is stored in *AH* (05) and *AL* (06).

```
0000   B0 08      MOV   AL,08H      ;AL = 08H
0002   B3 07      MOV   BL,07H      ;BL = 07H
0004   F6 E3      MUL   BL          ;AL = AL x BL
0006   D4 0A      AAM               ;ASCII adjust
```

Figure 4.37 Example of unpacked BCD multiplication using ASCII adjust for multiplication, AAM

BCD Division

Consider the following decimal division:

```
      9     = quotient
   6 ⌐56
     54
     ──
      2     = remainder
```

Recall that the unsigned binary division instruction *DIV* divides the (binary) contents of *AX* by *reg8* (e.g. *BL*) and stores the quotient in *AL* and the remainder in *AH*. If you store the decimal value 56 as two unpacked BCD digits in *AH* and *AL* (05 in *AH* and 06 in *AL*) then the ASCII adjust instruction *AAD* (D5 0A) will convert this value in *AX* (0506) to the corresponding binary value (0036H). If the BCD divisor 06 is stored in *BL* then the normal (unsigned) binary division will produce the correct quotient (09) and remainder (02) in *AL* and *AH* respectively.

The program shown in Figure 4.38 will perform this BCD division. Note that unlike the ASCII adjust for addition, subtraction, and multiplication, which are executed *after* the arithmetic operation, the ASCII adjust for division instruction, *AAD*, is executed *before* the *DIV* instruction. Single step the program in Figure 4.38 and note how the *AAD* instruction modifies the contents of *AX* and how the final quotient is in *AL* and the remainder is in *AH*.

```
0000   B8 06 05     MOV   AX,0506H     ;AX = 0506H
0003   B3 06        MOV   BL,06        ;BL = 06H
0005   D5 0A        AAD                ;Adjust AX for
                                       ;  BCD div
0007   F6 F3        DIV   BL           ;divide
```

Figure 4.38 Example of unpacked BCD division using
ASCII adjust for division, AAD

4.5 BASIC LOGICAL INSTRUCTIONS

The basic logical operators are *AND*, *OR*, and *NOT*. The *EXCLUSIVE-OR* operation (which can be defined in terms the basic three logical operators) was defined earlier in this chapter in the section on carry and overflow. In Chapter 3 we saw that the 8086 *NOT* instruction took the one's complement of a byte or word; that is, it changed the state of each bit. The 8086 instructions *AND*, *OR*, and *XOR* perform the logical operations *AND*, *OR*, and *XOR* on a bit-by-bit basis according to Table 4.10. In this table b_R represents a register bit and b_M can be a memory or a register bit. We can also *AND*, *OR* and *XOR* immediate data with the contents of a register or memory.

For example, the instruction

```
24 F0     AND AL,0F0H
```

will *AND* the value in accumulator *AL* with the value F0H. Notice that we have written F0H as 0F0H in the instruction. This is because the assembler (to be described in the next chapter) requires all immediate values to begin with a digit (0 - 9). Otherwise, it will treat F0H as a possible label or variable name.

Table 4.10 Logical Operations				
b_R	b_M	b_R AND b_M	b_R OR b_M	b_R XOR b_M
0	0	0	0	0
0	1	0	1	1
1	0	0	1	1
1	1	1	1	0

The opcodes associated with all instructions can be found from Table A.2 in Appendix A. This table shows the opcode space for the 8086. For example, the opcode for *AND AL,0F0H* is found from the entry *AND AL,imm* in row 2, column 4. Thus, the opcode is 24. Therefore, the two program bytes 24 F0 will AND accumulator *AL* with the immediate value 0F0H. Note from Table A.2 that some of the instructions are byte (*b*) instructions which involve 8 bit data and registers. Others are word (*w*) instructions which involve 16 bit data and registers.

The instruction *AND* performs a bit-by-bit AND operation of the contents of register *R* with the contents of memory location *M*, where *M* is specified by the addressing mode. In general, the result may be stored in the register *R* or memory location *M*. For the immediate mode, *M* will be the byte following the opcode and the result will be stored in the register *R*. Type in the two instructions in Figure 4.39 and execute them in the single step mode. Note that after executing the instruction *AND AL,0F0H* the value in accumulator *AL* will be 50H. That is, the lower nibble (the four bits 1010=A) has been masked to zero. This is because ANDing anything with a zero produces a zero, while ANDing any bit with a 1 leaves the bit unchanged (see Table 4.10).

```
0000    B0 5A      MOV    AL,5AH
0002    24 F0      AND    AL,0F0H
```

Figure 4.39 ANDing a byte with F0H will mask the lower nibble

A particular bit can be set to 1 by using the *OR* instruction. For example, the instructions in Figure 4.40 will set bit 7 of accumulator *AL* by ORing the contents of *AL* (13H) with 80H. The resulting value of *AL* will be 93H. Type in these two instructions and execute them by single stepping. Do you see where the opcode 0C comes from in Table A.2?

```
0000    B0 13      MOV    AL,13H
0002    0C 80      OR     AL,80H
```

Figure 4.40 Bit 7 of accumulator A can be set by executing OR AL,80H

Note from Table 4.10 that *0 XOR 1 = 1* and *1 XOR 1 = 0*. Thus, if you exclusive-OR the contents of *AL* with FFH you will obtain the one's complement of *AL*. For example, type in the two instructions in Figure 4.41 and execute them by single stepping. Note that the value 55H becomes AAH when exclusive-ORed with FFH. The same result is achieved with the two-byte instruction *NOT AL* (F6 D0).

```
0000    B0 55      MOV    AL,55H
0002    34 FF      XOR    AL,0FFH
```

Figure 4.41 The one's complement of *AL* can be found by executing *XOR AL,0FFH*

PROGRAMMING PROBLEMS

Problem 4.1 – 8086 Instructions

a. Fill in the column labeled *Machine Code* in the following table by looking up the opcodes in Appendix A.

| | | Register Value After Execution | | |
Instruction	Machine Code	BINARY	HEX	Carry
MOV AL,0A7H	B0 A7	AL=10100111	A7	---
SHL AL,1		AL=		
RCL,AL,1		AL=		
NOT AL		AL=		
NEG AL		AL=		
SAR AL,1		AL=		
MOV AH,AL		AX=		
INC AX		AX=		
DEC AH		AX=		
MOV CX,AX		CX=		
SHR AH,1		AX=		
MOV SI,AX		SI=		
XCHG SI,CX		SI=		
MOV AX,CX		AX=		
MOV CL,4		CX=		
ROR AX,CL		AX=		
SHL AL,1		AX=		
RCR AX,1		AX=		
MOV DI,AX		DI=		
INC DI		DI=		
XCHG DI,AX		AX=		

b. Enter all of the machine code into the computer starting at offset address 0000 using the TUTOR command /MH. After entering the code go to offset address 0000 and then type /UP. This will disassemble your code on the right side of the screen and you can easily check to make sure you didn't make any errors in entering the code. To disassemble a longer block of code, you can type /LP. This will replace the TUTOR memory display with the disassembled code. Press the right arrow key (on the keypad digit 6) to disassemble another page. Press the *Enter* key to go back to TUTOR.

c. Fill in the *binary* and *hex* values of the indicated registers that will result when each instruction is executed. Also fill in the resulting value of the carry flag C. Verify each result by single stepping the instructions using the *F1* function key and observing the registers on the TUTOR screen.

Problem 4.2 – 8086 Arithmetic

a. Key in and single step through the program in Figure 4.11. Modify the program so as to perform the additions in Figures 4.11, 4.12 and 4.13. Explain the value of the carry and overflow flags in each case.

b. Key in and single step through the programs in Figures 4.16, 4.17, 4.18 and 4.19. Key in a program that will subtract the hex number B3CF from 73D9. Single step the program and observe the value of the carry and overflow flags. Explain the results. Verify the subtraction by doing it by hand.

c. Key in and single step through the multiplication and division programs in Figures 4.22, 4.24, 4.25 and 4.28. Modify the program in Figure 4.30 to perform *signed* division by using *IDIV*. Use this program to carry out the following divisions:

$$26/7 \qquad -26/7 \qquad 26/-7 \qquad -26/-7$$

What is the relationship between the sign of the remainder and the sign of the dividend and/or divisor?

d. One high resolution graphics screen on a PC is made up of a rectangular array of 640 x 200 dots. The horizontal, or *x*, coordinate increases from left to right (0 - 639). The vertical, or *y*, coordinate increases from top to bottom (0 - 199). Thus, the upper left-hand corner of the screen is coordinate (0,0).

A rectangular box on the screen can be defined by giving its top-left and bottom-right coordinates. Assume that *AX* contains the value of *TOP*, *BX* contains *LEFT*, *CX* contains *BOTTOM*, and *DX* contains *RIGHT*. Write a routine that will leave the area of the rectangle in *DX:AX*. Assume that the area *contains* the coordinate points *TOP*, *LEFT*, *BOTTOM*, and *RIGHT*. For example, the width of the rectangle is (*RIGHT* - *LEFT* + 1).

Test your program by entering the following values in the four general registers using */R*:

```
TOP        AX = 0015H
LEFT       BX = 0022H
BOTTOM     CX = 00BDH
RIGHT      DX = 01FAH
```

Single step through your program and find the hex value of the area of the rectangle.

EXERCISES

Exercise 4.1
Find the machine code instructions corresponding to the following assembly language instructions:

```
MOV     DL,CH
XCHG    AX,SI
XCHG    BL,DH
MOV     CX,DI
XCHG    DX,BX
```

Type in these instructions and single step through them.

Exercise 4.2
Single step through a program that loads the hex value 2C into accumulator *AL*, transfers the value to register *AH*, and then exchanges the contents of *AX* and *BP*.

Exercise 4.3

The opcodes for *STC* and *CLC* are F9 and F8 respectively. Enter the following bytes in memory starting at offset address 0000.

```
F9 F8 F9 F8 F9 F8 F9 F8
```

Single step through these instructions (by pressing key *F1*) and watch the carry flag.

Exercise 4.4

Repeat the exercise shown in Figure 4.5 using register *BL*. The opcode for *SHL BL,1* is D0 E3 (see Table 4.2).

Exercise 4.5

Store the hex value 7B in accumulator *AL* and execute the instruction *SHL AL,1* eight times. What is the value of the carry bit and the hex value in accumulator *AL* after executing each instruction?

Exercise 4.6

Store the hex value D5 in accumulator *AL* and execute the instruction *SHR AL,1* (D0 E8) eight times. What is the value in the carry bit and the hex value in accumulator *AL* after executing each instruction? Repeat using register *DL* (D0 EA).

Exercise 4.7

Store the hex value 2C in accumulator *AL* and a 1 in the carry bit. (you can store a 1 in the carry bit by typing */RF* 0001). Execute the instruction *RCL AL,1* (D0 D0) eight times. What is the value in the carry bit and the hex value in accumulator *AL* after executing each instruction? Repeat using register *CL* (D0 D1).

Exercise 4.8

Store the hex value 69 in accumulator *AL* and a 1 in the carry bit. Execute the instruction *RCR AL,1* (D0 D8) eight times. What is the value in the carry bit and the hex value in accumulator *AL* after executing each instruction? Repeat using register *BH* (D0 DF).

Exercise 4.9

Store the hex value 85 in accumulator *AL*. Execute the instruction *ROL AL,1* (D0 C0) eight times. What is the value in the carry bit and the hex value in accumulator *AL* after executing each instruction? Repeat using the instruction *ROR AL,1* (D0 C8).

Exercise 4.10

Store the hex value B1 in accumulator *AL* and execute the instruction *SAR AL,1* (D0 F8) eight times. What is the value in the carry bit and the hex value in accumulator *AL* after executing each instruction? Repeat using register *BH* (D0 FF).

Exercise 4.11

Store the hex value 05 in *AL* and execute the two instructions

```
MOV   CL,3
SHL   AL,CL
```

Do these two instructions multiply by 8?

Exercise 4.12
Store the hex value 6A34 in *DX* and execute the two instructions

```
MOV   CL,0AH
SHR   DX,CL
```

Do these two instructions divide by 1024?

Exercise 4.13
Modify the program in Figure 4.18 to perform the following subtractions. In each case explain the answer in accumulator *AL* and the value of the carry flag *C* and the overflow flag *O*.

a)	73H - A1H	c)	BBH - F2H
b)	D3H - 47H	d)	E1H - C3H

Exercise 4.14
Modify the programs in Figures 4.18 and 4.19 to perform the following additions and subtractions.

a)	31A4H + B120H	c)	4BCFH - 182AH
b)	ABCDH - 813CH	d)	015DH + 3AFFH

Exercise 4.15
Single step through a program that will perform each of the following multiplications and divisions. Verify the results in each case.

a)	4FH X 31H	c)	4217H / AAH
b)	183CH X 209FH	d)	135A2C1BH / D1C4H

Exercise 4.16
Modify the program in Figure 4.32 to perform the following decimal additions. In each case indicate the answer in accumulator AL and the value of the carry flag *C*.

a)	49 + 34	c)	29 + 36
b)	73 + 47	d)	55 + 69

Exercise 4.17
Modify the program in Figure 4.33 to perform the following decimal subtractions. In each case indicate the answer in accumulator *AL* and the value of the carry flag *C*.

a)	89 - 35	c)	46 - 63
b)	63 - 27	d)	23 - 47

Exercise 4.18
Modify the programs in Figures 4.33 – 4.36 to perform the following unpacked BCD arithmetic operations.

a)	4 + 8	c)	7 - 5
b)	8 X 6	d)	37 / 5

CHAPTER 5

8086 Programs

In the last chapter you became familiar with a number of the 8086 instructions. You were able to execute these instructions in short programs that you entered using the TUTOR monitor. We now want to see how these instructions can be used to form larger programs. For a program to be useful we need to be able to alter the order of execution of the instructions based on what has previously occurred in the program. In 8086 programs we use branching instructions to accomplish this and we will look at these instructions in Section 5.1.

The secret to writing large assembly language programs is to break the program into lots of little programs that are written in terms of modules. One form of module is the subroutine that we will look at in Section 5.2. Another type of module is the software interrupt call such as the BIOS and DOS calls. We will see how these work in Section 5.3.

You will learn the most about assembly language programming by debugging your own programs. In Section 5.4 we will see how the TUTOR monitor makes it easy for you to debug programs that are assembled using a macro assembler. In this chapter you will learn:

- The 8086 conditional and unconditional jump instructions
- How to calculate branching displacements
- How to use the *LOOP* instruction
- How a stack works
- How to use the *PUSH* and *POP* instructions
- How subroutines and software interrupts work
- The general structure of an 8086 assembly language program
- How to load .EXE files into TUTOR, set breakpoints and debug programs
- How to generate an object file using a macro assembler and to link one or more of these object modules to produce an executable .EXE file

5.1   BRANCHING INSTRUCTIONS

A computer program achieves its apparent power by being able to conditionally branch to different parts of a program. The 8086 microprocessor uses branching, or conditional jump, instructions for this purpose. A conditional jump instruction can cause a branch in the program to occur, depending on the state of one or more of the bits in the status register. In this section we will look at the 8086 instructions related to branching.

The Conditional Jump Instructions

The 8086 has a large number of conditional branching instructions. The instructions shown in Table 5.1 test the state of one of the status flags. Other branching instructions, that will be described later in this section, test some combination of the status flags.

A branching instruction will cause a branch to occur if the branch test is true. For example, the branching instruction *JE* (jump on equal) will cause a branch in the program if the *Z* flag in the status register is 1. This will be the case if the result of the previous instruction produced a result of zero.

The conditional jump instructions shown in Table 5.1 are all two bytes long. The first byte is the opcode, whose values for the eight branching instructions shown in Table 5.1 are give in the table. The second byte of the instruction is the *relative displacement* of the branch destination. This is the two's complement number that must be added to the value of the instruction pointer + 2 (the offset address of the next instruction) to obtain the offset address of the instruction to be executed if the branch test is *true*. If the branch test is *false*, then the instruction following the branching instruction is executed. This is illustrated in Figure 5.1. Note that if *Z* = 1 when the *JE* instruction is executed, the program will branch to the offset address formed by adding the displacement (06) to the offset address of the next instruction (0014); that is, to offset address 001A = 0014 + 06.

<table>
<tr><td colspan="4" align="center">Table 5.1</td></tr>
<tr><td colspan="4" align="center">Some Conditional Jump Instructions</td></tr>
<tr><td>Operation</td><td>Mnemonic</td><td>Opcode</td><td>Branch Test</td></tr>
<tr><td>Jump on equal zero</td><td>JE/JZ</td><td>74</td><td>Z = 1</td></tr>
<tr><td>Jump on not equal zero</td><td>JNE/JNZ</td><td>75</td><td>Z = 0</td></tr>
<tr><td>Jump on not sign</td><td>JNS</td><td>79</td><td>S = 0</td></tr>
<tr><td>Jump on sign</td><td>JS</td><td>78</td><td>S = 1</td></tr>
<tr><td>Jump on not below (not carry)</td><td>JNB/JAE/JNC</td><td>73</td><td>C = 0</td></tr>
<tr><td>Jump on below (carry)</td><td>JB/JNAE/JC</td><td>72</td><td>C = 1</td></tr>
<tr><td>Jump on overflow</td><td>JO</td><td>70</td><td>O = 1</td></tr>
<tr><td>Jump on not overflow</td><td>JNO</td><td>71</td><td>O = 0</td></tr>
<tr><td>Jump on parity (even)</td><td>JP/JPE</td><td>7A</td><td>P = 1</td></tr>
<tr><td>Jump on not parity (odd)</td><td>JNP/JPO</td><td>7B</td><td>P = 0</td></tr>
</table>

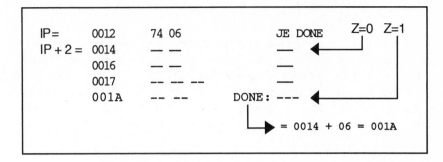

Figure 5.1 The displacement (06) in a branching instruction is added
to the instruction pointer + 2 to obtain the destination
offset address of the branch

If a branching instruction branches backward in memory, the displacement must be negative. It is just the two's complement of the number of bytes between the offset address of the next instruction (*IP* + 2) and the branch destination offset address. Note that since the branch displacement is a single 8-bit byte, a branching instruction can branch forward only a maximum of 127 bytes (7FH) and backward a maximum of −128 bytes (80H). The counting of these bytes always begins at the offset address of the instruction *following* the branching instruction. These displacements are automatically calculated by the assembler. Note that all conditional jumps take place within a given segment.

The Unconditional Jump Instructions

The instructions in Table 5.1 are *conditional* jump instructions that may or may not cause a branch to occur depending upon the value of one of the status flags. Sometimes you may want to jump no matter what. This is called an unconditional jump. Three different versions of the unconditional jump instruction are shown in Table 5.2.

The short *JMP* instruction (opcode = EB) has an 8-bit displacement as an operand. This is the same two's complement displacement described above for conditional jump instructions. It will allow an unconditional jump a maximum of 127 bytes forward or 128 bytes backward.

If you need to jump a farther distance within a segment you can use the long form of the *JMP* instruction (opcode = E9). This requires a two-byte operand which represents a 16-bit two's complement number that must be added to the offset address of the next instruction to obtain the destination offset address.

Table 5.2			
Some Unconditional Jump Instructions			
Operation	Mnemonic	Opcode	Operand
Short Jump	JMP	EB	8-bit displacement
Long Jump	JMP	E9	16-bit displacement
Absolute Jump	JMP	EA	segment address : offset address

All the branching instructions described so far use a *relative* displacement in the operand. This will allow a branch to any offset address within a given segment. Most conditional branch instructions are to nearby addresses so that a one byte (8-bit) displacement is sufficient. If, on occasion, you need to jump conditionally to a distant location within the segment you can use the long *JMP* instruction. For example, the instruction

```
        JE distant
next: -----
```

can be replaced with

```
        JNE next
        JMP distant
next: -----
```

where *distant* is a 16-bit displacement. A 16-bit displacement can have values between +32,767 (7FFFH) and −32,728 (8000H). These displacements, when added to the value in the instruction pointer + 2, will produce on offset address that will wrap around within the current segment. That is, branching instructions that use relative displacements in the operand can not jump out of the current segment.

To jump to a new segment you must use a different form of the *JMP* statement. One version is the absolute *JMP* instruction (opcode = EA) shown in Table 5.2. The operand for this instruction contains a new offset address plus a new segment address. For example, suppose you want to jump to the absolute address 0123:4567. The following instruction will do this.

```
        EA 67 45 23 01     JMP 0123:4567
```

Note that the opcode (EA) is followed first by the destination offset address (low byte, high byte) and then by the destination segment address (low byte, high byte).

Within a given segment both short and long jump instructions use a *relative* displacement in the instruction. Since this is the number that is *added* to the offset address of the following instruction, it is independent of the destination offset address. This means that if the entire program is moved within the segment, this relative displacement does not change. The use of relative displacements for determining a destination address will allow you to write *position-independent code*. This means that a program within a given segment can be moved to any location in memory and still run.

Calculating Branching Displacements

If you are entering short programs using the TUTOR monitor you can calculate the branching displacements either by hand or automatically using the /J TUTOR monitor command. Suppose a branching instruction is to branch backward -8 bytes from the address of the next instruction. Since -8 is represented as a two's complement hexadecimal number by F8H, the branching displacement will be F8 as shown in Figure 5.2. Note that this subtraction is done by subtracting the address of the next instruction (*IP* + 2) from the destination offset address. The result, FFF8H, is the 16-bit hexadecimal representation of -8_{10}. When a two's complement, 8-bit hexadecimal number such as F8 is stored as a 16-bit number, the sign bit (1 in this case) is extended to the left through the high order byte. Thus, F8H and FFF8H both represent the negative number -8_{10}. When using a short jump instruction, the displacement F8H is used; when using a long jump instruction, the displacement FFF8H is used.

```
              000C    --              LOOP1:  ---
              000D    -- --                   ---
              000F    -- -- --                 ---
   IP =       0012    75 F8                   JNE LOOP1
   IP + 2 =   0014    -- --                   ---
              0016    -- -- --
                                  000C    LOOP1
                                 -0014    IP + 2
                                  FFF8
```

Figure 5.2 Negative branches can be found by subtracting the offset address
of the next instruction from the destination offset address

If you are entering a machine language program into memory using TUTOR and you don't know the branching displacements, you can have TUTOR calculate these displacements for you. When entering a machine language program with TUTOR (by using /MH), and you come to the location of a jump displacement, just type 00 if it is a short jump instruction and 00 00 if it is a long jump instruction. This will leave one or two bytes where the displacement is to go. Then go back to each of these displacement locations and type /J. The command line will display

JUMP DISPLACEMENT: L S

Type L for a long jump or S for a short jump. The command line will then display

ENTER DESTINATION OFFSET ADDRESS

Enter the destination offset address and the correct displacement will automatically be inserted at the current position cursor location (that is, at the location of the displacement byte) when you press the *Enter* key. If you had pressed S, one displacement byte is inserted. If you had pressed L, two displacement bytes are inserted.

Try this by going to location 0013. Then type */JS 000C*. The displacement F8H should be inserted at 0013 as shown in Figure 5.2. If you now type */JS 001A*, the displacement 06H will be inserted at 0013 as shown in Figure 5.1.

Branching Examples

The following short examples will illustrate branching on the state of the Z, S, and C flags.

Branching on the Zero Flag Z

Type in the program shown in Figure 5.3 starting at offset address 0000. You should verify the displacements FD (at offset address 0004) and F8 (at offset address 0007) by using the /J displacement calculation feature of the TUTOR monitor described above.

```
0000    B9 03 00        LOOP1:   MOV    CX,3
0003    49              LOOP2:   DEC    CX
0004    75 FD                    JNE    LOOP2
0006    74 F8                    JE     LOOP1
```

Figure 5.3 JNE and JE branch on Z=0 and Z=1 respectively

Now single step through this program starting at offset address 0000. After executing the instruction *DEC CX* (at 0003) the first time, the value of *CX* is 02H and the value of the zero flag *Z* is zero. Therefore, the *JNE* instruction at address 0004 will branch back to address 0003 and execute *DEC CX* again. The value of *CX* will now be 01H and the *Z* flag will still be zero. Therefore, the *JNE* instruction will branch back to address 0003 again. This time the *DEC CX* instruction will cause the value of *CX* to go to zero. This will cause the *Z* flag to be set to one. The test *Z* = 0 of the *JNE* instruction will fail so that another branch will not occur. The next instruction at address 0006 will therefore be executed. This is a *JE* instruction that will branch if *Z* = 1. But the *Z* flag will be equal to 1 (otherwise, the *JNE* instruction would have jumped) and therefore the program will jump to address 0000 and you can single step through the program again. Single step through this program several times, observing the value of the *Z* flag and the contents of *CL*.

Branching on the Sign Flag S

The program shown in Figure 5.4 will test the branching instructions *JNS* and *JS*. Type in this program and single step through it. The value in *CL* is set to 7DH at address 0000 and then incremented by one (to 7EH) at address 0002. The *S* flag will be zero (7EH is a positive number) so that the JNS instruction will branch back to address 0002. Register *CL* will then be incremented to 7FH (still positive) so that the *JNS* instruction will branch back again to the *INC CL* instruction. This time *CL* will be incremented to 80H which is a negative number (-128_{10}) because bit 7 is set to 1. This will cause the sign flag *S* in the status register to be set to 1 so that the *JNS* test (*S* = 0) will fail. The *JS* instruction at address 0006 will then be executed which will always (because *S* = 1) branch back to address 0000. Single step through this program several times and observe the value of the *S* flag and the contents of *CL*.

```
0000    B1 7D           LOOP1:   MOV    CL,7DH
0002    FE C1           LOOP2:   INC    CL
0004    79 FC                    JNS    LOOP2
0006    78 F8                    JS     LOOP1
```

Figure 5.4 JNS and JS branch on S = 0 and S = 1 respectively

Branching on the Carry Flag C

The example given in Figure 5.3 decrements register *CL* until it becomes zero. The example given in Figure 5.4 increments register *CL* until to becomes negative (equal to 80H). Suppose you wanted to decrement register *AL* until it became less than a particular value, say 2BH. The program shown in Figure 5.5 will do this. Type in the program and single step through it.

```
0000    B0  2E        LOOP1:   MOV   AL,2EH
0002    FE  C8        LOOP2:   DEC   AL
0004    3C  2B                 CMP   AL,2BH
0006    73  FA                 JNB   LOOP2
0008    72  F6                 JC    LOOP1
```

Figure 5.5   JNB and JB branch on C = 0 and C = 1 respectively

The *CMP* (compare) instruction at address 0004 will subtract the value 2BH from the current value of *AL*. Recall from Section 4.4 that the carry flag, *C*, will be set to 1 if the magnitude of *AL* (considered to be an 8-bit positive number from 0 through 255_{10}) is less than 2BH. If *AL* is greater than or equal to 2BH then the carry flag will be cleared to zero. Thus, the *JNB* (jump on not below or jump on not carry) instruction at address 0006 will branch if the value of *AL* is "not below" 2BH. That is, if *AL* is larger than or equal to 2BH a branch will occur. The *JC* (jump on carry or jump on below) instruction at address 0008 will always branch because the carry flag will have to be set to get to the instruction. Single step through this program several times and observe the value of the *C* flag and the contents of accumulator *AL*.

An example that branches on the *overflow flag* is left as an exercise at the end of the chapter.

Other Conditional Jump Instructions

The conditional jump instructions given in Table 5.1 are the ones most commonly used. In fact, you can get by using only these. However, sometimes it is convenient to use the additional conditional jump instructions given in Tables 5.3 and 5.4. You must, however, be careful. It is very easy to make a mistake when using these conditional jump instructions. The instructions in Table 5.3 must only be used when you are thinking about *unsigned* numbers; that is, 8-bit numbers with decimal values between 0 and 255 (00H-FFH), or 16-bit numbers with decimal values between 0 and 65,535 (0000H-FFFFH).

Table 5.3			
Conditional Jump Instructions to Use Following a Comparison of UNSIGNED Numbers			
Operation	Mnemonic	Opcode	Branch Test
Jump on Above (Not Below or equal)	JA/JNBE	77	C + Z = 0
Jump on Below or Equal (Not Above)	JBE/JNA	76	C + Z = 1
Jump on Above of Equal (Not Below, Not Carry)	JAE/JNB/JNC	73	C = 0
Jump on Below (Carry) (Not Above or Equal)	JB/JNAE/JC	72	C = 1

Table 5.4

**Conditional Jump Instructions to Use Following a
Comparison of SIGNED Numbers**

Operation	Mnemonic	Opcode	Branch Test
Jump on Greater Than or equal (Not Less)	JGE/JNL	7D	S + O = 0
Jump on Less Than (Not Greater or Equal)	JL/JNGE	7C	S + O = 1
Jump on Greater Than (Not Less than or Equal)	JG/JNLE	7F	Z + (S+O)=0
Jump on Less than or Equal (Not Greater)	JLE/JNG	7E	Z + (S+O)=1

The branching instructions in Table 5.4 must only be used when you are thinking about *signed* numbers; that is, 8-bit signed numbers with decimal values between -128 (80H) and +127, (7FH), or 16-bit signed numbers with decimal values between -32,768 (8000H) and +32,767 (7FFFH).

It is very easy to confuse the instructions in Tables 5.3 and 5.4. This can lead to execution errors that are sometimes hard to find. For example, suppose register *CL* is used as a counter and you want to go through a loop 200_{10} (C8H) times. You might think that the following loop will work:

```
        MOV CL,0        ;set CL = 0
LOOP:   INC CL          ;increment CL
        CMP CL,C8H      ;compare CL to C8H
        JL  LOOP        ;loop if CL < 200
```

It won't! The branching instruction *JL LOOP* will fail the first time. This is because the value of *CL* is 1 and the value of C8H is not 200_{10} but is -56_{10}. Remember that the *JL* instruction (and all the instructions in Table 5.4) consider all numbers to be two's complement *signed* numbers. Inasmuch as 1 (the value of *CL*) is greater than -56_{10} the instruction *JL* will not branch.

The instruction you really want to use is *JB* (jump on below). This instruction, and all instructions in Table 5.3 treat all numbers as unsigned numbers, so that C8H is considered to be 200_{10} and not -56_{10}.

In Table 5.3 note that the instructions *JAE/JNB* and *JB/JNAE* test only the carry flag. All other instructions in Tables 5.3 and 5.4 use branch tests that involve more than one status flag.

The Loop Instructions

The 8086 has three versions of a *LOOP* instruction that make it easy to form loops. These loop instructions are given in Table 5.5. The statement

```
LOOP  disp8
```

decrements *CX* and jumps if $CX \neq 0$. The value of *disp8* is an 8-bit two's complement displacement calculated the same as for the conditional jump instructions.

```
                    Table 5.5

              The LOOP Instructions
```

Opcode	Assembly Language Instruction	Operation
E2	`LOOP    disp8`	Dec CX and jump if CX ≠ 0
E1	`LOOPZ   disp8` or `LOOPE   disp8`	Dec CX and jump if CX ≠ 0 and Z=1
E0	`LOOPNZ  disp8` or `LOOPNE  disp8`	Dec CX and jump if CX ≠ 0 and Z=0
E3	`JCXZ    disp8`	Jump if CX=0

As an example, the program in Figure 5.6 is equivalent to the program in Figure 5.3. Note that the *LOOP* instruction loops on itself. This is OK because *CX* is decremented by one each time the *LOOP* instruction is executed. Type in this program and single step through it several times.

```
0000   B9 03 00      L1:     MOV   CX,3
0003   E2 FE         L2:     LOOP  L2
0005   EB F9                 JMP   L1
```

Figure 5.6   Using a LOOP instruction to form an equivalent loop to that in Figure 5.3

The *LOOP* instruction can be thought of as implementing a *repeat while* $CX \neq 0$ or a *repeat until* $CX = 0$ loop as shown in Figure 5.7. Sometimes you would like to implement a *do while* loop which is not executed at all if *CX* is equal to 0 at the beginning of the loop. The *JCXZ* instruction in Table 5.5 can be used at the beginning of a loop to accomplish this as shown in Figure 5.8.

Two other forms of the *LOOP* instruction are shown in Table 5.5. The *LOOPZ* (or *LOOPE*) instruction will decrement *CX* and jump if $CX \neq 0$ *and* $Z = 1$. Thus, an early exit from the loop will occur if the instruction preceding *LOOPZ* produced a non-zero result.

The *LOOPNZ* (or *LOOPNE*) instruction will decrement *CX* and jump if $CX \neq 0$ *and* $Z = 0$. That is, an early exit from the loop will occur if the instruction preceding *LOOPNZ* produced a zero result.

```
L1:    ---            L1:    ---            L1:    ---
       ---                   ---                   ---
       ---     =             ---      =            ---
                             CX = CX-1             CX = CX-1
    LOOP L1           repeat while CX≠0     repeat until CX=0
```

Figure 5.7   The LOOP instruction can implement a *repeat while* or *repeat until* loop

```
           JCXZ NEXT             do while CX ≠ 0
    L1:    ---                        ---
           ---                        ---

           ---          =            ---
                                   CX = CX - 1
           LOOP L1               enddo
    NEXT:  ---                   next: ---
```

Figure 5.8 Implementing a *do while* CX ≠ 0 loop

5.2 THE STACK AND SUBROUTINES

The stack is a group of memory locations in which temporary data can be stored. A stack is different from any other collection of memory locations in that data is put on and taken from the *top* of the stack. The process is similar to stacking dinner plates on top of one another, where the last plate put on the stack is always the first one removed from it. We sometimes refer to this as a *last in-first out* or LIFO stack.

The offset memory address corresponding to the top of the stack (the last full location) is stored in the stack pointer, *SP*. The actual stack address is found by combining the offset address in the stack pointer with the segment address in the stack segment register, *SS*. When data are put on the stack, the stack pointer is *decremented*. This means that the stack grows *backward* in memory. As data values are put on the stack they are put into memory locations with lower addresses. Data can be put on and taken off the stack two bytes at a time using *PUSH* and *POP* instructions.

PUSH and POP Instructions

The *PUSH* and *POP* instructions of the 8086 are given in Table 5.6. The *PUSH* and *POP* instructions always move 2 bytes (16 bits) at a time to and from the stack. As shown in Table 5.6 any 16-bit register can be pushed on (or popped from) the stack using a 1-byte opcode. A 2-byte opcode can be used to push (or pop) data directly from (or to) a memory location. The postbytes |mod|110|r/m| and |mod|000|r/m| determine the memory locations involved using the addressing modes described in Chapter 6. In this chapter we will illustrate pushing and popping the contents of registers.

For example, suppose you want to push the value of register *AX* on the stack. From Table 5.6 the opcode for *PUSH AX* is 50H. When you first run TUTOR the stack pointer, *SP*, contains the value 0FFF. The stack segment, *SS*, will be the same as the code segment in which the current memory is being displayed. These value are displayed on the far right side of the TUTOR screen beside the word STACK. Note that the stack is empty (no values are displayed under the word STACK).

The program shown in Figure 5.9 will load *AX* with the value 1234H, and then push *AX* on the stack. Type in this program and single step through it. Note that when the *PUSH AX* instruction at address 0003 is executed, the value 1234H is pushed on the stack and the value of the stack pointer (the address of the top of the stack) has been decremented to 0FFD as shown in Figure 5.10. When the instruction *PUSH AX* is executed the following steps occur:

Table 5.6

PUSH and POP Instructions

Operation	Mnemonic	Opcode Encoding
Push register on stack	PUSH reg	01010rrr
Push segment reg on stack	PUSH segreg	000ss110
Push status reg on stack	PUSHF	9C
Push 16 bits from memory	PUSH mem	FF |mod|110|r/m|
Pop register from stack	POP reg	01011rrr
Pop segment reg from stack	POP segreg	000ss111
Pop status reg from stack	POPF	9D
Pop 16 bits to memory	POP mem	8F |mod|000|r/m|

rrr	reg		ss	segreg
000	AX		00	ES
001	CX		01	CS (can not POP to CS)
010	DX		10	SS
011	BX		11	DS
100	SP			
101	BP			
110	SI			
111	DI			

```
0000    B8 34 12        MOV   AX,1234H
0003    50              PUSH  AX
```

Figure 5.9 Program to push AX on the stack

```
        8086 Microprocessor TUTOR          Press F7 for Help

    AH AL     BH BL     CH CL      DH DL      DATA SEG   08 19 2A 3B 4C 5D 6E 7F
 AX 12 34  BX 11 C5  CX 00 C5  DX 3A EE      1574:0000  B8 34 12 50 00 00 00 00
                                             1574:0008  00 00 00 00 00 00 00 00
    SP 0FFD       SI 0000      IP 0004        1574:0010  00 00 00 00 00 00 00 00
    BP 0000       DI 0000                     1574:0018  00 00 00 00 00 00 00 00
    SS 1574       DS 1574      CS 1574        1574:0020  00 00 00 00 00 00 00 00
 SP+SS 1673D   SI+DS 15740     ES 1574        1574:0028  00 00 00 00 00 00 00 00
 BP+SS 15740   DI+DS 15740  IP+CS 15744       1574:0030  00 00 00 00 00 00 00 00
 STATUS FLAGS 7206 0111001000000110           1574:0038  00 00 00 00 00 00 00 00
                   ODITSZ A P C               1574:0040  00 00 00 00 00 00 00 00
 1574:0004 0000      ADD   [BX+SI],AL         1574:0048  00 00 00 00 00 00 00 00

 SEG 1574:  08 19 2A 3B 4C 5D 6E 7F                        1574: STACK
      FFE8  00 00 00 00 00 00 00 00    . . . . . . . .     0FFD  1234
      FFF0  00 00 00 00 00 00 00 00    . . . . . . . .
      FFF8  00 00 00 00 00 00 00 00    . . . . . . . .
      0000  B8 34 12 50>00 00 00 00    . 4 . P . . . .
      0008  00 00 00 00 00 00 00 00    . . . . . . . .
      0010  00 00 00 00 00 00 00 00    . . . . . . . .
      0018  00 00 00 00 00 00 00 00    . . . . . . . .


                                       / : Command     > : Go To Memory
                                       Use Cursor Keys to Scroll thru Memory
```

Figure 5.10 Screen display after executing the program in Figure 5.9

1. The stack pointer *SP* is decremented by 1 (to 0FFEH).
2. The contents of *AH* are stored at the address in *SP* (0FFEH).
3. The stack pointer *SP* is decremented by 1 again (to 0FFDH).
4. The contents of *AL* are stored at the address in *SP* (0FFDH).

The result is that the value in *AH* (12H) is stored in location 0FFEH and the value in *AL* (34H) is stored in location 0FFDH, and the value of *SP* has been decremented by 2 to 00FDH as shown in Figure 5.11. Go to offset address 0FFDH in the current segment and verify that, in fact, this is where the value 1234H was stored.

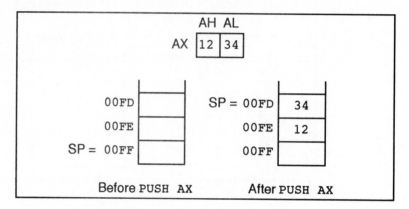

Figure 5.11 Pushing AX on the stack

If the statement

```
0004   5B       POP   BX
```

is added to the program in Figure 5.9 then the same two values pushed on the stack will be popped off the stack and stored in register *BX*. This statement causes the following steps to occur:

1. The value at the offset address stored in *SP* is loaded into register *BL*.
2. The stack pointer is incremented by 1.
3. The value at the new address stored in *SP* is loaded into register *BH*.
4. The stack pointer is incremented by 1.

Therefore, the final value of *SP* will be 0FFF.

Note that the values pushed on the stack in Figure 5.9 can be popped off into another register. Try this by adding the above statement to the program in Figure 5.9 and then single step this one statement (assuming that the value 1234H is still on the stack from single stepping the statements in Figure 5.9).

Subroutines

A subroutine is a segment of code that is normally written to perform a particular function or task. A subroutine is called by executing a *CALL* instruction. A subroutine is exited by executing a *return from subroutine* (*RET*) instruction. This will cause the program to return to the instruction following the *CALL* instruction that called the subroutine.

The computer knows where to go when an *RET* instruction is executed because it stored the return address on the stack when the *CALL* instruction was executed. To see how this works, key in all of the instructions shown in Figure 5.12. Note that this is three separate modules: a main program starting at offset address 0000 and two subroutines starting at offset addresses 0008 and 0010.

```
0000    E8 05 00            CALL 0008H
0003    E8 0A 00            CALL 0010H
0006    CC                  INT  3
----------------------------------------
0008    E8 05 00            CALL 0010H
000B    C3                  RET
----------------------------------------
0010    C3                  RET
```

Figure 5.12 Illustrating the CALL and RET instructions

The first instruction is *CALL 0008H*. This form of the *CALL* statement (opcode = E8) uses a 16-bit relative displacement as an operand. This is the same type of two's complement relative displacement used in the long *JMP* instruction described in Section 5.1. You can use the */JL* TUTOR command to calculate the displacement 0005 stored at offset address 0001 in Figure 5.12. This displacement (0005) is added to the offset address of the next instruction (0003) to obtain the destination offset address 0008 = 0003 + 0005. If you single step this instruction the program will jump to offset address 0008H and the offset address 0003H will be pushed on the stack as shown in Figure 5.13.

```
        8086 Microprocessor TUTOR           Press F7 for Help

      AH AL     BH BL     CH CL     DH DL    DATA SEG    08 19 2A 3B 4C 5D 6E 7F
   AX 00 00  BX 11 C5  CX 00 C5  DX 3A EE    1574:0000   E8 05 00 E8 0A 00 CC 00
                                             1574:0008   E8 05 00 C3 00 00 00 00
      SP 0FFD      SI 0000      IP 0008       1574:0010   C3 00 00 00 00 00 00 00
      BP 0000      DI 0000                    1574:0018   00 00 00 00 00 00 00 00
      SS 1574      DS 1574      CS 1574       1574:0020   00 00 00 00 00 00 00 00
   SP+SS 1673D  SI+DS 15740     ES 1574       1574:0028   00 00 00 00 00 00 00 00
   BP+SS 15740  DI+DS 15740  IP+CS 15748      1574:0030   00 00 00 00 00 00 00 00
   STATUS FLAGS 7206 0111001000000110         1574:0038   00 00 00 00 00 00 00 00
                     ODITSZ A P C             1574:0040   00 00 00 00 00 00 00 00
   1574:0008 E80500      CALL   0010H         1574:0048   00 00 00 00 00 00 00 00


   SEG 1574:    08 19 2A 3B 4C 5D 6E 7F                      1574: STACK
        FFF0    00 00 00 00 00 00 00 00    . . . . . . . .   0FFD   0003
        FFF8    00 00 00 00 00 00 00 00    . . . . . . . .
        0000    E8 05 00 E8 0A 00 CC 00    . . . . . . . .
        0008   >E8 05 00 C3 00 00 00 00    . . . . . . . .
        0010    C3 00 00 00 00 00 00 00    . . . . . . . .
        0018    00 00 00 00 00 00 00 00    . . . . . . . .
        0020    00 00 00 00 00 00 00 00    . . . . . . . .

                                            / : Command      > : Go To Memory
                                            Use Cursor Keys to Scroll thru Memory
```

Figure 5.13 Screen display after executing CALL 0008H at address 0000

The offset address of the next instruction is 0003H. This is the address stored on the stack. When a *RET* instruction (opcode = C3) is executed it pops the top offset address from the stack, and puts it in the instruction pointer. This will cause the program to return to the instruction following the *CALL* instruction that called the subroutine.

The first instruction of the subroutine at offset address 0008H is another *CALL* instruction that jumps to offset address 0010H. If you single step this instruction the screen display will be as shown in Figure 5.14. Note that the program jumps to offset address 0010H and the return offset address 000BH is pushed on the stack.

```
        8086 Microprocessor TUTOR          Press F7 for Help

    AH AL    BH BL    CH CL    DH DL    DATA SEG    08 19 2A 3B 4C 5D 6E 7F
 AX 00 00  BX 11 C5  CX 00 C5  DX 3A EE   1574:0000  E8 05 00 E8 0A 00 CC 00
                                          1574:0008  E8 05 00 C3 00 00 00 00
    SP 0FFB     SI 0000      IP 0010      1574:0010  C3 00 00 00 00 00 00 00
    BP 0000     DI 0000                   1574:0018  00 00 00 00 00 00 00 00
    SS 1574     DS 1574    CS 1574        1574:0020  00 00 00 00 00 00 00 00
 SP+SS 1673B  SI+DS 15740   ES 1574       1574:0028  00 00 00 00 00 00 00 00
 BP+SS 15740  DI+DS 15740  IP+CS 15750    1574:0030  00 00 00 00 00 00 00 00
 STATUS FLAGS 7206 0111001000000110       1574:0038  00 00 00 00 00 00 00 00
                      ODITSZ A P C        1574:0040  00 00 00 00 00 00 00 00
 1574:0010 C3         RET                 1574:0048  00 00 00 00 00 00 00 00

 SEG 1574:   08 19 2A 3B 4C 5D 6E 7F                   1574: STACK
    FFF8   00 00 00 00 00 00 00 00    . . . . . . . .    0FFB   000B
    0000   E8 05 00 E8 0A 00 CC 00    . . . . . . . .    0FFD   0003
    0008   E8 05 00 C3 00 00 00 00    . . . . . . . .
    0010  >C3 00 00 00 00 00 00 00    . . . . . . . .
    0018   00 00 00 00 00 00 00 00    . . . . . . . .
    0020   00 00 00 00 00 00 00 00    . . . . . . . .
    0028   00 00 00 00 00 00 00 00    . . . . . . . .
                                      / : Command     > : Go To Memory
                                      Use Cursor Keys to Scroll thru Memory
```

Figure 5.14 Screen display after executing CALL 0010H at address 0003

The instruction at offset address 0010H is *RET*. If you single step this instruction the program will return to offset address 000BH as shown in Figure 5.15. Note that the most recent return offset address has been popped from the stack.

If you single step the *RET* instruction at offset address 000BH, the program will return to offset address 0003H. Note that the program found its way back to offset address 0003H by popping the last return offset address from the stack.

The instruction at offset address 0003H is another *CALL 0010H* instruction. Single step this instruction and note how the *RET* instruction at 0010H will return this time to offset address 0006H.

Table 5.7 shows all the different forms of the *CALL* and *RET* instructions. The form of the *CALL* statement illustrated in Figure 5.12 is

CALL *displ6*

where *displ6* is the 16-bit relative displacement. This means that you can jump to a subroutine anywhere within the current segment (intrasegment). Suppose you want to jump to a subroutine in a different segment (intersegment). In this case you could use the form

CALL *addr*

shown in Table 5.7. For example, to call a subroutine at the absolute memory location 1234:5678 you could use the following instruction:

9A 78 56 34 12   CALL 1234:5678

```
        8086 Microprocessor TUTOR          Press F7 for Help

    AH AL    BH BL    CH CL    DH DL     DATA SEG    08 19 2A 3B 4C 5D 6E 7F
 AX 00 00 BX 11 C5 CX 00 C5 DX 3A EE     1574:0000   E8 05 00 E8 0A 00 CC 00
                                         1574:0008   E8 05 00 C3 00 00 00 00
    SP 0FFD       SI 0000      IP 000B    1574:0010   C3 00 00 00 00 00 00 00
    BP 0000       DI 0000                 1574:0018   00 00 00 00 00 00 00 00
    SS 1574       DS 1574      CS 1574    1574:0020   00 00 00 00 00 00 00 00
 SP+SS 1673D  SI+DS 15740      ES 1574    1574:0028   00 00 00 00 00 00 00 00
 BP+SS 15740  DI+DS 15740   IP+CS 1574B   1574:0030   00 00 00 00 00 00 00 00
 STATUS FLAGS 7206 0111001000000110       1574:0038   00 00 00 00 00 00 00 00
                        ODITSZ A P C      1574:0040   00 00 00 00 00 00 00 00
 1574:000B C3           RET               1574:0048   00 00 00 00 00 00 00 00

 SEG 1574:   08 19 2A 3B 4C 5D 6E 7F                 1574: STACK
      FFF0   00 00 00 00 00 00 00 00                 0FFD  0003
      FFF8   00 00 00 00 00 00 00 00      . . . . . . . .
      0000   E8 05 00 E8 0A 00 CC 00      . . . . . . . .
      0008   E8 05 00>C3 00 00 00 00      . . . . . . . .
      0010   C3 00 00 00 00 00 00 00      . . . . . . . .
      0018   00 00 00 00 00 00 00 00      . . . . . . . .
      0020   00 00 00 00 00 00 00 00      . . . . . . . .

 _____  / : Command    > : Go To Memory
                                            Use Cursor Keys to Scroll thru Memory
```

Figure 5.15 Screen display after executing RET at location address 0010H

Table 5.7		
CALL and RET Instructions		
Operation	Mnemonic	Opcode Encoding
Intrasegment		
Call subroutine	CALL *disp16*	E8 disp_lo disp_hi
Call subroutine	CALL *mem*	FF |mod|010|r/m|
Return from subroutine	RET	C3
Return and add to SP	RET *disp16*	C2 disp_lo disp_hi
Intersegment		
Call subroutine	CALL *mem*	FF |mod|011|r/m|
Call subroutine	CALL *addr*	9A segment:offset
Return from subroutine	RET	CB
Return and add to SP	RET *disp16*	C2 disp_lo disp_hi

Note that the operand contains 4 bytes. The first two are the destination offset address and the next two are the destination segment address. This instruction jumps to the destination address by storing the first two bytes of the operand in *IP* and the next two bytes in *CS*. How can the program find its way back to the statement following *CALL*? This *CALL* statement must not only store the offset address (*IP*) of the next instruction but also the current contents of *CS*. It pushes *CS* on the stack first, then it pushes *IP+5* (the offset address of the next instruction) on the stack.

To return from an intersegment subroutine the program must pop four bytes off the stack. The first two go into *IP* and the next two go into *CS*. The *RET* statement (opcode = C3) used in Figure 5.12 only popped two bytes off the stack. This is the one to use for intrasegment CALLs. The intersegment *RET* statement (opcode = CB) shown in Table 5.7 will pop four bytes off the stack and return to the segment from which the CALL was made.

Table 5.7 shows an intersegment and intrasegment CALL of the form

```
CALL mem
```

This is an indirect call to a memory location using the addressing modes described in Chapter 6.

The return statement of the form

```
RET disp16
```

shown in Table 5.7 adds the 16-bit value *disp16* to the stack pointer after the return has occurred. This is sometimes useful as a method of adjusting the stack pointer if parameters were passed to the subroutine on the stack. An example of this will be given in Chapter 6.

5.3 SOFTWARE INTERRUPTS

Another type of software module, similar to subroutines, is the software interrupt such as the *INT 16H* BIOS call we used to read the keyboard in Chapter 9 or the *INT 21H* DOS call we used to display a character on the screen. Where does the program jump when these instructions are executed? The answer is that the programmer must have stored the address of the software interrupt routine in a special table of interrupt routine addresses, called interrupt vectors. This interrupt vector table occupies the first 1024 bytes of memory in the computer; that is, addresses 0000:0000 – 0000:03FF. Each entry in the table occupies four bytes: the first two bytes contain the offset address to be loaded into the instruction pointer, *IP*, and the next two bytes contain the segment address to be loaded into the segment register *CS*. This means that there can be a total of 256 (FFH) interrupt vectors in the table as shown in Figure 5.16. The *CS:IP* pairs in the interrupt vector table represent the starting addresses of the various interrupt routines.

Software interrupts are called using the instruction

```
INT n
```

where *n* is the interrupt type number (00H – FFH) given in Figure 5.16. When *INT n* is executed the following interrupt sequence takes place:

1. The current status register is pushed on the stack.
2. The interrupt enable flag, *I*, and the trap flag, *T*, in the status register are cleared to mask further hardware interrupts.
3. The current values of *CS* and *IP* are pushed on the stack.
4. New values for CS_n and IP_n are loaded from the interrupt vector table.

Thus, after executing *INT n* the six bytes shown in Figure 5.17 will be pushed on the stack and the interrupt service routine at $CS_n:IP_n$ will start executing. This same sequence occurs for hardware interrupts which we will describe in Chapter 14.

The address $CS_n:IP_n$ is called an interrupt vector and you must store this address in the special locations shown in Figure 5.16. This would be the starting address of your interrupt service routine. The last statement in an interrupt service routine must be the *IRET* (return from interrupt) instruction (opcode = CF). This statement pops the instruction pointer (first two bytes), the *CS* register (next two bytes), and the status register (next two bytes) off the stack. The program will therefore continue at the point in the program where the interrupt occurred. For a software interrupt this would be the statement following the *INT n* statement.

Each entry in the interrupt vector table shown in Figure 5.16 has an interrupt type number associated with it. This is a number between 0 and 255 (00H - FFH). The address of the interrupt vector is found by multiplying the interrupt type number by 4. For example, interrupt type number 5 has its interrupt vector located at address 5 x 4 = 20 = 014H as shown in Figure 5.16. Note that each interrupt vector consists of 4 bytes -- the first two contain *IP* and the next two contain *CS*.

The first few entries in the interrupt vector table are used for special purposes as indicated in Figure 5.16. The type 0 interrupt is automatically requested if a division instruction results in a quotient that is too large to fit into the quotient register (*AL* or *AX*). This is called a *divide by zero* error even though you don't have to divide by zero to produce this interrupt. The type 1 interrupt is a special interrupt used for single stepping, which we will describe below. The type 2 interrupt is always the vector address for the non-maskable hardware interrupt (NMI) which we will describe in Chapter 14. If you want an interrupt to occur when the overflow flag is set (see Chapter 10) you can follow the arithmetic instruction with the instruction *INTO*, interrupt on overflow, (opcode = CE). This will cause a type 4 interrupt.

Interrupt types 10H – 1CH shown in Figure 5.16 are the BIOS ROM routines for handling basic I/O operations. We have already used *INT 16H* for reading the keyboard and *INT 10H* for setting the screen cursor. We will consider the video I/O routines in more detail in Chapter 7 and some of the other BIOS routines in Chapters 10 – 13.

In addition to the interrupt routines that are built into the BIOS ROM, the disk operating system, DOS, which is loaded into RAM when you boot up the system, also contains a number of interrupt routines that you can use. Some of these are shown in Figure 5.16. The most important one is *INT 21H*. This is a function request that handles many useful DOS functions depending upon the value in *AH* when *INT 21H* is called. A list of these functions is given in Appendix D. We have already used the character output and string output routines in Chapter 3. We will cover a number of the most important DOS calls related to disk I/O in Chapter 10.

Software interrupts can be used much like subroutines where the starting address of the routine, *CS:IP*, is stored in the interrupt vector table.

The other difference between an interrupt service routine and a subroutine is that a software interrupt saves the status flag as well as *CS* and *IP* on the stack. As a result, three words must be popped from the stack at the end of an interrupt service routine (using *IRET*) rather than one (for a near *RET*) or two (for a far *RET*) for a subroutine. We will show you how to write your own interrupt service routines in Chapter 11.

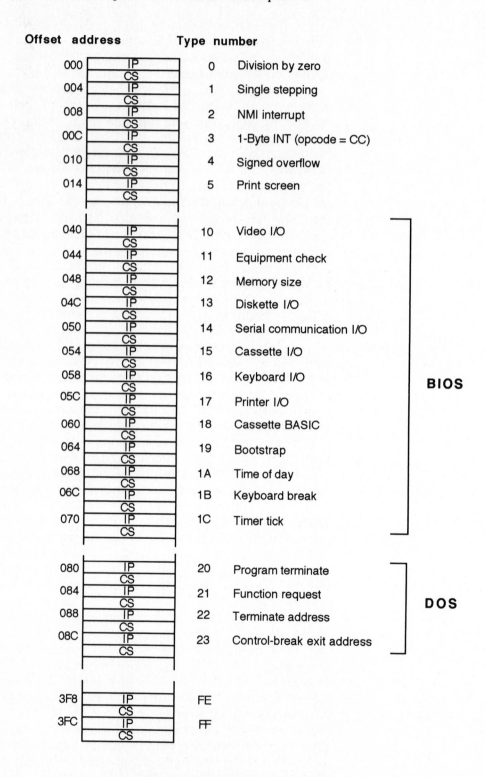

Offset address		Type number	
000	IP / CS	0	Division by zero
004	IP / CS	1	Single stepping
008	IP / CS	2	NMI interrupt
00C	IP / CS	3	1-Byte INT (opcode = CC)
010	IP / CS	4	Signed overflow
014	IP / CS	5	Print screen
040	IP / CS	10	Video I/O
044	IP / CS	11	Equipment check
048	IP / CS	12	Memory size
04C	IP / CS	13	Diskette I/O
050	IP / CS	14	Serial communication I/O
054	IP / CS	15	Cassette I/O
058	IP / CS	16	Keyboard I/O
05C	IP / CS	17	Printer I/O
060	IP / CS	18	Cassette BASIC
064	IP / CS	19	Bootstrap
068	IP / CS	1A	Time of day
06C	IP / CS	1B	Keyboard break
070	IP / CS	1C	Timer tick
080	IP / CS	20	Program terminate
084	IP / CS	21	Function request
088	IP / CS	22	Terminate address
08C	IP / CS	23	Control-break exit address
3F8	IP / CS	FE	
3FC	IP / CS	FF	

(Interrupt types 10–1C grouped as **BIOS**; types 20–23 grouped as **DOS**)

Figure 5.16 Interrupt vector table

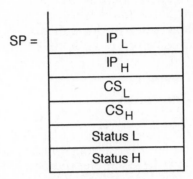

Figure 5.17 Interrupts push the status register, *CS*, and *IP* onto the stack

Breakpoints and Single Stepping

Note that software interrupts require two bytes: CD, the opcode for *INT* plus the type number. When setting a breakpoint as we do in the TUTOR monitor (by typing */BS*) you need to be able to replace only a single byte. A special software interrupt, *INT 3*, uses the single opcode, CC (see Figure 5.16). We have used this instruction to end many of our programs. This is because the TUTOR monitor has an interrupt service routine, whose vector address is stored in the type 3 location of the interrupt vector table, that displays the current register contents and then jumps back to the TUTOR monitor.

The single stepping feature of the TUTOR monitor uses the type 1 interrupt which will occur one instruction after the trap flag, *T*, in the status register is set to 1. The *T* flag can be set to 1 by pushing the status register on the stack (perhaps as the result of an interrupt) and ORing the high byte of the status register (in the stack) with 10H. Assuming that *CS* and *IP* have also been pushed on the stack then an *IRET* instruction will cause the modified status register (with *T*=1) to be popped from the stack. After one instruction is executed a type 1 interrupt will occur.

In the TUTOR monitor this interrupt service routine resets to zero the *T*-flag that was just pushed onto the stack. (The 8086 automatically resets the *T*-flag in the actual status register to zero after it pushes it on the stack. Otherwise, you would single step each instruction in the interrupt service routine!) It then displays the current contents of all the registers.

5.4 WRITING AND DEBUGGING COMPLETE PROGRAMS

We will now take a look at complete programs — how to write them, assemble them, link them, run them and debug them. To write a program you will need some type of text editor or word processor. Any kind that will generate straight ASCII text files will do. A full screen editor such as EMACS will work just fine. You will also need a macro assembler such as the IBM PC Macro Assembler (MASM), Microsoft's Macro Assembler (MASM) or Borland's Turbo Assembler (TASM). We will describe how to use a macro assembler later in this section.

If you don't have an editor or assembler handy you can still learn a lot about assembly language programming by studying, running and debugging the programs in this book that we have already edited and assembled for you. The source listings (.ASM and .LST files), object code (.OBJ files) and executable (.EXE) files for many of the programs in this book are included on the TUTOR disk. We will show you in this section how you can load these .EXE files into TUTOR, set breakpoints and execute part or all of the programs.

General Structure of an 8086 Assembly Language Program

The general structure of an 8086 assembly language program is shown in Figure 5.18. The program is made up of a collection of segments that begin with the assembler directive *SEGMENT* and end with the *ENDS* directive. A stack segment is required to produce a valid .EXE file that can be run. The data segment will contain the definitions of data variables.

The code segment will contain the main program and subroutines which must begin with the assembler directive *PROC* and end with the directive *ENDP*. The directive *PROC* is followed by either *NEAR* or *FAR*, which determines the version of *RET* to be used in that procedure. The attribute *NEAR* will use the intrasegment version of *RET* (opcode = C3) and the attribute *FAR* will use the intersegment version (opcode = CB; see Table 5.7).

The assembly language program must end with the *END* directive. This can be followed by an optional expression which identifies the label corresponding to the starting offset address of the program.

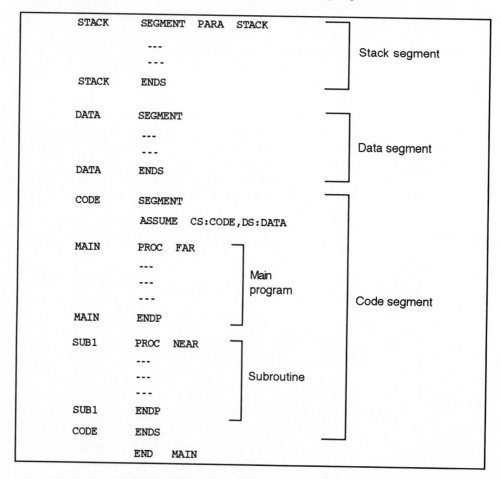

Figure 5.18 General structure of an 8086 assembly language program

Note from Figure 5.18 that the labels associated with each *SEGMENT* directive must be the same labels used with the corresponding *ENDS* directive. Similarly, the labels associated with each *PROC* directive must also be used with the corresponding *ENDP* directive.

The main program is normally given the type attribute *FAR* in the *PROC* directive. This means that you can end the main program with an intersegment *RET* instruction that will transfer control to another segment. Of course, you must have pushed the destination code segment (*CS*) and instruction pointer (*IP*) on the stack so that they will be popped off the stack when the *RET* instruction is executed. While this is somewhat awkward it was the standard way to quit programs in earlier versions of DOS. With DOS versions 2.0 and above it is better (and easier) to return to DOS from the main program by executing the following DOS function call:

```
MOV    AX,4C00H        ;quit to DOS
INT    21H
```

Consider the program shown in Listing 5.1a for finding the two's complement of a double (32-bit) word.

```
Listing 5.1a  neg2word.asm
        title  Two's complement of a double word

stack   segment        para    stack
                db      64 dup(?)
stack   ends

data    segment
dnum    dd      12345678h
negnum  dd      ?
data    ends

code    segment public
                assume cs:code,ds:data

main    proc    far
                mov     ax,data
                mov     ds,ax              ;set ds=data
                mov     ax,word ptr dnum   ;ax=low word
                mov     dx,word ptr dnum+2 ;dx=high word
                call    dnegate            ;2's compl
                mov     word ptr negnum,ax   ;store lo word
                mov     word ptr negnum+2,dx ;store hi word
                int     3
main    endp

;       negate double word dx:ax
dnegate         proc    near
                push    bx                 ;save regs
                push    cx
                mov     bx,dx              ;bx=hi word
                mov     cx,ax              ;cx=lo word
                xor     ax,ax              ;ax=0
                mov     dx,ax              ;dx=0
                sub     ax,cx              ;dx:ax =
                sbb     dx,bx              ; 0:0 - bx:cx
                pop     cx                 ;restore regs
                pop     bx
                ret
dnegate         endp
code    ends
                end     main
```

This program is designed to be run only from TUTOR so we will end the main program with the *INT 3* breakpoint instruction. Listing 5.1a is exactly as you would type it using an editor such as EMACS and is stored on the TUTOR disk under the filename *neg2word.asm*. All of your assembly language source files must have the filename extension *asm*. This file becomes the input to the macro assembler.

The assembler will produce two output files: *neg2word.obj* and *neg2word.lst*. The .OBJ file is the object file that will be the input to the linker. The .LST file is shown in Listing 5.1b.

Listing 5.1b   *neg2word.lst*

```
IBM Personal Computer MACRO Assembler   Version 2.00      Page   1-1
Two's complement of a double word                         07-12-91


                          title  Two's complement of a double word

0000                      stack  segment        para    stack
0000      40 [                     db     64 dup(?)
          ??
             ]

0040                      stack  ends

0000                      data   segment
0000   78 56 34 12        dnum            dd       12345678h
0004   ????????           negnum         dd       ?
0008                      data   ends


0000                      code   segment public
                          assume cs:code,ds:data


0000                      main   proc    far
0000   B8 ---- R            mov    ax,data
0003   8E D8                mov    ds,ax                ;set ds=data
0005   A1 0000 R            mov    ax,word ptr dnum     ;ax=low word
0008   8B 16 0002 R         mov    dx,word ptr dnum+2   ;dx=high word
000C   E8 0017 R            call   dnegate                ;2's compl
000F   A3 0004 R            mov    word ptr negnum,ax   ;store lo word
0012   89 16 0006 R         mov    word ptr negnum+2,dx ;store hi word
0016   CC                   int    3
0017                      main   endp

                          ;      negate double word dx:ax
0017                      dnegate proc   near
0017   53                   push   bx                   ;save regs
0018   51                   push   cx
0019   8B DA                mov    bx,dx                ;bx=hi word
001B   8B C8                mov    cx,ax                ;cx=lo word
001D   33 C0                xor    ax,ax                ;ax=0
001F   8B D0                mov    dx,ax                ;dx=0
0021   2B C1                sub    ax,cx                ;dx:ax =
0023   1B D3                sbb    dx,bx                ; 0:0 - bx:cx
0025   59                   pop    cx                   ;restore regs
0026   5B                   pop    bx
0027   C3                   ret
0028                      dnegate        endp

0028                      code   ends
                          end    main
```

Listing 5.1b (continued)

```
IBM Personal Computer MACRO Assembler    Version 2.00  Page Symbols - 1
Two's complement of a double word                      07-12-91


Segments and Groups:

          N a m e                      Size   Align  Combine Class

CODE . . . . . . . . . . . . . . .     0028   PARA   PUBLIC
DATA . . . . . . . . . . . . . . .     0008   PARA   NONE
STACK. . . . . . . . . . . . . . .     0040   PARA   STACK

Symbols:

          N a m e                      Type   Value  Attr

DNEGATE. . . . . . . . . . . . . .     N PROC  0017   CODE  Length =0011
DNUM . . . . . . . . . . . . . . .     L DWORD 0000   DATA
MAIN . . . . . . . . . . . . . . .     F PROC  0000   CODE  Length =0017
NEGNUM . . . . . . . . . . . . . .     L DWORD 0004   DATA

50092 Bytes free


Warning Severe
Errors   Errors
  0   0
```

The .LST file is the same source listing as the .ASM file in Listing 5.1a with the addition of the offset addresses (within the code segment) and the machine code displayed to the left of each assembly language instruction. In addition there is a symbol table at the end of the .LST file that gives the offset addresses of all variables and labels. This .LST file will help you find any particular instruction when the machine code has been loaded into TUTOR.

Note that in the stack segment in Listing 5.1 the statement

```
db      64 dup(?)
```

will reserve 64 bytes of memory for the stack. This stack segment will be located immediately following the program starting at the next paragraph (16 byte increments) boundary.[1] (This is the meaning of the *PARA* option in the stack *SEGMENT* directive).

The statement

```
assume        cs:code,ds:data
```

must appear at the beginning of a code segment to tell the assembler to assume that the code segment register, *CS*, will contain the address of the segment *CODE* and the data segment register, *DS*, will contain the address of the segment *DATA*. The program must explicitly set the data segment register *DS* to *DATA* and this is done with the first two statements in the program:

```
0000   B8 ---- R     mov  ax,data
0003   8E D8         mov  ds,ax            ;set ds=data
```

---

[1] The stack segment may not always immediately follow the code segment. It will depend on the names of the segments. Unless overridden, the linker will arrange the segments alphabetically in memory. The .MAP file, produced by the linker, will show you where all the segments in a given program are located.

Note that the first statement is assembled as a *MOV ax,immed* instruction (opcode = B8H) but the immediate value to move into *AX* isn't known and is left in the listing as two unknown bytes ---- *R*. Even after the linker produces the executable file *neg2word.exe* from the object file *neg2word.obj* (we will describe how to do this later in this section) this immediate value of *DATA* will still not be known. This value represents the segment address of the data segment for this program. But this data segment value can't be known until the program is loaded into memory. When you execute an .EXE file from DOS by typing its name (such as *neg2word*) DOS will load in the file and then compute and insert all of the relocatable addresses such as the value of *DATA* in the above example before it executes the program. We will now show you how TUTOR can do the same thing which will allow you to load, execute and debug any .EXE program.

Debugging .EXE Programs Using TUTOR

The TUTOR monitor can be used to explore the structure of .EXE files and to debug programs that you have written as .EXE files. With the position cursor of TUTOR set to offset address 0000 in a free memory segment (such as the one displayed when you first execute TUTOR), load the file *neg2word.exe* using /SL.[2] The header of the .EXE file will be loaded at offset address 0000. This header will always begin with the two bytes 4D 5A. The meanings of the other bytes in the header are given in Figure 5.19. Note that the header contains information from the linker about where the code segment and stack segment should be (relative to where the .EXE file was loaded into memory) and the values of the stack pointer and instruction pointer. When DOS loads an .EXE file it sets *CS*, *SS*, *SP*, and *IP* using these values. It creates a 256-byte *program segment prefix* (PSP) in front of the program and sets *DS* and *ES* to the segment address of this program segment prefix. The .EXE header also contains relocation information needed, for example, to locate the data segment relative to the code segment.

.EXE File Header

	08	19	2A	3B	4C	5D	6E	7F
0000	4D	5A	last page size		file size		#reloc items	
0008	header size		min alloc		max alloc		SS offset	
0010	initial SP		checksum		initial IP		CS offset	
0018	reloc tbl offset		overlay #		|		|	
0020	|		|		|		|	
	offset		segment		offset		segment	

Figure 5.19 Description of an .EXE file header

The .EXE header in the file *neg2word.exe* that you have just loaded into memory contains 512 (200H) bytes. Go to offset address 0200 and you should find the object code for the program shown in Listing 5.1b. However, the first statement will be

```
MOV  AX,0003H
```

---

[2] In response to the prompt *LOAD: <pathname>* you can enter any pathname such as *c:\progs\neg2word.exe*. For earlier TUTOR versions less than Version 4.01 the file must be in the current directory.

This value of 0003H is not going to be the final value for *DATA*. Note the value of the current segment address *SEG*. Go back to offset address 0000 and *press function key F10*. Note that the segment address has changed and the position cursor is pointing to the first instruction of the program at offset address 0000. In addition, the value to be moved into *AX* in the first instruction has also been changed and is equal to the current segment address *SEG* plus 0003 (this was the 0003 that was in the original .EXE file). Pressing function key *F10* has just performed the loading function that DOS does everytime you run an .EXE program. It has computed the real value of the data segment once we know where you actually loaded in the program.

The program needs to actually set the data segment register, *DS*, to this value by executing the first two instructions. Single step these two instructions by pressing function key *F1* twice. Note that the data segment memory displayed in the upper-right part of the screen changes to this new value of *DS* and displays the values

```
78 56 34 12
```

in the first four bytes of the data segment. This is just the 32-bit value 12345678H that was defined in the program by the statement

```
dnum        dd      12345678h
```

in Listing 5.1a. Note from the listing file in Listing 5.1b that the assembler actually stores this 32-bit number in memory at offset address 0000 in the data segment. We have just found these data using TUTOR!

The assembler directive *dd* means *define double word* and will reserve 32-bits in the data segment for the variable we have called *dnum*, and will assign an initial value of 12345678H to this variable. The second statement in the data segment portion of Listing 5.1 is

```
negnum       dd      ?
```

This statement defines a second variable called *negnum* that also contains 32-bits (*dd*) but has an unspecified initial value (?). The contents of this variable are stored at offset addresses 0004 – 0007 in the data segment. These will be the last four bytes in the top row of the data segment memory in TUTOR and may contain all zeros at this point. The program is going to compute the two's complement of 12345678H and store the result in this second variable *negnum*.

The third statement in the main program of Listing 5.1b is

```
0005  A1 0000 R      mov ax,word ptr dnum      ;ax=low word
```

This statement will load the low word of *dnum* (5678H) into *ax*. Because we have defined *dnum* as a 32-bit value using *dd* we cannot just load *dnum* into the 16-bit register *ax*. The assembler expects only 16-bit variables (defined with the directive *dw – define word*) to be loaded into 16-bit registers and only 8-bit variables (defined with the directive *db – define byte*) to be loaded into 8-bit registers. We can tell the assembler to load the 16-bit value starting at the address of *dnum* (0000) into *ax* by including the assembler directive *word ptr* before the variable *dnum* as shown. This tells the assembler that notwithstanding the fact that we defined *dnum* to be 32-bits, for this operation treat it as a 16-bit value starting at *dnum*. Therefore, if we execute this instruction the value 5678H (stored low-byte first at offset address 0000 in the data segment) should be loaded into *ax*. Single step this instruction with *F1* and see if it does.

The next statement is

```
0008  8B 16 0002 R  mov  dx,word ptr dnum+2   ;dx=high word
```

This will move the 16-bit value at dnum+2 (1234H) into *dx*. Verify this by pressing *F1* again.

The next statement is

```
000C  E8 0017 R    call dnegate              ;2's compl
```

This is a call to the subroutine *dnegate* which will take the two's complement of the 32-bit number in *dx:ax* and leave the result in *dx:ax*. If you press *F1* at this point you will enter this subroutine and could single step through each instruction in the subroutine. You can do this later. For now press function key *F2* which will execute the entire subroutine and return to the instruction following *call dnegate*. The two's complement of 12345678H should now be stored in *dx:ax* (the high word will be in *dx* and the low word in *ax*). You should verify that this is the correct two's complement.

The next two statement will move this 32-bit value in *dx:ax* into the variable *negnum*. Press *F1* twice and watch it go! Note the order that the bytes are stored in *negnum*.

The subroutine *dnegate* in Listing 5.1 takes the two's complement of *dx:ax* by subtracting this value from 0:0. It does this by first moving *dx:ax* into *bx:cx* and then setting *dx:ax* = 0:0. Note that the statement

```
        xor   ax,ax
```

will set *ax* to zero. Verify this. Also note that the second subtraction in this subroutine must be a *subtract with borrow* instruction in order to handle a possible borrow from the first subtraction.

Go back to the beginning of the program by pressing *Home* and single step the program again — this time single stepping through the subroutine by pressing *F1*. Make sure you understand how the program works.

Suppose you had single stepped through the program using *F2* and when you called the subroutine it produced the wrong answer. Inasmuch as the values in *ax* and *dx* going into the subroutine were correct the problem must have been within the subroutine. Perhaps we mistyped the instruction at offset address 001FH and typed *mov ax,dx* instead of *mov dx,ax*. This would have produced the machine code 8B C2 at this offset address instead of 8B D0. Change D0 to C2 at offset address 0020 using /MH.

To find this mistake, we will set a breakpoint at offset address 0019H. This is within the subroutine but before where we expect the error to be. To set the breakpoint move the position cursor to address 0019H and then type */BS*. This will set a breakpoint by replacing the opcode with CCH. Now press *Home* to go to the beginning of the program and execute the program by pressing */EG*. Note that the program will execute up to the breakpoint and replace the original opcode at that address. You can now begin to single step from here. Note that at this point the correct values are in *ax* and *dx* but when you single step the incorrect instruction it will be obvious that the zero in *ax* is not being moved to *dx* and you will have discovered the error.

This technique of setting a breakpoint as far into the program as possible without causing the error and then single stepping until the error is discovered is an important debugging tool. By using this technique you should be able to discover most run time errors in your programs.

When you load an .EXE file into TUTOR and then press function key *F10* the program will be ready to execute. In addition to fixing up all the relocation addresses TUTOR stores the correct values of *CS*, *DS*, *ES*, *SS*, *SP*, and *IP* for this .EXE file in these registers.

You can therefore load any .EXE file into any convenient place in memory, press key *F10*, and execute the program. You can therefore use TUTOR to debug your programs by setting breakpoints and single stepping. When the program is completely debugged, it should work from DOS without change.

If you press key *F10*, set a breakpoint, and then execute the program, the program will stop with the data segment register and the stack pointer in general changed to some values that are different from their initial values. If you want to go back and execute the program again from the beginning, these values should be restored to their original values. This can normally be done by pressing function key *F9*.

Using a Macro Assembler

When using the IBM PC macro assembler (or similar assembler) you will carry out the following steps:

1. Create a source code file with a filename extension .ASM using any convenient editor.
2. Use the assembler to convert the .ASM file to an object file (with an .OBJ extension) and to produce a listing file (with an extension .LST).
3. Use the linker to produce an executable file (with an extension .EXE) from one or more .OBJ files.
4. Run the program by typing the name of the .EXE file.

We will consider each of these steps by means of the example program shown in Listing 5.2a.

This program will clear the screen and then display on the screen any key you type from the keyboard. The cursor will automatically be advanced one space as each character is typed. If you press the *Enter* key the cursor will advance to the beginning of the next line. (We call this a carriage return, *CR*, and a line feed, *LF*). If you press the *ESC* key the screen will clear and the program will return to DOS.

The program in Listing 5.2 uses four external subroutines that are stored in the file *screen.asm* that is on your TUTOR disk. We will study how all of these subroutines work in Chapter 7. For now we will use only the four given in Table 5.8.

The file *screen.asm* has been assembled to produce the object file *screen.obj*. This object file must be linked with the object file produced by assembling Listing 5.2a. We will show you how to do this later in this section. To use the subroutines in Table 5.8 we must include the statements

```
extrn clrscn:near,chrout1:near
extrn crlf:near,getkey:near
```

Listing 5.2a *typescn.asm*

```
title     Type characters to screen

;         LINK with screen
stack     segment para stack
          db      64 dup(?)
stack     ends

;         screen subroutines
          extrn   clrscn:near,chrout1:near
          extrn   crlf:near,getkey:near

code      segment  public
          assume cs:code
main      proc    far
          call    clrscn              ;clear screen
keyscn:   call    getkey              ;wait for key
          cmp     al,1bh              ;if esc key
          jne     chkcr
          call    escape              ;quit to DOS
          int     21h
chkcr:    cmp     al,0dh              ;if enter key
          jne     dspchr
          call    crlf                ;do cr lf
          jmp     keyscn              ; & loop back
dspchr:   call    chrout1             ;else display char
          jmp     keyscn              ; & do again
main      endp

;         return to DOS
escape    proc    near
          call    clrscn              ;clear screen
          mov     ax,4C00h            ;terminate
          int     21h                 ; process
escape    endp

code      ends
          end     main
```

Table 5.8

Some *screen.asm* Subroutines

Subroutine	Input	Output	Regs. modified	Description
clrscn	none	none	none	Clear screen
getkey	none	AL = ASCII code of key	AX	Wait for key and get key value
crlf	none	none	none	Carriage return line feed
chrout1	AL = ASCII code of char to display	none	none	Output a char to screen with current attribute

at the beginning of the program as shown in Listing 5.2a. These statements tell the assembler to consider the subroutines *clrscn*, *chrout1*, *crlf* and *getkey* as near subroutines whose actual offset address won't be resolved until the two object files *typescn.obj* and *screen.obj* are linked. The main program in Listing 5.2a calls these four external subroutines as well as the internal subroutine *escape* which will return to DOS when the *Enter* key is pressed. Note in the main program that ordinary labels used for branching must end with a colon (:) while segment and procedure names do not.

We will assume that the assembler is on the hard disk drive *C* and that you will write your programs to a floppy disk in drive *A*. First type in the program shown in Listing 5.2a using any text editor. You should use the tab key to tab to the various columns. Start typing the labels in the left-most column on the screen.

The directory containing the macro assembler MASM should be in the *PATH* command in the *AUTOEXEC.BAT* file. This will mean that DOS can always find MASM regardless of your current directory. Assuming you have the file *typescn.asm* on your disk in drive *A* and the current directory is *A>*, then type

```
masm typescn
```

This will load the assembler from drive *C* and prompt you. Respond to each prompt with

```
a:
```

or simply press *Enter* as shown in Figure 5.20. If there are any errors in the source program they will be listed on the screen. At the end of the assembly process the number of errors will be displayed as shown in Figure 5.20.

```
A:\ >masm typescn
IBM Personal Computer MACRO Assembler    Version 2.00
(C)Copyright IBM Corp 1981, 1984
(C)Copyright Microsoft Corp 1981, 1983, 1984

Object filename [typescn.OBJ]: a:
Source listing  [NUL.LST]: a:
Cross reference [NUL.CRF]:

50092 Bytes free

Warning Severe
Errors  Errors
0       0

A:\ >
```

Figure 5.20 Example of using the assembler

In addition to the object file *testprog.obj* you have also created the listing file *typescn.lst*. shown in Listing 5.2b. You can see the contents of this file by typing

```
type testprog.lst
```

Press the two keys *Ctrl PrtSc* before typing the line above to get the listing sent to the printer. Press *Ctrl PrtSc* again to stop the printing.

Note that the machine code is printed in the .LST listing. However, the machine code in this listing is not exactly the same as the executable code that is stored in memory. For example, the value 001D at offset address 000B will actually be stored in memory as 1D 00. Similarly, the value 4C00 at offset address 0021 will actually be stored in memory as 00 4C. Any 16-bit value written in the listing file without a space such as 1234 will be stored in memory "backward" as 34 12.

Before you can run the program you must link it using the linker.

```
Listing 5.2b      typescn.lst


IBM Personal Computer MACRO Assembler    Version 2.00       Page   1-1
Type characters to screen                                          07-14-91

                          title  Type characters to screen

                        ;   LINK with screen
0000                    stack       segment para stack
0000    40 [                        db      64 dup(?)
           ??
        ]

0040                    stack       ends

                        ;   screen subroutines
                                    extrn   clrscn:near,chrout1:near
                                    extrn   crlf:near,getkey:near

0000                    code        segment  public
                                    assume cs:code
0000                    main        proc    far
0000    E8 0000 E                   call    clrscn              ;clear screen
0003    E8 0000 E       keyscn:     call    getkey              ;wait for key
0006    3C 1B                       cmp     al,1bh              ;if esc key
0008    75 05                       jne     chkcr
000A    E8 001D R                   call    escape              ;quit to DOS
000D    CD 21                       int     21h
000F    3C 0D           chkcr:      cmp     al,0dh              ;if enter key
0011    75 05                       jne     dspchr
0013    E8 0000 E                   call    crlf                ;do cr lf
0016    EB EB                       jmp     keyscn              ; & loop back
0018    E8 0000 E       dspchr:     call    chrout1             ;display char
001B    EB E6                       jmp     keyscn              ; & do again
001D                    main        endp

                        ;   return to DOS
001D                    escape      proc    near
001D    E8 0000 E                   call    clrscn              ;clear screen
0020    B8 4C00                     mov     ax,4C00h            ;terminate
0023    CD 21                       int     21h                 ; process
0025                    escape      endp

0025                    code        ends
                                    end     main
```

Using the Linker LINK

The linker is stored in the DOS file LINK.EXE. The directory containing this file should also be in the PATH command in the AUTOEXEC.BAT file. You will need to copy the object file *screen.obj* from the TUTOR disk to your current directory containing your assembled object file *typescn.obj*. Then type

```
link
```

The linker will be executed and will prompt you. Respond to the first prompt (for the .OBJ filename) with the two object files

```
typescn screen
```

Simply press *Enter* for the last three prompts as shown in Figure 5.21. This will create the default executable file *typescn.exe*. You are now ready to run the program.

You must always use the linker to produce an .EXE file even if you are not linking in any external subroutines. You would just list you own program name when asked for the .OBJ file to link.

```
A:\ >link

Microsoft (R) Personal Computer Linker  Version 2.40
Copyright (C) Microsoft Corp 1983, 1984, 1985.  All rights reserved.

Object Modules [.OBJ]: typescn screen
Run File [TYPESCN.EXE]:
List File [NUL.MAP]:
Libraries [.LIB]:

A:\ >
```

Figure 5.21 Linking the subroutines in *screen.obj* to your program *typescn.obj*

Running the Program

To run the program *typescn.exe*, simply type

```
typescn
```

This will cause the file *typescn.exe* to be loaded into memory, a program segment prefix to be created, and any relocation to be done. The program will then be executed beginning at the start address (as specified in the *END* statement of the assembly language program).

When you run *typescn.exe* you should be able to type anything you want on the screen and return to DOS by pressing the *ESC* key as shown in Figure 5.22.

```
The program typescn.exe is now running.  Anything you type on the keyboard will
be displayed on the screen.  When you press the enter key the cursor will move t
o the beginning of the next line like this.
If you reach the end of the screen line, the typing will automatically continue
on the next line.
If you press the ESC key the screen will clear and you will return to DOS.
```

Figure 5.22 An example of running the program *typescn.exe*

In Listing 5.2, the statement

```
code        segment      public
```

defines the code segment to have the name *code* and to be *public*. The file *screen.asm* has this same statement for its code segment. The public declaration in each statement means that these two code segments will be concatenated in memory by the linker in the order that you specified them when running the linker. In the example shown in Figure 5.21 the object code for *typescn.obj* will be stored in memory first followed by the object code for *screen.obj*. If you load the file *typescn.exe* into TUTOR and press *F10* you will be at the beginning of the program *typescn*. The subroutines in *screen.asm* will follow this code in memory.

In the file *screen.asm* the statements

```
public      clrscn,chrout1,crlf,getkey
```

must be included to make the addresses of these subroutines available to the linker so that they can be linked with other programs.

PROGRAMMING PROBLEMS

Problem 5.1 – Mixed Double Multiply

In this programming problem you will write an 8086 subroutine that will multiply an unsigned 32-bit multiplicand by an unsigned 16-bit multiplier and produce a 32-bit product.

a. The 8086 instruction *MUL* can multiply a 16-bit integer in *AX* by another 16-bit integer producing a 32-bit product in *DX:AX*. Sometimes we need to multiply a 32-bit value (double word) by a 16-bit value (word). In general, this could produce a 48-bit product as follows, where *A*, *B*, *C*, *D*, *E* and *F* are 16-bit values.

```
            A     B
        x         C
          BCH   BCL
    ACH   ACL
      D     E     F
```

The values *BCH* and *BCL* are the high word and low word of the partial product *B* x *C* and the values *ACH* and *ACL* are the high word and low word of the partial product *A* x *C*. Even though this product can contain 48 bits, we often know that the result will, in fact, fit in 32 bits. That is, the product will be less than 4,294,967,296. If this is the case then *D* = *ACH* will equal zero and the 32-bit product will consist of the high word *PH* = *E* = *BCH* + *ACL* and the low word *PL* = *F* = *BCL*.

Write a subroutine called *mdmul* that will multiply *dx:ax* by *bx* and leave the 32-bit product in *dx:ax*.

b. Write a main program module that includes a stack segment, a data segment and a code segment. The data segment should be as follows

```
data        segment
prod        dd      ?
oper1       dd      123456h
oper2       dw      100h
data        ends
```

The first two statements of your main program should be

```
mov     ax,data
mov     ds,ax
```

This will establish the value *ds* to be your data segment. Write a main program that will read the values of *oper1* and *oper2* from the data segment, calculate the mixed double product by calling the subroutine *mdmul* and store the result in the variable *prod* in the data segment. Stop the program by executing *INT 3*.

c.   Load the .EXE file of your program into TUTOR at offset address 0000. The position cursor will be pointing to the beginning of the .EXE file header which starts with 4D 5A. Press function key *F10*. Single step the first two instructions and note that your data segment will be displayed. Single step the remainder of your program and watch 123456H x 100H being calculated. What is the answer?

d.   Change the values in *oper1* and *oper2* so as to calculate ABCDEFH x ABH. What is the answer?

Problem 5.2 – Double Word Division

In this programming problem you will write an 8086 subroutine that will divide an unsigned 32-bit dividend by an unsigned 16-bit divisor and produce a 32-bit quotient and a 16-bit remainder.

a.   The 8086 instruction *DIV* can divide a 32-bit integer in *DX:AX* by a 16-bit integer leaving the 16-bit quotient in *AX* and the 16-bit remainder in *DX*. If the 32-bit dividend is too large or the 16-bit divisor is too small, the quotient may not fit into 16 bits. If this occurs, a divide-by-zero trap (interrupt) will occur. To keep this from happening, what is needed is a divide routine that will return a 32-bit quotient rather than a 16-bit quotient. This is easy to do by using multiple-word division. When doing long division you divide the divisor into the "high part" of the dividend to get the "high part" of the quotient. The "high remainder" becomes part of the remaining dividend that is divided by the divisor to yield the "low part" of the quotient and the final remainder.

In particular, if *num* is a 32-bit numerator with high word *numH* and low word *numL*, then to divide *num* by the 16-bit denominator *denom*, first divide *0:numH/denom* to give *quotH* and *remH*.   Then divide *remH:numL/denom* to give *quotL* and *rem*.

Write a subroutine called *ddiv* that will divide *dx:ax* by *bx* and leave the quotient in *dx:ax* and the remainder in *bx*.

b.   Write a main program module that includes a stack segment, a data segment and a code segment. The data segment should be as follows

```
data       segment
num        dd     12345678h
denom      dw     10h
rem        dw     ?
quot       dd     ?
data       ends
```

The first two statements of your main program should be

```
mov    ax,data
mov    ds,ax
```

This will establish the value *ds* to be your data segment. Write a main program that will read the values of the numerator and denominator from the data segment, calculate the double division by calling the subroutine *ddiv* and store the result in the variables *quot* and *rem* in the data segment. Stop the program by executing *INT 3*.

c. Load the .EXE file of your program into TUTOR at offset address 0000. The position cursor will be pointing to the beginning of the .EXE file header which starts with 4D 5A. Press function key *F10*. Single step the first two instructions and note that your data segment will be displayed. Single step the remainder of your program and watch 12345678H/10H being calculated. What is the answer?

d. Change the values in *num* and *denom* so as to calculate ABCDEF12H/BADH. What is the answer?

Problem 5.3 – Keyboard Inputs

The subroutine *getkey* in Table 5.8 returns the ASCII code of the key pressed. However, if you look at Table 9.4 in Chapter 9 you will note that the function keys and some of the keys on the numeric keypad have keyboard ASCII codes of zero. When this occurs the subroutine *getkey* adds (or ORs) the hex value 80H to the scan code given in Table 9.4. For example, if you press the *Del* key (with scan code = 53H) the subroutine *getkey* will return the value 53H + 80H = D3H.

Modify Listing 5.2a given is Section 5.4 so that if you press the *Del* key the program will clear the screen and you can begin typing in characters again. Assemble, link and run this new program.

EXERCISES

Exercise 5.1

Type in the following program and single step through it several times. Explain how each instruction affects the contents of accumulator *AL* and the value of the carry flag *C*.

```
0000   B0 13    LOOP1:   MOV   AL,13H
0002   FE C0    LOOP1:   INC   AL
0004   3C 16             CMP   AL,16H
0006   72 FA             JB    LOOP2
0008   73 F6             JNB   LOOP1
```

Exercise 5.2

Type in the following program and single step through in several times. Explain how each instruction affects the accumulator *AL* and the value of the overflow flag *O*.

```
0000   B0 7A    LOOP1:   MOV   AL,7AH
0002   04 02    LOOP2:   ADD   AL,2
0004   71 FC             JNO   LOOP2
0006   70 F8             JO    LOOP1
```

Exercise 5.3

Type in the following program and single step through it several times. Explain what you observe.

```
0000   B0 83    LOOP1:  MOV   AL,83H
0002   FE C8    LOOP2:  DEC   AL
0004   3C 7E            CMP   AL,7EH
0006   77 FA            JA    LOOP2
0008   76 F6            JBE   LOOP1
```

Change the instructions *JA* to *JG* and *JBE* to *JLE* and single step through the program several times. Explain what you observe.

Exercise 5.4

```
L1:    MOV    CX,5
       MOV    BX,3
L2:    DEC    BX
       LOOPNE L2
       JMP    L1
```

a) Write the machine code for the program given above.
b) Type in the program starting at offset address 0000 and single step through it several times. Explain what you observe.
c) Change the first statement to *MOV CX,2* and repeat (b).
d) Change the statement *LOOPNE L2* to *LOOPE L2* and repeat (b).

Exercise 5.5

Write a program that will push the values of *AX* and *CX* on the stack and then *POP* these values into *SI* and *DI*.

CHAPTER **6**

More Addressing Modes

In previous chapters we have executed a number of 8086 instructions, either by single stepping (using key *F1*) or by executing a program using */E*. Most 8086 instructions operate on some kind of data. For example, the contents of accumulator *AX* may be incremented. This is an example of a single operand instruction. Some instructions, such as *ADD*, contain two operands. The operands specify where the data to be used in the instruction are to be obtained. There are many different forms that these operands can take. These are known as the *operand addressing modes*.

You have already learned to use register addressing and immediate addressing in Chapter 4. In this chapter you will learn to use the following 8086 addressing modes:

- Direct
- Register indirect
- Indexed, with possible displacement
- Based
- Indexed plus based, with possible displacement
- Stack addressing

6.1 THE ADDRESSING MODE POSTBYTE

Many 8086 instructions include a *postbyte* in addition to the primary opcode byte. This postbyte, as we saw in Chapter 4, can have one of the two forms shown in Figure 6.1.

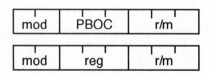

Figure 6.1 Two forms of the 8088 addressing mode postbyte

In the first of the two forms in Figure 6.1, PBOC is a 3-bit postbyte opcode which, together with the primary opcode, determines the instruction. For example, in Table A.2a in Appendix A an asterisk in a particular opcode location indicates that a secondary postbyte opcode is needed to specify the instructions. These are listed in Table A.2b of Appendix A. The postbyte opcodes are only 3 of the bits that form the entire postbyte. The remaining 5 bits are divided between a 2-bit *mod* field and a 3-bit *r/m* field as shown in Figure 6.1. The meanings of these two fields are given in Table 6.1. Although this table looks complicated, it, together with Table 6.2, defines all of the 8086 addressing modes. Tables 6.1 and 6.2 are reproduced in Appendix A as Tables A.3 and A.4.

The second form of the postbyte shown in Figure 6.1 includes the field *reg* instead of a postbyte opcode. The meaning of *reg* is shown in Table 6.2. When *mod* = 11 the *r/m* code refers to a register. This means that the instruction is a *register to register* instruction such as the *MOV* instructions we looked at in Section 4.2. If *mod* is *not* 11 then one of the operands in the instruction will refer to a memory location. Table 6.1 is rearranged in Table 6.3 to give the names of these operand addressing modes. We will look at each of these addressing modes in the following sections. Before doing that, however, let's look at a few more examples of the addressing mode postbyte for some register and immediate addressing.

Table 6.1

Postbyte *mod,r/m* Fields

r/m	mod = 11 byte	mod = 11 word	mod = 00	mod = 01	mod = 11
000	AL	AX	BX + SI	BX + SI + disp8	BX + SI + disp16
001	CL	CX	BX + DI	BX + DI + disp8	BX + DI + disp16
010	DL	DX	BP + SI	BP + SI + disp8	BP + SI +disp16
011	BL	BX	BP + DI	BP + DI + disp8	BP + DI +disp16
100	AH	SP	SI	SI + disp8	SI + disp16
101	CH	BP	DI	DI + disp8	DI + disp16
110	DH	SI	Direct	BP + disp8	BP + disp16
111	BH	DI	BX	BX + disp8	BX + disp16

Table 6.2

Postbyte *reg* Field

reg	byte (b)	word (w)
000	AL	AX
001	CL	CX
010	DL	DX
011	BL	BX
100	AH	SP
101	CH	BP
110	DH	SI
111	BH	DI

Table 6.3
8086 Operand Addressing Modes

Addressing Mode	r/m	mod = 00	mod = 01	mod = 10
Direct	110	Direct		
Register Indirect	100	SI		
	101	DI		
	111	BX		
Indexed	100		SI + disp8	SI + disp16
	101		DI + disp8	DI + disp16
Based	111		BX + disp8	BX + disp16
Based Stack	110		BP + disp8	BP + disp16
Based + Indexed	000	BX + SI	BX + SI + disp8	BX + SI + disp16
	001	BX + DI	BX + DI + disp8	BX + DI + disp16
Based + Indexed Stack	010	BP + SI	BP + SI + disp8	BP + SI + disp16
	011	BP + DI	BP + DI + disp8	BP + DI + disp16

Immediate Addressing

To see how Table 6.1 is used with the immediate mode instructions in Table A.2, suppose you want to code the instruction

```
ADD  BL,19H
```

From Table A.2 you see that the only single opcode immediate *ADD* instruction involves registers *AL* or *AX*. The instruction

```
ADD b r/m,imm
```

uses the opcode 80 plus the postbyte

mod	0	0	0	r/m

From Table 6.1 you see that a value of *mod* = 11 corresponds to an operation on a *register*. The value of *r/m* then specifies the register. A value of *r/m* = 011 corresponds to *BL* for a byte instruction. Therefore, the postbyte for the instruction *ADD BL,19H* is

```
     mod      reg       r/m
    | 1  1 | 0  0  0 | 0  1  1 |
     reg      ADD       BL
```

or C3H. Therefore, the coding for the instruction will be

```
80 C3 19    ADD  BL,19H
```

To try this, type in the program shown in Figure 6.2. This is the same program as in Figure 4.9 that adds 35H to 19H except that register *BL* is used in Figure 6.2. Single step this instruction and observe the result (4E) in *BL*.

```
0000   B3 35          MOV   BL,35H
0002   80 C3 19       ADD   BL,19H
```

Figure 6.2 Program to add 35H and 19H using *BL*

Register Addressing

In *register addressing* the data is found in a register. For example, the instruction

```
DEC CL
```

decrements the contents of register *CL*. This is an example of a single operand instruction. From Table A.2a in Appendix A you see that there is no single opcode for this instruction. You can *DEC* the 16-bit register *CX* with the opcode 49 but to *DEC CL* you must use the opcode FE plus a postbyte. The postbyte can be found from Tables A.1a and A.3 to be

```
 mod       reg        r/m
┌─────┬───────────┬──────────┐
│ 1  1│ 0   0   1 │ 0   0   1│
└─────┴───────────┴──────────┘
 reg       DEC         CL
           (FE)
```

or C9H. Therefore, the coding for *DEC CL* is FE C9.

Register addressing can also involve two operands as we saw in Chapter 4. For example, the instruction

```
MOV  AX,SI
```

moves the contents of register *SI* to register *AX*. Opcodes 88 – 8B in Table A.2 correspond to the instructions shown in Table 6.4. These instructions can be used to move data from one register to another register, from a register to a memory location, or from a memory location to a register. The second form of the postbyte shown in Figure 6.1 is used to determine the source and destination in this instruction.

Table 6.4
General MOV Instructions

Opcode	Instruction
88	MOV b r/m,reg
89	MOV w r/m,reg
8A	MOV b reg,r/m
8B	MOV w reg,r/m

For example, to code

```
MOV  AX,SI
```

you can choose *AX* to be the *reg* and *SI* to be the *r/m* (with *mod* = 11). You would then choose the form *MOV w reg,r/m* with the primary opcode 8B and the postbyte (see Tables 6.1 and 6.2)

```
         mod      reg      r/m
        ┌──┬──┬──┬──┬──┬──┬──┬──┐
        │ 1│ 1│ 0│ 0│ 0│ 1│ 1│ 0│
        └──┴──┴──┴──┴──┴──┴──┴──┘
         reg      AX       SI
```

or C6H. Therefore, the coding of the instruction is

         8B C6   MOV   AX,SI

Note that this instruction could also be coded as

         89 F0   MOV   AX,SI

by using *r/m* as the destination and *reg* as the source. In this case the postbyte is

```
         mod      reg      r/m
        ┌──┬──┬──┬──┬──┬──┬──┬──┐
        │ 1│ 1│ 1│ 1│ 0│ 0│ 0│ 0│
        └──┴──┴──┴──┴──┴──┴──┴──┘
         reg      SI       AX
```

or F0H.

The reason that there are two ways to code the same instruction is that both the source and destination in this example are registers. However, in Table 6.4 the operand *r/m* can, in general, be a *memory* location. The operand *reg* is always a register. We will now look at how to move data between a register and a memory location.

6.2   DIRECT ADDRESSING MODE

The direct addressing mode uses a two-byte operand that can represent any offset address. This offset address is combined with the value in the *data segment register*, *DS*, to form the actual address of the data.

An example of using the direct addressing mode was given in Listing 5.1 in Chapter 5. In that example *dnum* and *negnum* were defined to be 32-bit values in the data segment using the assembler directive *dd*. As another example, consider the program shown in Listing 6.1. This program stores the value FDH in memory location *joe* (direct mode) and then increments this memory location (direct mode) until the value becomes 00 (is no longer negative). The offset address 0000 within the data segment is given the name *joe* using the *define-byte* (*DB*) assembler directive. This means that *joe* is a variable name whose offset address within the data segment is 0000. The value of *joe* will be the byte stored at this address. The *?* in the *DB* statement means that the assembler doesn't have to assign an initial value to *joe*.

Linking the assembly language program shown in Listing 6.1 will produce the executable file *joe.exe*. Load this .EXE file into TUTOR (using */SL*) and then press function key *F10*. Single step the first two instructions by pressing function key *F1* twice. This will set *DS* to the data segment containing *joe* and will display the contents of *joe* in the first byte of the data segment displayed in the upper-right part of the screen. When you press *F1* again you will execute the instruction *mov joe,0fdh* which will store the hex value FD in offset address 0000 in the data segment as shown in Figure 6.3.

```
Listing  6.1  joe.lst

                              title   Direct addressing example

        0000                          stack   segment para stack
        0000      40 [                         db      64 dup(?)
                      ??
                         ]
        0040                          stack   ends

        0000                          data    segment public
        0000   ??                     joe     db      ?
        0001                          data    ends

        0000                          code    segment public
                                              assume  cs:code,ds:data
        0000                          main    proc    far
        0000   B8 ---- R                       mov     ax,data         ;set ds
        0003   8E D8                           mov     ds,ax
        0005   C6 06 0000 R FD        m1:      mov     joe,0fdh        ;joe = fd
        000A   FE 06 0000 R           m2:      inc     joe             ;joe = joe + 1
        000E   78 FA                           js      m2              ;repeat until joe=0
        0010   74 F3                           je      m1              ;do again
        0012                          main    endp

        0012                          code    ends
                                              end     main
```

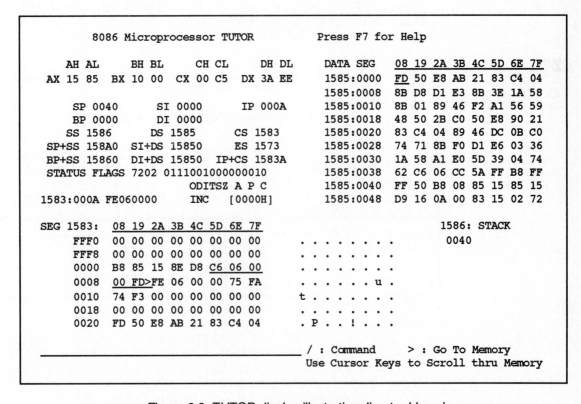

```
        8086 Microprocessor TUTOR              Press F7 for Help

    AH AL      BH BL      CH CL      DH DL    DATA SEG    08 19 2A 3B 4C 5D 6E 7F
 AX 15 85   BX 10 00   CX 00 C5   DX 3A EE    1585:0000   FD 50 E8 AB 21 83 C4 04
                                              1585:0008   8B D8 D1 E3 8B 3E 1A 58
     SP 0040       SI 0000       IP 000A      1585:0010   8B 01 89 46 F2 A1 56 59
     BP 0000       DI 0000                    1585:0018   48 50 2B C0 50 E8 90 21
     SS 1586       DS 1585       CS 1583      1585:0020   83 C4 04 89 46 DC 0B C0
 SP+SS 158A0   SI+DS 15850       ES 1573      1585:0028   74 71 8B F0 D1 E6 03 36
 BP+SS 15860   DI+DS 15850   IP+CS 1583A      1585:0030   1A 58 A1 E0 5D 39 04 74
 STATUS FLAGS 7202 0111001000000010           1585:0038   62 C6 06 CC 5A FF B8 FF
                      ODITSZ A P C            1585:0040   FF 50 B8 08 85 15 85 15
 1583:000A FE060000      INC   [0000H]        1585:0048   D9 16 0A 00 83 15 02 72

 SEG 1583:   08 19 2A 3B 4C 5D 6E 7F                      1586: STACK
    FFF0      00 00 00 00 00 00 00 00    . . . . . . . .      0040
    FFF8      00 00 00 00 00 00 00 00    . . . . . . . .
    0000      B8 85 15 8E D8 C6 06 00    . . . . . . . .
    0008      00 FD>FE 06 00 00 75 FA    . . . . . . u .
    0010      74 F3 00 00 00 00 00 00    t . . . . . . .
    0018      00 00 00 00 00 00 00 00    . . . . . . . .
    0020      FD 50 E8 AB 21 83 C4 04    . P . . ! . . .

                                          / : Command      > : Go To Memory
                                          Use Cursor Keys to Scroll thru Memory
```

Figure 6.3 TUTOR display illustrating direct addressing

Continue to single step through this program several times while watching the contents of DS:0000. Note that the instruction

```
MOV   JOE,0FDH
```

will move the value FDH into memory location DS:0000. Similarly, the instruction

```
INC   JOE
```

will increment the contents of memory location DS:0000.

The second instruction in Figure 6.3 is

```
MOV   DS,AX
```

which moves the contents of *AX* to the segment register *DS*. The segment registers are not included in the register lists in Tables 6.1 and 6.2 and therefore cannot be used for *reg* or *r/m* in the postbytes in Figure 6.1. Rather, special instructions are required that involve the segment registers. Table 6.5 shows the *MOV* instructions that use the segment registers. The postbyte D8 in Listing 6.1 is found as follows:

You can move the contents of *CS* to *r/m* but you can *not* move the contents of *r/m* to *CS*. The only way you should change the contents of *CS* is with the instructions *JMP, CALL, RET, IRET,* and *INT*.

Table 6.5		
Segment Register MOV Instructions		
Operation	Mnemonic	Opcode encoding
Move segment register to register or memory	MOV r/m,segreg	8C |mod|0ss|r/m|
Move register or memory to segment register	MOV segreg,r/m	8E |mod|0ss|r/m|
ss	segreg	
00	ES	
01	CS (MOV CS,r/m *not* allowed)	
10	SS	
11	DS	

Note that there are no instructions for loading immediate data directly into the segment registers. The immediate data must first be moved into another register (such as *AX*) and then into the segment register as shown by the first two instructions in Listing 6.1.

The coding of the third instruction in Listing 6.1,

```
C6 06 0000 FD    m1:   mov    joe,0fdh
```

is determined as follows. The opcode C6 is for the general instruction

```
C6    MOV b  r/m,imm
```

We want *r/m* to be *direct addressing*. From Table 6.1 this requires a postbyte with *mod* = 00 and *r/m* = 110. The three *reg* bits in the middle are not used and are just set to 000. Thus, the postbyte is

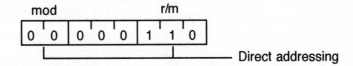

or 06H. For direct addressing the postbyte is followed by the 16-bit offset address in the low-byte, high-byte format. The immediate data will then follow these bytes. Thus, the complete coding will be

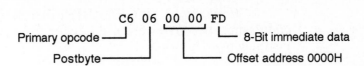

If *joe* had been given a *word* type by using the *DW* (*define word*) assembler directive in Listing 6.1, then the instruction

```
MOV   JOE,0FDH
```

will store the value FDH in *joe* and the value 00H in *joe*+1. The assembler now considers *joe* to be a 16-bit value. When the value FDH is incremented it will change to FEH but this is now considered to be the positive value 00FDH and not a negative value. Therefore, the sign flag will not be set and the JS instruction in Listing 6.1 will fail. This is an example where changing the type attribute of *joe* from *byte* to *word* makes the program bomb.

When *joe* is given the type *word*, the assembler will code the instruction

```
MOV   JOE,0FDH
```

as follows:

```
                   C7 06 00 00 FD 00
Primary opcode────┘   │  └──┘  └── 16-Bit immediate data
Postbyte──────────────┘       └──── Offset address 0000H
```

If *joe* has been defined as type *word*, but you really want to store FDH only in a single byte, you can type

```
MOV   BYTE PTR JOE,0FDH
```

This will override the declared type and assemble the byte opcode C6 rather than the word opcode C7. On the other hand, if *joe* has been defined as type *byte*, you can override this declaration by typing

```
MOV   WORD PTR JOE,0FDH
```

In this case the value FDH will be stored in *joe* and the value 00H will be stored in *joe*+1.

Table 6.6 shows the instructions that can be used to directly increment or decrement a memory location. When applied to direct addressing, the postbyte for *INC* will be 06.

```
┌─────────────────────────────────────────────────────┐
│                      Table 6.6                        │
│                                                       │
│             INC and DEC Instructions                  │
│               for Register or Memory                  │
├─────────────┬─────────────────┬───────────────────────┤
│   Opcode    │    Postbyte     │      Instruction      │
├─────────────┼─────────────────┼───────────────────────┤
│     FE      │ |mod|000|r/m|   │  INC BYTE PTR r/m     │
│     FF      │ |mod|000|r/m|   │  INC WORD PTR r/m     │
│     FE      │ |mod|001|r/m|   │  DEC BYTE PTR r/m     │
│     FF      │ |mod|001|r/m|   │  DEC WORD PTR r/m     │
└─────────────┴─────────────────┴───────────────────────┘
```

When word (*WORD PTR*) instructions are applied to direct addressing, two bytes are used at the offset address. For example, the instruction

```
FF 06 00 00        INC   WORD PTR JOE
```

will increment the 16-bit word stored at the offset addresses 0000H (low-byte) and 0001H (high-byte).

If *joe* has been defined as type *byte* using *DB* and you then type the instruction

```
MOV  AX,JOE
```

the assembler will produce the error message *operand types must match.* Both parts of the operand must be of the same type--*byte* or *word*. You could correct this error by typing

```
MOV  AX,WORD PTR JOE
```

which would move the value of *joe* into *AL* and the value of *joe*+1 into *AH*.

Suppose that instead of the *contents* of *joe* and *joe*+1 you want to store the *offset address* of *joe* in *AX*. The statement

```
MOV  AX,OFFSET JOE
```

will do this and the assembler will use the immediate mode of addressing. For example, if *joe* is at offset address 0000H, then the above instruction will be coded as follows:

```
B8 00 00        MOV  AX,OFFSET JOE
```

Note that the offset address 0000H is stored as immediate data in the program.

The *load effective address*, LEA, instruction can also be used to produce the same result. The general form of the LEA instruction is

```
LEA  reg,r/m
```

where the offset address associated with *r/m* (as given in Table 6.1) is stored in *reg* (as given in Table 6.2).

For example, the instruction

```
8D 06 00 00        LEA  AX,JOE
```

will produce the same result as

            B8 00 00   MOV   AX,OFFSET JOE

where 0000H is the offset address of *JOE*.

6.3   REGISTER INDIRECT ADDRESSING

Register indirect addressing stores the address of a data item in a register. The 8086 index registers *SI* and *DI* and the *base* register *BX* can be used to point to various memory locations. The actual address pointed to by these registers is formed by using the contents of the data segment register *DS* as the segment address and the contents of *SI*, *DI*, or *BX* as the offset address.

As an example of using register indirect addressing, the program shown in Listing 6.2 will move *CX* (4) bytes from the offset address pointed to by *SI* (*source*) to the offset address pointed to by *DI* (*dest*). The first two instructions set *DS* to point to the data segment. The next three instructions load *CX* with 4, *SI* with the offset address of *source* (0000), and *DI* with the offset address of *dest* (0004). The instruction

            ml: mov   al,[si]

will move the contents of 0000H (the offset address stored in *SI*) into accumulator *AL*. The coding of this instruction can be found from Tables 6.4 and 6.1 as follows:

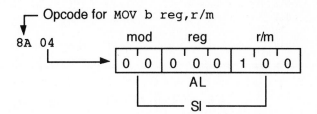

The instruction

            88 05   mov   [di],al

will move the contents of *AL* to the memory location pointed to by *DI* (initially 0004H). The coding of this instruction can also be found from Tables 6.4 and 6.1 as follows:

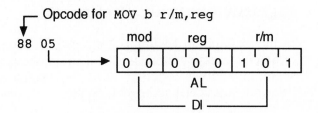

The next two instructions in Listing 6.2 increment *SI* and *DI* so they will point to offset addresses 0001H and 0005H respectively. The *loop ml* instruction will decrement *CX* and branch back to *ml* if *CX* is not equal to zero. Thus, this loop will be executed 4 times with *SI* and *DI* incremented each time through the loop.

```
        Listing  6.2 movbyte1.lst

                                    title     Register Indirect Addressing

        0000                        stack     segment para stack
        0000      40 [                 db        64 dup(?)
                         ??
                       ]

        0040                        stack     ends

        0000                        data      segment public
        0000   11 22 33 44          source    db        11h,22h,33h,44h
        0004      04 [              dest      db        4 dup(?)
                         ??
                       ]
        0008                        data      ends

        0000                        code      segment  public
                                              assume  cs:code,ds:data
        0000                        main      proc      far
        0000  B8 ---- R                       mov       ax,data           ;set ds
        0003  8E D8                           mov       ds,ax
        0005  B9 0004                         mov       cx,4              ;4 bytes
        0008  BE 0000 R                       mov       si,offset source
        000B  BF 0004 R                       mov       di,offset dest
        000E  8A 04               m1:         mov       al,[si]           ;get next byte
        0010  88 05                           mov       [di],al           ;& move it
        0012  46                              inc       si
        0013  47                              inc       di
        0014  E2 F8                           loop      m1                ;do 4 times
        0016  CC                              int       3
        0017                        main      endp

        0017                        code      ends
                                              end       main
```

The executable file for this program, *movbyte1.exe*, is on the TUTOR disk. Load the program into TUTOR (using */SL*) and press function key *F10*. Press *F1* twice to single step the first two instructions. This will set *DS* and display the data segment at the upper-right part of the screen. Note that the initial values, 11 22 33 44, specified for *source* in the data segment of Listing 6.2 are already stored at offset addresses 0000 through 0003 as shown in Figure 6.4. Now continue to single step through this program and note how the four values 11 22 33 44 get moved to offset addresses 0004 through 0007.

Segment Override Prefix

In the example in Listing 6.2 the default segment used with the register indirect addressing mode is *DS*. That is, the contents of *DS* are used as the segment address together with the offset addresses in *SI* and *DI* to determine the actual address of the data in the instructions

```
        MOV   AL,[SI]
```
and
```
        MOV   [DI],AL
```

It is possible to override this default segment register by using a *segment override prefix* given in Figure 6.5. For example, the instruction

```
26 88 05          MOV  ES:[DI],AL
```

will use the extra segment register *ES* instead of *DS* in forming the actual address from the offset address in *DI*.

```
        8086 Microprocessor TUTOR          Press F7 for Help

    AH AL    BH BL    CH CL    DH DL    DATA SEG   08 19 2A 3B 4C 5D 6E 7F
 AX 15 85 BX 10 00 CX 00 C5 DX 3A EE    1585:0000  11 22 33 44 00 00 00 00
                                        1585:0008  04 89 46 FC F6 46 FA 08
    SP 0040      SI 0000      IP 0005    1585:0010  74 18 8B 76 FA 81 E6 03
    BP 0000      DI 0000                 1585:0018  00 8A 84 F2 50 98 89 46
    SS 1586      DS 1585    CS 1583      1585:0020  F6 8A 84 66 51 88 46 F8
 SP+SS 158A0  SI+DS 15850    ES 1573     1585:0028  EB 18 8A 46 FA 24 03 88
 BP+SS 15860  DI+DS 15850 IP+CS 15835    1585:0030  46 F8 B8 00 04 50 2B C0
 STATUS FLAGS 7202 0111001000000010      1585:0038  50 E8 64 30 83 C4 04 89
                   ODITSZ A P C          1585:0040  46 F6 80 7E 85 15 85 15
 1583:0005 B90400     MOV  CX,0004H      1585:0048  D9 16 05 00 83 15 02 72

 SEG 1583:  08 19 2A 3B 4C 5D 6E 7F                 1586: STACK
    FFE8  00 00 00 00 00 00 00 00    . . . . . . . .    0040
    FFF0  00 00 00 00 00 00 00 00    . . . . . . . .
    FFF8  00 00 00 00 00 00 00 00    . . . . . . . .
    0000  B8 85 15 8E D8>B9 04 00    . . . . . . . .
    0008  BE 00 00 BF 04 00 8A 04    . . . . . . . .
    0010  88 05 46 47 E2 F8 CC 00    . . F G . . . .
    0018  00 00 00 00 00 00 00 00    . . . . . . . .

                                       / : Command      > : Go To Memory
                                       Use Cursor Keys to Scroll thru Memory
```

Figure 6.4 Initial values specified in the data segment of Listing 6.2

Segment register	Segment override prefix
ES	26
CS	2E
SS	36
DS	3E

Figure 6.5 Segment override prefixes

String Primitive Instructions

The 8086 has a number of *string primitive instructions* that makes it easy to manipulate a sequence of bytes in memory. For example, the entire loop *m1* in Listing 6.2 can be replaced with the *single instruction*

```
F3 A4          rep movsb
```

The instruction *MOVSB* is one of the string primitive instructions given in Table 6.7. It will move a byte of data from the offset address pointed to by *SI* in the *data* segment to an offset address pointed to by *DI* in the *extra* segment. The values of *SI* and *DI* will then either be incremented or decremented depending upon whether the direction flag *D* in the status register is a 0 (increment) or a 1 (decrement).

Table 6.7
String Primitive Instructions

Opcode	Instruction	Meaning
A4	MOVS b	Move byte of data from [SI] in the data segment (DS) to [DI] in the *extra segment* (ES). Adjust SI and DI.
A5	MOVS w	Move word of data from [SI] in the data segment (DS) to [DI] in the *extra segment* (ES). Adjust SI and DI.
A6	CMPS b	Compare byte of data at [SI] in the data segment (DS) with byte of data at [DI] in the *extra* segment (ES). Adjust SI and DI.
A7	CMPS w	Compare word of data at [SI] in the data segment (DS) with word of data at [DI] in the *extra* segment (ES). Adjust SI and DI.
AA	STOS b	Store contents of AL in [DI] in the *extra* segment (ES). Adjust DI.
AB	STOS w	Store contents of AX in [DI] in the *extra* segment (ES). Adjust DI.
AC	LODS b	Load byte from [SI] in the data segment (DS) into AL. Adjust SI.
AD	LODS w	Load word from [SI] in the data segment (DS) into AX. Adjust SI.
AE	SCAS b	Compare contents of AL with byte of data at [DI] in the *extra* segment (ES). Adjust DI.
AF	SCAS w	Compare contents of AX with word of data at [DI] in the *extra* segment (ES). Adjust DI.

The *REP* prefix when used before the string primitive instruction *MOVS* (or *LODS* or *STOS*) repeats the string primitive instruction *CX* times. Following each execution of the string primitive instruction, *CX* is decremented by 1 and the *REP* prefix tests *CX*. If *CX* = 0 then the program continues with the instruction following the string primitive instruction.

As an example of using a string primitive instruction, the program shown in Listing 6.3 performs the same operation as the program in Listing 6.2. Note that the instruction

```
        rep movsb
```

has replaced the entire *m1* loop in Listing 6.2. Also note that the data segment address *data* has to be moved into the *extra* segment register *ES* because the *DI* register used by the string primitive instructions *always* uses the extra segment register. It cannot be overridden with a segment override prefix. The instruction *CLD* will clear the direction flag in the status register so that the values of *SI* and *DI* will automatically be *incremented* each time *MOVSB* is executed.

The executable file for this program, *movbyte2.exe*, is on the TUTOR disk. Load the program into TUTOR (using */SL*) and press function key *F10*. Press *F1* twice to single step the first two instructions. This will set *DS* and display the initial values, 11 22 33 44, in the data segment at the upper-right part of the screen. Now continue to single step through this program. Note that you must single step the instruction

```
        F3 A4          rep movsb
```

four times in order to move all four bytes.

```
Listing  6.3  movbyte2.lst
                                    title    String Primitive Example

         0000                       stack    segment para stack
         0000      40 [             db       64 dup(?)
                        ??
                            ]

         0040                       stack    ends

         0000                       data     segment  public
         0000  11 22 33 44          source   db       11h,22h,33h,44h
         0004      04 [             dest     db       4 dup(?)
                        ??
                            ]

         0008                       data     ends

         0000                       code     segment public
                                             assume  cs:code,ds:data
         0000                       main     proc     far
         0000  B8 ---- R                     mov      ax,data            ;set ds
         0003  8E D8                         mov      ds,ax
         0005  8E C0                         mov      es,ax              ;es = ds
         0007  B9 0004                       mov      cx,4               ;4 bytes
         000A  BE 0000 R                     mov      si,offset source
         000D  BF 0004 R                     mov      di,offset dest
         0010  FC                            cld                         ;inc si and di
         0011  F3/ A4                        rep      movsb              ;move 4 bytes
         0013  CC                            int      3
         0014                       main     endp

         0014                       code     ends
                                             end      main
```

When used before the string primitive instructions *CMPS* and *SCAS* two forms of the REP prefix are possible as shown in Figure 6.6. As an example, the program shown in Listing 6.4 will scan the 8 bytes starting at offset address 0000 in the data segment (also the extra segment) looking for the byte 55H (stored in *AL*). This is all done by the instruction

```
F2 AE          repne scasb
```

This loop can terminate in one of two ways. If the byte 55H is not one of the bytes from 0000 to 0007 then the loop will end because *CX* went to zero. No match will be found so the *Z*-flag will be 0.

Opcode	Instruction	Meaning
F2	REPNE/REPNZ	Following CMPS or SCAS loop will terminate if Z-flag is 1
F3	REPE/REPZ	Following CMPS or SCAS loop will terminate if Z-flag is 0

Figure 6.6 *REP* prefix will affect the *Z*-flag when used before *CMPS* or *SCAS*

On the other hand, suppose that the byte 55H is at offset address 0004 in the data segment (as it is in Listing 6.4). In this case, the loop will terminate when the match is found (*DI* = 0004) because the *Z*-flag goes to

1. After that *SCASB* instruction is executed *DI* will automatically be incremented by 1. That is, *DI* will point to the byte following the one where a match was found. A *JE* branching instruction can be used following the instruction

```
F2 AE          repne scasb
```

to jump to a particular section of code if a match is found.

```
┌──────────────────────────────────────────────────────────────────────┐
│  Listing  6.4  scan8.lst                                               │
├──────────────────────────────────────────────────────────────────────┤
│                                  title   Scan String Example           │
│                                                                        │
│   0000                           stack   segment para stack            │
│   0000     40 [                          db      64 dup(?)             │
│                   ??                                                    │
│                     ]                                                   │
│                                                                        │
│   0040                           stack   ends                          │
│                                                                        │
│   0000                           data    segment public                │
│   0000   11 22 33 44             buff    db      11h,22h,33h,44h        │
│   0004   55 66 77 88                     db      55h,66h,77h,88h        │
│   0008                           data    ends                          │
│                                                                        │
│   0000                           code    segment  public               │
│                                          assume cs:code,ds:data         │
│   0000                           main    proc    far                   │
│   0000   B8 ---- R                       mov     ax,data      ;set ds   │
│   0003   8E D8                           mov     ds,ax                  │
│   0005   8E C0                           mov     es,ax        ;es = ds  │
│   0007   B9 0008                         mov     cx,8         ;8 bytes  │
│   000A   BF 0000 R                       mov     di,offset buff ;di -> 1st byte │
│   000D   FC                              cld                  ;inc di   │
│   000E   B0 55                           mov     al,55h       ;look for 55h │
│   0010   F2/ AE                          repne scasb          ;scan bytes │
│   0012   CC                              int     3                      │
│   0013                           main    endp                          │
│                                                                        │
│   0013                           code    ends                          │
│                                          end     main                  │
└──────────────────────────────────────────────────────────────────────┘
```

The executable file for this program, *scan8.exe*, is on the TUTOR disk. Load the program into TUTOR (using */SL*) and press function key *F10*. Press *F1* twice to single step the first two instructions. This will set *DS* and display the initial values, 11 22 33 44 55 66 77 88, in the data segment at the upper-right part of the screen. Now continue to single step through this program. Note that after you single step the instruction

```
F2 AE          repne scasb
```

five times the loop exits with the *Z*-flag in the status register equal to 1 and *DI* = 0005 (the byte following the match).

Now change the value in location DS:0004 to 00. (To do this remember the code segment, *CS*, and change the segment *SEG* to the data segment using >*S*. Make the change using */MH* and then return to the code segment.) Single step through the program again. Note that this time you will execute the instruction

```
F2 AE          repne scasb
```

eight times after which the value of *DI* will be 0008 and the *Z*-flag in the status register will be 0, indicating that no match was found.

6.4   INDEXED ADDRESSING

The 8086 has a number of addressing modes that make it easy to access data elements within an array. The *indexed addressing mode* uses *SI* or *DI* to index into an array starting at the offset address *disp8* or *disp16* within the data segment (*DS*). This is illustrated in Figure 6.7.

For example, consider the array of weights (given in hex) shown in Figure 6.8. These are stored in the data segment of the program in Listing 6.5 using the statements

```
0008   86 7B C5 CD      wt    db    134,123,197,205
000C   6E 9B B7 AF            db    110,155,183,175
```

Note that the weights are entered in decimal (without the H) following the *define byte* directive. The assembler will convert the values to hex as shown. The first weight is stored at offset address 0008. This is the offset address of the label *wt*. You can use *SI* (or *DI*) to index into the array to find a particular weight. For example, in Listing 6.5 the two statements

```
BE 0004           mov  si,4       ;index = 4
8A 84 0008 R      mov  al,wt[si]  ;get wt[4]
```

will move the value of *WT(4)* = 6E into *AL*.

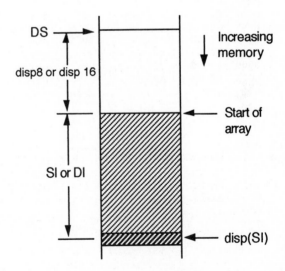

Figure 6.7 Accessing an array element *disp(SI)* or *disp(DI)*

I	WT(I)
0	86
1	7B
2	C5
3	CD
4	6E
5	9B
6	B7
7	AF

Figure 6.8 An array of weights *WT(I)*

The postbyte 84H used in the second statement is found from Tables 6.2 and 6.3 as follows:

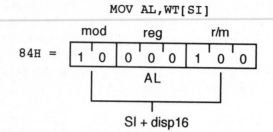

MOV AL,WT[SI]

Note that the array name, *WT*, is associated with the displacement, *disp16*, and has the value 0008 in the example shown.

```
Listing  6.5 weights.lst

                          title   Indexed Addressing Example

0000                      stack   segment para stack
0000      40 [                    db      64 dup(?)
               ??
              ]

0040                      stack   ends

0000                      data    segment public
0000  11 22 33 44         buff    db      11h,22h,33h,44h
0004  55 66 77 88                 db      55h,66h,77h,88h
0008  86 7B C5 CD         wt      db      134,123,197,205
000C  6E 9B B7 AF                 db      110,155,183,175
0010                      data    ends

0000                      code    segment  public
                                  assume  cs:code,ds:data
0000                      main    proc    far
0000  B8 ---- R                   mov     ax,data          ;set ds
0003  8E D8                       mov     ds,ax
0005  BE 0004                     mov     si,4             ;index = 4
0008  8A 84 0008 R                mov     al,wt[si]        ;get wt[4]
000C  CC                          int     3
000D                      main    endp

000D                      code    ends
                                  end     main
```

The executable file for this program, *weights.exe*, is on the TUTOR disk. Load the program into TUTOR (using /SL) and press function key *F10*. Press *F1* twice to single step the first two instructions. This will set *DS* and display the weights, 86 7B C5 CD 6E 9B B7 AF, on the second line of the data segment (starting at offset address 0008) at the upper-right part of the screen. Continue to single step through this program and note how the byte at *wt[4]* (6E) gets loaded into *AL*. Change the value of *SI* at offset address 0006 in the program from 04 to 07 and see if the weight value AFH gets loaded into *AL* when the instruction *mov al,wt[si]* is executed. Try some different values of *SI*.

Sometimes it is more convenient to use the value in a register as the *base* address of an array and to use a displacement such as *disp8* or *disp16* as the index into the array. This is called *based addressing*.

```
        8086 Microprocessor TUTOR          Press F7 for Help

        AH AL    BH BL    CH CL    DH DL    DATA SEG   08 19 2A 3B 4C 5D 6E 7F
    AX 15 6E  BX 10 00  CX 00 C5  DX 3A EE  1584:0000  11 22 33 44 55 66 77 88
                                            1584:0008  86 7B C5 CD 6E 9B B7 AF
        SP 0040     SI 0004     IP 000C     1584:0010  2B C0 50 E8 9A 30 83 C4
        BP 0000     DI 0000                 1584:0018  04 89 46 FC F6 46 FA 08
        SS 1585     DS 1584     CS 1583     1584:0020  74 18 8B 76 FA 81 E6 03
    SP+SS 15890  SI+DS 15844     ES 1573    1584:0028  00 8A 84 F2 50 98 89 46
    BP+SS 15850  DI+DS 15840  IP+CS 1583C   1584:0030  F6 8A 84 66 51 88 46 F8
    STATUS FLAGS 7202 0111001000000010      1584:0038  EB 18 8A 46 FA 24 03 88
                          ODITSZ A P C      1584:0040  46 F8 B8 00 6E 15 84 15
    1583:000C CC          INT3              1584:0048  D9 16 0C 00 83 15 02 72

    SEG 1583:  08 19 2A 3B 4C 5D 6E 7F                   1585: STACK
       FFF0    00 00 00 00 00 00 00 00    . . . . . . . .   0040
       FFF8    00 00 00 00 00 00 00 00    . . . . . . . .
       0000    B8 84 15 8E D8 BE 04 00    . . . . . . . .
       0008    8A 84 08 00>CC 00 00 00    . . . . . . . .
       0010    11 22 33 44 55 66 77 88    . " 3 D U f w .
       0018    86 7B C5 CD 6E 9B B7 AF    . { . . n . . .
       0020    2B C0 50 E8 9A 30 83 C4    + . P . . 0 . .

                                          / : Command      > : Go To Memory
                                          Use Cursor Keys to Scroll thru Memory
```

Figure 6.9 The value 6E at offset address 0008 + 0004 is moved to *AL*

6.5   BASED ADDRESSING

A *record* is a collection of data items, possibly of different types (ASCII data, integer data, etc.) that are related in some way. For example, suppose you want to store an address book in the computer. Each entry (different person) in the book would be a record. This record would contain the person's name, address, and phone number as shown in Table 6.8. Note that each record is 40H bytes long and is made up of the six record items shown in Table 6.9.

The important point in Table 6.8 is that the starting location of a particular record item (e.g. *PHONE*) is at the same relative displacement from the beginning of the record for all records in the address book.

Table 6.8						
Record Layout for an Address Book						
	00 0F	10 1F	20 2C	2D 30	31 35	36 3F
Record 0	NAME	STREET	CITY	STATE	ZIP	PHONE
Record 1						
Record 2						
• • • •						
Record n						

Table 6.9 Location of Record Items within Record			
Record Item	Displacement within Record	Length of Record Item	Type of Data
NAME	00H	10H	ASCII
STREET	10H	10H	ASCII
CITY	20H	0DH	ASCII
STATE	2DH	04H	ASCII
ZIP	31H	05H	ASCII
PHONE	36H	0AH	ASCII

Suppose that register *BX* contains the starting address (base address) of a particular record. The *PHONE* number associated with that record will always be found by adding 36H (the displacement of *PHONE*) to the contents of *BX*. To find the phone number of a different record you only have to change the contents of *BX*. This is called *based addressing*.

Note that whereas the indexed addressing form *disp*(*SI*) uses the *disp* as the starting address of an array, the based addressing form *BX*(*disp*) uses *disp* as the displacement into a record whose starting address is in *BX*.

From Tables 6.1, 6.2, and 6.3 the first digit of the phone number can be loaded into *AL* using the statement

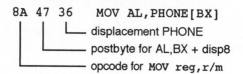

The postbyte 47H is determined as follows:

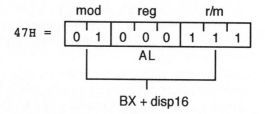

More powerful methods of accessing the data in Table 6.8 can be obtained by combining indexed and based addressing.

6.6 INDEXED PLUS BASED ADDRESSING

It is possible to use *SI* and *DI* as an index variable into a based array of the form *BX*(*SI*) or *BX*(*DI*). These forms of addressing are listed as *BX+SI* and *BX+DI* in the *mod* = 00 column in Table 6.3. In addition you can add either an 8-bit or 16-bit displacement as shown in the last two columns of Table 6.3.

As an example of when you may want to do this consider the address book records shown in Table 6.8. A collection of such records is sometimes called a *file*. You may have more than one such file. For example, you might have a Christmas list address book, and perhaps others for different members of the family. Each address book would start at a different offset address in memory (within a given data segment). The base address stored in *BX* would select a particular address book. Since each record is 40H bytes long, record *n* will start at 40H x *n* bytes from the base address. This value could be stored in *SI*. A constant displacement can then access a particular record item.

An example of using this addressing mode is shown in Listing 6.6. This listing illustrates the use of a assembler directive called *STRUC*. The purpose of *STRUC* is to define a particular data structure that can be duplicated at other locations within the program. We will use *STRUC* to define the structure of a particular record in Listing 6.6. The two statements *adbook struc* and *adbook ends* at the beginning of Listing 6.6 define a dummy segment in which the labels *name, street, city, state, zip,* and *phone* define the lengths of each of these fields within the record. Later in the data segment we can duplicate these records by using *adbook* as a assembler directive in the form *rec0 adbook* or *rec1 adbook*.

Look at the data segment in Listing 6.6 and notice how the three records *rec0, rec1,* and *rec2* have been defined. The definition of *adbook* using the *STRUC* assembler directive has initialized all of the bytes to ASCII blanks. The lengths of each field were adjusted by using the DB assembler directive with an ASCII string of blanks of the proper length. When defining a specific instance of the address book record in the data segment using *adbook*, any or all of these blank fields may be overwritten by using the *angle bracket* operand as shown in Listing 6.6. The angle bracket operand contains parameter fields separated by commas, corresponding to each field defined by *STRUC* to be in *adbook*. For example, *rec0* is defined to have the initial name, *Joe Doe*, the street, *123 Main St.*, the city, *Rochester*, and the State, *Mich.* All the other fields will maintain their default blank values. You can leave any field within the record with its default value by including commas within the angle bracket operand. For example, in *rec1* the operand <*'Mary',,,,,'521-8934'*> will define the name field to be *Mary* and the phone field to be *521-8934*. All other fields will remain blank.

The program in Listing 6.6 will get the phone number in record 2 (831-4321) and store this phone number in the 10 byte phone buffer, *phbuff*, at the beginning of the data segment. The start of the address book is at offset address *rec0* within the data segment. This offset address (000AH) is stored in *BX* in the instruction at offset address 0008 within the code segment. The start of record 2 is found by adding 40H x 2 to *BX*. The value 40H x 2 is stored in *SI* in the instruction at location *CS:0014*. The statement

```
8A 40 36        MOV  AL,PHONE[BX][SI]
```

at location *CS:0019* moves the first digit (ASCII code) of the phone number into *AL*. Note that it adds the contents of *BX* (the start of the address book), *SI* (the beginning of record 2) and 36H (the beginning of *PHONE*) to get the final offset address of *PHONE*. This value is stored at address *ES:DI* using the *STOSB* instruction at *CS:001D*. The *m1* loop will transfer the entire phone number (the length of *PHONE*, 0AH, is in *CX*) from the address book to the phone buffer at location *DS:0000–DS:0009*.

You could have used the *REP MOVSB* instruction to perform the entire loop in Listing 6.6 if you had moved the starting address of *PHONE* into *SI*. However, this example is to illustrate the use of the based plus indexed addressing mode.

Listing 6.6 *adbook.lst*

```
                                title   Address Book

0000                            stack   segment para stack
0000      40 [                  db      64 dup(?)
               ??
                 ]

0040                            stack   ends

                                adbook  struc
0000   20 20 20 20 20 20        name    db      '                   '
       20 20 20 20 20 20
       20 20 20 20
0010   20 20 20 20 20 20        street  db      '                  '
       20 20 20 20 20 20
       20 20 20 20
0020   20 20 20 20 20 20        city    db      '             '
       20 20 20 20 20 20
       20
002D   20 20 20 20             state   db      '   '
0031   20 20 20 20 20           zip     db      '    '
0036   20 20 20 20 20 20        phone   db      '       '
       20 20 20 20
0040                            adbook  ends

0000                            data    segment public
0000      0A [                  phbuff  db      10 dup(0)
              00
                 ]

000A   4A 6F 65 20 44 6F        rec0    adbook  <'Joe Doe','123 Main St.','Roch
       65 20 20 20 20 20                        ester','Mich'>
       20 20 20 20
001A   31 32 33 20 4D 61
       69 6E 20 53 74 2E
       20 20 20 20
002A   52 6F 63 68 65 73
       74 65 72 20 20 20
       20
0037   4D 69 63 68
003B   20 20 20 20 20
0040   20 20 20 20 20 20
       20 20 20 20

004A   4D 61 72 79 20 20        rec1    adbook  <'Mary',,,,,'521-8934'>
       20 20 20 20 20 20
       20 20 20 20
005A   20 20 20 20 20 20
       20 20 20 20 20 20
       20 20 20 20
006A   20 20 20 20 20 20
       20 20 20 20 20 20
       20
0077   20 20 20 20
007B   20 20 20 20 20
0080   35 32 31 2D 38 39
       33 34 20 20

008A   4A 6F 68 6E 20 20        rec2    adbook  <'John',,,,,'831-4321'>
       20 20 20 20 20 20
       20 20 20 20
```

Listing 6.6 (continued)

```
009A  20 20 20 20 20 20
      20 20 20 20 20 20
      20 20 20 20
00AA  20 20 20 20 20 20
      20 20 20 20 20 20
      20
00B7  20 20 20 20
00BB  20 20 20 20 20
00C0  38 33 31 2D 34 33
      32 31 20 20

00CA                       data    ends

0000                       code    segment public
                                   assume cs:code,ds:data,es:data
0000                       main    proc    far
0000  B8 ---- R                    mov     ax,data           ;set ds
0003  8E D8                        mov     ds,ax
0005  8E C0                        mov     es,ax             ; and es
0007  FC                           cld                       ;di increases
0008  BB 000A R                    mov     bx,offset rec0    ;start of file
000B  B9 000A                      mov     cx,10             ;phone = 10 char
000E  B0 02                        mov     al,2              ;record 2
0010  B4 40                        mov     ah,64             ;64 char/rec
0012  F6 E4                        mul     ah
0014  8B F0                        mov     si,ax             ;si=64*rec#
0016  BF 0000 R                    mov     di,offset phbuff  ;di-> buffer
0019  8A 40 36          ml:        mov     al,phone[bx][si]  ;get digit
001C  46                           inc     si
001D  AA                           stosb                     ;move to buffer
001E  E2 F9                        loop    ml                ;get all digits
0020  CC                           int     3
0021                       main    endp
0021                       code    ends
                                   end     main
```

The executable file for this program, *adbook.exe*, is on the TUTOR disk. Load the program into TUTOR (using */SL*) and press function key *F10*. Press *F1* twice to single step the first two instructions. This will set *DS* and display the beginning of the data segment at the upper-right part of the screen. Note that the first ten bytes are zeros, corresponding to the initial values in *phbuff* and the following bytes contain the contents of rec0 as shown in the TUTOR screen display in Figure 6.10. The program will move the phone number from *rec2* that begins at offset address 008A in the data segment. This part of the data segment isn't visible on the TUTOR screen. However, you can display any part of memory in the upper-right part of the screen by using the TUTOR command */G*. If you type */G* the command line will display

        DATA SEGMENT: S O D

Type *O* and then enter the offset address 8A. This will display the data segment starting at offset address 008A and you will be able to see the phone number starting at offset address 00C0 as shown in Figure 6.11.

Type */GD* to go back to the beginning of the current data segment where *phbuff* is located. (*/GS* will allow you to display a different segment in the upper-right part of the screen.) Now continue to single step through this program and note how each byte of the phone number of *rec2* is moved to *phbuff*.

```
        8086 Microprocessor TUTOR          Press F7 for Help

      AH AL    BH BL    CH CL    DH DL    DATA SEG   08 19 2A 3B 4C 5D 6E 7F
   AX 15 86  BX 10 00  CX 00 C5  DX 3A EE  1586:0000  00 00 00 00 00 00 00 00
                                           1586:0008  00 00 4A 6F 65 20 44 6F
      SP 0040     SI 0000     IP 0005      1586:0010  65 20 20 20 20 20 20 20
      BP 0000     DI 0000                  1586:0018  20 20 31 32 33 20 4D 61
      SS 1593     DS 1586     CS 1583      1586:0020  69 6E 20 53 74 2E 20 20
   SP+SS 15970  SI+DS 15860      ES 1573   1586:0028  20 20 52 6F 63 68 65 73
   BP+SS 15930  DI+DS 15860   IP+CS 15835  1586:0030  74 65 72 20 20 20 20 4D
   STATUS FLAGS 7202 0111001000000010      1586:0038  69 63 68 20 20 20 20 20
                         ODITSZ A P C      1586:0040  20 20 20 20 20 20 20 20
   1583:0005 8EC0        MOV   ES,AX       1586:0048  20 20 4D 61 72 79 20 20

   SEG 1583:  08 19 2A 3B 4C 5D 6E 7F                 1593: STACK
       FFE8  00 00 00 00 00 00 00 00     . . . . . . . .    0040
       FFF0  00 00 00 00 00 00 00 00     . . . . . . . .
       FFF8  00 00 00 00 00 00 00 00     . . . . . . . .
       0000  B8 86 15 8E D8>8E C0 FC     . . . . . . . .
       0008  BB 0A 00 B9 0A 00 B0 02     . . . . . . . .
       0010  B4 40 F6 E4 8B F0 BF 00     . @ . . . . . .
       0018  00 8A 40 36 46 AA E2 F9     . . @ 6 F . . .

   _____  / : Command    > : Go To Memory
                                             Use Cursor Keys to Scroll thru Memory
```

Figure 6.10 The first ten bytes of the data segment (*phbuff*) initially contain all zeros

```
        8086 Microprocessor TUTOR          Press F7 for Help

      AH AL    BH BL    CH CL    DH DL    DATA SEG   08 19 2A 3B 4C 5D 6E 7F
   AX 15 86  BX 10 00  CX 00 C5  DX 3A EE  1586:008A  4A 6F 68 6E 20 20 20 20
                                           1586:0092  20 20 20 20 20 20 20 20
      SP 0040     SI 0000     IP 0005      1586:009A  20 20 20 20 20 20 20 20
      BP 0000     DI 0000                  1586:00A2  20 20 20 20 20 20 20 20
      SS 1593     DS 1586     CS 1583      1586:00AA  20 20 20 20 20 20 20 20
   SP+SS 15970  SI+DS 15860      ES 1573   1586:00B2  20 20 20 20 20 20 20 20
   BP+SS 15930  DI+DS 15860   IP+CS 15835  1586:00BA  20 20 20 20 20 20 38 33
   STATUS FLAGS 7202 0111001000000010      1586:00C2  31 2D 34 33 32 31 20 20
                         ODITSZ A P C      1586:00CA  51 0A 50 FF 76 F6 E4 4D
   1583:0005 8EC0        MOV   ES,AX       1586:00D2  DF 83 C4 06 0A C0 74 04

   SEG 1583:  08 19 2A 3B 4C 5D 6E 7F                 1593: STACK
       FFE8  00 00 00 00 00 00 00 00     . . . . . . . .    0040
       FFF0  00 00 00 00 00 00 00 00     . . . . . . . .
       FFF8  00 00 00 00 00 00 00 00     . . . . . . . .
       0000  B8 86 15 8E D8>8E C0 FC     . . . . . . . .
       0008  BB 0A 00 B9 0A 00 B0 02     . . . . . . . .
       0010  B4 40 F6 E4 8B F0 BF 00     . @ . . . . . .
       0018  00 8A 40 36 46 AA E2 F9     . . @ 6 F . . .

   _____  / : Command    > : Go To Memory
                                             Use Cursor Keys to Scroll thru Memory
```

Figure 6.11 The phone number of *rec2* starts at offset address 00C0 in the data segment

6.7 STACK ADDRESSING

The *based* and *based plus indexed* addressing described in the previous two sections involve the use of the base register *BX*. When this register is used the actual address is found in the data segment. That is, the data segment register *DS* is used to calculate the actual address.

Sometimes it is useful to use these same addressing modes when accessing data in the stack segment rather than the data segment. This may occur, for example, when passing parameters on the stack to subroutines. The base pointer register, *BP*, can be used instead of *BX* to hold a base address within the stack segment. Table 6.3 shows the *based stack* and *based plus indexed stack* addressing modes that are available on the 8086. These modes work just like the *based* and *based plus indexed* modes just described except that *BP* replaces *BX* and *SS* replaces *DS*. That is, the data is accessed in the *stack segment.*

As an example of passing parameters on the stack we will modify the program shown in Listing 5.1a in Chapter 5 that uses the subroutine *neg2word* to find the two's complement of a double word. Instead of passing the double word to the subroutine in the registers *dx:ax* we will push the double word on the stack before calling the subroutine *dneg2* as shown in the main program in Listing 6.7. The instruction call *dneg2* will push the return (offset) address on the stack before jumping to the subroutine *dneg2*. The first four instructions of *dneg2* will push *bp* on the stack, set *bp* to *sp*, and then push *bx* and *cx* on the stack. At this point the stack will therefore look like Figure 6.12.

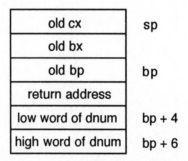

Figure 6.12 Stack picture after executing the first four instructions in the subroutine *dneg2*

The double word, *dnum*, is now on the stack at location *bp* + 4 and *bp* + 6. We can move these values into *bx* and *cx* using the instructions

```
mov    bx,6[bp]     ;bx=hi word
mov    cx,4[bp]     ;cx=lo word
```

as shown in Listing 6.7. Note that when using this stack addressing mode the data is accessed in the stack segment. This subroutine will pass the answer (the two's complement of *dnum*) back to the main program in the registers *dx:ax*.

After executing the three *pop* instructions at the end of the subroutine *dneg2* the stack pointer will be pointing to the word containing the return address. If we execute the instruction *ret* at this point the program will return to the main program but the stack pointer will be pointing to the address *bp* + 4 in Figure 6.12. The main program should then add 4 to the stack pointer to put it back to its location prior to pushing the parameters on the stack. Alternatively, the subroutine itself can fix up the stack by using the form of the return statement given by

```
                         ret     4                ;fix stack
```

which will add 4 to the stack pointer after popping the return address from the stack.

Listing 6.7   *stkpara.asm*

```
        title   Two's complement of a double word
        ;       Example of passing parameters on the stack
        stack   segment         para    stack
                db      64 dup(?)
        stack   ends

        data    segment
        dnum    dd      12345678h
        negnum  dd      ?
        data    ends

        code    segment public
                assume  cs:code,ds:data

        main    proc    far
                mov     ax,data
                mov     ds,ax               ;set ds=data
                mov     ax,word ptr dnum    ;ax=low word
                mov     dx,word ptr dnum+2  ;dx=high word
                push    dx                  ;push high word
                push    ax                  ;push low word
                call    dneg2               ;2's compl
                mov     word ptr negnum,ax    ;store lo word
                mov     word ptr negnum+2,dx  ;store hi word
                int     3
        main    endp

        ;       negate double word passed on stack
        dneg2   proc    near
                push    bp                  ;save bp
                mov     bp,sp               ;index with bp
                push    bx                  ;save regs
                push    cx
                mov     bx,6[bp]            ;bx=hi word
                mov     cx,4[bp]            ;cx=lo word
                xor     ax,ax               ;ax=0
                mov     dx,ax               ;dx=0
                sub     ax,cx               ;dx:ax =
                sbb     dx,bx               ; 0:0 - bx:cx
                pop     cx                  ;restore regs
                pop     bx
                pop     bp                  ;restore bp
                ret     4                   ;fix stack
        dneg2   endp

        code    ends
                end     main
```

This technique of passing parameters to a subroutine on the stack is used by most high-level languages when they want to access an assembly language routine. Languages differ in the order that their parameters are pushed on the stack and whether the calling program or the subroutine should be responsible for fixing up the stack after the return. If the subroutine is passing no more than four bytes of information back to the calling program it will normally use registers *ax* and *dx* for this purpose. Otherwise, it may pass the segment and offset addresses of the returned data in *dx:ax* (as in C) or the calling program may have included the offset address (within the data segment) where the resulting data is to be deposited as the last parameter pushed on the stack prior to the subroutine call (as in FORTRAN, BASIC and PASCAL).

PROGRAMMING PROBLEMS

Problem 6.1 – Macros and Threaded Languages
a. In this problem you will learn how to use *macros*, and how a stack-oriented, threaded interpretive language works. You will also see a good example of register indirect addressing associated with the *PUSH* and *POP* instructions.

Programming is made easier if you break up your programs into small modules. You can do this by using lots of subroutines. Your program might then look something like this:

```
call  sub1
call  sub2
call  sub3
call  sub4
```

Suppose that *every* statement in your program was of this form. Then you wouldn't really need to include the opcode for the *CALL* statement since every statement would be understood to be a *CALL* statement. This would save you a byte of memory for every statement and the program would reduce to a list of addresses of the subroutines:

```
sub1
sub2
sub3
sub4
```

This is the idea behind threaded interpretive languages such as *Forth*. The language is made up entirely of *words* (which are like subroutines) which are made up of a list of other words (that you have previously defined). This list of words is just a list of the addresses to be executed when the word is called or executed. Thus, in the list above *sub1* might itself consist of another list of *word* addresses which must be "executed" every time *sub1* is called. Of course, eventually some real 8086 machine code must be executed for anything to happen. Words which contain real machine code, rather than just a list of addresses of other words, are called *primitive* or *kernel* words.

b. Data is passed from one word to the next on the stack. Every word has a stack picture associated with it that shows the items on the stack before the word is called and after the word is called. The stack picture looks like this:

```
( stack items before -- stack items after )
```

For example, the word *DUP* duplicates the top stack item and the stack picture looks like this:

```
DUP  ( w -- w w )
```

This means that before *DUP* is executed a value *w* is on the stack and after *DUP* has been executed there are two values of *w* on the stack. In these pictures the top of the stack is on the right. The word *DUP* is a primitive that can be implemented in 8086 assembly language as

```
dup:  mov  bx,sp
      push 0[bx]
```

The word *OVER* (*w1 w2 -- w1 w2 w1*) copies the second stack item to the top of the stack. It can be implemented as

```
over: mov  bx,sp
      push 2[bx]
```

The word *DROP* (*w --*) discards the top stack item. It can be implemented as

```
drop: inc  sp
      inc  sp
```

The word *SWAP* (*w1 w2 -- w2 w1*) exchanges the top two stack items. It can be implemented as

```
swap: pop  bx
      pop  ax
      push bx
      push ax
```

c. Write assembly language code that will implement the following words:

store (w a --)   Store the word *w* at offset address *a*.
                      (This word is written as ! in Forth)

at (a -- w)   Fetch the word value *w* stored at the
                      address *a*.
                      (This word is written as @ in Forth)

plus (w w -- w)   Add the top two items on the stack.
                      (This word is written as + in Forth)

d. The word *PSTOR* (*n a --*) adds *n* to the contents of address *a*. In Forth this word is written as *+!* and pronounced "*plus-store.*" Note that *PSTOR* can be defined in terms of our previous words as

```
: pstor     ( n a -- )
            swap        ( a n     )
            over        ( a n a   )
            at          ( a n val )
            plus        ( a val+n )
            swap        ( val+n a )
            store ;     (         )
```

e. In assembly language we can implement *pstor* by writing

```
pstor:      dw    swap,over,at
            dw    plus,swap,store
```

The assembler will assemble this word as a list of the offset addresses of the six words making up the definition. Suppose that *si* is pointing to *pstor* (that is, it is pointing to an address that contains the address of *swap*). The two statements

```
            lodsw
            jmp   ax
```

will load *si* with the address of *swap* and then jump to this address (that is, *swap* will be executed). The value of *si* will automatically be incremented by 2 (by *lodsw*) and will therefore be pointing to the word containing the address of *over*. After executing each of the words in *pstor* we need to execute the above two statements to go to the next word. We can do this by introducing the following *macro*:

```
            $next macro
                  lodsw
                  jmp   ax
            endm
```

We would then include this macro at the end of each primitive definition. For example,

```
            dup:  mov   bx,sp
                  push  0[bx]
                  $next
```

When this code is assembled, the actual code in the macro *$next* is inserted at the end of the definition of *dup*.

f. Write a program that includes the following:

1. The statement

```
            spp   equ   3e7eh
```

2. The macro definition of *$next*.
3. A single code segment containing the assume statement

```
            assume      cs:code,ds:code,ss:code
```

4. The following main program

```
main:   mov   ax,cs
        mov   ds,ax
        mov   ss,ax
        mov   sp,ssp
        cld
again:  mov   ax,2
        push  ax
        mov   ax,offset addr1
        push  ax
        mov   si,offset pstor
        $next

addr1   dw    0
```

5. Add definitions for all of the primitives discussed above as well as the definition of *pstor*. Add the statement

```
        dw    again
```

to the definition of *pstor*.

   g. Assemble, link and load this program into TUTOR. Single step through the program and watch the value 2 be added to the contents of *addr1* as all of the words in *pstor* are executed.

EXERCISES

Exercise 6.1
Code the following instructions:

```
a) SUB  AX,1234H      c) MOV  DX,5432H
b) XOR  CH,3CH        d) CMP  AH,0CH
```

Exercise 6.2
Code the following instructions:

```
a) MOV  DH,CL         c) MOV  DI,AX
b) MOV  SP,AX         d) MOV  BL,AH
```

Exercise 6.3
Code the following instructions assuming that *SAM* is a label at offset address 0005H.

```
a) DEC  BYTE PTR SAM  c) MOV  BYTE PTR SAM,13H
b) MOV  ES,AX         d) MOV  SS,SAM
```

Exercise 6.4
Write a program that will store the value AAH in 256 consecutive memory locations starting at location *DS:0100*.
   Hint: The instruction *REP STOSB* will store the same value in consecutive memory locations.

Exercise 6.5
After executing the program in Exercise 6.4, write and execute a program that will transfer 256 bytes starting at location *DS:0100* to another location starting at location *DS:0200*.

Exercise 6.6

The word *CAT* can be stored in memory as the three ASCII bytes 43 41 54. Store these values at some location between *DS:0100* and *DS:0200*. Write and execute a program that will search for the word *CAT* in this memory range and determine the address where it is stored.

Exercise 6.7

Enter three names, addresses, and phone numbers in *rec0, rec1*, and *rec2* in Listing 6.6. Change *phbuff* to be a 16-byte buffer. Modify the program in Listing 6.6 to move the following data to this new buffer region.

a) the name in record 1   d) the street in record 0
b) the zip code in record 0 e) the state in record 2
c) the city in record 2   f) the phone number in record 1

CHAPTER 7

Screen Display

The PC screen display is controlled by a plug-in board in the PC. When IBM introduced the first PC in 1981 it provided two different types of screen display boards: a *monochrome display adapter* (MDA) and a *color graphics adapter* (CGA). Each adapter required its own separate monitor. The monochrome monitor displayed only text: 25 rows of 80 characters each. The color graphics adapter could display either 40 characters per row or 80 characters per row of text as well as limited color graphics. In 1982 Hercules Computer Technology introduced its first graphics card which allowed monochrome graphics to be displayed on the monochrome monitor. We will study how this is done in Chapter 12. A number of other companies introduced color graphics cards that provided better resolution and more colors than CGA graphics. In 1984 IBM introduced its *enhanced graphics adapter* (EGA) and later brought out its *video graphics array* (VGA) board both of which provided high resolution color graphics and text.

This chapter will be concerned with text display. The use of graphics will be covered in Chapter 12. In this chapter you will learn:

- How a raster scan display works
- How character data is stored in a video RAM
- How to display characters using BIOS routines
- How to write a number of useful subroutines for controlling the screen display and keyboard inputs
- How to allocate and deallocate memory

7.1 RASTER SCAN DISPLAYS

A video monitor screen works by causing an electron beam to scan the screen in a raster format, that is, in a series of horizontal lines moving down the screen. The electron beam impinging on a phosphor coated screen causes light to be emitted. The electron beam scans the entire screen

144

in 1/60 second. Home TV images are displayed in an *interlaced* format in which every other scan line is displayed in the first 1/60 second, and the remaining alternate scan lines are displayed in the next 1/60 second. It therefore takes 1/30 second to display the entire image. Although only one spot on the screen is being hit by the electron beam at any instant of time, if the entire screen is rewritten every 1/30 second, the eye will retain the image from one screen scan to the next. It will therefore look as if an image fills the entire screen, even though only one spot is really being displayed.

When using a color graphics adapter (CGA) the PC scans the same 200 horizontal lines every 1/60 second. Eight consecutive horizontal lines are used to display a single character. Therefore, 25 (200/8) lines of text can be displayed on the screen. Each character displayed on the screen is in the form of a 5 x 7 dot matrix located within an 8 x 8 dot area on the screen.

The IBM monochrome monitor will display 25 rows of 80 characters each. The monochrome characters are a 7 x 9 dot matrix within a 9 x 14 character box as shown in Figure 7.1. Therefore, 350 (25 x 14) horizontal lines are scanned every 1/60 second on the monochrome display.

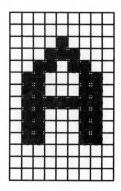

Figure 7.1   A 7 x 9 dot matrix character within a 9 x 14 dot area on the screen

A dot will be displayed on the screen if the electron beam is turned on when it is at the location on the screen where the dot is to be displayed. If the electron beam is turned off then no dot will be displayed on the screen. The video signal that is fed into the video monitor is a signal that turns the electron beam on and off at the proper timing to produce the desired effect on the screen.

For example, to display the A shown in Figure 7.1 we must control the electron beam for fourteen consecutive scan lines. The third scan line (the top of the A) contains a single dot surrounded by four blanks on each side. If we represent a dot by 1 and a blank by 0 then the top of the A is represented by 000010000. The next two scan lines of the A would be represented by 000111000 and 001101100 respectively.

With the color graphics adapter (CGA) the PC can display either 40 or 80 characters per line. If we use 40 characters per line, 320 (40 x 8) dot positions will occur on each line. To display an entire line of 40 characters we must display the top row of each character, then the second row of each character, then the third row, and so on. It will take eight horizontal scan lines to display one line of 40 characters.

The way that this is done is shown in Figure 7.2. Suppose that you want to display the three characters *T H E* at the upper left-hand corner of the screen. The screen ASCII codes for these characters are stored in the first three even address locations of a video RAM. Each byte containing a screen ASCII code is followed by a byte containing a character attribute code. To display the top bar of the T (in row 0) the ASCII code for T (54) and the row number (00) are used to form an input address to the character generator. The character generator is really a read only memory (ROM) that contains the dot patterns used to form the various characters. For example, the top bar of the T is represented by the dot pattern 11111000. This will be the output of the character generator when the input is the ASCII code for T and the row select value 00. This dot pattern code is put into a shift register from which it is shifted out one bit at a time to form the video signal as shown in Figure 7.2. This video signal goes to the video monitor where it controls the electron beam.

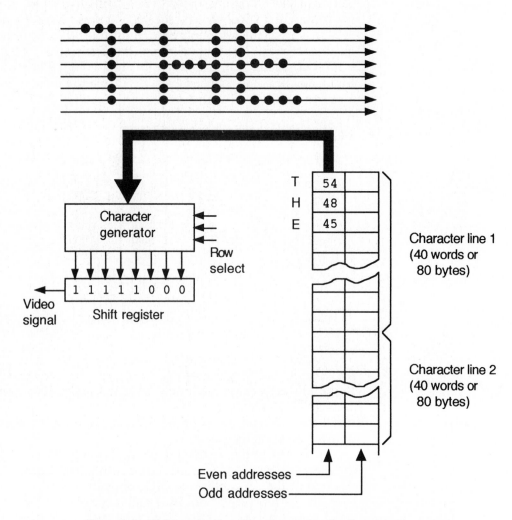

Figure 7.2 ASCII codes for characters to be displayed on the screen are stored in a video RAM

After the top of the T is displayed the top of the H must be displayed next. The ASCII code for H (stored in the next even address of the video RAM) is moved to the input of the character generator. The row select input remains at 00. The output of the character generator will be 10001000, corresponding to the top part of the H. This code then gets shifted out of the shift register and becomes the next part of the video signal.

This process continues until the first 40 ASCII codes, stored in the first 40 even bytes of the video RAM, have all been cycled to the character generator. At this point the top of all characters will have been displayed. This will all have taken place in less than one ten-thousandth of a second. The row select input is then incremented by 1 and the same 40 ASCII codes stored in the first 40 even bytes of the video RAM are recycled to the character generator. This will cause the proper dot pattern for row 1 of all 40 characters to be displayed on the screen.

After eight rows of dots have been displayed (corresponding to row select inputs of 0 through 7), a complete line of 40 characters will have been displayed. To display the next line of 40 characters, the same process is repeated using 40 new bytes in the video RAM. These 40 bytes will contain the ASCII codes for the 40 characters to be displayed on line 2 of the video screen.

To display 25 lines of 40 characters each will require $25 \times 40 = 1000$ bytes of memory in which to store the ASCII codes of the characters to be displayed. Changing a character on the screen is then simply a matter of changing the ASCII code that is stored in a particular memory location in the video RAM. The next time this ASCII code is cycled to the character generator (within 1/60 second) this new character will be displayed on the screen. To use the video RAM we must therefore know what memory locations are associated with each printing location on the screen.

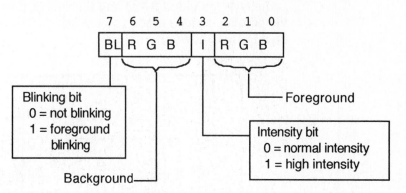

Background	Foreground	Monochrome Display	Color Graphics Display
0 0 0	1 1 1	Normal display	Normal display
1 1 1	0 0 0	Reverse video	Reverse video
0 0 0	0 0 0	Non display (black)	Non display (black)
1 1 1	1 1 1	Non display (white)	Non display (white)
0 0 0	0 0 1	Underline	Blue character

Foreground/Background Color Codes		
R G B	Color	
0 0 0	Black	
0 0 1	Blue	Setting the I-bit
0 1 0	Green	will result in 8
0 1 1	Cyan	additional shades of
1 0 0	Red	these 8 colors for
1 0 1	Magenta	the foreground color.
1 1 0	Yellow	
1 1 1	White	

Figure 7.3 The attribute byte

Each ASCII code stored in the video RAM has an associated *attribute byte* stored in the following odd address. For a monochrome display this attribute byte determines whether the character will be displayed in normal or reverse video and if the character will be underlined, blinking and/or displayed in high intensity. For a color display the attribute will determine the foreground and background color of each character. The definitions of the bits within this attribute byte are shown in Figure 7.3.

It is important to note that the attribute byte must contain some non-zero value. If the attribute byte is zero then the character will not be displayed on the screen regardless of the value of the ASCII code. If you want to display a blank on the screen you should store the ASCII code for a blank (20H) followed by the normal attribute byte (07H).

7.2 THE VIDEO RAM

You saw in Chapter 3 (see Section 3.5) that the video RAM for storing text on a PC screen begins at memory location B000:0000 for a monochrome display and at memory location B800:0000 for a graphics monitor display. Each character location on the screen is associated with two consecutive bytes in memory. The first byte (even memory address) contains the ASCII code for the character to be displayed. The second byte (odd memory address) contains the attribute byte given in Figure 7.3. The segment address of the video RAM and the size of the character cell will depend on the particular video mode you are using. The standard text modes available on a PC are shown in Table 7.1.

Table 7.1				
Text Modes				
Mode	Type	Col. x Rows	Video RAM Seg. Addr.	Character Cell Size
0	CGA EGA VGA	40 x 25	B800	8 x 8 8 x 14 9 x 16
1	CGA EGA VGA	40 x 25	B800	8 x 8 8 x 14 9 x 16
2	CGA EGA VGA	80 x 25	B800	8 x 8 8 x 14 9 x 16
3	CGA EGA VGA	80 x 25	B800	8 x 8 8 x 14 9 x 16
7	MDA VGA	80 x 25	B000	9 x 14 9 x 16

The first graphics board provided with the early IBM PCs was a color graphics adapter (CGA) that allowed you to display text in either black and white (modes 0 and 2) or color (modes 1 and 3). The color graphics adapter will display text in either a 40 x 25 format or an 80 x 25 format. Since each character requires two bytes (one for the ASCII code and one for the attribute) the video RAM must contain either 2000 bytes (40 x 25 x 2) or 4000 bytes (80 x 25 x 2). The original color graphics adapter board contained 16K bytes of RAM used for the video RAM. This means that either eight pages of a 40 x 25 screen, or four pages of an 80 x 25 screen could simultaneously be stored in the computer. Which page is being displayed depends on the starting address of the video RAM. This can be changed under software control. The starting segment address of each page is given in Figure 7.4. Within each page the offset address associated with each screen position is shown in Figure 7.5 for a 40 column display and Figure 7.6 for an 80 column display.

40 x 25 Screen		80 x 25 Screen	
Page	Starting Segment Address	Page	Starting Segment Address
0	B800	0	B800
1	B880	1	B900
2	B900	2	BA00
3	B980	3	BB00
4	BA00		
5	BA80		
6	BB00		
7	BB80		

Figure 7.4   Starting segment addresses for the video RAM
in a color graphics adapter

The monochrome display adapter (MDA) always displays 80 x 25 characters. The MDA video RAM starts at segment address B000H. The offset addresses for the various characters on the screen are those shown in Figure 7.6. Note from Table 7.1 the character cell size for a monochrome display is 9 x 14 while that for VGA text is 9 x 16. The cell size for CGA text is 8 x 8 and for EGA text is 8 x 14.

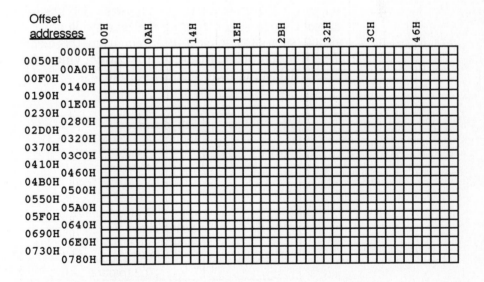

Figure 7.5 Memory map for video RAM associated with a 40 column text screen

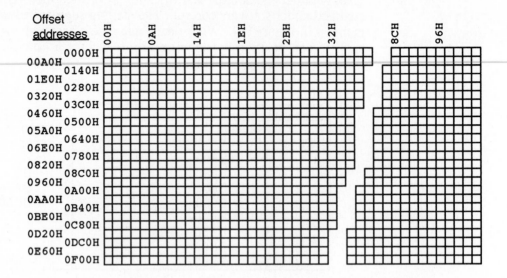

Figure 7.6 Memory map for video RAM associated with an 80 column text screen

7.3 BIOS SCREEN DISPLAY ROUTINES

These video routines are stored in the Basic Input-Output System (BIOS) ROM that is built into the PC. The particular function that gets performed depends on the contents of various registers when the software interrupt *INT 10H* is executed. Register *AH* is used to define various video functions.

Figure 7.7 shows the values of *AX* to use to set the text mode and select the active display page. The *AH* = 15 function can be used to find the current video state. Setting the text mode always clears the screen. A simple subroutine to clear the screen using this technique is shown in Figure 7.8. The subroutine first reads the current video state and then sets it again. This will clear the screen and it is quite fast.

AH = 0	*Set text mode*
	Input: AL (See Table 7.1)
	            0 - 40x25 BW
	            1 - 40x25 COLOR
	            2 - 80x25 BW
	            3 - 80x25 COLOR
	            7 - Monochrome

AH = 5	*Select active display page*
	Input: AL = new page value
	            0-7 (modes 0-1)
	            0-3 (modes 2-3)

AH = 15 (0FH)	*Get current video state*
	Output: AL = current mode (see AH=0)
	            AH = number of characters per row
	            BH = current active display page

Figure 7.7 Setting the text mode using INT 10H

```
;           clear screen
clrscn      proc        near
            push        ax
            mov         ah,15           ;read vid mode
            int         10h
            mov         ah,0            ;and set again
            int         10h
            pop         ax
            ret
clrscn      endp
```

Figure 7.8 Subroutine to clear the screen

As you saw in Chapter 3 you can print a character on the screen simply by storing the ASCII code and attribute for the character in the proper location in the video RAM. The built-in video routines called by *INT 10H* do a lot of these details for you.

First of all, to display a character at a particular location you must know the address in the video RAM associated with that location. The PC has a *cursor* that can be positioned anywhere on the screen. All characters are then printed at the current cursor position. The cursor can be controlled using the *INT 10H* routines given in Figure 7.9.

AH = 1	*Set cursor type* Input: CH = start line of cursor CL = stop line of cursor
AH = 2	*Set cursor position* Input: DH = row number DL = column number BH = page number
AH = 3	*Read cursor position* Input: BH = page number Output: DH = row number of current cursor CH = start line of current cursor CL = stop line of current cursor

Figure 7.9 Cursor control options using INT 10H

The form, or type, of the cursor can be controlled using the *AH* = 1 instruction in Figure 7.9. The cursor is always blinking. Normally it looks like an underline. When using a monochrome monitor this is really a double line in rows 11 and 12 of the 9 x 14 character box in each character location. You can change this cursor form by specifying the start line and stop line for the cursor in *CH* and *CL*. For example, if you make the start line 0 (*CH* = 00H) and the stop line 13 (*CL* = 0DH) then the cursor will be a 9 x 14 blinking rectangle rather than an underline.

The position of the cursor is set by using *AH* = 2 before calling *INT 10H* as shown in Figure 7.9. The row number is stored in *DH* (00H is the top row and 18H is the bottom row) and the column number is stored in *DL* (00H is the left-most column). The page number defined in Figure 7.4 is stored in *BH*. Using *AH* = 3 when calling *INT 10H* allows you to read the current cursor position as shown in Figure 7.9.

A number of useful subroutines can be written using the cursor control BIOS routines in Figure 7.9. For example, the subroutine *setcur* shown in Figure 7.10 will set the cursor at row *dh* and column *dl*. The subroutine *rdcurs* in Figure 7.10 will read the current cursor position and leave the row in *dh* and the column in *dl*. These subroutines can then be used to write the subroutines *inccur* and *deccur* shown in Figure 7.11 which will increment and decrement the cursor. Note that these subroutines do not check for the end or the beginning of the line. We will see later how to perform a carriage return/line feed when the end of the line is reached.

```
;          set cursor at dx=row:col
setcur     proc      near
           push      ax
           push      bx
           mov       bh,0              ;page 0
           mov       ah,2
           int       10h               ;set cursor
           pop       bx
           pop       ax
           ret
setcur     endp

;          read cursor
;          output: dh=row  dl=col
rdcurs     proc      near
           push      ax
           push      bx
           push      cx
           mov       bh,0              ;page 0
           mov       ah,3
           int       10h               ;read cursor
           pop       cx
           pop       bx
           pop       ax
           ret
rdcurs     endp
```

Figure 7.10 Subroutines to set and read the cursor

```
;          inc cursor
inccur     proc      near
           push      dx
           call      rdcurs            ;read cursor
           inc       dl                ;inc dl
           call      setcur            ;set cursor
           pop       dx
           ret
inccur     endp

;          dec cursor
deccur     proc      near
           push      dx
           call      rdcurs            ;read cursor
           dec       dl                ;inc dl
           call      setcur            ;set cursor
           pop       dx
           ret
deccur     endp
```

Figure 7.11 Subroutines to increment and decrement the cursor

The subroutine *home* shown in Figure 7.12 will set the cursor to the upper left-hand corner of the screen (row 0, column 0). The subroutine *tab* shown in Figure 7.12 will increment the cursor by 5 column spaces. Again note that this subroutine does not check for the end of a line.

```
;          home cursor
home       proc      near
           push      dx
           mov       dx,0                    ;row=0 col=0
           call      setcur
           pop       dx
           ret
home       endp

;          tab
tab        proc      near
           push      ax
           push      bx
           push      dx
           mov       bh,0
           mov       ah,3                    ;read cursor
           int       10h
           add       dl,5                    ;mov cursor +5
           mov       ah,2
           int       10h                     ;set cursor
           pop       dx
           pop       bx
           pop       ax
           ret
tab        endp
```

Figure 7.12 Subroutines to home and tab the cursor

Character Output Routines

Once the cursor position is set you can read or write character and attribute bytes using the video routines shown in Figure 7.13. The $AH = 9$ routine allows you to write at the current cursor position the character whose ASCII code is in AL and whose attribute is in BL. The value in CX determines how many of these characters to write. If you want to display only one character (the normal case) you must set $CX = 1$. On the other hand you could draw a dashed line all the way across an 80 column screen by setting $CX = 50H$ and putting the ASCII code for a dash (2DH) in AL.

AH = 8	Read character/attribute at current cursor position
	Input: BH = page number
	Output: AL = ASCII code of character read
	AH = Attribute of character read
AH = 9	Write character/attribute at current cursor position
	Input: BH = page number
	CX = count of characters to write
	AL = ASCII code of character to write
	BL = attribute of character to write
AH = 10 (0AH)	Write character only at current cursor position
	Input: BH = page number
	CX = count of characters to write
	AL = ASCII code of character to write
AH = 14 (0EH)	Write character (teletype mode)
	Input: AL = ASCII code of character to write
	BL = foreground color (in graphics mode)
	BH = page number
	Cursor position is automatically incremented and screen width is specified by most recent mode set.

Figure 7.13 Character handling routines using INT 10H

The subroutine *chrout* shown in Figure 7.14 will print a character (with a given attribute) at the current cursor position and then advance the cursor one character position on the screen. The subroutine uses the $AH = 3$ option in Figure 7.9 to read the current cursor position. When calling this subroutine the ASCII code of the character to write is in AL and the attribute of the character is in BL (see the $AH = 9$ option in Figure 7.13). After writing the character/attribute at the current cursor position the column number of the cursor (in DL) is incremented. If it exceeds the line length (taken as 80 in Figure 7.14) then DL is set to 0 (a carriage return) and the row number (in DH) is incremented (a line feed). When the row number exceeds 24 the entire screen is scrolled up one line using the $AH = 6$ scroll option given in Figure 7.15.

```
            ;              character output
chrout      proc near
            push    ax
            push    bx                      ;save regs
            push    cx
            push    dx
            push    ax
            mov     bh,0
            mov     ah,3
            int     10h                     ;read cursor
            mov     cx,1
            pop     ax                      ;get char
            cmp     al,0dh                  ;check for CR
            je      chr1
            cmp     al,20h                  ;ignore ctrl
            jb      chr3                    ; characters
            mov     ah,9
            int     10h                     ;write char/att
            inc     dl                      ;inc cursor
            cmp     dl,80                   ;if end of line
            jb      chr2
chr1:       mov     dl,0                    ;do CR
            inc     dh                      ; LF
            cmp     dh,25                   ;if end of
            jb      chr2                    ; screen
            mov     cx,0                    ;scroll
            mov     dx,184fh                ; entire
            mov     bh,07h                  ; screen
            mov     ax,0601h                ; up
            int     10h                     ; 1 line
            mov     dx,1800h                ;CR
            mov     bh,0                    ;reset page no.
chr2:       mov     ah,2
            int     10h                     ;set new cursor
chr3:       pop     dx                      ;restore regs
            pop     cx
            pop     bx
            pop     ax
            ret
chrout      endp
```

Figure 7.14 A character output subroutine

A simpler character output subroutine, called *chrprt*, is given in Figure 7.16. This routine uses the teletype mode option ($AH = 0EH$) in Figure 7.13. This option will print a character whose ASCII code is in AL at the current cursor position. It automatically increments the cursor position after each character is written. The screen width (either 40 or 80) is determined by the most recent mode set and the screen will scroll when the cursor increments past the bottom line. The subroutine in Figure 7.16 seems to do everything that the one in Figure 7.14 does. The difference is that the attribute of individual characters can be set (in *BL*) by the subroutine in Figure 7.14. On the other hand, characters printed using the subroutine in Figure 7.16 will acquire whatever attribute has previously been assigned to that screen location. If the attribute byte happens to be 00 (non display, see Figure 7.3), then the subroutine in Figure 7.16 will appear *not* to print a character. You must be careful about this. In addition, you can easily modify the subroutine in Figure 7.14 to write characters in a pre-defined window on the screen, and scroll the characters only within that window.

AH = 6	Scroll active page up
	Input: AL = number of lines to scroll
	(e.g. AL=1 scrolls page up 1 line)
	AL=0 will blank entire window
	(CH,CL) = row,column of upper left corner of scroll
	(DH,DL) = row,column of lower right corner of scroll
	BH = attribute to use on blank bottom line
AH = 7	Scroll active page down
	Input: AL = number of lines to scroll
	(e.g. AL=1 scrolls page down 1 line)
	AL=0 will blank entire window
	(CH,CL) = row,column of upper left corner of scroll
	(DH,DL) = row,column of lower right corner of scroll
	BH = attribute to use on blank top line

Figure 7.15 Scroll options using INT 10H

```
;              print a char using teletype mode
chrprt         proc        near
               push        ax
               push        bx
               mov         bh,0              ;page 0
               mov         ah,0eh            ;write char in
               int         10h               ; al on screen
               pop         bx
               pop         ax
               ret
chrprt         endp
```

Figure 7.16 Alternate subroutine to print a character at the
current cursor location

We can write our own subroutine to print a character on the screen at the current cursor position with the current attribute by first reading the character and attribute at the current cursor location using the *AH* = 8 function in Figure 7.13, storing that attribute value in *BL* and then calling the *chrout* routine in Figure 7.14. The subroutine *chrout1* shown in Figure 7.17 will do this. This subroutine will be convenient to use when you want to write a character on the screen using the current attribute at the cursor location. All you need to do is load the ASCII code of the character to write into AL and then call *chrout1*.

```
;          display char with current attribute
chrout1    proc      near
           push      ax
           push      bx
           push      ax                     ;save char
           mov       bh,0                   ;page 0
           mov       ah,8
           int       10h                    ;read attribute
           mov       bl,ah
           pop       ax                     ;get char
           call      chrout                 ;& display
           pop       bx
           pop       ax
           ret
chrout1    endp
```

Figure 7.17 Subroutine to print a character with the current attribute

The subroutine *clrwin* shown in Figure 7.18 will clear a window on the screen by using the *AL* = 0 option of the scroll *INT 10H* function (*AH* = 6) given in Figure 7.15. This subroutine is useful if you need to blank only a portion of the screen.

```
;          clear window
;          ch:cl = row:col of upper left corner
;          dh:dl = row:col of lower right corner
clrwin     proc      near
           push      ax
           push      bx
           mov       bh,7                   ;normal attr
           mov       ah,6                   ;scroll func
           mov       al,0                   ;blank window
           int       10h
           pop       bx
           pop       ax
           ret
clrwin     endp
```

Figure 7.18 Subroutine to clear a rectangular area on the screen

7.4 SCREEN SUBROUTINES

In the last section we wrote a number of subroutines to clear the screen, set and move the cursor, and write a character on the screen. These subroutines were based on the *INT 10h* video BIOS routines. All of these subroutines are included in the file *screen.asm* which is included on the TUTOR disk. A list of all of the subroutines included in this file is given in Table 7.2. A complete listing of this file is given in Appendix C. In this section we will look at some of the other screen subroutines that are included in the *screen.asm* file.

You can use any of these subroutines in your own programs by assembling the file *screen.asm* to produce the object file *screen.obj*. You would then link this object file with the object file of your program as described in Section 5.4. You would need to include an *extrn* statement in your program for each of the screen subroutines that you use as illustrated in the example in Listing 5.2a in Chapter 5.

Table 7.2
Screen Subroutines

Subroutine	Function
stvseg	set video RAM segment address, *vidseg*, to B000H or B800H.
chrout	output a character to the screen at the current cursor position.
mess	display a message on the screen.
chrout1	character output with the current attribute.
mess2	display a message on the screen at the current cursor position.
fmess	fast message display by writing directly to the screen
setcur	set cursor at *row,col*
rdcurs	read cursor position
inccur	increment cursor position
deccur	decrement cursor position
clrscn	clear screen
home	move cursor to upper-left corner of screen
crlf	carriage return, line feed
tab	move cursor 5 positions to the right
getatt	get the attribute of character at the current cursor position
chgatt	change attribute of character at the current cursor position
invatt	invert attribute of word at the current cursor position
togatt	invert attribute of character at the current cursor
invline	invert line of text at current cursor position
blank	blank one row
clrwin	clear window
curoff	hide cursor
chrprt	print a character on the screen using the teletype mode
hexasc	hex to ascii conversion for single hex digit
pbyte	print a byte as two hex digits
delay	delay *ax* ticks (18.2 ticks per second)
tone	make a tone
beep	beep a tone
getkey	wait for key and get key value
dokey	process a key
query	buffered keyboard input at current cursor position
svinit	allocate save screen buffer (16000 bytes for 4 screens)
resize	resize memory
relssb	release save screen buffer
savescr	save screen (can be nested 4 deep)
restscr	restore screen
quit	quit to DOS

Printing a Message

Suppose you want to print a message, consisting of a string of characters, at some arbitrary location on the screen. The first thing to do is to store the message as a sequence of ASCII codes in consecutive memory locations. The message can be printed on the screen by moving this block of ASCII codes into the proper area of the video RAM.

The subroutine *mess* shown in Figure 7.19 will write a message on the screen starting at location *DH* (row), *DL* (col) using the character output

subroutine *chrout* given in Figure 7.14. The message must end with a byte
containing 00H. The starting address of the message must be stored in *SI*
and the attribute to be used for each character in the message must be stored
in *BL*.

```
;          message display
mess       proc     near
           push     ax
           push     bx
           push     cx
           push     si
           mov      bh,0            ;page 0
           mov      ah,2            ;set cursor
           int      10h             ; at dh,dl
           mov      cx,1            ;1 character
           cld                      ;si increases
ms1:       lodsb                    ;[si]-->al
           cmp      al,0            ;message done?
           je       ms2             ;if so, return
           call     chrout          ;display char
           jmp      ms1             ;and continue
ms2:       pop      si
           pop      cx
           pop      bx
           pop      ax
           ret
mess       endp
```

Figure 7.19 Subroutine to print message from *[SI]* at row = *DH*, col = *DL*
with attribute in *BL*

As an example, the program shown in Listing 7.1 will print the
message *Hello World* in reverse video near the center of a cleared screen.
Note that the message *Hello World* is stored in a separate data segment
using the *db* assembler directive. If the message is included between single
quotes the ASCII code for each character in the message will be stored in
consecutive bytes in memory. The message must end with a byte
containing 00H. Note that this program must be linked with the *screen.obj*
file to produce an executable .EXE file.

An alternate message display subroutine is shown in Figure 7.20.
The subroutine *mess2* will display a message on the screen at the *current
cursor position* with the *current attribute*. The message must be stored at *si*
in the data segment. Note that this subroutine first reads the current cursor
position and the current attribute and then calls the subroutine *mess*.

Fast Message Printing Subroutine

Sometimes it is necessary to write to the screen at a faster rate than is
possible by using the BIOS (or DOS) routines. This is the case if data is
being updated continuously. For example, in the logic analyzer program,
logic2.asm, which you have used in earlier chapters, the input lines from
the printer port are displayed on the screen in real time. If the subroutine
mess given above is used to display these input bits, the cursor will be
observed jumping around under these bits. This is because the cursor
constantly has to be moved from the output bits to the input bits while the
program continually prints the input bits and waits for the cursor in the
output bits to be moved.

```
   Listing 7.1      messtest.lst
                                    title    Message test
                         ;          LINK with screen

0000                                stack    segment para stack
0000      40 [                               db       64 dup(?)
              ??
          ]
0040                                stack    ends

0000                                data     segment public
0000  48 65 6C 6C 6F 20 msg1        db       'Hello World',0
      57 6F 72 6C 64 00
000C                                data     ends


                         ;          screen subroutines
                                    extrn    mess:near,clrscn:near

0000                                code     segment public
                                             assume cs:code,ds:data
0000                                main     proc     far
0000  B8 ---- R                              mov      ax,data         ;set ds
0003  8E D8                                  mov      ds,ax
0005  E8 0000 E                              call     clrscn          ;clear screen
0008  B6 0B                                  mov      dh,11           ;row 11
000A  B2 20                                  mov      dl,32           ;column 32
000C  B3 70                                  mov      bl,70h          ;reverse video
000E  BE 0000 R                              mov      si,offset msg1  ;si -> message
0011  E8 0000 E                              call     mess            ;print message
0014  B4 00                                  mov      ah,0            ;wait for
0016  CD 16                                  int      16h             ; any key
0018  E8 0000 E                              call     clrscn          ;clear screen
001B  B8 4C00                                mov      ax,4C00h
001E  CD 21                                  int      21h             ;return to DOS
0020                                main     endp
0020                                code     ends
                                             end      main
```

```
;          message display with current attribute
;          at current cursor position
mess2      proc      near
           push      ax
           push      bx
           push      dx
           call      rdcurs              ;read cursor
           mov       bh,0                ;page 0
           mov       ah,8
           int       10h                 ;read attribute
           mov       bl,ah
           call      mess                ;& display mess
           pop       dx
           pop       bx
           pop       ax
           ret
mess2      endp
```

Figure 7.20 Subroutine to display a message with the current attribute
at the current cursor position

An alternative is to replace the subroutine *mess* with the subroutine
fmess, which will write directly to the screen. In this case the cursor is
never actually moved to the location on the screen where the message is

printed. Rather, the *row* (*DH*) and *column* (*DL*) values are used to compute the offset address (to be stored in *DI*) in the video RAM where the message is to start. From Figure 7.6 this offset address will be given by the equation

$$offset\ address = 160 * row + 2 * col$$

or

$$di = 160 * dh + 2 * dl \qquad (7.1)$$

To compute the value *di* in Eq. (7.1) as fast as possible we will not use the *MUL* instruction but rather will use the subroutine *setdi* shown in Figure 7.21. Note that to compute 160 * *dh* we use the fact that

$$160 * dh = 128 * dh + 32 * dh$$

where we can compute 128 * *dh* and 32 * *dh* by fast shifting operations. Note that we can always use this technique to multiply by any constant because we can write the constant as the sum of numbers that are powers of two (its binary representation). In Figure 7.21 we put the row value in *ax* and then shift it left 5 bits (to multiply by 32) and then two more bits (to multiply by 128). These two values are added to get the value 160 * *row*.

```
;              set di to video RAM offset address
;              di = row * 160 + col
setdi   proc      near
        push      cx
        mov       ah,0
        mov       al,dh              ;ax=row
        mov       cl,5
        shl       ax,cl              ;ax=32*row
        mov       di,ax              ;di=32*row
        shl       ax,1
        shl       ax,1               ;ax=128*row
        add       di,ax              ;di=160*row
        mov       ah,0
        mov       al,dl              ;ax=col
        shl       ax,1               ;ax=2*col
        add       di,ax              ;di=video offset
        pop       cx
        ret
setdi   endp
```

Figure 7.21 Fast subroutine to compute video RAM offset address

The subroutine *fmess* is shown in Figure 7.22. After storing the video RAM offset address of the first character of the message in *di* (by calling *setdi*) the attribute of the message (in *bl*) is stored in *ah*. The instruction *lodsb* in the *fms1* loop will read each ASCII code of the message from the string in the data segment and the instruction *stosw* will store both the ASCII code (in *al*) and the attribute (in *ah*) at the next location in the video RAM. The loop will terminate when the zero at the end of the message is read.

When writing directly to the screen the segment address of the video RAM must be known and stored in the variable *vidseg*. This can be done by calling the subroutine *stvseg* shown in Figure 7.23.

The subroutine *stvseg* in Figure 7.23 first gets the current video state using the *INT 10H* (*AH* = 15) BIOS call and then sets the variable *vidseg* to B000H for a monochrome monitor or to B800H for all others (such as VGA).

```
;              fast message routine
;              si -> message in data segment
;              dh = row, dl = col
;              bl = attribute of message
fmess          proc       near
               push       ax
               push       di
               call       setdi           ;di->vidRAM offset
               mov        ah,bl           ;ah=attribute
               mov        es,vidseg       ;es->video RAM
               cld
fms1:          lodsb
               cmp        al,0
               je         fms2
               stosw
               jmp        fms1
fms2:          pop        di
               pop        ax
               ret
fmess          endp
```

Figure 7.22 Message subroutine that writes directly to the screen

```
;              set video RAM segment address
stvseg         proc       near
               push       ax
               mov        ah,15
               int        10h             ;get video state
               cmp        al,7            ;if monochrome
               jne        svg1
               mov        vidseg,0b000h   ; vidseg=b000
               jmp        svg2            ;else
svg1:          mov        vidseg,0b800h   ; vidseg=b800
svg2:          pop        ax
               ret
stvseg         endp
```

Figure 7.23 Subroutine to set the video RAM segment address

Keyboard Control

In Chapter 3 you saw that *INT 16H* can be used to read the keyboard. All
of the options available with this interrupt call are given in Figure 7.24. In
addition to waiting for a key to be pressed (*AH* = 0) you can check to see if
a key has been pressed (*AH* = 1), and if so (*Z* = 0), read the value in *AX*,
or if not (*Z* = 1), go do something else. This would be useful, for example,
in a terminal emulation program where you want to alternate between
checking the keyboard and checking the RS-232 serial port (see Chapter
13).

The third option in Figure 7.24 (*AH* = 2) allows you to interrogate
the state of some special keys. Memory location 0040:0017 is called the
kb_flag and the bits in this byte are set according to the state of certain
special keys as indicated in Figure 7.25.

To see how these bits get set, go to location 0040:0017 in the
TUTOR monitor. The memory locations (and registers) in TUTOR get
updated only when you make a change such as moving the position cursor
(>) forward or backward. Move the position cursor forward and backward
and watch memory location 0040:0017 as you press the following keys:

Ins, Caps Lock, Num Lock, Scroll Lock, Left Shift, Right Shift. Note that the forward and backward cursor keys will not work while pressing the *Ctrl* or *Alt* keys.

AH = 0	*Wait for key to be pressed* Output: AH = scan code of key pressed AL = ASCII code of key pressed
AH = 1	*Check to see if key has been pressed and set Z-flag* Output: Z = 1 no key was pressed Z = 0 key has been pressed and AH = scan code AL = ASCII code
AH = 2	*Check special keys* Output: AL = kb_flag (0040:0017)

Figure 7.24 Keyboard control options using INT 16H

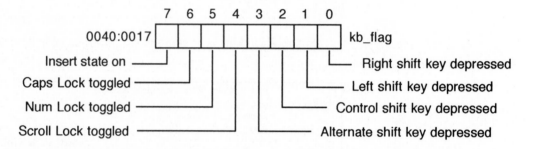

Figure 7.25 Definition of the *kb_flag* at location 0040:0017

From Table 3.4 in Chapter 3 note that the ASCII codes for certain keys such as the function keys and the cursor keys are all zero. This means that the scan code is the only way to distinguish between these keys. It will be useful to assign these keys a modified ASCII code that is formed by ORing their scan code with 80H. This will provide a unique ASCII code inasmuch as all "normal" ASCII codes are 7-bit codes with values between 00H and 7FH. The subroutine *getkey* shown in Figure 7.26 will do this. Note from Table 3.4 that pressing the alternate key with a key on the numeric keypad produces a scan code of zero. These keys are ignored in the subroutine *getkey*.

```
;              wait for key and get key value
;              output: al = ascii code of key
;                      function & cursor keys have
;                      al = scan code OR 80H
getkey    proc      near
gk1:      mov       ah,0
          int       16h              ;wait for key
          cmp       ah,0             ;ignore Alt-keypd
          je        gk1
          cmp       al,0
          jne       gk2              ;if ascii = 0
          mov       al,ah            ;use scan code
          or        al,80h           ; OR 80h
gk2:      ret
getkey    endp
```

Figure 7.26 The subroutine *getkey*

Use of a Jump Table

Many programs will wait for a key to be pressed and then execute a particular subroutine depending upon the key pressed. For example, the use of pop-up menus is described in the exercises at the end of this chapter. In this program certain keys such as the cursor keys and some of the letter keys perform particular tasks.

In programs of this sort a jump table made up of a list of key ASCII codes and subroutine offset addresses is a useful technique for executing the appropriate routine. For example, the subroutine *dokey* shown in Figure 7.27 will process a key whose ASCII code (as obtained from the subroutine getkey in Figure 7.26) is stored in register *al*. Before calling the subroutine *dokey* register *di* contains the offset address of a jump table in the code segment and dx contains the offset address of the default subroutine to call if the key ASCII code is not in the jump table. Note that the jump table is made up of bytes (*db*) containing the key ASCII code of different keys followed by a word (*dw*) containing the label (offset address) of the subroutine to call if that key is pressed. For example, if the key with an ASCII code *key1* is pressed, then the subroutine *sub1* will be called. Similarly, if the key with an ASCII code *key2* is pressed, then the subroutine *sub2* will be called. The jump table ends with a byte containing 00H.

```
;              process a key
;              input: al = ascii code of key
;                     di -> jump table
;                     dx -> default subroutine
dokey      proc    near
dk1:       cmp     al,cs:[di]            ;chk next code
           jne     dk2                   ;if a match
           call    word ptr cs:1[di]     ;call sub
           ret                           ;and quit
dk2:       cmp     byte ptr cs:[di],0    ;if not
           je      dk3                   ;end of table
           add     di,3                  ;chk next entry
           jmp     dk1                   ; in table
dk3:       call    dx                    ;else call
           ret                           ;default sub
dokey      endp


;              jump table
jmptbl     db      key1                  ;<-- di points here
           dw      sub1
           db      key2
           dw      sub2
           db      key3
           dw      sub3
           db      0


;              default subroutine
deflt      proc    near                  ;<-- dx points here
           ---
           ---
           ---
           ret
deflt      endp
```

Figure 7.27 Processing a key using a jump table

The subroutine *dokey* compares the ASCII code in *al* with each entry in the jump table until a match is found (at which point the following subroutine in the jump table is executed after which the subroutine *dokey* is exited). If no match is found in the jump table, the program jumps to *dk3* which will call the subroutine whose offset address is in register *dx*. Study the subroutine *dokey* and make sure you understand how it works.

The advantage of using a jump table like the one shown in Figure 7.27 is that it is easy to add new key functions and change what keys do by simply adding or changing the entries in the jump table. To assemble a jump table without errors you must tell the assembler the location of all the subroutines in the jump table. You could just use the *extrn* assembler directive to indicate that the subroutine will be assembled in a separate module. Regardless of whether the subroutine in an internal or external subroutine you can begin by just making a stub for each subroutine of the form

```
sub1    proc    near
        ret
sub1    endp
```

You can then assemble and link all modules to produce an executable file that you can begin to debug. You can then write and debug each subroutine one by one. This is an example of *top-down programming*.

Buffered Keyboard Input

In many programs it is necessary to type a string of characters into a buffer for further processing. We will look at two ways to do this. The first is a DOS function call and the second is the subroutine *query* that is part of our screen subroutine file, *screen.asm*.

Function call 0AH (i.e., *AH* = 0AH in *INT 21H*) is used for a buffered keyboard input. The setup for using this function is shown in Figure 7.28. Load *DS* and *DX* such that *DS:DX* points to the beginning of an input buffer. Store the length of this buffer in the first byte. After calling *INT 21H*, characters typed on the keyboard will be stored in the buffer starting with the third byte as shown in Figure 7.28. Some basic editing features can be used while filling this buffer. The interrupt function exits when you press *Enter*. At that point the second byte of the buffer will contain the number of characters actually stored in the input buffer. If you try to type past the next to last byte in the buffer, the bell will sound and the extra characters will be ignored.

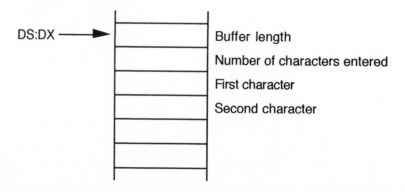

Figure 7.28 Setup for using the buffered keyboard input (*AH* = 0AH) in *INT 21H*

The subroutine *query* in the file *screen.asm* is a buffered keyboard input routine that stores the input characters in the buffer *kbuf* which is an 80-byte buffer defined in the data segment in the *screen.asm* file as shown in Figure 7.29. The label *bufend* in Figure 7.29 defines the byte following the end of the input keyboard buffer.

```
data        segment   public
kbuf        db        80 dup(?)
bufend      db        ?
span        dw        ?
sisave      dw        ?
svseg       dw        0
data        ends
```

Figure 7.29 The data segment used by the screen subroutines in the file *screen.asm*

```
;           buffered keyboard input
;           at current cursor position
;           input asciiz string is at kbuf
;           # of character entered at span
;           output: none
query       proc      near
            mov       sisave,si
            mov       si,offset kbuf        ;si->kbuf
qy1:        call      getkey               ;get key
            mov       di,offset jmptbq
            mov       dx,offset tobuff      ;default
            call      dokey                ;process key
            jmp       qy1
query       endp


;           query jump table
jmptbq      db        _bksp                 ;backspace
            dw        backsp
            db        _enter                ;enter
            dw        enterq
            db        _esc                  ;esc
            dw        quit
            db        0


;           display & store char in kbuf
tobuff      proc      near
            cmp       si,offset bufend
            jb        tb1                   ;if end.of.buf
            call      beep                  ; beep &
            ret                             ; quit
tb1:        mov       [si],al               ;store char
            inc       si                    ;inc ptr
            call      chrout1               ;display char
            ret
tobuff      endp
```

Figure 7.30 The subroutine *query*

The subroutine *query* is shown in Figure 7.30. The subroutine *dokey* given in Figure 7.27 is used together with the jump table *jmptbq* to process each key pressed. The jump table handles the *backspace*, *Enter* and *ESC* keys while the subroutine *tobuff* is the default subroutine that stores any other key in the buffer *kbuf* and displays the character on the screen. Note that in the subroutine *tobuff* the index register *si* gets incremented to point to the next available byte in the keyboard input buffer, *kbuf*. In the jump table in Figure 7.30 the variables *_bksp*, *_enter* and *_esc* have been equated to the key ASCII codes 8, 13 and 27 respectively. These three keys will call the subroutines *backsp*, *enterq* and *quit* respectively. These three subroutines are given in Figure 7.31.

The subroutine *backsp* in Figure 7.31 decrements the *kbuf* pointer, *si*, (unless the buffer in empty) and stores a blank ASCII code (20H) in that byte. It also decrements the cursor on the screen and erases the character by writing a blank character on the screen. Note that after calling the subroutine *chrout1*, which advances the cursor, the cursor needs to be decremented again.

```
;               backspace
backsp          proc        near
                cmp         si,offset kbuf
                ja          bk1                 ;if 1st char
                call        beep                ;beep & ret
                ret
bk1:            dec si                          ;back up & put
                mov         byte ptr [si],20h   ;20h in kbuf
                call        deccur              ;back up & put
                mov         al,20h              ;blank on
                call        chrout1             ;screen
                call        deccur
                ret
backsp          endp


;               enter from query
;               exits from query
enterq          proc        near
                mov         byte ptr [si],0     ;make asciiz
                sub         si,offset kbuf      ;store #char
                mov         span,si             ;in span
                mov         si,sisave           ;restore si
                pop         ax                  ;>enterq
                pop         ax                  ;>dokey
                ret                             ;>query
enterq          endp


;               quit to dos
quit            proc        near
                mov         ax,4C00h
                int         21h
quit            endp
```

Figure 7.31 *Query* jump table subroutines

The subroutine *enterq* in Figure 7.31 is a little tricky. This is the subroutine that is called when the *Enter* key is pressed while you are typing characters into *kbuf* in *query*. We therefore want to leave *query* at this point. But note in Figure 7.30 that the subroutine *query* does not have any *RET* statement. It is just a continuous loop that calls *getkey* and *dokey*. We must rely on *dokey* to exit *query* when the *Enter* key is pressed. How can we do this? Remember that every time we call a subroutine the return address of the next instruction is pushed on the stack. Therefore, when we execute *call query* the return address of the next instruction (call it *addr1*) will be pushed on the stack. This is the address we want to get back to when we press the *Enter* key. When we press the *Enter* key we will execute the statement *call dokey* in the subroutine *query* in Figure 7.30. This will push the return address of the next instruction (call it *addr2*) on the stack. At this point the two addresses *addr1* and *addr2* are on the stack. But the subroutine *dokey* given in Figure 7.27 will call the subroutine *enterq* in Figure 7.31 by executing the statement *call word ptr cs:1[di]*. This will push the return address of the next instruction (call it *addr3*) on the stack. At this point the three addresses *addr1*, *addr2* and *addr3* will be on the stack. The RET instruction in *enterq* will normally return to *addr3*, which is the address on the top of the stack. But we really want to return to *addr1* (the address following the *call query* instruction), which is the third address on the stack. To get to this address we just pop the top two addresses from the stack using the two *pop ax* instructions just before the *RET* instruction in the subroutine *enterq* in Figure 7.31. The *RET* instruction will then pop the address *addr3* into the instruction pointer and return to the instruction following the *call query* instruction. Before leaving *enterq* a zero is inserted at the end of the string in *kbuf* to make it an ASCIIZ string. In addition the number of characters entered into *kbuf* by *query* is stored in the variable *span* which is defined in the data segment in Figure 7.29. Also note that the value of *si* that was saved in the variable *sisave* at the beginning of the subroutine *query* is restored in *enterq*.

The subroutine *quit* in Figure 7.31, executed when the *ESC* key is pressed, just returns to DOS using the *AH* = 4C function call. You could add a *call clrscn* instruction to the beginning of this subroutine if you wanted the screen to be cleared before returning to DOS.

```
Listing 7.2     typscn.asm
                title   type characters to screen


        ;       LINK with screen
        stack   segment para stack
                db      64 dup(?)
        stack   ends


        data    segment  public
        data    ends


        ;       screen subroutines
                extrn   clrscn:near,query:near
                extrn   crlf:near


        code    segment  public
                assume  cs:code,ds:data
        main    proc    far
                mov     ax,data                 ;set ds
                mov     ds,ax
                call    clrscn                  ;clear screen
        mn1:    call    query                   ;type next line
                call    crlf                    ;carriage return
                jmp     mn1                     ;keep going
        main    endp


        code    ends
                end     main
```

Typing Characters on the Screen

As an example of using the subroutine *query* consider the program shown in Listing 7.2 which will type any characters on the screen. Note that after assembling this program the object file *typscn.obj* must be linked with *screen.obj* to make available the subroutines *clrscn*, *query* and *crlf*.

The subroutine *query* allows you to type any characters on a single line of the screen and use the *backspace* key to make any corrections. When you press the *Enter* key the subroutine *query* will be exited as described above and the subroutine *crlf*, shown in Figure 7.32, will be executed. This subroutine will cause the cursor to move to the beginning of the next line and scroll the screen when the bottom of the screen in reached.

Note that the main program is just a loop that continually calls the two subroutines *query* and *crlf*. When the *ESC* key is pressed the subroutine *query* causes the program to return to DOS using the subroutine *quit* in Figure 7.31.

```
;          carriage return line feed
crlf       proc      near
           push      ax
           push      bx
           push      cx
           push      dx
           call      rdcurs          ;read cursor
           mov       dl,0            ;do CR
           inc       dh              ; LF
           cmp       dh,25           ;if end of
           jb        crl             ; screen
           mov       cx,0            ;scroll
           mov       dx,184fh        ; entire
           mov       bh,07h          ; screen
           mov       ax,0601h        ; up
           int       10h             ; 1 line
           mov       dx,1800h        ;CR
           mov       bh,0            ;page 0
crl:       call      setcur          ;set cursor
           pop       dx
           pop       cx
           pop       bx
           pop       ax
           ret
crlf       endp
```

Figure 7.32 Subroutine to perform a screen carriage return/line feed

Attribute Control

Sometimes it is useful to know the attribute of a particular character on the screen and to be able to change the attribute of any character. The subroutines *getatt* and *chgatt* shown in Figure 7.33 will do this. These subroutines just use the basic *INT 10H* BIOS calls given in Figure 7.13.

The subroutine *togatt* shown in Figure 7.34 will toggle the attribute of the character at the current cursor position between normal and inverse. Suppose you want to toggle the attribute of an entire word. You can do this by toggling the attribute of each character in the word until a blank character on the screen is encountered. The subroutine *invatt* shown in Figure 7.35 will do this. This subroutine might be useful if you are selecting menu

```
;             get attribute of character at
;             dx = row:col and store in bl
getatt        proc         near
              push         ax
              call         setcur                 ;set cursor
              mov          bh,0                   ;page 0
              mov          ah,8                   ;read char/attr
              int          10h
              mov          bl,ah                  ;bl = attrib
              pop          ax
              ret
getatt        endp


;             change attribute of character at
;             current cursor position to bl
chgatt        proc         near
              push         ax
              push         bx
              push         cx
              mov          bh,0                   ;page 0
              mov          ah,8                   ;read char/attr
              int          10h
              mov          cx,1
              mov          ah,9
              int          10h                    ;write char/att
              pop          cx
              pop          bx
              pop          ax
              ret
chgatt        endp
```

Figure 7.33 Subroutines to get and change the attribute of characters
on the screen

```
;             toggle attribute of character
;             at current cursor position
togatt        proc         near
              push         ax
              push         bx
              push         cx
              mov          bh,0                   ;page 0
              mov          ah,8                   ;read char/attr
              int          10h
              cmp          ah,07h                 ;if normal
              jne          ta1
              mov          bl,70h                 ;make inverse
              jmp          ta2                    ;else
ta1:          mov          bl,07h                 ;make normal
ta2:          mov          cx,1
              mov          ah,9
              int          10h                    ;write char/att
              pop          cx
              pop          bx
              pop          ax
              ret
togatt        endp
```

Figure 7.34 Subroutine to toggle the attribute of a character
from normal to inverse

items by moving the cursor up and down and the selected item is displayed in reverse video. However, suppose the menu items contain more than one word. How can you invert a line of text containing more than one word? You could continue to invert words (together with the blanks between them) until two consecutive blanks are encountered. The subroutine *invline* shown in Figure 7.36 will do this.

Note that the subroutine *invatt* leaves the cursor at the first blank following the word. The subroutine *invline* just calls *invatt* (which inverts the attribute of a word) and *togatt* (which inverts the blank following the word) until a second blank following a word is found. In this way *invline* will invert the attribute of a group of words including a blank at the end of the line of text. This will be useful in making menus including pop-up menus. (See Problems 7.1 and 7.2 at the end of this chapter.)

```
;           invert attribute of word at current
;           cursor position
invatt      proc      near
            push      ax
            push      bx
            push      cx
            mov       bh,0              ;page 0
ia1:        mov       ah,8              ;read char/attr
            int       10h
            cmp       al,20h            ;if blank
            je        ia4               ; quit
            cmp       ah,07h            ;if normal
            jne       ia2
            mov       bl,70h            ;make inverse
            jmp       ia3               ;else
ia2:        mov       bl,07h            ;make normal
ia3:        mov       cx,1
            mov       ah,9
            int       10h               ;write char/att
            call      inccur            ;adv cursor
            jmp       ia1               ;repeat
ia4:        pop       cx
            pop       bx
            pop       ax
            ret
invatt      endp
```

Figure 7.35 Subroutine to toggle the attribute of a word from normal to inverse

```
;           invert line of text at
;           current cursor position
invline     proc      near
            push      ax
ivl1:       call      invatt            ;invert word
            call      togatt            ;invert blank
            call      inccur            ;inc cursor
            mov       ah,8              ;read chr/attr
            int       10h
            cmp       al,20h            ;repeat until
            jne       ivl1              ;blank
            pop       ax
            ret
invline     endp
```

Figure 7.36 Subroutine to toggle the attribute of a line of text from normal to inverse

7.5 MEMORY MANAGEMENT

As we have seen the data segment is used to store variables including arrays, strings and tables. These are all static data structures that we define (and therefore reserve space for) before we run the program. Sometimes it is more convenient to use dynamic data structures where we allocate and deallocate memory "on the fly" during the execution of the program. We may not know how much memory we need for some application or we may need to reuse the same physical memory for different purposes in a program because we don't have enough memory to allocate it all ahead of time. Finally, we may simply want to allocate a large block of memory in a separate segment for some special purpose.

We can use certain DOS *INT 21H* function calls to allocate and deallocate memory. These DOS functions are shown in Figure 7.37. When a program is run DOS will normally allocate all available memory to the program. There is usually a lot more memory allocated than the program actually needs. This means that if you want to allocate additional memory in your program for some particular function this additional memory will not be available. To make it available you will need to modify the memory allocation by calling the *AH* = 4AH DOS *INT 21H* function. As shown in Figure 7.37 this requires that you know how many total paragraphs of memory your program really needs and the segment address corresponding to the beginning of your program.

AH = 4AH	*Modify memory allocation*
	Input: BX = new requested block size in paragraphs
	            ES = segment of block to be modified
	Output: If carry = 0, successful
	            If carry = 1, then
	                AX = error codes
	                    7 memory control blocks destroyed
	                    8 insufficient memory
	                    9 invalid segment in ES
	                BX = maximum block size available

AH = 48H	*Allocate memory*
	Input: BX = number of paragraphs of memory needed
	Output: If carry = 0, successful
	                AX = initial segment of allocated block
	            If carry = 1, then
	                AX = error codes
	                    7 memory control blocks destroyed
	                    8 insufficient memory
	                BX = size of largest available block

AH = 49H	*Release memory*
	Input: ES = segment of block to be released
	Output: If carry = 0, successful
	            If carry = 1, then
	                AX = error codes
	                    7 memory control blocks destroyed
	                    9 invalid segment in ES

Figure 7.37 Allocating and deallocating memory using INT 21H

In memory, your program will consist of a program segment prefix (PSP), the code segment, the data segment and the stack segment. When the program is first run the extra segment register will point to the beginning of the program segment prefix and the stack segment register will point to the stack segment. The value *SS – ES* will therefore be the number of paragraphs of memory used by the program excluding the stack. We normally reserve 64 bytes (or four paragraphs) of memory for the stack. Therefore, if we add five paragraphs to (*SS – ES*) we should have a block size larger than is needed by the program. The subroutine *resize* shown in Figure 7.38 can be called at the beginning of a program (immediately after setting the data segment register) to release all excess memory and make it available to allocate by the user. Note from Figure 7.37 that if this resize operation is not successful the carry flag will be set to 1 and *AX* will contain one of three possible error codes. You should check this carry flag after calling *resize* to make sure the excess memory got released.

```
;           resize memory
resize      proc      near
            mov       ax,es           ;ax=psp seg
            mov       bx,ss           ;bx=stack seg
            sub       bx,ax           ;reserve psp-ss
            add       bx,5            ; + stack size
            mov       ah,4Ah
            int       21h             ;resize mem
            ret
resize      endp
```

Figure 7.38 Subroutine to release excess memory at the beginning of a program

To allocate memory you just set *BX* to the number of paragraphs you want and call *INT 21H* with *AH* = 48H as shown in Figure 7.37. If this function call is successful the carry flag will be zero and *AX* will contain the initial segment address of the block of memory allocated. You can save this segment address in some convenient place (such as a variable name) for future use.

To deallocate memory that has previously been allocated using the *AH* = 48H function call you just set *ES* to the segment address of the block to be released and call *INT 21H* with *AH* = 49H as shown in Figure 7.37.

As an example suppose we want to reserve 16,000 bytes of memory to hold up to four video screens of data. Recall that one screen contains 80 x 25 = 2,000 characters and each character needs two bytes – one for the ASCII code and one for the attribute byte. The subroutine *svinit* shown in Figure 7.39 can be used to allocate this 16,000-byte screen buffer and the subroutine *relssb* also shown in Figure 7.39 will release these same 16,000 bytes. Note that the variable *svseg* (defined in the data segment in Figure 7.29) is used to store the segment address of the 16,000-byte buffer allocated by *svinit*. If the value of this variable is zero then no bytes are allocated. We will use this 16,000-byte buffer to save up to four different screen images.

To save a screen to our 16,000-byte buffer we can just call the subroutine *savescr* shown in Figure 7.40. This subroutine always moves the 2,000 words of the video RAM to the first 2,000 words (4,000 bytes) of the 16,000-byte save buffer. However, before moving these 2,000 words it first moves the first 12,000 bytes of the buffer up in memory by 4,000 bytes to make room for the new screen. This means that you can store up to four different screens in the buffer by simply calling *savescr* four times.

```
;             allocate save screen buffer
svinit        proc          near
              mov           svseg,0                ;svseg = 0
              mov           bx,1000                ;request 16000
              mov           ah,48h                 ; bytes
              int           21h
              jc            sv1                    ;if no error
              mov           svseg,ax               ;svseg = seg
sv1:          ret
svinit        endp


;             release save screen buffer
relssb        proc          near
              cmp           svseg,0                ;if allocated
              je            rel1
              mov           ax,svseg               ;deallocate
              mov           es,ax                  ;es = svseg
              mov           ah,49h
              int           21h                    ;release mem
rel1:         ret
relssb        endp
```

Figure 7.39 Subroutines to allocate and deallocate memory

```
;             save screen
savescr       proc          near
              push          ax                     ;save regs
              push          cx
              push          si
              push          di
              push          ds
              push          es
              cmp           svseg,0                ;if buff exists
              je            svsc1
              std                                  ;move 12000
              mov           ax,svseg               ; bytes up
              mov           ds,ax                  ; 4000 bytes
              mov           es,ax                  ; to make hole
              mov           cx,6000                ; in buffer
              mov           si,11998
              mov           di,15998
              rep movsw
              mov           ax,vidseg              ;move video ram
              mov           ds,ax                  ; to svseg
              mov           si,0                   ; buffer
              mov           di,0
              mov           cx,2000
              cld
              rep movsw
svsc1:        pop           es                     ;restore regs
              pop           ds
              pop           di
              pop           si
              pop           cx
              pop           ax
              ret
savescr       endp
```

Figure 7.40 The subroutine *savescr*

The last screen saved can be restored by calling the subroutine *restscr* shown in Figure 7.41. This subroutine will move the first 2,000 words in the save screen buffer to the video RAM and then move the last 12,000 bytes in the buffer down by 4,000 bytes. This will put the data of the next-to-last screen saved at the beginning of the buffer so that if the subroutine *restscr* is called again the next-to-last screen saved will be redisplayed. This technique can by used in Experiment 29 at the end of this chapter to make pop-up menus. If the subroutine *savescr* is called before a sub-menu is displayed on top of a main menu then the subroutine restscr will cause the sub-menu to be erased and the main menu to be redisplayed. You can nest these sub-menus four deep (that is, call *savescr* four times before you need to call *restscr*).

```
;           restore screen
restscr     proc        near
            push        ax                  ;save regs
            push        cx
            push        si
            push        di
            push        ds
            push        es
            cmp         svseg,0             ;if buff exists
            je          rsts1
            mov         ax,vidseg           ;move 1st 4000
            mov         es,ax               ; bytes from
            mov         ax,svseg            ; svseg buffer
            mov         ds,ax               ; to tv ram
            mov         si,0
            mov         di,0
            mov         cx,2000
            cld
            rep movsw
            mov         ax,data
            mov         ds,ax               ;ds = data
            mov         ax,svseg            ;move last
            mov         es,ax               ; 12000 bytes
            mov         ds,ax               ; in buffer
            mov         si,4000             ; down 4000
            mov         di,0                ; bytes
            mov         cx,6000
            rep movsw
rsts1:      pop         es                  ;restore regs
            pop         ds
            pop         di
            pop         si
            pop         cx
            pop         ax
            ret
restscr     endp
```

Figure 7.41 The subroutine *restscr*

PROGRAMMING PROBLEMS

Problem 7.1 – Menus and Transaction Control
In this experiment you will learn to use the screen display subroutines in the file *screen.asm* that you can link with your own programs.

Write a main program that displays the following initial screen:

```
┌─────────────────────────────────────────────────┐
│                                                   │
│                                                   │
│                  Menu display example             │
│                                                   │
│                  First screen display             │
│                                                   │
│                  Second screen display            │
│                                                   │
│                  Text display                     │
│                                                   │
│                                                   │
│       Press ESC to return to DOS                  │
│                                                   │
└─────────────────────────────────────────────────┘
```

The first menu item *First screen display* should be displayed in reverse video. This indicates a *selected* menu item. Pressing the up and down cursor keys should move the *selected* item up and down. Pressing the *Enter* key should cause the selected item (the one displayed in reverse video) to be executed. As an alternate method of selecting a menu item, allow the menu item to be executed by typing the first letter of the item. That is, *F* or *f* should select the first item, *S* or *s* should select the second item, and *T* or *t* should select the third item.

The three menu items should perform the following functions when executed:

Item 1: *First screen display*
Clear the screen and display the message *This is the first screen* in the center of the screen. The message should be *blinking* in *normal* video. Display the message *Press ESC to return to previous screen* at the bottom of the screen and have the program return to the main menu if you press the *ESC* key.

Item 2: *Second screen display*
Clear the screen and display the message *This is the second screen* in the center of the screen. The message should be *blinking* in *reverse* video. Display the message *Press ESC to return to previous screen* at the bottom of the screen and have the program return to the main menu if you press the *ESC* key.

Item 3: *Text display*
Clear the screen and display any characters that you type from the keyboard. Pressing the *Enter* key should produce a carriage return and line feed. When you reach the bottom of the screen, the entire screen should scroll up one line. Have the program return to the main menu if you press the *ESC* key.

Problem 7.2 – Pop-up Menus

In this experiment you will learn to make pop-up menus, to use the struc assembler directive and to use jump tables to control what your program does in response to different key pressings. You should use the subroutines in a file *screen.asm* and link these subroutines with your program.

A menu will be defined by the following data structure:

```
menudat    struc
ulx        db      0           ;upper-left x-coord of menu
uly        db      0           ;upper-left y-coord of menu
wid        db      0           ;width of menu
attrib     db      70h         ;reverse video attribute
no_item    db      0           ;no. of items in menu
curpos     db      0           ;cursor position of selected item
items      dw      0           ;list of message addresses of items
enttbl     dw      0           ;enter table for menu
jmptbl     dw      0           ;jump table for menu
menudat    ends
```

Use character graphics to draw a box around each menu and sub-menu. Each menu will have the following behavior:

1. The up and down cursor keys will be used to select a menu item. A selected menu item will appear with its attribute complemented.

2. Pressing the *Enter* key will execute the selected item by calling the appropriate subroutine.

3. Pressing the first letter of a menu item will cause that item to be selected and executed.

Write a main program that displays the following initial menu:

```
First  item

Second item

Quit to DOS
```

This main menu should have its upper-left corner located at column 25, row 6 and have a width of 25. You can define this menu with the statement

```
menu1  menudat <25,6,25,,3,,,,>
```

The three menu items should perform the following functions when executed:

Item 1: *First Item*
Display the following sub-menu at column 30, row 8 superimposed on top of the main menu:

```
First  sub1  item

Second sub1 item
```

Include stubs for these subroutines. Pressing the *ESC* key should remove this sub-menu and return to the main menu.

Item 2: *Second Item*
Display the following sub-menu at column 30, row 10 superimposed on top of the main menu:

```
First  sub2  item

Second sub2 item
```

Include stubs for these subroutines. Pressing the *ESC* key should remove this sub-menu and return to the main menu.

Item 3: *Quit to DOS*
Clear the screen, release any memory you allocated and go to DOS.

Use the subroutines *savescr* and *restscr* (see Figures 7.40 and 7.41) from *screen.asm* to save the screen before a sub-menu is displayed and restore the screen when the sub-menu is to be erased.

Problem 7.3 – Text Editor
In this experiment you will write a program that will allow you to enter any text you want within a 64 x 16 character text window on the screen. You will then create a full screen editor within this window that will allow you to insert and delete characters and move text to different parts of the window.
The text window will contain 1024 (1 Kbyte) characters. Some versions of the FORTH programming language use such 1-Kbyte screens to store the source listings of its programs. You could also use such 1-Kbyte blocks to store any kind of useful information. In Chapter 10 we will see how to store these 1-Kbyte blocks of information on disk.

a. The main program for this full screen editor should use the subroutines *getkey* and *dokey* to process the keys using a jump table (see Figures 7.26 and 7.27). Begin by writing an initial display subroutine that will display the screen shown in Figure 7.42.
Use the subroutine *mess* given in Figure 7.19 to print the text in Figure 7.42. Display the window border using reverse video spaces. Recall from Figure 7.13 that you can display an entire horizontal bar by using the *AH* = 9, *INT 10H* function call with *CX* equal to the number of reverse video spaces to print. Pressing the *ESC* key should exit to DOS.

b. Implement the four cursor keys on the numeric keypad and the *Home* key (key 7 of the numeric keypad). The four cursor keys should move the cursor nondestructively to any position within the text editor window. The *up* and *down* cursor keys should cause the cursor to stop at the top and bottom of the window. At the right edge of the window the right cursor key should advance the cursor to the beginning of the following line. At the left edge of the window the left cursor key should move the cursor to the end of the previous line. The *Home* key should move the cursor to the top-left position of the text window.

c. Implement the *default* subroutine called by *dokey* when the key ASCII code is not in the jump table. This routine should *insert* any text typed at the current location of the cursor and advance the cursor to the next location within the text window. To implement this routine, store an image of the text window as 1024 contiguous words (ASCII code, attribute byte) in a text buffer in memory. When a character is to be inserted in the text, insert one word at the cursor position in the text buffer and then rewrite the text buffer to the screen. To work at an acceptable speed you will need to write directly to the video RAM rather than go through the BIOS ROM. Write a subroutine that will copy row number *row* from the text buffer to the screen window. This subroutine can be used to form other subroutines that will copy to the screen either the remaining characters in the text buffer or the entire text buffer.

Implement the *tab* key by having it insert five spaces at the current cursor location. Implement the *Enter* key by having it insert spaces to the end of the current line and move the cursor to the beginning of the following line.

d. Implement the six function keys shown below the text window in the figure in Part 1. Pressing *F1* will cause the character at the current cursor position to be displayed in reverse video. Subsequent pressings of the cursor keys will make all text between the original and final cursor positions reverse video. This is called *selecting* text characters. Selected text can be deselected by pressing key *F1* again. Selected text can be erased by pressing the backspace key. Selected text can be copied or cut (erased) to the clipboard (another 1024-word buffer in memory) by pressing *F1* or *F2*. Text on the clipboard can be inserted (pasted) at the current cursor position by pressing *F4*. Key *F5* will clear the entire window and key *F6* will undo the most recent change that deleted any characters.

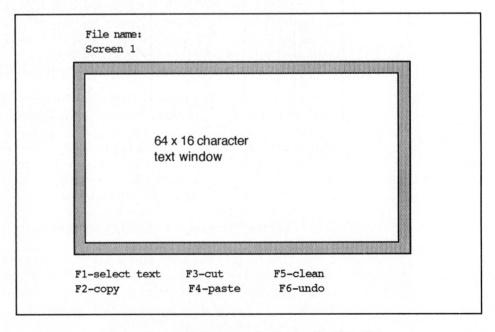

Figure 7.42 Initial screen display for Problem 7.3

EXERCISES

Exercise 7.1
Give the hex value of the attribute byte on a monochrome display for each of the following:

       (a) normal video
       (b) reverse video
       (c) blinking normal video
       (d) blinking reverse video
       (e) high-intensity normal video
       (f) high-intensity reverse video

Exercise 7.2
Give the hex value of the attribute byte on a color display for each of the following:

       (a) yellow character on a blue background
       (b) yellow character on a black background
       (c) red character on a green background
       (d) red character on a blue background
       (e) white character on a blue background
       (f) white character on a red background

Exercise 7.3
In the video RAM of an 80-character/row display find the offset address containing the ASCII code of a character located at each of the following screen locations:

       (a) column 13, row 0
       (b) column 25, row 5
       (c) column 0, row 8
       (d) column 40, row 15
       (e) column 5, row 24

Exercise 7.4
Using any subroutines in the file *screen.asm* (see Table 7.2), write instructions to set the cursor to column 10, row 5.

Exercise 7.5
Using any subroutines in the file *screen.asm* (see Table 7.2), write instructions to print the message "8086 Microprocessor" centered on the top row of the screen.

Exercise 7.6
Using any subroutines in the file *screen.asm* (see Table 7.2), write instructions to blank the lower-right quarter of the screen.

Exercise 7.7
Write instructions that use the shift and add method of multiplying by a constant (see Figure 7.21) to compute the following:

       (a) $ax = ax * 10$
       (b) $ax = ax * 30$
       (c) $ax = ax * 50$
       (d) $ax = ax * 100$

Exercise 7.8

Go to address 0040:0017 in TUTOR. You should be able to verify the operation of 6 of the 8 bits shown in Figure 7.25 by pressing the various keys and moving the TUTOR position cursor back and forth to update the TUTOR screen. Which two keys cannot be verified in this way?

Exercise 7.9

If *al* contains the value *key2* when the subroutine *dokey* in Figure 7.27 is called, how many times will the instruction *cmp al,cs:[di]* at the label *dk1:* be executed before the subroutine *sub2* is executed?

Exercise 7.10

Write a subroutine called *query2* that uses the buffered keyboard input DOS function (*AH* = 0AH) to perform the same function as the subroutine *query* given in Figure 7.30.

CHAPTER 8

Computer Arithmetic

The arithmetic instructions available in the 8086 were described in Chapter 4. In that chapter you saw how 8-bit and 16-bit binary addition and subtraction can be carried out and how binary multiplication and division work. In addition, you learned how both packed and unpacked BCD arithmetic can be done. When arithmetic involving larger numbers is required, it is necessary to use multiple bytes (or multiple words) to store the data.

In this chapter you will learn:

- How to add and subtract binary data stored in multiple words
- How to convert an ASCII number string to a binary number
- How to convert a binary number to an ASCII number string
- How to make a calculator for 16-bit integers
- How to make a calculator for 32-bit double numbers
- How to perform multiple-byte unpacked BCD arithmetic
- How to use general subroutines for performing packed, multiple-byte BCD addition, subtraction, multiplication, and division

8.1   BINARY ARITHMETIC

Binary Addition

Suppose you want to perform the following hexadecimal addition:

```
5A87A4B9    augend
23581C6F    addend
7DDFC128    sum
```

You will need four bytes, or two words, to store each number as shown in Figure 8.1. Note that the least significant byte must be stored in memory first. The program to add these two numbers is given in Listing 8.1.

181

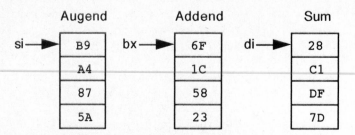

Figure 8.1 Adding two 8-digit hexadecimal numbers

```
        Listing 8.1    multiadd.asm
              title    multi-byte add

stack    segment para stack
         db       64 dup(?)
stack    ends

data     segment          public
augend   dd       5a87a4b9h
addend   dd       23581c6fh
sum      dd       ?
data     ends

code     segment          public
         assume   cs:code,ds:data
main     proc     far
         mov      ax,data                    ;set ds
         mov      ds,ax
         mov      es,ax                      ; and es
         mov      si,offset augend           ;si -> augend
         mov      bx,offset addend           ;bx -> addend
         mov      di,offset sum              ;di -> sum
         mov      cx,2                       ;do 2 words
         cld
         clc                                 ;clear carry
mn1:     lodsw                               ;get next word
         adc      ax,word ptr [bx]           ;add to addend
         stosw                               ;store to sum
         inc      bx
         inc      bx                         ;inc pointers
         loop     mn1
         int      3                          ;tutor break
main     endp

code     ends
         end      main
```

The two numbers to be added are stored in the data segment at offset addresses 0000 – 0003 (the *augend*) and 0004 – 0007 (the *addend*). The answer will be stored in the *sum* at offset addresses 0008 – 000B. The first three instructions in Listing 8.1 store the value of the data segment *data* in the segment registers *DS* and *ES* and the next three instructions load *SI*, *BX*, and *DI* with the three offset addresses associated with the *augend*, *addend*, and *sum*. Note that these offset addresses are the addresses of the least-significant byte in each case. This will allow us to access a word at a time when adding the two numbers.

The statement *mov cx,2* loads *CX* with the number of (16-bit) words needed to store the numbers. The direction flag is set to 0 (*CLD*) and the carry bit is cleared to 0 (*CLC*). The *mn1:* loop in Listing 8.1 adds the two words of the *addend* (pointed to by *BX*) to the two words of the *augend* (pointed to by *SI*) and stores the sum in locations pointed to by *DI*. Note that *LODSW* loads the word pointed to by *SI* (in the *augend*) into *AX* and increments *SI* by 2. Similarly, *STOSW* stores the contents of *AX* in the word pointed to by *DI* (in the *sum*) and increments *DI* by 2. Remember that the *LOOP* statement automatically decrements *CX*.

Load the .EXE file produced by assembling and linking this program (available on the TUTOR disk) into TUTOR and press function key *F1*. Single step through this program and note how the addition is carried out one word at a time. The two numbers to be added will initially be in the first eight bytes in the data segment.

Binary Subtraction

Suppose you want to perform the following hexadecimal subtraction:

```
5A87A4B9    minuend
23581C6F    subtrahend
372F884A    difference
```

The *minuend* and *subtrahend* are the same values as the *augend* and *addend* in Figure 8.1. The program given in Listing 8.1 is easily modified to perform this multiple-byte subtraction by changing the instruction

```
13 07    ADC  AX,WORD PTR [BX]
```

at offset address 0016 in the code segment to

```
1B 07    SBB  AX,WORD PTR [BX]
```

Make this modification by changing the opcode 13H at offset address 0016H to 1BH and single step through the program again. Note that the carry bit is used as a borrow in 8086 subtraction. At the end of the subtraction the carry bit is 0 because the magnitude of the minuend is larger than the magnitude of the subtrahend.

Binary Multiplication

Problem 5.1 in Chapter 5 involved writing a mixed double multiply subroutine called *mdmul* that multiplies an unsigned 32-bit multiplicand by an unsigned 16-bit multiplier and produces a 32-bit product. In general, this could produce a 48-bit product as follows, where A, B, C, D, E and F are 16-bit values.

```
          A    B
     x         C
         BCH  BCL
   ACH  ACL
     D    E    F
```

The values *BCH* and *BCL* are the high word and low word of the partial product $B \times C$ and the values *ACH* and *ACL* are the high word and low word of the partial product $A \times C$. Even though this product can contain 48 bits, we often know that the result will, in fact, fit in 32 bits. That is, the product will be less than 4,294,967,296. If this is the case then

$D = ACH$ will equal zero and the 32-bit product will consist of the high word $PH = E = BCH + ACL$ and the low word $PL = F = BCL$.

The subroutine *mdmul* shown in Figure 8.2 will multiply *dx:ax* by *bx* and leave the 32-bit product in *dx:ax*. This subroutine is included in the file *number.asm* which contains a collection of number conversion subroutines that will be described in this chapter.

```
;       mixed double multiply
;       dx:ax = dx:ax * bx
;             = A B * C = PH PL
;       PL = BCL
;       PH = BCH + ACL
mdmul   proc  near
        push  cx                    ;save cx
        mov   cx,dx                 ;cx = A
        mul   bx                    ;dx=BCH ax=BCL
        push  ax                    ;save BCL
        push  dx                    ;save BCH
        mov   ax,cx                 ;ax = A
        mul   bx                    ;dx=ACH ax=ACL
        pop   dx                    ;dx=BCH
        add   dx,ax                 ;dx=BCH+ACL
        pop   ax                    ;ax=BCL
        pop   cx                    ;restore cx
        ret
mdmul   endp
```

Figure 8.2 Listing of the subroutine *mdmul*

More generally, if you want to multiply a 32-bit multiplicand by a 32-bit multiplier and obtain the full 64-bit product you would use the following scheme where *A*, *B*, *C* and *D* are 16-bit values.

```
                 A   B
          x      C   D
          _____
                DBH DBL
            DAH DAL
            CBH CBL
      CAH CAL
      _____
        E   F   G   H
```

Multiplying *B* by *D* will produce the 32-bit value *DBH:DBL*. Similarly, $A \times D = DAH:DAL$, $C \times B = CBH:CBL$ and $C \times A = CAH:CAL$. The 64-bit product will be *E:F:G:H* where $E = CAH$, $F = DAH + CBH + CAL$, $G = DBH + DAL + CBL$ and $H = DBL$.

The subroutine *mdmul* performs unsigned multiplication. To do signed multiplication you need to check the sign of the product. This can be done by XORing the multiplier (*C*) by the high word (*A*) of the multiplicand. The sign of this result will be the sign of the product; i.e. it will be negative if one of the numbers to be multiplied is negative. You would then take the absolute value of the multiplicand and the multiplier and use *mdmul* to find the unsigned product. Then adjust the sign based on the XOR operation performed earlier.

Binary Division

Recall that the 8086 instruction *DIV* can divide a 32-bit integer in *DX:AX* by a 16-bit integer leaving the 16-bit quotient in *AX* and the 16-bit remainder in *DX*. If the 32-bit dividend is too large or the 16-bit divisor is too small, the quotient may not fit into 16 bits. If this occurs, a divide-by-zero trap (interrupt) will occur. To keep this from happening, what is needed is a divide routine that will return a 32-bit quotient rather than a 16-bit quotient. The subroutine *ddiv* developed in Problem 5.2 in Chapter 5 will divide an unsigned 32-bit dividend by an unsigned 16-bit divisor and produces a 32-bit quotient and a 16-bit remainder. This is done by using multiple-word division. When doing long division you divide the divisor into the "high part" of the dividend to get the "high part" of the quotient. The "high remainder" becomes part of the remaining dividend that is divided by the divisor to yield the "low part" of the quotient and the final remainder.

In particular, if *num* is a 32-bit numerator with high word *numH* and low word *numL*, then to divide *num* by the 16-bit denominator *denom*, first divide *0:numH/denom* to give *quotH* and *remH*. Then divide *remH:numL/denom* to give *quotL* and *rem*. The subroutine *ddiv* shown in Figure 8.3 divides *dx:ax* by *bx* and leaves the quotient in *dx:ax* and the remainder in *bx*.

```
;        divide double word dx:ax by bx
;        quot in dx:ax     rem in bx
ddiv     proc   near
         push   cx                           ;save reg
         push   ax                           ;save numL
         mov    ax,dx                         ;ax=numH
         mov    dx,0
         div    bx                            ;0 numH / bx
         mov    cx,ax                         ;cx=quotH
         pop    ax                            ;get numL
         div    bx                            ;rH numL / bx
         mov    bx,dx                         ;bx=rem
         mov    dx,cx                         ;dx:ax=quot
         pop    cx                            ;restore reg
         ret
ddiv     endp
```

Figure 8.3 Listing of the subroutine *ddiv*

The most common method used to divide a 32-bit dividend by a 32-bit divisor is the so-called *shift and subtract* algorithm. To understand this algorithm, which can be used with any size numbers, consider how the 8086 *div* instruction might be implemented. The 8-bit version of this instruction divides the contents of *ax* by (for example) *bl* and stores the quotient in *al* and the remainder in *ah*. The setup for implementing this division using the *shift and subtract* algorithm is shown in Figure 8.4. The 16-bit dividend is stored in *ax* and the 8-bit divisor is stored in *bx*. The remainder register *dl* is initially cleared to zero. The algorithm for this division is given in Figure 8.5.

The subroutine *bindiv* given in Listing 8.2 will perform the same operation as the 8-bit *div* instruction using the *shift and subtract* algorithm shown in Figure 8.5. Note that we must use the full 16-bit registers *dx* and *bx* for the remainder and quotient because a shift into the remainder from the dividend might move a bit into *dh* before the remainder becomes greater than the divisor.

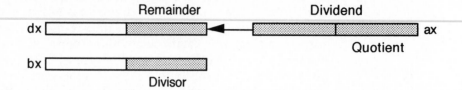

Figure 8.4 Setup for performing division using the shift and subtract algorithm

```
         Listing  8.2    bindiv.asm
              title   Binary divide
       ;              using shift & subtract algorithm
       stack  segment para stack
              db      64 dup(?)
       stack  ends

       data   segment public
       numer  dw      0bc2fh
       denom  db      0eeh
       quot   db      ?
       rem    db      ?
       data   ends

       code   segment public
              assume  cs:code,ds:data
       main   proc    far
              mov     ax,data             ;set ds
              mov     ds,ax
              mov     ax,numer            ;ax = dividend
              mov     bl,denom            ;bl = divisor
              call    bindiv
              mov     quot,al             ;quot in al
              mov     rem,ah              ;rem in ah
              int     3
       main   endp

       ;      binary divide
       bindiv proc    near
              mov     dx,0                ;rem=0
              mov     bh,0
              mov     cx,16               ;shift 16 bits
       bd1:   shl     ax,1                ;shift dividend left
              rcl     dx,1                ; into remainder
              cmp     dx,bx               ;if rem >= divisor
              jb      bd2
              sub     dx,bx               ;rem = rem - divisor
              or      al,1                ;add 1 to quotient
       bd2:   loop    bd1                 ;do 16 times
              cmp     ah,0                ;if overflow
              je      bd3
              mov     ax,0ffffh           ;set quot & rem to ffh
              jmp     bd4
       bd3:   mov     ah,dl               ;rem in ah, quot in al
       bd4:   ret
       bindiv endp

       code   ends
              end     main
```

```
Clear remainder to zero
Do 16 times
          Shift dividend left 1 bit into remainder
          If        remainder >= divisor
          Then      Subtract divisor from remainder
                    Add 1 to quotient (al)
Endo
```

Figure 8.5 Shift and subtract algorithm for division

The program given in Listing 8.2 is in the file *bindiv.asm* on the TUTOR disk. This program will divide the dividend BC2FH by the divisor EEH to produce the quotient CAH and the remainder 63H. This was the example of binary division given in Section 4.5. The .EXE file of this program should be loaded into TUTOR and the instructions single stepped using function key *F1* to see how the quotient CAH and the remainder 63H are formed.

8.2 NUMBER STRING CONVERSIONS

When we enter a number (such as 34671) from the keyboard (e.g. using the subroutine *query* discussed in Chapter 7) the characters in the number are stored in a buffer (*kbuf*) as an ASCII string. If we want to store the *value* of this number in some register or memory location we must convert the ASCII number string to a binary number. After performing some calculation it will be necessary to convert the binary number to an ASCII number string before the result can be displayed on the screen. Subroutines to carry out these conversions will be developed in this section.

ASCII Number String to Binary Conversion

The decimal value 34671 can be represented as

$$34671 = 3 \times 10^4 + 4 \times 10^3 + 6 \times 10^2 + 7 \times 10 + 1$$
$$= 1 + 10(7 + 10(6 + 10(4 + 10(3)))) \qquad (8.1)$$

This form of representing a number can be used to convert an ASCII number string to a binary number. The ASCII code for a given character can be checked to see if it is a valid character in the current base using the algorithm given in Figure 8.6. The current base is stored in the variable *base*.

The subroutine *digit* given in Figure 8.7 implements the algorithm shown in Figure 8.6. Note that if the character is a valid digit the contents of *al* will contain the valid hex value. For example, if *al* contains 35H (the ASCII code for the character 5) when the subroutine *digit* is called, it will return the hex value 05H in *al* and clear the carry flag. If the character is not a valid digit in the current base the carry flag will be set and *al* will contain the original invalid ASCII code.

The algorithm to convert an ASCII number string to a 32-bit double number is given in Figure 8.8. This algorithm follows from the nested representation of the number given in Eq. (8.1). This algorithm is implemented as the subroutine *convert* in Figure 8.9. When calling this subroutine *di* points to a 32-bit binary buffer that will contain the converted number and *si* points to the number string to be converted. When the subroutine is exited the value in *si* will point to the first invalid digit in the number string. This will normally be the character following the number and may be a *blank* or a *carriage return*.

```
DIGIT:   input:    al = ascii code of char
         output:  if carry = 0  al = valid hex value of char
                  if carry = 1  al = invalid char in current base

         al = al – 30h                    ; ascii codes < '0'
         if al < 0
         then fail                        ; are invalid
         if al > 9                        ; ascii codes > '9'
         then    if al < 17               ; and < 'A'
                 then fail                ; are invalid
                 else al = al – 7         ; fill gap between 9 and A
         if al >= base                    ; hex value must be < base
         then fail
         else al = valid hex digit (clear carry)

         fail: set carry  al = original ascii digit
```

Figure 8.6 Algorithm to check for a valid digit in the current base

```
;           convert ascii digit to value in base
;           input:  al=char (ascii code)
;           output: carry=0 al=valid hex value
;                   carry=1 al=invalid ascii code
digit      proc  near
           push  bx                        ;save regs
           push  ax
           mov   bx,base                   ;bx=base
           sub   al,'0'                    ;ascii codes<30
           jb    fail                      ; are invalid
           cmp   al,9                      ;char between
           jbe   dgt1                      ; 9 and A
           cmp   al,17                     ; are invalid
           jb    fail                      ;fill gap
           sub   al,7                      ; between 9&A
dgt1:      cmp   al,bl                     ;digit must be
           jae   fail                      ; < base
           clc                             ;valid digit
           pop   bx                        ;pop old ax
           pop   bx                        ;restore bx
           ret
fail:      pop   ax                        ;invalid digit
           pop   bx
           stc
           ret
digit      endp
```

Figure 8.7 Listing of the subroutine *digit*

```
CONVERT:   input:    si -> number string
                     di -> binary number buffer
           output:   si -> invalid digit


clear binary number buffer (dnum)
loop:   get next digit
        call digit
while: digit is valid
        multiply dnum by base and
        add digit value
        store result in dnum
repeat:
```

Figure 8.8 Algorithm to convert an ASCII string to a 32-bit double number

```
;         ascii number to binary conversion
;         input:  di -> bin buf
;                 si -> number string
;         output: si -> invalid digit
convert proc   near
        push   ax                    ;save regs
        push   bx
        push   cx
        push   dx
        cld
cvt1:   lodsb                        ;get next digit
        call   digit                 ;conv to value
        jc     cvt2                   ;if valid digit
        mov    ah,0                   ;ax=digit value
        push   ax                    ;save value
        mov    bx,base               ;mult dnumH by
        mov    ax,word ptr 2[di]     ; base
        mul    bx
        mov    cx,ax                 ;cx=lo word
        mov    ax,word ptr [di]      ;mult dnumL by
        mul    bx                    ; base
        pop    bx                    ;get value
        add    ax,bx                 ;add to prodL
        adc    dx,cx                 ;+ cx to prodH
        mov    word ptr [di],ax      ;store in dnum
        mov    word ptr 2[di],dx
        cmp    decflg,0              ;if . occurred
        je     cvt1
        inc    dpl                   ; inc dpl
        jmp    cvt1                  ;do until
cvt2:   dec    si                    ; invalid digit
        pop    dx                    ;restore regs
        pop    cx
        pop    bx
        pop    ax
        ret
convert endp
```

Figure 8.9 Listing of the subroutine convert

The subroutine *convert* contains a check of the variable *decflg* (which gets set by the subroutine *number* to be described below if a decimal point is encountered in an ASCII number string) and will increment the variable *dpl* (which will represent the number of digits to the right of the decimal point) if *decflg* is set.

A real number which may contain a leading minus sign and an embedded decimal point can be converted to a binary number using the subroutine *number* shown in Figure 8.10. When calling this subroutine *si* will point to the number string to be converted. The subroutine will return the converted double number in *dx:ax* (ignoring any decimal point) and the number of digits to the right of the decimal (radix) point in *cx*. Register *si* will be pointing to the first invalid digit following the number.

```
;       convert real number
;       input:  si -> number string
;       output: dx:ax = double number
;               cx = # to right of dp
;               si -> invalid digit
number  proc  near
        push  di
        mov   di,offset dnum
        mov   word ptr [di],0        ;clr bin buf
        mov   word ptr 2[di],0
        mov   dpl,0                  ;clr dpl
        mov   decflg,0               ;clr decflg
        mov   negflg,0               ;clear negflg
        cld
        lodsb                        ;get 1st char
        cmp   al,'-'                 ;if - sign
        jne   nb1
        not   negflg                 ;set neg flag
        jmp   nb2
nb1:    dec   si                     ;->1st digit
nb2:    call  convert                ;convert number
        lodsb                        ; get next byte
        cmp   al,'.'                 ; if .
        jne   nb3
        not   decflg                 ; set decflg
        call  convert                ;conv rest
        lodsb                        ;dummy load
nb3:    dec   si                     ;si->invalid dg
        mov   ax,[di]                ;dx:ax=number
        mov   dx,2[di]
        cmp   negflg,0               ;if negative
        je    nb4
        call  dnegate                ;negate it
nb4:    mov   cx,dpl                 ;cx=dpl
        pop   di
        ret
number  endp
```

Figure 8.10 Listing of the subroutine *number*

The subroutine *getnum* shown in Figure 8.11 will wait for a number string to be entered from the keyboard and convert the number string to a double number stored in *dx:ax* with the number of digits to the right of the decimal point stored in *cx*. If an invalid number is entered the carry flag will be set to 1.

All of the subroutines discussed in this section are part of the subroutine file *number.asm*. This file can be assembled and linked with your own programs.

```
;        get number from keyboard
;        number can have a decimal point (dp)
;          and can be prceded by a minus sign
;        input:  none
;        output: dx:ax = double number
;                cx = # to right of dp
;                carry = 1 if invalid number
getnum proc  near
       push  si
       push  di
       call  query              ;get string
       mov   si,offset kbuf      ;si->string
       call  number             ;conv.to.binary
       cmp   byte ptr [si],0     ;if invalid
       je    gtn1               ; digit not 0
       stc                      ; set carry
gtn1:  pop   di
       pop   si
       ret
getnum endp
```

Figure 8.11 Listing of the subroutine *getnum*

Binary Number to ASCII String Conversion

To display the value of a 32-bit double number on the screen it is first necessary to convert this double number to a string of ASCII characters that can the be written to the screen using a string display subroutine such as *mess* described in Chapter 7. The steps used to create this string of ASCII characters are illustrated in Figure 8.12. Note that the algorithm consists of dividing the number by the base and converting the remainder to an ASCII character.

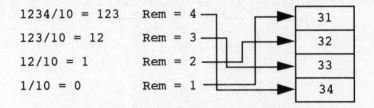

Figure 8.12 Steps for creating an ASCII number string

Figure 8.13 shows the algorithm for the subroutine *sharp* which will convert the next digit of a double number according to the steps in Figure 8.12. The 8086 listing of this subroutine is given in Figure 8.14.

Note that when this subroutine is called *si* is pointing to the double number to be converted and *di* is pointing to the position in the ASCII string where the next ASCII digit will be stored. The subroutine will decrement *di* by one so that it will be left pointing to the position in the ASCII output string where the next digit is to be stored.

The algorithm for the subroutine *sharps* is also given in Figure 8.13 and the 8086 listing of *sharps* is given in Figure 8.15.[1] This subroutine will convert all of the remaining digits in a double number.

```
SHARP: convert the next digit of a double number to ASCII
        input:  si --> double number
                di --> position in ASCII string to store next digit
        output: di is decremented by 1
        The digits are converted least significant digit first
        and stored  in memory starting at the end of the string.

        Divide double number pointed to by si by base
        If rem > 9 then add 7 to rem
        Add '0' to rem to convert to ASCII
        Store ASCII digit at [di]
        Decrement di

SHARPS: convert all (remaining) digits in the double number

        loop:   call SHARP
        repeat until double number quotient = 0
```

Figure 8.13 Algorithms to convert a double number to an ASCII string

---

```
;       convert 1 digit & add to ascii string
;       si->bin buf   di->ascii buf
sharp   proc near
        push    ax                      ;save regs
        push    bx
        push    dx
        mov     dx,2[si]
        mov     ax,[si]
        mov     bx,base
        call    ddiv                    ;dnum/base
        mov     [si],ax                 ; = dnum
        mov     2[si],dx
        cmp     bl,9                    ;if rem>9
        jbe     shp1
        add     bl,7                    ; add 7
shp1:   add     bl,'0'                  ;conv to ascii
        mov     [di],bl                 ;store digit
        dec     di                      ;->next digit
        pop     dx                      ;restore regs
        pop     bx
        pop     ax
        ret
sharp   endp
```

Figure 8.14 Listing of the subroutine *sharp*

---

[1] The names *sharp* and *sharps* for these subroutines are used because the programming language *Forth* uses the two words # ("sharp") and #S ("sharp-S") to perform similar functions.

```
;        convert all digits to ascii
;        si->bin buf    di->ascii buf
sharps proc near
shs1:  call    sharp                       ;do next digit
       cmp     word ptr [si],0             ;repeat until
       jne     shs1                        ; quot=0
       cmp     word ptr 2[si],0
       jne     shs1
       ret
sharps endp
```

Figure 8.15 Listing of the subroutine *sharps*

As an example of using *sharps* the subroutine *dot* shown in Figure 8.16 will convert the 16-bit signed value in *ax* to an ASCII number string and leave *si* pointing to this string. The subroutine *pax* shown in Figure 8.17 will then print the signed value in *ax* on the screen.

```
;        convert ax to signed number string
;        output: si -> number asciiz string
dot      proc    near
         push    ax
         push    bx
         push    di
         mov     bx,ax                     ;bx has sign
         call    absol
         mov     word ptr dnum,ax          ;dnum=ax
         mov     word ptr dnum+2,0
         mov     si,offset dnum
         mov     di,offset bufend-1
         mov     byte ptr 1[di],0          ;bufend=0
         call    sharps                    ;conv to ascii
         or      bx,bx                     ;if negative
         jns     dt1
         mov     byte ptr [di],'-'         ;add - sign
         dec     di
dt1:     inc     di
         mov     si,di                     ;->1st digit
         pop     di
         pop     bx
         pop     ax
         ret
dot      endp
```

Figure 8.16 Listing of the subroutine *dot*

```
;        print signed value in ax
pax      proc    near
         push    ax
         push    si
         call    dot                       ;signed string
         call    mess2                     ;print it
         pop     si
         pop     ax
         ret
pax      endp
```

Figure 8.17 Listing of the subroutine *pax*

The subroutines described above are contained in the file *number.asm*. All of the subroutines in this file are listed in Table 8.1. The complete listing of this file is given in Appendix C. The file is included on the TUTOR disk and can be assembled and linked with your own programs.

Table 8.1	
Number Subroutines	
Subroutine	Function
getnum	get real number from the keyboard
pax	print signed value in *ax* on the screen
upax	print unsigned value in *ax* on the screen
pdxax	print 32-bit signed value in *dx:ax* on the screen
updxax	print 32-bit unsigned value in *dx:ax* on the screen
udot	convert *ax* to an unsigned number string
uddot	convert *dx:ax* to an unsigned number string
dot	convert *ax* to a signed number string
ddot	convert *dx:ax* to a signed number string
home	move cursor to upper-left corner of screen
absol	absolute value of *ax*
dabsol	absolute value of *dx:ax*
convert	convert an ASCII number string to a double number
digit	convert an ASCII digit to its hex value in the current base
sharp	convert one digit and add it to an ASCII number string
sharps	convert all remaining digits and add to an ASCII number string
ddiv	divide double word *dx:ax* by *bx*. quotient in *dx:ax*, rem in *bx*
dnegate	negate the double word in *dx:ax*
mdmul	mixed double multiply: *dx:ax = dx:ax * bx*
number	convert an ASCII real number string to a double binary number
float	convert ASCII floating point number string to a 64-bit FP number
binflt	convert significand and exponent to 64-bit floating point number
tenx	compute 10**ST where ST is the top of the 8087 stack
fpdec	convert a floating point number to F*10**E
pst	print the top of the 8087 stack as a FP number on the screen
fdump	dump the 8087 stack to the buffer *fdumpb*

8.3 AN RPN CALCULATOR

In this section we will learn to parse an input stream of characters entered from the keyboard by making a Reverse Polish Notation (RPN) calculator for adding, subtracting, multiplying and dividing 16-bit integers. An RPN calculator is one that works like a Hewlett-Packard calculator.

The general form of the input will be of the following form:

35   27   +   .

When this line is processed it should do the following:

1. The number 35 is put on a data stack.
2. The number 27 is put on the data stack.
3. The plus operator (+) adds the top two elements on the data stack and leaves the result on the data stack.
4. The dot operator (.) displays the top element on the data stack.

if you enter the above line the value 62 should be displayed.
rations can be strung together as follows:

```
35   27   +   2   *   58   -   23   5   *   /   .
```

s and operators entered must be separated by one or more blank

must establish a data stack that is separate from the normal 8086
k used for holding subroutine return addresses. We will do this
the stack segment 128 bytes long and then initializing *BP* to
e will then use *BP* for the data stack pointer. The data stack will
below the system stack. To push a value on the data stack, we
following macro:

```
bpush macro   val
      xchg    bp,sp
      push    val
      xchg    bp,sp
      endm
```

ample, the statement *bpush ax* will push the contents of *ax* on
k. Similarly, to pop values from the data stack we will use the
acro:

```
bpop  macro   val
      xchg    bp,sp
      pop     val
      xchg    bp,sp
      endm
```

These macros are defined at the beginning of the RPN calculator program
given in Listing 8.3.

```
┌─────────────────────────────────────────────────────────────┐
│  Listing  8.3    rpncalc.asm                                  │
├─────────────────────────────────────────────────────────────┤
│           title   RPN calculator                              │
│                                                               │
│   stack   segment para    stack                               │
│           db      128 dup(?)                                   │
│   stack   ends                                                │
│                                                               │
│   data    segment public                                      │
│   to_in   dw      ?                                           │
│   here    db      16 dup(?)                                    │
│   msg1    db      ' <-- What??',0                              │
│   bptop   dw      ?                                           │
│   data    ends                                                │
│                                                               │
│   bpush   macro   val                                         │
│           xchg    bp,sp            ;push val                   │
│           push    val              ;on bp stack               │
│           xchg    bp,sp                                        │
│           endm                                                │
│   bpop    macro   val                                         │
│           xchg    bp,sp            ;pop val                    │
│           pop     val              ;from bp stack             │
│           xchg    bp,sp                                        │
│           endm                                                │
└─────────────────────────────────────────────────────────────┘
```

Listing 8.3 (continued)

```
            extrn   clrscn:near,dokey:near
            extrn   query:near,number:near
            extrn   pax:near,crlf:near
            extrn   mess2:near,chrout1:near
            extrn   kbuf:byte
            extrn   span:word

    code    segment public
            assume  cs:code,ds:data

    main    proc    far
            mov     ax,data
            mov     ds,ax                   ;set ds
            mov     es,ax                   ;es=ds
            mov     bp,sp
            sub     bp,128                  ;set data stack
            mov     bptop,bp                ;top of data stack
            cld                             ;dir increase
            call    clrscn                  ;clear screen
    mn1:    mov     to_in,0                 ;t0_in=0
            call    crlf                    ;do crlf
            call    query                   ;get input
    mn2:    call    gtword                  ;get next word
            cmp     here,0                  ;if no word
            je      mn1                     ; get new input
            call    doword                  ;eval word
            jmp     mn2
    main    endp


    ;       parse string for blanks between words
    ;       input:  si -> string
    ;               cx -> length of string
    ;       output: si -> 1st char of parsed word
    ;               di -> 1st blank after word
    parse   proc    near
            mov     di,si                   ;di->string
            push    ds
            pop     es                      ;es=ds
            cld                             ;di increases
            mov     al,20h                  ;look for blank
            jcxz    pr2                     ;skip no string
            repe scasb                      ;skip leading
            je      pr1                     ; blanks
            inc     cx                      ;back up to 1st
            dec     di                      ; non blank
    pr1:    mov     si,di                   ;si->next word
            jcxz    pr2                     ;skip no string
            repne scasb                     ;find 1st blank
            jne     pr2                     ; after word
            inc     cx                      ;back up to 1st
            dec     di                      ; blank
    pr2:    ret
    parse   endp


    ;       parse next word & move to here
    gtword  proc    near
            mov     si,offset kbuf
            add     si,to_in                ;si->to_in
            mov     cx,span                 ;cx = # of
            sub     cx,to_in                ;chars left
            jcxz    wd1                     ;if 0 do again
            call    parse                   ;get next word
            mov     cx,di                   ;cx=# char
            sub     cx,si                   ; in word
            mov     ax,di
```

Listing 8.3 (continued)

```
          sub     ax,offset kbuf
          mov     to_in,ax              ;set to_in
wd1:      mov     di,offset here        ;move word
          mov     [di],cl               ; as $string
          inc     di                    ; to here
          jcxz    wd2
          rep movsb
wd2:      mov     al,0                  ; make asciiz
          stosb
          ret
gtword endp

;         process word at here
doword proc     near
          mov     al,here               ;al=count
dwd1:     mov     si,offset here        ;si->$string
          inc     si                    ;si->1st char
          cmp     al,1                  ;if not 1 char
          je      dwd2
          call    cknum                 ;check for number
          ret
dwd2:     mov     di,offset jmptbo      ;di->jump table
          mov     dx,offset cknum       ;default check number
          mov     al,[si]               ;al = char (operator)
          call    dokey                 ;use dokey
          ret
doword endp

jmptbo db      '+'                      ;add
       dw      plus
       db      '-'                      ;subtract
       dw      minus
       db      '*'                      ;multiply
       dw      times
       db      '/'                      ;divide
       dw      slash
       db      '.'                      ;print value
       dw      dott
       db      0

;      add top 2 elements on data stack
plus   proc    near
       bpop    ax
       bpop    bx
       add     ax,bx
       bpush   ax
       ret
plus   endp

;      subtract top 2 elements on data stack
minus  proc    near
       bpop    bx
       bpop    ax
       sub     ax,bx
       bpush   ax
       ret
minus  endp

;      multiply top 2 elements on data stack
times  proc    near
       bpop    ax
       bpop    bx
       mul     bx                       ;signed prod
       bpush   ax                       ;is in ax!
       ret
```

Listing 8.3   (continued)

```
times   endp

;       divide 2nd element on data stack
;       by the top element on data stack
slash   proc    near
        bpop    bx                      ;bx=denom
        bpop    ax
        or      ax,ax                   ;if negative
        jns     sl1
        mov     dx,0ffffh               ;sign extend
        jmp     sl2                     ;else
sl1:    mov     dx,0                    ;0:ax=numer
sl2:    idiv    bx                      ;signed divide
        bpush   ax
        ret
slash   endp

;       display top element on stack
dott    proc    near
        mov     al,20h
        call    chrout1                 ;print blank
        bpop    ax                      ;get value
        call    pax                     ;print it
        ret
dott    endp

;       check word for number
cknum   proc    near
        push    si
        push    di
        mov     si,offset here          ;si->$string
        mov     al,[si]
        mov     ah,0                    ;ax = count
        inc     si
        mov     bx,si
        add     bx,ax                   ;bx->00(end)
        call    number                  ; get number
        cmp     si,bx                   ;bx->00
        jne     ck1                     ;if valid
        bpush   ax                      ; push ax
        jmp     ck2                     ;else
ck1:    call    errmsg                  ;error message
ck2:    pop     di
        pop     si
        ret
cknum   endp

;       print error message
errmsg  proc    near
        call    crlf
        mov     si,offset here
        inc     si
        call    mess2                   ;print word
        mov     si,offset msg1
        call    mess2                   ; <-- What??
        mov     bp,bptop                ;reset data sp
        ret
errmsg  endp

code    ends
        end     main
```

The variable *to_in* is a pointer that will point to the next character to be parsed in the input stream. We initialize this pointer to zero at the label *mn1:* in the main program in Listing 8.2. We use the subroutine *query* in *screen.asm* to input the line of characters into *kbuf*. Recall that pressing the *ESC* key in *query* returns to DOS. Pressing the *Enter* key will exit *query* and leave the number of characters entered in *kbuf* in the variable *span*.

Each group of characters separated by blanks in the input buffer *kbuf* is called a *word*. Thus, in Figure 8.18 the numbers 345 and 12 as well as the operators *plus* (+) and *dot* (.) are all words. The subroutine *gtword* in Listing 8.3 will get the next word in *kbuf* and move it to a 16-byte buffer in the data segment called *here*. It will store the word at *here* as a *counted* ASCIIZ string. This means that the first character at here will be the number of characters in the string and the string will be terminated with a nul (00) byte. Thus, for example, the input number 345 would be stored at *here* as the five bytes: 03H, 33H, 34H, 35H, 00H.

The subroutine *gtword* calls the subroutine *parse* to parse each word. The subroutine *parse* will parse a string (pointed to by *si*) of length *cx* to the blank following the next word in the string. Leading blanks are ignored. Figure 8.18 shows the values of *si*, *cx* and *di* before and after parsing the first word, 345. After parsing a word *cx* is the length of the remaining string and *di* points to the first character following the parsed word. If *si* is set to *di* then *parse* can be called again to parse the next word. If *cx* = 0 then the last word has been parsed and a zero length string will be moved to *here*. Thus, if the count byte at *here* is zero the entire input string has been parsed.

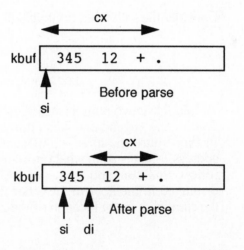

Figure 8.18 Pointers to *kbuf* before and after calling the subroutine *parse*

After each word is moved to *here* by the subroutine *gtword* it is processed by the subroutine *doword*. If the parsed word contains a single character it could be one of the operators (+, −, *, / or .) or a single digit number. These five single character operators are processed using a jump table, *jmptbo*, and the subroutine *dokey* described in Chapter 7. Although we processed key ASCII codes in Chapter 7 the subroutine *dokey* only needs the value to be processed to be in *al*. The default subroutine to be called if the character is not in the jump table is the subroutine *chnum* which will check to see if the character at *here* is a valid number in the current base by calling the subroutine *number*. If it is a valid number its value is pushed on the data stack; otherwise, an error message is displayed. This same *chnum* subroutine is called by *doword* if the parsed word contains more than one character.

The subroutines *plus*, *minus*, *times*, *slash* and *dott* are used to process the five operators (+, –, *, / and .). The first four operate on the top two values on the data stack and leave the result on the data stack. The subroutine *dott* will print the value on top of the data stack on the screen by calling the subroutine *pax* given in Figure 8.17.

The program given in Listing 8.3 is stored on the TUTOR disk as the file *rpncalc.asm.* This program can be modified to handle double numbers using the technique described in Problem 8.3 at the end of this chapter.

8.4 MULTIPLE-BYTE UNPACKED BCD ARITHMETIC

In Chapter 5 you saw how to add, subtract, multiply, and divide unpacked BCD numbers by using the ASCII adjust instructions *AAA*, *AAS*, *AAM*, and *AAD*. In this section we will generalize these results to add and subtract two unpacked BCD numbers of arbitrary size. The generalization of multiplication to the multiple-byte case is fairly straightforward but the generalization of division is not so straightforward, and we will defer the discussion of multiple-byte BCD multiplication and division until we treat the packed BCD case.

Decimal Addition

Consider the following decimal addition:

```
 71428    augend
+37845    addend
109273    sum
```

To add these two numbers using unpacked BCD addition we will store each digit of the augend and addend in a separate byte as shown in Figure 8.19. In this figure the most significant digit is stored in the lowest memory address. This is somewhat opposite to the standard Intel format but we will follow this convention in our BCD examples so that the digits will be displayed in memory in the order they occur in the number. We will store the sum back in the location of the augend.

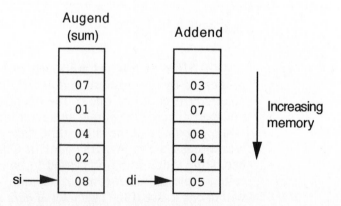

Figure 8.19 Performing the unpacked BCD addition 71428 + 37845

The program to add these two numbers is shown in Listing 8.4. The two initial values are stored in the variables *augend* and *addend* in the data segment. The number of characters in each digit (5) is stored in the variable *nochar*. The main program sets *si* and *di* to the least-significant digit of the augend and addend respectively. The ASCII adjust instruction will add a decimal carry to *AH*. For this reason *AH* must be set to zero each time around the loop. A final carry will then be stored in the sum by the instruction *mov [si],ah*. This program is on the TUTOR disk as the file *bcdupack.exe*. Load this program into TUTOR and press function key *F10*. Single step through this program. Study the algorithm in Listing 8.4 and note carefully how each partial sum is formed and how the final value in *AH* becomes the most significant byte in the sum.

```
      Listing  8.4    bcdupack.asm
            title    add two unpacked bcd numbers
      stack   segment para stack
              db       64 dup(?)
      stack   ends

      data    segment public
      augend  db       00h,07h,01h,04h,02h,08h
      addend  db       00h,03h,07h,08h,04h,05h
      nochar  dw       5
      data    ends

      code    segment public
              assume cs:code,ds:data
      main    proc     far
              mov      ax,data            ;set ds
              mov      ds,ax
              mov      cx,nochar          ;no. digits = 5
              mov      si,offset augend   ;si ->
              add      si,cx              ; LSB of augend
              mov      di,offset addend   ;di ->
              add      di,cx              ; LSB of addend
              std                         ;decrement si
              clc                         ;clear carry
      mn1:    mov      ah,0               ;ah = 0
              lodsb                       ;get next byte
              adc      al,[di]            ;add to addend
              aaa                         ;ASCII adjust
              mov      1[si],al           ;store sum
              dec      di                 ;decrement di
              loop     mn1
              mov      [si],ah            ;ah = MSB of sum
              int      3
      main    endp
      code    ends
              end      main
```

Decimal Subtraction

Suppose that the two unpacked BCD numbers shown in Figure 8.19 are to be subtracted to produce the difference

```
 71428   minuend
-37845   subtrahend
 33583
```

This subtraction can be performed by changing the two instructions

```
adc   al,[di]              ;add to addend
aaa                        ;ASCII adjust
```

in Listing 8.4 to

```
1A 05   sbb   al,[di]      ;subtract subtrahend
3F      aas                ;ASCII adjust
```

Load the program *bcdupack.exe* into TUTOR and press function key *F10*. Then go to offset address 0018H and change the next three bytes to 1A 05 3F. Press the *Home* key and single step through the program and observe the multiple-byte BCD subtraction produce the difference 33583.

8.5 MULTIPLE-BYTE PACKED BCD ARITHMETIC

Packed binary coded decimal (BCD) addition and subtraction were discussed in Chapter 4. In this section we will introduce a collection of subroutines that will perform addition, subtraction, multiplication, and division of packed BCD numbers of arbitrary size. The subroutines use parameters that are passed on the stack (see Section 6.7).

The subroutines are stored on the TUTOR disk under the file name *bcdmath.asm*. A listing of these subroutines is given in Listing 8.5. You can assemble this file and link it to your own programs using the techniques described in Chapter 5. We will illustrate the use of these routines by means of specific examples.

Multiple-byte BCD Addition

Suppose you want to perform the following BCD addition:

```
123456   augend
789123   addend
912579   sum
```

You can store the *augend* and *addend* anywhere in memory, two BCD digits per byte with the most-significant digits stored first, as shown in Figure 8.20. These can be thought of as two 3-byte BCD registers, *REG1* and *REG2*. The length of these registers is *RLEN* = 3. The two pointers *PTRR1* and *PTRR2* point to the least significant byte of *REG1* and *REG2* respectively.

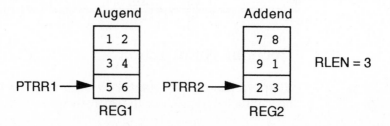

Figure 8.20 BCD numbers to be added are stored in multiple-byte BCD registers

Listing 8.5   *bcdmath.asm*

```
            title   bcd math routines

            public  bcdadd,clrmem,bcdsub,bcdmul,bcddiv
code        segment public
            assume  cs:code
add:        jmp     bcdadd
sub:        jmp     bcdsub
mul:        jmp     bcdmul
div:        jmp     bcddiv

;           bcd addition
;           reg1=reg1+reg2
bcdadd      proc near
            push    ax
            push    si                      ;save regs
            push    di
            push    cx
            push    bp
            mov     bp,sp
            add     bp,12                   ;point to parameters
            mov     cx,[bp]                 ;cx=rlen
            mov     di,2[bp]                ;di=ptrr2
            mov     si,4[bp]                ;si=ptrr1
            std
            clc                             ;clear carry
add1:       lodsb
            adc     al,[di]
            daa                             ;dec adjust
            mov     1[si],al                ;[si]=[si]+[di]
            dec     di
            loop    add1                    ;repeat rlen times
            pop     bp
            pop     cx
            pop     di
            pop     si
            pop     ax
            ret 6
bcdadd      endp

;           bcd subtraction
;           reg1=reg1-reg2
bcdsub      proc near
            push    ax
            push    si                      ;save regs
            push    di
            push    cx
            push    bp
            mov     bp,sp
            add     bp,12                   ;point to parameters
            mov     cx,[bp]                 ;cx=rlen
            mov     di,2[bp]                ;di=ptrr2
            mov     si,4[bp]                ;si=ptrr1
            std
            clc                             ;clear carry
sub1:       lodsb
            sbb     al,[di]
            das                             ;dec adjust
            mov     1[si],al                ;[si]=[si]-[di]
            dec     di
            loop    sub1                    ;repeat rlen times
            pop     bp
            pop     cx                      ;restore regs
            pop     di
            pop     si
```

Listing 8.5 (continued)

```
        pop     ax
        ret 6
bcdsub  endp

;       clear cx bytes starting at di
clrmem  proc near
        push    cx
        push    es
        push    ds
        pop     es                      ;es=ds
        cld
        mov     al,0
        rep stosb
        pop     es
        pop     cx
        ret
clrmem  endp

;       logic shift right reg1
lsrreg  proc near
        push    ax                      ;save regs
        push    si
        push    cx
        push    bp
        mov     bp,sp
        add     bp,10                   ;point to parameters
        mov     si,2[bp]                ;si=ptrr
        mov     cx,[bp]                 ;cx=rlen
        inc     si
        sub     si,cx                   ;si->msb
        clc                             ;clear carry
lsr1:   rcr     byte ptr [si],1         ;rotate [si]
        inc     si
        loop    lsr1                    ;repeat rlen times
        pop     bp                      ;restore regs
        pop     cx
        pop     si
        pop     ax
        ret 4
lsrreg  endp
        page


;       logic shift left reg1
lslreg  proc near
        push    ax                      ;save regs
        push    si
        push    cx
        push    bp
        mov     bp,sp
        add     bp,10                   ;point to parameters
        mov     si,2[bp]                ;si=ptrr
        mov     cx,[bp]                 ;cx=rlen
        clc                             ;clear carry
lsl1:   rcl     byte ptr [si],1         ;rotate l [si]
        dec     si
        loop    lsl1                    ;repeat rlen times
        pop     bp                      ;restore regs
        pop     cx
        pop     si
        pop     ax
        ret 4
lslreg  endp

;       bcd multiplication
bcdmul  proc near
```

Listing 8.5   (continued)

```
                push    ax                      ;save regs
                push    bx
                push    cx
                push    dx
                push    di
                push    bp
                mov     bp,sp
                add     bp,14                   ;point to parameters
                mov     ax,[bp]
                shl     ax,1
                mov     cx,ax
                mov     di,6[bp]                ;di=prod
                sub     di,cx
                inc     cx
                mov     dx,cx                   ;dx=2*rlen+1
                call    clrmem                  ;clr prod
                dec     cx                      ;cx=2*rlen
mul1:           mov     di,2[bp]
                mov     al,[di]
                and     al,0fh
                je      mul3
                mov     bl,al                   ;bl=bcnt
mul2:           mov     ax,6[bp]
                sub     ax,[bp]
                push    ax                      ;ptrr1=prod-rlen
                push    4[bp]                   ;ptrr2=op1
                mov     ax,[bp]
                inc     ax
                push    ax                      ;rlen+1
                call    bcdadd                  ;bcd add op1 & prod
                dec     bl                      ;repeat bcnt times
                jne     mul2
mul3:           mov     bh,4
mul4:           push    6[bp]                   ;rotate
                push    dx                      ; prod
                call    lsrreg
                push    2[bp]                   ; & op2
                push    [bp]
                call    lsrreg                  ; right
                dec     bh                      ; 4 bits
                jne     mul4
                loop    mul1                    ;repeat 2*rlen times
                pop     bp                      ;restore regs
                pop     di
                pop     dx
                pop     cx
                pop     bx
                pop     ax
                ret 8
bcdmul          endp

;               bcd division
bcddiv          proc near
                sub     sp,2                    ;2 temp locations
                push    ax                      ;save regs
                push    bx
                push    cx
                push    di
                push    bp
                mov     bp,sp
                add     bp,10                   ;point to equot
                mov     ax,4[bp]                ;rlen
                shl     ax,1
                mov     cx,ax                   ;cx=2*rlen
                call    normal                  ;normalize
```

206   CHAPTER 8

Listing 8.5   (continued)

```
              mov     di,10[bp]                ;quot
              mov     bx,di
              sub     di,cx
              inc     di                       ;di=quot-2*rlen+1
              call    clrmem                   ;clear quot
              mov     di,bx
              dec     di                       ;di=quot-1
div1:         push    8[bp]                    ;push num
              push    6[bp]                    ;push denom
              mov     bx,4[bp]
              inc     bx
              push    bx                       ;push rlen+1
              call    bcdsub                   ;sub denom from num
              jb      div2                     ; until a borrow (C=1)
              inc     byte ptr [di]            ;else +quot
              jmp     div1                     ; & repeat
div2:         push    8[bp]                    ;add denom
              push    6[bp]                    ; to num
              push    bx                       ;rlen+1
              call    bcdadd
              dec     cx                       ;do 2*rlen times
              je      div4
              mov     ah,4                     ;rotate
div3:         push    di                       ; quot
              push    4[bp]
              call    lslreg
              push    8[bp]                    ; & num
              push    bx
              call    lslreg                   ; left
              dec     ah                       ; 4 bits
              jne     div3
              jmp     div1                     ;repeat all
div4:         mov     ax,[bp]                  ;adj dec. pt.
              sub     ax,1[bp]
              shl     bx,1                     ;2*(rlen+1)
              sub     ax,bx                    ;equot=enum-eden
              add     ax,3                     ;  -2*rlen+5
              mov     1[di],al                 ;exp in quot
              pop     bp                       ;restore regs
              pop     di
              pop     cx
              pop     bx
              pop     ax
              add     sp,2                     ;fix stack
              ret     8
bcddiv        endp

;             normalize num and denom
normal        proc near
              push    ax                       ;save regs
              push    cx
              push    si
              mov     byte ptr [bp],0          ;enum=0
              mov     byte ptr 1[bp],0         ;eden=0
              push    cx                       ;save 2*rlen
nm1:          mov     si,6[bp]                 ;si=denom
              sub     si,4[bp]
              mov     al,1[si]                 ;al=msb of denom
              and     al,0f0h
              jne     nm4                      ;if =0 &
              dec     cx                       ; 2*rlen<>0
              jne     nm2                      ; if denom=0
              mov     byte ptr 1[si],10h       ;set to 1
              jmp     nm4
nm2:          dec     byte ptr 1[bp]           ;then dec eden
```

Listing 8.5   (continued)

```
              mov      ah,4                      ; rotate
      nm3:    push     6[bp]                     ;  denom
              push     4[bp]
              call     lslreg                    ;  left
              dec      ah                        ;   4 bits
              jne      nm3
              jmp      nm1                       ;repeat
      nm4:    pop      cx                        ;cx=2*rlen
      nm5:    mov      si,8[bp]                  ;si=num
              sub      si,4[bp]
              mov      al,1[si]                  ;al=msb of num
              and      al,0f0h
              jne      nm7                       ;if =0 &
              dec      cx                        ; 2*rlen<>0
              je       nm7
              dec      byte ptr [bp]             ;dec enum
              mov      ah,4                      ; rotate
      nm6:    push     8[bp]                     ;  num
              push     4[bp]
              call     lslreg                    ;  left
              dec      ah                        ;   4 bits
              jne      nm6
              jmp      nm5                       ;repeat
      nm7:    pop      si                        ;restore regs
              pop      cx
              pop      ax
              ret
      normal  endp
      code    ends
              end
```

The subroutine *bcdadd* in Listing 8.5 will add the BCD number in *REG1* to that in *REG2* and store the result in *REG1*. This routine can be entered at offset address 0000 (add:) at the beginning of Listing 8.5. Before calling this routine *PTRR1*, *PTTR2*, and *RLEN* must be pushed on the stack in the order shown in Figure 8.21. After returning from the subroutine *bcdadd* the stack has already been fixed up with the instruction *RET 6* at the end of the subroutine .

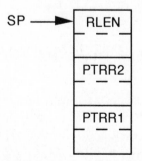

Figure 8.21 Set up of stack before calling the subroutine BCDADD

The subroutine *bcdadd* in Listing 8.5 first saves the registers *AX*, *SI*, *DI*, *CX*, and *BP* on the stack. The stack will then look like that shown in Figure 8.22. Note that the five statements

```
mov   bp,sp
add   bp,12
mov   cx,0[bp]
mov   di,2[bp]
mov   si,4[bp]
```

can then be used to load *CX* with *RLEN*, *DI* with *PTRR2*, and *SI* with *PTRR1*. These statements make use of the base pointer, *BP*, which will access the stack segment. The remainder of the *bcdadd* subroutine is straightforward.

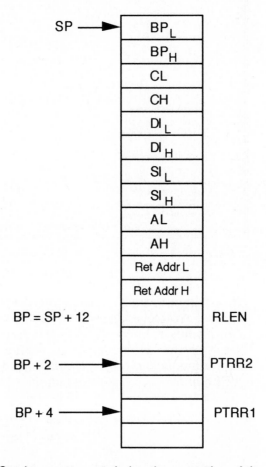

Figure 8.22 Stack arrangement during the execution of the *bcdadd* subroutine

As an example of using this subroutine, the program shown in Listing 8.6 will add the two numbers given in Figure 8.20. This program is on the TUTOR disk as the file *bcdadd.exe*. Load this program into TUTOR and press function key *F10*. Single step through this program using function key *F2* which will execute through the subroutine *bcdadd*. The sum (912579) should be stored at offset 0000 in the data segment. Note that when using *bcdadd* the carry flag will be set to 1 if the sum exceeds the number of digits that will fit into *REG1*.

```
┌─────────────────────────────────────────────────────────────────────┐
│   Listing 8.6    bcdadd.asm                                           │
├─────────────────────────────────────────────────────────────────────┤
│           title    add two packed BCD numbers                         │
│   stack   segment  para stack                                         │
│           db       64 dup(?)                                          │
│   stack   ends                                                        │
│   data    segment  public                                             │
│   augend  db       12h,34h,56h                                        │
│   addend  db       78h,91h,23h                                        │
│   rlen    dw       3                                                  │
│   data    ends                                                        │
│           extrn    bcdadd:near                                        │
│   code    segment  public                                             │
│           assume   cs:code,ds:data                                    │
│   main    proc     far                                                │
│           mov      ax,data                      ;set ds               │
│           mov      ds,ax                                              │
│           mov      ax,offset augend                                   │
│           add      ax,2                                               │
│           push     ax                           ;push PTRR1           │
│           mov      ax,offset addend                                   │
│           add      ax,2                                               │
│           push     ax                           ;push PTRR2           │
│           mov      ax,rlen                                            │
│           push     ax                           ;push RLEN            │
│           call     bcdadd                       ;BCD add              │
│           int      3                                                  │
│   main    endp                                                        │
│           code     ends                                               │
│           end      main                                               │
└─────────────────────────────────────────────────────────────────────┘
```

Multiple-byte BCD Subtraction

The BCD subtraction routine, *bcdsub*, in Listing 8.5 uses the same stack set up procedure as used for *bcdadd* (see Figure 8.21). The subroutine *bcdsub* subtracts the contents of *REG2* (pointed to by *PTR2*) from the contents of *REG1* (pointed to by *PTR1*) and stores the result in *REG1*. As an example, the program shown in Listing 8.7 will perform the subtraction

$$
\begin{array}{ll}
789123 & \text{minuend} \\
\underline{-123456} & \text{subtrahend} \\
665667 & \text{difference}
\end{array}
$$

This program is on the TUTOR disk as the file *bcdsub.exe*. Load this program into TUTOR and press function key *F10*. Single step through this program using function key *F2*, which will execute through the subroutine *bcdsub*. The difference (665667) should be stored at offset 0000 in the data segment.

The subroutine *bcdsub* adjusts the carry flag so that it will be set if the subrahend is larger than the minuend. That is, the carry flag will behave like a borrow flag.

Multiple-byte BCD Multiplication

The BCD multiplication routine, *bcdmul*, in Listing 8.5 multiplies two BCD numbers (*operand1* and *operand2*) and stores the product in a different memory area. The situation is shown in Figure 8.23. The number of bytes in each operand must be the same, *RLEN* + 1, where 2 x *RLEN* is the maximum number of BCD digits to be multiplied. Each operand must contain the same number of bytes and in each operand the memory location with an address one less than the most significant byte (MSB) must be set to 00. This is the top byte in each operand in Figure 8.23.

```
   Listing  8.7    bcdsub.asm
                title  subtract two packed BCD numbers

   stack     segment para stack
             db       64 dup(?)
   stack     ends

   data      segment public
   minuend   db       78h,91h,23h
   subtra    db       12h,34h,56h
   rlen      dw       3
   data      ends

             extrn  bcdsub:near

   code      segment public
             assume cs:code,ds:data
   main      proc   far
             mov    ax,data                      ;set ds
             mov    ds,ax
             mov    ax,offset minuend
             add    ax,2
             push   ax                           ;push PTRR1
             mov    ax,offset subtra
             add    ax,2
             push   ax                           ;push PTRR2
             mov    ax,rlen
             push   ax                           ;push RLEN
             call   bcdsub                       ;BCD subtract
             int    3
   main      endp

   code      ends
             end    main
```

The pointers *OP1* and *OP2* point to the least significant byte of *operand1* and *operand2* respectively. The product will be stored in a group of memory locations pointed to by the pointer *PROD* as shown in Figure 8.23. You should reserve 2 x *RLEN* + 1 memory locations for this product area. The pointers *PROD*, *OP1*, and *OP2* and the value of *RLEN* are pushed on the stack before calling *bcdmul* as shown in Figure 8.24. The subroutine *bcdmul* automatically fixes the stack by executing the return instruction *RET 8* at the end of the subroutine.

As an example of using this BCD multiplication routine the program shown in Listing 8.8 will multiply

$$35 \times 277 = 9695$$

This program is on the TUTOR disk as the file *bcdmul.exe*. Load this program into TUTOR and press function key *F10*. Single step through this program using function key *F2* which will execute through the subroutine *bcdmul*. The product (9695) should be stored at offset 000D in the data segment.

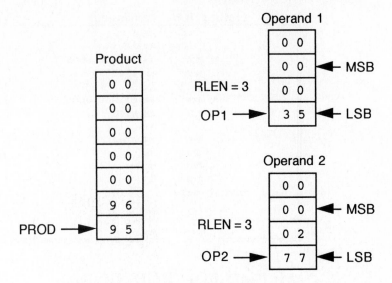

Figure 8.23 *Operand1* x *Operand2* = *Product*

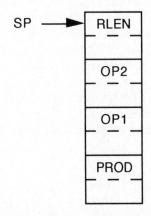

Figure 8.24 Setup of stack before calling the subroutine *bcdmul*

```
Listing  8.8    bcdmul.asm
            title   multiply two packed BCD numbers

stack   segment para stack
        db      64 dup(?)
stack   ends

data    segment public
oper1   db      00h,00h,00h,35h
oper2   db      00h,00h,02h,77h
prod    dw      7 dup(?)
rlen    dw      3
data    ends

        extrn   bcdmul:near

code    segment public
        assume  cs:code,ds:data
main    proc    far
        mov     ax,data                 ;set ds
        mov     ds,ax
        mov     ax,offset prod
```

Listing 8.8   (continued)

```
        add    ax,6
        push   ax                      ;push PROD
        mov    ax,offset oper1
        add    ax,rlen
        push   ax                      ;push OP1
        mov    ax,offset oper2
        add    ax,rlen
        push   ax                      ;push OP2
        mov    ax,rlen
        push   ax                      ;push RLEN
        call   bcdmul                  ;BCD multiply
        int    3
main    endp

code    ends
        end    main
```

Multiple-byte BCD Division

The BCD division routine, *bcddiv*, in Listing 8.5 divides a BCD numerator by a BCD denominator to produce a BCD quotient. The pointers *NUM*, *DENOM*, and *QUOT* point to the numerator, denominator, and quotient as shown in Figure 8.25. The value of *RLEN* is the number of bytes needed to store the BCD numerator and denominator. An extra byte containing 00 must also be reserved below the MSB of the numerator and denominator as was done with the multiplication routine.

The pointers *QUOT*, *NUM*, and *DENOM*, and the value of *RLEN* are pushed on the stack befor calling *bcddiv* as shown in Figure 8.26. The subroutine *bcddiv* fixes the stack by executing the return instruction *RET 8*.

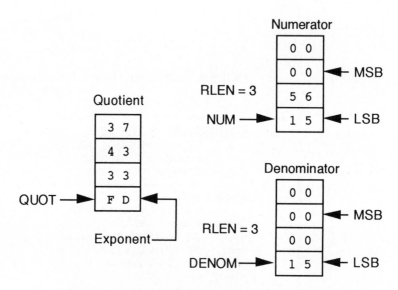

Figure 8.25 *Numerator / Denominator = Quotient*

As an example of using this BCD division routine the program shown in Listing 8.9 will divide

$$5615/15 = 374.333$$

This program is on the TUTOR disk as the file *bcddiv.exe*. Load this program into TUTOR and press function key *F10*. Single step through this program using function key *F2* which will execute through the subroutine *bcddiv*. The quotient (374.333) should be stored at offset 0008 in the data segment. The division routine automatically adjusts the decimal point and displays the exponent in the least-significant byte of the quotient. Thus, the exponent FD (-3) is stored at offset address 000B in the data segment. The quotient is therefore 374333E-3. When entering the numerator and denominator you must take care to locate the decimal point of each in the same relative position.

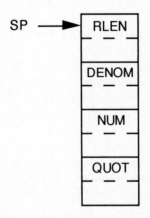

Figure 8.26 Setup of stack before calling the subroutine *bcddiv*

```
     Listing  8.9    bcddiv.asm
          title   divide two packed BCD numbers
stack   segment para stack
          db      64 dup(?)
stack   ends

data    segment public
numer   db      00h,00h,56h,15h
denom   db      00h,00h,00h,15h
quot    dw      4 dup(?)
rlen    dw      3
data    ends


          extrn   bcddiv:near
code    segment public
          assume  cs:code,ds:data
main    proc    far
          mov     ax,data                    ;set ds
          mov     ds,ax
          mov     ax,offset quot
          add     ax,3
          push    ax                         ;push QUOT
          mov     ax,offset numer
          add     ax,rlen
          push    ax                         ;push NUM
          mov     ax,offset denom
          add     ax,rlen
          push    ax                         ;push DENOM
          mov     ax,rlen
          push    ax                         ;push RLEN
          call    bcddiv                     ;BCD divide
          int     3
main    endp
          code    ends
          end     main
```

PROGRAMMING PROBLEMS

Problem 8.1 – 32-Bit Multiplication

Write a subroutine called *mul32* that will multiply the 32-bit positive integer in *dx:ax* by the 32-bit positive integer in *cx:bx*. Return the high 32 bits of the 64-bit product in *cx:bx* and the low 32 bits of the 64-bit product in *dx:ax*. Write a main program to test the subroutine. How would you modify the subroutine to perform a 32-bit signed multiplication?

Problem 8.2 – 32-Bit Division

Write a subroutine called *div32* that will use the *shift and subtract* algorithm to divide the 32-bit positive integer in *dx:ax* by the 32-bit positive integer in *cx:bx*. Return the 32-bit quotient in *dx:ax* and and the 32-bit remainder in *cx:bx*. Write a main program to test the subroutine. How would you modify the subroutine to perform a 32-bit signed division?

Problem 8.3 – Design of a Word-based Jump Table

In the RPN calculator program given in Listing 8.3 we used a jump table and the subroutine *dokey* to execute a particular subroutine when a certain operator (+, -, *, / or .) occurred in the input stream. This scheme only worked because each operator contained a single character. Suppose you used more general operators, called *words*, made up of one or more characters (e.g. *SWAP*, *D+*, *MU/MOD*). In this problem you will make a generalized jump table in which the entries can be words, rather than single characters. You will modify the RPN calculator program given in Listing 8.3 to handle double word arithmetic.

a. Consider the following macro:

```
       _link = 0
$head macro lex,name,sub
       dw    sub
       dw    _link
       _link = $
       db    lex,name
       endm
```

The two entries

```
$head 1,'+',plus
$head 2,'D+',dplus
```

will then produce the following 2-entry word-based jump table:

```
0066  00E9        +    dw    plus
0068  0000        +    dw    _link
006A  01 2B       +    db    1,'+'

006C  010C        +    dw    dplus
006E  006A        +    dw    _link
0070  02 44 2B    +    db    2,'D+'
```

The first line of the macro, *dw sub*, will store the address of the subroutine to be called if the word is "executed." For example, the subroutine *plus* will be at offset address 00E9H and the subroutine *dplus* will be at offset address 010CH. The second line of the macro, *dw _link*, will store the address of the name of the previous word defined. The first word defined has a *_link* address of zero. The third line of the macro, *_link = $*, sets the value of *_link* to the current offset address in the assembly. This will be the address of the name of the word, and will be used as the link address for the next word defined. The last line in the macro, *db lex,name*, stores the number of characters in the name as well as the ASCII codes for each character in the name. Note that we have created a linked list of word names together with their subroutine addresses. The offset addresses shown in the above example are arbitrary and the actual offset addresses will depend on where in the assembly language listing the *$head* macros are called.

   b. Make a word-based jump table using *$head* that will contain all of the operators in Listing 8.3 plus the following double-word operators:

D+ (d1 d2 -- dsum)	Add the top 2 double words (32-bits) on the data stack and leave the double sum.
D- (d1 d2 -- dsum)	Subtract the top double word (d2) on the the stack from the 2nd double word (d1) and leave the double difference.
MU/MOD (ud un -- rem dquot)	Divide the unsigned double number (ud) by the unsigned single number (un) and leave the single remainder (rem) and the double quotient (dquot). Use *ddiv*.
UM* (un1 un2 -- ud)	Multiply the unsigned single number (un1) by the unsigned single number (un2) and leave the unsigned double number (ud) on the data stack. Use *MUL*.
D. (d --)	Print the signed double number on top of the data stack. Use *pdxax*.
UD. (d --)	Print the unsigned double number on top of the data stack. Use *updxax*.

   c. Modify the subroutine *doword* in Listing 8.3 so that it will search for a word in the linked-list "dictionary" and execute the appropriate subroutine. If the word is not in the dictionary, it should be checked to see if it is a valid number. If the number contains a decimal point, it should be stored on the stack as a double number. Otherwise, it should be stored on the stack as a single number.

EXERCISES

Exercise 8.1
Modify the program in Listing 8.1 to add the two hex numbers 3A52714A39H and 81F3D1B37AH. Verify your result.

Exercise 8.2
Write a program to subtract the hex number 3A52714A39H from the hex number 81F3D1B37AH. Verify your result.

Exercise 8.3
Use the program in Listing 8.4 to perform the following decimal addition: 3174279 + 8315942.

Exercise 8.4
Use the program in Listing 8.6 to perform the decimal addition given in Exercise 8.3.

Exercise 8.5
Write a program to add the two BCD numbers 31527549 and 47820135.

Exercise 8.6
Write a program that will subtract 31528746 from 82105379.

Exercise 8.7
Use the program in Listing 8.8 to perform the following multiplications:

```
a) 2658 x 17953 = 47719074
b) 735 x 68520 = 50362200
c) 95 x 187632 = 17825040
d) 25.4 x 499 = 12674.6
e) 16.33 x 5.123 = 83.65859
```

Exercise 8.8
Use the program in Listing 8.9 to perform the following divisions:

```
a) 2659/43 = 61.837
b) 65.2/45 = 1.448
c) 5.45/0.7 = 7.785
d) 73502/12.5 = 5880.16
```

CHAPTER 9

Floating Point Arithmetic

In Chapter 8 we learned how the 8086 can be used to perform multiple-byte addition, subtraction, multiplication and division. The routines covered in that chapter can probably take care of most of our calculation needs. Sometimes, however, we deal with problems in which the size of the numbers involved extend over a wide range. We may also need to compute such things as square roots, logarithms or trigonometric functions. For these types of problems it is convenient to use *floating point numbers* in which the location of the radix point is automatically taken care of by the computer.

Floating point calculations can either be done in software (slow) or by using a floating point coprocessor (fast) which is a hardware implementation of the floating point calculations. In this chapter we will look at how the Intel 8087 coprocessor can be used to perform floating point calculations on the PC. To execute the programs described in this chapter your computer must have an 8087 (or 80297 or 80387) coprocessor installed on the motherboard.

In this chapter you will learn:

- How a real number is represented as a floating point number in the computer
- How to convert real numbers to their floating point representation
- The architecture of the 8087 floating point coprocessor
- The data types supported by the 8087 coprocessor
- To use the 8087 floating point instructions
- ASCII string to floating point conversion routines

9.1 FLOATING POINT NUMBERS

A *floating point number* contains two main parts: a *mantissa* or *significand*, and an *exponent*. For example, the number 123.45 could be written as

$$123.45 = 1.2345 \times 10^2$$

where 1.2345 is the *mantissa* and 2 is the *exponent*. Similarly, the number 0.004321 could be written as

$$0.004321 = 4.321 \times 10^{-3}$$

In these examples the exponent corresponds to a power of 10. When storing floating point numbers in the computer for use with the 8087 coprocessor the exponent will represent *powers of 2*. We therefore first must represent a number as a binary number. For example, the decimal number 5.375 can be written as follows

$$
\begin{aligned}
5.375_{10} &= 101.011_2 \\
&= 1.01011 \times 2^2 \\
&= 1.01011E2
\end{aligned}
\tag{9.1}
$$

where the symbol *E* represents *times 2 to the*. In this floating point number the mantissa, or significand, is 1.01011 and the exponent is 2.

There are three different formats in which this floating point number can be stored in the computer depending on the number of bits used to store the number. The *short real format* stores the number in 32 bits, the *long real format* stores the number in 64 bits and the *temporary real format* stores the number in 80 bits. We will consider each of these formats separately.

Short Real Format

The *short real format* stores a floating point number in a 32-bit field made up of a 23-bit significand, an 8-bit exponent and a single sign bit as shown in Figure 9.1. The sign bit is zero for a positive number and 1 for a negative number. The sign of the exponent is built into the 8-bit exponent field but *not* by representing the exponent as a two's complement value. Rather the signed exponent is added to the bias value 7FH to obtain the 8-bit exponent used in Figure 9.1. This biased form of the exponent makes it easier to compare the values of two floating point numbers.

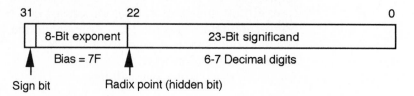

Figure 9.1 Short real format used to store a floating point number

The 23-bit significand assumes that the radix point precedes bit position 22. It is assumed that the significand contains a 1 preceding the radix point. This is a hidden bit which is not actually stored in the 32-bit field shown in Figure 9.1.

As an example, the number 5.375 shown in Eq. (9.1) has the significand 1.01011. The leading 1 will be hidden so that the 23-bit significand will be 01011000000000000000000. The exponent is 2 which is added to the bias 7FH. The resulting exponent is therefore 2H + 7FH = 81H = 10000001. The sign bit will be 0 so that the complete 32-bit binary format will be

0100 0000 1010 1100 0000 0000 0000 0000

which is equivalent to the hex value

```
40 AC 00 00
```

By including the statement *.8087* at the beginning of an assembly language listing the macro assembler *masm* will convert the real number 5.375 to the 32-bit floating point value 40 AC 00 00 by using the statement

```
val1    dd      5.375
```

in the data segment as shown in Figure 9.2. Note that this 32-bit value is stored least-significant byte first in the form 00 00 AC 40.

```
                                  .8087

0000                          data      segment   public
0000    00 00 AC 40           val1      dd        5.375
0004    00 A0 45 43           val2      dd        197.625
0008    4E 61 BC 00           val3      dd        12345678
000C    2B 52 9A 44           val4      dd        1234.5678
0010    2B 52 9A 44           val5      dd        123456.78E-2
0014                          data      ends
```

Figure 9.2   Floating point numbers can be assembled in the data segment
by using the directive .8087

As a second example, consider the number 197.625 shown in Figure 9.2. This can be written as a binary number as follows:

$$197.625_{10} = 11000101.101_2$$
$$= 1.1000101101 \times 2^7$$
$$= 1.1000101101E7 \qquad (9.2)$$

Therefore, excluding the hidden bit, the significand will be 1000101101 and the exponent will be 7 + 7FH = 86H = 10000110. The sign bit is 0 so that the 32-bit floating point representation will be

```
0100 0011 0100 0101 1010 0000 0000 0000
```

which is equivalent to the hex value

```
43 45 A0 00
```

which is stored as 00 A0 45 43 in Figure 9.2.

The last three examples shown in Figure 9.2 involve the digits 12345678. Written without a decimal point this is treated as the integer

$$12345678_{10} = 00BC614E_{16}$$

Note that *masm* will assemble this 32-bit value into memory. However, if a decimal point is included in the number, as in 1234.5678, then the floating point representation is used to store the number. Note that you can write the number in floating point notation so that the two entries

```
000C    2B 52 9A 44           val4      dd    1234.5678
0010    2B 52 9A 44           val5      dd    123456.78E-2
```

produce the same 32-bit floating point representation 44 9A 52 2B stored in memory.

Let's work backward from the floating point number 44 9A 52 2B to see if it is equivalent to the decimal number 1234.5678. The first step is to write it as the binary number

```
0100 0100 1001 1010 0101 0010 0010 1011
```

The 8-bit exponent 10001001 = 89H corresponds to an exponent value of 89H - 7FH = $0A_{16}$ = 10_{10}. Adding the hidden bit, the value of the number can be written as

$$
\begin{aligned}
1.&00110100101001000101011 \times 2^{10} \\
&= 10011010010.1001000101011 \\
&= 4D2.9158_{16}
\end{aligned}
$$

(9.3)

The integer part $4D2_{16}$ is equal to 1234_{10}, which is correct. However, the fractional part 0.9158_{16} is equal to

```
      9/16 = 0.5625
 +   1/256 = 0.0039062
 +  5/4096 = 0.0012207
 + 8/65536 = 0.000122
           = 0.5677489
```

which is only an approximation to 0.5678. This is because the 23-bit significand in Figure 9.1 can represent only 6-7 decimal digits of precision. The number 1234.5678 contains 8 decimal digits so we should not be surprised that it cannot be represented accurately in the short real format. To get a better floating point representation of 1234.5678 we can use the 64-bit long real format described next.

Long Real Format

The *long real format* stores a floating point number in a 64-bit field made up of a 52-bit significand, an 11-bit exponent and a single sign bit as shown in Figure 9.3. The 11-bit exponent uses a bias value of 3FFH. A hidden 1 bit precedes the radix point which is followed by the 52-bit significand.

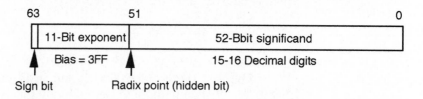

Figure 9.3 Long real format used to store a floating point number

The assembler directive *dq* can be used to define a quadword (8 bytes = 64 bits) as shown in Figure 9.4. Note that the numbers are stored least-significant byte first so that the number 1234.5678 is stored as the floating point number

```
40 93 4A 45 6D 5C FA AD
```

$$= 01000000\ 10010011\ 01001010\ 01000101$$
$$\quad\quad 01101101\ 01011100\ 11111010\ 10101101$$

The 11-bit exponent $10000001001 = 409H$ corresponds to the exponent $409H - 3FFH = 0AH = 10_{10}$. The floating point number can then be written as

$$1.0011\ 01001010\ 01000101\ 01101101$$
$$\quad\quad 01011100\ 11111010\ 10101101 \times 2^{10}$$

$$= 10011010010.10010001\ 01011011\ 01010111$$
$$\quad\quad 00111110\ 10101011\ 0100$$

$$= 4D2.915B573EAB4_{16} \qquad\qquad (9.4)$$

Comparing this value with that given in Eq. (9.3) we see that the integer parts and the first three digits of the fractional parts are the same. The remaining fractional digits in Eq. (9.4) will add to produce a very accurate representation of the decimal value 0.5678.

```
                                    .8087

        0000                        data      segment   public
        0000  AD FA 5C 6D 45 4A     val4      dq        1234.5678
              93 40
        0008  AD FA 5C 6D 45 4A     val5      dq        123456.78E-2
              93 40
        0010                        data      ends
```

Figure 9.4   Long real format floating point numbers can be stored using the *dq* assembler directive

Temporary Real Format

The *temporary real format* stores a floating point number in an 80-bit field made up of a 64-bit significand, a 15-bit exponent and a single sign bit as shown in Figure 9.5. The 15-bit exponent uses a bias value of 3FFFH. The 1 bit preceding the radix point is *not* hidden in the temporary real format but rather is explicitly stored as part of the 64-bit significand.

The assembler directive *dt* can be used to define a ten-byte word (80 bits) as shown in Figure 9.6.[1] Note that the numbers are stored least-significant byte first so that the number 1234.5678 is stored as the floating point number

```
40 09 9A 52 2B 6A E7 D5 66 CF
```

$$= 01000000\ 00001001\ 10011010\ 01010010\ 00101011$$
$$\quad\quad 01101010\ 11100111\ 11010101\ 01100110\ 11001111$$

---

[1] If the *dt* directive is used with a number without a decimal point the number is stored in the packed BCD format with two BCD digits per byte -- least significant digit first. The most significant byte contains the sign bit.

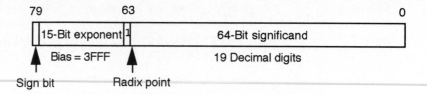

Figure 9.5 Temporary real format used to store a floating point number

The 15-bit exponent 100000000001001 = 4009H corresponds to the exponent 4009H – 3FFFH = 0AH = 10_{10}. The floating point number can then be written as

```
1.0011010 01010010 00101011 01101010
 11100111 11010101 01100110 11001111 x 2^10

= 10011010010.10010001 01011011 01010111 00111110
              10101011 00110110 01111000

= 4D2.915B573EAB3678_16                          (9.5)
```

Comparing this value with that given in Eq. (9.4) we see that the integer parts and the first ten digits of the fractional parts are the same. The remaining fractional digits (3678_{16} in Eq. (9.5) compared with 4_{16} in Eq. (9.4)) will produce an even more accurate representation of the decimal value 0.5678.

```
                                .8087

0000                            data     segment   public
0000  CF 66 D5 E7 6A 2B         val6     dt        1234.5678
      52 9A 09 40
000A  CF 66 D5 E7 6A 2B         val7     dt        123456.78E-2
      52 9A 09 40
0014                            data     ends
```

Figure 9.6 Temporary real format floating point numbers can be stored using the *dt* assembler directive

The temporary real format is the format used by the Intel 8087 floating point coprocessor (to be described in the following section) to store floating point data in the 80-bit data stack registers. Using this 80-bit format to carry out the floating point operations will minimize any rounding errors.

To understand the range of numbers that can be represented by this format we note that the exponent bias 3FFFH is added to the actual exponent to form the 15-bit exponent field. A maximum 15-bit exponent equal to 7FFFH – 3FFFH = 4000H = 16384_{10}. This means that the maximum size of a number is of the order $2^{+16384} \approx 1.19$ x 10^{4932}. This is a *very* large number. For example, the radius of the universe is estimated to be approximately 13 x 10^9 light years ≈ 1.23 x 10^{28} cm. The volume of the universe is then about 7.77 x 10^{84} cm^3. The radius of the hydrogen nucleus is of the order of 10^{-13} cm or the volume of the hydrogen nucleus is about 10^{-39} cm^3. This means that the ratio of the volume of the universe to the volume of a hydrogen nucleus is 7.77 x 10^{84} / $10^{-39} \approx 10^{124}$ which is roughly the number of hydrogen nuclei needed to fill the entire universe! This is a small fraction of the largest number ($\approx 1.2 \times 10^{4932}$) that will fit in the 8087 coprocessor. The value 1.2×10^{4932} is about 1754! (factorial). Most calculators can't compute a factorial greater than 69! $\approx 1.7 \times 10^{98}$.

The 64 digits of the significand in Figure 9.5 means that the precision of a number stored in this format will be 1 part in 2^{64} which is approximately the ratio of the diameter of the hydrogen atom to the circumference of the moon orbit about the earth. This represents about 19 decimal digits.

9.2   THE 8087 FLOATING POINT COPROCESSOR

The 8087 floating point coprocessor is a separate 40-pin chip[2] that sits beside the 8086 microprocessor on the mother board and monitors the instructions that are being received by the 8086 as shown in Figure 9.7. If the instruction has an opcode between D8H and DFH (that is, the first five bits are 11011, called the *escape sequence*), the 8087 will recognize the instruction as a floating point instruction that it will execute. Note from the 8086 instruction opcode map in Table A.2 in Appendix A that these opcodes correspond to the 8086 instructions *ESC 0 – ESC 7*. This means that the 8086 knows that these instructions will be executed by a different coprocessor. However, if the instruction needs some operand data from memory the 8086 will compute the effective memory address using its usual addressing modes and read a byte of data from this address. The 8087 will then use this address to read or write data associated with its floating point instruction.

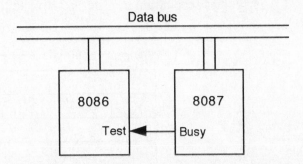

Figure 9.7 The 8087 reads the instructions being fetched by the 8086

While the 8087 coprocessor is executing a floating point instruction the 8086 will continue to execute the instructions in the program. Before fetching another floating point instruction it must be sure that the 8087 has completed any previous floating point instruction. It does this by executing the *WAIT* instruction (opcode = 9BH) which will wait until the *Test* line shown in Figure 9.7 goes low. This line is connected to the *Busy* line of the 8087 which remains high while an 8087 floating point instruction is being executed. The *WAIT* opcode 9BH is automatically included by the assembler as the first byte of each floating point instruction as shown in Table 9.1.[3]

If an 8087 floating point instruction references a memory location (such as storing a floating point result in a particular memory location) you as the programmer must ensure that the 8086 does not try to read the result before the 8087 has finished its instruction. You do this by including the instruction *FWAIT* (which is the same as *WAIT* with the opcode 9BH) between any 8087 floating point instruction and an 8086 instruction that accesses the same memory location. This will cause the 8086 to wait for the 8087 instruction to be completed before it accesses the data in memory.

The 8087 Registers

The 8087 contains eight 80-bit data registers, *R0 – R7*, which are arranged as a floating point stack as shown in Figure 9.8. The stack pointer is a 3-bit number (corresponding to register *Ri*) that is stored in bits 11 – 13 of the 8087 *status word* shown in Figure 9.9. The register corresponding to the top of the stack is called *ST(0)*, or simply *ST*. When a value is pushed on this floating point stack the 3-bit stack pointer is decremented by 1 and the value is stored in the register *Ri* pointed to by this new stack pointer. This means that the register corresponding to the top of the stack *ST* is not always the same register. Rather, *ST* moves to lower register numbers when a value is pushed on the stack and moves to higher register numbers when a value is popped from the stack. When the top of the stack reaches register *R0* it will wrap around to register *R7*.

The register containing the second value on the stack is labeled *ST(1)*; the register containing the third value on the stack is labeled *ST(2)* and so forth as illustrated in Figure 9.8. Floating point instructions generally operate on the value on top of the stack at *ST*, or on the two top values on the stack at *ST* and *ST(1)*. However, some instructions allow you to specify any register, relative to the top of the stack, such as *ST(3)*.

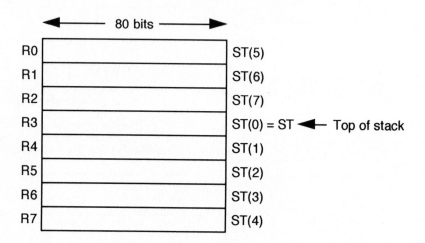

Figure 9.8 Structure of the 8087 stack

In addition to containing the top of stack pointer the 8087 status word shown in Figure 9.9 contains four condition codes, *C0 – C3*, which indicate the result of certain floating point compare and examine

---

.287 directive at the beginning of an assembly language program will cause Microsoft's MASM assembler, Version 5.0 and later, to omit the 9BH WAIT opcode from the floating point instructions and will allow additional 80287 instructions to be assembled.

instructions. The status word can be examined by storing it in an 8086 register or a memory location using the instruction *FSTSW*. Bits 0 – 5 in the 8087 status word contain exception flags that are set to 1 when certain errors occur in the computation. The interrupt request bit 7 is set to 1 if any unmasked exception bit (bits 0 – 5) is set to 1. An exception bit can be masked by setting the corresponding exception mask bit (bits 0 – 5) in the 8087 control word shown in Figure 9.10. Bit 15 is a busy flag that is 1 if the 8087 is executing an instruction.

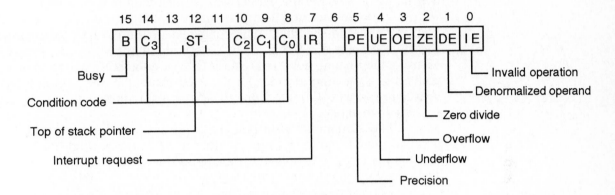

Figure 9.9 The 8087 Status Word

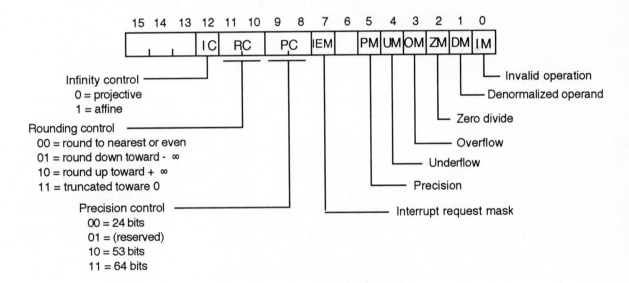

Figure 9.10 The 8087 Control Word

8087 Data Types and Instructions

The 8087 supports seven data types: 3 integer types, 3 floating point real types, and 1 packed BCD type. The three integer types are a 16-bit word integer (*dw*), a 32-bit short integer (or double word, *dd*), and a 64-bit long integer (or quadword, *dq*). The three real types are the 32-bit short real, the 64-bit long real and the 80-bit temporary real whose formats are given in Figures 9.1, 9.3, and 9.5 respectively. The packed BCD type is 80 bits long (ten bytes, *dt*). The most-significant byte contains the sign of the number as its most-significant bit (0 for a positive number and 1 for a negative number). The remaining nine bytes contain 18 packed BCD digits.

All numbers stored in the 8087 stack shown in Figure 9.8 are stored in the 80-bit temporary real format shown in Figure 9.5. If an integer stored in some memory location (using *dw*, *dd*, or *dq*) is loaded into *ST* (using the instruction *fild*) the 8087 will automatically convert these integer values to the 80-bit temporary real format before storing the number in *ST*. Similarly, if the result of some floating point calculation in *ST* is stored in an integer variable (using the instruction *fist*) the 8087 will automatically convert the 80-bit temporary real format to the appropriate integer format depending on whether the integer was defined with *dw*, *dd*, or *dq*.

Variables defined using *dd*, *dq*, or *dt* can be used to store floating point numbers in the short real, long real or temporary real formats as shown in Figures 9.2, 9.4 and 9.6. These real numbers can be loaded into *ST* using the floating point instruction *fld* where the 8087 will automatically convert to the temporary real format used inside the 8087. Similarly, the instruction *fst* will store the value in *ST* as a real number (*dd*, *dq*, or *dt*) in a variable in memory.

The statements *fbld* and *fbstp* are used to load a packed BCD number into *ST* and to store the number in *ST* into a packed BCD number. In the latter case, the number is then popped from the floating point stack. These loading and storing instructions are illustrated in Table 9.1

The operands of the instructions in Table 9.1 refer either to the floating point stack (e.g., *ST* and *ST(3)*) or to the external memory variables defined in the data segment at the beginning of Table 9.1. The variables *d1* and *d2* are 32-bit short real variables, the variable *exp* is a 16-bit word integer, the variable *sig* is a 32-bit short integer and *bcd* is a 10-byte packed bcd variable.

Suppose you want to add two numbers using the 8087. One of the operands (the destination) must be one of the 8087 stack registers, *ST(i)*, while the second operand (the source) can be either another stack register (one must be *ST*) or an external memory location. The sum is always stored in the destination operand. The floating point instruction *FADD* can be used to add an external real operand to *ST* while the instruction *FIADD* can be used to add an external integer operand to *ST*.

The following examples are given in Table 9.1. The instruction *FADD* (with no operands) will add the contents of *ST(1)* to *ST* and leave the sum in *ST*. The instruction *FADD d1* will add the real floating point value in variable *d1* to *ST* and leave the sum in *ST*. The instruction *FADD ST(3),ST* will add *ST* to *ST(3)* and leave the sum in *ST(3)*. The instruction *FADDP ST(1),ST* will add *ST* to *ST(1)*, leave the sum in *ST(1)* and then pop the top of the stack *(ST)*. This will leave the sum, which was in *ST(1)*, on top of the stack -- that is, it is now at *ST*. Finally, the instruction *FIADD sig* will add the integer value stored in *sig* to the value in *ST* and leave the sum in *ST*. Note that if you want to access *integer* values in memory you must use the versions of the instructions that begin with *fi*, as in *fild*, *fist* and *fiadd*.

The subtract instructions *FSUB* and *FISUB* are used for subtractions involving real and integer operands respectively. In these instructions the source is subtracted from the destination with the difference stored in the destination. Adding the suffix *R* will cause the operands to be reversed so that the destination is subtracted from the source. The suffix *P* will cause the top of the stack to be popped after the subtraction occurs. For example, the instruction *FSUBRP ST(1),ST* will cause the destination *ST(1)* to be subtracted from the source *ST* with the difference stored in *ST(1)*. The top of the stack is then popped so that the difference will end up on the new top of the stack, namely *ST*.

Table 9.1

8087 Floating Point Instructions

```
0000                           data    segment
0000   2B 52 9A 44             d1      dd        1234.5678
0004   2B 52 9A 44             d2      dd        123456.78E-2
0008   FFFC                    exp     dw        -4
000A   4E 61 BC 00             sig     dd        12345678
000E   ????????                fdbuf   dd        ?
0012   0001                    one     dw        1
0014   0002                    two     dw        2
0016   ????                    ctrl    dw        ?
0018   ????                    status  dw        ?
001A   ????????????????????    bcdbuf  dt        ?
0024      0E [ ?? ]            environ db        14 dup(?)
0032      5E [ ?? ]            buf     db        94 dup(?)
0090      08 [ ?? ]            fdumpb  dq        8 dup(?)
0290                           data    ends
```

Machine code	Instruction	Operation
9B D9 F0	f2xm1	(2**st)-1
9B D9 E1	fabs	|st|
9B DE C1	fadd	st=st+st(1)
9B D8 06 0000 R	fadd d1	st=st+d1
9B DC C3	fadd st(3),st	st(3)=st(3)+st
9B DE C1	faddp st(1),st	st=st(1)+st pop
9B DF 26 001A R	fbld bcdbuf	st=bcdbuf
9B DF 36 001A R	fbstp bcdbuf	bcdbuf=st pop
9B D9 E0	fchs	st=-st
9B DB E2	fclex	clear exceptions
9B D8 D1	fcom	cmp st,st(1)
9B D8 16 0000 R	fcom d1	cmp st,d1
9B D8 D9	fcomp	cmp st,st(1) pop
9B D8 1E 0000 R	fcomp d1	cmp st,d1 pop
9B DE D9	fcompp	cmp st,st(1) 2pop
9B D9 F6	fdecstp	dec stack ptr
9B DB E1	fdisi	disable intr
9B DE F9	fdiv	st=st/st(1)
9B DC FA	fdiv st(2),st	st(2)=st(2)/st
9B D8 36 0000 R	fdiv d1	st=st/d1
9B DE F9	fdivp st(1),st	st=st(1)/st pop
9B DE F1	fdivr	st=st(1)/st
9B D8 FA	fdivr st,st(2)	st=st(2)/st
9B DC F2	fdivr st(2),st	st(2)=st/st(2)
9B D8 3E 0000 R	fdivr d1	st=d1/st
9B DE F1	fdivrp st(1),st	st=st/st(1) pop
9B DB E0	feni	enable interrupts
9B DD C1	ffree st(1)	free register
9B DA 06 000A R	fiadd sig	st=st+sig
9B DA 16 000A R	ficom sig	cmp st,sig
9B DA 1E 000A R	ficomp sig	cmp st,sig pop
9B DA 36 000A R	fidiv sig	st=st/sig
9B DA 3E 000A R	fidivr sig	st=sig/st
9B DB 06 000A R	fild sig	st=sig push
9B DA 0E 000A R	fimul sig	st=st*sig
9B D9 F7	fincstp	inc stack ptr
9B DB E3	finit	initialize 8087
9B DB 16 000A R	fist sig	sig=st
9B DB 1E 000A R	fistp sig	sig=st pop st
9B DA 26 000A R	fisub sig	st=st-sig
9B DA 2E 000A R	fisubr sig	st=sig-st
9B D9 C3	fld st(3)	st=st(3) push
9B D9 06 0000 R	fld d1	st=d1 push
9B D9 E8	fld1	st=1 push

Table 9.1 (continued)

9B D9 2E 0016 R	fldcw ctrl	load control word
9B D9 26 0024 R	fldenv environ	load environment
9B D9 EA	fldl2e	st=log2 e
9B D9 E9	fldl2t	st=log2 10
9B D9 EC	fldlg2	st=log10 2
9B D9 ED	fldln2	st=ln 2
9B D9 EB	fldpi	st=pi
9B D9 EE	fldz	st=0
9B DE C9	fmul	st=st*st(1)
9B D8 0E 0000 R	fmul d1	st=st*d1
9B D8 CA	fmul st,st(2)	st=st*st(2)
9B DC CA	fmul st(2),st	st(2)=st(2)*st
9B DE C9	fmulp st(1),st	st=st(1)*st pop
9B D9 D0	fnop	no operation
9B D9 F3	fpatan	st=arctan(st/st(1))
9B D9 F8	fprem	st=mod(st/st(1))
9B D9 F2	fptan	Y/X=tan(st)->Y\X
9B D9 FC	frndint	round to integer
9B DD 26 0032 R	frstor buf	restore state
9B DD 36 0032 R	fsave buf	save state
9B D9 FD	fscale	st=st*2**st(1)
9B D9 FA	fsqrt	st=sqrt(st)
9B DD D3	fst st(3)	st(3)=st
9B D9 16 0000 R	fst d1	d1=st
9B D9 3E 0016 R	fstcw ctrl	ctrl=control word
9B D9 36 0024 R	fstenv environ	store environment
9B DD DB	fstp st(3)	st(3)=st pop st
9B D9 1E 0000 R	fstp d1	d1=st pop st
9B DD 3E 0018 R	fstsw status	status=status word
9B DE E9	fsub	st=st-st(1)
9B DC EB	fsub st(3),st	st(3)=st(3)-st
9B D8 E3	fsub st,st(3)	st=st-st(3)
9B D8 26 0000 R	fsub d1	st=st-d1
9B DE E9	fsubp st(1),st	st=st(1)-st pop
9B DE E1	fsubr	st=st(1)-st
9B D8 2E 0000 R	fsubr d1	st=d1-st
9B DC E3	fsubr st(3),st	st(3)=st-st(3)
9B D8 EB	fsubr st,st(3)	st=st(3)-st
9B DE E1	fsubrp st(1),st	st=st-st(1) pop
9B D9 E4	ftst	test st,0
9B	fwait	wait (8088 wait)
9B D9 E5	fxam	examine st
9B D9 C9	fxch	swap st & st(1)
9B D9 CB	fxch st(3)	swap st & st(3)
9B D9 F4	fxtract	st->exp\signif
9B D9 F1	fyl2x	st=st(1)*log2 st
9B D9 F9	fyl2xp1	st=st(1)*log2(st+1)

The multiplication instructions *FMUL* and *FIMUL* are used to multiply a multiplicand on the 8087 stack by a real or integer multiplier respectively. The instruction *FMUL* (with no operands) will multiply the contents of *ST* by *ST(1)* and leave the product in *ST*. The instruction *FMUL d1* will multiply the real floating point value in variable *d1* by *ST* and leave the product in *ST*. The instruction *FMUL ST(2),ST* will multiply *ST* by *ST(2)* and leave the product in *ST(2)*. The instruction *FMULP ST(1),ST* will multiply *ST* by *ST(1)*, leave the product in *ST(1)* and then pop the top of the stack *(ST)*. This will leave the product, which was in *ST(1)*, on top of the stack -- that is, it is now at *ST*. Finally, the instruction *FIMUL sig* will multiply the integer value stored in *sig* by the value in *ST* and leave the product in *ST*.

The division instructions *FDIV* and *FIDIV* are used to perform floating point divisions involving real and integer values respectively. The instruction *FDIV* (with no operands) will divide the contents of *ST* by *ST(1)* and leave the quotient in *ST*. The instruction *FDIV d1* will divide *ST* by the real floating point value in variable *d1* and leave the quotient in *ST*. The suffix *R* will cause the source to be divided by the destination. Thus, the instruction *FDIVR ST(2),ST* will divide *ST* by *ST(2)* and leave the quotient in *ST(2)*. The instruction *FDIVP ST(1),ST* will divide *ST(1)* by *ST*, leave the quotient in *ST(1)* and then pop the top of the stack *(ST)*. This will leave the quotient, which was in *ST(1)*, on top of the stack -- that is, it is now at *ST*. Finally, the instruction *FIDIV sig* will divide the value in *ST* by the integer value stored in *sig* and leave the quotient in *ST*.

The TUTOR monitor does not support the 8087 in the sense of displaying the contents of the 8087 stack or in disassembling 8087 instructions. When single stepping through a program containing floating point instructions, these instructions will be disassembled as the 8086 *WAIT* and *ESC* instructions. If you want to examine the contents of the 8087 stack you can dump all eight values to an 8 quadword (64 bits) buffer using the subroutine *fdump* shown in Figure 9.11. The buffer *fdumpb* must be defined as 8 quadwords as shown in the data segment at the beginning of Table 9.1. Note in Figure 9.11 that the floating point statement *fst   qword ptr fdumpb[bx]* will store the value at *ST* in the quadword pointed to by *bx* in *fdumpb* in the long word format. The 8087 stack pointer is then incremented (8 times) in the *fdp1* loop using the floating point instruction *fincstp*. Therefore, after completing the loop the location of *ST* will be back where it started.

```
;           dump 8087 stack to fdumpb
fdump       proc         near
            push         bx
            push         cx
            mov          bx,0
            mov          cx,8
fdp1:       fst          qword ptr fdumpb[bx]
            fincstp
            add          bx,8
            loop         fdp1
            pop          cx
            pop          bx
            ret
fdump       endp
```

Figure 9.11 Subroutine to dump the contents of the 8087 stack
to the buffer *fdumpb*

9.3 BINARY TO FLOATING POINT CONVERSIONS

We have seen that the 8087 will perform floating point operations on 80-bit floating point numbers stored in its internal data stack. In transferring data values to and from external memory, the 8087 will automatically convert between this 80-bit temporary real format and the various real and integer formats described in the previous section. We saw in Section 9.1 that if you enter a number with a decimal point in an assembly language listing (and use the .8087 directive) the assembler will convert this number to its floating point representation. However, if we want to enter floating point numbers from the keyboard and display floating point numbers on the screen we will need to convert an ASCII string to a floating point representation and vice versa. We will develop these conversion routines in this section.

ASCII String to Floating Point Conversion

Suppose you enter the decimal floating point number

```
1.234E2
```

from the keyboard. By this you mean the number $1.234 \times 10^2 = 123.4 = 1234 \times 10^{-1}$. If you use the subroutine *query* described in Chapter 7 to enter this number the ASCII string representing this number will be in the buffer *kbuf*. The subroutines to convert this ASCII string to a floating point number are included in the file *number.asm* described in Chapter 8. The data segment from this file is shown in Figure 9.12. The double word *sig* is used to hold the significand (1234 in the above example) and the word *exp* is used to hold the final exponent (-1 in the above example after shifting the decimal point all the way to the right).

```
.8087

data        segment public
base        dw          10
dnum        dd          ?
dpl         dw          ?
negflg      db          ?
decflg      db          ?
one         dw          1
two         dw          2
exp         dw          ?
sig         dd          ?
fdbuf       dd          ?
ctrl        dw          ?
ten8        dd          100000000
E           dd          ?
F           dt          ?
negeflg     db          ?
fdumpb      dq          8 dup(?)
data        ends
```

Figure 9.12 The data segment from the file *number.asm*

The subroutine float shown in Figure 9.13 will convert an ASCII string pointed to by *si* to a quadword floating point number pointed to by *di*. The subroutine *number* (discussed in Chapter 8) is first used to convert the significand to a double number and store the result (1234 in the above example) in the variable *sig*. The negative of the number of digits following the decimal point (-3 in the above example) is stored in the variable *exp*. If the next digit is an *E* or an *e*, the subroutine *number* is used to convert the exponent to a 16-bit integer (in *ax*) which is then added to *exp* to produce the final value of the exponent (-3 + 2 = -1 in the above example).

The significand *sig* is pointed to by *si* and the exponent *exp* is pointed to by *bx* and the subroutine *binflt* is called which will convert the number represented by *sig* and *exp* to a long real floating point number that is stored in the quadword pointed to by *di*.

How does the subroutine *binflt*, which is shown in Figure 9.14, work? If we let z represent the floating point number then we can write

$$z = \text{sig} \times 10^{exp}$$

```
;           convert to floating point
;           si --> ascii fp number string
;           di --> floating point buffer (qword)
float   proc    near
        push    ax
        push    bx
        push    cx
        push    dx
        cld
        call    number                      ;get signif
        mov     word ptr sig,ax
        mov     word ptr sig+2,dx
        neg     cx                          ;move -dpl
        mov     exp,cx                      ; to exp
        lodsb                               ;get char
        or      al,20h                      ;E or e
        cmp     al,'e'                      ;if not e
        je      flt1                        ; quit
        dec     si
        jmp     short flt2
flt1:   call    number                      ;get exp
        add     exp,ax                      ; + to exp
flt2:   push    si                          ;save si
        mov     si,offset sig               ;convert to
        mov     bx,offset exp               ; fpoint
        call    binflt
        pop     si                          ;restore si
        pop     dx
        pop     cx
        pop     bx
        pop     ax
        ret
float   endp
```

Figure 9.13 The subroutine *float* will convert an ASCII string to a
floating point number

```
;           binary to floating point
;           si -> significand (dword)
;           bx -> exponent    (word)
;           di -> result      (qword)
binflt  proc    near
        push    bx                          ;save regs
        push    si
        push    di
        fild    word ptr [bx]               ;X
        call    tenx                        ;10**X=2**Y
        fimul   dword ptr [si]              ;sig*2**Y
        fstp    qword ptr [di]              ;store ans
        fwait                               ;synchronize
        pop     di                          ;restore regs
        pop     si
        pop     bx
        ret
binflt  endp
```

Figure 9.14 The subroutine *binflt* will compute the floating point number
$z = \text{sig} \times 10^{exp}$

If we could compute 10^{exp} using the 8087 and then multiply the result by *sig* we would have computed z and the 8087 would automatically convert this to the long real format when the result is stored in memory. This, in fact, is what the subroutine *binflt* shown in Figure 9.14 does. The only problem is that there is no 8087 instruction that will compute, for example, 10ST that we could use to compute 10^{exp}. There is, however, the instruction *F2XM1* that computes the value $2^{ST} - 1$. We can use this instruction to write a subroutine called *tenx* that will compute 10ST.

Suppose we want to compute 10^X. We can write this as

$$10^X = 2^Y \tag{9.6}$$

where Y can be found by taking the logarithm to the base 2 of both sides of the equation. That is,

$$X \log_2 10 = Y \tag{9.7}$$

Combining Eqs. (9.6) and (9.7) we can write

$$10^X = 2^{X \log_2 10} \tag{9.8}$$

Therefore, if we could compute $X \log_2 10$ we could use the instruction *F2XM1* to compute $2^Y - 1$ from which we could compute 10^X from Eq. (9.6). The 8087 instruction *FLDL2T* will load the constant value $log_2 10 \approx 2.302585$ into ST. It looks as if we could just multiply this value by X and then use the instruction *F2XM1* to compute $2^Y - 1$. However, if you look at Note 8 of Table 5 in the 8087 data sheet in Appendix E you will see that the value of ST must be between 0 and 0.5 when using the instruction *F2XM1* to compute $2^{ST} - 1$. This presents a further complication.

As an example, suppose we want to compute 10^2. From Eq. (9.8) we can write this as

$$
\begin{aligned}
10^2 &\approx 2^{2 \times 2.3} = 2^{4.6} \\
&= 2^4 \times 2^{0.6} \\
&= 2^4 \times 2^{0.6/2} \times 2^{0.6/2} \tag{9.9}
\end{aligned}
$$

We have succeeded in writing 10^2 as the product of three factors involving powers of 2. The last two factors have exponents that will always be less than 0.5 so that we can use the instruction *F2XM1*. In the first factor, the exponent of 2 will always be an integer and this factor can be computed using the 8087 instruction *FSCALE*, which computes $ST = ST \times 2^{ST(1)}$ where $ST(1)$ must be an integer.

The subroutine *tenx*, which will compute 10ST, is shown in Figure 9.15. The first instruction stores the 8087 control word in the variable *ctrl* given in the data segment in Figure 9.12. Note that this must be followed by the instruction *fwait* before the 8086 changes the contents of *ctrl* by setting bit 10 and clearing bit 11. This will cause the 8087 to round down as shown in Figure 9.10. This is necessary so that the 8087 instruction *frndint* will round to the next lower integer. For example, in Figure 9.15 the statement *fldl2t* will load (push) the value $log_2 10$ on the top of the 8087 stack. The value of X, which was on the top of the stack (in ST) when the subroutine *tenx* is called, is pushed to $ST(1)$. The values on the stack are shown in the comments on the right of Figure 9.15. The top of the stack is to the right.

```
;              10**ST
tenx           proc    near
               fstcw ctrl                              ;round down
               fwait
               and     ctrl,0f3ffh                     ; ctrl reg
               or      ctrl,0400h                      ; bit 10=1
               fldcw ctrl                              ; bit 11=0
               fldl2t                                  ;X\log2 10
               fmulp st(1),st(0)                       ;X*log2 10 = Y
               fld     ST                              ; Y \ Y
               frndint                                 ; Y \ I
               fxch                                    ; I \ Y
               fld     st(1)                           ; I\Y\I
               fsubp   st(1),st(0)                     ;I\(Y-I=F)
               fidiv   two                             ;I\F/2
               f2xm1                                   ;I\2**F/2 - 1
               fiadd   one                             ;I\2**F/2=T2
               fld     ST                              ;I\T2\T2
               fmulp   st(1),st(0)                     ;I\2**F
               fscale                                  ;I\2**(F+I)
               fstp    st(1)                           ;2**Y = 10**X
               fwait
               ret
tenx           endp
```

Figure 9.15 The subroutine *tenx* will compute 10ST

The instruction *fmulp st(1),st(0)* will multiply X by $log_2 10$ and pop $log_2 10$ from the top of the stack leaving only $Y = X*log_2 10$ on top of the stack. The next instruction, *fld ST*, will duplicate the top of the stack so that both ST and $ST(1)$ will contain Y. The instruction *frndint* will then replace the value of Y on top of the stack with its integer value, I. For example, if Y was 4.6 as in Eq. (9.9), then the value of I will be 4. The next instruction, *fxch*, swaps the top two values on the stack and the instruction *fld st(1)* copies the second element on the stack to the top. At this point the stack will contain the three values $I\backslash Y\backslash I$. The instruction *fsubp st(1),st(0)* will subtract the I on top of the stack from Y in $ST(1)$ and then pop I leaving the difference, equal to the fractional part of Y (called F), on top of the stack. In Eq. (9.9) the value of F is 0.6. We must now divide this fractional part of Y by 2 using the instruction *fidiv two* (two is the constant 2 given in the data segment in Figure 9.12) before executing the instruction *f2xm1* to compute $2^{F/2} - 1$. Adding 1 to this value will produce $2^{F/2} = T2$. The next instruction duplicates $T2$ and the following instruction multiplies these two values to produce the result 2^F. The instruction *fscale* will then multiply this value by 2^I to yield the final result $2^F \times 2^I = 2^{(F+I)} = 2^Y = 10^X$. The instruction *fstp st(1)* has the effect of removing the value I as the second element on the stack and leaving the value 10^X on top of the stack.

Floating Point to ASCII String Conversion

The problem of printing the value stored at ST on the screen is the opposite of converting an ASCII string from the keyboard to a floating point number. In this case we already have a floating point number, z, on top of the 8087 stack and we want to convert it to the form $F \times 10^E$ where F is the mantissa with a single decimal digit to the left of the decimal point and the exponent E is an integer. We can write

$$
\begin{aligned}
z &= F \times 10^E \\
&= 10^{E'}
\end{aligned}
$$

(9.10)

where E' is the sum of the integer part E plus a fractional part. Taking the logarithm to the base 2 of both sides of Eq. (9.10) we obtain

$$\log_2 z = E' \times \log_2 10$$

from which

$$E' = \log_2 z \ / \ \log_2 10$$

(9.11)

The 8087 instruction *FYL2X* computes $ST = ST(1) \times log_2 ST$ and can be used to compute $log_2 z$ by storing a 1 in $ST(1)$ and $|z|$ in ST. After computing E' from Eq. (9.11) the value of E in Eq. (9.10) is found by rounding E' to the next lower integer. Once E is found the value of F can be computed from Eq. (9.10) as

$$F = z \times 10^{-E}$$

(9.12)

These calculations are all carried out in the subroutine *fpdec* which is shown in Figure 9.16. The value of F computed by Eq. (9.12) will be a real number with a single decimal digit to the left of the decimal point. If we multiply this value by 10^8 (a constant stored in the variable *ten8* in Figure 9.12) using the instruction *fimul ten8*, the result can be stored as a packed BCD number in the variable F (defined with *dt* in Figure 9.12) using the instruction *fbstp F*. This will allow floating point numbers to be displayed on the screen with eight digits following the decimal point in the mantissa. The subroutine *pst* given in Figure 9.17 will print the floating point number on the top of the 8087 stack on the screen in the format *–s.ssssssssE–ee*.

```
;          floating point to F*10**E
fpdec      proc    near                    ;z
           fld     st(0)                   ;z\z
           fld     st(0)                   ;z\z\z
           fabs                            ;z\z\|z|
           fld1                            ;z\z\|z|\1
           fxch    st(1)                   ;z\z\1\|z|
           fyl2x                           ;z\z\log₂z
           fldl2t                          ;z\z\log₂z\log₂10
           fdivp   st(1),st(0)             ;z\z\E'
           frndint                         ;z\z\E
           fist    E                       ;z\z\E
           fchs                            ;z\z\-E
           call    tenx                    ;z\z\10**-E
           fmulp   st(1),st(0)             ;z\F (1-9)
           fimul   ten8                    ;z\F*10**8
           fbstp   F                       ;z\bcd store
           fwait                           ;z
           ret
fpdec      endp
```

Figure 9.16 The subroutine *fpdec* will convert the floating point number *z* on top of the 8087 stack to $F \times 10^E$ and store the results in *F* and *E*

```
;              print F*10**E
pst            proc   near
               push   ax
               push   cx
               push   si
               push   di
               push   es
               push   ds
               pop    es                         ;es=ds
               call   fpdec                      ;calc F*10**E
               std
               mov    di,offset bufend-1
               mov    byte ptr 1[di],0           ;bufend=0
               mov    si,offset E
               mov    negeflg,0                  ;convert E
               test   byte ptr E+3,80h           ;if E neg
               jns    pf2
               call   negE                       ;negate E
               not    negeflg                    ;set flag
pf2:           call   sharps
               cmp    negeflg,0                  ;if E neg
               je     pf0
               mov    al,'-'                     ; add -
               stosb
pf0:           mov    al,'E'
               stosb                             ;add E
               mov    al,' '
               stosb                             ;add blank
               mov    si,offset F
               mov    base,16                    ;bcd is hex
               mov    cx,8
pf3:           call   sharp                      ;do 8 digits
               loop   pf3
               mov    al,'.'                     ;add .
               stosb
               mov    al,byte ptr F+4
               and    al,0fh
               or     al,30h                     ;add units
               stosb                             ; digit
               mov    al,byte ptr F+9            ;check sign
               test   al,80h                     ;if neg
               jns    pf1
               mov    al,'-'                     ;add -
               stosb
pf1:           inc    di
               mov    si,di                      ;si->string
               call   mess2
               mov    base,10                    ;base=10
               pop    es                         ;restore regs
               pop    di
               pop    si
               pop    cx
               pop    ax
               ret
pst            endp
```

Figure 9.17 The subroutine *pst* will print the value of *ST* on the screen

The subroutine *pst* in Figure 9.17 first calls *fpdec* to compute and store the values of the mantissa and exponent in *F* and *E* respectively as described above. It then builds the appropriate ASCIIZ string to be printed by the subroutine *mess2* by calling the conversion subroutines *sharps* and *sharp* that were described in Chapter 8. If the value of *E* is negative (its sign bit is 1) then the flag *negeflg* is set and *E* is negated using the subroutine *negE* given in Figure 9.18. This is necessary because we want to display the absolute value of the exponent with a preceding minus sign if it is a negative number. Note that the sign of the floating point number will be stored in the most-significant byte of *F* (packed BCD format). Also note that we must change the base to 16 before converting the eight fractional digits of the mantissa in *F* because if we treat the packed BCD format as a hex number the converted digits will represent the decimal digits.

```
;         negate E
negE      proc      near
          push      dx
          mov       ax,word ptr E
          mov       dx,word ptr E+2
          call      dnegate
          mov       word ptr E,ax
          mov       word ptr E+2,dx
          pop       dx
          ret
negE      endp
```

Figure 9.18 Subroutine *negE* to negate the value of *E*

PROGRAMMING PROBLEMS

Problem 9.1 – RPN Floating Point Calculator
Modify Problem 8.3 in Chapter 8 by adding the following floating point operations to your dictionary of recognized words.

F+ (f1 f2 -- fsum)	Add the top two elements on the floating point stack.
F- (f1 f2 -- fdiff)	Subtract the top two elements on the floating point stack (f1 - f2).
F* (f1 f2 -- fprod)	Multiply the top two elements on the floating point stack.
F/ (f1 f2 -- fquot)	Divide the top two elements on the floating point stack(f1/f2).
FSQRT (f1 -- f2)	Take the square root of the top element on the floating point stack.
E. (f --)	Print the top value on the floating point stack.

To multiply two floating point numbers, you would enter

```
3215E-1 12.8E2 F* E.
```

When you press the *Enter* key, the product should be displayed in the form

```
3215E-1 12.8E2 F* E. 4.11520000 E5
```

Make a separate floating point stack that stores all numbers in the long, real floating point format. If you type the word *FLOATS*, push all numbers entered (single, double or floating point) on the floating point stack. Type *DOUBLES* to go back to the case of Problem 8.3 where numbers were pushed on the regular data stack.

Try the following examples:

```
1234.56E5 84.2 F/ E. 1.46622328 E6

1234.5 543.33 F+ E. 1.77783000 E3

8.44E7 22.3E6 F- E. 6.21000000 E7
```

Problem 9.2 – Full-Screen Floating Point Calculator

In this problem you will write a full-screen calculator that will simultaneously calculate and display the sum, difference, product and quotient of the contents of two registers displayed on the screen.

   a. Write a subroutine that will produce the following screen display where the shaded areas are displayed in reverse video.

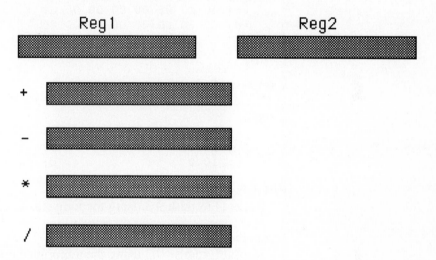

The cursor will be located at the beginning of *Reg1*. The program you write should allow you to enter floating point numbers in *Reg1*. Pressing the *Tab* key should move the cursor to the other register. Pressing the *Enter* key should move the cursor to the other register and display the sum, difference, product, and quotient in the appropriate fields.

   b. The numbers that you enter can be any floating point number in the form

$$-374.333E-7$$

After entering a number in *Reg1* and pressing the *Tab* key, the subroutine *tab* should move the cursor to *Reg2*, convert the number entered in *Reg1* to a long real format floating point number, and store this result in *fdbuf1*. If you have entered a number in *Reg2*, then calling *tab* should move the cursor to *Reg1*, convert the number entered in *Reg2* to a long real format floating point number, and store this result in *fdbuf2*. When you press the *Enter* key after entering both numbers, the subroutine *tabclc* should first call *tab* and then calculate and display the floating point sum, difference, product and quotient.

EXERCISES

Exercise 9.1

What decimal number is represented by each of the following short real floating point numbers?

a) 42 C1 28 00   d) 42 A4 B0 A4
b) 41 20 00 00   e) C2 85 33 33
c) C1 F6 00 00   f) 46 1C 40 00

Exercise 9.2

What decimal number is represented by each of the following long real floating point numbers?

a) 40 6E 70 00 00 00 00 00
b) 40 39 80 00 00 00 00 00
c) 40 C3 88 00 00 00 00 00
d) C0 3E C0 00 00 00 00 00
e) C0 80 F9 AE A4 7A E1 48
f) 40 54 96 14 7A E1 47 AE

Exercise 9.3

Write the following decimal numbers in the short real floating point format.

a) 1000.0   d) −74.8
b) 255.0   e) −543.21
c) 10.0   f) −66.6

Exercise 9.4

Repeat Exercise 9.3 using the long real floating point format.

Exercise 9.5

Repeat Exercise 9.3 using the temporary real floating point format.

Exercise 9.6

Write the following decimal numbers in the long real floating point format.

a) 10000.0   d) −30.75
b) 243.5   e) 82.345
c) 25.5   f) 100.0

Exercise 9.7

Repeat Exercise 9.6 using the short real floating point format.

Exercise 9.8

Repeat Exercise 9.6 using the temporary real floating point format.

Exercise 9.9

Write an equation that indicates what calculation is performed by each of the following instructions.

a) fadd s(2),st
b) fsub s(1),st
c) fsubr st(2),st
d) fsubr st,st(4)
e) fmul st(1),st
f) fmulp st(1),st
g) fdiv st(1),st
h) fdivr st(s),st

Exercise 9.10
Consider the following data segment:

```
data    segment public
val1    dd      64
val2    dd      64.0
val3    dq      64
val4    dq      64.0
val5    dt      64
val6    dt      64.0
val7    dt      -64
val8    dt      123456789123456789
data    ends
```

If these statements are assembled with the .8087 directive what values will be stored in memory for each of the variables *val1 – val8*?

Exercise 9.11
What 8087 instructions would you use to load to the top of the 8087 stack each of the values *val1 – val8* shown in the data segment in Exercise 9.10?

Exercise 9.12
What 8087 instructions would you use to store the value on top of the 8087 stack into each of the variables *val1 – val8* shown in the data segment in Exercise 9.10?

CHAPTER 10

Disk Input/Output

The user interacts with a personal computer by means of various input/output devices. We have seen how to use the IBM PC screen and keyboard in Chapters 3 and 7. We will look at the printer and sound interfaces in Chapter 11. In this chapter we will look at how the PC handles input/output (I/O) operations associated with the disk drives. In particular, in this chapter you will learn:

- The various disk formats used in the PC
- How to access the boot sector using DOS interrupts
- The directory structure of disk files
- How to use DOS functions to
  - a. open and close files
  - b. read from and write data to disk files
  - c. search the dictionary for a file name
- How to make a *terminate-and-stay-resident* (TSR) program that will write the screen to a disk file when you press *Shift-Print Screen*

10.1 DISK FORMATS AND FILE STRUCTURE

Floppy disk drives used in the PC come in two sizes, 5.25 inches and 3.5 inches. The diskettes used in the 5.25-inch drives can be either single-sided or double-sided and double-density or high-density. The 3.5-inch diskettes are double-sided and may be high-density. This situation leads to five different types of diskettes with different capacities as shown in Table 10.1. A single-sided 5.25-inch drive (now obsolete) can read only single-sided diskettes. A double-density diskette has 40 circular tracks per side with either 8 (DOS 1.1 and below) or 9 (DOS 2.0 and above) sectors per track. Each sector contains 512 bytes; therefore, each track contains 4,096 (DOS 1.1) or 4,608 (DOS 2.0) bytes and each side of the diskette contains 163,840 bytes (160 KBytes) for 8 sectors/track or 184,320 bytes (180 KBytes) for 9 sectors/track. A double-sided disk drive has two separate reading heads and a double-sided, double-density diskette contains a total of 327,680 bytes (320 KBytes) or 368,640 bytes (360 KBytes). Double-sided drives can read disks formatted on single-sided drives, but not vice versa. High-capacity 5.25-inch drives can use double-sided, high-density diskettes that have 80 tracks/side and 15 sectors/track with each sector containing 512 bytes. This means that these high-density diskettes can contain 1,228,800 bytes (1.2 MBytes). A high-capacity drive can read double-density or single-sided diskettes, but not vice versa.

The 3.5-inch diskettes contain 80 tracks/side and may have either 9 or 18 sectors/track. With 512 bytes/sector this means that these diskettes can contain either 737,280 bytes (720 KBytes) or 1,474,560 bytes (1.44 MBytes). A 1.44-MByte drive can read 720-KByte diskettes, but not vice versa. Given a choice, you should use high-density disk drives which can access data on diskettes with a lower capacity. Of course, you can't use 5.25-inch diskettes in 3.5-inch drives or vice versa. The best option is to have both size drives in the same computer.

Table 10.1				
Types of PC Diskettes				
Size (inches)	Description	# tracks per side	# sectors per track	Capacity (bytes)
5.25	single-sided (SS) double-density (DD)	40	8 or 9	160KB/180KB
5.25	double-sided (DS) double-density (DD)	40	8 or 9	320KB/360KB
5.25	double-sided (DS) high-density (HD)	80	15	1.2MB
3.5	double-sided (DS)	80	9	720KB
3.5	double-sided (DS) high-density (HD)	80	18	1.44MB

In addition to floppy disk drives, most PCs today also have some type of fixed, or hard disk drive. The capacity of these fixed disk drives varies widely from perhaps 20 Mbytes to hundreds of Mbytes.

The DOS software interrupt statements *INT 25H* and *INT 26H* can be used to read and write specific sectors on a disk using the options shown in Figure 10.1. When returning from either of these routines the stack will still contain the status register pushed on the stack by these instructions. Two bytes should therefore be added to *SP* to keep the stack from growing. If the disk access operation is successful, the carry flag will be cleared to zero. Otherwise, the carry flag will be set and the reason for the error is given in *AH* according to the error codes in Table 10.2.

You will seldom use the interrupt calls given in Figure 10.1 because DOS provides much safer ways to access the disk by using *INT 21H* function calls. We will look in detail at how to use these function calls later in this chapter. However, as an example of using the *INT 25H* absolute disk read routine, suppose you want to read the boot sector which is sector number 0 on the disk. From the point of view of DOS, all sectors on the disk are numbered sequentially from track to track. These logical sector numbers therefore become independent of the number of sectors per track for a particular disk format. The boot sector is logical sector number 0 which is the first sector on track zero of side 1 on the disk.

INT 25H	Absolute Disk Read
	Input: CX = no. of sectors to read
	AL = drive no. (0 = A, 1 = B, 2 = C, etc.)
	DX = starting logical sector no.
	DS:BX = buffer address
	Output: carry=0 successful operation
	carry=1 failed operation (reason in AH)
INT 26H	Absolute Disk Write
	Input: CX = no. of sectors to write
	AL = drive no. (0 = A, 1 = B, 2 = C, etc.)
	DX = starting logical sector no.
	DS:BX = buffer address
	Output: carry=0 successful operation
	carry=1 failed operation (reason in AH)

Figure 10.1 Absolute disk read and write operations using *INT 25H* and *INT 26H*

Table 10.2

Disk Error Codes in AH

Value	Status
01H	Bad command
02H	Bad address mark
03H	Write protected disk
04H	Sector not found
08H	DMA failure
10H	CRC error
20H	Disk controller error
40H	Seek error
80H	Time-out error

The program shown in Listing 10.1 will read this boot sector into the 512-byte buffer *dbuff* in the data segment. An example of running this program when drive A is a 1.2-MByte 5.25-inch disk drive is shown in Figure 10.2. The first 80 bytes read from the boot sector are shown in the data segment at the upper-right portion of the screen.

Listing 10.1 *int25.lst*

```
                          title   Absolute disk read
              ;           read boot sector

0000              stack segment para stack
0000   40 [                    db      64 dup(?)
          ??
                 ]
0040              stack ends

0000              data  segment  public
0000   0200 [     buff  db      512 dup(?)          ;disk buffer
          ??
                 ]
0200              data  ends

0000              code  segment  public
                        assume cs:code,ds:data
```

Listing 10.1 (continued)

```
0000                  main   proc far
0000  B8 ---- R              mov    ax,data            ;set ds
0003  8E D8                  mov    ds,ax
0005  BB 0000 R              mov    bx,offset buff     ;disk transfer area
0008  B9 0001                mov    cx,1               ;# sectors to read
000B  B0 01                  mov    al,0               ;drive # (A)
                                                       ;use 1 for drive B
                                                       ;use 2 for drive C
000D  BA 0000                mov    dx,0               ;relative sector 0
0010  CD 25                  int    25h                ;disk read
0012  72 03                  jc     mn1                ;jump if error
0014  83 C4 02               add    sp,2               ;fix stack
0017  CC             mn1:    int 3                     ;breakpoint
0018                  main   endp

0018                  code   ends
                             end    main
```

```
              8086 Microprocessor TUTOR              Press F7 for Help

       AH AL    BH BL    CH CL    DH DL      DATA SEG   08 19 2A 3B 4C 5D 6E 7F
   AX  01 00 BX 00 00 CX 00 00 DX 00 00      1587:0000  EB 34 90 4D 53 44 4F 53
                                             1587:0008  33 2E 33 00 02 01 01 00
       SP 0040     SI 01B6      IP 0017       1587:0010  02 E0 00 60 09 F9 07 00
       BP 7420     DI 0001                   1587:0018  0F 00 02 00 00 00 00 00
       SS 15A7     DS 1587    CS 1585        1587:0020  00 00 00 00 00 00 00 00
   SP+SS 15AB0  SI+DS 15A26      ES 1575     1587:0028  00 00 00 00 00 00 00 12
   BP+SS 1CE90  DI+DS 15871  IP+CS 15867     1587:0030  00 00 00 00 01 00 FA 33
   STATUS FLAGS 7212 0111001000010010        1587:0038  C0 8E D0 BC 00 7C 16 07
                         ODITSZ A P C        1587:0040  BB 78 00 36 C5 37 1E 56
   1585:0017 CC          INT3                1587:0048  16 53 BF 2B 7C B9 0B 00


   SEG 1585:  08 19 2A 3B 4C 5D 6E 7F                   15A7: STACK
      FFF8  00 00 00 00 00 00 00 00     . . . . . . . .     0040
      0000  B8 87 15 8E D8 BB 00 00     . . . . . . . .
      0008  B9 01 00 B0 00 BA 00 00     . . . . . . . .
      0010  CD 25 72 03 83 C4 02>CC     . % r . . . . .
      0018  00 00 00 00 00 00 00 00     . . . . . . . .
      0020  EB 34 90 4D 53 44 4F 53     . 4 . M S D O S
      0028  33 2E 33 00 02 01 01 00     3 . 3 . . . . .

   ───────────────────────────────────   / : Command      > : Go To Memory
                                          Use Cursor Keys to Scroll thru Memory
```

Figure 10.2 Example of running the program in Listing 10.1 to read the boot sector

The first three bytes in the boot sector are a *JMP* instruction to the bootstrap program which will read into memory the disk files containing the operating system. In Figure 10.2 these three bytes are

```
EB 34        JMP    0036H
90           NOP
```

The beginning of the bootstrap program can be seen at offset address 0036H beginning with the instruction FA (*CLI*). The next eight bytes in the boot sector contain the manufacturer's identification. In Figure 10.2 these contain the bytes *MSDOS3.3* as can be seen in the code segment starting at offset address 0023H which is the same as offset address 0003H in the data segment.

Bytes 000BH – 001DH in the boot sector (shown underlined in the data segment in Figure 10.2) contain the information in Table 10.3 concerning the physical layout of the disk. Bytes 000BH – 0017H are called the BIOS parameter block (BPB). Note that this disk contains a total of 2400 sectors. At 512 bytes/sector this means that the total capacity of the disk is 2400 x 512 = 1,228,800 which agrees with the high-density 5.25-inch diskette given in Table 10.1. The media descriptor byte (at offset address 0015H) in Table 10.3 indicates the type of media currently in the disk drive according Table 10.4.

DOS files are allocated disk space in file allocation units called *clusters*. A cluster may consist of one or more (2, 4 or 8) sectors depending on the type of disk. From Table 10.3 we see that the high-density diskette used in the example of Figure 10.2 uses 1 sector per cluster. Each cluster is associated with one entry in the *file allocation table* (FAT) which occupies a number of sectors following the boot sector. From Table 10.3 we see that the FAT uses 7 sectors on the high-density disk of Figure 10.2.

Table 10.3

Boot Sector Information

Offset Address	Description	Size (bytes)	Figure 10.2 Example Hex	Dec
000BH	Bytes/sector	2	0200	512
000DH	Sectors/cluster	1	01	1
000EH	Reserved sectors	2	0001	1
0010H	No. of FATs	1	02	2
0011H	No of root directory entries	2	00E0	224
0013H	Total no. of sectors	2	0960	2400
0015H	Media descriptor byte	1	F9	249
0016H	No. sectors/FAT	2	0007	7
0018H	No. sectors/track	2	000F	15
001AH	No. of heads	2	0002	2
001EH	No. of hidden sectors	2	0000	0

Table 10.4

Media Descriptor Byte

Descriptor	Media Type
0F8H	Fixed disk
0F0H	3.5-inch, 2-sided, 18 sector
0F9H	3.5-inch, 2-sided, 9 sector
0F9H	5.25-inch, 2-sided, 15 sector
0FCH	5.25-inch, 1-sided, 9 sector
0FDH	5.25-inch, 2-sided, 9 sector
0FEH	5.25-inch, 1-sided, 8 sector
0FFH	5.25-inch, 2-sided, 8 sector

Each entry in the FAT consists of 12 bits (fixed disks may have 16-bit FAT entries) containing a link to another FAT entry. This means that every three bytes in the FAT contain two FAT entries. The first two entries in the FAT contain information about the type of disk being used. The remaining bytes in the FAT are initially filled with zeros. When a file is created it is allocated a cluster of disk space and the FAT entry corresponding to this cluster is filled with FFFH (or any value between FF8H and FFFH) indicating it is the last cluster of a file. The FAT entry number is stored in the directory entry for that file. Each directory entry contains the 32 bytes shown in Figure 10.3 The root directory occupies space on the disk following the FAT. From Table 10.3 we see that the high-density 5.25-inch disk contains 224 root directory entries (double-sided, double-density disks contain 112 root directory entries). The size of this directory will therefore be 224 x 32 = 7,168 bytes or 14 sectors. When a file is enlarged it is allocated additional clusters and the FAT entries corresponding to these clusters are linked into the FAT to form a FAT chain. For example, if a file contains three clusters, the first cluster number will be stored at offset 1AH within the file directory entry as shown in Figure 10.3. This first cluster number is also a FAT entry number. The contents of this FAT entry will contain the cluster number of the second cluster in the file which is also the FAT entry number of the next entry in the chain. This second entry will contain the cluster number of the third cluster in the file which points to the third FAT entry in the chain. This third FAT entry will contain FFFH indicating that it is the last cluster in the file.

Bytes	Contents
00H-07H	Filename (E5H in byte 0 means directory entry not used)
08H-0AH	Filename extension
0BH	File attribute
	01H = read only
	02H = hidden file
	04H = system file
	08H = volume label
	10H = subdirectory
	20H = archive bit
0CH-15H	Reserved
16H-17H	Time of last update
	Bits 0-4 2-second increment (binary)
	Bits 5-10 minutes, 0-59 (binary)
	Bits 11-15 hours, 0-23 (binary)
18H-19H	Date of last update
	Bits 0-4 day, 1-31 (binary)
	Bits 5-8 month, 1-12 (binary)
	Bits 9-15 year, 0-119 (1980-2099) (binary)
1AH-1BH	Starting cluster number (points to the logical sector of the start of the file)
1CH-1FH	File size in bytes

Figure 10.3 Format of each directory entry

Subdirectories

The root directory of the high-density disk given in the example in Table 10.3 can contain a maximum of 224 entries. Some of these entries can be subdirectories. When this is the case, the file attribute byte at offset 0BH in the directory entry has bit 4 set to 1. A subdirectory will have a file size of zero and its cluster will contain additional directory entries of the form shown in Figure 10.3. A subdirectory will always contain at least two directory entries. The first has the filename consisting of a single dot (.) (2EH) which refers to the subdirectory itself. The second entry will have the filename consisting of two dots (..) (2EH 2EH) and represents the parent directory.

Subdirectories are only available on versions of DOS of 2.0 and higher. The earlier versions of DOS (1.1) did not allow subdirectories and accessed files using a cumbersome file control block (FCB). This technique has been superseded by a simpler and more general file access method that uses file handles. In this book we will use only the file handle method.

A particular file is specified by an *ASCIIZ string* which is a string containing the pathname followed by a zero byte. You can think of the directory as made up of a tree structure in which the primary filenames are attached to a root directory (designated by a backslash \). Each of these primary filenames can have one or more subdirectories, and these subdirectories can have their own subdirectories. This makes it easy for you to organize all of your files in a logical manner. Figure 10.4 shows a simple example of subdirectories. To access the file *neg2word.asm* on a disk in drive *B* you would specify the pathname with the following ASCIIZ string:

```
'b:\programs\chap11\neg2word.asm',0
```

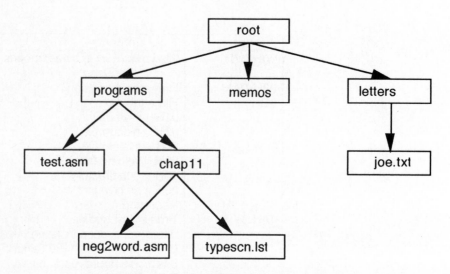

Figure 10.4 An example of subdirectories

To create, or make, the subdirectory *programs* you would go to the root directory and type

```
md programs
```

To change the current directory from the root directory to the subdirectory programs you can type

```
cd programs
```

To remove a subdirectory (the subdirectory must contain no files) you can type

```
rd programs
```

The statement

```
prompt $p$g
```

will cause the prompt to look like this.

```
B:\PROGRAMS >
```

This is useful because it will tell you what subdirectory you are in. If you include this statement in the *autoexec.bat* file in the root directory, then the statement will be executed every time you turn on the computer.

Another statement that should be in your *autoexec.bat* file is the *path* statement that will tell DOS what subdirectories to check when searching for a filename. For example, if you type the statement

```
path c:\;c:\dos;b:\programs
```

then if a file is not found in the current or specified directory, DOS will look for the file in the root directory of drive *C*, the subdirectory \DOS in drive *C* and the subdirectory \PROGRAMS in drive *B*.

The *INT 21H* functions shown in Figure 10.5 can be used to make, remove, and change subdirectories. If an error occurs when calling one of these *INT 21H* functions, the carry flag will be set to 1 and the value in *AX* will contain a standard error code whose meaning is given in Table 10.5. The error codes in Table 10.5 are available in DOS 2.0 and later versions. Additional error codes were introduced with DOS 3.0 and later versions. These extended error codes also provide suggestions for taking corrective action. (See DOS *INT 21H* function call *AH* = 59H).

AH = 39H	*Make directory* Input: DS:DX points to ASCIIZ string Output: AX = standard error codes (3 or 5) (see Figure 10.47) If no errors, carry flag = 0
AH = 3AH	*Remove directory* Input: DS:DX points to ASCIIZ string Output: AX = standard error codes (3 or 5)
AH = 3BH	*Change current directory* Input: DS:DX points to ASCIIZ string Output: AX = standard error codes (3)

Figure 10.5 Subdirectory options using INT 21H

10.2 DISK FILE I/O ROUTINES

DOS provides a series of disk I/O routines that allow you to access files by name without having to worry about where the file is actually stored on the disk. Early versions of DOS (1.1) required that you first set up a *file control block* (FCB) before accessing a file. With the introduction of DOS 2.0 a new method of accessing files using file handles was provided that eliminated the need to set up a FCB. The use of file handles is becoming the standard way of accessing MS DOS disk files and it is the only method that we will consider in this chapter.

In this section we will study a number of the *INT 21H* DOS function calls that are used to access data in a disk file. Using these DOS function calls we will write a number of useful subroutines for handling disk I/O. All of these subroutines are contained in a file called *dos.asm* whose complete source listing is given in Appendix C. This file is on the disk accompanying this book and can be assembled and linked with your own programs.

Table 10.5	
Standard Error Codes	
Error code	Meaning
1	Invalid function number
2	File not found
3	Path not found
4	No handle available: all in use
5	Access denied
6	Invalid handle
7	Memory control blocks destroyed
8	Insufficient memory
9	Invalid memory block address
A	Invalid environment (see DOS SET command)
B	Invalid format
C	Invalid access code
D	Invalid data
E	Not used
F	Invalid drive specification
10	Attempt to remove current directory
11	Not same device
12	No more files to be found

Opening and Closing Files

Before you can read and write data to a disk file you must open the file. If the file does not exist, it must first be created. The functions shown in Figure 10.6 are used to create, open, and close a file. When a file is opened DOS assigns it a *handle* which is just a 16-bit number used to identify the file to other functions. There are five standard handles that are available to every file. These are given in Figure 10.7.

The function $AH = 3CH$ shown in Figure 10.6 will create a new file of zero length with a filename given by the ASCIIZ string at *DS:DX*. If a file with this filename already exists its contents will be lost. On the other hand the function $AH = 3DH$ given in Figure 10.6 will open an existing file whose filename is an ASCIIZ string at *DS:DX*. If a file with this filename does not exist, a *file not found* error (*error code* = 2) will occur.

The subroutine shown in Figure 10.8 will open an existing file or, if the file does not exist, will create a new file. When calling this subroutine *dx* points to an ASCIIZ string in the data segment containing the pathname of the file. After leaving the subroutine the handle of the opened file will be in *bx*. Note that the subroutine first tries to open an existing file using the $AH = 3DH$ function call. If this is successful, the file handle is put in *bx* and the subroutine is exited. On the other hand, if error code 2 occurs (file not found) a new file is created using the $AH = 3CH$ function call. Any other error will produce a call to the subroutine *open_err* shown in Figure 10.9. The error message, *em1*, called in the subroutine in Figure 10.9 is contained in the *dos.asm* data segment shown in Figure 10.10.

The subroutine shown in Figure 10.11 will ask for a filename to be entered (using *query* from the *screen.asm* subroutines) from the keyboard and will then open the file and store the handle in the word variable *handle* in the data segment of Figure 10.10.

The subroutine in Figure 10.12 will close the file whose handle is in *bx* by calling the *AH* = 3EH DOS function call. An error will produce a close-error message by calling the subroutine *close_err* which is similar to the *open_err* subroutine in Figure 10.9 and is given in the *dos.asm* file in Appendix C.

Sometimes you may need to replace an existing file with a new file of the same name. Calling the subroutine *create* shown in Figure 10.13 will create a file of zero length which will allow you to write over old data in a previous file of the same name without having any of the old data still around.

AH = 3CH	*Open/Create file* Input: DS:DX points to ASCIIZ string 　　　CX = file attribute: 　　　　　01H=read only 　　　　　02H=hidden 　　　　　04H=system 　　　　　08H=volume label 　　　　　10H=subdirectory 　　　　　20H=archive Output: AX = file handle 　　　If carry = 1, then 　　　　　AX = standard error codes (3, 4 or 5)
AH = 3DH	*Open file* Input: DS:DX points to ASCIIZ string 　　　AL = access code: 　　　　　0=open for reading 　　　　　1=open for writing 　　　　　2=open for reading and writing Output: AX = file handle 　　　If carry = 1, then 　　　　　AX = standard error codes (2, 4, 5 or C)
AH = 3EH	*Close file handle* Input:　BX = file handle Output: AX = standard error codes (6)

Figure 10.6　Open and Close functions using INT 21H

Handle	Use
0	Standard input (normally keyboard)
1	Standard output (normally screen)
2	Standard error output (always screen)
3	Standard auxiliary device
4	Standard printer

Figure 10.7　Standard handles available to all files

Reading and Writing Data to a File

To read or write to a file or device the functions given in Figure 10.14 are used. You just specify a file handle (given to you when you opened the file), point to the buffer address with *DS:DX*, and store the number of bytes to read or write in *CX*. This is an example of stream-oriented I/O in which a given number of bytes is sent to or read from the file in a serial fashion. The "file" need not be a file on disk but could be a device associated with one of the standard handles in Figure 10.7. For example, a serial I/O port

```
;          open or create file
;          input:  dx -> asciiz string
;          output: bx = handle
open       proc    near
           push    cx
           mov     al,2                          ;read & write
           mov     ah,3dh
           int     21h                           ;open file
           jnc     op2
           cmp     ax,2                          ;if file
           jne     op1                           ; not found
           mov     ah,3ch                        ;create
           mov     cx,0                          ; normal attr
           int     21h                           ; file
           jnc     op2
op1:       call    open_err                      ;error mess
           stc
           jmp     op3
op2:       mov     bx,ax                         ;bx=handle
op3:       pop     cx
           ret
open       endp
```

Figure 10.8 Subroutine to open an existing file or create a new one

```
open_err   proc    near
           push    bx
           push    dx
           push    si
           call    beep
           mov     bx,ax                         ;bx=err code
           mov     dx,1801h                      ;bottom line
           call    setcur
           mov     si,offset em1                 ;print
           call    mess2                         ; error message
           mov     al,bl
           call    pbyte                         ; & error code
           mov     al,'H'
           call    chrprt
           pop     si
           pop     dx
           pop     bx
           ret
open_err   endp
```

Figure 10.9 Subroutine to print a disk open error message

```
data       segment public
handle     dw      ?
bytbuf     db      ?
fnmsg      db      'Enter filename: ',0
em1        db      'Disk open error: ',0
em2        db      'Disk close error: ',0
em3        db      'Disk read error: ',0
em4        db      'Disk write error: ',0
em5        db      'Disk file error: ',0
data       ends
```

Figure 10.10 Data segment used by the *dos.asm* subroutines

```
;           enter filename and open
;           input:  none
;           output: handle is in 'handle'
;                   carry = 1 if not opened
openfn      proc    near
            push    bx
            push    dx
            push    si
            mov     si,offset fnmsg
            call    mess2                       ;display mess
            call    query                       ;enter filename
            cmp     span,0                      ;if no chars
            jne     of0                         ; set carry
            stc                                 ; and quit
            jmp     of1
of0:        mov     dx,offset kbuf
            call    open                        ;open it
            jc      of1                         ;if error,quit
            mov     handle,bx                   ;store handle
of1:        pop     si
            pop     dx
            pop     bx
            ret
openfn      endp
```

Figure 10.11 Subroutine to enter a filename and open the file

```
;           close file
;           input: bx = handle
close       proc    near
            mov     ah,3eh
            int     21h                         ;close file
            jnc     cl1                         ;if error
            call    close_err                   ; print it
            stc
cl1:        ret
close       endp
```

Figure 10.12 Subroutine to close a file

```
;           create file
;           (set length to zero to write over)
;           input:  dx -> asciiz string
;           output: bx = handle
create      proc    near
            push    cx
            mov     ah,3ch                      ;create
            mov     cx,0                        ; normal attr
            int     21h                         ; file
            jnc     ct2
ct1:        call    open_err                    ;error mess
            stc
            jmp     ct3
ct2:        mov     bx,ax                       ;bx=handle
ct3:        pop     cx
            ret
create      endp
```

Figure 10.13 Subroutine to create a new file

AH = 3FH	Read from file or device
	Input: BX = file handle
	        CX = count of bytes to read
	        DS:DX points to buffer to receive data
	Output: AX = actual number of bytes read
	        (AX=0 means end of file read)
	        If carry = 1, then
	                AX = standard error codes (5 or 6)

AH = 40H	Write to file or device
	Input: BX = file handle
	        CX = count of bytes to write
	        DS:DX points to buffer containing data
	Output: AX = actual number of bytes written
	        (must equal CX for no error)
	        If carry = 1, then
	                AX = standard error codes (5 or 6)

AH = 42H	Move file pointer
	Input: BX = file handle
	        CX:DX = offset value (CX is high-order word)
	        AL = method code:
	                0=move pointer to start of file + offset
	                1=increase pointer by offset
	                2=move pointer to end of file + offset
	Output: DX:AX = new value of file pointer
	        If carry = 1, then
	                AX = standard error codes (1 or 6)

Figure 10.14 File read and write options using INT 21H

could be the standard auxiliary device with a handle of 3. The use of a handle makes it easy to redirect data to different files or devices by simply changing the handle value.

The *read* and *write* subroutines shown in Figure 10.15 allow you to read *cx* bytes from a file into a buffer at *DS:DX* and to write *cx* bytes from such a buffer to a file. The *read* subroutine will return a value of zero in *AX* if an *end-of-file mark* was read. This will occur if there are no more data bytes in the file. If an error occurs when using these subroutines an error message similar to the one shown in Figure 10.9 will be written at the bottom of the screen. The subroutines *read_err* and *write_err* are given in the file *dos.asm* in Appendix C.

The subroutine *gtbyte* shown in Figure 10.16 is a useful subroutine that returns the next byte in the file in register *al*. It only needs the file handle in *bx* when the subroutine is called. The subroutine indicates an *end-of-file* condition by setting the carry flag.

The subroutine *sndbyte* shown in Figure 10.17 will write the byte in *al* to a file whose handle is in *bx*. An example of using this subroutine is shown in Figure 10.18 where the subroutine *sndcrlf* will send a carriage return (0DH) and a line feed (0AH) to the disk file.

It is up to you to structure the file in any logical manner you wish. You can position the file pointer (where you begin to read or write) within a file using the *AH* = 42H option given in Figure 10.14. This function call is incorporated in the general subroutine *movptr* shown in Figure 10.19. When calling this subroutine, *bx* contains the file handle, *cx:dx* is a 32-bit offset value and *al* contains the method code. If *al* = 0, the pointer is moved from the start of the file plus the offset. If *al* = 1, the pointer is incremented by the offset from its current location. If $al = 2$, the pointer is moved to the end of the file plus the offset. While this last case may seem useless it actually is useful in finding the length of a file. Because the DOS function $AH = 42H$ returns the new value of the pointer in $dx:ax$ if we set the offset $cx:dx$ to zero before calling the function with $al = 2$, the length of the file will be returned in $dx:ax$. The subroutine *getlen* shown in Figure 10.20 will do this.

```
;            read file
;            input:  bx = handle
;                    cx = # of bytes to read
;                    dx -> buffer address
;            output: ax = # of bytes read
;                    ax = 0 if EOF
read         proc    near
             mov     ah,3fh
             int     21h                          ;read file
             jnc     rd1                          ;if error
             call    read_err                     ; print it
             stc
rd1:         ret
read         endp

;            write file
;            input:  bx = handle
;                    cx = # of bytes to write
;                    dx -> buffer address
write        proc    near
             mov     ah,40h
             int     21h                          ;write file
             jnc     wt1                          ;if error
             call    write_err                    ; print it
             stc
wt1:         ret
write        endp
```

Figure 10.15 Subroutines to read and write file data

```
;            get next byte
;            input:  bx = handle
;            output: al = byte
;                    carry = 1 if EOF
gtbyte       proc    near
             push    cx
             push    dx
             mov     cx,1                          ;read 1 byte
             mov     dx,offset bytbuf
             call    read
             cmp     ax,0                          ;if EOF
             jne     gb1
             stc                                   ; set carry
             jmp     gb2                           ;else
gb1:         mov     al,bytbuf                     ;al=byte
             clc                                   ;clear carry
gb2:         pop     dx
             pop     cx
             ret
gtbyte       endp
```

Figure 10.16 The subroutine *gtbyte* will read the next byte into *al*

```
;           send byte
;           input: bx = handle
;                  al = byte
sndbyte     proc    near
            push    cx
            push    dx
            mov     bytbuf,al                    ;bytbuf=byte
            mov     dx,offset bytbuf
            mov     cx,1                         ;1 byte
            call    write                        ;send it
            pop     dx
            pop     cx
            ret
sndbyte     endp
```

Figure 10.17 The subroutine *sndbyte* will send the byte in *al* to the file whose handle is in *bx*

```
;           send crlf
sndcrlf     proc    near
            mov     al,13                        ;send cr
            call    sndbyte
            mov     al,10                        ;send lf
            call    sndbyte
            ret
sndcrlf     endp
```

Figure 10.18 The subroutine *sndcrlf*

```
;           move pointer
;           input: bx = handle
;                  cx:dx = offset value
;                  al = 0 - start of file + offset
;                       1 - inc ptr by offset
;                       2 - end of file + offset
;           output: dx:ax = new value of ptr
movptr      proc    near
            mov     ah,42h                       ;move ptr
            int     21h
            jnc     mpt1
            call    ptr_err
            stc
mpt1:       ret
movptr      endp
```

Figure 10.19 The subroutine *movptr* is used to move the file pointer

If an error occurs in *movptr* or *getlen* an error message similar to the one shown in Figure 10.9 will be written at the bottom of the screen. The subroutine *ptr_err* is given in the file *dos.asm* in Appendix C.

If you write data to a file, the file pointer will be pointing to the end of the file where any new data will be added. If you want to read the data that you just wrote to the file, you will first need to move the pointer back to the beginning of the file. The subroutine *rewind* shown in Figure 10.21 will do this. Note that it calls the move pointer DOS function $AH = 42H$ in Figure 10.14 with an offset and method code of zero.

```
;          get length of file
;          input:  bx = handle
;          output: dx:ax = length of file
getlen     proc     near
           push     cx
           mov      cx,0
           mov      dx,0                      ;offset=0
           mov      al,2                      ;mov ptr from
           mov      ah,42h                    ; end of file
           int      21h
           jnc      gl1                       ;if error
           call     ptr_err                   ; print it
           stc
gl1:       pop      cx
           ret
getlen     endp
```

Figure 10.20 The subroutine *getlen* will return the length of a file in *dx:ax*

```
;          rewind file
;          input: bx = handle
rewind     proc     near
           push     cx
           push     dx
           mov      cx,0
           mov      dx,0                      ;offset=0
           mov      al,0                      ;mov ptr from
           mov      ah,42h                    ; start of file
           int      21h
           jnc      rw1                       ;if error
           call     ptr_err                   ; print it
           stc
rw1:       pop      dx
           pop      cx
           ret
rewind     endp
```

Figure 10.21 The subroutine *rewind* will move the pointer to the beginning of the file

Finding Directory Entries

Suppose you want to make a list of the filenames in the directory. To do this you can use the DOS *INT 21H* functions shown in Figure 10.22. You must first set up a *disk transfer area* (DTA) in the data segment by setting *DX* to the offset address of the DTA and calling *INT 21H* with *AH* = 1AH. To find the first entry in the root directory of drive C you would have *DX* point to the following ASCIIZ file specification in the data segment:

'C:*.*'

If you wanted to find the first entry in subdirectory *programs* of drive A you would use the file specification

'A:\programs*.*'

Then call *INT 21H* with *AH* = 4EH and *CX* equal to the file attribute given in Figure 10.6. If CX is set to zero then the first ordinary file in the directory will be found and data associated with that file will be stored in the DTA as shown in Figure 10.23. The filename found will be located at offset 30 (1EH) within the DTA in the form of an ASCIIZ string with a period inserted between the filename and the extension. If the file attribute, *CX*, contains the value 10H then both ordinary files and subdirectories will be included in the search.

Once the first match is found (the specification *.* will match all files in the directory) the next match can be found by calling *INT 21H* with *AH* = 4FH. This call will use the same attribute and file specification used in the previous *AH* = 4EH call. Information about the next file will then be found in the DTA. If no more files are found then the carry flag will be set to 1 and *AX* will contain the error code 12H. This test can be used to find all filenames in the directory.

AH = 1AH	*Set disk transfer area address* Input: DS:DX points to disk transfer area (DTA) Output: none

AH = 4EH	*Search directory for first match*
	Input: CX = attribute to use in search
	              DS:DX points to ASCIIZ file specification
	Output: If carry = 0
	                          DTA contains data in Figure 10.23
	              If carry = 1, then
	                          AX = standard error codes (2 or 12H)

AH = 4FH	*Search directory for next match*
	Input: none
	Output: If carry = 0
	                          DTA contains data in Figure 10.23
	              If carry = 1, then
	                          AX = standard error codes (12H)

Figure 10.22 DOS INT 21H functions for finding directory entries

Byte offset within DTA	Contents
0 – 20	reserved for future use
21	attribute of matched file
22 – 23	file time
24 – 25	file date
26 – 27	file size (least significant word)
28 – 29	file size (most significant word)
30 – 42	filename and extension (ASCIIZ string)

Figure 10.23 Contents of disk transfer area (DTA) after finding a directory match

10.3 SAVING THE SCREEN DISPLAY TO DISK

It is sometimes useful to save everything on the screen to disk. To do this we will change the *Print Screen* interrupt so that when you press *Shift Print Screen* the contents of the screen will go to a disk file rather than to the printer. You could then edit this data, move it to another computer and print it out later. Interrupt type number 5 is used for the print screen interrupt service routine as shown in Figure 5.16 in Chapter 5. We will need to replace the interrupt vector stored in the interrupt table by DOS for sending the screen to the printer with the interrupt vector for our own interrupt service routine for sending the screen to a disk file.

To be useful, this interrupt service routine must be in memory all the time so that regardless of what program you are currently running the screen will be sent to disk if you press *Shift Print Screen*. To do this, we must make our interrupt service routine a so-called *Terminate-and-Stay-Resident* (or TSR) program. We do this by using the DOS *INT 21H* function with *AH* = 31H as shown in Figure 10.24. The use of this DOS function is illustrated in Listing 10.2 which is a listing of the file *ss.asm*. This assembled file is linked with the object files *screen.obj* and *dos.obj* to produce the executable file *ss.exe*. When the program *ss* is executed from DOS it will execute the main program shown at the end of Listing 10.2. Notice that this main program is in a separate code segment called *transient_main*. The purpose of the main program is to store the address of the interrupt service routine *snc2fil*, which will write the screen to a disk file, in the interrupt vector table (type 5) and then exit to DOS without releasing the memory associated with the interrupt service routine. Note that the current value of *CS* when this main program is being executed will be the segment address of *transient_main*. We don't need to keep this. The value in *ES* will be the segment address of the program segment prefix which precedes our entire program. Therefore, the value $DX = CS - ES$ will be the number of paragraphs to save which will include all of the segments *code*, *data* and *stack* (including the *code* and *data* segments included in the files *screen.asm* and *dos.asm*). This is because the order of these segments in memory is in alphabetical order as can be seen from the file *ss.map* (created when calling LINK) shown in Figure 10.25.

AH = 31H	*Terminate and stay resident*
	Input: AL = return code
	DX = memory size to save (in paragraphs)

Figure 10.24 DOS INT 21H function for terminating a process without releasing its memory

The interrupt service routine, *scn2fil*, will save the current screen to disk. After saving the video RAM segment address in the variable *vidseg* by calling the *screen.asm* subroutine *stvseg*, the program saves the bottom row of the screen in *tempbuf* using the subroutine *save24*. The user is then asked to enter a filename on this bottom row using the *screen.asm* subroutine *openfn*. The subroutine *get24* then restores the bottom row on the screen.

```
Listing 10.2    ss.asm
        title   Save screen to disk
        ;               Terminate and stay resident
        ;               Use Shift-PrtScn to save screen

        ;       LINK with screen and disk

        data    segment  public
        tempbuf         dw      80 dup(?)
        curpos dw       ?
        data    ends

        ;       screen subroutines
                extrn   setcur:near,rdcurs:near
                extrn   stvseg:near,vidseg:word
```

Listing 10.2   (continued)

```
;        dos subroutines
         extrn   close:near,sndbyte:near
         extrn   openfn:near,handle:word


code     segment  public
         assume cs:code,ds:data


;        interrupt 5 service routine
scn2fil         proc    near
         sti
         push    ax
         push    bx
         push    cx
         push    dx
         push    si
         push    di
         push    es
         push    ds
         assume ds:data
         mov     ax,seg data
         mov     ds,ax
         call    stvseg              ;set vidseg
         call    save24              ;save row 24
         mov     dh,24
         mov     dl,0
         call    setcur
         call    openfn              ;open filename
         call    get24               ;restore row 24
         mov     ax,vidseg           ;save screen
         mov     es,ax
         mov     si,0
         mov     cx,25
         mov     bx,handle
s2f1:    call    sndline             ;send 25 lines
         loop    s2f1
         call    close
         pop     ds
         pop     es
         pop     di
         pop     si
         pop     dx
         pop     cx
         pop     bx
         pop     ax
         iret
scn2fil         endp


;        save row 24 in tempbuf
save24 proc    near
         push    ds
         push    ds
         pop     es
         mov     ax,vidseg
         mov     ds,ax
         mov     di,offset tempbuf
         mov     si,0f00h
         mov     cx,80
         rep movsw
         assume ds:data
         mov     ax,data
         mov     ds,ax
         call    rdcurs
         mov     curpos,dx           ;save curs pos
         pop     ds
```

Listing 10.2 (continued)

```
        ret
save24  endp


;       restore row 24 from tempbuf
get24   proc    near
        mov     ax,vidseg
        mov     es,ax
        mov     si,offset tempbuf
        mov     di,0f00h
        mov     cx,80
        rep movsw
        mov     dx,curpos
        call    setcur
        ret
get24   endp


;       send line of 80 characters from screen
;       inputs:  bx = handle
;                es = vidseg
;                si = offset addr of row to send
;       outputs: si = offset addr of next row
sndline         proc    near
        push    cx
        mov     cx,80                   ;send 80 chars.
sl1:    mov     al,es:[si]
        cmp     al,32                   ;if ascii code
        jb      sl2                     ;is < 20H
        cmp     al,128                  ;or > 7FH
        jb      sl3
sl2:    mov     al,'.'                  ;send a '.'
sl3:    call    sndbyte
        add     si,2
        loop    sl1
        mov     al,13                   ;send crlf
        call    sndbyte
        mov     al,10
        call    sndbyte
        pop     cx
        ret
sndline         endp
code    ends


transient_main          segment para public
        assume  cs:transient_main,ss:stack
main    proc    far
        mov     ax,seg scn2fil          ;set int 5
        mov     ds,ax
        mov     dx,offset scn2fil
        mov     al,5
        mov     ah,25h
        int     21h
        mov     dx,cs                   ;dx=end of resident portion
        mov     ax,es                   ;es = psp segment
        sub     dx,ax                   ;dx=size of resident portion
        mov     ax,3100h                ;terminate and stay resident
        int     21h
main    endp
transient_main          ends


stack   segment para stack
        db      64 dup(?)
stack   ends


        end     main
```

```
Start   Stop    Length  Name                        Class
00000H  00A01H  00A02H  CODE
00A10H  00D0FH  00300H  DATA
00D10H  00D4FH  00040H  STACK
00D50H  00D68H  00019H  TRANSIENT_MAIN

Program entry point at 00D5:0000
```

Figure 10.25 Contents of the file *ss.map*

The *s2f1* loop in Listing 10.2 sends the characters on the screen to the disk by calling the subroutine *sndline* 25 times. The subroutine *sndline*, also given in Listing 10.2, will send a single line of 80 characters to the screen using the *dos.asm* subroutine *sndbyte*.

PROGRAMMING PROBLEMS

Problem 10.1 – Typing Characters to a Disk File
Write a program that will send each line typed on the screen to a disk file. When the program is first run it should ask for a filename to open. When you press the *Enter* key without typing any characters on the line the program should close the file before exiting to DOS.

Write a second program that will read the file containing your data and display the contents on the screen. When the program is run it should ask for a filename to open, read all the data from the disk and display it on the screen, close the file and exit to DOS.

Problem 10.2 – Saving Text Editor Files
a.   Modify the program written in Problem 7.3 in Chapter 7 by adding the capability to read and save disk files. The disk files will consist of 1,024 byte blocks of data each of which will fill the 64 x 16 window on the screen. The first block on the disk will contain data for Screen 1, the second block will contain data for Screen 2, etc. The screen number should be displayed above the window on the screen as shown in Figure 7.42.

When function key *F7* is pressed the program should ask for a filename at the top of the screen and create the file if it does not exist. If the file does exist, the first block of 1,024 bytes of data should be loaded into the text buffer and displayed in the window on the screen where it can be edited.

When function key *F8* is pressed the screen number displayed on the screen should be saved. If no file is open, a new filename should be entered to save the data.

b.   Use the *Page up* and *Page down* cursor keys to display different blocks of data on the screen. The program should increase or decrease the screen number displayed on the screen by one each time the *Page up* or *Page down* cursor keys are pressed. When you press one of these keys the program should save the current screen data and then load the new screen data from disk.

When you press the *ESC* key the program should save the current screen, close the file and exit to DOS.

Problem 10.3 – Disk Directory and File Display

In this problem you will write a program that will display the disk directory and allow you to select a particular file to display on the screen.

Write a program that will display the directory on a disk as a list of up to 15 filenames in a window. When the directory is first displayed, the first filename should be displayed in reverse video; all of the others in normal video. This *reverse video cursor* will be moved from filename to filename by using the *up* and *down* cursor keys plus the *Home* and *End* keys. When you press the *Enter* key the program should print out on the screen the contents of the file whose filename is currently displayed in reverse video. When the file is printed to the screen, have the output pause each time the screen fills up until a key is pressed. Pressing the *ESC* key should take you back to DOS.

Hints:

a. Use a jump table in your main program to handle the cursor keys, the *Home* and *End* keys, and the *Enter* key.

b. Display the directory by searching for all files using a *.* pathname. Use the DOS functions 4EH and 4FH to search for a filename.

c. Keep track of the file number corresponding to the filename displayed in reverse video.

Extra Credit:

Modify the program so as to display subdirectories as well as normal filenames. When you press the *Enter* key with a subdirectory selected the program should display the directory (filenames) of the subdirectory. Any of these files (including additional subdirectories) should be displayed by selecting with the cursor keys and pressing the *Enter* key. When displaying the files in a subdirectory, pressing function key *F1* should bring you back to the next higher directory in the path.

Problem 10.4 – Browsing and Printing Text Files

Write a program that is controlled by a menu display (see Problems 7.1 and 7.2 in Chapter 7). One menu item should select a filename from a menu (see Experiment 34) and display the contents of the file on the screen. Display a screenful at a time and use the *page up* and *page down* cursor keys to scroll through the file.

A second menu item should select a filename from a menu (see Problem 10.3) and print the contents of the file to a printer. Use the standard handle number 4 to redirect the file contents to the printer.

EXERCISES

Exercise 10.1

Modify the program in Listing 10.1 to read the boot sector for a disk in your disk drive. Find the information in Table 10.3 for your disk.

Exercise 10.2

Modify the program in Listing 10.1 to read sector 1 (the first sector of the FAT). The first byte will be the media descriptor byte and the next two bytes will each contain FFH. The next three bytes will contain two 12-bit FAT entries. For example, the three bytes 03 40 00 correspond to the two FAT entries 003 and 004. An FAT entry of FFF indicates the last cluster in a file. Make a list of the cluster numbers for the first file on your disk.

Exercise 10.3

Using the boot sector information for your disk found in Exercise 10.1 find the logical sector number for the first file on your disk. The first file will be located after the FAT and the root directory. The number of sectors per FAT, the number of FATs and the number of root directory entries will tell you how many sectors to skip. (Each directory entry uses 32 bytes so there can be 16 directory entries per sector.) Modify the program in Listing 10.1 to read the sector corresponding to the first cluster of the first file on your disk.

CHAPTER 11

PC Hardware

The user interacts with a personal computer by means of various input/output devices. We have seen how to use the PC keyboard and video screen in Chapters 3 and 7. In Chapter 3 we studied software interrupts. External devices can produce hardware interrupts. When a hardware interrupt occurs the normal execution of a program is suspended and control is transferred to a special part of the program called an interrupt service routine. After executing this interrupt service routine, control returns to the point at which the program was interrupted.

In this chapter we will take a closer look at how the 8086 microprocessor handles interrupts and input/output (I/O) operations. In particular, you will learn:

- How hardware interrupts are generated and processed by the 8086
- How to display a real-time clock on the PC
- The meaning of the 8086 IN and OUT instructions
- The I/O address space associated with the PC
- How to use the parallel printer interface
- How the PC logic analyzer program works
- How to use the IBM PC speaker interface

11.1   INTERRUPTS

The 8086 microprocessor can handle three different types of interrupts -- *reset*, *hardware interrupts*, and *software interrupts*. Software interrupts were described in Chapter 5 and occur when the *INT* instruction (opcode = CC or CD) is executed. In this section we will discuss the reset and hardware interrupts.

Reset

When the *reset* pin on an 8086 goes high, normal microprocessor functions are suspended. When this pin returns low, the microprocessor will set the status register, the instruction pointer, and the segment registers *DS*, *SS*, and *ES* to 0000H. It will set the code segment register to FFFFH. Execution will therefore begin at location FFFF:0000.

The PC has a power-up reset circuit that causes this reset pin to go high and then low after power (5 volts) has been applied to the 8086. Location FFFF:0000 in the BIOS (Basic Input Output System) ROM contains an intersegment JMP instruction to the code in ROM that is executed when the computer is turned on.

The reset routine is executed only in response to power on. Pressing the combination *Ctrl, Alt, Del* keys will (normally) execute the equivalent of a system reset (reboot) without the power-on diagnostics.

Hardware Interrupts

There are two hardware interrupt pins on the 8086 -- INTR and NMI. NMI is a *non-maskable interrupt.* When this pin goes from low to high, the instruction being executed is completed, and the following interrupt sequence takes place:

1. The status register, code segment register (*CS*), and instruction pointer (*IP*) are pushed on the stack (see Figure 11.1).
2. The program jumps to CS_2:IP_2 where the instruction pointer IP_2 is stored in locations 0000:0008 – 0000:0009 and the code segment CS_2 is stored in locations 0000:000A – 0000:000B. Thus a non-maskable interrupt is a Type 2 interrupt. (see Figure 5.16 in Chapter 5).

The address CS_2:IP_2 is called an interrupt vector and you must store this address in the interrupt vector table shown in Figure 5.16. This would be the starting address of your interrupt service routine.

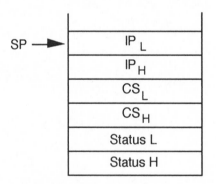

Figure 11.1   Hardware interrupts push the status register, CS, and IP onto the stack

The last statement in an interrupt service routine must be the *IRET* (return from interrupt) instruction (opcode = CF). This statement pops the instruction pointer (first two bytes), the *CS* register (next two bytes), and the status register (next two bytes) off the stack. The program will therefore continue at the point in the program where the interrupt occurred.

Only the instruction pointer, the *CS* register, and the status register are saved on the stack when an interrupt occurs. If your interrupt service routine uses other registers, you must also save these values by pushing them on the stack. At the end of the interrupt service routine, you must *POP* any saved registers off the stack.

The *INTR* pin on the 8086 is used for processing *maskable* hardware interrupts. These interrupts can be masked by clearing the interrupt enable flag, *I*, in the status register to zero. This can be done with the *clear interrupt flag* instruction, *CLI* (opcode = FA). To enable hardware interrupts on the *INTR* pin you must set the interrupt enable flag, *I*, in the status register to 1 by using the instruction *STI* (opcode = FB).

When an enabled *INTR* hardware interrupt occurs, you want a particular interrupt service routine to be executed. You may have several different sources of hardware interrupts, each of which has its own interrupt service routine. This means you will need several different interrupt vectors (*CS:IP* pairs) that point to the starting address of the interrupt service routine. The hardware interrupt vectors are stored in the same interrupt vector table used for software interrupts that is shown in Figure 5.16. This interrupt vector table occupies the first 1024 bytes of memory (in segment 0000).

How does the 8086 know which of the 256 interrupt vectors to use when it receives an *INTR* hardware interrupt? The answer is that the interrupting source must send the interrupt type number on the data bus after the 8086 has acknowledged (via the INTA pin or status lines *S0–S2*) the interrupt. Thus, the device causing the interrupt tells the 8086 where to find the interrupt vector. The 8086 simply multiplies the type number sent on the data bus by 4 to obtain the address of the interrupt vector.

External circuitry is required to generate these interrupt type numbers when hardware interrupts occur. The PC uses a special programmable interrupt controller (PIC) chip (Intel 8259A) for this purpose (see Figure 11.2). It can generate eight different hardware interrupts with type numbers from 8 to F. Some of these eight interrupt numbers are used by the PC, while others are available for the user to use. These are shown in Table 11.1.

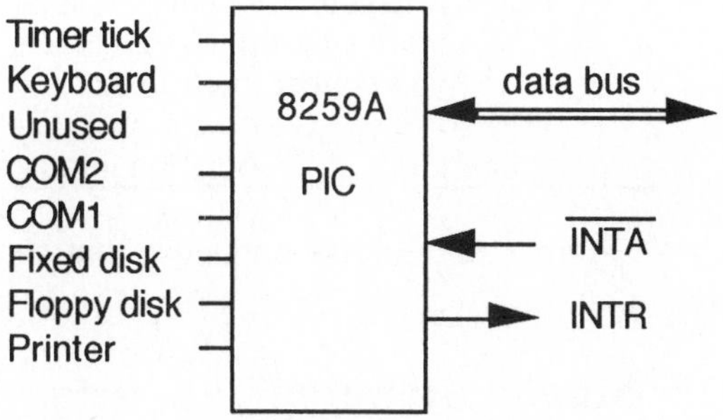

Figure 11.2 The programmable interrupt controller sends one
of eight interrupts to the PC

After an interrupt has been acknowledged and the location of the interrupt vector determined, the interrupt is processed by carrying out the steps shown in Figure 11.3. After pushing the status register onto the stack, the *I*-flag and *T*-flag are cleared to zero. This has the effect of masking interrupts. (The *T*-flag is associated with single-stepping and will be described below.) The instruction pointer, *IP*, and code segment register, *CS*, are also pushed onto the stack so that the program can pick up from where it left off. The stack will look like Figure 11.1. Loading *IP* and *CS* from the interrupt vector table will cause execution to begin at the beginning of the interrupt service routine.

Table 11.1
PC Hardware Interrupts

Interrupt Type No.	Interrupt Vector Hex Offset Address	Name
8	20	Timer Tick
9	24	Keyboard
A	28	Unused
B	2C	Reserved for COM2 Serial I/O
C	30	Reserved for COM1 Serial I/O
D	34	Unused
E	38	Disk I/O
F	3C	Reserved for Printer

When the interrupt service routine executes the *return from interrupt* instruction, *IRET*, it pops *IP*, *CS*, and the *status register* off the stack. These were the values pushed on the stack when the interrupt occurred, so the program will pick up from where it left off. Note that the status register popped from the stack will have the *I*-flag set to 1, because that was its value when the status register was pushed on the stack. It is therefore not necessary to execute the statement *STI* before returning from an interrupt service routine. Sometimes (particularly in software interrupt routines) you may want to enable hardware interrupts while the interrupt service routine is being executed. You would then include the *STI* instruction at the beginning of the interrupt service routine.

---

1. Push the current status register on the stack.
2. Clear the interrupt enable flag, I, and the trap flag, T, in the status register to mask further interrupts.
3. Push IP and CS on the stack.
4. Load IP and CS from the interrupt vector table.

Figure 11.3 Interrupt sequence that causes a jump to an interrupt service routine

Single Stepping

A type 1 interrupt will occur one instruction after the trap flag, *T*, in the status register is set to 1. The *T* flag can be set to 1 by pushing the status register on the stack (perhaps as the result of an interrupt) and ORing the high byte of the status register (in the stack) with 10H. Assuming that *CS* and *IP* have also been pushed on the stack, then an *IRET* instruction will cause the modified status register (with *T* = 1) to be popped from the stack. After one instruction is executed, a type 1 interrupt will occur.

In the TUTOR monitor this interrupt service routine resets the *T*-flag that was just pushed onto the stack to zero. (The 8086 automatically resets the *T*-flag in the actual status register to zero after it pushes it on the stack. Otherwise, you would single step each instruction in the interrupt service routine!) It then displays the current contents of all the registers.

Setting the Interrupt Vector

If you write an interrupt service routine you must store the segment and offset addresses of your interrupt service routine in the interrupt vector table. Before you do this it is a good idea to save the current segment and offset addresses that are at that particular interrupt number location in the interrupt vector table so that you can restore these values before you leave your program. The best way to set the interrupt vector is to use the DOS *INT 21H* functions shown in Figure 11.4. These routines will take care of turning interrupts off while the new values are being stored so that an interrupt won't occur before both the segment address and the offset address have been changed. Otherwise, the system could crash if the interrupt occurred with the wrong segment or offset address.

AH = 35H	*Get Interrupt Vector* Inputs: AL = interrupt number Outputs: ES:BX = segment:offset of current Type AL interrupt handler
AH = 25H	*Set Interrupt Vector* Inputs: AL = interrupt number DS:DX = segment:offset of interrupt handler

Figure 11.4 DOS *INT 21H* functions for getting and setting the interrupt vector

As an example, the code shown in Figure 11.5 will save the interrupt vector currently stored for the type 1CH interrupt and replace it with the interrupt service routine labeled *intser* in the current code segment. We will use this code in the following example of a real-time clock.

```
        push    ds                  ;save ds
        mov     ah,35h              ;save 1Ch int vec
        mov     al,1Ch
        int     21h
        mov     vecseg,es
        mov     vecoff,bx
        push    cs                  ;store int vec
        pop     ds
        mov     dx,offset intser
        mov     ah,25h
        int     21h
        pop     ds                  ;restore ds
```

Figure 11.5 Code to store the interrupt vector in the type 1CH location

Real-time Clock

In this section we will write a program that displays a real-time clock on the screen using the hardware interrupt type 8 (see Table 11.1). The 8253-5 Programmable Interval Timer chip produces a hardware interrupt (type 8) approximately 18.2 times per second. The interrupt service routine for this type 8 interrupt is stored in ROM at the segment and offset addresses stored in the interrupt vector table at address 0000:0020. This interrupt service routine increments a 32-bit counter stored in locations 0040:006C –

0040:006D (low word) and 0040:006E – 0040:006F (high word). The built-in software interrupt, *INT 1AH*, (time of day) allows you to read and set this 32-bit counter as shown in Figure 11.6.

After incrementing the 32-bit counter, the type 8 hardware interrupt checks for a time-out of the disk drive motor and then calls interrupt type 1CH using *INT 1CH*. This is a user-defined interrupt routine that normally contains only an *IRET* instruction (see Figure 5.16). You can write any interrupt service routine you like and store the starting address in locations 0000:0070 – 0000:0073 (vector address for a type 1CH interrupt). Your routine will then be executed on every hardware interrupt (18.2 times per second).

AH = 0	*Read the 32-bit counter clock setting* Output: CX = high word of count DX = low word of count AL = 0 if count has not exceeded 24 hours since last read = 1 if 24 hours has passed
AH = 1	*Set the 32-bit counter clock* Input: CX = high word of count DX = low word of count

Figure 11.6 Time of day options using INT 1AH

We will use the type 1CH interrupt for our interrupt service routine. The algorithm for this interrupt service routine is shown in Figure 11.7. The time will be displayed in reverse video in the upper right-hand corner of the screen in the form

HOURS:MINS:SECS

Since there are 18.2 interrupts per second we will count 18 interrupts before incrementing the SECS. Every 5th second we will use a count of 19 interrupts. This should make the clock gain only about 1.3 seconds/hour.

```
dec count (count is initially set to 18)
if count > 0
then return from interrupt
else inc SECS
   if SECS = 60
   then inc MINS
        reset SECS = 00
        if MINS = 60
        then inc HOURS
             reset MINS = 00
             if HOURS = 13
             then set HOURS = 01
             endif
        endif
   endif
   display time
   set count to 18 (or 19 every 5th time)
endif
```

Figure 11.7 Algorithm for real-time clock interrupt service routine

We will write a main program that reads in and displays the current time, stores the interrupt vector address, and then returns to the TUTOR monitor (using *INT 3*) with the hardware interrupts enabled. The clock should continue to tick along on the screen as you go about using the TUTOR monitor.

We will use the buffered keyboard input subroutine *query* available in our *screen.asm* subroutines (see Chapter 7). The keyboard buffer will start at location *data:kbuf* and after entering the time 10:24:37, the *HOURS*, *MINS*, and *SECS* will be stored in the keyboard buffer as shown in Figure 11.8. The complete real-time clock program is given in Listing 11.1

kbuf	3 1	HOURS
	3 0	
	3 A	:
kbuf + 3	3 2	MINS
	3 4	
	3 A	:
kbuf + 6	3 3	SECS
	3 7	

Figure 11.8 Storing the time 10:24:37 in the keyboard buffer

Note that the data entered from the keyboard in Figure 11.8 is ASCII data. This makes it easy to display this data in the upper right-hand corner of the screen. The eight bytes from *kbuf* are simply stored in the eight even bytes of the video RAM starting at offset address 008C (see Figure 13.6) and the appropriate attribute code (70H for reverse video) is stored in the first eight odd bytes. The subroutine *dsptim* shown at the end of Listing 11.1 will display the time.

The interrupt service routine is given in Listing 11.1 as the routine *intser*. It follows the algorithm given earlier. Note that since the time data is stored in the keyboard buffer in ASCII form it is convenient to use the ASCII adjust addition, *AAA*, instruction (see Chapter 4) when incrementing SECS, MINS, and HOURS.

An executable version of the program shown in Listing 11.1 is stored on your tutor disk under the filename *clock.exe*. You can load this program into TUTOR by typing /SL and then entering the filename *clock.exe*. If you press function key F10 you will note that the main program starts at offset address 0011. Execute the program starting at this location by typing */EG*. After entering the time, the clock should begin working. While it is keeping time you can move around in TUTOR.

To stop the clock you must replace the interrupt vector for the type 1CH interrupt with the values saved in *vecoff* and *vecseg* at the end of the main program. The procedure *clkoff* given at the beginning of Listing 11.1 will do this. Just go to this location by pressing *Home* and execute the code by typing */EG* and the clock will stop. If you don't stop the clock, it will continue to be displayed even when you return to DOS!

Listing 11.1   clock.*asm*

```
title   real-time clock
;       Link with screen

stack   segment para stack
        db      64 dup (?)
stack   ends

        extrn   mess2:near,setcur:near
        extrn   query:near
        extrn   kbuf:byte,blank:near

data    segment public
msg1    db      'Enter current time '
        db      '<hour:min:sec>: ',0
count   db      ?
cnt5    db      ?
vidseg  dw      ?       ;video segment address
vecseg  dw      ?       ;save int vector segment addr
vecoff  dw      ?       ;save int vector offset addr
data    ends
;
code    segment public
        assume  cs:code,ds:data

;       turn clock off
clkoff  proc near
        push    ds                      ;save ds
        mov     dx,vecoff               ;restore old
        mov     ds,vecseg               ; 1Ch int vec
        mov     al,1Ch
        mov     ah,25h
        int     21h
        pop     ds
        int 3
clkoff  endp

;       main program
clock   proc far
        mov     ax,data
        mov     ds,ax                   ;ds=data
        mov     ah,15                   ;get video state
        int     10h
        cmp     al,7                    ;if mode 7
        jne     clk1
        mov     vidseg,0b000h           ;vidseg=b000
        jmp     clk2                    ;else
clk1:   mov     vidseg,0b800h           ;vidseg=b800
clk2:   mov     dh,24                   ;row=24
        call    blank                   ;blank row 24
        mov     dl,0                    ;col=0
        call    setcur                  ;set cursor
        mov     si,offset msg1
        call    mess2                   ;enter
        call    query                   ; starting time
        call    dsptim                  ;display time
        mov     count,18                ;count=18
        mov     cnt5,5                  ;cnt5=5
        push    ds                      ;save ds
        mov     ah,35h                  ;save 1Ch int vec
        mov     al,1Ch
        int     21h
        mov     vecseg,es
        mov     vecoff,bx
        push    cs                      ;store int vec
```

Listing 11.1 (continued)

```
        pop     ds
        mov     dx,offset intser
        mov     ah,25h
        int     21h
        pop     ds                      ;restore ds
        int 3                           ; stay in tutor
clock   endp

;       interrupt service routine
intser  proc near
        push    ax                      ;save regs
        push    cx
        push    si
        push    ds
        mov     ax,data
        mov     ds,ax                   ;ds=data
        dec     count                   ;dec count
        jne     out2                    ;if = 0
        mov     si,offset kbuf          ;point to time
        mov     ax,6[si]                ;ax=secs
        xchg    al,ah
        add     al,1                    ;inc secs
        aaa                             ;ascii adjust
        or      al,30h
        mov     6[si],ah
        mov     7[si],al
        cmp     ax,3630h                ;if secs=60
        jne     out1                    ;then
        mov     word ptr 6[si],3030h    ;  secs=00
        mov     ax,3[si]
        xchg    al,ah
        add     al,1                    ;   inc mins
        aaa
        or      al,30h
        mov     3[si],ah
        mov     4[si],al
        cmp     ax,3630h                ;  if mins=60
        jne     out1                    ;  then
        mov     word ptr 3[si],3030h    ;    mins=00
        mov     ax,[si]
        xchg    al,ah
        add     al,1                    ;    inc hours
        aaa
        or      al,30h
        mov     [si],ah
        mov     1[si],al
        cmp     ax,3133h                ;     if hours=13
        jne     out1                    ;     then
        mov     word ptr [si],3130h     ;        hours=01
out1:   call    dsptim                  ;display time
        mov     count,18                ;count=18
        dec     cnt5                    ;  (or every
        jne     out2                    ;    5th time,
        inc     count                   ;    count=19)
        mov     cnt5,5                  ; reset cnt5=5
out2:   pop     ds                      ;restore regs
        pop     si
        pop     cx
        pop     ax
out3:   iret
intser  endp

;       display time
dsptim  proc near
        push    ax                      ;save regs
```

Listing 11.1   (continued)

```
            push    si
            push    di
            push    cx
            push    es
            mov     ax,vidseg           ;point to video
            mov     es,ax               ; RAM with es
            mov     di,008ch            ;end of 1st row
            mov     cx,8                ;move 8 bytes
            mov     si,offset kbuf      ;point to time
            mov     ah,70h              ;reverse video
            cld
dpt1:       lodsb                       ;load byte
            stosw                       ;store word
            loop    dpt1                ;do 8 times
            pop     es                  ;restore regs
            pop     cx
            pop     di
            pop     si
            pop     ax
            ret
dsptim  endp

code    ends
        end     clock
```

A Delay Subroutine

As mentioned above, a timer tick occurs 18.2 times per second and produces the Type 8 hardware interrupt listed in Table 11.1. The *INT 1AH* time of day software interrupt shown in Figure 11.6 can be used to delay a given number of ticks. The subroutine given in Figure 11.9 will delay *ax* ticks.

```
;           delay
;           input:   ax = no. of ticks to delay
;                    18.2 ticks per second
delay       proc     near
            push     ax                 ;save regs
            push     cx
            push     dx
            push     ax                 ;push #ticks
            mov      ah,0               ;time of day
            int      1Ah                ; interrupt
            push     cx                 ;push hi count
            push     dx                 ;push lo count
            mov      bp,sp              ;bp -> lo count
dly1:       mov      ah,0
            int      1Ah                ;get new count
            sub      dx,[bp]
            sbb      cx,2[bp]           ;calc diff
            cmp      dx,4[bp]           ;repeat until
            jb       dly1               ;diff > #ticks
            add      sp,6               ;fix stack
            pop      dx                 ;restore regs
            pop      cx
            pop      ax
            ret
delay       endp
```

Figure 11.9 A delay subroutine

After calling this subroutine with the number of ticks to delay in register *ax*, the registers *ax*, *cx* and *dx* are saved on the stack. Then *ax* is pushed on the stack again. This is the number of ticks to delay and this value on the stack will be used as a local variable in the subroutine. The 32-bit counter is then read using the *AH* = 0 option in Figure 11.6. The high count and low count that are returned in registers *cx* and *dx* are pushed on the stack and the value of the stack pointer is then stored in register *bp*. At this point the stack will look like that shown in Figure 11.10.

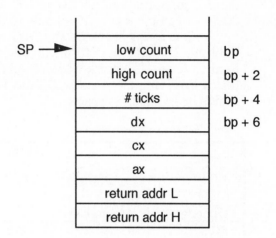

Figure 11.10 Stack contents at instruction labeled dly1 in Figure 11.9

Note that the original low count is stored at [*bp*], the original high count is stored at 2[*bp*] and the number of ticks to delay is stored at 4[*bp*]. These are all local variables that will disappear when we leave the subroutine. The 32-bit counter is then continually read in the *dly1* loop until the new value minus the original value is greater than or equal to the number of ticks to delay. Note that when the loop is exited the stack pointer must be incremented by 6 so as to jump over our three local variables before we pop the three registers from the stack and return from the subroutine.

11.2 IN AND OUT INSTRUCTIONS

As you have seen in previous chapters of this book, the 8086 microprocessor has a large number of instructions that access data in various memory locations. Some memory locations are read-only memory (ROM) and some are read/write memory (RAM).

Personal computers typically access external devices by means of various peripheral interface chips. Some of these are programmable chips that contain various registers. The microprocessor must store data in some of these registers and read data from others. These registers therefore look like memory locations to the microprocessor.

It is possible to connect these peripheral chips in such a way that they occupy the same memory space used by RAM and ROM. This is called *memory-mapped I/O*. The advantage of this method is that all of the instructions that access memory can be used to access the I/O registers. No special instructions are needed to do I/O processing. A disadvantage of memory-mapped I/O is that the I/O devices take up memory space that could otherwise be used for RAM or ROM. Some microprocessors, such as those from Motorola, use memory-mapped I/O exclusively.

The 8086 microprocessor has two special instructions, *IN* and *OUT*, that are used only for I/O operations. When one of these instructions is executed a certain line will go low. This line can be used to ensure that a programmable peripheral chip will respond only to *IN* and *OUT* instructions and not to other memory access instructions. The 16 address lines used to form the normal memory offset address can also be used to form a 64-Kbyte memory space that is devoted entirely to I/O. This means that *in addition* to the 1 Mbyte address space of the 8086 described in Chapter 3, there is an additional 64-Kbyte I/O address space, with addresses from 0000H – FFFFH that respond only to the *IN* and *OUT* instructions.

The forms of the *IN* and *OUT* instructions for the 8086 are given in Table 11.2. The 2-byte forms involving the I/O port number *data8* can be used to access I/O ports with I/O addresses between 00H and FFH. The forms involving the register *DX* can be used to access any I/O port in the 64-Kbyte I/O address space.

Table 11.2

IN and OUT Instructions

Opcode	Mnemonic	Operation
EC	IN AL,DX	Input I/O port [DX] to AL
ED	IN AX,DX	Input I/O ports [DX] and [DX]+1 to AX
E4 *data8*	IN AL,*data8*	Input I/O port *data8* to AL
E5 *data8*	IN AX,*data8*	Input I/O port *data8* and *data8+1* to AX
EE	OUT DX,AL	Output AL to I/O port [DX]
EF	OUT DX,AX	Output AX to I/O port [DX] and [DX]+1
E6 *data8*	OUT *data8*,AL	Output AL to I/O port *data8*
E7 *data8*	OUT *data8*,AX	Output AX to I/O port *data8* and *data8+1*

PC I/O Address Space

The I/O address space used in a typical IBM PC is shown in Table 11.3. Note that the addresses in the lower half of the table (>FFH) can be accessed only by using the *DX* form of the *IN* and *OUT* instructions in Table 11.2.

We will describe the operation of some of the programmable peripheral interface devices listed in Table 11.3 in this and subsequent chapters. We will look at the printer interface in the following section and the speaker interface in Section 11.4. The use of the 6845 CRT controller chip to create Hercules graphics will be discussed in Chapter 12. The 8250 Universal Asynchronous Receiver/Transmitter (UART) and the 8259A Programmable Interrupt Controller (PIC) will be described in Chapter 13 where we will see how to use these chips to program an interrupt-driven serial communications program.

11.3 THE PRINTER INTERFACE

The printer interface is a parallel I/O port. This means that data is sent to the printer a byte (8-bits) at a time. The printer must have a parallel interface capable of receiving this data. Some printers have serial interfaces and they cannot be used with the PC parallel printer interface. Most printers used with personal computers, however, come with parallel interfaces.

Table 11.3	
IBM PC I/O Address Map	

Hex addresses	Device
00 - 0F	8237-2 DMA Controller
20 - 21	8259A Programmable Interrupt Controller
40 - 43	8253-5 Programmable Interval Timer
60 - 63	8255A-5 Programmable Peripheral Interface (PPI)
80 - 83	DMA Page Reg
A0	NMI Mask Reg
200 - 20F	Game I/O Adapter
378 - 37F	Parallel Printer Port
3B0 - 3BF	IBM Monochrome Display (6845) and Parallel Printer Adapter
3D0 - 3DF	Color/Graphics Adapter (6845)
3F0 - 3F7	NEC PD765 Floppy Disk Controller
3F8 - 3FF	8250 Universal Asynchronous Receiver/Transmitter (UART)

To use a printer you must have a parallel printer adapter on a board plugged into one of the peripheral I/O slots in the computer. A parallel printer adapter is often included as part of some other board such as a monochrome display board. The parallel printer adapter will have a 25-pin "D" connector that comes out the back of the computer. The pins on this connector contain the signals shown in Figure 11.11.

To print a character on the printer, the PC puts the ASCII code for the character to be printed on the data pins 2 – 9. It then checks to see that the *BUSY* line (pin 11) is low (that is, the printer is not busy printing the previous character). If the printer is not busy, then the PC pulses the *STROBE* line (pin 1) low then high. When this *STROBE* line goes low, the printer will bring the *BUSY* line high, read the data byte, and print the character. After the character has been printed (or stored in the printer buffer waiting to be printed), the printer will bring the *BUSY* line low indicating that it can receive another data byte. This basic handshake operation is shown in Figure 11.12.

The PC uses three consecutive bytes of I/O memory to communicate with the printer. The I/O address (port number) of the first of these bytes (called *printer_base*) is stored in memory locations 0040:0008 – 0040:0009 for printer number 0. You can use up to four printers and locations 0040:0008 – 0040:000F will store the *printer_base* addresses for the four printers.

Go to memory location 0040:0008 using the TUTOR monitor and see what the *printer_base* address is. If it is 0000H then you have no printer attached. It will be 0378H for the IBM parallel printer adapter and 03BCH for the printer adapter on the IBM monochrome display card.

The three bytes starting at the *printer_base* address have the meanings shown in Figure 11.13. The *data out* port is the I/O port used to store the data byte being sent to the printer. Bit 7 of the *printer status byte* port is used to test for the printer being busy. This bit has the opposite polarity of the *BUSY* signal in Figure 11.12. Thus, the printer will not be busy when bit 7 of the *printer status byte* is high.

Pin No.	Signal	Direction
1	Strobe	Out
2	Data bit 0	Out
3	Data bit 1	Out
4	Data bit 2	Out
5	Data bit 3	Out
6	Data bit 4	Out
7	Data bit 5	Out
8	Data bit 6	Out
9	Data bit 7	Out
10	Acknowledge	In
11	Busy	In
12	Out of paper	In
13	Select	In
14	Auto feed	Out
15	I/O error	In
16	Initialize printer	Out
17	Select in	Out
18–25	Ground	

Figure 11.11 Connector used for the parallel printer interface

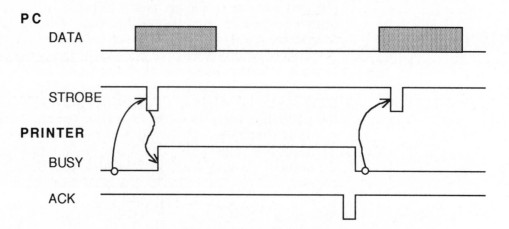

Figure 11.12 Basic handshake used by the parallel printer interface

The *STROBE* signal in Figure 11.12 can be pulsed *low* then *high* by bringing bit 0 in the *printer control byte* port in Figure 11.13 *high* then *low*. This is because bit 0 in the *printer control byte* port has the opposite polarity of the *STROBE* signal in Figure 11.12.

You can initialize the printer by bringing bit 2 of the *printer control byte* port low for at least 50 microseconds. The *acknowledge* signal (pin 10) in Figure 11.11 will pulse *low* then *high* just before the *busy* signal goes low. That is, it pulses low after each character is printed. If the IRQ enable bit (bit 4) in the *printer control byte* port in Figure 11.13 is set to 1 then a type 0FH interrupt (see Table 11.1) will occur on a high to low transition of the *acknowledge* signal (pin 10 in Figure 11.11 or bit 6 in the *printer status byte* port in Figure 11.13). Using the above information you could write your own printer I/O driver routines. The basic algorithm for printing a character is given in Figure 11.14.

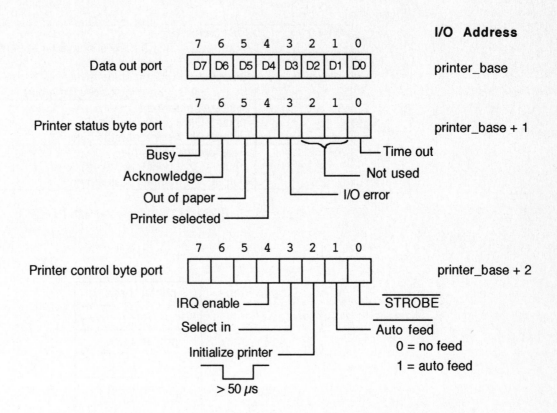

Figure 11.13 The three I/O ports used in the parallel printer interface

```
Store ASCII code of character to be
    printed in data out port.
Wait for bit 7 of the printer status byte
    port (BUSY) to go high.
Bring bit 0 of the printer control byte
    (STROBE) high (1) then low (0).
```

Figure 11.14 Algorithm to send a character to the printer

Alternatively, you can use the built-in BIOS routines which are called using the software interrupt 17H (see Figure 5.16). The options available with these printer I/O routines are given in Figure 11.15. Before calling these routines you must set *DX* to the printer number (0, 1, 2, or 3) of the printer to use. If you have only one printer, use *DX* = 0. The value of *DX* used will select one of four possible *printer_base* addresses from the table at locations 0040:0008 – 0040:000F as shown in Figure 11.16.

As an example of using these printer routines, the program shown in Listing 11.2 will

1. Clear the screen and "home" the cursor
2. Use the buffered keyboard input subroutine *query* to type a line on the screen
3. Print the line just typed on the printer
4. Repeat steps (2) and (3) until only *Enter* is pressed, which will quit the program and return to DOS.

AH = 0	*Print character* Input: AL = ASCII code of character to print DX = printer no. (0 - 3) Output: AH = printer status byte bit 0 = 1 if printer busy (time out)
AH = 1	*Initialize printer port* Input: DX = printer no. (0 - 3) Output: AH = printer status byte
AH = 2	*Read printer status byte* Input: DX = printer no. (0 - 3) Output: AH = printer status byte

Figure 11.15 Printer I/O options used with INT 17H

DX

0040:0008	printer_base 0	0
0040:000A	printer_base 1	1
0040:000C	printer_base 2	2
0040:000E	printer_base 3	3

Figure 11.16 The value of DX will select one of four possible *printer_base* address values for use in the INT 17H printer I/O routines

You can try out this program, which is on your disk. Remember to turn on the printer. If you try to print a character and the printer can't do it within 5 – 15 seconds (depending on the speed of your computer), bit 0 of the *printer status byte* (Figure 11.13) will be set to 1. If this occurs in the program in Listing 11.2 the program will return to DOS. Try this by keeping the ON-LINE button on the printer turned off. After entering the first line on the screen, the program will "hang-up" but will return to DOS following the timeout.

11.4 THE SOUND INTERFACE

Two programmable interface chips, a PPI and an interval timer, are involved in the speaker interface as shown in Figure 11.17. The basic sound signal sent to the speaker amplifier is a square wave produced by the interval timer. The period of the square wave (or pitch of the sound) depends on a 16-bit value stored in the counter register of the interval timer. This counter register (all 16 bits) has the I/O address 0042H. You have to store 8 bits at a time in this register. Whether the byte you store in I/O port 0042H goes to the least significant byte (LSB) or the most significant byte

(MSB) of the counter register depends on how you set up the control register at I/O port 0043H. For the speaker interface you should store the value B6H in the control register. The meanings of the various bits in this value are given in Figure 11.18. The interval timer has three 16-bit counters and a control register. The control register is used to select a particular counter and mode of operation. Six different modes of operation are possible including event counting, one-shot operation, rate generator, square wave generator, and software and hardware triggered strobes.

```
Listing 11.2    prntype.asm
                title type to printer

stack           segment para stack
                db      64 dup(?)
stack           ends

;               screen subroutines
                extrn   crlf:near,quit:near
                extrn   clrscn:near,query:near
                extrn   kbuf:byte,span:word

data            segment public
data            ends

code            segment public
                assume cs:code,ds:data
prntyp          proc far
                mov     ax,data
                mov     ds,ax                   ;ds=data
                call    clrscn                  ;clear screen
                mov     dx,0
                mov     ah,1
                int     17h                     ;init printer
pt1:            call    query                   ;get line of text
                cmp     span,0                  ; typed
                je      pt3                     ;exit to DOS
                mov     cx,span                 ;cx = #char
                mov     dx,0                    ;printer # = 0
                mov     si,offset kbuf          ;point to char
                cld
pt2:            lodsb                           ;al=next char
                mov     ah,0
                int     17h                     ;print char
                test    ah,01h                  ;if time out
                jne     pt3                     ; goto DOS
                loop    pt2
                mov     al,0ah                  ;at end of line
                mov     ah,0
                int     17h                     ;printer cr/lf
                call    crlf                    ;screen cr/lf
                jmp     pt1
pt3:            call    quit                    ;goto DOS
prntyp          endp
code            ends
                end     prntyp
```

In the square wave generator mode used in the speaker interface the output (*CLKOUT 2*) remains high for half the count and low for half the count (even number counts). The counter register is decremented by 2 on each falling edge of the 1.19 MHz *CLOCK IN 2* signal. When the counter register reaches zero it is reloaded with the original count and the state of the *CLKOUT 2* signal is changed.

The counter register can be inhibited from decrementing by means of the *GATE* input. This input must be high for the counter to decrement. As seen in Figure 11.17 this gate input is connected to bit 0 of port B in the 8255A-5 PPI. The PPI is a *programmable parallel interface* chip that contains three 8-bit I/O ports. Bits 0 and 1 of port B (I/O address 0061H) must be set to 1 for the speaker to produce a tone. These bits can be used to turn the speaker on and off.

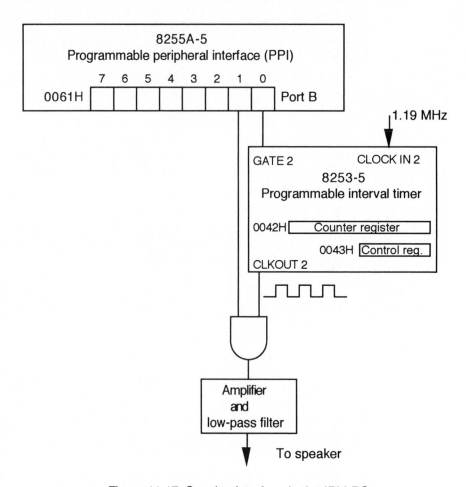

Figure 11.17 Speaker interface in the IBM PC

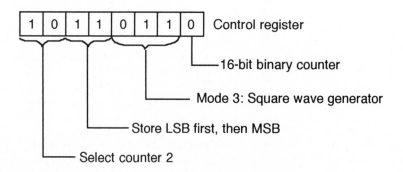

Figure 11.18 Interval timer control register setup used for the speaker interface

The *tone* subroutine included in the *screen.asm* file is given in Figure 11.19 with comments describing the meaning of each instruction. Notice how the *IN* and *OUT* instructions are used to access the control and counter registers in the interval timer and the port B register in the PPI. This subroutine uses the value of *DX* as the pitch (the value stored in the counter register) and the value in *BX* as the length of the tone. The *beep* subroutine, also included in the *screen.asm* file, uses a pitch value of 300h and a tone length of four timer ticks as shown in Figure 11.20.

```
;              make a tone
;              dx = pitch of tone
;              bx = length of tone
tone     proc     near
         push     ax                          ;save regs
         push     bx
         push     cx
         push     dx
         mov      al,0b6h
         out      43h,al                      ;B6 in ctrl reg
         mov      al,dl                       ;LSB pitch ->
         out      42h,al                      ; counter reg
         mov      al,dh                       ;MSB pitch ->
         out      42h,al                      ; counter reg
         in       al,61h                      ;PPI port B
         mov      ah,al                       ; -> AH
         or       al,03h                      ;speaker on
         out      61h,al                      ;set bits 0,1
         push     ax
         mov      ax,bx                        ;delay bx ticks
         call     delay
         pop      ax
         mov      al,ah                       ;speaker off
         out      61h,al
         pop      dx                          ;restore regs
         pop      cx
         pop      bx
         pop      ax
         ret
tone     endp
```

Figure 11.19 The subroutine *tone*

```
;              beep a tone
beep     proc     near
         push     bx
         push     dx
         mov      dx,0300h                    ;set pitch
         mov      bx,4                        ;delay .22 s
         call     tone
         pop      dx
         pop      bx
         ret
beep     endp
```

Figure 11.20 The subroutine *beep*

PROGRAMMING PROBLEMS

Problem 11.1 – Morse Code Generator

In this problem you will write a program to generate and display the Morse code for all of the letters in the alphabet.

The International Morse Code is

```
A .-      E .       I ..      M --      Q --.-     U ..-     Y -.--
B -...    F ..-.    J .---    N -.      R .-.      U ...-    Z --..
C -.-.    G --.     K -.-     O ---     S ...      W .--
D -..     H ....    L .-..    P .--.    T -        X -..-
```

To store the International Morse Code in memory, design a sequential table containing the Morse code for each letter (in order) using the following format:

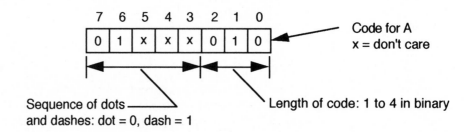

Write an assembly language program for the PC that, for any letter key pressed, will display the letter and corresponding Morse code on the bottom line of the screen in the format shown above, and then sound the Morse code. The program should default to uppercase, ignore non-letter keys and return to DOS when the *ESC* key is pressed.

Use any appropriate subroutines in the file *screen.asm* including the subroutine *tone* to produce the sound of the Morse code.

EXERCISES

Exercise 11.1

Using the TUTOR monitor, find the address in ROM that is executed on power-up. Disassemble the first dozen or so instructions that are executed.

Exercise 11.2

Using the TUTOR monitor, find the address in ROM of the first instruction that is executed when the timer tick hardware interrupt occurs. Disassemble the first dozen or so instructions of this interrupt service routine.

Exercise 11.3

Using the TUTOR monitor, find the address in ROM of the first instruction that is executed when the keyboard hardware interrupt occurs. Disassemble the first dozen or so instructions of this interrupt service routine.

Exercise 11.4

Using the TUTOR monitor, find the address in ROM of the first instruction that is executed when an *INT 21H* DOS function call is made. Disassemble the first dozen or so instructions of this software interrupt service routine.

Exercise 11.5

Using the TUTOR monitor, go to the low byte of the 32-bit timer tick counter at location 0040:006C. Each time you move the position cursor back and forth the value of the counter will be updated. Do this and observe the contents of the counter. Observe the elapsed tick time if you wait 15 seconds between position cursor moves. What should the value be?

Exercise 11.6

Modify the *clock.asm* program (included on the TUTOR disk) so that it will display the clock at the beginning of the second row on the screen. Assemble and link the program with *screen.obj* and run the program from TUTOR.

Exercise 11.7

Write a subroutine called *seconds* that will delay *ax* seconds. How accurate is your delay routine? Make it as accurate as you can.

Exercise 11.8

The *printer_base* address(es) for any printer ports in your computer will be stored in memory starting at address 0040:0008 as shown in Figure 11.16. Examine these memory locations using the TUTOR monitor and find the *printer_base* addresses for all printer ports in your computer. Write a subroutine called *gtport* that will read the *printer_base* address from location 0040:0008 and store the result in the data segment variable *pport*.

Exercise 11.9

The frequencies associated with the musical scale are shown in the following table. Calculate the pitch values to use for *DX* in the tone subroutine in Figure 11.19 for each of the notes. Write a program that will play the major musical scale when you press keys A, S, D, F, G, H, J, K on the keyboard.

Note	Freq. Hz
Middle C	261.6
$C^\#$ D^b	277.2
D	293.7
$D^\#$ E^b	311.1
E	329.6
F	349.2
$F^\#$ G^b	370.0
G	392.0
$G^\#$ A^b	415.3
A	440.0
$A^\#$ B^b	466.2
B	493.9
C	523.3
$C^\#$ D^b	554.4
D	587.3
$D^\#$ E^b	622.3
E	659.3

CHAPTER 12

Graphics

You learned how to display text on the screen in Chapter 7. In this chapter we will look at how to display graphics on the PC. In particular you will learn:

- How to select the CGA, EGA and VGA graphics modes
- How to plot a dot
- How to plot a line
- How the 6845 CRT controller is used to display Hercules graphics
- How to set the Hercules graphics mode
- How to display characters using Hercules graphics

12.1 GRAPHICS MODES

As discussed in Chapter 7, IBM provided two different types of screen display boards, a monochrome display adapter (MDA) and a color graphics adapter (CGA) with its first PC in 1981. The MDA displayed only text on a monochrome monitor. The color graphics adapter could display color graphics on a separate color TV or color monitor. In 1982 Hercules Computer Technology introduced its first graphics card which allowed monochrome graphics to be displayed on the monochrome monitor. We will show you how to do this later in this chapter. In 1984, IBM introduced its *enhanced graphics adapter* (EGA) and later brought out its *video graphics array* (VGA) board both of which provide high resolution color graphics and text.

The graphics modes on the PC are set using *INT 10H* with *AH* = 0 and *AL* set to one of the mode numbers given in Table 12.1. Modes 4, 5 and 6 are the original CGA modes. These modes are also available on the newer EGA and VGA boards. Mode 4 is a medium resolution (320 x 200) mode that supports four colors. Mode 6 has higher resolution (640 x 200) but only two colors (black and white). Note that the video RAM containing this graphic data begins at segment address B800H.

EGA graphics introduced modes 0D, 0E, 0F and 10 which provided more colors (16) and higher resolution (up to 640 x 350). VGA graphics supports these EGA modes plus adds modes 11, 12 and 13 which provide even higher resolution (640 x 480) plus a new medium resolution mode (320 x 200) that can display 256 different colors. Most VGA boards also support some extended VGA modes that can display 132 columns of text and 800 x 600 resolution color graphics with 16 colors. Note that the video RAM for the EGA and VGA graphics modes begins at segment address A000H.

Most high performance graphics programs require writing the graphics data directly to the video RAM to increase speed. We will show how to do this later in the chapter when we describe Hercules graphics. There are *INT 10H* BIOS routines that allow you to set a graphics mode, select colors and read and write dots to the screen. In addition, the character display BIOS functions described in Chapter 7 can be used to write text on the screen when in any of the graphics modes in Table 12.1.

Table 12.1						
Graphics Modes						
Mode	Type	Resolution Col. x Rows	No. of Colors	Video RAM Seg. Addr.	Character Cell Size
4	CGA,EGA,VGA	320 x 200	4	B800	8 x 8
5	CGA,EGA,VGA	320 x 200	4	B800	8 x 8
6	CGA,EGA,VGA	640 x 200	2	B800	8 x 8
0D	EGA,VGA	320 x 200	16	A000	8 x 8
0E	EGA,VGA	640 x 200	16	A000	8 x 8
0F	EGA,VGA	640 x 350	2	A000	8 x 14
10	EGA,VGA	640 x 350	16	A000	8 x 14
11	VGA	640 x 480	2	A000	8 x 16
12	VGA	640 x 480	16	A000	8 x 16
13	VGA	320 x 200	256	A000	8 x 8

The graphics data is stored in the video RAM. In mode 6 there are 640 x 200 = 128,000 picture elements (pixels or pels) displayed on the screen. The information about eight consecutive pixels is stored in a single byte. This means that 128,000/8 = 16,000 bytes of memory are required to contain all of the graphics information. Each plot position on the screen is associated with a single *bit* in one of the memory buffer bytes. A 1 in a bit position will produce a white spot on the screen, while a 0 in a bit position will produce a black spot on the screen. Bit position 7 in each byte is plotted first. The graphics memory buffer for mode 6 is actually divided into two 8000 byte banks. The bank from B800:0000 – B800:1F3F contains data for the even scan lines (0, 2, 4, ..., 198). The bank from B800:2000 - B800:3F3F contains data for the odd scan lines (1, 3, 5, ..., 199).

The CGA graphics mode 4 has 320 x 200 = 64,000 pixels in an image. Its memory buffer still contains 16,000 bytes which means that only four pixels are associated with each byte. That is, each pixel uses two bits in a byte. These two bits are used to encode one of four possible colors to be plotted. If the two bits are 00, it means the background color is to be plotted. The background can be one of 16 different colors and the other 3 colors can be selected from one of two color palettes.

The background color and the color palette selection can be done using *INT 10H* with *AH* = 11 (0BH) as shown in Figure 12.1. Note that one of 16 background colors can be selected using *BH* = 0. Setting *BH* = 1 selects one of two possible color palettes depending upon the value in *BL*. For color palette 0, the three possible foreground pixel colors are green, red, and yellow. For color palette 1, the three possible foreground pixel colors are cyan, magenta, and white.

The program shown in Listing 12.1 will switch to graphics mode 4 and display the background as black. Each time you press the space bar the background will cycle through all 16 colors shown in Figure 12.1. Pressing any other key will return to the text mode and to DOS. This program is included on the TUTOR disk. Alternatively, you can just enter the machine code shown in Listing 12.1 using TUTOR and execute the program from there.

The VGA mode 13 is a medium resolution graphics mode that can display 256 colors. In this mode the graphics data is stored as one byte per pixel where the byte contains one of 256 possible color values. The other EGA and VGA graphics modes store data for eight pixels in each byte — i.e. one bit per pixel. The way they are able to represent up to 16 different colors is to use up to four bit-planes where a given bit (or byte) in each plane can be at the same address but can store different color data. Special map mask and latch registers are used write different colors to different pixel locations.

AH = 11 (0BH)	Select background color and palette
	Input: BH = 0 Select background color
	BL = background color (bits 0 – 3)
	BH = 1 Select palette
	BL = 0 palette 0
	BL = 1 palette 1

Background Colors		Color Palettes		
		Color No.	Palette 0	Palette 1
0 0 0 0	Black	1	green	cyan
0 0 0 1	Blue	2	red	magenta
0 0 1 0	Green	3	yellow	white
0 0 1 1	Cyan			
0 1 0 0	Red			
0 1 0 1	Magenta			
0 1 1 0	Brown			
0 1 1 1	Light gray			
1 0 0 0	Dark gray			
1 0 0 1	Light blue			
1 0 1 0	Light green			
1 0 1 1	Light cyan			
1 1 0 0	Light red			
1 1 0 1	Light magenta			
1 1 1 0	Yellow			
1 1 1 1	White			

Figure 12.1 Color options for CGA mode 4 using *INT 10H*

```
          Listing 12.1      colorb.lst
                     title    CGA color background
0000                 stack    segment para stack
0000       40 [               db      64 dup(?)
           ??  ]
0040                 stack    ends

0000                 code     segment public
                     assume   cs:code
0000                 main     proc    far
0000   B4 0F                  mov     ah,15        ;get video mode
0002   CD 10                  int     10h
0004   50                     push    ax           ;and save it
0005   B4 00                  mov     ah,0
0007   B0 04                  mov     al,4         ;switch to
0009   CD 10                  int     10h          ;graphics mode 4
000B   BB 0000                mov     bx,0         ;start with black
000E   B4 0B        again:    mov     ah,0bh       ;change
0010   CD 10                  int     10h          ;background color
0012   B4 00                  mov     ah,0
0014   CD 16                  int     16h          ;wait for key
0016   3C 20                  cmp     al,20h       ;if space bar
0018   75 04                  jne     done         ;then inc
001A   FE C3                  inc     bl           ;background color
001C   EB F0                  jmp     again        ;& change again
001E   58           done:     pop     ax           ;get text mode
001F   B4 00                  mov     ah,0         ;and reset it
0021   CD 10                  int     10h
0023   B8 4C00                mov     ax,4c00h     ;quit to DOS
0026   CD 21                  int     21h
0028                 main     endp
0028                 code     ends
                     end      main
```

12.2 PLOTTING A DOT

To plot a dot on the screen you can use $AH = 12$ (0CH) with *INT 10H* as given in Figure 12.2. The row number (0 – 199, 0 – 349 or 0 – 479) and column number (0 – 319 or 0 – 639) are stored in registers *DX* and *CX* respectively. The color value is stored in *AL*. The EGA/VGA modes 0D, 0E, 0F and 10 contain 8, 4, 2 and 2 pages of memory respectively. This means that separate graphic images can be stored simultaneously on these different pages. When plotting a dot in these modes you must set *BH* to this page number. If you are using only one page, this will be zero.

If bit 7 of *AL* is set to 1 when a dot is plotted, the color value in *AL* will be exclusive ORed with the color value of the current dot. For example, suppose a red dot (color value = 2) is plotted on the screen. If you plot another red dot on top of it, with bit 7 in *AL* set to 1, the actual dot plotted will be 2 *XOR* 2 (10 XOR 10 = 00) or 0. This will plot the background color, or erase the red dot.

The program shown in Listing 12.2 will fill the screen with a series of vertical lines (by plotting a dot in each row of a column) using all 16 colors in the EGA/VGA mode 0Dh. The result will be a set of vertical bands of colors. After plotting all of the vertical lines, the program will wait for you to press any key before returning to the text mode and to DOS. Running this program will give you a good idea of how long it takes to plot dots using these BIOS routines. This program is included on the TUTOR disk. Alternatively, you can just enter the machine code shown in Listing 12.2 using TUTOR and execute the program from there. You can easily modify this program to use different graphics modes with different resolutions. (See the exercises at the end of the chapter.)

AH = 12 (0CH)	Write dot Input: DX = row number CX = column number BH = page no. (EGA and VGA only) AL = color number If bit 7 of AL equals 1, the color value is exclusive OR'd with the color value of the current dot. If both color values are the same, the dot will be erased.
AH = 13 (0DH)	Read dot Input: DX = row number CX = column number BH = page no. (EGA and VGA only) Output: AL = color value of dot read

Figure 12.2 Reading and writing a graphics dot using INT 10H

12.3   LINE DRAWING ROUTINE

The built-in graphics routines associated with *INT 10H* do not include a routine for plotting a line. Suppose you want to plot a straight line from one point on the screen to another. You can plot a straight line by plotting a series of dots between the two points. But how do you know where to plot the dots? You could calculate the slope of the line and use this value to calculate the location of each point. Efficient algorithms involving only addition and subtraction have been developed for this purpose.[1] An alternate approach is described by Beetem in the October 1980 issue of *Byte* magazine.[2]

The basic idea of the Beetem approach is to calculate the midpoint between the two endpoints of the line as shown in Figure 12.3. This operation requires only one addition and a divide by 2 (*SHR,1*) for each component (*x* and *y*). If the midpoint (*mid.x*, *mid.y*) does not coincide with the origin (*x1,y1*) then the midpoint becomes the new endpoint and the new half-length line segment is bisected again to form a new midpoint. This process is continued until the midpoint falls on the origin (this will happen using integer arithmetic) and then the origin is plotted. As this subdivision process takes place, the midpoints and endpoints are saved by pushing them on the stack. After each new origin is plotted, a new origin and endpoint are popped from the stack and the process continues until all points along the line have been plotted.

A pseudocode version of the algorithm for plotting this line is given in Figure 12.4. For the algorithm to work the *orig* must always be to the left of the *endp*. If it isn't, the algorithm automatically interchanges them at the beginning. When computing the midpoint, it is necessary to ensure that the values of *mid.x* and *mid.y* are truncated to the *orig* side of *midp*. Since *orig* is always to the left of *endp*, this will be the case for *mid.x*. If *orig.y*

[1] See, for example, Bresenham, J.E., "Algorithm for computer control of a digital plotter," *IBM Systems J.* 4, pp 25-30, (1965).

[2] Beetem, J., "Vector graphics for raster displays," *Byte*, 5, pp 286-293, Oct. 1980.

< *endp.y* then *mid.y* is truncated; otherwise, *mid.y* is rounded. This is easy to test by checking the carry flag after dividing by 2 (shifting right) when calculating *mid.y*.

```
        Listing  12.2        colors.lst
                             title   Color graphics
0000                         stack   segment para stack
0000     40 [                db      64 dup(?)
              ?? ]
0040                         stack   ends

0000                         code    segment         public
                                     assume  cs:code
0000                         main    proc    far
0000     B4 0F                       mov     ah,15           ;get video mode
0002     CD 10                       int     10h
0004     50                          push    ax              ;and save it
0005     B4 00                       mov     ah,0
0007     B0 0D                       mov     al,0Dh          ;switch to
0009     CD 10                       int     10h             ;graphics mode 0D
000B     B7 00                       mov     bh,0            ;page 0
000D     B9 013F                     mov     cx,319          ;cx = col no.
0010     B0 0F                       mov     al,15           ;al - color no.
0012     BA 00C7          mn1:        mov     dx,199          ;dx = row no.
0015     B4 0C           mn2:        mov     ah,0ch
0017     CD 10                       int     10h             ;plot dot
0019     4A                          dec     dx
001A     79 F9                       jns     mn2             ;plot 1 col
001C     FE C8                       dec     al              ;change color
001E     79 02                       jns     mn3             ;if < 0
0020     B0 0F                       mov     al,15           ;reset to 15
0022     E2 EE           mn3:        loop    mn1             ;do all cols.
0024     B4 00                       mov     ah,0
0026     CD 16                       int     16h             ;wait for key
0028     58                          pop     ax              ;get text mode
0029     B4 00                       mov     ah,0            ;and reset it
002B     CD 10                       int     10h
002D     B8 4C00                     mov     ax,4c00h        ;quit to DOS
0030     CD 21                       int     21h
0032                         main    endp
0032                         code    ends
                                     end     main
```

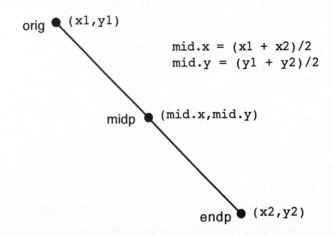

$$mid.x = (x1 + x2)/2$$
$$mid.y = (y1 + y2)/2$$

Figure 12.3 Calculating the midpoint of a line segment

```
save registers
if orig.x > endp.x
then interchange orig and endp
push endp
push endp
loop: compute midp
          if midp = orig
          then  plot orig
                pop orig
                pop endp
          else  push endp
                push midp
                endp = midp
repeat until stack is empty
plot orig
restore registers
```

Figure 12.4 Algorithm for plotting a straight line in Figure 12.3 from x1,y1 to x2,y2

An 8086 implementation of this algorithm is given in Listing 12.3. To use this subroutine, the values of *x1*, *y1*, *x2*, and *y2* are stored in registers *CX*, *DX*, *AX*, and *BX* respectively. The subroutine *plot* called by *line* in Listing 12.3 must be a subroutine that plots a dot at $x = DX$, $y = CX$. For example, the subroutine *plot* given at the end of Listing 12.3 will plot a white dot ($AL = 3$) in graphics mode 6. These line and plot subroutines are given in the file *plotline.asm* that is included on the TUTOR disk and can be linked with your own programs.

```
Listing  12.3  plotline.asm
        title   plot line subroutine
;       inputs: ax = x2 = endp.x
;               bx = y2 = endp.y
;               cx = x1 = orig.x
;               dx = y1 = orig.y
        public line
code    segment public
        assume cs:code

;       plot line
line    proc near
        push    ax                      ;save registers
        push    bx
        push    cx
        push    dx
        push    si
        push    di
        push    bp
        push    ax                      ;make space for yflg
        mov     bp,sp                   ;bp=initial sp
        mov     byte ptr 1[bp],0        ;yflg=0
        cmp     cx,ax                   ;if orig.x1>orig.x2
        jb      la                      ;then interchange
        xchg    cx,ax                   ;orig and endp
        xchg    dx,bx
la:     cmp     bx,dx                   ;if bx<dx then set
        ja      lb                      ; yflg=80h
        mov     byte ptr 1[bp],80h
lb:     push    ax                      ;push endp:x
        push    bx                      ;push endp:y
        push    ax                      ;push endp:x
        push    bx                      ;push endp:y
```

Listing 12.3   (continued)

```
        ln1:    mov     si,cx                   ;compute midp.x
                add     si,ax
                shr     si,1                    ;si=(x1+x2)/2
                mov     di,dx                   ;compute midp.y
                add     di,bx
                shr     di,1                    ;di=(y1+y2)/2
                jnb     ln2                     ;if carry set
                cmp     byte ptr 1[bp],0
                je      ln2                     ;then if yflg set
                inc     di                      ;round midp.y
        ln2:    cmp     si,cx                   ;if midp=orig
                jne     ln3
                cmp     di,dx
                jne     ln3                     ;then
                call    plot                    ;plot orig
                pop     dx                      ;pop orig.y
                pop     cx                      ;         .x
                pop     bx                      ;pop endp.y
                pop     ax                      ;         .x
                jmp     ln4
        ln3:    push    ax                      ;push endp.x
                push    bx                      ;          .y
                push    si                      ;push midp.x
                push    di                      ;          .y
                mov     ax,si
                mov     bx,di
        ln4:    cmp     bp,sp
                jne     ln1
                call    plot                    ;plot orig
        ln5:    pop     ax                      ;restore yflg
                pop     bp                      ;restore regs
                pop     di
                pop     si
                pop     dx
                pop     cx
                pop     bx
                pop     ax
                ret
        line    endp

        ;       plot point at x=dx, y=cx
        plot    proc near
                push    ax
                mov     ax,0c03h                ;color=white
                int     10h                     ;write dot
                pop     ax
                ret
        plot    endp
        code    ends
                end
```

As an example of using this line plotting subroutine, suppose you want to plot the star shown in Figure 12.5. Store the number of lines to plot (5) followed by the *x,y* pairs of each vertex in a data segment as shown at the beginning of the program in Listing 12.4. In the main program to plot the star given in Listing 12.4, register *SI* points to the beginning of the memory buffer containing the vertex data and is incremented by 4 (2 words per vertex) after each line is plotted.

The line subroutine given in Listing 12.3 and the program to plot the star given in Listing 12.4 can be assembled separately and then linked. It is clear that the program in Listing 12.4 can be used to plot any figure whose vertices can be pre-stored in memory.

Listing 12.4 *star.asm*

```
            title   star
stack    segment          para stack
            db      64 dup(?)
stack    ends

data     segment
points   dw      05                      ;no. of lines
            dw      101,191                 ;x1,y1
            dw      160,10                  ;x2,y2
            dw      219,191                 ;x3,y3
            dw      65,79                   ;x4,y4
            dw      255,79                  ;x5,y5
            dw      101,191                 ;x1,y1
data     ends

            extrn   line:near

code     segment public
            assume  cs:code,ds:data

;           plot star
star     proc far
            mov     ax,data
            mov     ds,ax                   ;ds=data
            mov     ah,15                   ;get video mode
            int     10h
            push    ax                      ;and save it
            mov     ax,0004h                ;switch to med-res
            int     10h                     ;    graphics
            mov     ah,0bh
            mov     bx,0101h
            int     10h                     ;select palette 1
            mov     bx,0
            mov     ah,0bh
            int     10h                     ;background black
            mov     si,offset points        ;star data
            mov     bp,[si]                 ;bp=# of lines to plot
            add     si,2                    ;point to first point
st1:        mov     cx,[si]                 ;cx=orig.x
            mov     dx,2[si]                ;dx=orig.y
            mov     ax,4[si]                ;ax=endp.x
            mov     bx,6[si]                ;bx=endp.y
            call    line                    ;plot next line
            add     si,4                    ;point to next point
            dec     bp                      ;if more lines
            jne     st1                     ;keep going
            mov     ah,0
            int     16h                     ;wait for key
            pop     ax                      ;get text mode
            mov     ah,0                    ;& switch to it
            int     10h
            mov     ax,4c00h                ;return to DOS
            int     21h
star     endp
code     ends
            end     star
```

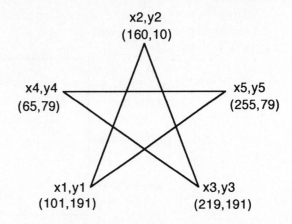

Figure 12.5 To plot the star store the coordinates of the vertices
in a data segment in memory

12.4   THE MC6845 CRT CONTROLLER

Figure 7.2 in Chapter 7 illustrated how a raster scan display works. We
saw that the ASCII codes of the characters displayed on the screen are
stored in a video RAM and continuously cycled to a character generator.
This character generator has a set of row-select inputs in addition to the
character ASCII code and outputs the bit pattern corresponding to the
selected row in the character. This output goes to a shift register which
becomes the video signal to the monitor. Graphics displays work in a
similar manner except the character generator is bypassed. That is, the bit
pattern for each row of 8 dots on the screen must be stored in a byte in the
video RAM. This means that the video RAM for graphics must be much
larger than that for text.

Implementing the raster scan process shown in Figure 7.2 requires
critical timing to read the ASCII codes and generate the proper row select
signals at just the right time. This function is performed by a CRT (Cathode
Ray Tube) controller chip. The original IBM PC used the Motorola
MC6845 CRT controller chip (CRTC) for this purpose. This chip is also
used to display Hercules graphics on a monochrome monitor. We will
show how this is done in the next section. In this section we will describe
the basic function of the MC6845 CRTC and show how it is configured for
monochrome text display. EGA and VGA display boards use special
graphics display chips with many additional features. However, they also
include registers which replicate the functions of the MC6845 CRTC
described in this section.

The MC6845 CRTC is a 40-pin chip whose principal signals are
shown in Figure 12.6. The data sheet for the MC6845 is included in
Appendix E. The MC6845 communicates with the host microprocessor
over the 8-bit data bus shown in Figure 12.6. The register select signal *RS*
shown in Figure 12.6 is connected to address line A0. This means that the
MC6845 CRTC looks like two consecutive memory locations to the host
processor. In the Hercules graphics examples we will present, these two
memory locations are the addresses 03B4H and 03B5H in the I/O space
(read and written to with the *IN* and *OUT* instructions). The MC6845
actually contains 18 internal registers. An indirect addressing scheme is
used to address these 18 registers with only two different external
addresses. The first address (03B4H) is used to store the register number
selected (0 – 17) and then the data to read or write to that register is read

from or stored in the second address (03B5H). This process will be illustrated in the next section.

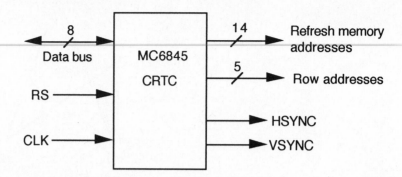

Figure 12.6 Principal signals associated with the MC6845 CRT controller

The CLK input signal to the MC6945 CRTC is a *character* clock signal whose period, T_c, is equal to the time it takes to display one row of dots in a character. For a monochrome display with a 9 x 14 character cell, this will be the time to display 9 dots. This character time, T_c, for a monochrome display is 553 ns (553×10^{-9} seconds) corresponding to a dot frequency of $(9/0.553) = 16.27$ MHz.

The 14 refresh memory address lines shown in Figure 12.6 are used to address up to $2^{14} = 16$ Kbytes of video RAM memory. The 5 row address lines shown in Figure 12.6 are used to select up to $2^5 = 32$ row select lines on a character generator. The HSYNC and VSYNC signals are the horizontal and vertical sync signals that are generated by the MC6845 CRTC and used by the video monitor to control the horizontal and vertical scan times.

The MC6845 CRTC is a programmable device in which the user can select such things as the number of characters per row, the number of rows displayed on the screen and the cell size of the characters. To program the MC6845 for the monochrome text mode (80 characters x 25 rows) we can store the values shown in Table 12.2 in the first 16 registers in the MC6845 (the last two registers are used to read a light pen location). The meanings of most of these registers are shown in Figure 12.7. The first four registers, *R0 – R3*, control the horizontal timing. The values stored in these registers are multiples of the character time, T_c. The number of characters displayed on a line is stored in *R1*. The total horizontal scan time (including the horizontal retrace) is *R0* + 1. In Figure 12.7 this corresponds to a time of 98 x .553 μs = 54.2 μs. The position and width of the horizontal sync signal shown in Figure 12.7 are controlled by registers *R2* and *R3* respectively.

The vertical scan timing is controlled by registers *R4 – R7*. The number of rows of characters to display on the screen is stored in register *R6*. The total vertical scan time (including the vertical retrace) is given by *(R4 + 1) rows + R5 scan lines*. This vertical scan time normally corresponds to a vertical scan frequency of 60 Hz (cycles per second) or 50 Hz. The monochrome display uses a vertical scan frequency of 50 Hz. The value stored in register *R5* is the number of horizontal scan lines needed to make the total vertical scan time as close to 1/50 second as possible. The position of the vertical sync pulse is stored in register *R7*. Its width is constant and equal to 16 horizontal scan lines.

Table 12.2			
CRTC Register Values for Monochrome Text Mode			
Reg. #	Register Name	Programmed Value Decimal	Hex
R0	H. Total	97	61H
R1	H. Displayed	80	50H
R2	H. Sync Position	82	52H
R3	H. Sync Width	15	0FH
R4	V. Total	25	19H
R5	V. Scan Line Adjust	6	06H
R6	V. Displayed	25	19H
R7	V. Sync Position	25	19H
R8	Interlace Mode	2	02H
R9	Max. Scan Line Address	13	0DH
R10	Cursor Start	11	0BH
R11	Cursor End	12	0CH
R12	Start Address (H)	0	00H
R13	Start Address (L)	0	00H
R14	Cursor (H)	0	00H
R15	Cursor (L)	0	00H

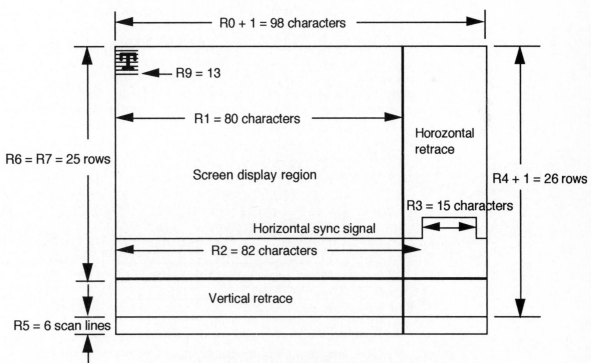

Figure 12.7 Meanings of MC6845 CRT controller registers

The other register value shown in Figure 12.7 is *R9*, which is the maximum scan line address for a given character cell. For a monochrome display with a 9 x 14 character cell, the row addresses for each character are numbered 0 – 13. This last row number is the one that is stored in register *R9*. Register *R8* is an interlace mode and the value of 2 given in Table 12.2 corresponds to normal interlace (see the data sheet in Appendix E). The cursor start and cursor end values stored in registers *R10* and *R11* define the shape of the cursor. The values 11 and 12 given in Table 12.2 mean that the cursor will be an underline starting in row 11 of the character cell and ending in row 12. The address within the video RAM (as addressed by the refresh memory addresses of the MC6845 CRTC) corresponding to the upper left-hand corner of the screen is stored in registers *R12* and *R13*. The initial location of the cursor within the video RAM is stored in registers *R14* and *R15*. The value of zero means that the cursor will be in the upper right-hand corner of the screen (corresponding to address 0000 in the video RAM).

The process of setting the monochrome text mode (by calling *INT 10H* with *AH* = 0 and *AL* = 7) will include writing the values shown in Table 12.2 to the MC6845 CRTC registers. In the next section we will show how a Hercules graphics display can be produced by changing the values of the MC6845 CRTC registers.

12.5 HERCULES GRAPHICS ROUTINES

In this section we will show you how to set the Hercules graphics mode (by programming the MC6845 CRTC) and to write subroutines to plot and erase dots, draw lines and display characters on the screen. The resolution of a Hercules graphics screen is 720 x 348 as shown in Figure 12.8. The 720 dots on a given row are stored in 90 consecutive bytes of memory (90 x 8 = 720) as shown in Figure 12.8. This means that the video RAM must contain 90 x 348 = 31,320 bytes. This is almost 32 Kbytes of memory which will require 15 address lines (2^{15} = 32,768). But note from Figure 12.6 that the MC6845 CRTC has only 14 refresh memory address lines. The solution to this problem is to use some of the five row address lines as video RAM address lines inasmuch as we are no longer using a character generator. Hercules graphics uses the first 13 address lines from the refresh address lines in Figure 12.6 for the video RAM address lines *A0 – A12*. The first two row address lines in Figure 12.6 are then connected to the video RAM address lines *A13* and *A14*. The resulting memory map is shown in Figure 12.9.

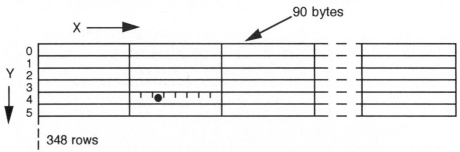

Figure 12.8 Video display layout for Hercules graphics

RA1	RA0			Refresh	Memory	Addresses									
A15	A14	A13	A12	A11	A10	A9	A8	A7	A6	A5	A4	A3	A2	A1	A0	Address range
0	0	0	X	X	X	X	X	X	X	X	X	X	X	X	X	0000 - 1FFF
0	0	1	X	X	X	X	X	X	X	X	X	X	X	X	X	2000 - 3FFF
0	1	0	X	X	X	X	X	X	X	X	X	X	X	X	X	4000 - 5FFF
0	1	1	X	X	X	X	X	X	X	X	X	X	X	X	X	6000 - 7FFF

Figure 12.9 Memory map associated with Hercules graphics

Note that as the row address lines *RA1* and *RA0* (connected to address lines *A14* and *A13*) take on the values 00, 01, 10 and 11 the resulting video RAM address increases by 0000H, 2000H, 4000H and 6000H as shown in Figure 12.9. Using two row address lines is like having a character generator with characters that are four scan lines high. Recalling how a raster scan display works, this means that the row address lines *RA1* and *RA0* will be incremented through the values 00, 01, 10 and 11 on four consecutive scan lines on the screen. Therefore, the video RAM addresses of the first byte of the first four scan lines will be 0000H, 2000H, 4000H and 6000H. The 90 bytes in row number 0 will have addresses, 0000H – 0059H. The 90 bytes in row number 1 will have addresses, 2000H – 2059H. Row number 4 (the fifth line on the screen) will begin with video RAM address 005AH. In general, the video RAM address of the first byte in row *Y* is given by

```
first.byte.address =
          [2000H * (Y MOD 4)] + [90 * INT(Y/40)]     (12.1)
```

For speed we will compute these first byte addresses for all 348 rows and store them in a table called *row_table*. This can be done automatically when you assemble a program by including the macro shown in Figure 12.10. This macro is included in the file *graph.asm* which contains all of the Hercules graphics subroutines described in this section. A listing of the file *graph.asm* is included in Appendix C.

```
        row_table  label   word                    ;define row add
        line_num = 0
        rept 87                                     ;348/4
            dw  line_num * 90
            dw  2000h + line_num * 90
            dw  4000h + line_num * 90
            dw  6000h + line_num * 90
            line_num = line_num + 1                 ;next row
        endm
```

Figure 12.10 Macro used to build a table containing the address
of the first byte in each row

Inasmuch as each of the 90 bytes in a row contains 8 bits corresponding to 8 consecutive dots on the screen, a dot located at position (*X,Y*) on the screen will be located in a byte whose address is

```
byte.address = first.byte.address + [INT(X/8)]     (12.2)
```

where *first.byte.address* is given by Eq. (12.1).

To set the Hercules graphics mode, we must store the appropriate values in the 16 MC6845 CRTC registers. The values used for Hercules graphics are given in Table 12.3. Note that the *H. Displayed* value in *R1* is 45. This is because Hercules graphics reads two bytes at a time into a 16-bit shift register. Therefore, the 90 bytes on each line are like 45 characters that are 16 bits wide. Note that the value in *R9* is 3, which means that the "characters" are 4 scan lines high. This is because we are using the two row address lines, *RA1* and *RA0*, as described above. The *V. Displayed* value in *R6* is 87, which means that 87 "characters" that are 4 lines high are displayed on the screen. Therefore, the number of displayed scan lines is 87 x 4 = 348.

Table 12.3				
CRTC Register Values for Hercules Graphics Mode				
Reg. #	Register Name	Programmed Value		
		Decimal	Hex	
R0	H. Total	53	35H	
R1	H. Displayed	45	2DH	
R2	H. Sync Position	46	2EH	
R3	H. Sync Width	7	07H	
R4	V. Total	91	5BH	
R5	V. Scan Line Adjust	2	02H	
R6	V. Displayed	87	57H	
R7	V. Sync Position	87	57H	
R8	Interlace Mode	2	02H	
R9	Max. Scan Line Address	3	03H	
R10	Cursor Start	0	00H	
R11	Cursor End	0	00H	
R12	Start Address (H)	0	00H	
R13	Start Address (L)	0	00H	
R14	Cursor (H)	0	00H	
R15	Cursor (L)	0	00H	

In addition to filling the MC6845 registers with the values given in Table 12.3 the two Hercules graphics registers shown in Figure 6.11 must also be set. The *config switch* at address 03BFH must have bit 0 set to 1 to enable graphics. The *display control port* at address 03B8H must be set to 0AH to enable the video and graphics on page 0.

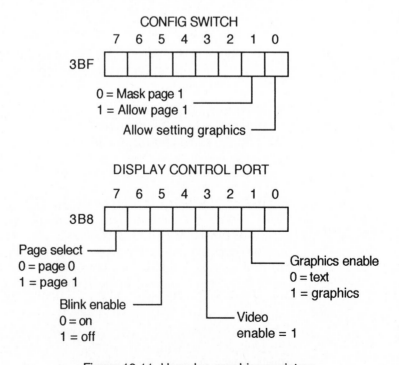

Figure 12.11 Hercules graphics registers

The subroutine *stherc* given in Figure 12.12 will set Hercules graphics. This subroutine is included in the file *graph.asm.* Note that the table *vidtbl* in the data segment contains the 16 values given in Table 12.3 to be stored in the MC6845 registers. This is done in the *sg1:* loop where the consecutive register numbers (*ah*) are stored in the MC6845 address 03B4H and the internal register values (read with *lodsb*) are stored in the MC6845 address 03B5H. Note that the screen is cleared by filling the video RAM with zeros.

```
data        segment public
vidtbl      db        53,45,46,7,91,2,87,87
            db        2,3,0,0,0,0,0,0
data        ends

code        segment public
            assume cs:code,ds:data
;           set up hercules graphics
stherc      proc      near
            push      ax                      ;save regs
            push      cx
            push      dx
            push      di
            mov       dx,03bfh                ;config switch
            mov       al,1
            out       dx,al                   ;allow graphics
            mov       ax,0b000h               ;seg b000h
            mov       es,ax
            mov       cx,8000h                ;word count
            mov       di,0
            cld
            xor       ax,ax                   ;ax=0
            rep stosw                         ;clear video ram
            mov       dx,03b4h                ;6845 port
            mov       si,offset vidtbl        ;si->values
            mov       cx,16                   ;16 regs
            xor       ax,ax                   ;ah=0
sg1:        mov       al,ah                   ;reg no.
            out       dx,al                   ;select reg
            inc       dx                      ;dx=03b5h
            lodsb                             ;get value
            out       dx,al                   ;store it
            dec       dx                      ;dx=03b4h
            inc       ah                      ;next reg
            loop      sg1                     ;do all 16
            mov       dx,03b8h                ;control port
            mov       al,0ah                  ;enable video
            out       dx,al                   ; & graphics
            pop       di                      ;restore regs
            pop       dx
            pop       cx
            pop       ax
            ret
stherc      endp
code        ends
            end
```

Figure 12.12 Subroutine to set Hercules graphics

To plot a dot on the screen we simply need to write a 1 to the appropriate bit position in the appropriate byte in the video RAM. The address of this byte is given by Eq. 12.2. The bit position within this byte is given by

$$\text{bit.position} = 7 - (\text{X MOD 8}) \hspace{3cm} (12.3)$$

The subroutine *plotad* given in Figure 12.13 will find the address and bit position of the dot to be plotted. The *X* and *Y* coordinates of the dot to be plotted are stored in *CX* and *DX* before calling the subroutine. The subroutine will return the byte address of the dot in *DI* and the appropriate mask byte in *BL*. For example, if bit 5 in the byte corresponds to the dot then the value of *BL* will be 00100000. The value of *ES* will also be set to the segment address of the video RAM.

```
;              calculate plot addr at x=cx, y=dx
;              di --> addr  bl=mask  es=B000

plotad     proc near
           push    ax
           push    cx
           push    dx
           mov     di,dx               ;y-table
           shl     di,1                ; index
           mov     di,row_table[di]    ;di->y-table
           mov     ax,cx               ;ax = x
           shr     ax,1
           shr     ax,1
           shr     ax,1                ;int(x/8)
           add     di,ax               ;byte addr
           mov     bl,80h              ;mask
           and     cx,7                ;x mod 8
           shr     bl,cl               ;get mask
           mov     ax,0b000h
           mov     es,ax               ;seg b000h
           pop     dx
           pop     cx
           pop     ax
           ret
plotad     endp
```

Figure 12.13 Subroutine to find the video RAM plot address

The subroutines *plot* and *erase* given in Figure 12.14 will plot and erase a dot at location *X = CX* and *Y = DX*. Note that in each case the subroutine *plotad* is called to find the byte (in *DI*) and the mask (in *BL*) corresponding to the dot location. The 1 in the mask is simply ORed into the byte to plot the dot. To erase the dot the mask is complemented to produce a zero at the dot position which is then ANDed into the byte.

The subroutine *line* given earlier in this chapter in Listing 12.3 is included in the file *graph.asm*. In this case the plot subroutine called by *line* will be the Hercules graphics plot routine given in Figure 12.14. To use the Hercules graphics subroutines in *graph.asm* you must either have a Hercules graphics card installed in your computer or switch to the Hercules monochrome mode that is available on many VGA cards. There is normally a program you run (such as *vgaplus*) that allows you to select the Hercules mode. Once you are in the Hercules mode you can switch to Hercules graphics by calling the subroutine *stherc* in Figure 12.12.

Once you switch to the Hercules graphics mode you are in a bit-mapped environment in which the character generator is no longer available for displaying characters. If you want to display a character you must plot all of the dots that make up the character! While this may seem like a lot of work (and it is) it has the advantage that you can make the character look like anything you want (any font), have any size and be displayed anywhere on the screen. For example, the monochrome uppercase A has the bit-mapped layout shown in Figure 12.15 where the hex byte associated with each row is given on the right. Note that a 1 in the byte corresponds to a dot being plotted in the character.

```
;            plot point at x=cx, y=dx
plot         proc    near
             push    bx
             push    di
             push    es
             call    plotad              ;calc addr
             or      es:[di],bl          ;or in 1
             pop     es
             pop     di
             pop     bx
             ret
plot         endp

;            erase point at x=cx, y=dx
erase        proc    near
             push    bx
             push    di
             push    es
             call    plotad              ;calc addr
             not     bl                  ;not mask
             and     es:[di],bl          ;and in 0
             pop     es
             pop     di
             pop     bx
             ret
erase        endp
```

Figure 12.14 Subroutines to plot and erase a dot

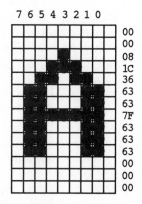

Figure 12.15 Bit-mapped values for the letter A

The bit-mapped values for all 256 characters in the monochrome character set are included at the end of the data segment of *graph.asm* in Appendix C as the table *charset*. The data are stored as 16 bytes per character in the order of their ASCII code. Groups of 16 characters are labeled separately. If you go to ASCII code 41H you will find the 14 bytes shown in Figure 12.15. By modifying this table you could easily change the font of any character.

To write a character on the screen you need to move the first 14 bytes from the *charset* table (the ones shown in Figure 12.15 for the letter A) for the character to be displayed to the appropriate memory in the video RAM. Because there are 90 bytes per row but only 80 monochrome characters per row (9 bits wide) each row of bits in most characters will actually be stored in two consecutive video RAM bytes rather than one. This somewhat complicates the process of writing the characters to the screen. The subroutine for doing this, called *charwt*, is shown in Figure 12.16 and is included in the file *graph.asm*. Before calling this subroutine, you load *AL* with the ASCII code of the character to write and (*CX*,*DX*) with the *X* and *Y* coordinate of the upper-left dot in the character. The subroutine will leave *DX* unchanged and *CX* increased by 9. This will be the location of the next adjacent character.

From Table 3.3 in Chapter 3 note that the graphics characters whose ASCII codes begin with *C* or *D* extend to the right-most bit position in the 9 x 14 character cell. These are the only characters that are actually 9 dots wide. In the subroutine *charwt* in Figure 12.16 the variable *bit9flg* is set (to FFH) for the character graphics ASCII codes. This flag is checked later in the subroutine to see if a 1 in the 8th pixel should by copied into the 9th pixel location.

The other complication in the subroutine *charwt* is due to the fact that the character data will normally need to be stored in two consecutive bytes. The way this is done is that two bytes are read into *AX* from the video RAM at the location where the character is to be plotted and information about the bit position of the left-most dot in the character is stored in *CL* (*X MOD* 8). The problem is that when two bytes are read from memory into *AX* the low memory byte goes to *AL* and the high memory byte goes to *AH*. To make the pair *AH:AL* contain the dots as they appear on the screen it is necessary to exchange these two bytes. Once this is done *AX* is rotated *CL* bits to get all bits corresponding to dots in other characters (i.e. ones we don't want to change) into *AL*. Note that at this point bit 7 in *AL* will correspond to bit 9 (the right-most bit) in the new character. The new data from the *charset* table is then read into *AH* and then *AX* is rotated back to its previous position. Finally, *AH* and *AL* are exchanged again and *AX* is then written back into the video RAM. This will write one row of the character. The process is repeated 14 times in the *cw2:* loop in Figure 12.16 to write each row in the character.

```
;           character write
;           input:  al = ascii code of char
;                   cx = x-coord. upper-left
;                   dx = y-coord. upper-left
;           output: cx = cx(input)+9 = x-coord+9
;                   dx = dx(input) = y-coord
charwt      proc    near
            push    ax
            push    bx
            push    si                      ;save regs
            push    di
            push    bp
            mov     bx,cx                   ;bx = x
            mov     es,video_seg            ;es->video ram
            cld
            mov     bit9flg,0               ;default no
            cmp     al,0c0h                 ; line draw
            jb      cw1                     ;check for
            cmp     al,0dfh                 ; line draw
            ja      cw1                     ; characters
```

```
              not      bit9flg              ;yes, set flag
cw1:          xor      ah,ah                ;ah = 0
              shl      ax,1                 ;mult by 16
              shl      ax,1                 ;16 bytes per
              shl      ax,1                 ; char in table
              shl      ax,1
              mov      si,offset charset    ;si->char set
              add      si,ax                ;offset in tbl
              mov      bp,14                ;char height=14
cw2:          mov      cx,bx                ;cx = x
              mov      di,dx                ;di = y
              shl      di,1                 ;2 bytes/entry
              mov      di,row_table[di]     ;row offset
              mov      ax,cx                ;ax = col
              shr      ax,1
              shr      ax,1
              shr      ax,1                 ;int(x/8)
              add      di,ax                ;char pos byte
              and      cl,7                 ;x mod 8
              mov      ax,es:[di]           ;get 2 bytes
              xchg     ah,al                ;ah = [di]
              rol      ax,cl                ;mov char to al
              mov      ah,byte ptr [si]     ;ah= char line
              cmp      bit9flg,0
              je       cw3
              test     ah,1                 ;if 8th pixel
              je       cw3                  ; on, duplicate
              or       al,80h               ; 8th bit
              jmp      cw4
cw3:          and      al,07fh              ;erase pixel 9
cw4:          ror      ax,cl                ;restore word
              xchg     ah,al                ;restore order
              stosw                         ;write word
              inc      dx                   ;next row
              inc      si                   ;next tbl byte
              dec      bp                   ;do all 14 rows
              jne      cw2
              sub      dx,14                ;restore orig y
              add      bx,9                 ;inc col by 9
              mov      cx,bx
              pop      bp
              pop      di                   ;restore regs
              pop      si
              pop      bx
              pop      ax
              ret
charwt        endp
```

Figure 12.16 Subroutine to write a character to the screen

All of the Hercules graphics subroutines that are included in the file *graph.asm* are shown in Table 12.4. Note that in addition to the subroutines described above there is a message writing subroutine, *messg*, that will write messages on the screen. The message must be stored in the data segment as an ASCIIZ string as was done with the subroutine *mess* in *screen.asm*. The subroutine *cpconv* will convert a character cursor position in terms of character rows and columns into a graphics dot location on the screen where the subroutine *charwt* can display the character.

The subroutines *sinax* and *cosax* will return the sine and cosine (times 1000) of the angle *AX* (in degrees) using a table lookup. These subroutines can be useful for plotting graphic figures where you may want to plot a line at some particular angle and you need to compute the endpoint coordinates to use the subroutine *line*.

Table 12.4
Hercules Graphics Subroutines

stherc	*set up hercules graphics* input:　none output: es = B000H
line	*plot line* input:　　ax = x-coordinate of endpoint 　　　　　bx = y-coordinate of endpoint 　　　　　cx = x-coordinate of origin 　　　　　dx = y-coordinate of origin output:　none
plot	*plot dot* input:　　cx = x-coordinate of point to plot 　　　　　dx = y-coordinate of point to plot output:　none
erase	*erase dot* input:　　cx = x-coordinate of point to erase 　　　　　dx = y-coordinate of point to erase output:　none
plotad	*calculate plot addr at coordinate x,y* input:　　cx = x-coordinate of point 　　　　　dx = y-coordinate of point output: di = offset address of byte containing point 　　　　　bl = mask with 1 in bit position of point 　　　　　es = B000H
messg	*message display* input:　　si = offset address of asciiz message 　　　　　cx = x-coordinate of start of message 　　　　　dx = y-coordinate of start of message output:　none
charwt	*character write* input:　　al = ascii code of char 　　　　　cx = x-coord. upper-left 　　　　　dx = y-coord. upper-left output:　cx = cx(input)+9 = x-coord+9 　　　　　dx = dx(input) = y-coord
cpconv	*cursor position conversion* input:　　dl = col = character column position (0 - 79) 　　　　　dh = row = character row position (0 - 24) output:　cx = x-coordinate = 9*col 　　　　　dx = y-coordinate = 14*row
sinax	compute sin ax input:　　ax = degrees output:　ax = sine value x 1000
cosax	compute cos ax input:　　ax = degrees output:　ax = cosine value x 1000

PROGRAMMING PROBLEMS

Problem 12.1 – Drawing Graphic Pictures

In this problem you will write a program that will allow you to plot graphic figures interactively.

a. Write a program that will set Hercules graphics and display a single dot (the cursor) at the center of the screen. Moving the eight cursor keys around the 5 on the numeric keypad should move the dot in 8 possible directions (up, down, left, right, NE, SE, SW, NW). If the *Num Lock* key is on, the dots should remain plotted as you move the cursor. If the *Num Lock* key is off, the dots are not plotted. Pressing the *ESC* key should clear the screen and take you back to DOS.

b. Modify your program so that you type out Hercules graphics characters when you press any key. The graphics dot cursor should be adjusted so that it always follows the character just displayed.

c. Add some additional feature of your own choice. For example, you might move the dot cursor so as to set the two end points of a line and then have the LINE subroutine plot the line between these two points. You could use various function keys for this purpose.

Problem 12.2 – Plotting Sine and Cosine Waves

a. Using the subroutine *sinax* plot six cycles of a sine wave on the screen. Include both horizontal and vertical labeled axes. Use the subroutine *line* to plot a line between adjacent points on the graph.

b. Add a plot of a cosine wave to the sine wave plotted is part (a).

Problem 12.3 – Plotting Graphic Figures

a. Write a subroutine called *BOX* that will draw a square box on the screen by starting at location $X = CX$, $Y = DX$ and drawing a line of length BX at an angle AX to the horizontal. Continue plotting the box counterclockwise by adding 90 degrees to AX for each of the other three sides.

b. Plot a figure made up of 18 boxes of the same size. All boxes should share a common vertex at the center of the screen and the initial angle of each box should be 20 degrees more than the previously drawn box.

c. Plot a figure made up of 10 concentric boxes at a 45 degree angle (diamonds) with sides ranging from 15 dots to 150 in steps of 15.

d. Use multiple calls to the subroutine *BOX* to draw some unique graphic figure of your choice.

EXERCISES

Exercise 12.1
Modify the program in Listing 12.2 to fill the screen with bands of all 16 colors in the EGA/VGA mode 0EH.

Exercise 12.2
Modify the program in Listing 12.2 to fill the screen with bands of all 16 colors in the EGA/VGA mode 10H.

Exercise 12.3
Modify the program in Listing 12.2 to fill the screen with bands of all 16 colors in the VGA mode 12H.

Exercise 12.4
Modify the program in Listing 12.2 to plot 256 vertical lines on the screen displaying each of the 256 colors in the VGA mode 13H.

Exercise 12.5
Modify the program in Listing 12.2 to make horizontal bands. Change the program to display horizontal lines for the graphics modes in Exercises 12.1 – 12.4.

Exercise 12.6
Write 8086 instructions that will plot a green dot on a red background at the center of the screen in graphics mode 04.

Exercise 12.7
The *line* subroutine in Listing 12.3 is called with the following values in the general registers: $AX = 0065H$, $BX = 002CH$, $CX = 0062H$, $DX = 002FH$. How many times will the subroutine *plot* be executed?

Exercise 12.8
Modify the program in Listing 12.4 to plot a polygon with
    a) 5 equal sides
    b) 8 equal sides
    c) 12 equal sides

Exercise 12.9
Modify the program in Listing 12.4 so that each vertex of the star is connected to all other vertices.

Exercise 12.10
The MC6845 CRTC register values for monochrome text are given in Table 12.2. Assume that the character time, T_c, is 553 ns. What is the time, T_{sl}, to scan a single line? What is the time, T_{cr}, to display a single row of characters? What is the total time for a single vertical scan?

Exercise 12.11
Find the Hercules graphics video RAM address and bit position for a dot to be plotted at the following coordinates:

    a) X = 244, Y = 139   c) X = 500, Y = 210
    b) X = 125, Y = 300   d) X = 53, Y = 25

Exercise 12.12

Using the *charset* table in the file *graph.asm* in Appendix C, find the 14 bytes representing the bit mapped values for the following characters:

```
E, J, q, %, 9
```

Exercise 12.13

Draw a diagram to show the steps used in the subroutine *charwt* to plot each row of a character.

Exercise 12.14

Write 8086 instructions that will find the Hercules graphics dot coordinates corresponding to a character to plot in character row 10, character column 15. Leave the *X*-coordinate in *CX* and the *Y*-coordinate in *DX*.

CHAPTER 13

Serial Communication

Parallel I/O as used in the printer interface described in Chapter 11 requires eight data lines to transmit a byte (8 bits) of data. This becomes expensive when data has to be sent a long distance. It is much less expensive to use a single data line over which the eight bits are sent one bit at a time. This is called *serial communication* and will obviously be considerably slower than sending the eight bits in parallel.

In this chapter you will learn:

- The basic format of asynchronous serial communication
- The PC BIOS functions that can be used for serial I/O
- To program the 8250 UART
- How to write an interrupt-driven terminal program

13.1 SERIAL I/O

There are two basic types of serial communication: *synchronous* and *asynchronous*. In synchronous communication, data are normally sent in blocks that often contain error checking. The timing is controlled by a standard clock at both the transmitter and receiver ends. On the other hand, the timing for asynchronous communication is handled one character at a time, and while the clocks at the transmitter and receiver must be approximately the same, they are resynchronized with each character. Because each character requires these additional synchronizing bits, asynchronous communication is slower than synchronous communication. However, it is simpler to implement and is in widespread use. In this chapter we will consider only asynchronous communication.

Asynchronous serial communication uses a *start bit* to tell when a particular character is being sent. This is illustrated in Figure 13.1 which shows the transmitted waveform when the character "*T*" (ASCII code = 54H) is sent with odd parity. Before a character is sent, the line is in the high, or *mark* state. The line is then brought low (called a *space*) and held low for a time *t* called the bit time. This first space is called the *start bit*. It is typically followed by seven or eight data bits. The least significant bit *D0* is transmitted first. For example, in Figure 13.1 the seven bits corresponding to the ASCII code 54H (the character *"T"*) are sent starting with *D0*. These seven bits are followed by a *parity bit*. This bit is set to a 1 or a 0 such that the sum of the number of 1's transmitted is either even or odd. We have used odd parity in Figure 13.1. Since three 1's were sent (*D2*, *D4*, and *D6*) the parity bit is zero. Sometimes a character is sent with no parity in which case the parity bit is ignored. The parity bit is followed by one or two stop bits which are always high (a *mark*). The next character will be indicated by the presence of the next start bit.

The reciprocal of the bit time is called the *baud rate*. Common baud rates used in serial communication are given in Table 13.1. The 110 baud rate uses two stop bits. This means that 11 bit times per character are used (7 data bits + 1 parity bit + 1 start bit + 2 stop bits). Therefore, 10 characters per second are transmitted at 110 baud. The remaining baud rates in Table 13.1 use 1 stop bit and therefore use 10 bit times per character.

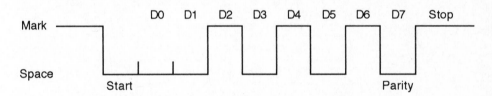

Figure 13.1   ASCII code 54H = 1010100 ("T") sent with odd parity

<table>
<tr><td colspan="5" align="center">**Table 13.1**</td></tr>
<tr><td colspan="5" align="center">**Common Serial Baud Rates**</td></tr>
<tr><td>Baud rate</td><td>Bit time (msec)</td><td>No. of STOP bits</td><td>Char. time (msec.)</td><td>Char./sec.</td></tr>
<tr><td>110</td><td>9.09</td><td>2</td><td>100.00</td><td>10</td></tr>
<tr><td>150</td><td>6.67</td><td>1</td><td>66.67</td><td>15</td></tr>
<tr><td>300</td><td>3.33</td><td>1</td><td>33.3 3</td><td>30</td></tr>
<tr><td>600</td><td>1.67</td><td>1</td><td>16.67</td><td>60</td></tr>
<tr><td>1200</td><td>0.833</td><td>1</td><td>8.33</td><td>120</td></tr>
<tr><td>2400</td><td>0.417</td><td>1</td><td>4.17</td><td>240</td></tr>
<tr><td>4800</td><td>0.208</td><td>1</td><td>2.08</td><td>480</td></tr>
<tr><td>9600</td><td>0.104</td><td>1</td><td>1.04</td><td>960</td></tr>
</table>

13.2   THE BIOS RS-232 COMMUNICATIONS INTERFACE

The *Asynchronous Communications Adapter* (ACA) was the original serial communications board provided by IBM that plugged into one of the I/O peripheral slots. This card uses a special programmable I/O chip called the *8250 Universal Asynchronous Receiver/Transmitter* (UART) manufactured by National Semiconductor. We will describe this chip in more detail in Section 13.3. Many manufacturers provide serial boards for the PC that use this UART chip.

A functional block diagram of the Asynchronous Communications Adapter (ACA) is shown in Figure 13.2. This communications adapter will have a 25-pin "D" connector (sometimes a 9-pin connector is used) that comes out of the back of the computer. The pins on this connector contain the signals shown in Figure 13.3. This connector is compatible with the standard RS-232C serial interface. The serial bit patterns sent over the transmit and receive pins (pins 2 and 3) are represented by +12 volt (bit = 0) and -12 volt (bit = 1) signals. These voltages are transformed from the corresponding 0 and 5 volt levels used in the computer by the ACA.

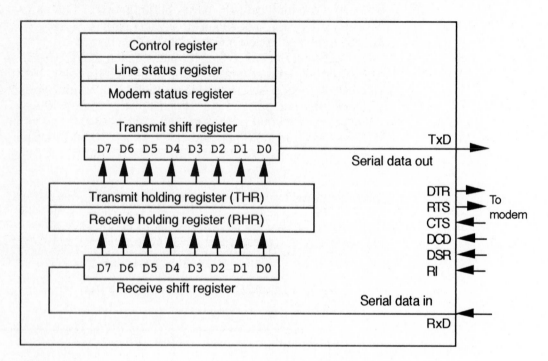

Figure 13.2 Functional diagram of an Asynchronous Communications Adapter (ACA)

Pin No.	Signal	Direction
1	NC	
2	Transmit data (TxD)	Out
3	Receive data (RxD)	In
4	Request to send (RTS)	Out
5	Clear to send (CTS)	In
6	Data set ready (DSR)	In
7	Signal ground	
8	Carrier detect (CD)	In
9	+Transmit current loop return (20 ma)	Out
10	NC	
11	-Transmit current loop data (20 ma)	Out
12-17	NC	
18	+Receive current loop data (20 ma)	In
19	NC	
20	Data terminal ready (DTR)	Out
21	NC	
22	Ring indicate	In
23-24	NC	
25	-Receive current loop return (20 ma)	In

Figure 13.3 Connector used for the RS-232C serial communications interface

In addition to the standard RS-232C voltage interface, a different interface, the EAI 20 milliampere (ma) current loop, represents a 0 and 1 bit by the absence or presence of a 20 ma current rather than a voltage level. The IBM asynchronous communications adapter board allows you to select either the voltage (RS-232C) or current loop option by changing the direction in which you plug in a shunt module.

The main function of the ACA is to transform parallel data from the 8086 into serial data and send it out through the transmit data pin *TxD*, and to receive serial data through the receive data pin *RxD* and transform it to parallel data that can be read by the 8086.

You can access the ACA by means of the BIOS software interrupt *INT 14H*. These communications routines make use of a control register and two status registers. The control register is shown in Figure 13.4. This control register allows you to select the baud rate, the parity, the number of stop bits, and the word length. You initialize the communications port by setting *AH* = 0 and calling *INT 14H* with the appropriate control register in *AL*. This and the other options available with *INT 14H* are shown in Figure 13.5.

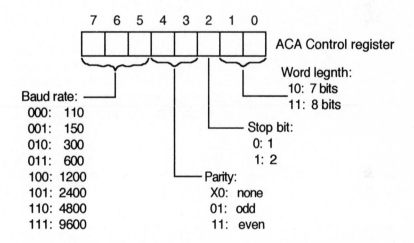

Figure 13.4 Control register used by the communications port

AH = 0	*Initialize communications port*
	Input: AL = ACA control register (Figure 13.4)
	            DX = RS-232 card no. (0 - 3)
	Output: AH = Line status register (Figure 13.6)
	            AL = Modem status register (Figure 13.7)

AH = 1	*Send serial character* Input: AL = character to send DX = RS-232 card no. (0 - 3) Output: AH = Line status register (Figure 13.6)
AH = 2	*Receive a serial character* Input: DX = RS-232 card no. (0 - 3) Output: AL = character received AH = Line status register (Figure 13.6)
AH = 3	*Read status register* Input: DX = RS-232 card no. (0 - 3) Output: AH = Line status register (Figure 13.6) AL = Modem status register (Figure 13.7)

Figure 13.5 RS-232 communications options used with INT 14H

As with the printer I/O routines described in Chapter 11, you must set *DX* to the RS-232C card number you want to use. If you have only one serial port, use *DX* = 0. The starting I/O port addresses for up to four RS-232C adapters are stored at locations 0040:0000 – 0040:0007.

When you initialize an RS-232C communications port by calling *INT 14H* with *AH* = 0, the initialization routine will return with *AH* containing the *line status register* and *AL* containing the *modem status register*. The definitions of these status registers are given in Figures 13.6 and 13.7.

Bit 0 of the line status register is the *data ready* bit. This bit is set to 1 when the *receive shift register* has filled up with a complete byte and transferred this byte to the *receive holding register* (RHR) (see Figure 13.2). The *receive holding register* can then be read by using *INT 14H* with *AH* = 2 (see Figure 13.5).

Reading the *receive holding register* will clear the *DR* bit in the line status register. If you call *INT 14H* with *AH* = 2, the software interrupt routine will wait for a serial character to be received. Alternatively, you can poll the *DR* bit to see if the *receive holding register* is full, and if not, go do something else. A typical polling sequence is shown in Figure 13.8. If the *DR* bit is set to 1, then the *receive holding register* is read using *INT 14H* with *AH* = 2. Otherwise the program branches to *next* which might check the keyboard and then returns to *recv* to check the *DR* bit again.

You must make sure that you check the *DR* bit often enough not to miss any incoming bytes. If the *receive shift register* gets full before the previous data in the *receive holding register* has been read, the *overrun error flag* (bit 1) in the line status register will be set to 1. The overrun error flag is cleared by reading the line status register.

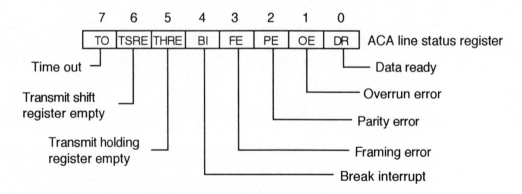

Figure 13.6 Line status register

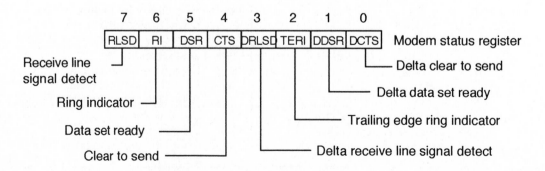

Figure 13.7 Modem status register

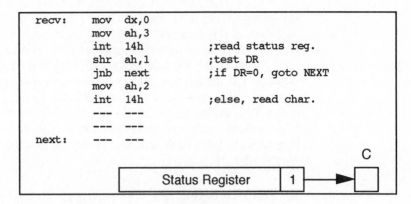

```
recv:    mov  dx,0
         mov  ah,3
         int  14h         ;read status reg.
         shr  ah,1        ;test DR
         jnb  next        ;if DR=0, goto NEXT
         mov  ah,2
         int  14h         ;else, read char.
         ---  ---
         ---  ---
next:    ---  ---
```

Figure 13.8 Polling the *Receive Holding Register*

All asynchronous serial data must end with at least one stop bit. If a stop bit does not occur where expected, a framing error is indicated and the *FE* flag (bit 3) in the status register is set to 1. This flag is set or reset after each byte is received. You must therefore test this bit between the time that a character is received and the next character fills the *receive shift register*.

When a data character has been received in the *receive holding register* the parity error flag, *PE*, (bit 2) in the line status register will be set to 1 if the number of ones in the byte does not agree with the preselected parity (odd or even). The parity error flag is cleared whenever the line status register is read.

Bit 5 of the line status register is the *transmit holding register empty* (*THRE*) bit. This bit is set to 1 when data from the *transmit holding register* (*THR*) is transferred to the *transmit shift register*. This data is then shifted out through *TxD* at the baud rate, preceded by a start bit and ending with a parity bit (if selected) and one or two stop bits (see Figure 13.2). While this data is being shifted out, another byte can be stored in the *transmit holding register*. When this is done the *THRE* bit is cleared to zero and will remain zero until the *transmit shift register* has finished shifting out the previous character. When the shift register is free to accept another byte, the *transmit shift register empty* flag (bit 6) will be set to 1 and the contents of the *THR* are transferred to the shift register and the *THRE* flag (bit 5) in the line status register is set to 1 again.

A *break* signal occurs on an asynchronous serial line when a *space* (logic 0) occurs for longer than a full character transmission time. When this occurs the *break interrupt* flag (bit 4) in the line status register is set to 1.

To send a serial character, all you have to do is store the character in *AL* and call *INT 14H* with *AH* = 1 (see Figure 13.5). This BIOS routine will take care of checking the *transmit holding register empty* flag to make sure it is set to 1 before sending your character. If it is unable to send your character then the *time out* flag (bit 7) in the line status register will be set to 1.

The *modem status register* shown in Figure 13.7 is associated with the use of a *modem*. A modem is used to modulate (and demodulate) a serial, digital signal so that is can be transmitted over telephone lines.

The *clear to send* (*CTS*) flag (bit 4) and the *data set ready* (*DSR*) flag (bit 5) in the modem status register are the complements of the *CTS* and *DSR* signals from a modem. These flags must both be 1 in order to send a character over the communications line.

The *receive line signal detect* (*RLSD*) flag (bit 7) in the modem status register is the complement of the *Carrier Detect* (*CD*) signal from the modem. If this flag is 0 it indicates that a carrier is not present at the modem and therefore valid data cannot be sent or received.

When the *ring indicator* (*RI*) flag (bit 6) in the modem status register is set to 1 it means that a telephone ringing signal has been received by the modem. The *trailing edge ring indicator* (*TERI*) flag (bit 2) will be set to 1 if the *RI* input to the ACA has changed from on to off. Bits 0, 1, and 3 in the modem status register get set if the *CTS*, *DSR*, or *RLSD* signals respectively have changed state since the last time the modem status register was read.

A BIOS-Based PC Terminal Program

In this section we will write a program that will turn the PC into a dumb terminal. A typical dumb terminal will check to see if a key has been pressed. If it has, it will send the character to the host computer. It will then check to see if the host computer is sending a character. If it is, it will display the character on the screen. Otherwise, it will check the keyboard again.

This algorithm for a dumb terminal is given in Figure 13.9. This algorithm is for *full-duplex* communication in which the host computer echoes each character that it receives. Therefore, the PC will not display a character typed on the keyboard until the character has been sent to the host computer and returned. The user will think that it is being displayed immediately, but actually it makes a round trip to the host computer. In *half-duplex* communication, the PC would display each character as it is typed, and the host computer would not echo the characters that it receives.

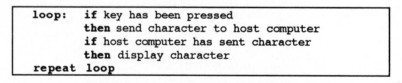

```
loop:    if key has been pressed
         then send character to host computer
         if host computer has sent character
         then display character
repeat loop
```

Figure 13.9 Algorithm for a dumb terminal

The assembly language program for this dumb terminal is shown in Listing 13.1. The program continually alternates between checking the keyboard and checking the asynchronous communications adapter (ACA). The communications port is initialized to 1200 baud, no parity, 1 stop bit, and 8-bit word length by using the control byte 83H in *AL* and calling *INT 14H* with *AH* = 0. The characters are displayed on the screen using the *chrout* subroutine given in the file *screen.asm* (see Chapter 7).

The dumb terminal program given in Listing 13.1 is limited to baud rates below 1200 baud. The reason for this is that if we don't check the status register before another character is received into the receive holding register the previously received character will be overrun and lost. Therefore, we can't spend too much time in *chrout* displaying the character on the screen. This is generally not a problem if we only display a single character. However, when the characters reach the bottom of the screen the entire screen needs to be scrolled and this takes enough time so that characters will be lost at baud rates above about 1200 baud.

Listing 13.1   *dumbterm.asm*

```
                title  PC Dumb Terminal

;               link with screen
stack           segment para stack
                db  64 dup(?)
stack           ends

extrn           clrscn:near,chrout:near,quit:near
code            segment public
                assume cs:code

term            proc far
                call clrscn                ;clear screen
                mov  dx,0                  ;1200 baud
                mov  ax,0083h              ;no parity
                int  14h                   ;1 stop/8 bits
key:            mov  ah,1                   ;if key not
                int  16h                   ; pressed,
                je   recv                  ; goto recv
                mov  ah,0
                int  16h                   ;read key
                cmp  al,1bh                ;if esc key
                je   done                  ;goto DOS
                mov  ah,1                   ;al=ascii code
                int  14h                   ;send character
recv:           mov  ah,3
                int  14h                   ;read status
                shr  ah,1                  ;if no char
                jnb  key                   ;check keyboard
                mov  ah,2                  ;otherwise,
                int  14h                   ;read character
                and  al,7fh                ;clear parity bit
                mov  bl,7                   ;normal video
                call chrout                ;display char
                jmp  key                   ;repeat again
done:           call quit                  ;goto DOS
term            endp
code            ends
                end  term
```

The solution to this problem is to have each received character produce a hardware interrupt which will simply read the character from the receive holding register and put it in a circular queue data structure from which it can be read at our leisure. Thus, more than one character could be received during the scrolling operation but these characters will not be lost because they would be in the queue — put there by the interrupt service routine that interrupted the scrolling process.

We cannot use most of the BIOS *INT 14H* serial I/O functions when using hardware interrupts. This is because some of these explicitly turn off the interrupts. To use interrupts we must program the 8250 asynchronous communications element chip directly. We will describe how the 8250 is connected to the 8086 in the next section and will then write an interrupt-driven communications program in Section 13.4.

13.3 THE 8250 UNIVERSAL ASYNCHRONOUS RECEIVER/TRANSMITTER

The *8250 Universal Asynchronous Receiver/Transmitter* (UART) is a 40-pin chip that is used on serial I/O cards for the PC. The functional block diagram for the 8250 UART chip is the same as for the ACA shown in Figure 13.2. The 8250 UART has the ten internal registers shown in Table 13.2. The I/O space addresses of these registers for the two serial ports, COM1 and COM2, are given in Table 13.2. Note that the first three registers in Table 13.2 have the same I/O address. If bit 7 of the *line control register* is set to 1 then the address 3F8H (COM1) will be the *divisor low register* (which is used to set the baud rate). On the other hand, if bit 7 of the *line control register* is zero, the address 3F8H (COM1) will be the *receive data buffer* for a read operation and the *transmit data buffer* for a write operation. These are the same as the receive and transmit holding registers in Figure 13.2. The *interrupt enable register* and the *divisor high register* in Table 13.2 also share the same I/O address and are distinguished by the value of bit 7 in the *line control register*.

<table>
<tr><td colspan="6" align="center">Table 13.2

8250 UART Registers</td></tr>
<tr><td colspan="2">Register Addr.
COM1   COM2</td><td>Bit 7
LCR</td><td>Read/
Write</td><td>8250 Register
Name</td><td>Symbol</td></tr>
<tr><td>3F8H</td><td>2F8H</td><td>0</td><td>R</td><td>Receive Data Buffer</td><td>RECDATA</td></tr>
<tr><td>3F8H</td><td>2F8H</td><td>0</td><td>W</td><td>Transmit Data Buffer</td><td>TXDATA</td></tr>
<tr><td>3F8H</td><td>2F8H</td><td>1</td><td>R/W</td><td>Divisor Low Register</td><td>DIVLOW</td></tr>
<tr><td>3F9H</td><td>2F9H</td><td>0</td><td>R/W</td><td>Interrupt Enable Register</td><td>IER</td></tr>
<tr><td>3F9H</td><td>2F9H</td><td>1</td><td>R/W</td><td>Divisor High Register</td><td>DIVHI</td></tr>
<tr><td>3FAH</td><td>2FAH</td><td>X</td><td>R</td><td>Interrupt ID Register</td><td>INTID</td></tr>
<tr><td>3FBH</td><td>2FBH</td><td>X</td><td>R/W</td><td>Line Control Register</td><td>LCR</td></tr>
<tr><td>3FCH</td><td>2FCH</td><td>X</td><td>R/W</td><td>Modem Control Register</td><td>MCR</td></tr>
<tr><td>3FDH</td><td>2FDH</td><td>X</td><td>R/W</td><td>Line Status Register</td><td>LSR</td></tr>
<tr><td>3FEH</td><td>2FEH</td><td>X</td><td>R/W</td><td>Modem Status Register</td><td>MSR</td></tr>
</table>

The 8250 UART *line control register* (LCR) is similar to the *ACA control register* shown in Figure 13.4 except that the baud rate is not set with this register. The lower five bits are the same as in Figure 13.4 and bit 7 is used as a register address discrimination bit as described above. The 8250 UART *line status register* (LSR) is similar to the *ACA line status register* shown in Figure 13.6 except that bit 7 (time out) is always zero. The 8250 UART *modem status register* (MSR) is the same as the *ACA modem status register* shown in Figure 13.7. The INS8250 data sheet is included in Appendix E.

The way in which the *8259A Priority Interrupt Controller* (PIC) is used to process hardware interrupts on the PC was discussed in Section 11.1. The interrupt line from the 8250 UART chip is connected to the COM1 (*irq4*) line of the PIC as shown in Figure 13.10. Note that this interrupt line goes through a buffer that is enabled when the *OUT2** line of the 8250 goes low. This line is controlled by bit 3 in the 8250 UART *modem control register* that is shown in Figure 13.11. This bit must be set to 1 to enable 8250 interrupts. To have a hardware interrupt occur every time the receive data ready bit in the *line status register* gets set (meaning a new value has been loaded into the *receive data buffer*) we must set bit 0 of the 8250 *interrupt enable register* shown in Figure 13.12.

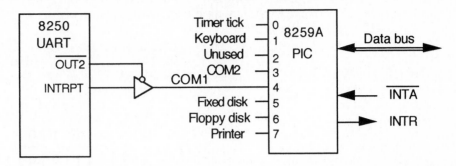

Figure 13.10 The 8250 must have $\overline{OUT2}$ low to enable COM1 interrupts

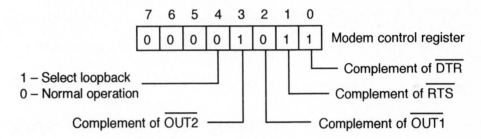

Figure 13.11 The 8250 Modem control register

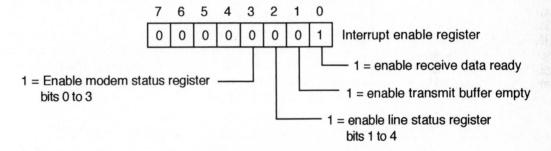

Figure 13.12 The 8250 Interrupt enable register

Even after setting the *modem control register* and the *interrupt enable register* to the values shown in Figures 13.11 and 13.12 the interrupt signal will still not get through the PIC to the 8086 microprocessor. That is because the PIC has an *interrupt mask register* that can mask any of the eight possible hardware interrupts shown in Figure 13.10. Bit 4 of this *interrupt mask register* (which has the I/O address 21H) controls the COM1 interrupt signal and must be cleared to zero to enable this interrupt as shown in Figure 13.13. The timer, keyboard and disk drives will normally be enabled already while the printer and the two serial ports will generally be masked. Therefore, to enable COM1 while keeping all the other bits in the *interrupt mask register* unchanged we can use the instructions

```
in     al,imask
and    al,0efh          ;enable irq4
out    imask,al
```

where *imask* is equated to 21H, the I/O address of the *interrupt mask register.* To turn off the COM1 interrupt we can set bit 4 of the *interrupt mask register* with the following instructions:

```
in     al,imask
or     al,10h           ;disable irq4
out    imask,al
```

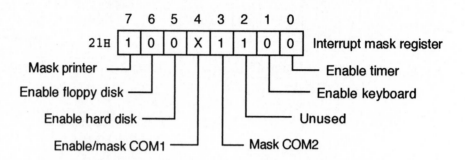

Figure 13.13 The 8259A PIC Interrupt mask register

13.4   AN INTERRUPT-DRIVEN PC TERMINAL PROGRAM

In this section we will write a PC terminal program in which a hardware interrupt occurs each time a character is received in the serial port. The interrupt service routine will read this character and store the value in the *circular queue* shown in Figure 13.14. Multiple values can be stored in this queue before they are removed (in the same order they were stored). Therefore, characters will not be lost if they are received faster than they can be displayed while scrolling. Of course, if the queue is full and another character is received, it will be lost; but we will make the queue big enough so that this will not happen.

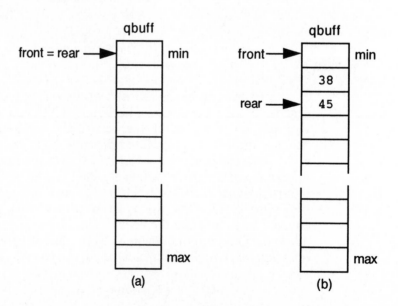

Figure 13.14 A circular queue: (a) empty; (b) containing two values

Using this queue the main program will then be that shown at the beginning of Listing 13.2. You should compare the instructions between the labels *key:* and *done:* with those in Listing 13.1 for our dumb terminal using the BIOS functions. Note that instead of checking the *line status register* to see if a character has been received we simply check the queue to see if a hardware interrupt has deposited a character for us to read.

The queue is defined to be a 256-byte buffer called *qbuff* in the data segment. The first byte in the queue has the offset address *min* and the last byte has the offset address *max*. The pointers *front* and *rear* are initialized to *min* in the subroutine *initq* in Listing 13.2. To store a value in the queue the pointer *rear* is incremented and the value is stored at *rear*. However, when *rear* exceeds *max* it must wrap around to *min*. If *rear* ever runs into *front*, then the queue is full and we will back up *rear* and not store the new value. The complete algorithm for storing a value in the queue is given in Figure 13.15 and is implemented by the subroutine *qstore* in Listing 13.2 which stores the value in *al* in the queue.

```
inc rear
if rear > max
then rear = min
if front = rear
then queue is full
        dec rear
        if rear < min
        then rear = max
else store value at rear
```

Figure 13.15 Algorithm to store a value in the circular queue in Figure 13.14

To read a value from the queue the pointer *front* is incremented and that value is read. This will guarantee that the first value stored in the queue will be the first one read from the queue. The queue will be empty any time that *front = rear*. The algorithm to check the queue is given in Figure 13.16 and is implemented by the subroutine *checkq* in Listing 13.2.

```
if front = rear
then queue is empty (Z flag = 1)
else  disable interrupts
      inc front
      if front > max
      then front = min
      read byte at front into al
      clear Z flag
      enable interrupts
```

Figure 13.16 Algorithm to check queue for a value

The subroutine *checkq* is called in the main program at the beginning of Listing 13.2. If the queue is empty, *checkq* will return the Z flag set to 1 and the main program jumps back to check the keyboard. If the queue is not empty, *checkq* reads a value from the queue into register *al* and clears the Z flag so that the main program will display the character on the screen. When the subroutine *checkq* reads a value from the queue, interrupts are disabled (with the instruction *CLI*) so that the subroutine *qstore* in the interrupt service routine will not be called while the variable *front* is being modified. This is prudent even though you may get away with it in this case (see Exercise 13.3). Remember that interrupts are automatically masked while an interrupt service routine is being executed so that the subroutine *qstore*, which is called from within the interrupt service routine *intser*, cannot itself be interrupted.

The subroutine *isetup*, called near the beginning of the main program in Listing 13.2, initializes the modem control register and the interrupt enable register with the values shown in Figures 13.11 and 13.12. It then stores the address of the interrupt service routine, *intser*, in the interrupt vector table at interrupt type number 0CH (see Table 11.1 in Chapter 11).

```
Listing  13.2     ibmterm.asm
              title   IBM PC terminal using interrupts

      stack      segment      para stack
                 db       64 dup(?)
      stack      ends

      data       segment
      qbuff      db       256  dup(?)
      front      dw       ?
      rear       dw       ?
      min        dw       ?
      max        dw       ?
      m0         db       'Select Baud Rate',0
      m1         db       '1.  300',0
      m2         db       '2.  600',0
      m3         db       '3. 1200',0
      m4         db       '4. 2400',0
      m5         db       '5. 4800',0
      m6         db       '6. 9600',0
      vecseg     dw       ?                  ;save int vector
      vecoff     dw       ?
      txdata     equ      3f8h
      recdat     equ      3f8h
      mcr        equ      3fch
      ier        equ      3f9h
      lsr        equ      3fdh
      intvec     equ      0ch
      imask      equ      21h
      eoi        equ      20h
      ocw2       equ      20h
      data       ends

      extrn      chrout:near,mess:near
      extrn      clrscn:near,quit:near

      code       segment  public
                 assume  cs:code,ds:data

      main       proc     far
                 mov      ax,data            ;set ds
                 mov      ds,ax
                 call     initq              ;queue init
                 call     gtbaud             ;get baud
                 call     isetup             ;int setup
                 in       al,imask
                 and      al,0efh            ;enable irq4
                 out      imask,al
```

Listing 13.2 (continued)

```
        key:    mov     ah,1            ;if key not
                int     16h             ; pressed
                je      recv            ; goto recv
                mov     ah,0            ;else
                int     16h             ;read key
                cmp     ah,1            ;if esc key
                je      done            ;goto DOS
                call    send            ;send character
        recv:   call    checkq          ;check queue
                je      key             ;if empty,rdkey
                mov     bl,07h          ;normal video
                and     al,7fh          ;strip parity
                call    chrout          ;display char
                jmp     key             ;repeat again
        done:   in      al,imask
                or      al,10h          ;disable irq4
                out     imask,al
                push    ds              ;save ds
                mov     dx,vecoff       ;restore old
                mov     ds,vecseg       ; 0ch int vec
                mov     al,intvec
                mov     ah,25h
                int     21h
                pop     ds              ;restore ds
                call    quit            ;goto DOS
        main    endp

        ;       display menu
        menu    proc    near
                call    clrscn          ;clear screen
                mov     dx,0510h        ;row 5,col 16
                mov     si,offset m0
                mov     bl,07h          ;normal video
                call    mess            ;mess 0
                add     dh,2            ;row=row+2
                add     dl,4            ;col=col+4
                mov     si,offset m1
                call    mess            ;mess 1
                inc     dh              ;inc row
                mov     si,offset m2
                call    mess            ;mess 2
                inc     dh
                mov     si,offset m3
                call    mess            ;mess 3
                inc     dh
                mov     si,offset m4
                call    mess            ;mess 4
                inc     dh
                mov     si,offset m5
                call    mess            ;mess 5
                inc     dh
                mov     si,offset m6
                call    mess            ;mess 6
                mov     dh,5            ;row=5
                mov     dl,33           ;col=33
                mov     ah,2
                int     10h             ;set cursor
                ret
        menu    endp

        ;       get baud rate
        gtbaud  proc    near
                call    menu            ;display menu
        gb1:    mov     ah,0            ;wait for key
                int     16h
```

Listing 13.2 (continued)

```
                cmp     al,31h              ; between 1
                jb      gb1
                cmp     al,36h              ; and 6
                ja      gb1
                and     al,0fh              ;baud code
                inc     al                  ;between 2-7
                mov     cl,5                ;move to
                shl     al,cl               ; bits 5-7
                mov     cl,3                ;no parity
                or      al,cl               ; 8 bits
                mov     ah,0
                mov     dx,0
                int     14h                 ;set ACA ctrl reg
                call    clrscn              ;clear screen
                ret
        gtbaud  endp

        ;       initialize queue
        initq   proc    near
                mov     ax,offset qbuff
                mov     front,ax            ;front->qbuff
                mov     rear,ax             ;rear->qbuff
                mov     min,ax              ;min->qbuff
                add     ax,255              ;max ->
                mov     max,ax              ; qbuff+255
                ret
        initq   endp

        ;       check queue
        checkq  proc    near
                mov     si,front
                cmp     si,rear             ;if front=rear
                je      cq2                 ;then empty
                cli                         ;disable int
                inc     si                  ;inc front
                cmp     si,max              ;if front>max
                jbe     cq1                 ;then
                mov     si,min              ; front=min
        cq1:    mov     front,si            ;get byte
                mov     al,[si]             ; @ front
                test    al,0ffh             ;clear Z flag
                sti                         ;enable int
        cq2:    ret
        checkq  endp

        ;       store al in queue
        qstore  proc    near
                inc     rear                ;inc rear
                mov     si,rear             ;if rear>max
                cmp     si,max              ;then
                jbe     qs1
                mov     si,min              ;rear=min
                mov     rear,si
        qs1:    cmp     si,front            ;if front=rear
                jne     qs3                 ;then full
                dec     si                  ; dec rear
                cmp     si,min              ; if rear<min
                jae     qs2                 ; then rear=max
                mov     si,max
                mov     rear,si
        qs2:    ret                         ;else store
        qs3:    mov     [si],al             ; at rear
                ret
        qstore  endp
```

Listing 13.2 (continued)

```
        ;          send char in al to 8250
        send    proc    near
                push    ax                      ;save char
                mov     dx,lsr
        sd1:    in      al,dx                   ;wait for
                test    al,20h                  ; trans buff
                je      sd1                     ; to be empty
                mov     dx,txdata
                pop     ax                      ;get char &
                out     dx,al                   ; send it
                ret
        send    endp

        ;          interrupt setup
        isetup  proc    near
                mov     dx,mcr                  ;modem cr
                mov     al,0bh                  ;out2 lo
                out     dx,al                   ;DTR,RTS lo
                mov     dx,ier
                mov     al,1                    ;enable recv
                out     dx,al                   ; interrupts
                push    ds                      ;save ds
                mov     ah,35h                  ;save 0Ch int vec
                mov     al,intvec
                int     21h
                mov     vecseg,es
                mov     vecoff,bx
                mov     dx,offset intser
                push    cs
                pop     ds
                mov     ah,25h                  ;set int type
                int     21h                     ; vector
                pop     ds
                ret
        isetup  endp

        ;          interrupt service routine
        intser  proc    near
                push    ax                      ;save regs
                push    si
                push    dx
                push    ds
                mov     ax,data
                mov     ds,ax                   ;ds=data
                mov     dx,lsr                  ;if char ready
                in      al,dx
                test    al,01h
                je      ints1
                mov     dx,recdat               ;read it
                in      al,dx
                call    qstore                  ;put in queue
        ints1:  pop     ds
                pop     dx
                pop     si
                mov     al,eoi                  ;8259 EOI
                out     ocw2,al
                pop     ax
                iret
        intser  endp

        code    ends
                end     main
```

At the beginning of the main program in Listing 13.2 the baud rate is set using the subroutine *gtbaud*. This subroutine displays a menu from which six different baud rates can be selected. The selected baud rate is set by initializing the communications port (by calling *INT 14H* with *AH* = 0) with the appropriate value in the ACA control register in Figure 13.4. Inasmuch as this call to the BIOS function *INT 14H* will disable the 8250 interrupts it is necessary to call the subroutine *gtbaud* before calling the subroutine *isetup*. For the same reason, we cannot use the *INT 14H* function (*AH* = 1) to send a character out the serial line. We must therefore write our own *send* subroutine that waits for bit 5 in the *line status register* in Figure 13.6 to go high before writing the character to the transmit holding register.

Setting the baud rate by storing a value in the ACA control register in Figure 13.4 using the *INT 14H* BIOS function will limit you to a maximum baud rate of 9600 baud. You can also set the baud rate by writing values directly to the 8250 UART *divisor high* and *divisor low* registers given in Table 13.2. The values to store in these registers for various baud rates are given in Table 13.3.

Table 13.3		
8250 UART Baud Rate Divisors		
Baud Rate	Divisor-High	Divisor-Low
110	04H	17H
150	03H	00H
300	01H	80H
600	00H	0CH
1,200	00H	60H
2,400	00H	30H
4,800	00H	20H
9,600	00H	0CH
19,200	00H	06H
38,400	00H	03H
57,600	00H	02H
115,200	00H	01H

The interrupt service routine, *intser*, given at the end of Listing 13.2, checks to make sure a character is really there and then reads it from the receive data buffer and stores it in the queue by calling *qstore*. Note that the data segment register, *ds*, must be set to *data* at the beginning of the interrupt service routine because there is no guarantee that it will have this value when the interrupt service routine is called. For example, if a character is being displayed on the screen and is in the middle of an *INT 10H* BIOS call when the interrupt occurs, it is likely that the data segment will have been changed to 0040H, the data segment used by the BIOS routines. Of course, our interrupt service routine must save this value of *ds* and restore it before leaving.

Before leaving the interrupt service routine we must also execute the two instructions

```
mov     al,eoi                    ;8259 EOI
out     ocw2,al
```

where *eoi* is equal to 20H and *ocw2* is the I/O address 20H of the 8259A priority interrupt controller. Whenever a hardware interrupt occurs, a bit associated with that particular interrupt is stored in the 8259A in-service register. This bit must be cleared by writing a 20H value to I/O address 20H before leaving the interrupt service routine. This is called the *end of interrupt* (EOI) command. If you fail to do this, the interrupt will still be pending after leaving the interrupt service routine and it will be called again immediately. It will appear as if you never get out of the interrupt service routine!

PROGRAMMING PROBLEMS

Problem 13.1 – Communicating Between Two Computers
a. Connect two PCs together using a *null modem* between the two COM1 serial ports. A *null modem* is a serial cable in which pins 2 and 3 are crossed. That is, the transmit pin 2 of one computer is connected to the receive pin 3 of the other computer.

b. You will execute the same program on both computers. Modify the program given in Listing 13.2 so that when you press function key *F1* it switches to a double screen mode. In this mode, whatever you type on the first computer should be displayed on the lower half of the second computer and on the upper half of the first computer (after making a round trip to the second computer). Similarly, anything typed on the second computer should be displayed on the lower half of the first computer and on the upper half of the second computer (after making a round trip to the first computer). Both halves of the screen should scroll independently when they are full.

You need to be able to tell when a received character is one that originated at the other computer or is one that has made a round trip from your computer. To do this use the following algorithm:

```
      Send your own character with bit 7 = 0
      If    you receive a character with bit 7 = 0
      Then  display it on the bottom of the screen,
            make bit 7 = 1 and send it back
      Else  display it on the top of the screen
            and do not send it back
```

Extra credit:
c. Modify the program to download a file from one computer to another. That is, read a file from one disk, send it over the serial line, and store it on a disk in the other computer. Design a simple user interface of your choice.

d. Modify the program so as to communicate between the computers at a baud rate of 57,600 baud.

Problem 13.2 – A Smarter Communications Program
a. Add a pop-up menu front end to the program in Listing 13.2 by combining this program with the results of Problem 7.2 in Chapter 7. When the *Select baud rate* menu item is selected allow the user to select a baud rate from 300 to 9600 from a pop-up menu.

b. Add additional features to your communications program. These

can include
>   1. Automatically logging you on to a main computer or local area network by providing your user id and password.
>   2. Pressing function key *F1 turns capture on.* This will ask you for a filename and then store everything that comes in the serial port to this file on disk as well as display it on the screen. Pressing function key *F2* should *turn capture off* by closing the file.

EXERCISES

Exercise 13.1
Write a printer routine that will send characters to a serial printer using an ACA.

Exercise 13.2
Write a subroutine, *gtbaud*, that could be used in the program in Listing 13.2 to set the baud rate to any of the values given in Table 13.3. Modify the subroutine *menu* accordingly.

Exercise 13.3
Discuss what will happen if interrupts are not disabled in the subroutine *checkq* in Listing 13.2 and an interrupt occurs at various locations within the subroutine before and after the variable *front* is changed.

Exercise 13.4
What will the parity bit be for each of the following examples?
>   a) character Y, even parity   c) character K, odd parity
>   b) character S, even parity   d) character A, odd parity

Exercise 13.5
How long will it take to send a page of 4,096 characters over a 9600-baud asynchronous serial line?

Exercise 13.6
a) How long will it take to send a text file containing 100,000 characters over a 1200-baud asynchronous serial line?
b) How long will it take to send this same file between two computers at a baud rate of 57,600?

Exercise 13.7
What value should you store in the ACA control register to initialize the serial port for 300 baud, 7-bits and odd parity?

Exercise 13.8
What value should you store in the ACA control register to initialize the serial port for 9600 baud, 7-bits and even parity?

Exercise 13.9
Write a subroutine that will check the *line status register* for a *parity*, *overrun* or *framing* error and print the appropriate error message on the screen.

Exercise 13.10
How would you have to modify the program given in Listing 13.2 to have it use the COM2 serial port?

CHAPTER 14

Design of a Subroutine Threaded Language

In the RPN calculator program given in Listing 8.3 of Chapter 8 we used a jump table and the subroutine *dokey* to execute a particular subroutine when a certain operator (+, -, *, / or .) occurred in the input stream. A method to modify this jump table to handle word operators was suggested in Problem 8.3. In this chapter we will look at how this word dictionary is created and can be used to produce a subroutine threaded language that is similar to the programming language *Forth*. In particular, you will learn:

- How to use a macro to create a linked-list dictionary of predefined words
- How to search the dictionary for a word and execute it
- How to define new words using *colon definitions*
- The meaning of *immediate* or *compiler words*
- How to store *literals* in a word definition

14.1 THE WORD DICTIONARY

A threaded interpretive language such as Forth consists of a dictionary of words. With each word is associated a routine that is executed when the word is called. We will call a standard subroutine when a word is executed. This is called *subroutine threaded Forth*. (See Problem 6.1 for an example of *direct threaded Forth*).

Each word in the dictionary contains a header with the structure shown in Figure 14.1. The first entry is a 16-bit pointer to the offset address of the subroutine to be executed when the word is called. The second entry in the header is a pointer to the name of the most recently defined word in the dictionary. It points to the *name field address* (*NFA*) which contains the number of characters in the name followed by the ASCII codes for each character in the name. In the example shown in Figure 14.1, the name of the word is *BYE*, which will quit to DOS when executed. Therefore, the subroutine pointer at the beginning of the header will point to the subroutine *quit* given in the file *screen.asm* described in Chapter 7.

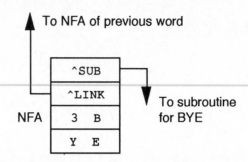

Figure 14.1 Header structure of a word in the dictionary

The header shown in Figure 14.1 can be produced using the macro *$head* given in Figure 14.2 with the following statement:

```
$head   3,'BYE',quit
```

Note that this macro requires three parameters corresponding to *lex*, *name* and *sub*. In our example, *lex* is 3 (the number of characters in the name), *name* is the ASCII string *'BYE'*, and *sub* is the name of the subroutine *quit*.

The first line of the macro, *dw sub*, will store the address of the subroutine to be called when the word is "executed" as the first entry in the header. The second line of the macro, *dw _link*, will store the address of the name of the previous word defined. The first word defined has a *_link* address of zero. The third line of the macro, *_link = $*, sets the value of *_link* to the current offset address in the assembly. This will be the address of the name of the word (the *name field address*, *NFA*), and will be used as the link address for the next word defined. The last line in the macro, *db lex,name*, stores the number of characters in the name as well as the ASCII codes for each character in the name. Note that this will create a linked list of word names together with their subroutine addresses.

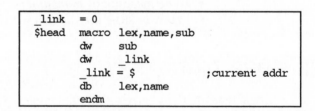

Figure 14.2 The macro *$head* used to create a header in the dictionary

As an example, the statements shown in Figure 14.3 will produce an initial dictionary containing the words for the RPN calculator described in Section 8.3 plus the 32-bit arithmetic words from Problem 8.3 that are defined in Figure 14.4. The parentheses following each word in Figure 14.4 show the stack picture for that word. For example, the word *D+* expects the two 32-bit double numbers *d1* and *d2* on the stack when it is executed and returns the 32-bit double sum *dsum* on the stack.

The dictionary shown in Figure 14.3 contains the word .S which will execute the subroutine *dots*. This subroutine will display the contents of the stack nondestructively. The subroutines *colon* (:) and *semis* (;) are used to define new words that can be added to the dictionary. These words will be described in Section 14.3.

```
$head          2,'D+',dplus
$head          2,'D-',dminus
$head          6,'MU/MOD',mumod
$head          3,'UM*',dtimes
$head          2,'D.',ddott
$head          3,'UD.',uddott
$head          1,'+',plus
$head          1,'-',minus
$head          1,'*',times
$head          1,'/',slash
$head          1,'.',dott
$head          2,'.S',dots
$head          1,':',colon
$head          IMMED+1,';',semis
$head          3,'BYE',quit
current        dw        link
```

Figure 14.3 Statements used to produce the initial dictionary

D+ (d1 d2 -- dsum)	Add the top 2 double words (32-bits) on the data stack and leave the double sum.
D- (d1 d2 -- dsum)	Subtract the top double word (*d2*) on the the stack from the 2nd double word (*d1*) and leave the double difference.
MU/MOD (ud un -- rem dquot)	Divide the unsigned double number (*ud*) by the unsigned single number (*un*) and leave the single remainder (*rem*) and the double quotient (*dquot*). Use *ddiv*.
UM* (un1 un2 -- ud)	Multiply the unsigned single number (*un1*) by the unsigned single number (*un2*) and leave the unsigned double number (*ud*) on the data stack. Use *MUL*.
D. (d --)	Print the signed double number on top of the data stack. Use *pdxax*.
UD. (d --)	Print the unsigned double number on top of the data stack. Use *updxax*.

Figure 14.4 Words used to perform 32-bit double word arithmetic

When the statements shown in Figure 14.3 are assembled, the *$head* macros will be expanded to produce the code shown in Figure 14.5. The variable *current* at offset address 00F3H is the head of the linked list dictionary and contains the value 00EFH, which is the NFA of the word *BYE*. The link field of *BYE* at address 00EDH contains the value 00E9H, which is the NFA of the word *;* (*semis*). The link field of this word in turn points to the word *:* (*colon*) and so forth through the entire dictionary until the first word *D+* is reached. This header has the value 0000 for a link pointer indicating the end of the dictionary.

We will write our small Forth language by modifying the program *rpncalc.asm* given in Listing 8.3 in Chapter 8 so that it will search for a word in the linked-list dictionary shown in Figure 14.5 and execute the appropriate subroutine. If the word is not in the dictionary, it will be checked to see if it is a valid number. If the number contains a decimal point, it will be stored on the stack as a double number. Otherwise, it should be stored on the stack as a single number.

```
                                    $head    2,'D+',dplus
      008A  0152 R                  +               dw       dplus
      008C  0000                    +               dw       _link
      008E  02 44 2B                +               db       2,'D+'
                                    $head    2,'D-',dminus
      0091  0175 R                  +               dw       dminus
      0093  008E R                  +               dw       _link
      0095  02 44 2D                +               db       2,'D-'
                                    $head    6,'MU/MOD',mumod
      0098  0198 R                  +               dw       mumod
      009A  0095 R                  +               dw       _link
      009C  06 4D 55 2F 4D 4F       +               db       6,'MU/MOD'
                                    $head    3,'UM*',dtimes
      00A3  01BA R                  +               dw       dtimes
      00A5  009C R                  +               dw       _link
      00A7  03 55 4D 2A             +               db       3,'UM*'
                                    $head    2,'D.',ddott
      00AB  01D1 R                  +               dw       ddott
      00AD  00A7 R                  +               dw       _link
      00AF  02 44 2E                +               db       2,'D.'
                                    $head    3,'UD.',uddott
      00B2  01E4 R                  +               dw       uddott
      00B4  00AF R                  +               dw       _link
      00B6  03 55 44 2E             +               db       3,'UD.'
                                    $head    1,'+',plus
      00BA  01F7 R                  +               dw       plus
      00BC  00B6 R                  +               dw       _link
      00BE  01 2B                   +               db       1,'+'
                                    $head    1,'-',minus
      00C0  0209 R                  +               dw       minus
      00C2  00BE R                  +               dw       _link
      00C4  01 2D                   +               db       1,'-'
                                    $head    1,'*',times
      00C6  021B R                  +               dw       times
      00C8  00C4 R                  +               dw       _link
      00CA  01 2A                   +               db       1,'*'
                                    $head    1,'/',slash
      00CC  022D R                  +               dw       slash
      00CE  00CA R                  +               dw       _link
      00D0  01 2F                   +               db       1,'/'
                                    $head    1,'.',dott
      00D2  024C R                  +               dw       dott
      00D4  00D0 R                  +               dw       _link
      00D6  01 2E                   +               db       1,'.'
                                    $head    2,'.S',dots
      00D8  02B1 R                  +               dw       dots
      00DA  00D6 R                  +               dw       _link
      00DC  02 2E 53                +               db       2,'.S'
                                    $head    1,':',colon
      00DF  02D8 R                  +               dw       colon
      00E1  00DC R                  +               dw       _link
      00E3  01 3A                   +               db       1,':'
                                    $head    IMMED+1,';',semis
      00E5  0320 R                  +               dw       semis
      00E7  00E3 R                  +               dw       _link
      00E9  81 3B                   +               db       IMMED+1,';'
                                    $head    3,'BYE',quit
      00EB  0000 E                  +               dw       quit
      00ED  00E9 R                  +               dw       _link
      00EF  03 42 59 45             +               db       3,'BYE'
      00F3  00EF R                  current         dw       link
```

Figure 14.5 Expanded view of the word dictionary

14.2 SEARCHING THE DICTIONARY

The file *forth.asm* contains the program shown in Listing 14.1. The main program is almost the same as that for the RPN calculator given in Listing 8.3 in Chapter 8. In particular, the main loop inputs each line of text using *query* and then parses each word using *gtword*, which moves the word to *here* as a counted string. This word is then processed using the subroutine *doword*. This subroutine is modified to search the dictionary for the word at *here* and if it is found the subroutine associated with that word is executed. Otherwise, the subroutine *chnum* tries to convert the string at *here* to a number.

```
      Listing  14.1    forth.asm
                 title   Colon definitions

      stack      segment para stack
                 db      256 dup(?)
      stack      ends

      IMMED      EQU     080H                    ;immediate precedence bit

      data       segment public
      to_in      dw      ?
      here       db      16 dup(?)
      msg1       db      ' <-- What??',0
      msgok      db      ' ok ',0
      bptop      dw      ?
      state      db      ?
      dp         dw      ?                       ;dictionary ptr
      last       dw      ?                       ;ptr to last name
      data       ends

      bpush      macro   val
                 xchg    bp,sp                   ;push val
                 push    val                     ;on bp stack
                 xchg    bp,sp
                 endm

      bpop       macro   val
                 xchg    bp,sp                   ;pop val
                 pop     val                     ;from bp stack
                 xchg    bp,sp
                 endm

      _link      = 0
      $head      macro   lex,name,sub
                 dw      sub
                 dw      _link
                 _link = $                       ;current addr
                 db      lex,name
                 endm

                 extrn   clrscn:near,dokey:near
                 extrn   query:near,number:near
                 extrn   pax:near,crlf:near
                 extrn   mess2:near,chrout1:near
                 extrn   kbuf:byte,beep:near
                 extrn   span:word,ddiv:near
                 extrn   pdxax:near,updxax:near
                 extrn   decflg:byte,quit:near

      code       segment public
```

Listing 14.1   (continued)

```
                assume  cs:code,ds:data

                main    proc far
                mov     ax,data
                mov     ds,ax                   ;set ds
                mov     es,ax                   ;es=ds
                mov     bp,sp
                sub     bp,128                  ;set data stack
                mov     bptop,bp                ;set bptop
                mov     state,0                 ;interpreting
                mov     ax,offset dict
                mov     dp,ax                   ;dp->dictionary
                mov     ax,cs:current
                mov     last,ax                 ;last->current
                cld                             ;dir increase
                call    clrscn                  ;clear screen
        mn1:    mov     to_in,0                 ;t0_in=0
                call    prompt                  ;ok prompt
                call    query                   ;get input
        mn2:    call    getword                 ;get next word
                cmp     here,0                  ;if no word
                je      mn1                     ; get new input
                call    doword                  ;eval word
                jmp     mn2
        main    endp

        ;       parse string for blanks between words
        ;       input:  si -> string
        ;               cx -> length of string
        ;       output: si -> 1st char of parsed word
        ;               di -> 1st blank after word
        parse   proc    near
                mov     di,si                   ;di->string
                push    ds
                pop     es                      ;es=ds
                cld                             ;di increases
                mov     al,20h                  ;look for blank
                jcxz    pr2                     ;skip no string
                repe scasb                      ;skip leading
                je      pr1                     ; blanks
                inc     cx                      ;back up to 1st
                dec     di                      ; non blank
        pr1:    mov     si,di                   ;si->next word
                jcxz    pr2                     ;skip no string
                repne scasb                     ;find 1st blank
                jne     pr2                     ; after word
                inc     cx                      ;back up to 1st
                dec     di                      ; blank
        pr2:    ret
        parse   endp

        ;       parse next word & move to here
        getword proc    near
                mov     si,offset kbuf
                add     si,to_in                ;si->to_in
                mov     cx,span                 ;cx = # of
                sub     cx,to_in                ;chars left
                jcxz    wd1                     ;if 0 do again
                call    parse                   ;get next word
                mov     cx,di                   ;cx=# char
                sub     cx,si                   ; in word
                mov     ax,di
                sub     ax,offset kbuf
                mov     to_in,ax                ;set to_in
        wd1:    mov     di,offset here          ;move word
```

Listing 14.1   (continued)

```
                mov     [di],cl                 ; as $string
                inc     di                      ; to here
                jcxz    wd2
                rep movsb
wd2:            mov     al,0                    ; make asciiz
                stosb
                ret
getword endp

$head    2,'D+',dplus
$head    2,'D-',dminus
$head    6,'MU/MOD',mumod
$head    3,'UM*',dtimes
$head    2,'D.',ddott
$head    3,'UD.',uddott
$head    1,'+',plus
$head    1,'-',minus
$head    1,'*',times
$head    1,'/',slash
$head    1,'.',dott
$head    2,'.S',dots
$head    1,':',colon
$head    IMMED+1,';',semis
$head    3,'BYE',quit
current dw      _link

;       find word in dictionary and execute it
doword proc     near
                push    cs
                pop     es                      ;es=cs
                mov     di,last                 ;di->last name
                mov     al,here                 ;al=count
dwd1:           mov     si,offset here          ;si->$string
                inc     si                      ;si->1st char
                mov     cl,cs:[di]
                and     cl,1fh                  ;cl=head cnt
                cmp     al,cl                   ;if cnts don't
                je      dwd2                    ; match
                mov     di,cs:-2[di]            ;follow link
                or      di,di                   ;if link=0
                jne     dwd1                    ; not found
                call    cknum                   ;chk number
                ret
dwd2:           mov     bx,di                   ;bx->name$
                mov     cl,al                   ;cx=count
                mov     ch,0
                inc     di                      ;di->1st char
                repe cmpsb                      ;compare $s
                je      found                   ;if not found
                mov     di,cs:-2[bx]            ;follow link
                or      di,di                   ;if link=0
                jne     dwd1                    ; not found
                call    cknum                   ;chk number
                ret
found:          mov     al,cs:[bx]             ;chk immed bit
                or      al,al                   ;if immed
                jns     dwd4                    ; execute
                cmp     state,0ffh              ; if compiling
                je      dwd5
                ret
dwd4:           cmp     state,0                 ;if interpret
                jne     dwd3
dwd5:           call    cs:-4[bx]              ; call sub
                ret                             ;else
dwd3:           mov     ax,cs:-4[bx]
```

Listing 14.1   (continued)

```
                    call     compile              ; compile sub
                    ret
      doword    endp

      dplus     proc     near
                bpop     dx
                bpop     ax                       ;get dx:ax
                bpop     cx
                bpop     bx                       ;get cx:bx
                add      ax,bx
                adc      dx,cx                    ;add
                bpush    ax
                bpush    dx                       ;push dx:ax
                ret
      dplus     endp

      dminus    proc     near
                bpop     cx
                bpop     bx                       ;get cx:bx
                bpop     dx
                bpop     ax                       ;get dx:ax
                sub      ax,bx
                sbb      dx,cx                    ;subtract
                bpush    ax
                bpush    dx                       ;push dx:ax
                ret
      dminus    endp

      ;         MU/MOD   ( ud un -- rem dquot )
      mumod     proc     near
                bpop     bx                       ;un
                bpop     dx                       ;udH
                bpop     ax                       ;udL
                call     ddiv                     ;ud/un
                bpush    bx                       ;push rem
                bpush    ax
                bpush    dx                       ;push dquot
                ret
      mumod     endp

      ;         UM*   ( un1 un2 -- ud )   ud = un1 * un2
      dtimes    proc     near
                bpop     ax
                bpop     bx
                mul      bx                       ;unsigned prod
                bpush    ax                       ;is in dx:ax
                bpush    dx
                ret
      dtimes    endp

      ;         print signed double number
      ddott     proc     near
                mov      al,20h
                call     chrout1
                bpop     dx
                bpop     ax                       ;get dvalue
                call     pdxax                    ;print it
                ret
      ddott     endp

      ;         print unsigned double number
      uddott    proc     near
                mov      al,20h
                call     chrout1
                bpop     dx
```

Listing 14.1   (continued)

```
                bpop    ax                              ;get dvalue
                call    updxax                          ;print it
                ret
uddott  endp

;       add top 2 elements on data stack
plus    proc    near
        bpop    ax
        bpop    bx
        add     ax,bx
        bpush   ax
        ret
plus    endp

;       subtract top 2 elements on data stack
minus   proc    near
        bpop    bx
        bpop    ax
        sub     ax,bx
        bpush   ax
        ret
minus   endp

;       multiply top 2 elements on data stack
times   proc    near
        bpop    ax
        bpop    bx
        mul     bx                              ;signed prod
        bpush   ax                              ;is in ax!
        ret
times   endp

;       divide 2nd element on data stack
;       by the top element on data stack
slash   proc    near
        bpop    bx                              ;bx=denom
        bpop    ax
        or      ax,ax                           ;if negative
        jns     sl1
        mov     dx,0ffffh                       ;sign extend
        jmp     sl2                             ;else
sl1:    mov     dx,0                            ;0:ax=numer
sl2:    idiv    bx                              ;signed divide
        bpush   ax
        ret
slash   endp

;       display top element on stack
dott    proc    near
        mov     al,20h
        call    chrout1
        bpop    ax                              ;get value
        call    pax                             ;print it
        ret
dott    endp

;       check word for number
cknum   proc    near
        push    si
        push    di
        mov     si,offset here                  ;si->$string
        mov     al,[si]
        mov     ah,0                            ;ax = count
        inc     si
        mov     bx,si
```

Listing 14.1   (continued)

```
                add    bx,ax                   ;bx->00(end)
                call   number                  ; get number
                cmp    si,bx                   ;bx->00
                jne    ck1                     ;if valid
                cmp    state,0                 ; & interp
                jne    ck0
                bpush  ax                      ; push ax
                cmp    decflg,0                ; if .
                je     ck2
                bpush  dx                      ; push dx
                jmp    ck2                     ;else
ck0:            call   litnum                  ; literal num
                jmp    ck2
ck1:            call   errmsg                  ;error message
ck2:            pop    di
                pop    si
                ret
cknum    endp

;        print error message
errmsg   proc   near
                call   crlf
                mov    si,offset here
                inc    si
                call   mess2                   ;print word
                mov    si,offset msg1
                call   mess2                   ; <-- What??
                ret
errmsg   endp

;        print ok prompt
prompt   proc   near
                mov    si,offset msgok
                call   mess2                   ; ok
                call   crlf
                ret
prompt   endp

;        display data stack
dots     proc   near
                push   ax
                push   cx
                push   si
                mov    cx,bptop                ;#items =
                sub    cx,bp                   ;(bptop-bp)
                mov    si,cx
                shr    cx,1                    ; /2
                sub    si,2                    ;si=index
                jcxz   dts2
dts1:           mov    ax,[bp][si]             ;next val
                push   ax
                mov    al,20h                  ;print
                call   chrout1                 ; blank
                pop    ax
                call   pax                     ;print it
                sub    si,2                    ;bump index
                loop   dts1                    ;do all items
dts2:           pop    si
                pop    cx
                pop    ax
                ret
dots     endp

;        colon definition
colon    proc   near
```

Listing 14.1   (continued)

```
              mov     state,0ffh              ;set state
              call    getword                 ;get name
              call    makehdr                 ;make header
              ret
colon    endp


;        compile address
;        input: ax = sub address
compile  proc    near
              push    cs
              pop     es                      ;es = cs
              mov     di,dp                   ;di=dp
              mov     byte ptr es:[di],0E8h
              inc     di                      ;CALL opcode
              sub     ax,di                   ;calc displ
              sub     ax,2
              stosw                           ;store displ
              mov     dp,di                   ;update di
              ret
compile  endp


;        make header of word at here
makehdr  proc    near
              push    cs
              pop     es                      ;es = cs
              mov     di,dp                   ;di=dp
              mov     bx,di                   ;bx=dp
              add     di,2                    ;store link
              mov     ax,last
              stosw
              mov     last,di                 ;update last
              mov     si,offset here
              mov     cl,[si]
              inc     cl                      ;move counted
              mov     ch,0                    ;string from
              rep movsb                       ;here
              mov     es:[bx],di              ;fill ^sub
              mov     dp,di                   ;update dp
              ret
makehdr  endp


;        semi-colon
semis    proc    near
              push    cs
              pop     es                      ;es=cs
              mov     state,0                 ;clear state
              mov     di,dp
              mov     al,0C3h                 ;store RET
              stosb
              mov     dp,di                   ;update dp
              ret
semis    endp


;        store literal number
litnum   proc    near
              push    dx                      ;save number
              push    ax
              cmp     decflg,0                ;if single
              jne     ln1
              mov     ax,offset lit           ;compile lit
              call    compile
              pop     ax                      ;and ax
              stosw
              pop     dx
              jmp     ln2                     ;else
```

Listing 14.1 (continued)

```
ln1:      mov     ax,offset dlit          ;compile dlit
          call    compile
          pop     ax
          stosw                           ;and dx:ax
          pop     dx
          stosw
ln2:      mov     dp,di                   ;update di
          ret
litnum    endp

;         runtime routine for single literals
lit       proc    near
          pop     di                      ;di->number
          mov     ax,cs:[di]              ;push number
          bpush   ax                      ;on data stack
          add     di,2                    ;jump over num
          push    di
          ret
lit       endp

;         runtime routine for double literals
dlit      proc    near
          pop     di                      ;di->number
          mov     ax,cs:[di]              ;push number
          bpush   ax                      ;on data stack
          add     di,2                    ;jump over num
          mov     ax,cs:[di]
          bpush   ax
          add     di,2
          push    di
          ret
dlit      endp

;         reserve dictionary space
dict      db      4000h dup(?)

code      ends
          end     main
```

The variable *last* contains the NFA of the last word defined. At the beginning of the main program this variable is initialized to the contents of *current*, which contains the NFA of the word *BYE*. The search in *doword* begins at *last* and continues through the linked list until either the word is found or the end of the list, signified by a link address of 0000, is reached. In searching for the name of a word, the number of characters in the name at *here* is compared with the number of characters in the name of the word in the header. If they match, the name at *here* is compared with the name in the header using the statement *repe cmpsb*.

If the word is found in the dictionary, the subroutine whose address is stored in the first entry of the header is executed. This is the operation when the program is being used as a calculator in the *interpret* mode. However, in the following section we will see how we can add new words to the dictionary by typing in *colon definitions*. This will require additional tests in *doword* when a name is found in the dictionary.

14.3   COLON DEFINITIONS

A colon definition is of the following form:

```
: name word1 word2 . . . wordn ;
```

where *name* is the name of a new word to add to your linked-list dictionary of names. The following list of words, *word1 word2 . . . wordn* are names of subroutines (previously defined words) that are to be called, in order, when *name* is called. The semicolon ends the definition.

If you enter the above line using *query*, the program must build a header to store the name of the new word, followed by calls to each subroutine in the definition. Thus, the code shown in Figure 14.6 must be generated in the code segment.

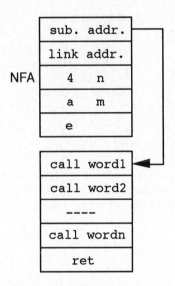

Figure 14.6 Code generated by a colon definition

Note that the following statement is included at the end of the code segment in Listing 14.1.

```
dict        db        4000h dup(?)
```

This will reserve 16 Kbytes of memory at the end of the code segment for adding new words to the language. The dictionary pointer, *dp*, is initialized to *offset dict* and points to the next available memory location where additions to the language can be added.

The word *:* (*colon*) is included in the *$head* list. The subroutine *colon* given in Listing 14.1 does the following:

1. Sets the variable *state* to true (0FFH). This indicates that the program is in the *compiling state* so that when the words in the definition are parsed, *doword* will not execute them, but instead will store them as *call word* statements following the name header.
2. Calls the subroutine *getword* to get the next word in the input stream and store it as a counted string at *here*.
3. Makes a header of this name at *dp* in the code segment by calling the subroutine *makehdr* which does the following:
    a. Stores the link address in *last* at *dp* + 2. Sets *last* to the address of the new name at *dp* + 4. This links the new header into the dictionary.
    b. Moves the counted name from *here* to *dp* + 4.
    c. Stores the next available offset address as the subroutine pointer in the first entry of the header as well as the new value of *dp*.

This is all that the subroutine *colon* will do. When the next word in the input stream, *word1*, is parsed, *doword* will note that the variable *state* is set and therefore *word1* needs to be compiled into the dictionary, rather than executed. The subroutine *compile* given in Listing 14.1 will do this. It does the following:

1. Stores E8H at the address in *dp*. This is the opcode for *CALL*.
2. Calculates and stores the 16-bit displacement to follow E8H that will cause the subroutine *word1* to be executed.

The subroutine *semis* given in Listing 14.1 that is called when *;* is executed does only two things:

1. Sets the variable *state* to zero to go back to the interpreting mode.
2. Add C3H, the opcode for *RET* to the end of the current definition.

There is only one problem. Since we are in the compiling mode (remember, *colon* set the variable *state*) the subroutine *semis* will just be compiled into the dictionary. This is not what we want. We need it to be executed so that it can turn the compiler off.

We will do this by setting bit 7 in the count byte in the name field of *semis*. This will flag it as an *immediate word* that must be executed immediately even if we are in the compiling mode. Note that when we defined the word *;* we used the following statement.

```
$head 81h,';',semis
```

which has bit 7 of the count byte set to 1.

Note that the subroutine *doword* checks this bit when a word is found. If the bit is set and the value of *state* is *true* (in the compiling state), the word is executed rather than compiled. If this bit is not set, the word is executed only if the value of *state* is zero; otherwise, the word is compiled into the dictionary.

Literals

Suppose we test the program by defining the following word:

```
: TEST   3 4 + . ;
```

If we then type *TEST*, the value 7 should be printed. But there is still a problem. How do the numbers 3 and 4 get compiled? They aren't the names of subroutines so we can't have *doword* compile them as we do for other words. What we want to happen is to have 3 and 4 put on the stack when the word *TEST* is later executed. We will therefore store the numbers in the definition of *TEST* as literals as shown in Figure 14.7.

We must modify the subroutine *cknum* (that checks for a number if *doword* doesn't find the word in the dictionary) from that given in Listing 8.3 for the RPN calculator so as to store the literal as shown in Figure 14.7 if *state* is set and the program is in the compiling mode. The subroutine *lit*, which is executed when *TEST* is called, must push the next word (the value of the number) on the stack. The subroutine shown in Figure 14.8 will do this. A similar subroutine, called *dlit*, which will handle double numbers that are entered with a decimal point, is also included in Listing 14.1

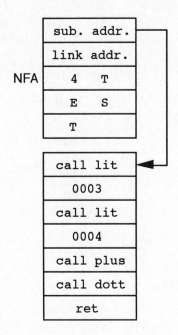

Figure 14.7 Code generated by the definition : TEST 3 4 + . ;

```
        lit    proc    near
               pop     di                  ;di->number
               mov     ax,cs:[di]          ;push number
               bpush   ax                  ; on data stack
               add     di,2                ;jump over number
               push    di
               ret
        lit    endp
```

Figure 14.8 Run time subroutine that will push a literal number on the stack

14.4 ADDING NEW CODE WORDS TO THE DICTIONARY

A *code word* is a word that is defined by an assembly language subroutine rather than by a colon definition. We can add new code words to the language by adding more *$head* statements to the list in Figure 14.3 and writing the appropriate subroutine for each new word. When Listing 14.1 is then reassembled, the new words will be in the dictionary. For example, the word *DUP* (*n -- n n*) duplicates the top element on the data stack and the word *DROP* (*n --*) drops the top element from the stack. The subroutines *dupp* and *drop* shown in Figure 14.9 will perform these functions. These words can be added to the dictionary using the following two statements:

```
        $head 3,'DUP',dupp
        $head 4,'DROP',drop
```

Immediate words can be used inside a colon definition to define various branching and looping instructions. For example, the two immediate words *FOR* and *NEXT* are used to produce a loop. For example, the statements

```
;          DUP       ( n -- n n )
dupp       proc      near
           bpop      ax
           bpush     ax
           bpush     ax
           ret
dupp       endp


;          DROP      ( n -- )
drop       proc      near
           inc       bp
           inc       bp
           ret
drop       endp
```

Figure 14.8 Subroutines to implement the Forth words *DUP* and *DROP*

```
            8 FOR . . . NEXT
```

will go through the loop 8 times. The word *I* is used to give the current value of the index within a *FOR . . . NEXT* loop. In the above example, the index will start at 8 and decrement by 1 each time through the loop. These three statements can be added to the dictionary using the following three statements.

```
$head 83h,'FOR',for
$head 84h,'NEXT',next
$head 1,'I',I
```

The subroutine *for* must do the following:

```
compile the code
    FF 76 00     PUSH 0[BP]
    45 45        INC BP   INC BP
```
and then *bpush* the current dictionary pointer
on the data stack.

Note that the loop count is stored on the system stack and the address of the first instruction following *FOR* is stored on the data stack. The listing for the subroutine *for* is shown in Figure 14.9.

The subroutine *next* must do the following:

```
compile the code
    59      POP  CX
    49      DEC  CX
    51      PUSH CX
    75      JNE
```
and then *bpop* the address *bpush*ed by *FOR* and
subtract the address of the next instruction from it to
find the 8-bit displacement to compile following
JNE. Then compile the code
```
    59      POP   CX
```

The listing of the subroutine *next* is shown in Figure 14.10 and the listing for the subroutine *I* is shown in Figure 14.11. See Problem 14.2 at the end of this chapter for an example of using these looping words to produce a turtle graphics system.

```
;       for ... next loop
;       for     ( n -- )  immediate word
for     proc    near
        push    cs
        pop     es
        mov     di,dp               ;compile >R
        mov     al,0FFH
        stosb                       ;FF 76 00
        mov     al,76h              ;PUSH 0[BP]
        stosb
        mov     al,0
        stosb
        mov     al,45h              ;45 45
        stosb                       ;INC BP
        mov     al,45h              ;INC BP
        stosb
        mov     dp,di
        bpush   di                  ;save loop addr
        ret
for     endp
```

Figure 14.9 The subroutine *for*

```
;       next    ( -- )    (R: sys1 -- sys1)
next    proc    near
        push    cs
        pop     es
        mov     di,dp               ;compile:
        mov     al,59h              ;pop cx
        stosb
        mov     al,49h              ;dec cx
        stosb
        mov     al,51h              ;push cx
        stosb
        mov     al,75h              ;jne
        stosb
        bpop    ax                  ;loop addr
        sub     ax,di
        dec     ax                  ;al=displ
        stosb
        mov     al,59h              ;pop cx
        stosb
        mov     dp,di               ;update dp
        ret
next    endp
```

Figure 14.10 The subroutine *next*

```
;       I       ( -- n )  R@
I       proc    near
        pop     ax                  ;ret addr
        pop     bx                  ;index
        push    bx                  ;put back
        push    ax
        bpush   bx                  ;index on data stack
        ret
I       endp
```

Figure 14.11 The subroutine *I*

PROGRAMMING PROBLEMS

Problem 14.1 – Loading Words and Saving .EXE Files

In this problem you will modify the program in Listing 14.1 to load and compile previously defined colon definitions from a disk file and to save a modified version of your program as a new .EXE file. You will use various file access subroutines that are in the file *dos.asm* discussed in Chapter 10.

    a. Add the following words to your dictionary:

```
$head 4,'LOAD',load
$head 8,'SAVE.EXE',savexe
```

You will use the word *LOAD* as follows:

```
LOAD myfile.4th
```

where *myfile.4th* is some file you have created that contains a list of colon definitions such as

```
: TEST  3 4 + . ;
```

When *LOAD* is executed, it will read the contents of *myfile.4th*, line by line, and compile (or execute) the words defined in the file just as if you typed in the entire file from within your program using *query*. Using this technique you can write entire programs in terms of colon definitions as separate files and then load, compile and execute them from your *Forth* program.

When you execute the word *SAVE.EXE* the current version of your program, including all new words added to your dictionary, will be saved as a new .EXE file. After typing *SAVE.EXE* you will be prompted to enter the name of a new .EXE filename.

When saving an .EXE file you must first save an .EXE header of the form shown in Figure 5.20 in Chapter 5. In your case, because the size of your dictionary space is set ahead of time, the size of your .EXE file will be the same, no matter how many words you add to your dictionary. This means that you can use the same .EXE header created when you linked your program. To save a copy of this .EXE header in a separate file called, for example, *exehead.tut*, go to TUTOR and load your .EXE file. *BEFORE* you press function key *F10*, save the .EXE header by typing

```
/SS
200           (number of hex bytes to save)
EXEHEAD.TUT   (filename)
```

This will save the 512-byte .EXE header in the file *EXEHEAD.TUT*.

Your subroutine *savexe* that is called when you type *SAVE.EXE* should do the following:

    1. Read the .EXE header from *EXEHEAD.TUT* into a 512-byte buffer.
    2. Fix all relocation addresses given in the header using the technique described below.
    3. Create and open a new .EXE filename and write the .EXE header to this new file.
    4. Compute the size of your program file from information in the .EXE header and write the entire program file to your new filename (following the .EXE header you just wrote).

The important fields within the .EXE header that you will need to use are as follows:

Byte offset	Data
2	No. of bytes in last 512-byte page of file -- NBLAST
4	Max. filesize in 512-byte pages -- FILESIZE
6	No. of relocation items -- NOITEMS
8	Header size in paragraphs -- HEADSIZE
18H	Offset to relocation table -- RELOFF
RELOFF	Table of NOTIMES offset:segment addresses from start of program that contain relocation data. Each word at these addresses has the value of the code segment added to it at load time. This means that in Step 2 above you must subtract the value of the code segment from the value at these addresses before saving the .EXE file. When you execute the .EXE file again, DOS will automatically fix these addresses again when it loads the program using the information in the .EXE header.

The size of your program that you must compute in Step 4 above is given by the equation

```
PROGSIZE = (FILESIZE - 1)*512 + NBLAST - HEADSIZE*16
```

b. Test your program by making a file containing some sample colon definitions. Load this file using *LOAD*, verify that the words got loaded by executing them, and then save your program using *SAVE.EXE*. Execute your new program and verify that the words are still there by executing them again.

Problem 14.2 – Turtle Graphics
In this problem you will modify the program in Listing 14.1 to do interactive turtle graphics. You will use various Hercules graphics subroutines that are in the file *graph.asm* described in Chapter 12. This *graph.asm* file also contains the subroutines *sinax* and *cosax* for finding the sine and cosine of the angle in *ax*.

a. Add the following words to your dictionary:

```
$head 3,'DUP',dupp
$head 4,'DROP',drop
$head 6,'TURTLE',turtle
$head 7,'FORWARD',forward
$head 6,'ROTATE',rotate
$head 83h,'FOR',for
$head 84h,'NEXT',next
$head 1,'I',I
```

The words *DUP* (*n -- n n*) and *DROP* (*n -- *) are the Forth words described in Section 14.4. The word *TURTLE* should call *stherc* to switch to Hercules graphics and plot a dot near the center of the screen. You should then go into an interpret loop that gets an input by calling *queryh* which is similar to *query* except that it will display the input on the bottom line of the screen when in the Hercules graphics mode.

The word *FORWARD* (*D -- *) will plot a line of length *D* in the current direction (whose angle is stored in the variable *deg*). The word *ROTATE* (*ang -- *) will add the angle *ang* to *deg*.

The words *FOR*, *NEXT*, and *I* are used to produce a loop as discussed in Section 14.4.

b. Test your program by typing in the following words:

```
: BOX    4 FOR DUP FORWARD 90 ROTATE NEXT DROP ;
: PIC1   18 FOR 20 ROTATE 80 BOX NEXT ;
: PIC2   10 FOR I 15 * BOX NEXT ;
```

These can by typed in either before or after typing *TURTLE*. After typing *TURTLE*, draw various size boxes by typing, for example,

```
40 BOX
80 BOX
```

and draw the pictures by typing

```
PIC1
PIC2
```

Extra Credit:
Store the above words together with additional ones that you make up in a separate text file and load them using the *LOAD* command from Problem 14.1. Add any additional features you wish, to make your graphics demonstration easier to use and more spectacular.

More Extra Credit:
Make a turnkey program in the form of an .EXE file that will plot some spectacular graphic figures when you run the program from DOS.

Bibliography

ABEL, PETER, *IBM PC Assembly Language and Programming*, 2nd Ed., Prentice-Hall, Inc., Englewood Cliffs, N.J., 1991.

AUGARTEN, STAN, *Bit by Bit – An Illustrated History of Computers*, Ticknor & Fields, New York, 1984.

BREY, BARRY B., *The Intel Microprocessors – 8086/8088, 80186, 80286, 80386, and 80486 – Architecture, Programming, and Interfacing*, Merrill/Macmillan Publishing Company, New York, 1991.

BRADLEY, DAVID J., *Assembly Language Programming for the IBM Personal Computer*, Prentice-Hall, Inc., Englewood Cliffs, N.J., 1984.

DUNCAN, RAY, *Advanced MS DOS*, Microsoft Press, Redmond, Wash., 1986.

EVANS, CHRISTOPHER, *The Making of the Micro – A History of the Computer*, Van Nostrand Reinhold Company, New York, 1981.

GILES, WILLIAM B., *Assembly Language Programming for the Intel 80XXX Family*, Macmillan Publishing Company, New York, 1991.

GOLDSTINE, HERMAN H., *The Computer from Pascal to von Neumann*, Princeton University Press, Princeton, N.J., 1972.

GRAY, ROBERT L., *Macro Assembler Programming – for the IBM PC and Compatibles*, SRA, Inc., Chicago, Ill., 1989.

JOURDAIN, ROBERT, *Programmer's Problem Solver for the IBM PC, XT & AT*, Brady Communications Company, Inc., New York, 1986.

MORGAN, CHRISTOPHER L. and WAITE, MITCHELL, *8086/8088 16-Bit Microprocessor Primer*, BYTE/McGraw-Hill, Peterborough, N.H., 1982.

MURRAY, WILLIAM H., III and PAPPAS, CHRIS H., *80386/80286 Assembly Language Programming*, Osborne, McGraw-Hill, Berkeley, Cal., 1986.

TRIEBEL, WALTER A. and SINGH, AVTAR, *The 8088 and 8086 Microprocessors – Programming, Interfacing, Software, Hardware, and Applications*, Prentice-Hall, Inc., Englewood Cliffs, N.J., 1991.

TRIEBEL, WALTER A., *The 80386DX Microprocessor – Hardware, Software, & Interfacing*, Prentice-Hall, Inc., Englewood Cliffs, N.J., 1992.

8086 Instruction Set

Table A.1

8086 Instruction Set

Effective address (EA) clock cycle values		Clocks
Displacement only	disp	6
Base or Index only	BX, SI, DI	5
Base + Displacement Index + Displacement	BX + disp, BP + disp SI + disp, DI + disp	9
Base + Index	BP + DI, BX + SI BP + SI, BX + DI	7 8
Base + Index + Displacement	BP + DI + disp, BX + SI + disp BP + SI + disp, BX + DI + disp	11 12

Add two clock cycles when segment override is used.

Key to status flag codes

x	Set or reset by instruction
u	Undefined
r	Replaced from memory or register
1	Always set to 1
0	Always cleared to 0
blank	Unchanged

Notes:

d = 1	"to" register
d = 0	"from" register
w = 1	word instruction
w = 0	byte instruction
s = 1	data byte sign extended to form 16-bit operand
v = 0	"count" = 1
v = 1	"count" in CL
x	don't care

AAA   *ASCII adjust for addition*   Flags   ODITSZAPC

| 0 0 1 1 0 1 1 1 |

Clocks = 4

u   uuxux

AAD   *ASCII adjust for division*   Flags   ODITSZAPC

| 1 1 0 1 0 1 0 1 | 0 0 0 0 1 0 1 0 |

Clocks = 60

u   xxuxu

AAM   *ASCII adjust for multiply*   Flags   ODITSZAPC

| 1 1 0 1 0 1 0 0 | 0 0 0 0 1 0 1 0 |

Clocks = 83

u   xxuxu

AAS   *ASCII adjust for subtraction*   Flags   ODITSZAPC

| 0 0 1 1 1 1 1 1 |

Clocks = 4

u   uuxux

ADC   *Add with carry*   Flags   ODITSZAPC
Register/memory with register to either

| 0 0 0 1 0 0 d w | mod   reg   r/m |

Clocks: register to register   3
         memory to register   9 + EA
         register to memory   16 + EA

x   xxxxx

Immediate to register/memory

| 1 0 0 0 0 0 s w | mod 0 1 0 r/m | data | data if s:w = 01 |

Clocks: immediate to register   4
         immediate to memory   17 + EA

Immediate to accumulator

| 0 0 0 1 0 1 0 w | data | data if w = 1 |

Clocks = 4

ADD   *Addition*   Flags   ODITSZAPC
Register/memory and register to either

| 0 0 0 0 0 0 d w | mod   reg   r/m |

Clocks: register to register   3
         memory to register   9 + EA
         register to memory   16 + EA

x   xxxxx

Immediate to register/memory

| 1 0 0 0 0 0 s w | mod 0 0 0 r/m | data | data if s:w = 01 |

Clocks: immediate to register   4
         immediate to memory   17 + EA

Immediate to accumulator

| 0 0 0 0 0 1 0 w | data | data if w = 1 |

Clocks = 4

AND   *Logical AND*   Flags   ODITSZAPC
Register/memory and register to either

| 0 0 1 0 0 0 d w | mod   reg   r/m |

Clocks: register to register   3
         memory to register   9 + EA
         register to memory   16 + EA

0   xxux0

Immediate to register/memory

| 1 0 0 0 0 0 0 w | mod 1 0 0 r/m | data | data if w = 1 |

Clocks: immediate to register   4
         immediate to memory   17 + EA

Immediate to accumulator

| 0 0 1 0 0 1 0 w | data | data if w = 1 |

Clocks = 4

CALL   *Call a procedure*   Flags   ODITSZAPC
Direct within segment

| 1 1 1 0 1 0 0 0 | disp-low | disp-high |

Clocks = 19

Indirect within segment

| 1 1 1 1 1 1 1 1 | mod 0 1 0 r/m |

Clocks = 21 + EA

Direct intersegment

| 1 0 0 1 1 0 1 0 | offset-low | offset-high |
| | segment-low | segment-high |

Clocks = 28

Indirect intersegment

| 1 1 1 1 1 1 1 1 | mod 0 1 1 r/m |

Clocks = 37 + EA

CBW   *Convert byte to word*   Flags   ODITSZAPC

| 1 0 0 1 1 0 0 0 |

Clocks = 2

CLC   *Clear carry flag*   Flags   ODITSZAPC
                                                                0

| 1 1 1 1 1 0 0 0 |

Clocks = 2

CLD   *Clear direction flag*   Flags   ODITSZAPC
                                                         0

| 1 1 1 1 1 1 0 0 |

Clocks = 2

CLI   *Clear interrupt flag*   Flags   ODITSZAPC
                                                          0

| 1 1 1 1 1 0 1 0 |

Clocks = 2

CMC   *Complement carry flag*   Flags   ODITSZAPC
                                                                x

| 1 1 1 1 0 1 0 1 |

Clocks = 2

CMP   *Compare*   Flags   ODITSZAPC
Register/memory and register   x   xxxxx

| 0 0 1 1 1 0 d w | mod reg r/m |

Clocks: register with register   3
         memory with register   9 + EA
         register with memory   9 + EA

Immediate with register/memory

| 1 0 0 0 0 0 s w | mod 1 1 1 r/m | data | data if s:w = 01 |

Clocks: immediate to register   4
         immediate to memory   17 + EA

Immediate with accumulator

| 0 0 1 1 1 1 0 w | data | data if w = 1 |

Clocks = 4

CMPS *Compare string*   Flags   ODITSZAPC
                                                      x   xxxxx

| 1 0 1 0 0 1 1 w |

Clocks = 22

CWD   *Convert word to double word*   Flags   ODITSZAPC

| 1 0 0 1 1 0 0 1 |

Clocks = 5

DAA   *Decimal adjust for addition*   Flags   ODITSZAPC

| 0 0 1 0 0 1 1 1 |

Clocks = 4   x   xxxxx

DAS   *Decimal adjust for subtraction*   Flags   ODITSZAPC

| 0 0 1 0 1 1 1 1 |

Clocks = 4   u   xxxxx

DEC   *Decrement by 1*   Flags   ODITSZAPC
Register/memory

| 1 1 1 1 1 1 1 w | mod 0 0 1 r/m | x   xxxxx

Clocks: register   2
         memory   15 + EA

Register

| 0 1 0 0 1 reg |

Clocks = 2

DIV   *Division (unsigned)*   Flags   ODITSZAPC

| 1 1 1 1 0 1 1 w | mod 1 1 0 r/m | u   uuuuu

Clocks: 8-bit register   80-90
         8-bit memory   (86-96) + EA
         16-bit register   144-162
         16-bit memory   (150-168) + EA

ESC   *Escape to external device*   Flags   ODITSZAPC

| 1 1 0 1 1 x x x | mod x x x r/m |

Clocks = 7 + EA

HLT   *Halt*   Flags   ODITSZAPC

| 1 1 1 1 0 1 0 0 |

Clocks = 2

IDIV   *Integer division (signed)*   Flags   ODITSZAPC

| 1 1 1 1 0 1 1 w | mod 1 1 1 r/m | u   uuuuu

Clocks: 8-bit register   101-112
         8-bit memory   (107-118) + EA
         16-bit register   165-184
         16-bit memory   (171-190) + EA

IMUL   *Integer multiplication (signed)*   Flags   ODITSZAPC

| 1 1 1 1 0 1 1 w | mod 1 0 1 r/m | x   uuuux

Clocks: 8-bit register   80-98
         8-bit memory   (86-104) + EA
         16-bit register   128-154
         16-bit memory   (134-160) + EA

IN   *Input to AL or AX from port*   Flags   ODITSZAPC
Fixed port

| 1 1 1 0 0 1 0 w | port |

Clocks = 10 (byte) or 14 (word)

Variable port (DX)

| 1 1 1 0 1 1 0 w |

Clocks = 8 (byte) or 12 (word)

INC   *Increment by 1*   Flags   ODITSZAPC
Register/memory   x   xxxxx

| 1 1 1 1 1 1 1 w | mod 0 0 0   r/m |

Clocks: register   2
         memory   15 + EA

Register

| 0 1 0 0 0 reg |

Clocks = 2

INT   *Interrupt*   Flags   ODITSZAPC
Type specified   00

| 1 1 0 0 1 1 0 1 | type |

Clocks = 51

Type 3

| 1 1 0 0 1 1 0 0 |

Clocks = 51

INTO   *Interrupt on overflow*   Flags   ODITSZAPC
                                                        00
| 1 1 0 0 1 1 1 0 |

Clocks = 52 or 4

IRET   *Interrupt return*   Flags   ODITSZAPC
                                                        rrrrrrrr
| 1 1 0 0 1 1 1 1 |

Clocks = 24

JA/JNBE   *Jump if above/not below or equal*   Flags   ODITSZAPC

| 0 1 1 1 0 1 1 1 | disp |

Clocks: jump taken   16
         jump not taken 4

JAE/JNB   *Jump if above or equal/not below*   Flags   ODITSZAPC

| 0 1 1 1 0 0 1 1 | disp |

Clocks: jump taken   16
         jump not taken 4

JB/JNAE   *Jump if below/not above or equal*   Flags   ODITSZAPC

| 0 1 1 1 0 0 1 0 | disp |

Clocks: jump taken   16
         jump not taken 4

JBE/JNA   *Jump if below or equal/not above*   Flags   ODITSZAPC

| 0 1 1 1 0 1 1 0 | disp |

Clocks: jump taken   16
         jump not taken 4

J C   *Jump if carry*   Flags   ODITSZAPC

| 0 1 1 1 0 0 1 0 | disp |

Clocks: jump taken   16
         jump not taken 4

JCXZ   *Jump if CX is zero*   Flags   ODITSZAPC

| 1 1 1 0 0 0 1 1 | disp |

Clocks: jump taken   18
         jump not taken 6

JE/JZ   *Jump if equal/zero*   Flags   ODITSZAPC

| 0 1 1 1 0 1 0 0 | disp |

Clocks: jump taken   16
         jump not taken 4

JG/JNLE   *Jump if greater/not less or equal*   Flags   ODITSZAPC

0 1 1 1 1 1 1 1	disp

Clocks: jump taken   16
        jump not taken 4

JGE/JNL   *Jump if greater or equal/not less*   Flags   ODITSZAPC

0 1 1 1 1 1 0 1	disp

Clocks: jump taken   16
        jump not taken 4

JL/JNGE   *Jump if less/not greater or equal*   Flags   ODITSZAPC

0 1 1 1 1 1 0 0	disp

Clocks: jump taken   16
        jump not taken 4

JLE/JNG   *Jump if less or equal/not greater*   Flags   ODITSZAPC

0 1 1 1 1 1 1 0	disp

Clocks: jump taken   16
        jump not taken 4

JMP   *Unconditional jump*   Flags   ODITSZAPC

Direct within segment

1 1 1 0 1 0 0 1	disp-low	disp-high

Clocks = 15

Direct within segment - short

1 1 1 0 1 0 1 1	disp

Clocks = 21 + EA

Indirect within segment

1 1 1 1 1 1 1 1	mod 1 0 0 r/m

Clocks: memory 18 + EA
        register 11

Direct intersegment

1 1 1 0 1 0 1 0	offset-low	offset-high
Clocks = 15	segment-low	segment-high

Indirect intersegment

1 1 1 1 1 1 1 1	mod 1 0 1 r/m

Clocks = 24 + EA

JNC   *Jump if not carry*   Flags   ODITSZAPC

0 1 1 1 0 0 1 1	disp

Clocks: jump taken   16
        jump not taken 4

JNE/JNZ   *Jump if not equal/not zero*   Flags   ODITSZAPC

0 1 1 1 0 1 0 1	disp

Clocks: jump taken   16
        jump not taken 4

JNO   *Jump if not overflow*   Flags   ODITSZAPC

0 1 1 1 0 0 0 1	disp

Clocks: jump taken   16
        jump not taken 4

JNP/JPO   *Jump if not parity/parity odd*   Flags   ODITSZAPC

0 1 1 1 1 0 1 1	disp

Clocks: jump taken   16
        jump not taken 4

JNS   *Jump if not sign*   Flags   ODITSZAPC

0 1 1 1 1 0 0 1	disp

Clocks: jump taken   16
         jump not taken 4

J O   *Jump if overflow*   Flags   ODITSZAPC

0 1 1 1 0 0 0 0	disp

Clocks: jump taken   16
         jump not taken 4

JP/JPE   *Jump if parity/parity even*   Flags   ODITSZAPC

0 1 1 1 1 0 1 0	disp

Clocks: jump taken   16
         jump not taken 4

J S   *Jump if sign*   Flags   ODITSZAPC

0 1 1 1 1 0 0 0	disp

Clocks: jump taken   16
         jump not taken 4

LAHF   *Load AH from flags*   Flags   ODITSZAPC

1 0 0 1 1 1 1 1

Clocks = 4

LDS   *Load pointer into reg and DS*   Flags   ODITSZAPC

1 1 0 0 0 1 0 1	mod reg r/m

Clocks = 16 + EA

LOCK   *Bus lock prefix*   Flags   ODITSZAPC

1 1 1 1 0 0 0 0

Clocks = 2

LODS   *Bus lock prefix*   Flags   ODITSZAPC

1 1 1 1 0 0 0 0

Clocks = 2

LOOP   *Loop CX times*   Flags   ODITSZAPC

1 1 1 0 0 0 1 0	disp

Clocks: jump taken   17
         jump not taken 5

LOOPE/LOOPZ   *Loop if equal/zero*   Flags   ODITSZAPC

1 1 1 0 0 0 0 1	disp

Clocks: jump taken   18
         jump not taken 6

LOOPNE/LOOPNZ   *Loop if not equal/not zero*   Flags   ODITSZAPC

1 1 1 0 0 0 0 0	disp

Clocks: jump taken   19
         jump not taken 5

LEA   *Load effective address to register*   Flags   ODITSZAPC

1 0 0 0 1 1 0 1	mod reg r/m

Clocks = 2 + EA

LES   *Load pointer to register and ES*   Flags   ODITSZAPC

1 1 0 0 0 1 0 0	mod reg r/m

Clocks = 16 + EA

MOV *Move*   Flags ODITSZAPC

Register/memory to/from register

1 0 0 0 1 0 d w	mod reg r/m

Clocks: register to register   2
        memory to register   8 + EA
        register to memory   9 + EA

Immediate to register/memory

1 1 0 0 0 1 1 w	mod 0 0 0 r/m	data	data if w = 1

Clocks: immediate to register   4
        immediate to memory   10 + EA

Immediate to register

1 0 1 1 w reg	data	data if w = 1

Clocks = 4

Memory to accumulator

1 0 1 0 0 0 0 w	addr-low	addr-high

Clocks = 10

Accumulator to memory

1 0 1 0 0 0 1 w	addr-low	addr-high

Clocks = 10

Register/memory to segment register

1 0 0 0 1 1 1 0	mod 0 reg r/m

Clocks: register to register   2
        memory to register   8 + EA

Segment register to register/memory

1 0 0 0 1 1 0 0	mod 0 reg r/m

Clocks: register to register   2
        register to memory   9 + EA

MOVS *Move string*   Flags ODITSZAPC

1 0 1 0 0 1 0 w

Clocks: byte   18
        word   26
        rep byte   9 + 17/rep
        rep word   9 + 25/rep

MUL *Multiply (unsigned)*   Flags ODITSZAPC
                                                                                    x   uuuux

1 1 1 1 0 1 1 w	mod 1 0 0 r/m

Clocks: 8-bit register   70-77
        8-bit memory   (76-83) + EA
        16-bit register   118-133
        16-bit memory (124-139) + EA

NEG *Negate (change sign)*   Flags ODITSZAPC
                                                                                    x   xxxx1

1 1 1 1 0 1 1 w	mod 0 1 1 r/m

Clocks: register 3
        memory 16 + EA

NOP *No operation*   Flags ODITSZAPC

1 0 0 1 0 0 0 0

Clocks = 3

NOT *Logical NOT*   Flags   ODITSZAPC
                                                                                     x   xxxx1

1 1 1 1 0 1 1 w	mod 0 1 0 r/m

Clocks: register 3
        memory 16 + EA

OR   *Logical inclusive OR*   Flags   ODITSZAPC
Register/memory and register to either   0   xxux0

| 0 0 0 0 1 0 d w | mod reg   r/m |

Clocks: register to register   3
         memory to register   9 + EA
         register to memory   16 + EA

Immediate to register/memory

| 1 0 0 0 0 0 0 w | mod 0 0 1 r/m | data | data if w = 1 |

Clocks: immediate to register   4
         immediate to memory   17 + EA

Immediate to accumulator

| 0 0 0 0 1 1 0 w | data | data if w = 1 |

Clocks = 4

OUT   *Output from AL or AX to port*   Flags   ODITSZAPC
Fixed port

| 1 1 1 0 0 1 1 w | port |

Clocks = 10 (byte) or 14 (word)

Variable port (DX)

| 1 1 1 0 1 1 1 w |

Clocks = 8 (byte) or 12 (word)

POP   *Pop word off stack*   Flags   ODITSZAPC
Register/memory

| 1 0 0 0 1 1 1 1 | mod 0 0 0 r/m |

Clocks: register   12
         memory   25 + EA

Register

| 0 1 0 1 1 reg |

Clocks = 12

Segment register

| 0 0 0 reg 1 1 1 |

Clocks = 12

POPF *Pop flags off stack*   Flags   ODITSZAPC
                                                                            rrrrrrrr

| 1 0 0 1 1 1 0 1 |

Clocks = 12

PUSH *Push word onto stack*   Flags   ODITSZAPC
Register/memory

| 1 1 1 1 1 1 1 1 | mod 1 1 0 r/m |

Clocks: register   15
         memory   24 + EA

Register

| 0 1 0 1 0 reg |

Clocks = 15

Segment register

| 0 0 0 reg 1 1 0 |

Clocks = 14

PUSHF   *Push flags onto stack*   Flags   ODITSZAPC

| 1 0 0 1 1 1 0 0 |

Clocks = 14

RCL　　*Rotate through carry left*　　　　　Flags　ODITSZAPC

1 1 0 1 0 0 v w	mod 0 1 0　r/m

　　　　　　　　　　　　　　　　　　　　　　　　　　　　　　x　　　　x

Clocks:　single-bit register　　2
　　　　　single-bit memory　　15 + EA (byte)　23 + EA (word)
　　　　　variable-bit register　8 + 4/bit
　　　　　variable-bit memory　20 + EA + 4/bit (byte)　28 + EA + 4/bit (word)

RCR　　*Rotate through carry right*　　　　Flags　ODITSZAPC

1 1 0 1 0 0 v w	mod 0 1 1　r/m

　　　　　　　　　　　　　　　　　　　　　　　　　　　　　　x　　　　x

Clocks:　single-bit register　　2
　　　　　single-bit memory　　15 + EA (byte)　23 + EA (word)
　　　　　variable-bit register　8 + 4/bit
　　　　　variable-bit memory　20 + EA + 4/bit (byte)　28 + EA + 4/bit (word)

REP　　*Repeat string operation*　　　　　Flags　ODITSZAPC

1 1 1 1 0 0 1 0

Clocks = 2

REPE/REPZ　　*Repeat string operation*　　Flags　ODITSZAPC
　　　　　　　　　　while equal/zero

1 1 1 1 0 0 1 1

Clocks = 2

REPNE/REPNZ　*Repeat string operation*　　Flags　ODITSZAPC
　　　　　　　　　　while not equal/hot zero

1 1 1 1 0 0 1 0

Clocks = 2

RET　　*Return from procedure*　　　　　　Flags　ODITSZAPC
Within segment

1 1 0 0 0 0 1 1

Clocks = 20

Within segment, add immediate to SP

1 1 0 0 0 0 1 0	data-low	data-high

Clocks = 24

Intersegment

1 1 0 0 1 0 1 1

Clocks = 32

Intersegment, add immediate to SP

1 1 0 0 1 0 1 0	data-low	data-high

Clocks = 31

ROL　　*Rotate left*　　　　　　　　　　　Flags　ODITSZAPC

1 1 0 1 0 0 v w	mod 0 0 0　r/m

　　　　　　　　　　　　　　　　　　　　　　　　　　　　　　x　　　　x

Clocks:　single-bit register　　2
　　　　　single-bit memory　　15 + EA (byte)　23 + EA (word)
　　　　　variable-bit register　8 + 4/bit
　　　　　variable-bit memory　20 + EA + 4/bit (byte)　28 + EA + 4/bit (word)

ROR　　*Rotate right*　　　　　　　　　　　Flags　ODITSZAPC

1 1 0 1 0 0 v w	mod 0 0 1　r/m

　　　　　　　　　　　　　　　　　　　　　　　　　　　　　　x　　　　x

Clocks:　single-bit register　　2
　　　　　single-bit memory　　15 + EA (byte)　23 + EA (word)
　　　　　variable-bit register　8 + 4/bit
　　　　　variable-bit memory　20 + EA + 4/bit (byte)　28 + EA + 4/bit (word)

SAHF　*Store AH into flags*　　　　　　　Flags　ODITSZAPC

1 0 0 1 1 1 1 0

　　　　　　　　　　　　　　　　　　　　　　　　　　　　　　　　rrrrr

Clocks = 4

SAL/SHL *Shift arithmetic left/logical left*   Flags ODITSZAPC

| 1 1 0 1 0 0 v w | mod 1 0 0 r/m |

                                                    x   x

Clocks: single-bit register   2
         single-bit memory   15 + EA (byte) 23 + EA (word)
         variable-bit register   8 + 4/bit
         variable-bit memory   20 + EA + 4/bit (byte) 28 + EA + 4/bit (word)

SAR *Shift arithmetic right*   Flags ODITSZAPC

| 1 1 0 1 0 0 v w | mod 1 1 1 r/m |

                                        x   x

Clocks: single-bit register   2
         single-bit memory   15 + EA (byte) 23 + EA (word)
         variable-bit register   8 + 4/bit
         variable-bit memory   20 + EA + 4/bit (byte) 28 + EA + 4/bit (word)

SBB *Subtract with borrow*   Flags ODITSZAPC
Register/memory and register from either   x   xxxxx

| 0 0 0 1 1 0 d w | mod reg r/m |

Clocks: register to register   3
         memory to register   9 + EA (byte) 13 + EA (word)
         register to memory   16 + EA (byte) 24 + EA (word)

Immediate from register/memory

| 1 0 0 0 0 0 s w | mod 0 1 1 r/m | data | data if s:w = 01 |

Clocks: immediate to register   4
         immediate to memory   17 + EA (byte) 25 + EA (word)

Immediate from accumulator

| 0 0 0 1 1 1 0 w | data | data if w = 1 |

Clocks = 4

SCAS *Scan string*   Flags ODITSZAPC

| 1 0 1 0 1 1 1 w |

                      x   xxxxx

Clocks: byte   15
         word   19
         rep byte   9 + 15/rep
         rep word   9 + 19/rep

SHR *Shift logical right*   Flags ODITSZAPC

| 1 1 0 1 0 0 v w | mod 1 0 1 r/m |

                                        x   x

Clocks: single-bit register   2
         single-bit memory   15 + EA (byte) 23 + EA (word)
         variable-bit register   8 + 4/bit
         variable-bit memory   20 + EA + 4/bit (byte) 28 + EA + 4/bit (word)

STC *Set carry flag*   Flags ODITSZAPC

| 1 1 1 1 1 0 0 1 |

                                              1

Clocks = 2

STD *Set direction flag*   Flags ODITSZAPC

| 1 1 1 1 1 1 0 1 |

                      1

Clocks = 2

STI *Set interrupt enable flag*   Flags ODITSZAPC

| 1 1 1 1 1 0 1 1 |

                        1

Clocks = 2

STOS *Store byte or word string*   Flags ODITSZAPC

| 1 0 1 0 1 0 1 w |

Clocks: byte   11
         word   15
         rep byte   9 + 10/rep
         rep word   9 + 14/rep

SUB *Subtractraction*   Flags   ODITSZAPC
Register/memory and register from either   x   xxxxx

0 0 1 0 1 0 d w	mod reg r/m

Clocks: register to register   3
         memory to register   9 + EA (byte) 13 + EA (word)
         register to memory   16 + EA (byte) 24 + EA (word)

Immediate from register/memory

1 0 0 0 0 0 s w	mod 1 0 1 r/m	data	data if s:w = 01

Clocks: immediate to register   4
         immediate to memory   17 + EA (byte) 25 + EA (word)

Immediate from accumulator

0 0 1 0 1 1 0 w	data	data if w = 1

Clocks = 4

TEST *Test (nondestructive logical AND)*   Flags   ODITSZAPC
Register/memory and register   0   xxux0

1 0 0 0 0 1 0 w	mod reg r/m

Clocks: register and register   3
         register and memory   9 + EA (byte) 13 + EA (word)

Immediate and register/memory

1 1 1 1 0 1 1 w	mod 0 0 0 r/m	data	data if w = 1

Clocks: immediate and register   4
         immediate and memory   11 + EA

Immediate and accumulator

1 0 1 0 1 0 0 w	data	data if w = 1

Clocks = 4

WAIT *Wait until TEST line active*   Flags   ODITSZAPC

1 0 0 1 1 0 1 1

Clocks = 3 + 5n

XCHG *Exchange*   Flags   ODITSZAPC
Register/memory with register

1 0 0 0 0 1 1 w	mod reg r/m

Clocks: register with register   4
         register with memory   17 + EA (byte) 25 + EA (word)

Register with accumulator

1 0 0 1 0 reg

Clocks = 3

XLAT *Translate byte to AL*   Flags   ODITSZAPC

1 1 0 1 0 1 1 1

Clocks = 11

XOR *Logical Exclusive OR*   Flags   ODITSZAPC
Register/memory and register to either   0   xxux0

0 0 1 1 0 0 d w	mod reg r/m

Clocks: register to register   3
         memory to register   9 + EA (byte) 13 + EA (word)
         register to memory   16 + EA (byte) 24 + EA (word)

Immediate to register/memory

1 0 0 0 0 0 0 w	mod 1 1 0 r/m	data	data if w = 1

Clocks: immediate to register   4
         immediate to memory   17 + EA (byte) 25 + EA (word)

Immediate to accumulator

0 0 1 1 0 1 0 w	data	data if w = 1

Clocks = 4

Table A.2a Instruction Opcode Map

The table reads with the high-order hex digit selecting the row and the low-order hex digit selecting the column.

	0	1	2	3	4	5	6	7	8	9	A	B	C	D	E	F
0	ADD r/m,reg	ADD w r/m,reg	ADD reg,r/m	ADD w reg,r/m	ADD b AL,imm	ADD w AX,imm	PUSH ES	POP ES	OR r/m,reg	OR w r/m,reg	OR reg,r/m	OR reg,r/m	OR b AL,imm	OR w AX,imm	PUSH CS	
1	ADC r/m,reg	ADC w r/m,reg	ADC reg,r/m	ADC w reg,r/m	ADC b AL,imm	ADC w AX,imm	PUSH SS	POP SS	SBB b r/m,reg	SBB w r/m,reg	SBB b reg,r/m	SBB w reg,r/m	SBB b AL,imm	SBB w AX,imm	PUSH DS	POP DS
2	AND r/m,reg	AND w r/m,reg	AND reg,r/m	AND w reg,r/m	AND b AL,imm	AND w AX,imm	SEGMENT ES	DAA	SUB b r/m,reg	SUB w r/m,reg	SUB b reg,r/m	SUB w reg,r/m	SUB b AL,imm	SUB w AX,imm	SEGMENT CS	DAS
3	XOR r/m,reg	XOR w r/m,reg	XOR reg,r/m	XOR w reg,r/m	XOR b AL,imm	XOR w AX,imm	SEGMENT SS	AAA	CMP b r/m,reg	CMP w r/m,reg	CMP b reg,r/m	CMP w reg,r/m	CMP b AL,imm	CMP w AX,imm	SEGMENT DS	AAS
4	INC AX	INC CX	INC DX	INC BX	INC SP	INC BP	INC SI	INC DI	DEC AX	DEC CX	DEC DX	DEC BX	DEC SP	DEC BP	DEC SI	DEC DI
5	PUSH AX	PUSH CX	PUSH DX	PUSH BX	PUSH SP	PUSH BP	PUSH SI	PUSH DI	POP AX	POP CX	POP DX	POP BX	POP SP	POP BP	POP SI	POP DI
6																
7	JO	JNO	JB/JNAE/JC	JNB/JAE/JNC	JE/JZ	JNE/JNZ	JBE/JNA	JNBE/JA	JS	JNS	JP/JPE	JNP/JPO	JL/JNGE	JNL/JGE	JLE/JNG	JNLE/JG
8	*	*	*	*	TEST r/m,reg	TEST r/m,reg	XCHG r/m,reg	XCHG r/m,reg	MOV b r/m,reg	MOV w r/m,reg	MOV b reg,r/m	MOV w reg,r/m	MOV r/m,seg	LEA reg,r/m	MOV seg,r/m	POP r/m
9	NOP	XCHG CX,AX	XCH DX,AX	XCH BX,AX	XCH SP,AX	XCHG BP,AX	XCHG SI,AX	XCHG DI,AX	CBW	CWD	CALL inter	WAIT	PUSHF	POPF	SAHF	LAHF
A	MOV b AL,mem	MOV w AX,mem	MOV mem,AL	MOV w mem,AX	MOVS b	MOVS w	CMPS b	CMPS w	TEST b AL,imm	TEST w AL,imm	STOS b	STOS w	LODS b	LODS w	SCAS b	SCAS w
B	MOV AL,imm	MOV CL,imm	MOV DL,imm	MOV BL,imm	MOV AH,imm	MOV CH,imm	MOV DH,imm	MOV BH,imm	MOV AX,imm	MOV CX,imm	MOV DX,imm	MOV BX,imm	MOV SP,imm	MOV BP,imm	MOV SI,imm	MOV DI,imm
C			RET intra+	RET intra	LE reg,r/m	LD reg,r/m	MOV b r/m,imm	MOV w r/m,imm			RET inter+	RET inter	INT type	INT	INTO	IRET
D	*	*	*	*	AAM	AAD		XLAT	ESC 0	ESC 1	ESC 2	ESC 3	ESC 4	ESC 5	ESC 6	ESC 7
E	LOOPNZ/LOOPNE	LOOPZ/LOOPE	LOOP	JCXZ	IN b AL,port	IN w AX,port	OUT b port,AL	OUT w port,AX	CALL intra	JMP intra	JMP inter	JMP short	IN b AL,DX	IN w AX,DX	OUT b DX,AL	OUT w DX,AX
F	LOCK		REP/REPNE/REPNZ	REPE/REPZ	HLT	CMC	*	*	CLC	STC	CLI	STI	CLD	STD	*	*

Table A.2b Instruction Opcode Map

mod	PBOC	r/m

Postbyte Opcodes (PBOC)

	000	001	010	011	100	101	110	111
80,82	ADD b r/m,imm	OR b r/m,imm	ADC b r/m,imm	SBB b r/m,imm	AND b r/m,imm	SUB b r/m,imm	XOR b r/m,imm	CMP b r/m,imm
81	ADD w r/m,imm	OR w r/m,imm	ADC w r/m,imm	SBB w r/m,imm	AND w r/m,imm	SUB w r/m,imm	XOR w r/m,imm	CMP w r/m,imm
83	ADD se r/m,imm		ADC se r/m,imm	SBB se r/m,imm		SUB se r/m,imm		CMP se r/m,imm
D0	ROL b r/m,1	ROR b r/m,1	RCL b r/m,1	RCR b r/m,1	SHL/SALb r/m,1	SHR b r/m,1		RAR b r/m,1
D1	ROL w r/m,1	RORw r/m,1	RCL w r/m,1	RCR w r/m,1	SHL/SALw r/m,1	SHR w r/m,1		RAR w r/m,1
D2	ROL b r/m,CL	ROR b r/m,CL	RCL b r/m,CL	RCR b r/m,CL	SHL/SALb r/m,CL	SHR b r/m,CL		RAR b r/m,CL
D3	ROL w r/m,CL	ROR w r/m,CL	RCL w r/m,CL	RCR w r/m,CL	SHL/SALw r/m,CL	SHR w r/m,CL		RAR w r/m,CL
F6	TEST b r/m,imm		NOT b r/m	NEG b r/m	MUL b r/m	IMUL b r/m	DIV b r/m	IDIV b r/m
F7	TEST w r/m,imm		NOT w r/m	NEG w r/m	MUL w r/m	IMUL w r/m	DIV w r/m	IDIV w r/m
FE	INC b r/m	DEC b r/m						
FF	INC w r/m	DEC w r/m	CALL intra	CALL inter	JMP intra	JMP inter	PUSH r/m	

Table A.3

Postbyte *mod,r/m* Fields

r/m	mod = 11 byte	mod = 11 word	mod = 00	mod = 01	mod = 11
000	AL	AX	BX + SI	BX + SI + disp8	BX + SI + disp16
001	CL	CX	BX + DI	BX + DI + disp8	BX + DI + disp16
010	DL	DX	BP + SI	BP + SI + disp8	BP + SI + disp16
011	BL	BX	BP + DI	BP + DI + disp8	BP + DI + disp16
100	AH	SP	SI	SI + disp8	SI + disp16
101	CH	BP	DI	DI + disp8	DI + disp16
110	DH	SI	Direct	BP + disp8	BP + disp16
111	BH	DI	BX	BX + disp8	BX + disp16

Table A.4

Postbyte *reg* Field

reg	byte (b)	word (w)
000	AL	AX
001	CL	CX
010	DL	DX
011	BL	BX
100	AH	SP
101	CH	BP
110	DH	SI
111	BH	DI

Table A.5

8086 Operand Addressing Modes

Addressing Mode	r/m	mod = 00	mod = 01	mod = 10
Direct	110	Direct		
Register Indirect	100	SI		
	101	DI		
	111	BX		
Indexed	100		SI + disp8	SI + disp16
	101		DI + disp8	DI + disp16
Based	111		BX + disp8	BX + disp16
Based Stack	110		BP + disp8	BP + disp16
Based + Indexed	000	BX + SI	BX + SI + disp8	BX + SI + disp16
	001	BX + DI	BX + DI + disp8	BX + DI + disp16
Based + Indexed	010	BP + SI	BP + SI + disp8	BP + SI + disp16
Stack	011	BP + DI	BP + DI + disp8	BP + DI + disp16

APPENDIX B

The TUTOR Monitor

The TUTOR monitor will run on a PC-compatible computer containing an 8088, 8086, 80286, 80386 or 80486 microprocessor. The last three microprocessors must be running in the *real* mode (the default) in which they behave like an 8086. The TUTOR monitor is stored in the file *tutor.exe* and can be executed from DOS by typing *tutor*.

When the program is executed, the starting segment address is displayed in *BX* and the starting offset address is displayed in *CX*. In Figure 3.3 this starting address of TUTOR is shown to be 13A3:00C5. The starting segment address will depend on which version of DOS you are using and whether you have any other resident software in your system. The actual starting address of TUTOR is stored in the type 60H software interrupt vector address. This means that *INT 60H* will execute the TUTOR monitor. The length of the TUTOR monitor is stored in *DX* when TUTOR is first executed. The initial segment of the memory displayed on the TUTOR monitor is the first free memory directly above the memory where TUTOR is stored. This is segment address 174FH in Figure 3.3 but will likely be different on your computer. However, this will be free memory where you can store your own programs.

Because the TUTOR monitor allows you to look anywhere in memory and change any value you want, you may sometimes inadvertently *bomb* the system. When this happens you will have to re-boot the system. You can usually do this by pressing the *Ctrl-Alt-Del* keys which will re-boot DOS. You will then have to execute the TUTOR monitor again. Sometimes, if you have inadvertently disabled interrupts, the keyboard will be dead and you will have to turn off the computer in order to re-boot the system. In this case you will lose all data in RAM including your program. You should make sure that you always have a copy of your programs on disk before executing any program.

A summary of the TUTOR monitor commands is given at the end of this appendix. The basic operation of the TUTOR monitor is introduced in Chapters 3 – 5. The following commands are described, with examples, at the indicated pages in the book.

363

/A	Display ASCII characters	page 35
/B	Set breakpoint	page 104
/E	Execute a program	page 40
/G	Change data segment	page 135
/J	Calculate a jump displacement	page 83
/M	Enter hex or ASCII values in memory	page 32
/R	Change the contents of a register	page 24
/S	Store (or retrieve) data on disk	page 102
/U	Unassemble a portion of memory on the right side of the display	page 33

The following TUTOR commands are not described elsewhere in the book:

/L   List a disassembled portion of memory

You can disassemble a program on the screen starting at the position cursor by typing /L. The command line will display

LIST: P B S

If you press *P* (for *Page*) a page of disassembled code will be listed on the screen. Press the forward (right cursor) key --> to disassemble a new page. You can continue to press the --> key to list a new page. Press the *Enter* key to go back to the TUTOR monitor.

If you want to disassemble only a fixed number of bytes, press /*LB*. You will be asked for an ending offset address. This should be the first offset address following the block of memory to be disassembled. When you press *Enter* only the disassembled block of memory will be displayed on the screen. Press *Enter* to return to the TUTOR monitor.

If you press /*LS* you can scroll through a program by disassembling one line at a time. When you type /*LS* the opcode at the position cursor location is disassembled and displayed on the top of the screen. Pressing the right cursor --> key will cause the next instruction to be disassembled. You can continue pressing the --> key to disassemble more instructions. Press the *Enter* key to return to the TUTOR monitor.

/P   Print a disassembled portion of memory

Prints a disassembled portion of memory on the printer using the same format as /L.

/D   Delete a block of bytes

Move the position cursor to the location in memory where bytes are to be deleted. In response to the prompt

DELETE: NO. OF BYTES

enter the number of bytes to be deleted. The prompt

DELETE: ENDING OFFSET ADDRESS

will then be displayed. Type the offset address following the last byte to be *moved up* when the deleted bytes are removed. When you press *Enter* the number of bytes indicated will be deleted, starting at the position cursor, and the remaining bytes up to the ending address will be moved up. Bytes can be deleted only within a single segment.

/F   Find a particular string of bytes

After the prompt

```
FIND: ENTER HEX VALUES
```

enter any number of 2-digit hex values. When you press *Enter* the cursor will move to the first byte in the sequence. The search occurs only within a single segment.

/I   Insert any number of hex bytes

Move the position cursor to the location in memory where bytes are to be inserted. In response to the prompt

```
INSERT: ENDING OFFSET ADDRESS
```

enter the offset address of the last byte that is to be shifted up in memory as bytes are inserted. Succeeding bytes will be overwritten as bytes are inserted.
After entering the ending address the prompt

```
ENTER HEX VALUES
```

will appear on the command line. Enter any number of 2-digit hex values. As each byte is entered it is inserted in memory, all bytes up to the ending address are moved up one byte in memory, and the position cursor is advanced to the next byte. Bytes can be inserted only within a single segment.

/T   Transfer a block of bytes

Move the position cursor to the location in memory of the first byte of the block to be transferred. In response to the prompt

```
TRANSFER: DESTINATION SEGMENT ADDRESS
```

enter the *segment* address of the destination. In response to the prompt

```
TRANSFER: DESTINATION OFFSET ADDRESS
```

enter the *offset* address of the destination. The destination address (*segment:offset*) is the address to which the first byte in the block (at the position cursor) is to be moved. After entering the destination address the prompt

```
TRANSFER: NO. OF BYTES
```

will appear on the command line. Enter the number of bytes to be moved. When you press *Enter* the block of bytes will be transferred to the new location and the cursor will move to the first byte of this new block. Any number of bytes can be moved either forward or backward in memory. If you try to move data into some parts of memory, such as that occupied by the TUTOR monitor or certain DOS addresses, the computer will *crash* and you will have to reload the TUTOR monitor.

/Q   Quit to DOS

In response to the prompt

```
QUIT: D R
```

pressing *D* will switch to DOS and display the DOS prompt. The memory occupied by TUTOR will be released by DOS. Pressing */QR* will also return to DOS but will keep TUTOR resident in memory. This means that a new .EXE file will be loaded by DOS above TUTOR. Such a program could call TUTOR for the purpose of debugging by executing an *INT 60H* instruction.

/X   Toggles data or stack segment on and off

In response to the prompt

```
SEGMENT ON/OFF: D S
```

pressing *D* will toggle the data segment display on and off. Pressing *S* will toggle the stack segment display on and off.

/Z   Displays the copyright message

```
(c) 1992 by Richard E. Haskell, Inc. v4
```

on the command line. Pressing any key will return to the TUTOR monitor.

Table B.1	
TUTOR Key Functions	
Key	*Function*
Right Cursor	Advance 1 byte
Left Cursor	Back up 1 byte
Down Cursor	Advance 1 row
Up Cursor	Back up 1 row
PgDn	Advance 7 rows
PgUp	Back up 7 rows
Home	Go to offset address 0000H
F1	Single step
F2	Single step over CALL or INT
F3	Execute breakpoint in loop
Ctrl F6	Execute TUTOR
F7	Help
F9	Reset DS and SP after F10
F10	Relocate operation on EXE file
>	Go To: Offset or Seg Address
/	TUTOR command

	Table B.2

TUTOR Commands

Command	Function
/A	Turn ASCII on/off

/B	Set breakpoints
	BREAKPOINT: S N F C
	  S: Set breakpoint at cursor location
	  N: Set breakpoint with no automatic removal
	  F: Find breakpoint
	  C: Clear breakpoint

/D	Delete bytes DELETE: NO. OF BYTES DELETE: ENDING OFFSET ADDRESS + 1

/E	Execute code
	EXECUTE: A G
	  A: Enter starting address
	  G: Go with address at cursor

/F	Find byte string FIND: ENTER HEX VALUES

/G	Change data segment display
	DATA SEGMENT: S O D
	  S: ENTER SEGMENT ADDRESS
	  O: ENTER OFFSET ADDRESS
	  D: Display segment DS

/I	Insert bytes INSERT: ENDING OFFSET ADDRESS + 1 ENTER HEX VALUES

/J	Calculate jump displacement
	JUMP DISPLACEMENT: L S
	  L: Long
	  S: Short
	  Enter destination and offset addresses

/L	Disassemble code
	LIST: P B S
	  P: Page
	    --> Next page
	    Enter
	  B: Block: Ending offset address + 1
	  S: Scroll
	    --> Advance
	    Enter

/M	Change memory
	CHANGE MEMORY: H A
	  H: Hex values
	  A: ASCII values

/P	Disassemble to printer
	PRINTER: P B S
	  P: Page
	    --> Next page
	    Enter
	  B: Block: Ending offset address + 1
	  S: Scroll
	    --> Advance
	    Enter

Table B.2 (continued)

/R	Change register value
	REGISTER CHANGE: G P I S F
	    G: Change general register: A B C D
	    P: Change pointer register: S B I
	    I: Change index register: S D
	    S: Change segment register: S D C E
	    F: Change status flags (HEX)

/S	Save or load disk file
	STORAGE: L S
	    L: Load: \<pathname\>
	    S: Save – No. of hex bytes to save
	        Enter \<pathname\>

/T	Transfer block of data TRANSFER: DESTINATION SEGMENT ADDRESS TRANSFER: DESTINATION OFFSET ADDRESS TRANSFER: NO. OF BYTES

/U	Unassemble on right of screen
	UNASSEMBLE: P B C
	    P: Page
	    B: Block: Enter ending address + 1
	    C: Clear right half of screen

/Q	Quit to DOS
	QUIT: D R
	    D: Return to DOS
	    R: Terminate and stay resident

/X	Turn data/stack segment on/off
	SEGMENT ON/OFF: D S
	    D: Toggle data segment on/off
	    S: Toggle stack segment on/off

/Z	Copyright (c) 1992 by Richard E. Haskell, Inc. v4 Press any key to return

APPENDIX C

Subroutine Listings

```
┌─────────────────────────────────────────────────────────────────┐
│    Listing C.1 – Screen Display Subroutines      File: screen.asm │
├─────────────────────────────────────────────────────────────────┤
│               title   Screen display subroutines                 │
│                                                                   │
│       ;       useful key ascii codes                             │
│       _esc     equ     27                                         │
│       _enter   equ     13                                         │
│       _bksp    equ     8                                          │
│                                                                   │
│       data     segment         public                            │
│       kbuf     db      80 dup(?)                                  │
│       bufend   db      ?                                          │
│       vidseg   dw      0b800h          ;video RAM segment         │
│       span     dw      ?                                          │
│       sisave   dw      ?                                          │
│       svseg    dw      0                                          │
│       pageno   db      0                                          │
│       data     ends                                              │
│                                                                   │
│               public  vidseg,stvseg                              │
│               public  savescr,restscr                           │
│               public  svinit,relssb,resize                      │
│               public  delay,tone,beep                           │
│               public  chrout,mess,chrout1,getatt                │
│               public  setcur,rdcurs,inccur,deccur                │
│               public  clrscn,home,tab,chgatt                     │
│               public  invatt,blank,clrwin,curoff                │
│               public  chrprt,hexasc,pbyte                        │
│               public  togatt,crlf,mess2,fmess                   │
│               public  getkey,dokey,invline                      │
│               public  query,kbuf,bufend,span                    │
│               public  enterq,sisave,pageno                      │
│                                                                   │
│       code     segment public                                   │
│               assume cs:code,ds:data                            │
│                                                                   │
│       ;       set video RAM segment address                      │
│       stvseg   proc    near                                      │
│               push    ax                                         │
│               mov     ah,15                                      │
│               int     10h              ;get video state          │
│               cmp     al,7             ;if monochrome            │
│               jne     svg1                                       │
│               mov     vidseg,0b000h     ; vidseg=b000            │
│               jmp     svg2             ;else                     │
│       svg1:   mov     vidseg,0b800h     ; vidseg=b800            │
│       svg2:   pop     ax                                         │
│               ret                                                │
│       stvseg   endp                                              │
└─────────────────────────────────────────────────────────────────┘
```

Listing C.1 (continued)

```
;          display char with current attribute
chrout1    proc    near
           push    ax
           push    bx
           push    ax                      ;save char
           mov     bh,pageno               ;page 0
           mov     ah,8
           int     10h                     ;read attribute
           mov     bl,ah
           pop     ax                      ;get char
           call    chrout                  ;& display
           pop     bx
           pop     ax
           ret
chrout1    endp

;          character output
chrout     proc near
           push    ax
           push    bx                      ;save regs
           push    cx
           push    dx
           push    ax
           mov     bh,pageno
           mov     ah,3
           int     10h                     ;read cursor
           mov     cx,1
           pop     ax                      ;get char
           cmp     al,0dh                  ;check for CR
           je      chr1
           cmp     al,20h                  ;ignore ctrl
           jb      chr3                    ; characters
           mov     ah,9
           int     10h                     ;write char/att
           inc     dl                      ;inc cursor
           cmp     dl,80                   ;if end of line
           jb      chr2
chr1:      mov     dl,0                    ;do CR
           inc     dh                      ; LF
           cmp     dh,25                   ;if end of
           jb      chr2                    ; screen
           mov     cx,0                    ;scroll
           mov     dx,184fh                ; entire
           mov     bh,07h                  ; screen
           mov     ax,0601h                ; up
           int     10h                     ; 1 line
           mov     dx,1800h                ;CR
           mov     bh,pageno               ;reset page no.
chr2:      mov     ah,2
           int     10h                     ;set new cursor
chr3:      pop     dx                      ;restore regs
           pop     cx
           pop     bx
           pop     ax
           ret
chrout     endp

;          message display
;          si -> message in data segment
;          dh = row, dl = col
;          bl = attribute of message
mess       proc    near
           push    ax
           push    bx
           push    cx
```

Listing C.1 (continued)

```
              push   si
              mov    bh,pageno           ;page 0
              mov    ah,2                ;set cursor
              int    10h                 ; at dh,dl
              mov    cx,1                ;1 character
              cld                        ;si increases
ms1:          lodsb                      ;[si]-->al
              cmp    al,0                ;message done?
              je     ms2                 ;if so, return
              call   chrout              ;display char
              jmp    ms1                 ;and continue
ms2:          pop    si
              pop    cx
              pop    bx
              pop    ax
              ret
mess          endp

;             message display with current attribute
;             at current cursor positon
;             si -> message in data segment
mess2         proc   near
              push   ax
              push   bx
              push   dx
              call   rdcurs              ;read cursor
              mov    bh,pageno           ;page 0
              mov    ah,8
              int    10h                 ;read attribute
              mov    bl,ah
              call   mess                ;display mess
              pop    dx
              pop    bx
              pop    ax
              ret
mess2         endp

;             fast message routine
;             si -> message in data segment
;             dh = row, dl = col
;             bl = attribute of message
fmess         proc   near
              push   ax
              push   di
              call   setdi               ;set di->vidRAM offset
              mov    ah,bl               ;ah=attribute
              mov    es,vidseg           ;es->video RAM
              cld
fms1:         lodsb
              cmp    al,0
              je     fms2
              stosw
              jmp    fms1
fms2:         pop    di
              pop    ax
              ret
fmess         endp

;             set di to video RAM offset address
;             di = row * 160 + col
setdi         proc   near
              push   cx
              mov    ah,0
              mov    al,dh               ;ax=row
              mov    cl,5
```

372   APPENDIX C

Listing C.1 (continued)

```
                shl     ax,cl                   ;ax=32*row
                mov     di,ax                   ;di=32*row
                shl     ax,1
                shl     ax,1                    ;ax=128*row
                add     di,ax                   ;di=160*row
                mov     ah,0
                mov     al,dl                   ;ax=col
                shl     ax,1                    ;ax=2*col
                add     di,ax                   ;di=video offset
                pop     cx
                ret
setdi           endp

;               set cursor at dx=row:col
setcur          proc    near
                push    ax
                push    bx
                mov     bh,pageno               ;page 0
                mov     ah,2
                int     10h                     ;set cursor
                pop     bx
                pop     ax
                ret
setcur          endp

;               read cursor
;               output: dh=row dl=col
rdcurs          proc    near
                push    ax
                push    bx
                push    cx
                mov     bh,pageno               ;page 0
                mov     ah,3
                int     10h                     ;read cursor
                pop     cx
                pop     bx
                pop     ax
                ret
rdcurs          endp

;               inc cursor
inccur          proc    near
                push    dx
                call    rdcurs                  ;read cursor
                inc     dl                      ;inc dl
                call    setcur                  ;set cursor
                pop     dx
                ret
inccur          endp

;               dec cursor
deccur          proc    near
                push    dx
                call    rdcurs                  ;read cursor
                dec     dl                      ;inc dl
                call    setcur                  ;set cursor
                pop     dx
                ret
deccur          endp

;               clear screen
clrscn          proc    near
                push    ax
                mov     ah,15                   ;read vid mode
                int     10h
```

Listing C.1 (continued)

```
                mov     ah,0                    ;and set again
                int     10h
                pop     ax
                ret
clrscn  endp

;       home cursor
home    proc    near
                push    dx
                mov     dx,0                    ;row=0 col=0
                call    setcur
                pop     dx
                ret
home    endp

;       carriage return line feed
crlf    proc    near
                push    ax
                push    bx
                push    cx
                push    dx
                call    rdcurs                  ;read cursor
                mov     dl,0                    ;do CR
                inc     dh                      ; LF
                cmp     dh,25                   ;if end of
                jb      cr1                     ; screen
                mov     cx,0                    ;scroll
                mov     dx,184fh                ; entire
                mov     bh,07h                  ; screen
                mov     ax,0601h                ; up
                int     10h                     ; 1 line
                mov     dx,1800h                ;CR
                mov     bh,pageno               ;page 0
cr1:    call    setcur                          ;set cursor
                pop     dx
                pop     cx
                pop     bx
                pop     ax
                ret
crlf    endp

;       tab
tab     proc    near
                push    ax
                push    bx
                push    dx
                mov     bh,pageno
                mov     ah,3                    ;read cursor
                int     10h
                add     dl,5                    ;mov cursor +5
                mov     ah,2
                int     10h                     ;set cursor
                pop     dx
                pop     bx
                pop     ax
                ret
tab     endp

;       get attribute of character at
;        dx = row:col and store in bl
getatt  proc    near
                push    ax
                call    setcur                  ;set cursor
                mov     bh,pageno               ;page 0
                mov     ah,8                    ;read char/attr
```

Listing C.1 (continued)

```
                    int     10h
                    mov     bl,ah                   ;bl = attrib
                    pop     ax
                    ret
        getatt      endp

        ;           change attribute of character at
        ;             current cursor position to bl
        chgatt      proc    near
                    push    ax
                    push    bx
                    push    cx
                    mov     bh,pageno               ;page 0
                    mov     ah,8                    ;read char/attr
                    int     10h
                    mov     cx,1
                    mov     ah,9
                    int     10h                     ;write char/att
                    pop     cx
                    pop     bx
                    pop     ax
                    ret
        chgatt      endp

        ;           invert attribute of word at current
        ;             cursor position
        invatt      proc    near
                    push    ax
                    push    bx
                    push    cx
                    mov     bh,pageno               ;page 0
        ia1:        mov     ah,8                    ;read char/attr
                    int     10h
                    cmp     al,20h                  ;if blank
                    je      ia4                     ; quit
                    cmp     ah,07h                  ;if normal
                    jne     ia2
                    mov     bl,70h                  ;make inverse
                    jmp     ia3                     ;else
        ia2:        mov     bl,07h                  ;make normal
        ia3:        mov     cx,1
                    mov     ah,9
                    int     10h                     ;write char/att
                    call    inccur                  ;adv cursor
                    jmp     ia1                     ;repeat
        ia4:        pop     cx
                    pop     bx
                    pop     ax
                    ret
        invatt      endp

        ;           toggle attribute of character
        ;           at current cursor position
        togatt      proc    near
                    push    ax
                    push    bx
                    push    cx
                    mov     bh,pageno               ;page 0
                    mov     ah,8                    ;read char/attr
                    int     10h
                    cmp     ah,07h                  ;if normal
                    jne     ta1
                    mov     bl,70h                  ;make inverse
                    jmp     ta2                     ;else
        ta1:        mov     bl,07h                  ;make normal
```

Listing C.1 (continued)

```
ta2:      mov     cx,1
          mov     ah,9
          int     10h                     ;write char/att
          pop     cx
          pop     bx
          pop     ax
          ret
togatt    endp

;         invert line of text at
;         current cursor position
invline   proc    near
          push    ax
ivl1:     call    invatt                  ;invert word
          call    togatt                  ;invert blank
          call    inccur                  ;inc cursor
          mov     ah,8                    ;read chr/attr
          int     10h
          cmp     al,20h                  ;repeat until
          jne     ivl1                    ;blank
          pop     ax
          ret
invline   endp

;         blank line dh
blank     proc    near
          push    ax
          push    bx
          push    cx
          push    dx
          mov     dl,0                    ;col 0
          call    setcur                  ;set cursor
          mov     cx,80                   ;80 blanks
          mov     al,20h                  ;ascii blank
          mov     bl,07h                  ;normal video
          mov     ah,9
          int     10h                     ;print all 80
          pop     dx
          pop     cx
          pop     bx
          pop     ax
          ret
blank     endp

;         clear window
;         ch:cl = row:col of upper left corner
;         dh:dl = row:col of lower right corner
clrwin    proc    near
          push    ax
          push    bx
          mov     bh,7                    ;normal attr
          mov     ah,6                    ;scroll func
          mov     al,0                    ;blank window
          int     10h
          pop     bx
          pop     ax
          ret
clrwin    endp

;         hide cursor
curoff    proc    near
          push    ax
          push    bx
          push    dx
          mov     bh,pageno               ;page 0
```

Listing C.1 (continued)

```
                    mov     dh,25                   ;row 25
                    mov     dl,0                    ;col 0
                    mov     ah,2                    ;set cursor
                    int     10h                     ; off screen
                    pop     dx
                    pop     bx
                    pop     ax
                    ret
        curoff      endp

        ;           print a char using teletype mode
        chrprt      proc    near
                    push    ax
                    push    bx
                    mov     bh,pageno               ;page 0
                    mov     ah,0eh                  ;write char in
                    int     10h                     ; al on screen
                    pop     bx
                    pop     ax
                    ret
        chrprt      endp

        ;           hex to ascii conversion
        hexasc      proc    near
                    cmp     al,0ah                  ;if >= 0ah
                    jb      ha1
                    add     al,37h                  ;add 37h
                    jmp     ha2
        ha1:        add     al,30h                  ;else add 30h
        ha2:        ret
        hexasc      endp

        ;           print a byte
        pbyte       proc    near
                    push    ax
                    push    cx
                    push    ax                      ;save byte
                    mov     cl,4
                    shr     al,cl                   ;hi nibble
                    call    hexasc                  ;conv to ascii
                    call    chrprt                  ;print char
                    pop     ax                      ;get byte
                    and     al,0fh                  ;lo nibble
                    call    hexasc                  ;con to ascii
                    call    chrprt                  ;print char
                    mov     al,20h                  ;print blank
                    call    chrprt
                    pop     cx
                    pop     ax
                    ret
        pbyte       endp

        ;           delay
        ;           input: ax = no. of ticks to delay
        ;                  18.2 ticks per second
        delay       proc    near
                    push    ax                      ;save regs
                    push    cx
                    push    dx
                    push    ax                      ;push #ticks
                    mov     ah,0                    ;time of day
                    int     1Ah                     ; interrupt
                    push    cx                      ;push hi count
                    push    dx                      ;push lo count
                    mov     bp,sp                   ;bp -> lo count
```

Listing C.1 (continued)

```
dly1:      mov     ah,0
           int     1Ah                     ;get new count
           sub     dx,[bp]
           sbb     cx,2[bp]                ;calc diff
           cmp     dx,4[bp]                ;repeat until
           jb      dly1                    ;diff > #ticks
           add     sp,6                    ;fix stack
           pop     dx                      ;restore regs
           pop     cx
           pop     ax
           ret
delay      endp


;          make a tone
;          dx = pitch of tone
;          bx = length of tone
tone       proc    near
           push    ax                      ;save regs
           push    bx
           push    cx
           push    dx
           mov     al,0b6h
           out     43h,al                  ;B6 in ctrl reg
           mov     al,dl                   ;LSB pitch ->
           out     42h,al                  ; counter reg
           mov     al,dh                   ;MSB pitch ->
           out     42h,al                  ; counter reg
           in      al,61h                  ;PPI port B
           mov     ah,al                   ; -> AH
           or      al,03h                  ;speaker on
           out     61h,al                  ;set bits 0,1
           push    ax
           mov     ax,bx                   ;delay bx ticks
           call    delay
           pop     ax
           mov     al,ah                   ;speaker off
           out     61h,al
           pop     dx                      ;restore regs
           pop     cx
           pop     bx
           pop     ax
           ret
tone       endp


;          beep a tone
beep       proc    near
           push    bx
           push    dx
           mov     dx,0300h                ;set pitch
           mov     bx,4                    ;delay .22 s
           call    tone
           pop     dx
           pop     bx
           ret
beep       endp


;          wait for key and get key value
;          output: al = ascii code of key
;                  function & cursor keys have
;                  al = scan code OR 80H
getkey     proc    near
gk1:       mov     ah,0
           int     16h                     ;wait for key
           cmp     ah,0                    ;ignore ^break
           je      gk1                     ;and Alt-keypd
```

Listing C.1 (continued)

```
                cmp     al,0
                jne     gk2                 ;if ascii = 0
                mov     al,ah               ;use scan code
                or      al,80h              ; OR 80h
gk2:            ret
getkey  endp

;       process a key
;       input: al = ascii code of key
;              di -> jump table
;              dx -> default subroutine
dokey   proc    near
dk1:            cmp     al,cs:[di]          ;chk next code
                jne     dk2                 ;if a match
                call    word ptr cs:1[di]   ;call sub
                ret                         ;and quit
dk2:            cmp     byte ptr cs:[di],0  ;if not
                je      dk3                 ;end of table
                add     di,3                ;chk next entry
                jmp     dk1                 ; in table
dk3:            call    dx                  ;else call
                ret                         ;default sub
dokey   endp

;       buffered keyboard input
;       at current cursor position
;       input asciiz string is at kbuf
;       # of character entered at span
;       output: none
query   proc    near
                mov     sisave,si
                mov     si,offset kbuf      ;si->kbuf
qy1:            call    getkey              ;get key
                mov     di,offset jmptbq
                mov     dx,offset tobuff    ;default
                call    dokey               ;process key
                jmp     qy1
query   endp

;       query jump table
jmptbq  db      _bksp                       ;backspace
        dw      backsp
        db      _enter                      ;enter
        dw      enterq
        db      _esc                        ;esc
        dw      quit
        db      0

;       display & store char in kbuf
tobuff  proc    near
                cmp     si,offset bufend
                jb      tb1                 ;if end.of.buf
                call    beep                ; beep &
                ret                         ; quit
tb1:            mov     [si],al             ;store char
                inc     si                  ;inc ptr
                call    chrout1             ;display char
                ret
tobuff  endp

;       backspace
backsp  proc    near
                cmp     si,offset kbuf
                ja      bk1                 ;if 1st char
                call    beep                ; beep & ret
```

Listing C.1 (continued)

```
                ret
bk1:            dec     si                              ;back up & put
                mov     byte ptr [si],20h               ;20h in kbuf
                call    deccur                          ;back up & put
                mov     al,20h                          ;blank on
                call    chrout1                         ;screen
                call    deccur
                ret
backsp          endp

;               enter from query
;               exits from query
enterq          proc    near
                mov     byte ptr [si],0                 ;make asciiz
                sub     si,offset kbuf                  ;store #char
                mov     span,si                         ;in span
                mov     si,sisave                       ;restore si
                pop     ax                              ;>enterq
                pop     ax                              ;>dokey
                ret                                     ;>query
enterq          endp

;               resize memory
resize          proc    near
                mov     ax,es                           ;ax=psp seg
                mov     bx,ss                           ;bx=stack seg
                sub     bx,ax                           ;reserve psp-ss
                add     bx,10                           ; + stack size
                mov     ah,4Ah
                int     21h                             ;resize mem
                ret
resize          endp

;               allocate save screen buffer
svinit          proc    near
                mov     svseg,0                         ;svseg = 0
                mov     bx,1000                         ;request 16000
                mov     ah,48h                          ; bytes
                int     21h
                jc      sv1                             ;if no error
                mov     svseg,ax                        ;svseg = seg
sv1:            ret
svinit          endp

;               release save screen buffer
relssb          proc    near
                cmp     svseg,0                         ;if allocated
                je      rel1
                mov     ax,svseg                        ;deallocate
                mov     es,ax                           ;es = svseg
                mov     ah,49h
                int     21h                             ;release mem
rel1:           ret
relssb          endp

;               save screen
savescr         proc    near
                push    ax                              ;save regs
                push    cx
                push    si
                push    di
                push    ds
                push    es
                cmp     svseg,0                         ;if buff exists
                je      svsc3
```

Listing C.1 (continued)

```
                std                          ;move 12000
                mov      ax,svseg            ; bytes up
                mov      ds,ax               ; 4000 bytes
                mov      es,ax               ; to make hole
                mov      cx,6000             ; in buffer
                mov      si,11998
                mov      di,15998
                rep movsw
                mov      ah,15
                int      10h                 ;get video state
                cmp      al,7
                je       svsc1               ;set ax =
                mov      ax,0b800h            ; video ram
                jmp      svsc2               ; segment
svsc1:          mov      ax,0b000h
svsc2:          mov      ds,ax               ; to svseg
                mov      si,0                ; buffer
                mov      di,0
                mov      cx,2000
                cld
                rep movsw
svsc3:          pop      es                  ;restore regs
                pop      ds
                pop      di
                pop      si
                pop      cx
                pop      ax
                ret
savescr         endp

;               restore screen
restscr         proc     near
                push     ax                  ;save regs
                push     cx
                push     si
                push     di
                push     ds
                push     es
                cmp      svseg,0             ;if buff exists
                je       rsts3
                mov      ah,15
                int      10h                 ;get video state
                cmp      al,7
                je       rsts1               ;set ax =
                mov      ax,0b800h            ; video ram
                jmp      rsts2               ; segment
rsts1:          mov      ax,0b000h           ;move 1st 4000
rsts2:          mov      es,ax               ; bytes from
                mov      ax,svseg            ; svseg buffer
                mov      ds,ax               ; to tv ram
                mov      si,0
                mov      di,0
                mov      cx,2000
                cld
                rep movsw
                mov      ax,data
                mov      ds,ax               ;ds = data
                mov      ax,svseg            ;move last
                mov      es,ax               ; 12000 bytes
                mov      ds,ax               ; in buffer
                mov      si,4000             ; down 4000
                mov      di,0                ; bytes
                mov      cx,6000
                rep movsw
rsts3:          pop      es                  ;restore regs
```

Listing C.1 (continued)

```
            pop     ds
            pop     di
            pop     si
            pop     cx
            pop     ax
            ret
restscr     endp

;           quit to dos
quit        proc    near
            mov     ax,4C00h
            int     21h
quit        endp

code        ends
            end
```

Listing C.2 *number.asm*

```
            title   Number conversion subroutines
        .8087
data        segment public
base        dw      10
dnum        dd      ?
dpl         dw      ?
negflg      db      ?
decflg      db      ?
one         dw      1
two         dw      2
exp         dw      ?
sig         dd      ?
fdbuf       dd      ?
ctrl        dw      ?
ten8        dd      100000000
E           dd      ?
F           dt      ?
negeflg     db      ?
fdumpb      dq      8 dup(?)
data        ends

            public  getnum,convert,digit
            public  sharp,sharps,ddiv
            public  dnegate,number,decflg
            public  base,negflg,dnum
            public  pax,upax,pdxax,updxax
            public  dot,udot,ddot,uddot
            public  absol,dabsol,mdmul
            public  float,pst,binflt,tenx,fdump
            extrn   query:near,kbuf:byte
            extrn   bufend:byte,span:word
            extrn   mess:near,mess2:near,crlf:near
            extrn   getkey:near,dokey:near
            extrn   beep:near,chrout1:near,deccur:near

code        segment public
            assume  cs:code,ds:data
;           get number from keyboard
;           number can have a decimal point (dp)
;             and can be prceded by a minus sign
;           input:  none
;           output: dx:ax = double number
;                   cx = # to right of dp
;                   carry = 1 if invalid number
getnum      proc    near
            push    si
            push    di
            call    query               ;get string
            mov     si,offset kbuf      ;si->string
            call    number              ;conv.to.binary
            cmp     byte ptr [si],0     ;if invalid
            je      gtn1                ; digit not 0
            stc                         ; set carry
gtn1:       pop     di
            pop     si
            ret
getnum      endp
```

Listing C.2 (continued)

```
;           print signed value in ax
pax        proc  near
           push  ax
           push  si
           call  dot                  ;signed string
           call  mess2                ;print it
           pop   si
           pop   ax
           ret
pax        endp

;           print unsigned value in ax
upax       proc  near
           push  ax
           push  si
           call  udot                 ;get string
           call  mess2                ;print it
           pop   si
           pop   ax
           ret
upax       endp

;           print signed value in dx:ax
pdxax      proc  near
           push  ax
           push  dx
           push  si
           call  ddot                 ;get string
           call  mess2                ;print it
           pop   si
           pop   dx
           pop   ax
           ret
pdxax      endp

;           print unsigned value in dx:ax
updxax     proc  near
           push  ax
           push  dx
           push  si
           call  uddot                ;get string
           call  mess2                ;print it
           pop   si
           pop   dx
           pop   ax
           ret
updxax     endp

;           convert ax to unsigned number string
;           output: si -> number asciiz string
udot       proc  near
           push  ax
           push  bx
           push  di
           mov   word ptr dnum,ax      ;dnum=ax
           mov   word ptr dnum+2,0
           mov   si,offset dnum
           mov   di,offset bufend-1
           mov   byte ptr 1[di],0      ;bufend=0
```

Listing C.2 (continued)

```
                call    sharps                  ;conv to ascii
                inc     di
                mov     si,di                   ;->1st digit
                pop     di
                pop     bx
                pop     ax
                ret
        udot    endp

        ;       convert dx:ax to unsigned number string
        ;       output: si -> number asciiz string
        uddot   proc    near
                push    ax
                push    bx
                push    di
                mov     word ptr dnum,ax         ;dnum=dx:ax
                mov     word ptr dnum+2,dx
                mov     si,offset dnum
                mov     di,offset bufend-1
                mov     byte ptr 1[di],0         ;bufend=0
                call    sharps                   ;conv to ascii
                inc     di
                mov     si,di                   ;->1st digit
                pop     di
                pop     bx
                pop     ax
                ret
        uddot   endp

        ;       convert ax to signed number string
        ;       output: si -> number asciiz string
        dot     proc    near
                push    ax
                push    bx
                push    di
                mov     bx,ax                   ;bx has sign
                call    absol
                mov     word ptr dnum,ax         ;dnum=ax
                mov     word ptr dnum+2,0
                mov     si,offset dnum
                mov     di,offset bufend-1
                mov     byte ptr 1[di],0         ;bufend=0
                call    sharps                   ;conv to ascii
                or      bx,bx                   ;if negative
                jns     dt1
                mov     byte ptr [di],'-'        ;add - sign
                dec     di
        dt1:    inc     di
                mov     si,di                   ;->1st digit
                pop     di
                pop     bx
                pop     ax
                ret
        dot     endp

        ;       convert dx:ax to signed number string
        ;       output: si -> number asciiz string
        ddot    proc    near
                push    ax
```

Listing C.2 (continued)

```
                push    bx
                push    di
                mov     bx,dx                   ;bx has sign
                call    dabsol
                mov     word ptr dnum,ax        ;dnum=dx:ax
                mov     word ptr dnum+2,dx
                mov     si,offset dnum
                mov     di,offset bufend-1
                mov     byte ptr 1[di],0        ;bufend=0
                call    sharps                  ;conv to ascii
                or      bx,bx                   ;if negative
                jns     ddt1
                mov     byte ptr [di],'-'       ;add - sign
                dec     di
ddt1:           inc     di
                mov     si,di                   ;->1st digit
                pop     di
                pop     bx
                pop     ax
                ret
ddot    endp

;               absolute value of ax
absol   proc    near
                or      ax,ax                   ;if ax is neg
                jns     ab1
                neg     ax                      ;negate it
ab1:            ret
absol   endp

;               absolute value of dx:ax
dabsol  proc    near
                or      dx,dx                   ;if dx:ax
                jns     da1                     ; is negative
                call    dnegate                 ;negate it
da1:            ret
dabsol  endp

;               ascii number to binary conversion
;               input:  di -> bin buf
;                       si -> number string
;               output: si -> invalid digit
convert proc    near
                push    ax                      ;save regs
                push    bx
                push    cx
                push    dx
                cld
cvt1:           lodsb                           ;get next digit
                call    digit                   ;conv to value
                jc      cvt2                    ;if valid digit
                mov     ah,0                    ;ax=digit value
                push    ax                      ;save value
                mov     bx,base                 ;mult dnumH by
                mov     ax,word ptr 2[di]       ; base
                mul     bx
                mov     cx,ax                   ;cx=lo word
                mov     ax,word ptr [di]        ;mult dnumL by
                mul     bx                      ; base
```

Listing C.2 (continued)

```
                pop     bx                          ;get value
                add     ax,bx                       ;add to prodL
                adc     dx,cx                       ;+ cx to prodH
                mov     word ptr [di],ax            ;store in dnum
                mov     word ptr 2[di],dx
                cmp     decflg,0                    ;if . occurred
                je      cvt1
                inc     dpl                         ; inc dpl
                jmp     cvt1                        ;do until
        cvt2:   dec     si                          ; invalid digit
                pop     dx                          ;restore regs
                pop     cx
                pop     bx
                pop     ax
                ret
        convert endp


        ;       convert ascii digit to value in base
        ;       al=char (ascii code)
        ;       output: carry=0 al=valid hex value
        ;               carry=1 al=invalid ascii code
        digit   proc    near
                push    bx                          ;save regs
                push    ax
                mov     bx,base                     ;bx=base
                sub     al,'0'                      ;ascii codes<30
                jb      fail                        ; are invalid
                cmp     al,9                        ;char between
                jbe     dgt1                        ; 9 and A
                cmp     al,17                       ; are invalid
                jb      fail                        ;fill gap
                sub     al,7                        ; between 9&A
        dgt1:   cmp     al,bl                       ;digit must be
                jae     fail                        ; < base
                clc                                 ;valid digit
                pop     bx                          ;pop old ax
                pop     bx                          ;restore bx
                ret
        fail:   pop     ax                          ;invalid digit
                pop     bx
                stc
                ret
        digit   endp


        ;       convert 1 digit & add to ascii string
        ;       si->bin buf   di->ascii buf
        sharp   proc near
                push    ax                          ;save regs
                push    bx
                push    dx
                mov     dx,2[si]
                mov     ax,[si]
                mov     bx,base
                call    ddiv                        ;dnum/base
                mov     [si],ax                     ; = dnum
                mov     2[si],dx
                cmp     bl,9                        ;if rem>9
                jbe     shp1
                add     bl,7                        ; add 7
```

Listing C.2 (continued)

```
shp1:   add    bl,'0'                   ;conv to ascii
        mov    [di],bl                  ;store digit
        dec    di                       ;->next digit
        pop    dx                       ;restore regs
        pop    bx
        pop    ax
        ret
sharp   endp


;       convert all digits to ascii
;       si->bin buf    di->ascii buf
sharps  proc near
shs1:   call   sharp                    ;do next digit
        cmp    word ptr [si],0          ;repeat until
        jne    shs1                     ; quot=0
        cmp    word ptr 2[si],0
        jne    shs1
        ret
sharps  endp


;       divide double word dx:ax by bx
;       quot in dx:ax    rem in bx
ddiv    proc   near
        push   cx                       ;save reg
        push   ax                       ;save numL
        mov    ax,dx                    ;ax=numH
        mov    dx,0
        div    bx                       ;0 numH / bx
        mov    cx,ax                    ;cx=quotH
        pop    ax                       ;get numL
        div    bx                       ;rH numL / bx
        mov    bx,dx                    ;bx=rem
        mov    dx,cx                    ;dx:ax=quot
        pop    cx                       ;restore reg
        ret
ddiv    endp


;       negate double word dx:ax
dnegate proc   near
        push   bx                       ;save regs
        push   cx
        mov    bx,dx                    ;bx=hi word
        mov    cx,ax                    ;cx=lo word
        xor    ax,ax                    ;ax=0
        mov    dx,ax                    ;dx=0
        sub    ax,cx                    ;dx:ax =
        sbb    dx,bx                    ; 0:0 - bx:cx
        pop    cx                       ;restore regs
        pop    bx
        ret
dnegate endp


;       mixed double multiply
;       dx:ax = dx:ax * bx
;             = A B * C = PH PL
;       PL = BCL
;       PH = BCH + ACL
mdmul   proc   near
        push   cx                       ;save cx
```

Listing C.2 (continued)

```
                  mov    cx,dx                   ;cx = A
                  mul    bx                      ;dx=BCH ax=BCL
                  push   ax                      ;save BCL
                  push   dx                      ;save BCH
                  mov    ax,cx                   ;ax = A
                  mul    bx                      ;dx=ACH ax=ACL
                  pop    dx                      ;dx=BCH
                  add    dx,ax                   ;dx=BCH+ACL
                  pop    ax                      ;ax=BCL
                  pop    cx                      ;restore cx
                  ret
        mdmul     endp


        ;         convert real number
        ;         input:  si -> number string
        ;         output: dx:ax = double number
        ;                 cx = # to right of dp
        ;                 si -> invalid digit
        number    proc   near
                  push   di
                  mov    di,offset dnum
                  mov    word ptr [di],0         ;clr bin buf
                  mov    word ptr 2[di],0
                  mov    dpl,0                   ;clr dpl
                  mov    decflg,0                ;clr decflg
                  mov    negflg,0                ;clear negflg
                  cld
                  lodsb                          ;get 1st char
                  cmp    al,'-'                  ;if - sign
                  jne    nb1
                  not    negflg                  ;set neg flag
                  jmp    nb2
        nb1:      dec    si                      ;->1st digit
        nb2:      call   convert                 ;convert number
                  lodsb                          ; get next byte
                  cmp    al,'.'                  ; if .
                  jne    nb3
                  not    decflg                  ; set decflg
                  call   convert                 ;conv rest
                  lodsb                          ;dummy load
        nb3:      dec    si                      ;si->invalid dg
                  mov    ax,[di]                 ;dx:ax=number
                  mov    dx,2[di]
                  cmp    negflg,0                ;if negative
                  je     nb4
                  call   dnegate                 ;negate it
        nb4:      mov    cx,dpl                  ;cx=dpl
                  pop    di
                  ret
        number    endp


        ;         convert to floating point
        ;         si --> ascii fp number string
        ;         di --> floating point buffer (qword)
        float     proc   near
                  push   ax
                  push   bx
                  push   cx
                  push   dx
```

Listing C.2 (continued)

```
                cld
                call    number                  ;get signif
                mov     word ptr sig,ax
                mov     word ptr sig+2,dx
                neg     cx                      ;move -dpl
                mov     exp,cx                  ; to exp
                lodsb                           ;get char
                or      al,20h                  ;E or e
                cmp     al,'e'                  ;if not e
                je      flt1                    ; quit
                dec     si
                jmp     short flt2
flt1:           call    number                  ;get exp
                add     exp,ax                  ; + to exp
flt2:           push    si                      ;save si
                mov     si,offset sig           ;convert to
                mov     bx,offset exp           ; fpoint
                call    binflt
                pop     si                      ;restore si
                pop     dx
                pop     cx
                pop     bx
                pop     ax
                ret
float           endp


;               binary to floating point
;               si -> significand (dword)
;               bx -> exponent    (word)
;               di -> result      (qword)
binflt          proc    near
                push    bx                      ;save regs
                push    si
                push    di
                fild    word ptr [bx]           ;Y
                call    tenx                    ;10**Y=2**E
                fimul   dword ptr [si]          ;sig*2**E
                fstp    qword ptr [di]          ;store ans
                fwait                           ;synchronize
                pop     di                      ;restore regs
                pop     si
                pop     bx
                ret
binflt          endp


;               10**ST
tenx            proc    near
                fstcw   ctrl                    ;round down
                fwait
                and     ctrl,0f3ffh             ; ctrl reg
                or      ctrl,0400h              ; bit 10=1
                fldcw   ctrl                    ; bit 11=0
                fldl2t                          ;Y\log2 10
                fmulp   st(1),st(0)             ;Y*log2 10 = E
                fld     ST                      ; E \ E
                frndint                         ; E \ I
                fxch                            ; I \ E
                fld     st(1)                   ; I\E\I
                fsubp   st(1),st(0)             ;I\(E-I=F)
```

Listing C.2 (continued)

```
                fidiv two                      ;I\F/2
                f2xm1                          ;I\2**F/2 - 1
                fiadd one                      ;I\2**F/2=T2
                fld   ST                       ;I\T2\T2
                fmulp st(1),st(0)              ;I\2**F
                fscale                         ;I\2**(F+I)
                fstp  st(1)                    ;2**E
                fwait
                ret
tenx    endp

;       floating point to F*10**E
fpdec   proc  near                     ;z
                fld   st(0)                    ;z\z
                fld   st(0)                    ;z\z\z
                fabs                           ;z\z\|z|
                fld1                           ;z\z\|z|\1
                fxch  st(1)                    ;z\z\1\|z|
                fyl2x                          ;z\z\log₂z
                fldl2t                         ;z\z\log₂z\log₂10
                fdivp st(1),st(0)              ;z\z\E'
                frndint                        ;z\z\E
                fist  E                        ;z\z\E
                fchs                           ;z\z\-E
                call  tenx                     ;z\z\10**-E
                fmulp st(1),st(0)              ;z\F (1-9)
                fimul ten8                     ;z\F*10**8
                fbstp F                        ;z\bcd store
                fwait                          ;z
                ret
fpdec   endp

;       negate E
negE    proc  near
                push  dx
                mov   ax,word ptr E
                mov   dx,word ptr E+2
                call  dnegate
                mov   word ptr E,ax
                mov   word ptr E+2,dx
                pop   dx
                ret
negE    endp

;       print F*10**E
pst     proc  near
                push  ax
                push  cx
                push  si
                push  di
                push  es
                push  ds
                pop   es                       ;es=ds
                call  fpdec                    ;calc F*10**E
                std
                mov   di,offset bufend-1
                mov   byte ptr 1[di],0         ;bufend=0
                mov   si,offset E
                mov   negeflg,0                ;convert E
```

Listing C.2 (continued)

```
                test    byte ptr E+3,80h        ;if E neg
                jns     pf2
                call    negE                    ;negate E
                not     negeflg                 ;set flag
        pf2:    call    sharps
                cmp     negeflg,0               ;if E neg
                je      pf0
                mov     al,'-'                  ; add -
                stosb
        pf0:    mov     al,'E'
                stosb                           ;add E
                mov     al,' '
                stosb                           ;add blank
                mov     si,offset F
                mov     base,16                 ;bcd is hex
                mov     cx,8
        pf3:    call    sharp                   ;do 8 digits
                loop    pf3
                mov     al,'.'                  ;add .
                stosb
                mov     al,byte ptr F+4
                and     al,0fh
                or      al,30h                  ;add units
                stosb                           ; digit
                mov     al,byte ptr F+9         ;check sign
                test    al,80h                  ;if neg
                jns     pf1
                mov     al,'-'                  ;add -
                stosb
        pf1:    inc     di
                mov     si,di                   ;si->string
                call    mess2
                mov     base,10                 ;base=10
                pop     es                      ;restore regs
                pop     di
                pop     si
                pop     cx
                pop     ax
                ret
        pst     endp

        ;       dump 8087 stack to fdumpb
        fdump   proc    near
                push    bx
                push    cx
                mov     bx,0
                mov     cx,8
        fdp1:   fst     qword ptr fdumpb[bx]
                fincstp
                add     bx,8
                loop    fdp1
                pop     cx
                pop     bx
                ret
        fdump   endp
        code    ends
                end
```

```
 Listing  C.3      dos.asm
                title   DOS subroutines

     data       segment public
     handle     dw      ?
     bytbuf     db      ?
     fnmsg      db      'Enter filename: ',0
     em1        db      'Disk open error: ',0
     em2        db      'Disk close error: ',0
     em3        db      'Disk read error: ',0
     em4        db      'Disk write error: ',0
     em5        db      'Disk file error: ',0
     ercode     db      'Invalid fnc no.',0
                db      'File not found ',0
                db      'Path not found ',0
                db      'No free handles',0
                db      'Access denied  ',0
                db      'Invalid handle ',0
                db      'Memory error   ',0
                db      'Out of memory  ',0
                db      'Invaled address',0
                db      'Bad environment',0
                db      'Invalid format ',0
                db      'Bad access code',0
                db      'Invalid data   ',0
                db      'Bad drive spec.',0
                db      'Current dir.   ',0
                db      'Not same device',0
                db      'No files found ',0
     data       ends

                extrn   mess:near,chrout:near,beep:near
                extrn   setcur:near,mess2:near
                extrn   curoff:near,digit:near
                extrn   convert:near,number:near
                extrn   dnegate:near,sharps:near
                extrn   clrscn:near,tab:near,query:near
                extrn   kbuf:byte,bufend:byte
                extrn   negflg:byte,dnum:dword
                extrn   span:word

                public  open,close,read,write,rewind
                public  gtbyte,gtdgt,gtnum,gtrnum
                public  sndbyte,sndnum,openfn,movptr
                public  getlen,sndcrlf,create,handle

     code       segment public
                assume  cs:code,ds:data

     ;          open or create file
     ;          input:  dx -> asciiz string
     ;          output: bx = handle
     open       proc    near
                push    cx
                mov     al,2                    ;read & write
                mov     ah,3dh
                int     21h                     ;open file
                jnc     op2
                cmp     ax,2                    ;if file
                jne     op1                     ; not found
                mov     ah,3ch                  ;create
                mov     cx,0                    ; normal attr
                int     21h                     ; file
```

Listing C.3 (continued)

```
                jnc     op2
op1:    call    open_err                ;error mess
                stc
                jmp     op3
op2:    mov     bx,ax                   ;bx=handle
op3:    pop     cx
                ret
open    endp

;       close file
;       input: bx = handle
close   proc    near
                mov     ah,3eh
                int     21h             ;close file
                jnc     cl1             ;if error
                call    close_err       ; print it
                stc
cl1:    ret
close   endp

;       create file
;       (set length to zero to write over)
;       input:  dx -> asciiz string
;       output: bx = handle
create  proc    near
                push    cx
                mov     ah,3ch          ;create
                mov     cx,0            ; normal attr
                int     21h             ; file
                jnc     ct2
ct1:    call    open_err                ;error mess
                stc
                jmp     ct3
ct2:    mov     bx,ax                   ;bx=handle
ct3:    pop     cx
                ret
create  endp

;       read file
;       input: bx = handle
;              cx = # of bytes to read
;              dx -> buffer address
;       output: ax = # of bytes read
;              ax = 0 if EOF
read    proc    near
                mov     ah,3fh
                int     21h             ;read file
                jnc     rd1             ;if error
                call    read_err        ; print it
                stc
rd1:    ret
read    endp

;       write file
;       input: bx = handle
;              cx = # of bytes to write
;              dx -> buffer address
write   proc    near
                mov     ah,40h
                int     21h             ;write file
                jnc     wt1             ;if error
                call    write_err       ; print it
                stc
wt1:    ret
write   endp
```

Listing C.3 (continued)

```
;         rewind file
;         input: bx = handle
rewind    proc    near
          push    cx
          push    dx
          mov     cx,0
          mov     dx,0                        ;offset=0
          mov     al,0                        ;mov ptr from
          mov     ah,42h                      ; start of file
          int     21h
          jnc     rw1                         ;if error
          call    ptr_err                     ; print it
          stc
rw1:      pop     dx
          pop     cx
          ret
rewind    endp

;         get length of file
;         input: bx = handle
;         output:         dx:ax = length of file
getlen    proc    near
          push    cx
          mov     cx,0
          mov     dx,0                        ;offset=0
          mov     al,2                        ;mov ptr from
          mov     ah,42h                      ; end of file
          int     21h
          jnc     gl1                         ;if error
          call    ptr_err                     ; print it
          stc
gl1:      pop     cx
          ret
getlen    endp

;         get next byte
;         input: bx = handle
;         output: al = byte
;                 carry = 1 if EOF
gtbyte    proc    near
          push    cx
          push    dx
          mov     cx,1                        ;read 1 byte
          mov     dx,offset bytbuf
          call    read
          cmp     ax,0                        ;if EOF
          jne     gb1
          stc                                 ; set carry
          jmp     gb2                         ;else
gb1:      mov     al,bytbuf                   ;al=byte
          clc                                 ;clear carry
gb2:      pop     dx
          pop     cx
          ret
gtbyte    endp

;         check for quote string
quote     proc    near
          cmp     al,'"'                      ;if "
          je      qt1
          ret
qt1:      call    gtbyte                      ;get byte
          cmp     al,'"'                      ;until
          jne     qt1                         ; another "
```

Listing C.3 (continued)

```
                call    gtbyte                  ;get next byte
                ret
quote           endp

;               get next digit (in current base)
;               input: bx = handle
;               output: al = ascii digit value
;                       carry = 1 if EOF
gtdgt           proc    near
gt1:            call    gtbyte                  ;get next byte
                jc      gt2                     ;until EOF
                call    quote                   ;check for "
                push    ax                      ;save ascii val
                call    digit                   ;or valid digit
                pop     ax                      ;get ascii val
                jc      gt1
gt2:            ret
gtdgt           endp

;               get next digit or a - sign
;               input: bx = handle
;               output: al = ascii digit value
;                       carry = 1 if EOF
gtdgtm          proc    near
gtm1:           call    gtbyte                  ;get next byte
                jc      gtm2                    ;until EOF
                call    quote                   ;check for "
                cmp     al,'-'                  ;if - sign
                je      gtm2                    ; quit
                push    ax                      ;save ascii val
                call    digit                   ;or valid digit
                pop     ax                      ;get ascii val
                jc      gtm1
gtm2:           ret
gtdgtm          endp

;               get next number (in current base)
;               input: bx = handle
;               output: dx:ax = double number
;                       carry = 1 if EOF
gtnum           proc    near
                push    si
                push    di
                push    ds
                pop     es                      ;es=ds
                cld
                mov     word ptr dnum,0         ;clear dnum
                mov     word ptr dnum+2,0
                mov     di,offset kbuf
                call    gtdgt                   ;get next digit
                jc      gn3                     ;while not EOF
                stosb                           ; save digit
gn1:            call    gtbyte                  ;get next byte
                jc      gn3
                call    quote                   ;check for "
                push    ax                      ;save ascii val
                call    digit                   ;while a digit
                pop     ax                      ;get ascii val
                stosb                           ; save it
                jc      gn2
                jmp     gn1
gn2:            mov     si,offset kbuf
                mov     di,offset dnum
                call    convert                 ;convert to
                mov     ax,word ptr dnum        ; double
```

Listing C.3 (continued)

```
                mov     dx,word ptr dnum+2      ; number
gn3:            pop     di
                pop     si
                ret
gtnum           endp

;               get next real number (in current base)
;               input: bx = handle
;               output: dx:ax = double number
;                       cx = # to right of dp
;                       carry = 1 if EOF or no number
gtrnum          proc    near
                push    si
                push    di
                push    ds
                pop     es                      ;es=ds
                cld
                mov     di,offset kbuf
                call    gtdgtm                  ;get digit or -
                jc      grn3                    ;while not EOF
                stosb                           ; save digit
grn1:           call    gtbyte                  ;get next byte
                jc      grn3
                call    quote                   ;check for "
                cmp     al,'.'                  ;save .
                je      grn4
                push    ax                      ;save ascii val
                call    digit                   ;save a digit
                pop     ax                      ;get ascii val
                jc      grn2
grn4:           stosb                           ; save it
                jmp     grn1
grn2:           stosb                           ;invalid digit
                mov     si,offset kbuf
                call    number                  ;convert
grn3:           pop     di
                pop     si
                ret
gtrnum          endp

;               send byte
;               input: bx = handle
;                      al = byte
sndbyte         proc    near
                push    cx
                push    dx
                mov     bytbuf,al               ;bytbuf=byte
                mov     dx,offset bytbuf
                mov     cx,1                    ;1 byte
                call    write                   ;send it
                pop     dx
                pop     cx
                ret
sndbyte         endp

;               send crlf
sndcrlf         proc    near
                mov     al,13                   ;send cr
                call    sndbyte
                mov     al,10                   ;send lf
                call    sndbyte
                ret
sndcrlf         endp

;               send number
```

Listing C.3 (continued)

```
;            input: bx = handle
;                   dx:ax = double number
sndnum   proc   near
         push   ax
         push   bx
         push   cx
         push   dx
         push   si
         push   di
         mov    negflg,0              ;clear negflg
         or     dx,dx                 ;if negative
         jns    sn1
         not    negflg               ;set negflg
         call   dnegate              ;negate dnum
sn1:     mov    di,offset bufend     ;di -> asc buf
         mov    si,offset dnum       ;si -> bin buf
         mov    [si],ax
         mov    2[si],dx
         call   sharps               ;conv digits
         cmp    negflg,0             ;if negative
         je     sn2
         mov    al,'-'               ;store -
         mov    [di],al              ; in buffer
         dec    di
sn2:     mov    dx,di                ;dx -> string
         inc    dx
         mov    cx,offset bufend
         sub    cx,di                ;cx=#digits
         call   write                ;send string
         pop    di
         pop    si
         pop    dx
         pop    cx
         pop    bx
         pop    ax
         ret
sndnum   endp


;            move pointer
;            input: bx = handle
;                   cx:dx = offset value
;                   al = 0 - start of file + offset
;                        1 - inc ptr by offset
;            output: dx:ax = new value of ptr
movptr   proc   near
         mov    ah,42h                ;move ptr
         int    21h
         jnc    mpt1
         call   ptr_err
         stc
mpt1:    ret
movptr   endp


;            enter filename and open
;            input: none
;            output:        handle is in 'handle'
;            carry = 1 if not opened
openfn   proc   near
         push   bx
         push   dx
         push   si
         mov    si,offset fnmsg
         call   mess2                 ;display mess
         call   query                 ;enter filename
         cmp    span,0                ;if no chars
```

Listing C.3 (continued)

```
                jne     of0                     ; set carry
                stc                             ; and quit
                jmp     of1
of0:    mov     dx,offset kbuf
                call    open                    ;open it
                jc      of1                     ;if error,quit
                mov     handle,bx               ;store handle
of1:    pop     si
                pop     dx
                pop     bx
                ret
openfn  endp

;               disk errors
open_err proc   near
                push    bx
                push    dx
                push    si
                call    beep
                mov     bl,7
                mov     dx,1801h                ;bottom line
                mov     si,offset em1           ;print
                call    mess                    ; error message
                mov     bx,ax                   ;bx=err code
                call    errmsg
                pop     si
                pop     dx
                pop     bx
                ret
open_err endp

close_err proc near
                push    bx
                push    dx
                push    si
                call    beep
                mov     bl,7
                mov     dx,1801h                ;bottom line
                mov     si,offset em2           ;print
                call    mess                    ; error message
                mov     bx,ax                   ;bx=err code
                call    errmsg
                pop     si
                pop     dx
                pop     bx
                ret
close_err endp

read_err proc   near
                push    bx
                push    dx
                push    si
                call    beep
                mov     bl,7
                mov     dx,1801h                ;bottom line
                mov     si,offset em3           ;print
                call    mess                    ; error message
                mov     bx,ax                   ;bx=err code
                call    errmsg
                pop     si
                pop     dx
                pop     bx
                ret
read_err endp
```

Listing C.3 (continued)

```
        write_err proc near
                push    bx
                push    dx
                push    si
                call    beep
                mov     bl,7
                mov     dx,1801h                ;bottom line
                mov     si,offset em4           ;print
                call    mess                    ; error message
                mov     bx,ax                   ;bx=err code
                call    errmsg
                pop     si
                pop     dx
                pop     bx
                ret
        write_err endp

        ptr_err proc    near
                push    bx
                push    dx
                push    si
                call    beep
                mov     bl,7
                mov     dx,1801h                ;bottom line
                mov     si,offset em5           ;print
                call    mess                    ; error message
                mov     bx,ax                   ;bx=err code
                call    errmsg
                pop     si
                pop     dx
                pop     bx
                ret
        ptr_err endp

        ;       error code message
        errmsg  proc    near
                mov     si,offset ercode
                mov     cl,4                    ;si->ercode
                dec     bx
                shl     bx,cl                   ; +16*code
                add     si,bx
                mov     bl,07h
                call    mess
                ret
        errmsg  endp

        code    ends
                end
```

Listing C.4 – Hercules Graphics Subroutines   File: *graph.asm*

```
                title   hercules graphics subroutines

                public  line,plot,stherc,erase
                public  messg,charwt,sinax,cosax
                public  cpconv

data            segment public
bit9flg         db      ?
video_seg       dw      0b000h                  ;video ram seg
vidtbl          db      53,45,46,7,91,2,87,87
                db      2,3,0,0,0,0,0,0

row_table       label   word                    ;define row add
            line_num = 0
            rept 87                             ;348/4
                dw      line_num * 90
                dw      2000h + line_num * 90
                dw      4000h + line_num * 90
                dw      6000h + line_num * 90
                line_num = line_num + 1         ;next row
            endm

sintbl  dw      00000,00175,00349,00524,00698       ;00 - 04
        dw      00872,01045,01219,01392,01571       ;05 - 09
        dw      01736,01908,02079,02250,02419       ;10 - 14
        dw      02588,02756,02924,03090,03256       ;15 - 19
        dw      03420,03584,03746,03907,04076       ;20 - 24
        dw      04226,04384,04540,04695,04848       ;25 - 29
        dw      05000,05150,05299,05446,05592       ;30 - 34
        dw      05736,05878,06018,06157,06293       ;35 - 39
        dw      06428,06561,06691,06820,06947       ;40 - 44
        dw      07071,07193,07314,07431,07547       ;45 - 49
        dw      07660,07771,07880,07986,08090       ;50 - 54
        dw      08192,08290,08387,08480,08572       ;55 - 59
        dw      08660,08746,08829,08910,08988       ;60 - 64
        dw      09063,09135,09205,09272,09336       ;65 - 69
        dw      09397,09455,09511,09563,09613       ;70 - 74
        dw      09659,09703,09744,09781,09816       ;75 - 79
        dw      09848,09877,09903,09925,09945       ;80 - 84
        dw      09962,09976,09986,09994,09998       ;85 - 89
        dw      10000                               ;90
axisv   dw      0,10000,0,-10000
signs   db      -1,-1,0,0

;       Monochrome display character set
;       16 bytes per character
;       ascii 00h - 0Fh
charset         db      000H,000H,000H,000H,000H,000H,000H,000H
        db      000H,000H,000H,000H,000H,000H,000H,000H
        db      000H,000H,07EH,081H,0A5H,081H,081H,0BDH
        db      099H,081H,07EH,000H,000H,000H,000H,000H
        db      000H,000H,07EH,0FFH,0DBH,0FFH,0FFH,0C3H
        db      0E7H,0FFH,07EH,000H,000H,000H,000H,000H
        db      000H,000H,000H,036H,07FH,07FH,07FH,07FH
        db      03EH,01CH,008H,000H,000H,000H,000H,000H
        db      000H,000H,000H,008H,01CH,03EH,07FH,03EH
        db      01CH,008H,000H,000H,000H,000H,000H,000H
        db      000H,000H,018H,03CH,03CH,0E7H,0E7H,0E7H
        db      018H,018H,03CH,000H,000H,000H,000H,000H
        db      000H,000H,018H,03CH,07EH,0FFH,0FFH,07EH
        db      018H,018H,03CH,000H,000H,000H,000H,000H
        db      000H,000H,000H,000H,000H,018H,03CH,03CH
        db      018H,000H,000H,000H,000H,000H,000H,000H
        db      0FFH,0FFH,0FFH,0FFH,0FFH,0E7H,0C3H,0C3H
```

Listing C.4 (continued)

```
        db      0E7H,0FFH,0FFH,0FFH,0FFH,0FFH,000H,000H
        db      000H,000H,000H,000H,03CH,066H,042H,042H
        db      066H,03CH,000H,000H,000H,000H,000H,000H
        db      0FFH,0FFH,0FFH,0FFH,0C3H,099H,0BDH,0BDH
        db      099H,0C3H,0FFH,0FFH,0FFH,0FFH,000H,000H
        db      000H,000H,00FH,007H,00DH,019H,03CH,066H
        db      066H,066H,03CH,000H,000H,000H,000H,000H
        db      000H,000H,03CH,066H,066H,066H,03CH,018H
        db      07EH,018H,018H,000H,000H,000H,000H,000H
        db      000H,000H,03FH,033H,03FH,030H,030H,030H
        db      070H,0F0H,0E0H,000H,000H,000H,000H,000H
        db      000H,000H,07FH,063H,07FH,063H,063H,063H
        db      067H,0E7H,0E6H,0C0H,000H,000H,000H,000H
        db      000H,000H,018H,018H,0DBH,03CH,0E7H,03CH
        db      0DBH,018H,018H,000H,000H,000H,000H,000H
;       ascii 10h - 1Fh
        db      000H,000H,040H,060H,070H,07CH,07FH,07CH
        db      070H,060H,040H,000H,000H,000H,000H,000H
        db      000H,000H,001H,003H,007H,01FH,07FH,01FH
        db      007H,003H,001H,000H,000H,000H,000H,000H
        db      000H,000H,018H,03CH,07EH,018H,018H,018H
        db      07EH,03CH,018H,000H,000H,000H,000H,000H
        db      000H,000H,033H,033H,033H,033H,033H,033H
        db      000H,033H,033H,000H,000H,000H,000H,000H
        db      000H,000H,07FH,0DBH,0DBH,0DBH,07BH,01BH
        db      01BH,01BH,01BH,000H,000H,000H,000H,000H
        db      000H,03EH,063H,030H,01CH,036H,063H,063H
        db      036H,01CH,006H,063H,03EH,000H,000H,000H
        db      000H,000H,000H,000H,000H,000H,000H,000H
        db      07FH,07FH,07FH,000H,000H,000H,000H,000H
        db      000H,000H,018H,03CH,07EH,018H,018H,018H
        db      07EH,03CH,018H,07EH,000H,000H,000H,000H
        db      000H,000H,018H,03CH,07EH,018H,018H,018H
        db      018H,018H,018H,000H,000H,000H,000H,000H
        db      000H,000H,018H,018H,018H,018H,018H,018H
        db      07EH,03CH,018H,000H,000H,000H,000H,000H
        db      000H,000H,000H,000H,00CH,006H,07FH,006H
        db      00CH,000H,000H,000H,000H,000H,000H,000H
        db      000H,000H,000H,000H,018H,030H,07FH,030H
        db      018H,000H,000H,000H,000H,000H,000H,000H
        db      000H,000H,000H,000H,000H,060H,060H,060H
        db      07FH,000H,000H,000H,000H,000H,000H,000H
        db      000H,000H,000H,000H,024H,066H,0FFH,066H
        db      024H,000H,000H,000H,000H,000H,000H,000H
        db      000H,000H,000H,008H,01CH,01CH,03EH,03EH
        db      07FH,07FH,000H,000H,000H,000H,000H,000H
        db      000H,000H,000H,07FH,07FH,03EH,03EH,01CH
        db      01CH,008H,000H,000H,000H,000H,000H,000H
;       ascii 20h - 2Fh  blank - '/'
        db      000H,000H,000H,000H,000H,000H,000H,000H
        db      000H,000H,000H,000H,000H,000H,000H,000H
        db      000H,000H,018H,03CH,03CH,03CH,018H,018H
        db      000H,018H,018H,000H,000H,000H,000H,000H
        db      000H,063H,063H,063H,022H,000H,000H,000H
        db      000H,000H,000H,000H,000H,000H,000H,000H
        db      000H,000H,036H,036H,07FH,036H,036H,036H
        db      07FH,036H,036H,000H,000H,000H,000H,000H
        db      00CH,00CH,03EH,063H,061H,060H,03EH,003H
        db      043H,063H,03EH,00CH,00CH,000H,000H,000H
        db      000H,000H,000H,000H,061H,063H,006H,00CH
        db      018H,033H,063H,000H,000H,000H,000H,000H
        db      000H,000H,01CH,036H,036H,01CH,03BH,06EH
        db      066H,066H,03BH,000H,000H,000H,000H,000H
        db      000H,030H,030H,030H,060H,000H,000H,000H
        db      000H,000H,000H,000H,000H,000H,000H,000H
```

Listing C.4 (continued)

```
                db      000H,000H,00CH,018H,030H,030H,030H,030H
                db      030H,018H,00CH,000H,000H,000H,000H,000H
                db      000H,000H,018H,00CH,006H,006H,006H,006H
                db      006H,00CH,018H,000H,000H,000H,000H,000H
                db      000H,000H,000H,000H,066H,03CH,0FFH,03CH
                db      066H,000H,000H,000H,000H,000H,000H,000H
                db      000H,000H,000H,018H,018H,018H,0FFH,018H
                db      018H,018H,000H,000H,000H,000H,000H,000H
                db      000H,000H,000H,000H,000H,000H,000H,000H
                db      018H,018H,018H,030H,000H,000H,000H,000H
                db      000H,000H,000H,000H,000H,000H,0FFH,000H
                db      000H,000H,000H,000H,000H,000H,000H,000H
                db      000H,000H,000H,000H,000H,000H,000H,000H
                db      000H,018H,018H,000H,000H,000H,000H,000H
                db      000H,000H,001H,003H,006H,00CH,018H,030H
                db      060H,040H,000H,000H,000H,000H,000H,000H
;               ascii 30h - 3Fh  '0' - '?'
                db      000H,000H,03EH,063H,067H,06FH,07BH,073H
                db      063H,063H,03EH,000H,000H,000H,000H,000H
                db      000H,000H,00CH,01CH,03CH,00CH,00CH,00CH
                db      00CH,00CH,03FH,000H,000H,000H,000H,000H
                db      000H,000H,03EH,063H,003H,006H,00CH,018H
                db      030H,063H,07FH,000H,000H,000H,000H,000H
                db      000H,000H,03EH,063H,003H,003H,01EH,003H
                db      003H,063H,03EH,000H,000H,000H,000H,000H
                db      000H,000H,006H,00EH,01EH,036H,066H,07FH
                db      006H,006H,00FH,000H,000H,000H,000H,000H
                db      000H,000H,07FH,060H,060H,060H,07EH,003H
                db      003H,063H,03EH,000H,000H,000H,000H,000H
                db      000H,000H,01CH,030H,060H,060H,07EH,063H
                db      063H,063H,03EH,000H,000H,000H,000H,000H
                db      000H,000H,07FH,063H,003H,006H,00CH,018H
                db      018H,018H,018H,000H,000H,000H,000H,000H
                db      000H,000H,03EH,063H,063H,063H,03EH,063H
                db      063H,063H,03EH,000H,000H,000H,000H,000H
                db      000H,000H,03EH,063H,063H,063H,03FH,003H
                db      003H,006H,03CH,000H,000H,000H,000H,000H
                db      000H,000H,000H,018H,018H,000H,000H,000H
                db      018H,018H,000H,000H,000H,000H,000H,000H
                db      000H,000H,000H,018H,018H,000H,000H,000H
                db      018H,018H,030H,000H,000H,000H,000H,000H
                db      000H,000H,006H,00CH,018H,030H,060H,030H
                db      018H,00CH,006H,000H,000H,000H,000H,000H
                db      000H,000H,000H,000H,000H,07EH,000H,000H
                db      07EH,000H,000H,000H,000H,000H,000H,000H
                db      000H,000H,060H,030H,018H,00CH,006H,00CH
                db      018H,030H,060H,000H,000H,000H,000H,000H
                db      000H,000H,03EH,063H,063H,006H,00CH,00CH
                db      000H,00CH,00CH,000H,000H,000H,000H,000H
;               ascii 40h - 4Fh  '@' - 'O'
                db      000H,000H,03EH,063H,063H,06FH,06FH,06FH
                db      06EH,060H,03EH,000H,000H,000H,000H,000H
                db      000H,000H,008H,01CH,036H,063H,063H,07FH
                db      063H,063H,063H,000H,000H,000H,000H,000H
                db      000H,000H,07EH,033H,033H,033H,03EH,033H
                db      033H,033H,07EH,000H,000H,000H,000H,000H
                db      000H,000H,01EH,033H,061H,060H,060H,060H
                db      061H,033H,01EH,000H,000H,000H,000H,000H
                db      000H,000H,07CH,036H,033H,033H,033H,033H
                db      033H,036H,07CH,000H,000H,000H,000H,000H
                db      000H,000H,07FH,033H,031H,034H,03CH,034H
                db      031H,033H,07FH,000H,000H,000H,000H,000H
                db      000H,000H,07FH,033H,031H,034H,03CH,034H
                db      030H,030H,078H,000H,000H,000H,000H,000H
                db      000H,000H,01EH,033H,061H,060H,060H,06FH
```

Listing C.4 (continued)

```
        db      063H,033H,01DH,000H,000H,000H,000H,000H
        db      000H,000H,063H,063H,063H,063H,07FH,063H
        db      063H,063H,063H,000H,000H,000H,000H,000H
        db      000H,000H,03CH,018H,018H,018H,018H,018H
        db      018H,018H,03CH,000H,000H,000H,000H,000H
        db      000H,000H,00FH,006H,006H,006H,006H,006H
        db      066H,066H,03CH,000H,000H,000H,000H,000H
        db      000H,000H,073H,033H,036H,036H,03CH,036H
        db      036H,033H,073H,000H,000H,000H,000H,000H
        db      000H,000H,078H,030H,030H,030H,030H,030H
        db      031H,033H,07FH,000H,000H,000H,000H,000H
        db      000H,000H,0C3H,0E7H,0FFH,0DBH,0C3H,0C3H
        db      0C3H,0C3H,0C3H,000H,000H,000H,000H,000H
        db      000H,000H,063H,073H,07BH,07FH,06FH,067H
        db      063H,063H,063H,000H,000H,000H,000H,000H
        db      000H,000H,01CH,036H,063H,063H,063H,063H
        db      063H,036H,01CH,000H,000H,000H,000H,000H
;       ascii 50h - 5Fh    'P' - '_'
        db      000H,000H,07EH,033H,033H,033H,03EH,030H
        db      030H,030H,078H,000H,000H,000H,000H,000H
        db      000H,000H,03EH,063H,063H,063H,063H,06BH
        db      06FH,03EH,006H,007H,000H,000H,000H,000H
        db      000H,000H,07EH,033H,033H,033H,03EH,036H
        db      033H,033H,073H,000H,000H,000H,000H,000H
        db      000H,000H,03EH,063H,063H,030H,01CH,006H
        db      063H,063H,03EH,000H,000H,000H,000H,000H
        db      000H,000H,0FFH,0DBH,099H,018H,018H,018H
        db      018H,018H,03CH,000H,000H,000H,000H,000H
        db      000H,000H,063H,063H,063H,063H,063H,063H
        db      063H,063H,03EH,000H,000H,000H,000H,000H
        db      000H,000H,0C3H,0C3H,0C3H,0C3H,0C3H,0C3H
        db      066H,03CH,018H,000H,000H,000H,000H,000H
        db      000H,000H,0C3H,0C3H,0C3H,0C3H,0DBH,0DBH
        db      0FFH,066H,066H,000H,000H,000H,000H,000H
        db      000H,000H,0C3H,0C3H,066H,03CH,018H,03CH
        db      066H,0C3H,0C3H,000H,000H,000H,000H,000H
        db      000H,000H,0C3H,0C3H,0C3H,066H,03CH,018H
        db      018H,018H,03CH,000H,000H,000H,000H,000H
        db      000H,000H,0FFH,0C3H,086H,00CH,018H,030H
        db      061H,0C3H,0FFH,000H,000H,000H,000H,000H
        db      000H,000H,03CH,030H,030H,030H,030H,030H
        db      030H,030H,03CH,000H,000H,000H,000H,000H
        db      000H,000H,040H,060H,070H,038H,01CH,00EH
        db      007H,003H,001H,000H,000H,000H,000H,000H
        db      000H,000H,03CH,00CH,00CH,00CH,00CH,00CH
        db      00CH,00CH,03CH,000H,000H,000H,000H,000H
        db      008H,01CH,036H,063H,000H,000H,000H,000H
        db      000H,000H,000H,000H,000H,000H,000H,000H
        db      000H,000H,000H,000H,000H,000H,000H,000H
        db      000H,000H,000H,000H,0FFH,000H,000H,000H
;       ascii 60h -6Fh    ''' - 'o'
        db      018H,018H,00CH,000H,000H,000H,000H,000H
        db      000H,000H,000H,000H,000H,000H,000H,000H
        db      000H,000H,000H,000H,000H,03CH,006H,03EH
        db      066H,066H,03BH,000H,000H,000H,000H,000H
        db      000H,000H,070H,030H,030H,03CH,036H,033H
        db      033H,033H,06EH,000H,000H,000H,000H,000H
        db      000H,000H,000H,000H,000H,03EH,063H,060H
        db      060H,063H,03EH,000H,000H,000H,000H,000H
        db      000H,000H,00EH,006H,006H,01EH,036H,066H
        db      066H,066H,03BH,000H,000H,000H,000H,000H
        db      000H,000H,000H,000H,000H,03EH,063H,07FH
        db      060H,063H,03EH,000H,000H,000H,000H,000H
        db      000H,000H,01CH,036H,032H,030H,07CH,030H
        db      030H,030H,078H,000H,000H,000H,000H,000H
```

Listing C.4 (continued)

```
                db      000H,000H,000H,000H,000H,03BH,066H,066H
                db      066H,03EH,006H,066H,03CH,000H,000H,000H
                db      000H,000H,070H,030H,030H,036H,03BH,033H
                db      033H,033H,073H,000H,000H,000H,000H,000H
                db      000H,000H,00CH,00CH,000H,01CH,00CH,00CH
                db      00CH,00CH,01EH,000H,000H,000H,000H,000H
                db      000H,000H,006H,006H,000H,00EH,006H,006H
                db      006H,006H,066H,066H,03CH,000H,000H,000H
                db      000H,000H,070H,030H,030H,033H,036H,03CH
                db      036H,033H,073H,000H,000H,000H,000H,000H
                db      000H,000H,01CH,00CH,00CH,00CH,00CH,00CH
                db      00CH,00CH,01EH,000H,000H,000H,000H,000H
                db      000H,000H,000H,000H,000H,0E6H,0FFH,0DBH
                db      0DBH,0DBH,0DBH,000H,000H,000H,000H,000H
                db      000H,000H,000H,000H,000H,06EH,033H,033H
                db      033H,033H,033H,000H,000H,000H,000H,000H
                db      000H,000H,000H,000H,000H,03EH,063H,063H
                db      063H,063H,03EH,000H,000H,000H,000H,000H
;               ascii 70h - 7Fh    'p' -
                db      000H,000H,000H,000H,000H,06EH,033H,033H
                db      033H,03EH,030H,030H,078H,000H,000H,000H
                db      000H,000H,000H,000H,000H,03BH,066H,066H
                db      066H,03EH,006H,006H,00FH,000H,000H,000H
                db      000H,000H,000H,000H,000H,06EH,03BH,033H
                db      030H,030H,078H,000H,000H,000H,000H,000H
                db      000H,000H,000H,000H,000H,03EH,063H,038H
                db      00EH,063H,03EH,000H,000H,000H,000H,000H
                db      000H,000H,008H,018H,018H,07EH,018H,018H
                db      018H,01BH,00EH,000H,000H,000H,000H,000H
                db      000H,000H,000H,000H,000H,066H,066H,066H
                db      066H,066H,03BH,000H,000H,000H,000H,000H
                db      000H,000H,000H,000H,000H,0C3H,0C3H,0C3H
                db      066H,03CH,018H,000H,000H,000H,000H,000H
                db      000H,000H,000H,000H,000H,0C3H,0C3H,0DBH
                db      0DBH,0FFH,066H,000H,000H,000H,000H,000H
                db      000H,000H,000H,000H,000H,063H,036H,01CH
                db      01CH,036H,063H,000H,000H,000H,000H,000H
                db      000H,000H,000H,000H,000H,063H,063H,063H
                db      063H,03FH,003H,006H,03CH,000H,000H,000H
                db      000H,000H,000H,000H,000H,07FH,066H,00CH
                db      018H,033H,07FH,000H,000H,000H,000H,000H
                db      000H,000H,00EH,018H,018H,018H,070H,018H
                db      018H,018H,00EH,000H,000H,000H,000H,000H
                db      000H,000H,018H,018H,018H,018H,000H,018H
                db      018H,018H,018H,000H,000H,000H,000H,000H
                db      000H,000H,070H,018H,018H,018H,00EH,018H
                db      018H,018H,070H,000H,000H,000H,000H,000H
                db      000H,000H,03BH,06EH,000H,000H,000H,000H
                db      000H,000H,000H,000H,000H,000H,000H,000H
                db      000H,000H,000H,000H,008H,01CH,036H,063H
                db      063H,07FH,000H,000H,000H,000H,000H,000H
;               ascii 80h - 8Fh
                db      000H,000H,01EH,033H,061H,060H,060H,061H
                db      033H,01EH,006H,003H,03EH,000H,000H,000H
                db      000H,000H,066H,066H,000H,066H,066H,066H
                db      066H,066H,03BH,000H,000H,000H,000H,000H
                db      000H,006H,00CH,018H,000H,03EH,063H,07FH
                db      060H,063H,03EH,000H,000H,000H,000H,000H
                db      000H,008H,01CH,036H,000H,03CH,006H,03EH
                db      066H,066H,03BH,000H,000H,000H,000H,000H
                db      000H,000H,066H,066H,000H,03CH,006H,03EH
                db      066H,066H,03BH,000H,000H,000H,000H,000H
                db      000H,030H,018H,00CH,000H,03CH,006H,03EH
                db      066H,066H,03BH,000H,000H,000H,000H,000H
                db      000H,01CH,036H,01CH,000H,03CH,006H,03EH
```

Listing C.4 (continued)

```
           db        066H,066H,03BH,000H,000H,000H,000H,000H
           db        000H,000H,000H,000H,03CH,066H,060H,066H
           db        03CH,00CH,006H,03CH,000H,000H,000H,000H
           db        000H,008H,01CH,036H,000H,03EH,063H,07FH
           db        060H,063H,03EH,000H,000H,000H,000H,000H
           db        000H,000H,066H,066H,000H,03EH,063H,07FH
           db        060H,063H,03EH,000H,000H,000H,000H,000H
           db        000H,030H,018H,00CH,000H,03EH,063H,07FH
           db        060H,063H,03EH,000H,000H,000H,000H,000H
           db        000H,000H,066H,066H,000H,038H,018H,018H
           db        018H,018H,03CH,000H,000H,000H,000H,000H
           db        000H,018H,03CH,066H,000H,038H,018H,018H
           db        018H,018H,03CH,000H,000H,000H,000H,000H
           db        000H,060H,030H,018H,000H,038H,018H,018H
           db        018H,018H,03CH,000H,000H,000H,000H,000H
           db        000H,063H,063H,008H,01CH,036H,063H,063H
           db        07FH,063H,063H,000H,000H,000H,000H,000H
           db        01CH,036H,01CH,000H,01CH,036H,063H,063H
           db        07FH,063H,063H,000H,000H,000H,000H,000H
;                    ascii 90h - 9Fh
           db        00CH,018H,030H,000H,07FH,033H,030H,03EH
           db        030H,033H,07FH,000H,000H,000H,000H,000H
           db        000H,000H,000H,000H,06EH,03BH,01BH,07EH
           db        0D8H,0DCH,077H,000H,000H,000H,000H,000H
           db        000H,000H,01FH,036H,066H,066H,07FH,066H
           db        066H,066H,067H,000H,000H,000H,000H,000H
           db        000H,008H,01CH,036H,000H,03EH,063H,063H
           db        063H,063H,03EH,000H,000H,000H,000H,000H
           db        000H,000H,063H,063H,000H,03EH,063H,063H
           db        063H,063H,03EH,000H,000H,000H,000H,000H
           db        000H,030H,018H,00CH,000H,03EH,063H,063H
           db        063H,063H,03EH,000H,000H,000H,000H,000H
           db        000H,018H,03CH,066H,000H,066H,066H,066H
           db        066H,066H,03BH,000H,000H,000H,000H,000H
           db        000H,030H,018H,00CH,000H,066H,066H,066H
           db        066H,066H,03BH,000H,000H,000H,000H,000H
           db        000H,000H,063H,063H,000H,063H,063H,063H
           db        063H,03FH,003H,006H,03CH,000H,000H,000H
           db        000H,063H,063H,01CH,036H,063H,063H,063H
           db        063H,036H,01CH,000H,000H,000H,000H,000H
           db        000H,063H,063H,000H,063H,063H,063H,063H
           db        063H,063H,03EH,000H,000H,000H,000H,000H
           db        000H,018H,018H,07EH,0C3H,0C0H,0C0H,0C3H
           db        07EH,018H,018H,000H,000H,000H,000H,000H
           db        000H,01CH,036H,032H,030H,078H,030H,030H
           db        030H,073H,07EH,000H,000H,000H,000H,000H
           db        000H,000H,0C3H,066H,03CH,018H,0FFH,018H
           db        0FFH,018H,018H,000H,000H,000H,000H,000H
           db        000H,0FCH,066H,066H,07CH,062H,066H,06FH
           db        066H,066H,0F3H,000H,000H,000H,000H,000H
           db        000H,00EH,01BH,018H,018H,018H,07EH,018H
           db        018H,018H,018H,0D8H,070H,000H,000H,000H
;                    ascii A0h - AFh
           db        000H,00CH,018H,030H,000H,03CH,006H,03EH
           db        066H,066H,03BH,000H,000H,000H,000H,000H
           db        000H,00CH,018H,030H,000H,038H,018H,018H
           db        018H,018H,03CH,000H,000H,000H,000H,000H
           db        000H,00CH,018H,030H,000H,03EH,063H,063H
           db        063H,063H,03EH,000H,000H,000H,000H,000H
           db        000H,00CH,018H,030H,000H,066H,066H,066H
           db        066H,066H,03BH,000H,000H,000H,000H,000H
           db        000H,000H,03BH,06EH,000H,06EH,033H,033H
           db        033H,033H,033H,000H,000H,000H,000H,000H
           db        03BH,06EH,000H,063H,073H,07BH,07FH,06FH
           db        067H,063H,063H,000H,000H,000H,000H,000H
```

Listing C.4 (continued)

```
        db      000H,03CH,06CH,06CH,03EH,000H,07EH,000H
        db      000H,000H,000H,000H,000H,000H,000H,000H
        db      000H,038H,06CH,06CH,038H,000H,07CH,000H
        db      000H,000H,000H,000H,000H,000H,000H
        db      000H,000H,018H,018H,000H,018H,018H,030H
        db      063H,063H,03EH,000H,000H,000H,000H,000H
        db      000H,000H,000H,000H,000H,000H,07FH,060H
        db      060H,060H,000H,000H,000H,000H,000H,000H
        db      000H,000H,000H,000H,000H,000H,07FH,003H
        db      003H,003H,000H,000H,000H,000H,000H,000H
        db      000H,060H,0E0H,063H,066H,06CH,018H,030H
        db      06EH,0C3H,006H,00CH,01FH,000H,000H,000H
        db      000H,060H,0E0H,063H,066H,06CH,018H,033H
        db      067H,0CFH,01FH,003H,003H,000H,000H,000H
        db      000H,000H,018H,018H,000H,018H,018H,03CH
        db      03CH,03CH,018H,000H,000H,000H,000H,000H
        db      000H,000H,000H,000H,01BH,036H,06CH,036H
        db      01BH,000H,000H,000H,000H,000H,000H,000H
        db      000H,000H,000H,000H,06CH,036H,01BH,036H
        db      06CH,000H,000H,000H,000H,000H,000H,000H
;       ascii B0h - BFh  character graphics
        db      011H,044H,011H,044H,011H,044H,011H,044H
        db      011H,044H,011H,044H,011H,044H,000H,000H
        db      055H,0AAH,055H,0AAH,055H,0AAH,055H,0AAH
        db      055H,0AAH,055H,0AAH,055H,0AAH,000H,000H
        db      0DDH,077H,0DDH,077H,0DDH,077H,0DDH,077H
        db      0DDH,077H,0DDH,077H,0DDH,077H,000H,000H
        db      018H,018H,018H,018H,018H,018H,018H,018H
        db      018H,018H,018H,018H,018H,018H,000H,000H
        db      018H,018H,018H,018H,018H,018H,018H,0F8H
        db      018H,018H,018H,018H,018H,018H,000H,000H
        db      018H,018H,018H,018H,018H,0F8H,018H,0F8H
        db      018H,018H,018H,018H,018H,018H,000H,000H
        db      036H,036H,036H,036H,036H,036H,036H,0F6H
        db      036H,036H,036H,036H,036H,036H,000H,000H
        db      000H,000H,000H,000H,000H,000H,000H,0FEH
        db      036H,036H,036H,036H,036H,036H,000H,000H
        db      000H,000H,000H,000H,000H,0F8H,018H,0F8H
        db      018H,018H,018H,018H,018H,018H,000H,000H
        db      036H,036H,036H,036H,036H,0F6H,006H,0F6H
        db      036H,036H,036H,036H,036H,036H,000H,000H
        db      036H,036H,036H,036H,036H,036H,036H,036H
        db      036H,036H,036H,036H,036H,036H,000H,000H
        db      000H,000H,000H,000H,000H,0FEH,006H,0F6H
        db      036H,036H,036H,036H,036H,036H,000H,000H
        db      036H,036H,036H,036H,036H,0F6H,006H,0FEH
        db      000H,000H,000H,000H,000H,000H,000H,000H
        db      036H,036H,036H,036H,036H,036H,036H,0FEH
        db      000H,000H,000H,000H,000H,000H,000H,000H
        db      018H,018H,018H,018H,018H,0F8H,018H,0F8H
        db      000H,000H,000H,000H,000H,000H,000H,000H
        db      000H,000H,000H,000H,000H,000H,000H,0F8H
        db      018H,018H,018H,018H,018H,018H,000H,000H
;       ascii C0h - CFh  character graphics
        db      018H,018H,018H,018H,018H,018H,018H,01FH
        db      000H,000H,000H,000H,000H,000H,000H,000H
        db      018H,018H,018H,018H,018H,018H,018H,0FFH
        db      000H,000H,000H,000H,000H,000H,000H,000H
        db      000H,000H,000H,000H,000H,000H,000H,0FFH
        db      018H,018H,018H,018H,018H,018H,000H,000H
        db      018H,018H,018H,018H,018H,018H,018H,01FH
        db      018H,018H,018H,018H,018H,018H,000H,000H
        db      000H,000H,000H,000H,000H,000H,000H,0FFH
        db      000H,000H,000H,000H,000H,000H,000H,000H
        db      018H,018H,018H,018H,018H,018H,018H,0FFH
```

Listing C.4 (continued)

```
          db      018H,018H,018H,018H,018H,018H,000H,000H
          db      018H,018H,018H,018H,018H,01FH,018H,01FH
          db      018H,018H,018H,018H,018H,018H,000H,000H
          db      036H,036H,036H,036H,036H,036H,036H,037H
          db      036H,036H,036H,036H,036H,036H,000H,000H
          db      036H,036H,036H,036H,036H,037H,030H,03FH
          db      000H,000H,000H,000H,000H,000H,000H,000H
          db      000H,000H,000H,000H,000H,03FH,030H,037H
          db      036H,036H,036H,036H,036H,036H,000H,000H
          db      036H,036H,036H,036H,036H,0F7H,000H,0FFH
          db      000H,000H,000H,000H,000H,000H,000H,000H
          db      000H,000H,000H,000H,000H,0FFH,000H,0F7H
          db      036H,036H,036H,036H,036H,036H,000H,000H
          db      036H,036H,036H,036H,036H,037H,030H,037H
          db      036H,036H,036H,036H,036H,036H,000H,000H
          db      000H,000H,000H,000H,000H,0FFH,000H,0FFH
          db      000H,000H,000H,000H,000H,000H,000H,000H
          db      036H,036H,036H,036H,036H,0F7H,000H,0F7H
          db      036H,036H,036H,036H,036H,036H,000H,000H
          db      018H,018H,018H,018H,018H,0FFH,000H,0FFH
          db      000H,000H,000H,000H,000H,000H,000H,000H
;         ascii D0h - DFh   character graphics
          db      036H,036H,036H,036H,036H,036H,036H,0FFH
          db      000H,000H,000H,000H,000H,000H,000H,000H
          db      000H,000H,000H,000H,000H,0FFH,000H,0FFH
          db      018H,018H,018H,018H,018H,018H,000H,000H
          db      000H,000H,000H,000H,000H,000H,000H,0FFH
          db      036H,036H,036H,036H,036H,036H,000H,000H
          db      036H,036H,036H,036H,036H,036H,036H,03FH
          db      000H,000H,000H,000H,000H,000H,000H,000H
          db      018H,018H,018H,018H,018H,01FH,018H,01FH
          db      000H,000H,000H,000H,000H,000H,000H,000H
          db      000H,000H,000H,000H,000H,01FH,018H,01FH
          db      018H,018H,018H,018H,018H,018H,000H,000H
          db      000H,000H,000H,000H,000H,000H,000H,03FH
          db      036H,036H,036H,036H,036H,036H,000H,000H
          db      036H,036H,036H,036H,036H,036H,036H,0FFH
          db      036H,036H,036H,036H,036H,036H,000H,000H
          db      018H,018H,018H,018H,018H,0FFH,018H,0FFH
          db      018H,018H,018H,018H,018H,018H,000H,000H
          db      018H,018H,018H,018H,018H,018H,018H,0F8H
          db      000H,000H,000H,000H,000H,000H,000H,000H
          db      000H,000H,000H,000H,000H,000H,000H,01FH
          db      018H,018H,018H,018H,018H,018H,000H,000H
          db      0FFH,0FFH,0FFH,0FFH,0FFH,0FFH,0FFH,0FFH
          db      0FFH,0FFH,0FFH,0FFH,0FFH,0FFH,000H,000H
          db      000H,000H,000H,000H,000H,000H,000H,0FFH
          db      0FFH,0FFH,0FFH,0FFH,0FFH,0FFH,000H,000H
          db      0F0H,0F0H,0F0H,0F0H,0F0H,0F0H,0F0H,0F0H
          db      0F0H,0F0H,0F0H,0F0H,0F0H,0F0H,000H,000H
          db      00FH,00FH,00FH,00FH,00FH,00FH,00FH,00FH
          db      00FH,00FH,00FH,00FH,00FH,00FH,000H,000H
          db      0FFH,0FFH,0FFH,0FFH,0FFH,0FFH,0FFH,000H
          db      000H,000H,000H,000H,000H,000H,000H,000H
;         ascii E0h - EFh
          db      000H,000H,000H,000H,000H,03BH,06EH,06CH
          db      06CH,06EH,03BH,000H,000H,000H,000H,000H
          db      000H,000H,000H,000H,03EH,063H,07EH,063H
          db      063H,07EH,060H,060H,020H,000H,000H,000H
          db      000H,000H,07FH,063H,063H,060H,060H,060H
          db      060H,060H,060H,000H,000H,000H,000H,000H
          db      000H,000H,000H,000H,07FH,036H,036H,036H
          db      036H,036H,036H,000H,000H,000H,000H,000H
          db      000H,000H,07FH,063H,030H,018H,00CH,018H
          db      030H,063H,07FH,000H,000H,000H,000H,000H
```

Listing C.4 (continued)

```
              db      000H,000H,000H,000H,000H,03FH,06CH,06CH
              db      06CH,06CH,038H,000H,000H,000H,000H,000H
              db      000H,000H,000H,000H,033H,033H,033H,033H
              db      03EH,030H,030H,060H,000H,000H,000H,000H
              db      000H,000H,000H,000H,03BH,06EH,00CH,00CH
              db      00CH,00CH,00CH,000H,000H,000H,000H,000H
              db      000H,000H,07EH,018H,03CH,066H,066H,066H
              db      03CH,018H,07EH,000H,000H,000H,000H,000H
              db      000H,000H,01CH,036H,063H,063H,07FH,063H
              db      063H,036H,01CH,000H,000H,000H,000H,000H
              db      000H,000H,01CH,036H,063H,063H,063H,036H
              db      036H,036H,077H,000H,000H,000H,000H,000H
              db      000H,000H,01EH,030H,018H,00CH,03EH,066H
              db      066H,066H,03CH,000H,000H,000H,000H,000H
              db      000H,000H,000H,000H,000H,07EH,0DBH,0DBH
              db      07EH,000H,000H,000H,000H,000H,000H,000H
              db      000H,000H,003H,006H,07EH,0DBH,0DBH,0F3H
              db      07EH,060H,0C0H,000H,000H,000H,000H,000H
              db      000H,000H,01CH,030H,060H,060H,07CH,060H
              db      060H,030H,01CH,000H,000H,000H,000H,000H
              db      000H,000H,000H,03EH,063H,063H,063H,063H
              db      063H,063H,063H,000H,000H,000H,000H,000H
;             ascii F0 - FFh
              db      000H,000H,000H,07FH,000H,000H,07FH,000H
              db      000H,07FH,000H,000H,000H,000H,000H,000H
              db      000H,000H,018H,018H,018H,0FFH,018H,018H
              db      018H,000H,0FFH,000H,000H,000H,000H,000H
              db      000H,000H,030H,018H,00CH,006H,00CH,018H
              db      030H,000H,07EH,000H,000H,000H,000H,000H
              db      000H,000H,00CH,018H,030H,060H,030H,018H
              db      00CH,000H,07EH,000H,000H,000H,000H,000H
              db      000H,000H,00EH,01BH,01BH,018H,018H,018H
              db      018H,018H,018H,018H,018H,018H,000H,000H
              db      018H,018H,018H,018H,018H,018H,018H,018H
              db      0D8H,0D8H,070H,000H,000H,000H,000H,000H
              db      000H,000H,018H,018H,000H,000H,0FFH,000H
              db      000H,018H,018H,000H,000H,000H,000H,000H
              db      000H,000H,000H,000H,03BH,06EH,000H,03BH
              db      06EH,000H,000H,000H,000H,000H,000H,000H
              db      000H,038H,06CH,06CH,038H,000H,000H,000H
              db      000H,000H,000H,000H,000H,000H,000H,000H
              db      000H,000H,000H,000H,000H,000H,018H,018H
              db      000H,000H,000H,000H,000H,000H,000H,000H
              db      000H,000H,000H,000H,000H,000H,000H,018H
              db      000H,000H,000H,000H,000H,000H,000H,000H
              db      000H,00FH,00CH,00CH,00CH,00CH,00CH,0ECH
              db      06CH,03CH,01CH,000H,000H,000H,000H,000H
              db      000H,0D8H,06CH,06CH,06CH,06CH,06CH,000H
              db      000H,000H,000H,000H,000H,000H,000H,000H
              db      000H,070H,0D8H,030H,060H,0C8H,0F8H,000H
              db      000H,000H,000H,000H,000H,000H,000H,000H
              db      000H,000H,000H,000H,03EH,03EH,03EH,03EH
              db      03EH,03EH,000H,000H,000H,000H,000H,000H
              db      000H,000H,000H,000H,000H,000H,000H,000H
              db      000H,000H,000H,000H,000H,000H,000H,000H
data          ends

code          segment public
              assume cs:code,ds:data

;             set up hercules graphics
stherc        proc    near
              push    ax                                ;save regs
              push    cx
              push    dx
```

Listing C.4 (continued)

```
                push    di
                mov     dx,03bfh                ;config switch
                mov     al,1
                out     dx,al                   ;allow graphics
                mov     ax,0b000h               ;seg b000h
                mov     es,ax
                mov     cx,8000h                ;word count
                mov     di,0
                cld
                xor     ax,ax                   ;ax=0
                rep stosw                       ;clear tv ram
                mov     dx,03b4h                ;6845 port
                mov     si,offset vidtbl        ;si->values
                mov     cx,16                   ;16 regs
                xor     ax,ax                   ;ah=0
sg1:            mov     al,ah                   ;reg no.
                out     dx,al                   ;select reg
                inc     dx                      ;dx=03b5h
                lodsb                           ;get value
                out     dx,al                   ;store it
                dec     dx                      ;dx=03b4h
                inc     ah                      ;next reg
                loop    sg1                     ;do all 16
                mov     dx,03b8h                ;control port
                mov     al,0ah                  ;enable video
                out     dx,al                   ; & graphics
                pop     di                      ;restore regs
                pop     dx
                pop     cx
                pop     ax
                ret
stherc  endp

;       plot line
line    proc near
                push    ax                      ;save registers
                push    bx
                push    cx
                push    dx
                push    si
                push    di
                push    bp
                push    ax                      ;make space for yflg
                mov     bp,sp                   ;bp=initial sp
                mov     byte ptr 1[bp],0        ;yflg=0
                cmp     cx,ax                   ;if orig.x1>orig.x2
                jb      la                      ;then interchange
                xchg    cx,ax                   ;orig and endp
                xchg    dx,bx
la:             cmp     bx,dx                   ;if bx<dx then set
                ja      lb                      ; yflg=80h
                mov     byte ptr 1[bp],80h
lb:             push    ax                      ;push endp:x
                push    bx                      ;push endp:y
                push    ax                      ;push endp:x
                push    bx                      ;push endp:y
ln1:            mov     si,cx                   ;compute midp.x
                add     si,ax
                shr     si,1                    ;si=(x1+x2)/2
                mov     di,dx                   ;compute midp.y
                add     di,bx
                shr     di,1                    ;di=(y1+y2)/2
                jnb     ln2                     ;if carry set
                cmp     byte ptr 1[bp],0
                je      ln2                     ;then if yflg set
```

Listing C.4 (continued)

```
              inc     di                          ;round midp.y
      ln2:    cmp     si,cx                       ;if midp=orig
              jne     ln3
              cmp     di,dx
              jne     ln3                         ;then
              call    plot                        ;plot orig
              pop     dx                          ;pop orig.y
              pop     cx                          ;         .x
              pop     bx                          ;pop endp.y
              pop     ax                          ;         .x
              jmp     ln4
      ln3:    push    ax                          ;push endp.x
              push    bx                          ;         .y
              push    si                          ;push midp.x
              push    di                          ;         .y
              mov     ax,si
              mov     bx,di
      ln4:    cmp     bp,sp
              jne     ln1
              call    plot                        ;plot orig
      ln5:    pop     ax                          ;restore yflg
              pop     bp                          ;restore regs
              pop     di
              pop     si
              pop     dx
              pop     cx
              pop     bx
              pop     ax
              ret
      line    endp

      ;       plot point at x=cx, y=dx
      plot    proc    near
              push    bx
              push    di
              push    es
              call    plotad                      ;calc addr
              or      es:[di],bl                  ;or in 1
              pop     es
              pop     di
              pop     bx
              ret
      plot    endp

      ;       erase point at x=cx, y=dx
      erase   proc    near
              push    bx
              push    di
              push    es
              call    plotad                      ;calc addr
              not     bl                          ;not mask
              and     es:[di],bl                  ;and in 0
              pop     es
              pop     di
              pop     bx
              ret
      erase   endp

      ;       calculate plot addr at x=cx, y=dx
      ;       di --> addr  bl=mask  es=B000
      plotad proc near
              push    ax
              push    cx
              push    dx
              mov     di,dx                       ;y-table
```

Listing C.4 (continued)

```
                shl    di,1                         ; index
                mov    di,row_table[di]             ;di->y-table
                mov    ax,cx                        ;ax = x
                shr    ax,1
                shr    ax,1
                shr    ax,1                         ;int(x/8)
                add    di,ax                        ;byte addr
                mov    bl,80h                       ;mask
                and    cx,7                         ;x mod 8
                shr    bl,cl                        ;get mask
                mov    ax,0b000h
                mov    es,ax                        ;seg b000h
                pop    dx
                pop    cx
                pop    ax
                ret
        plotad  endp

        ;       message display
        ;       input: si -> message
        ;                  cx = x
        ;                  dx = y
        messg   proc   near
                push   ax                           ;save regs
                push   si
                cld                                 ;si increases
        ms1:    lodsb                               ;[si]-->al
                cmp    al,0                          ;message done?
                je     ms2                           ;if so, return
                call   charwt                        ;display char
                jmp    ms1                           ;and continue
        ms2:    pop    si                            ;restore regs
                pop    ax
                ret
        messg   endp

        ;       character write
        ;       input: al = ascii code of char
        ;              cx = x-coord. upper-left
        ;              dx = y-coord. upper-left
        ;       output: cx = cx(input)+9 = x-coord+9
        ;               dx = dx(input) = y-coord

        charwt  proc   near
                push   ax
                push   bx
                push   si                           ;save regs
                push   di
                push   bp
                mov    bx,cx                         ;bx = x
                mov    es,video_seg                  ;es->tv ram
                cld
                mov    bit9flg,0                     ;default no
                cmp    al,0c0h                       ; line draw
                jb     cw1                           ;check for
                cmp    al,0dfh                       ; line draw
                ja     cw1                           ; characters
                not    bit9flg                       ;yes, set flag
        cw1:    xor    ah,ah                         ;ah = 0
                shl    ax,1                          ;mult by 16
                shl    ax,1                          ;16 bytes per
                shl    ax,1                          ; char in table
                shl    ax,1
                mov    si,offset charset             ;si->char set
                add    si,ax                         ;offset in tbl
```

Listing C.4 (continued)

```
              mov     bp,14                           ;char height=14
cw2:          mov     cx,bx                           ;cx = x
              mov     di,dx                           ;di = y
              shl     di,1                            ;2 bytes/entry
              mov     di,row_table[di]                ;row offset
              mov     ax,cx                           ;ax = col
              shr     ax,1
              shr     ax,1
              shr     ax,1                            ;int(x/8)
              add     di,ax                           ;char pos byte
              and     cl,7                            ;x mod 8
              mov     ax,es:[di]                      ;get 2 bytes
              xchg    ah,al                           ;ah = [di]
              rol     ax,cl                           ;mov char to ah
              mov     ah,byte ptr [si]                ;ah= char line
              cmp     bit9flg,0
              je      cw3
              test    ah,1                            ;if 8th pixel
              je      cw3                             ; on, duplicate
              or      al,80h                          ; 8th bit
              jmp     cw4
cw3:          and     al,07fh                         ;erase pixel 9
cw4:          ror     ax,cl                           ;restore word
              xchg    ah,al                           ;restore order
              stosw                                   ;write word
              inc     dx                              ;next row
              inc     si                              ;next tbl byte
              dec     bp                              ;do all 14 rows
              jne     cw2
              sub     dx,14                           ;restore orig y
              add     bx,9                            ;inc col by 9
              mov     cx,bx
              pop     bp
              pop     di                              ;restore regs
              pop     si
              pop     bx
              pop     ax
              ret
charwt        endp


;             cursor position conversion
;             input: dl = col
;                    dh = row
;             output: cx = x = 9*col
;                     dx = y = 14*row
cpconv        proc    near
              push    ax
              mov     cl,dl
              mov     ch,0                            ;cx = col
              mov     dl,dh
              mov     dh,0                            ;dx = row
              mov     ax,cx                           ;ax = col
              shl     ax,1
              shl     ax,1
              shl     ax,1                            ;col*8
              add     cx,ax                           ;cx = 9*col
              shl     dx,1                            ;row*2
              mov     ax,dx                           ;ax = 2*row
              shl     dx,1                            ;row*4
              add     ax,dx                           ;ax = 6*row
              shl     dx,1                            ;row*8
              add     dx,ax                           ;dx = 14*row
              pop     ax
              ret
cpconv        endp
```

Listing C.4 (continued)

```
;       sin ax
;       input:  ax = degrees
;       output: ax = sine value x 10000
sinax   proc    near
        push    bx                              ;save regs
        push    dx
        push    si
        or      ax,ax                           ;if negative
        jns     sn2
sn1:    add     ax,360                          ; add 360
        js      sn1                             ; until pos
        jmp     sn3
sn2:    mov     bx,360
        mov     dx,0
        div     bx
        mov     ax,dx                           ;ax=mod 360
sn3:    mov     bx,90                           ;find quad
        mov     dx,0
        div     bx                              ;ax = quad
        or      dx,dx                           ;if deg=0
        jne     sn4
        mov     si,ax                           ;find axis val
        shl     si,1                            ; ix*2
        mov     ax,axisv[si]
        jmp     sn7
sn4:    test    al,1                            ;in quad 1,3
        je      sn5
        sub     dx,90                           ;deg=90-deg
        neg     dx                              ;dx=deg
sn5:    mov     si,dx
        shl     si,1                            ;find sine
        mov     bx,sintbl[si]                   ; from table
        mov     si,ax                           ;find sign
        mov     dl,signs[si]                    ; from table
        or      dl,dl                           ;if negative
        jne     sn6
        neg     bx                              ;negate
sn6:    mov     ax,bx                           ;ax=sine
sn7:    pop     si                              ;restore regs
        pop     dx
        pop     bx
        ret
sinax   endp


;       cos ax
;       input:  ax = degrees
;       output: ax = cosine value x 10000
cosax   proc    near
        add     ax,90                           ;cos ax =
        call    sinax                           ;sin(ax+90)
        ret
cosax   endp

code    ends
        end
```

DOS Function Calls

Table D.1
DOS INT 21H Function Calls

AH = 00H	*Program terminate* Input: CS = segment address of PSP Output: none
AH = 01H	*Character input with echo* Input: none Output: AL = 8-bit character data
AH = 02H	*Character output* Input: DL = 8-bit character data Output: none
AH = 03H	*Auxiliary input from COM1* Input: none Output: AL = 8-bit input data
AH = 04H	*Auxiliary output from COM1* Input: DL = 8-bit output data Output: none
AH = 05H	*Printer output* Input: DL = 8-bit output data Output: none
AH = 06H	*Direct console I/O* Input: DL = character for output = 0FFH for input Output: for output: none for input: Z = 1 if no char ready Z = 0 if char ready AL = character data
AH = 07H	*Unfiltered character input without echo* Input: none Output: AL = 8-bit character data
AH = 08H	*Character input without echo* Input: none Output: AL = 8-bit character data
AH = 09H	*Output character string* Input: DS:DX --> string (end with $) Output: none
AH = 0AH	*Buffered keyboard input* Input: DS:DX --> input buffer Output: none
AH = 0BH	*Get input (keyboard) status* Input: none Output: AL = 00 if no character ready = 0FFH if character available
AH = 0CH	*Reset input buffer and then input* Input: AL = input function invoked (01H,06H,07H,08H or 0AH) if AL = 0AH DS:DX --> input buffer Output: AL = 8-bit character data except for function 0AH

AH = 0DH	*Disk reset* Input: none Output: none
AH = 0EH	*Set default disk drive* Input: DL = drive code (0 = A, etc.) Output: AL = no. of drives in system
AH = 0FH	*Open file* (uses file control block, FCB)
AH = 10H	*Close file* (uses file control block, FCB)
AH = 11H	*Search for first match* (uses file control block, FCB)
AH = 12H	*Search for next match* (uses file control block, FCB)
AH = 13H	*Delete file* (uses file control block, FCB)
AH = 14H	*Sequential read* (uses file control block, FCB)
AH = 15H	*Sequential write* (uses file control block, FCB)
AH = 16H	*Create or truncate file* (uses file control block, FCB)
AH = 17H	*Rename file* (uses file control block, FCB)
AH = 18H	*Reserved*
AH = 19H	*Get default disk drive* Input: none Output: drive code (0 = A, etc.)
AH = 1AH	*Set disk transfer area address* Input: DS:DX points to disk transfer area (DTA) Output: none
AH = 1BH	*Get allocation info for default drive* Input: none Output: AL = no. of sectors/cluster DS:BX --> FAT ID byte CX = size of sector in bytes DX = no. of clusters
AH = 1CH	*Get allocation info for specified drive* Input: DL = drive code (1 = A, etc.) Output: AL = no. of sectors/cluster DS:BX --> FAT ID byte CX = size of sector in bytes DX = no. of clusters
AH = 1DH	*Reserved*
AH = 1EH	*Reserved*
AH = 1FH	*Reserved*

AH = 20H	Reserved
AH = 21H	Random read (uses file control block, FCB)
AH = 22H	Random write (uses file control block, FCB)
AH = 23H	Get file size in records (uses file control block, FCB)
AH = 24H	Set random record number (uses file control block, FCB)
AH = 25H	Set interrupt vector Input: AL = interrupt type number DS:DX --> interrupt routine Output: none
AH = 26H	Create program segment prefix (PSP) Input: DX = segment of new PSP Output: none
AH = 27H	Random block read (uses file control block, FCB)
AH = 28H	Random block write (uses file control block, FCB)
AH = 29H	Parse filename (uses file control block, FCB)

AH = 2AH	Get system date
	Input: none
	Output: CX = year (1980 – 2099)
	          DH = month (1 – 12)
	          DL = day (1 – 31)
	          AL = day of week (0=Sunday)

AH = 2BH	Set system date
	Input: CX = year (1980 – 2099)
	          DH = month (1 – 12)
	          DL = day (1 – 31)
	Output: AL = 0 if successful
	          AL = 0FFH if date invalid

AH = 2CH	Get system time
	Input: none
	Output: CH = hour (0 – 23)
	          CL = minutes (0 – 59)
	          DH = seconds (0 – 59)
	          DL = hudredths of secs.(0 – 99)

AH = 2DH	Set system time
	Input: CH = hour (0 – 23)
	          CL = minutes (0 – 59)
	          DH = seconds (0 – 59)
	          DL = hudredths of secs.(0 – 99)
	Output: AL = 0 if successful
	          AL = 0FFH if time invalid

AH = 2EH	Set verify flag
	Input: AL = 00 if turning verfiy flag off
	          AL = 01 if turning verfiy flag on
	          DL = 00
	Output: none

AH = 2FH	Get disk transfer area (DTA) address Input: none Output: ES:BX --> disk transfer area
AH = 30H	Get MS-DOS version function Input: none Output: AL = major version number AH = minor version number

AH = 31H	Terminate and stay resident
	Input: AL = return code
	          DX = memory size to save
	            (in paragraphs)
	Output: none

AH = 32H	Reserved

AH = 33H	Get or set CTRL-Break flag
	Input: If getting status
	          AL = 00
	         If setting status
	          AL = 01
	          DL = 00 to turn checking off
	          DH = 01 to turn checking on
	Output: DL = 00 if Ctrl-Brk checking off
	          DL = 01 if Ctrl-Brk checking on

AH = 34H	Reserved
AH = 35H	Get interrupt vector Input: AL = interrupt number Output: ES:BX --> interrupt handler

AH = 36H	Get free disk space
	Input: DL = drive code (1 = A, etc.)
	Output: If drive valid
	          AX = sectors/cluster
	          BX = no. of available clusters
	          CX = bytes/sector
	          DX = clusters/drive
	         If drive invalid
	          AX = FFFFH

AH = 37H	Reserved
AH = 38H	Get or set country Input: get country
AH = 39H	Make directory Input: DS:DX points to ASCIIZ string Output: If carry = 1, then AX = error codes (3 or 5)
AH = 3AH	Remove directory Input: DS:DX points to ASCIIZ string Output: AX = error codes (3 or 5)
AH = 3BH	Change current directory Input: DS:DX points to ASCIIZ string Output: AX = error code (3)

AH = 3CH	Open/Create file
	Input: DS:DX points to ASCIIZ string
	          CX = file attribute:
	               01H=read only
	               02H=hidden
	               04H=system
	               08H=volume label
	               10H=subdirectory
	               20H=archive
	Output: AX = file handle
	          If carry = 1, then
	          AX = error codes (3, 4 or 5)

AH = 3DH	Open file
	Input: DS:DX points to ASCIIZ string
	          AL = access code:
	               0=open for reading
	               1=open for writing
	               2=open for reading
	                  and writing
	Output: AX = file handle
	          If carry = 1, then
	          AX = error codes (2, 4, 5 or C)

AH = 3EH	Close file handle Input: BX = file handle Output: If carry = 1, then AX = error code (6)

AH = 3FH	*Read from file or device*
	Input: BX = file handle
	           CX = count of bytes to read
	           DS:DX points to buffer to
	                  receive data
	Output: AX = actual number of bytes
	                  read
	           (AX=0 means end of file read)
	           If carry = 1, then
	           AX = error codes (5 or 6)

AH = 40H	*Write to file or device*
	Input: BX = file handle
	           CX = count of bytes to write
	           DS:DX points to buffer
	                  containing data
	Output: AX = actual number of bytes
	                  written
	           (must equal CX for no error)
	           If carry = 1, then
	           AX = error codes (5 or 6)

AH = 41H	*Delete file* Input: DS:DX points to ASCIIZ string Output: If carry = 1, then AX = error codes (2 or 5)

AH = 42H	*Move file pointer*
	Input: BX = file handle
	           CX:DX = offset value (CX is
	                  high-order word)
	           AL = method code:
	              0=move pointer to
	                  start of file + offset
	              1=increase pointer by offset
	              2=move pointer to
	                  end of file + offset
	Output: DX:AX = new value of file pointer
	           If carry = 1, then
	           AX = error codes (1 or 6)

AH = 43H	*Get or set file attibutes*
	Input: AL = 0 – get file attribute
	           AL = 1 – set file attribute
	           CX = new attribute (AL = 1)
	           DS:DX points to ASCIIZ string
	Output: If carry = 0, successful
	                  CX = attribute (AL = 0)
	           If carry = 1, then
	           AX = error code (1,2 ,3 , or 5)

AH = 44H	*Device-driver control (IOCTL)*
	Input: AL = subfunction
	           BX = handle
	                  (subfunc = 0,1,2,3,6,7,A)
	           BL = drive code
	                  (subfunc = 4,5,8,9)
	           CX = # of bytes to read or write
	           DS:DX points to buffer area
	                  (subfunc = 2 – 5)
	           DX = device information
	                  (subfunc=1)
	Output: If carry = 0, successful
	                  AX = # of bytes transferred
	                      (subfunc = 2 – 5)
	                  AX = value (subfunc = 8)
	                  AL = status (subfunc = 6,7)
	                  DX = device info(subf = 0)
	           If carry = 1, then
	           AX = err code (1,4 ,5 ,6,D or F)

AH = 45H	*Duplicate handle*
	Input: BX = file handle
	Output: If carry = 0, successful
	                  AX = new file handle
	           If carry = 1, then
	           AX = error code (4 or 6)

AH = 46H	*Force duplicate of handle*
	Input: BX = first file handle
	           CX = second file handle
	Output: If carry = 1, then
	           AX = error code (4 or 6)

AH = 47H	*Get current directory*
	Input: DL = drive code (1 = A, etc)
	           DS:SI points to 64-byte buffer
	Output: If carry = 0, successful
	                  buffer filled with
	                      complete pathname
	           If carry = 1, then
	           AX = error code (0FH)

AH = 48H	*Allocate memory*
	Input: BX = number of paragraphs of
	memory needed
	Output: If carry = 0, successful
	                  AX = initial segment of
	                      allocated block
	           If carry = 1, then
	                  AX = error codes
	                      7 memory control
	                          blocks destroyed
	                      8 insufficient memory
	                  BX = size of largest available
	                          block

AH = 49H	*Release memory*
	Input: ES = segment of block to be
	                  released
	Output: If carry = 0, successful
	           If carry = 1, then
	                  AX = error codes
	                      7 memory control
	                          blocks destroyed
	                      9 invalid seg. in ES

AH = 4AH	*Modify memory allocation*
	Input: BX = new requested block size
	                  in paragraphs
	           ES = segment of block to be
	                  modified
	Output: If carry = 0, successful
	           If carry = 1, then
	                  AX = error codes
	                      7 memory control
	                          blocks destroyed
	                      8 insufficient memory
	                      9 invalid seg in ES
	                  BX = maximum block size
	                          available

AH = 4BH	*Execute program*
	Input: AL = 00 if loading & executing
	                      program
	           AL = 03 if loading overlay
	           ES:BX --> parameter block
	           DS:DX --> ASCIIZ string
	Output: If carry = 0, successful
	                  all registers except
	                      CS & IP destroyed
	           If carry = 1, then
	           AX = error code (1,2,5,8,A or F)

AH = 4CH	Terminate with return code Input: AL = return code Output: none
AH = 4DH	Get return code Input: none Output: AH = exit type AL = return code

AH = 4EH	Search directory for first match
	Input: CX = attribute to use in search
	         DS:DX points to ASCIIZ file
	              specification
	Output: If carry = 0
	         DTA contains data in Fig. 15.23
	         If carry = 1, then
	         AX = error codes (2 or 12H)

AH = 4FH	Search directory for next match
	Input: none
	Output: If carry = 0
	         DTA contains data in Fig. 15.23
	         If carry = 1, then
	         AX = error codes (12H)

AH = 50H	Reserved
AH = 51H	Reserved
AH = 52H	Reserved
AH = 53H	Reserved
AH = 54H	Get verify flag Input: none Output: AL = 00 if verfiy flag off AL = 01 if verfiy flag on
AH = 55H	Reserved

AH = 56H	Rename file
	Input: DS:DX -> current ASCIIZ fname
	         ES:DI -> new ASCIIZ filename
	Output: If carry = 0, successful
	         If carry = 1, then
	         AX = error code (2,3,5 or 11H)

AH = 57H	Get or set file date and time
	Input: BX = handle
	         If getting date/time
	         AL = 00
	         If setting date/time
	         AL = 01
	         CX = time
	          Bits 0BH–0FH = hours (0-23)
	          Bits 05–0AH = minutes (0-59)
	          Bits 00–04 = # 2 sec inc (0-29)
	         DX = date
	          Bits 09–0FH = year (+ 1980)
	          Bits 05–08 = month (1-12)
	          Bits 00–04 = day of mos.(0-31)
	Output: If carry = 0, successful
	         If getting date/time
	         CX = time (see above format)
	         DX = date (see above format)
	         If carry = 1, then
	         AX = error code (1 or 6)

AH = 58H	Get or set allocation strategy
	Input: If getting strategy
	         AL = 00
	         If setting strategy
	         AL = 01
	         BX = strategy code
	          = 00 if first fit
	          = 01 if best fit
	          = 02 if last fit
	Output: If carry = 0, successful
	         If getting strategy code
	         AX = strategy code
	         If carry = 1, then
	         AX = error code (1)

AH = 59H	Get extended error information Input: BX = 0 Output: AX = extended error code

AH = 5AH	Create temporary file
	Input: CX = file attribute
	         DS:DX --> ASCIIZ path string
	Output: If carry = 0, successful
	         AX = handle
	         DS:DX --> ASCIIZ file spec.
	         If carry = 1, then
	         AX = error code (3 or 5)

AH = 5BH	Create new file
	Input: CX = file attribute
	         DS:DX --> ASCIIZ path string
	Output: If carry = 0, successful
	         AX = handle
	         If carry = 1, then
	         AX = error code (3,4,5 or 50H)
	         error 50H = file already exists

AH = 5CH	Control record access
	Input: AL = function code
	          00 if locking
	          01 if unlocking
	         BX = file handle
	         CX = region offset high
	         DX = region offset low
	         SI = region length high
	         DI = region length low
	Output: If carry = 0, successful
	         If carry = 1, then
	         AX = error code (1,6 or 21H)
	         error 21H = lock violation

AH = 5DH	Reserved
AH = 5EH	Network machine name/printer setup
AH = 5FH	Get/make assign-list entry
AH = 60H	Reserved
AH = 61H	Reserved
AH = 62H	Get program segment prefix address Input: none Output: BX = segment address of PSP

Table D.2 **Standard Error Codes**	
Error code	*Meaning*
1	Invalid function number
2	File not found
3	Path not found
4	No handle available: all in use
5	Access denied
6	Invalid handle
7	Memory control blocks destroyed
8	Insufficient memory
9	Invalid memory block address
A	Invalid environment
B	Invalid format
C	Invalid access code
D	Invalid data
E	Not used
F	Invalid drive specification
10	Attempt to remove current directory
11	Not same device
12	No more files to be found

APPENDIX E

Data Sheets

Intel 8087 Math Coprocessor
    (Reprinted courtesy of Intel Corporation)

Motorola MC6845 CRT Controller
    (Reprinted courtesy of Motorola, Inc.)

National INS8250A Universal Asynchronous Receiver/Transmitter
    (Reprinted courtesy of National Semiconductor)

8087
MATH COPROCESSOR

- ■ **Adds Arithmetic, Trigonometric, Exponential, and Logarithmic Instructions to the Standard 8086/8088 and 80186/80188 Instruction Set for All Data Types**

- ■ **CPU/8087 Supports 7 Data Types: 16-, 32-, 64-Bit Integers, 32-, 64-, 80-Bit Floating Point, and 18-Digit BCD Operands**

- ■ **Compatible with IEEE Floating Point Standard 754**

- ■ **Available in 5 MHz (8087), 8 MHz (8087-2) and 10 MHz (8087-1): 8 MHz 80186/80188 System Operation Supported with the 8087-1**

- ■ **Adds 8 x 80-Bit Individually Addressable Register Stack to the 8086/8088 and 80186/80188 Architecture**

- ■ **7 Built-In Exception Handling Functions**

- ■ **MULTIBUS® System Compatible Interface**

The Intel 8087 Math CoProcessor is an extension to the Intel 8086/8088 microprocessor architecture. When combined with the 8086/8088 microprocessor, the 8087 dramatically increases the processing speed of computer applications which utilize mathematical operations such as CAM, numeric controllers, CAD or graphics.

The 8087 Math CoProcessor adds 68 mnemonics to the 8086 microprocessor instruction set. Specific 8087 math operations include logarithmic, arithmetic, exponential, and trigonometric functions. The 8087 supports integer, floating point and BCD data formats, and fully conforms to the ANSI/IEEE floating point standard.

The 8087 is fabricated with HMOS III technology and packaged in a 40-pin cerdip package.

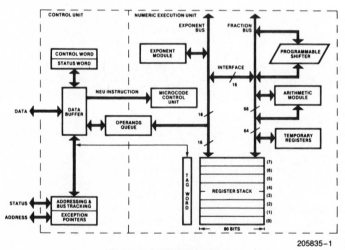

205835–1

Figure 1. 8087 Block Diagram

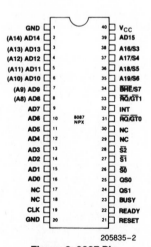

205835–2

Figure 2. 8087 Pin Configuration

intel

8087

Table 1. 8087 Pin Description

Symbol	Type	Name and Function
AD15–AD0	I/O	**ADDRESS DATA:** These lines constitute the time multiplexed memory address (T_1) and data (T_2, T_3, T_W, T_4) bus. A0 is analogous to the $\overline{BHE}$ for the lower byte of the data bus, pins D7–D0. It is LOW during T_1 when a byte is to be transferred on the lower portion of the bus in memory operations. Eight-bit oriented devices tied to the lower half of the bus would normally use A0 to condition chip select functions. These lines are active HIGH. They are input/output lines for 8087-driven bus cycles and are inputs which the 8087 monitors when the CPU is in control of the bus. A15–A8 do not require an address latch in an 8088/8087 or 80188/8087. The 8087 will supply an address for the T_1–T_4 period.
A19/S6, A18/S5, A17/S4, A16/S3	I/O	**ADDRESS MEMORY:** During T_1 these are the four most significant address lines for memory operations. During memory operations, status information is available on these lines during T_2, T_3, T_W, and T_4. For 8087-controlled bus cycles, S6, S4, and S3 are reserved and currently one (HIGH), while S5 is always LOW. These lines are inputs which the 8087 monitors when the CPU is in control of the bus.
BHE/S7	I/O	**BUS HIGH ENABLE:** During T_1 the bus high enable signed ($\overline{BHE}$) should be used to enable data onto the most significant half of the data bus, pins D15–D8. Eight-bit-oriented devices tied to the upper half of the bus would normally use $\overline{BHE}$ to condition chip select functions. $\overline{BHE}$ is LOW during T_1 for read and write cycles when a byte is to be transferred on the high portion of the bus. The S7 status information is available during T_2, T_3, T_W, and T_4. The signal is active LOW. S7 is an input which the 8087 monitors during the CPU-controlled bus cycles.
$\overline{S2}$, $\overline{S1}$, $\overline{S0}$	I/O	**STATUS:** For 8087-driven, these status lines are encoded as follows: $\overline{S2}$ $\overline{S1}$ $\overline{S0}$ 0 (LOW) X X Unused 1 (HIGH) 0 0 Unused 1 0 1 Read Memory 1 1 0 Write Memory 1 1 1 Passive Status is driven active during T_4, remains valid during T_1 and T_2, and is returned to the passive state (1, 1, 1) during T_3 or during T_W when READY is HIGH. This status is used by the 8288 Bus Controller (or the 82188 Integrated Bus Controller with an 80186/80188 CPU) to generate all memory access control signals. Any change in $\overline{S2}$, $\overline{S1}$, or $\overline{S0}$ during T_4 is used to indicate the beginning of a bus cycle, and the return to the passive state in T_3 or T_W is used to indicate the end of a bus cycle. These signals are monitored by the 8087 when the CPU is in control of the bus.
$\overline{RQ}/\overline{GT0}$	I/O	**REQUEST/GRANT:** This request/grant pin is used by the 8087 to gain control of the local bus from the CPU for operand transfers or on behalf of another bus master. It must be connected to one of the two processor request/grant pins. The request/grant sequence on this pin is as follows: 1. A pulse one clock wide is passed to the CPU to indicate a local bus request by either the 8087 or the master connected to the 8087 $\overline{RQ}/\overline{GT1}$ pin. 2. The 8087 waits for the grant pulse and when it is received will either initiate bus transfer activity in the clock cycle following the grant or pass the grant out on the $\overline{RQ}/\overline{GT1}$ pin in this clock if the initial request was for another bus master. 3. The 8087 will generate a release pulse to the CPU one clock cycle after the completion of the last 8087 bus cycle or on receipt of the release pulse from the bus master on $\overline{RQ}/\overline{GT1}$. For 80186/80188 systems the same sequence applies except $\overline{RQ}/\overline{GT}$ signals are converted to appropriate HOLD, HLDA signals by the 82188 Integrated Bus Controller. This is to conform with 80186/80188's HOLD, HLDA bus exchange protocol. Refer to the 82188 data sheet for further information.

int_el   8087

Table 1. 8087 Pin Description (Continued)

Symbol	Type	Name and Function
$\overline{RQ}/\overline{GT}1$	I/O	**REQUEST/GRANT:** This request/grant pin is used by another local bus master to force the 8087 to request the local bus. If the 8087 is not in control of the bus when the request is made the request/grant sequence is passed through the 8087 on the $\overline{RQ}/\overline{GT}0$ pin one cycle later. Subsequent grant and release pulses are also passed through the 8087 with a two and one clock delay, respectively, for resynchronization. $\overline{RQ}/\overline{GT}1$ has an internal pullup resistor, and so may be left unconnected. If the 8087 has control of the bus the request/grant sequence is as follows: 1. A pulse 1 CLK wide from another local bus master indicates a local bus request to the 8087 (pulse 1). 2. During the 8087's next T_4 or T_1 a pulse 1 CLK wide from the 8087 to the requesting master (pulse 2) indicates that the 8087 has allowed the local bus to float and that it will enter the "RQ/GT acknowledge" state at the next CLK. The 8087's control unit is disconnected logically from the local bus during "RQ/GT acknowledge." 3. A pulse 1 CLK wide from the requesting master indicates to the 8087 (pulse 3) that the "RQ/GT" request is about to end and that the 8087 can reclaim the local bus at the next CLK. Each master-master exchange of the local bus is a sequence of 3 pulses. There must be one dead CLK cycle after each bus exchange. Pulses are active LOW. For 80186/80188 system, the $\overline{RQ}/\overline{GT}1$ line may be connected to the 82188 Integrated Bus Controller. In this case, a third processor with a HOLD, HLDA bus exchange system may acquire the bus from the 8087. For this configuration, $\overline{RQ}/\overline{GT}1$ will only be used if the 8087 is the bus master. Refer to 82188 data sheet for further information.
QS1, QS0	I	**QS1, QS0:** QS1 and QS0 provide the 8087 with status to allow tracking of the CPU instruction queue. QS1 QS0 0 (LOW) 0 No Operation 0 1 First Byte of Op Code from Queue 1 (HIGH) 0 Empty the Queue 1 1 Subsequent Byte from Queue
INT	O	**INTERRUPT:** This line is used to indicate that an unmasked exception has occurred during numeric instruction execution when 8087 interrupts are enabled. This signal is typically routed to an 8259A for 8086/8088 systems and to INT0 for 80186/80188 systems. INT is active HIGH.
BUSY	O	**BUSY:** This signal indicates that the 8087 NEU is executing a numeric instruction. It is connected to the CPU's $\overline{TEST}$ pin to provide synchronization. In the case of an unmasked exception BUSY remains active until the exception is cleared. BUSY is active HIGH.
READY	I	**READY:** READY is the acknowledgement from the addressed memory device that it will complete the data transfer. The RDY signal from memory is synchronized by the 8284A Clock Generator to form READY for 8086 systems. For 80186/80188 systems, RDY is synchronized by the 82188 Integrated Bus Controller to form READY. This signal is active HIGH.
RESET	I	**RESET:** RESET causes the processor to immediately terminate its present activity. The signal must be active HIGH for at least four clock cycles. RESET is internally synchronized.
CLK	I	**CLOCK:** The clock provides the basic timing for the processor and bus controller. It is asymmetric with a 33% duty cycle to provide optimized internal timing.
V_{CC}		**POWER:** V_{CC} is the +5V power supply pin.
GND		**GROUND:** GND are the ground pins.

NOTE:
For the pin descriptions of the 8086, 8088, 80186 and 80188 CPUs, reference the respective data sheets (8086, 8088, 80186, 80188).

intel   8087

APPLICATION AREAS

The 8087 provides functions meant specifically for high performance numeric processing requirements. Trigonometric, logarithmic, and exponential functions are built into the coprocessor hardware. These functions are essential in scientific, engineering, navigational, or military applications.

The 8087 also has capabilities meant for business or commercial computing. An 8087 can process Binary Coded Decimal (BCD) numbers up to 18 digits without roundoff errors. It can also perform arithmetic on integers as large as 64 bits $\pm 10^{18}$).

PROGRAMMING LANGUAGE SUPPORT

Programs for the 8087 can be written in Intel's high-level languages for 8086/8088 and 80186/80188 Systems; ASM-86 (the 8086, 8088 assembly language), PL/M-86, FORTRAN-86, and PASCAL-86.

RELATED INFORMATION

For 8086, 8088, 80186 or 80188 details, refer to the respective data sheets. For 80186 or 80188 systems, also refer to the 82188 Integrated Bus Controller data sheet.

FUNCTIONAL DESCRIPTION

The 8087 Math CoProcessor's architecture is designed for high performance numeric computing in conjunction with general purpose processing.

The 8087 is a numeric processor extension that provides arithmetic and logical instruction support for a variety of numeric data types. It also executes numerous built-in transcendental functions (e.g., tangent and log functions). The 8087 executes instructions as a coprocessor to a maximum mode CPU. It effectively extends the register and instruction set of the system and adds several new data types as well. Figure 3 presents the registers of the CPU + 8087. Table 2 shows the range of data types supported by the 8087. The 8087 is treated as an extension to the CPU, providing register, data types, control, and instruction capabilities at the hardware level. At the programmer's level the CPU and the 8087 are viewed as a single unified processor.

System Configuration

As a coprocessor to an 8086 or 8088, the 8087 is wired in parallel with the CPU as shown in Figure 4. Figure 5 shows the 80186/80188 system configuration. The CPU's status (S0–S2) and queue status lines (QS0–QS1) enable the 8087 to monitor and decode instructions in synchronization with the CPU and without any CPU overhead. For 80186/80188 systems, the queue status signals of the 80186/80188 are synchronized to 8087 requirements by the 8288 Integrated Bus Controller. Once started, the 8087 can process in parallel with, and independent of, the host CPU. For resynchronization, the 8087's BUSY signal informs the CPU that the 8087 is executing an instruction and the CPU WAIT instruction tests this signal to insure that the 8087 is ready to execute subsequent instructions. The 8087 can interrupt the CPU when it detects an error or exception. The 8087's interrupt request line is typically routed to the CPU through an 8259A Programmable Interrupt Controller for 8086, 8088 systems and INT0 for 80186/80188.

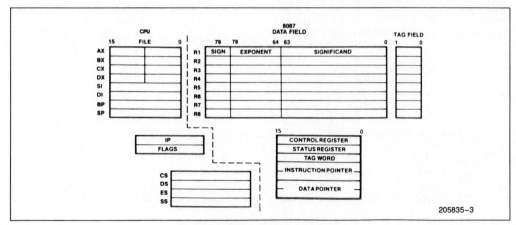

Figure 3. CPU + 8087 Architecture

intel   8087

The 8087 uses one of the request/grant lines of the 8086/8088 architecture (typically $\overline{RQ}/\overline{GT}0$) to obtain control of the local bus for data transfers. The other request/grant line is available for general system use (for instance by an I/O processor in LOCAL mode). A bus master can also be connected to the 8087's $\overline{RQ}/\overline{GT}1$ line. In this configuration the 8087 will pass the request/grant handshake signals between the CPU and the attached master when the 8087 is not in control of the bus and will relinquish the bus to the master directly when the 8087 is in control. In this way two additional masters can be configured in an 8086/8088 system; one will share the 8086/8088 bus with the 8087 on a first-come first-served basis, and the second will be guaranteed to be higher in priority than the 8087.

For 80186/80188 systems, $\overline{RQ}/\overline{GT}0$ and $\overline{RQ}/\overline{GT}1$ are connected to the corresponding inputs of the 82188 Integrated Bus Controller. Because the 80186/80188 has a HOLD, HLDA bus exchange protocol, an interface is needed which will translate $\overline{RQ}/\overline{GT}$ signals to corresponding HOLD, HLDA signals and vice versa. One of the functions of the 82188 IBC is to provide this translation. $\overline{RQ}/\overline{GT}0$ is translated to HOLD, HLDA signals which are then directly connected to the 80186/80188. The $\overline{RQ}/\overline{GT}1$ line is also translated into HOLD, HLDA signals (referred to as SYSHOLD, SYSHLDA signals) by the 82188 IBC. This allows a third processor (using a HOLD, HLDA bus exchange protocol) to gain control of the bus.

Unlike an 8086/8087 system, $\overline{RQ}/\overline{GT}$ is only used when the 8087 has bus control. If the third processor requests the bus when the current bus master is the 80186/80188, the 82188 IBC will directly pass the request onto the 80186/80188 without going through the 8087. The third processor has the highest bus priority in the system. If the 8087 requests the bus while the third processor has bus control, the grant pulse will not be issued until the third processor releases the bus (using SYSHOLD). In this configuration, the third processor has the highest priority, the 8087 has the next highest, and the 80186/80188 has the lowest bus priority.

Bus Operation

The 8087 bus structure, operation and timing are identical to all other processors in the 8086/8088 series (maximum mode configuration). The address is time multiplexed with the data on the first 16/8 lines of the address/data bus. A16 through A19 are time multiplexed with four status lines S3–S6. S3, S4 and S6 are always one (HIGH) for 8087-driven bus cycles while S5 is always zero (LOW). When the 8087 is monitoring CPU bus cycles (passive mode) S6 is also monitored by the 8087 to differentiate 8086/8088 activity from that of a local I/O processor or any other local bus master. (The 8086/8088 must be the only processor on the local bus to drive S6 LOW). S7 is multiplexed with and has the same value as $\overline{BHE}$ for all 8087 bus cycles.

Table 2. 8087 Data Types

Data Formats	Range	Precision	Most Significant Byte
Word Integer	10^4	16 Bits	I_{15} .... I_0 Two's Complement
Short Integer	10^9	32 Bits	I_{31} .... I_0 Two's Complement
Long Integer	10^{18}	64 Bits	I_{63} .... I_0 Two's Complement
Packed BCD	10^{18}	18 Digits	S — $D_{17}D_{16}$ .... D_1 D_0
Short Real	$10^{\pm38}$	24 Bits	S E_7 ... E_0 F_1 ... F_{23} F_0 Implicit
Long Real	$10^{\pm308}$	53 Bits	S E_{10} ... E_0 F_1 ... F_{52} F_0 Implicit
Temporary Real	$10^{\pm4932}$	64 Bits	S E_{14} ... E_0 F_0 ... F_{63}

Integer: I
Packed BCD: $(-1)^S(D_{17}...D_0)$
Real: $(-1)^S(2^{E-Bias})(F_0 \bullet F_1 ...)$
bias = 127 for Short Real
      1023 for Long Real
      16383 for Temp Real

intel   8087

The first three status lines, $\overline{S0}-\overline{S2}$, are used with an 8288 bus controller or 82188 Integrated Bus Controller to determine the type of bus cycle being run:

$\overline{S2}$	$\overline{S1}$	$\overline{S0}$	
0	X	X	Unused
1	0	0	Unused
1	0	1	Memory Data Read
1	1	0	Memory Data Write
1	1	1	Passive (no bus cycle)

Programming Interface

The 8087 includes the standard 8086, 8088 instruction set for general data manipulation and program control. It also includes 68 numeric instructions for extended precision integer, floating point, trigonometric, logarithmic, and exponential functions. Sample execution times for several 8087 functions are shown in Table 3. Overall performance is up to 100 times that of an 8086 processor for numeric instructions.

Any instruction executed by the 8087 is the combined result of the CPU and 8087 activity. The CPU and the 8087 have specialized functions and registers providing fast concurrent operation. The CPU controls overall program execution while the 8087 uses the coprocessor interface to recognize and perform numeric operations.

Table 2 lists the seven data types the 8087 supports and presents the format for each type. Internally, the 8087 holds all numbers in the temporary real format. Load and store instructions automatically convert operands represented in memory as 16-, 32-, or 64-bit integers, 32- or 64-bit floating point numbers or 18-digit packed BCD numbers into temporary real format and vice versa. The 8087 also provides the capability to control round off, underflow, and overflow errors in each calculation.

Computations in the 8087 use the processor's register stack. These eight 80-bit registers provide the equivalent capacity of 20 32-bit registers. The 8087 register set can be accessed as a stack, with instructions operating on the top one or two stack elements, or as a fixed register set, with instructions operating on explicitly designated registers.

Table 5 lists the 8087's instructions by class. All appear as ESCAPE instructions to the host. Assembly language programs are written in ASM-86, the 8086, 8088 assembly language.

Table 3. Execution Times for Selected 8086/8087 Numeric Instructions and Corresponding 8086 Emulation

Floating Point Instruction	Approximate Execution Time (μs)	
	8086/8087 (8 MHz Clock)	8086 Emulation
Add/Subtract	10.6	1000
Multiply (Single Precision)	11.9	1000
Multiply (Extended Precision)	16.9	1312
Divide	24.4	2000
Compare	−5.6	812
Load (Double Precision)	−6.3	1062
Store (Double Precision)	13.1	750
Square Root	22.5	12250
Tangent	56.3	8125
Exponentiation	62.5	10687

NUMERIC PROCESSOR EXTENSION ARCHITECTURE

As shown in Figure 1, the 8087 is internally divided into two processing elements, the control unit (CU) and the numeric execution unit (NEU). The NEU executes all numeric instructions, while the CU receives and decodes instructions, reads and writes memory operands and executes 8087 control instructions. The two elements are able to operate independently of one another, allowing the CU to maintain synchronization with the CPU while the NEU is busy processing a numeric instruction.

Control Unit

The CU keeps the 8087 operating in synchronization with its host CPU. 8087 instructions are intermixed with CPU instructions in a single instruction stream. The CPU fetches all instructions from memory; by monitoring the status ($\overline{S0}-\overline{S2}$, S6) emitted by the CPU, the control unit determines when an instruction is being fetched. The CPU monitors the data bus in parallel with the CPU to obtain instructions that pertain to the 8087.

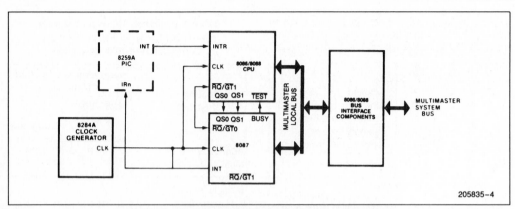

Figure 4. 8086/8087, 8088/8087 System Configuration

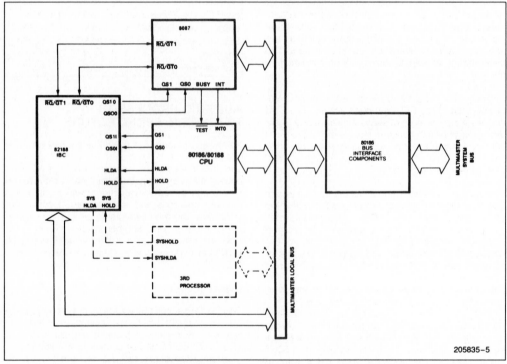

Figure 5. 80186/8087, 80188/8087 System Configuration

intel   8087

The CU maintains an instruction queue that is identical to the queue in the host CPU. The CU automatically determines if the CPU is an 8086/80186 or an 8088/80188 immediately after reset (by monitoring the $\overline{BHE}$/S7 line) and matches its queue length accordingly. By monitoring the CPU's queue status lines (QS0, QS1), the CU obtains and decodes instructions from the queue in synchronization with the CPU.

A numeric instruction appears as an ESCAPE instruction to the CPU. Both the CPU and 8087 decode and execute the ESCAPE instruction together. The 8087 only recognizes the numeric instructions shown in Table 5. The start of a numeric operation is accomplished when the CPU executes the ESCAPE instruction. The instruction may or may not identify a memory operand.

The CPU does, however, distinguish between ESC instructions that reference memory and those that do not. If the instruction refers to a memory operand, the CPU calculates the operand's address using any one of its available addressing modes, and then performs a "dummy read" of the word at that location. (Any location within the 1M byte address space is allowed.) This is a normal read cycle except that the CPU ignores the data it receives. If the ESC instruction does not contain a memory reference (e.g. an 8087 stack operation), the CPU simply proceeds to the next instruction.

An 8087 instruction can have one of three memory reference options: (1) not reference memory; (2) load an operand word from memory into the 8087; or (3) store an operand word from the 8087 into memory. If no memory reference is required, the 8087 simply executes its instruction. If a memory reference is required, the CU uses a "dummy read" cycle initiated by the CPU to capture and save the address that the CPU places on the bus. If the instruction is a load, the CU additionally captures the data word when it becomes available on the local data bus. If data required is longer than one word, the CU immediately obtains the bus from the CPU using the request/grant protocol and reads the rest of the information in consecutive bus cycles. In a store operation, the CU captures and saves the store address as in a load, and ignores the data word that follows in the "dummy read" cycle. When the 8087 is ready to perform the store, the CU obtains the bus from the CPU and writes the operand starting at the specified address.

Numeric Execution Unit

The NEU executes all instructions that involve the register stack; these include arithmetic, logical, transcendental, constant and data transfer instructions. The data path in the NEU is 84 bits wide (68 fractions bits, 15 exponent bits and a sign bit) which allows internal operand transfers to be performed at very high speeds.

When the NEU begins executing an instruction, it activates the 8087 BUSY signal. This signal can be used in conjunction with the CPU WAIT instruction to resynchronize both processors when the NEU has completed its current instruction.

Register Set

The CPU + 8087 register set is shown in Figure 3. Each of the eight data registers in the 8087's register stack is 80 bits and is divided into "fields" corresponding to the 8087's temporary real data type.

At a given point in time the TOP field in the control word identifies the current top-of-stack register. A "push" operation decrements TOP by 1 and loads a value into the new top register. A "pop" operation stores the value from the current top register and then increments TOP by 1. Like CPU stacks in memory, the 8087 register stack grows "down" toward lower-addressed registers.

Instructions may address the data registers either implicitly or explicitly. Many instructions operate on the register at the top of the stack. These instructions implicitly address the register pointed to by the TOP. Other instructions allow the programmer to explicitly specify the register which is to be used. Explicit register addressing is "top-relative."

Status Word

The status word shown in Figure 6 reflects the overall state of the 8087; it may be stored in memory and then inspected by CPU code. The status word is a 16-bit register divided into fields as shown in Figure 6. The busy bit (bit 15) indicates whether the NEU is either executing an instruction or has an interrupt request pending (B = 1), or is idle (B = 0). Several instructions which store and manipulate the status word are executed exclusively by the CU, and these do not set the busy bit themselves.

intel   8087

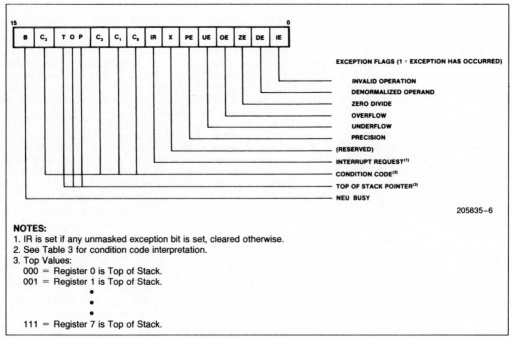

NOTES:
1. IR is set if any unmasked exception bit is set, cleared otherwise.
2. See Table 3 for condition code interpretation.
3. Top Values:
   000 = Register 0 is Top of Stack.
   001 = Register 1 is Top of Stack.
   •
   •
   •
   111 = Register 7 is Top of Stack.

Figure 6. 8087 Status Word

The four numeric condition code bits (C_0–C_3) are similar to flags in a CPU: various instructions update these bits to reflect the outcome of the 8087 operations. The effect of these instructions on the condition code bits is summarized in Table 4.

Bits 14–12 of the status word point to the 8087 register that is the current top-of-stack (TOP) as described above.

Bit 7 is the interrupt request bit. This bit is set if any unmasked exception bit is set and cleared otherwise.

Bits 5–0 are set to indicate that the NEU has detected an exception while executing an instruction.

Tag Word

The tag word marks the content of each register as shown in Figure 7. The principal function of the tag word is to optimize the 8087's performance. The tag word can be used, however, to interpret the contents of 8087 registers.

Instruction and Data Pointers

The instruction and data pointers (see Figure 8) are provided for user-written error handlers. Whenever the 8087 executes a math instruction, the CU saves the instruction address, the operand address (if present) and the instruction opcode. 8087 instructions can store this data into memory.

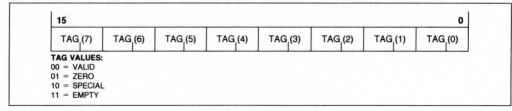

Figure 7. 8087 Tag Word

intel   8087

Table 4a. Condition Code Interpretation

Instruction Type	C₃	C₂	C₁	C₀	Interpretation
Compare, Test	0	0	X	0	ST > Source or 0 (FTST)
	0	0	X	1	ST < Source or 0 (FTST)
	1	0	X	0	ST = Source or 0 (FTST)
	1	1	X	1	ST is not comparable
Remainder	Q_1	0	Q_0	Q_2	Complete reduction with three low bits of quotient (See Table 4b)
	U	1	U	U	Incomplete Reduction
Examine	0	0	0	0	Valid, positive unnormalized
	0	0	0	1	Invalid, positive, exponent = 0
	0	0	1	0	Valid, negative, unnormalized
	0	0	1	1	Invalid, negative, exponent = 0
	0	1	0	0	Valid, positive, normalized
	0	1	0	1	Infinity, positive
	0	1	1	0	Valid, negative, normalized
	0	1	1	1	Infinity, negative
	1	0	0	0	Zero, positive
	1	0	0	1	Empty
	1	0	1	0	Zero, negative
	1	0	1	1	Empty
	1	1	0	0	Invalid, positive, exponent = 0
	1	1	0	1	Empty
	1	1	1	0	Invalid, negative, exponent = 0
	1	1	1	1	Empty

NOTES:
1. ST = Top of stack
2. X = value is not affected by instruction
3. U = value is undefined following instruction
4. Q_n = Quotient bit n

Table 4b. Condition Code Interpretation after FPREM Instruction As a Function of Divided Value

Dividend Range	Q_2	Q_1	Q_0
Dividend < 2 * Modulus	C_3[1]	C_1[1]	Q_0
Dividend < 4 * Modulus	C_3[1]	Q_1	Q_0
Dividend ≥ 4 * Modulus	Q_2	Q_1	Q_0

NOTE:
1. Previous value of indicated bit, not affected by FPREM instruction execution.

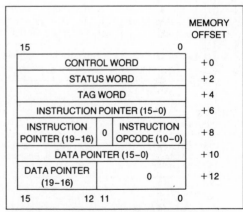

Figure 8. 8087 Instruction and Data Pointer Image in Memory

int_e_l   8087

Control Word

The 8087 provides several processing options which are selected by loading a word from memory into the control word. Figure 9 shows the format and encoding of the fields in the control word.

The low order byte of this control word configures 8087 interrupts and exception masking. Bits 5–0 of the control word contain individual masks for each of the six exceptions that the 8087 recognizes and bit 7 contains a general mask bit for all 8087 interrupts. The high order byte of the control word configures the 8087 operating mode including precision, rounding, and infinity controls. The precision control bits (bits 9–8) can be used to set the 8087 internal operating precision at less than the default of temporary real precision. This can be useful in providing compatibility with earlier generation arithmetic processors of smaller precision than the 8087. The rounding control bits (bits 11–10) provide for directed rounding and true chop as well as the unbiased round to nearest mode specified in the proposed IEEE standard. Control over closure of the number space at infinity is also provided (either affine closure, $\pm\infty$, or projective closure, ∞, is treated as unsigned, may be specified).

Exception Handling

The 8087 detects six different exception conditions that can occur during instruction execution. Any or all exceptions will cause an interrupt if unmasked and interrupts are enabled.

If interrupts are disabled the 8087 will simply continue execution regardless of whether the host clears the exception. If a specific exception class is masked and that exception occurs, however, the 8087 will post the exception in the status register and perform an on-chip default exception handling procedure, thereby allowing processing to continue. The exceptions that the 8087 detects are the following:

1. INVALID OPERATION: Stack overflow, stack underflow, indeterminate form ($0/0$, $\infty - \infty$, etc.) or the use of a Non-Number (NAN) as an operand. An exponent value is reserved and any bit pattern with this value in the exponent field is termed a Non-Number and causes this exception. If this exception is masked, the 8087's default response is to generate a specific NAN called IN-DEFINITE, or to propagate already existing NANs as the calculation result.

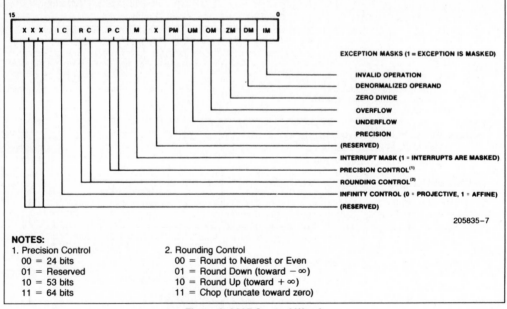

NOTES:

1. Precision Control	2. Rounding Control
00 = 24 bits	00 = Round to Nearest or Even
01 = Reserved	01 = Round Down (toward $-\infty$)
10 = 53 bits	10 = Round Up (toward $+\infty$)
11 = 64 bits	11 = Chop (truncate toward zero)

Figure 9. 8087 Control Word

int_e_l   8087

2. OVERFLOW: The result is too large in magnitude to fit the specified format. The 8087 will generate an encoding for infinity if this exception is masked.

3. ZERO DIVISOR: The divisor is zero while the dividend is a non-infinite, non-zero number. Again, the 8087 will generate an encoding for infinity if this exception is masked.

4. UNDERFLOW: The result is non-zero but too small in magnitude to fit in the specified format. If this exception is masked the 8087 will denormal-ize (shift right) the fraction until the exponent is in range. This process is called gradual underflow.

5. DENORMALIZED OPERAND: At least one of the operands or the result is denormalized; it has the smallest exponent but a non-zero significand. Normal processing continues if this exception is masked off.

6. INEXACT RESULT: If the true result is not exactly representable in the specified format, the result is rounded according to the rounding mode, and this flag is set. If this exception is masked, processing will simply continue.

ABSOLUTE MAXIMUM RATINGS*

Ambient Temperature Under Bias ......0°C to 70°C

Storage Temperature .... −65°C to + 150°C

Voltage on Any Pin with
   Respect to Ground.............. −1.0V to + 7V

Power Dissipation .... 3.0 Watt

Notice: Stresses above those listed under "Absolute Maximum Ratings" may cause permanent damage to the device. This is a stress rating only and functional operation of the device at these or any other conditions above those indicated in the operational sections of this specification is not implied. Exposure to absolute maximum rating conditions for extended periods may affect device reliability.

D.C. CHARACTERISTICS $T_A = 0°C$ to $70°C$, $V_{CC} = 5V \pm 5\%$

Symbol	Parameter	Min	Max	Units	Test Conditions
V_{IL}	Input Low Voltage	−0.5	0.8	V	
V_{IH}	Input High Voltage	2.0	V_{CC} + 0.5	V	
V_{OL}	Output Low Voltage (Note 8)		0.45	V	$I_{OL} = 2.5$ mA
V_{OH}	Output High Voltage	2.4		V	$I_{OH} = -400 \mu A$
I_{CC}	Power Supply Current		475	mA	$T_A = 25°C$
I_{LI}	Input Leakage Current		±10	μA	$0V \leq V_{IN} \leq V_{CC}$
I_{LO}	Output Leakage Current		±10	μA	$T_A = 25°C$
V_{CL}	Clock Input Low Voltage	−0.5	0.6	V	
V_{CH}	Clock Input High Voltage	3.9	V_{CC} + 1.0	V	
C_{IN}	Capacitance of Inputs		10	pF	fc = 1 MHz
C_{IO}	Capacitance of I/O Buffer (AD0−15, A_{16}−A_{19}, BHE, S2−S0, RQ/GT) and CLK		15	pF	fc = 1 MHz
C_{OUT}	Capacitance of Outputs BUSY INT		10	pF	fc = 1 MHz

8087

Table 5. 8087 Extensions to the 86/186 Instructions Sets

Data Transfer		Optional 8,16 Bit Displacement	Clock Count Range			
			32 Bit Real	32 Bit Integer	64 Bit Real	16 Bit Integer
FLD = LOAD	MF =		00	01	10	11
Integer/Real Memory to ST(0)	ESCAPE MF 1 │ MOD 0 0 0 R/M │ DISP		38–56 +EA	52–60 +EA	40–60 +EA	46–54 +EA
Long Integer Memory to ST(0)	ESCAPE 1 1 1 │ MOD 1 0 1 R/M │ DISP		60–68 +EA			
Temporary Real Memory to ST(0)	ESCAPE 0 1 1 │ MOD 1 0 1 R/M │ DISP		53–65 +EA			
BCD Memory to ST(0)	ESCAPE 1 1 1 │ MOD 1 0 0 R/M │ DISP		290–310 +EA			
ST(i) to ST(0)	ESCAPE 0 0 1 │ 1 1 0 0 0 ST(i)		17–22			
FST = STORE						
ST(0) to Integer/Real Memory	ESCAPE MF 1 │ MOD 0 1 0 R/M │ DISP		84–90 +EA	82–92 +EA	96–104 +EA	80–90 +EA
ST(0) to ST(i)	ESCAPE 1 0 1 │ 1 1 0 1 0 ST(i)		15–22			
FSTP = STORE AND POP						
ST(0) to Integer/Real Memory	ESCAPE MF 1 │ MOD 0 1 1 R/M │ DISP		86–92 +EA	84–94 +EA	98–106 +EA	82–92 +EA
ST(0) to Long Integer Memory	ESCAPE 1 1 1 │ MOD 1 1 1 R/M │ DISP		94–105 +EA			
ST(0) to Temporary Real Memory	ESCAPE 0 1 1 │ MOD 1 1 1 R/M │ DISP		52–58 +EA			
ST(0) to BCD Memory	ESCAPE 1 1 1 │ MOD 1 1 0 R/M │ DISP		520–540 +EA			
ST(0) to ST(i)	ESCAPE 1 0 1 │ 1 1 0 1 1 ST(i)		17–24			
FXCH = Exchange ST(i) and ST(0)	ESCAPE 0 0 1 │ 1 1 0 0 1 ST(i)		10–15			

Comparison

		Optional Displacement	32 Bit Real	32 Bit Integer	64 Bit Real	16 Bit Integer
FCOM = Compare						
Integer/Real Memory to ST(0)	ESCAPE MF 0 │ MOD 0 1 0 R/M │ DISP		60–70 +EA	78–91 +EA	65–75 +EA	72–86 +EA
ST(i) to ST(0)	ESCAPE 0 0 0 │ 1 1 0 1 0 ST(i)		40–50			
FCOMP = Compare and Pop						
Integer/Real Memory to ST(0)	ESCAPE MF 0 │ MOD 0 1 1 R/M │ DISP		63–73 +EA	80–93 +EA	67–77 +EA	74–88 +EA
ST(i) to ST(0)	ESCAPE 0 0 0 │ 1 1 0 1 1 ST(i)		45–52			
FCOMPP = Compare ST(1) to ST(0) and Pop Twice	ESCAPE 1 1 0 │ 1 1 0 1 1 0 0 1		45–55			
FTST = Test ST(0)	ESCAPE 0 0 1 │ 1 1 1 0 0 1 0 0		38–48			
FXAM = Examine ST(0)	ESCAPE 0 0 1 │ 1 1 1 0 0 1 0 1		12–23			

205835–17

intel   8087

Table 5. 8087 Extensions to the 86/186 Instructions Sets (Continued)

Constants	Encoding	Optional 8,16 Bit Displacement	Clock Count Range			
			32 Bit Real	32 Bit Integer	64 Bit Real	16 Bit Integer
	MF =		00	01	10	11
FLDZ = LOAD + 0.0 into ST(0)	ESCAPE 0 0 1 1 1 1 0 1 1 1 0		11–17			
FLD1 = LOAD + 1.0 into ST(0)	ESCAPE 0 0 1 1 1 1 0 1 0 0 0		15–21			
FLDPI = LOAD π into ST(0)	ESCAPE 0 0 1 1 1 1 0 1 0 1 1		16–22			
FLDL2T = LOAD $\log_2 10$ into ST(0)	ESCAPE 0 0 1 1 1 1 0 1 0 0 1		16–22			
FLDL2E = LOAD $\log_2 e$ into ST(0)	ESCAPE 0 0 1 1 1 1 0 1 0 1 0		15–21			
FLDLG2 = LOAD $\log_{10} 2$ into ST(0)	ESCAPE 0 0 1 1 1 1 0 1 1 0 0		18–24			
FLDLN2 = LOAD $\log_e 2$ into ST(0)	ESCAPE 0 0 1 1 1 1 0 1 1 0 1		17–23			

Arithmetic

FADD = Addition

	Encoding	Optional 8,16 Bit Displacement	32 Bit Real	32 Bit Integer	64 Bit Real	16 Bit Integer
Integer/Real Memory with ST(0)	ESCAPE MF 0 MOD 0 0 0 R/M	DISP	90–120 +EA	108–143 +EA	95–125 +EA	102–137 +EA
ST(i) and ST(0)	ESCAPE d P 0 1 1 0 0 0 ST(i)		70–100 (Note 1)			

FSUB = Subtraction

	Encoding	Optional 8,16 Bit Displacement	32 Bit Real	32 Bit Integer	64 Bit Real	16 Bit Integer
Integer/Real Memory with ST(0)	ESCAPE MF 0 MOD 1 0 R R/M	DISP	90–120 +EA	108–143 +EA	95–125 +EA	102–137 +EA
ST(i) and ST(0)	ESCAPE d P 0 1 1 1 0 R R/M		70–100 (Note 1)			

FMUL = Multiplication

	Encoding	Optional 8,16 Bit Displacement	32 Bit Real	32 Bit Integer	64 Bit Real	16 Bit Integer
Integer/Real Memory with ST(0)	ESCAPE MF 0 MOD 0 0 1 R/M	DISP	110–125 +EA	130–144 +EA	112–168 +EA	124–138 +EA
ST(i) and ST(0)	ESCAPE d P 0 1 1 0 0 1 R/M		90–145 (Note 1)			

FDIV = Division

	Encoding	Optional 8,16 Bit Displacement	32 Bit Real	32 Bit Integer	64 Bit Real	16 Bit Integer
Integer/Real Memory with ST(0)	ESCAPE MF 0 MOD 1 1 R R/M	DISP	215–225 +EA	230–243 +EA	220–230 +EA	224–238 +EA
ST(i) and ST(0)	ESCAPE d P 0 1 1 1 1 R R/M		193–203 (Note 1)			

	Encoding		Clock Count
FSQRT = Square Root of ST(0)	ESCAPE 0 0 1 1 1 1 1 1 0 1 0		180–186
FSCALE = Scale ST(0) by ST(1)	ESCAPE 0 0 1 1 1 1 1 1 1 0 1		32–38
FPREM = Partial Remainder of ST(0) ÷ ST(1)	ESCAPE 0 0 1 1 1 1 1 1 0 0 0		15–190
FRNDINT = Round ST(0) to Integer	ESCAPE 0 0 1 1 1 1 1 1 1 0 0		16–50

205835–18

NOTE:
1. If P = 1 then add 5 clocks.

8087

Table 5. 8087 Extensions to the 86/186 Instructions Sets (Continued)

		Optional 8,16 Bit Displacement	Clock Count Range
FXTRACT – Extract Components of St(0)	ESCAPE 0 0 1 1 1 1 1 0 1 0 0		27–55
FABS = Absolute Value of ST(0)	ESCAPE 0 0 1 1 1 1 0 0 0 0 1		10–17
FCHS = Change Sign of ST(0)	ESCAPE 0 0 1 1 1 1 0 0 0 0 0		10–17
Transcendental			
FPTAN = Partial Tangent of ST(0)	ESCAPE 0 0 1 1 1 1 1 0 0 1 0		30–540
FPATAN = Partial Arctangent of ST(0) ÷ ST(1)	ESCAPE 0 0 1 1 1 1 1 0 0 1 1		250–800
F2XM1 = $2^{ST(0)} - 1$	ESCAPE 0 0 1 1 1 1 1 0 0 0 0		310–630
FYL2X = $ST(1) \cdot Log_2 \|ST(0)\|$	ESCAPE 0 0 1 1 1 1 1 0 0 0 1		900–1100
FYL2XP1 = $ST(1) \cdot Log_2 [ST(0) + 1]$	ESCAPE 0 0 1 1 1 1 1 1 0 0 1		700–1000
Processor Control			
FINIT = Initialized 8087	ESCAPE 0 1 1 1 1 1 0 0 0 1 1		2–8
FENI = Enable Interrupts	ESCAPE 0 1 1 1 1 1 0 0 0 0 0		2–8
FDISI = Disable Interrupts	ESCAPE 0 1 1 1 1 1 0 0 0 0 1		2–8
FLDCW = Load Control Word	ESCAPE 0 0 1 MOD 1 0 1 R/M	DISP	7–14 + EA
FSTCW = Store Control Word	ESCAPE 0 0 1 MOD 1 1 1 R/M	DISP	12–18 + EA
FSTSW = Store Status Word	ESCAPE 1 0 1 MOD 1 1 1 R/M	DISP	12–18 + EA
FCLEX = Clear Exceptions	ESCAPE 0 1 1 1 1 1 0 0 0 1 0		2–8
FSTENV = Store Environment	ESCAPE 0 0 1 MOD 1 1 0 R/M	DISP	40–50 + EA
FLDENV = Load Environment	ESCAPE 0 0 1 MOD 1 0 0 R/M	DISP	35–45 + EA
FSAVE = Save State	ESCAPE 1 0 1 MOD 1 1 0 R/M	DISP	197 – 207 + EA
FRSTOR = Restore State	ESCAPE 1 0 1 MOD 1 0 0 R/M	DISP	197 – 207 + EA
FINCSTP = Increment Stack Pointer	ESCAPE 0 0 1 1 1 1 1 0 1 1 1		6–12
FDECSTP = Decrement Stack Pointer	ESCAPE 0 0 1 1 1 1 1 0 1 1 0		6–12

205835–19

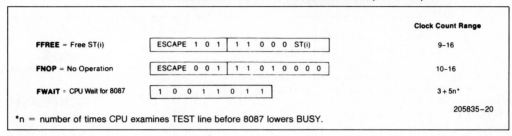

intel   8087

Table 5. 8087 Extensions to the 86/186 Instructions Sets (Continued)

		Clock Count Range
FFREE = Free ST(i)	ESCAPE 1 0 1 | 1 1 0 0 0 ST(i)	9–16
FNOP = No Operation	ESCAPE 0 0 1 | 1 1 0 1 0 0 0 0	10–16
FWAIT = CPU Wait for 8087	1 0 0 1 1 0 1 1	3 + 5n*
		205835–20

*n = number of times CPU examines TEST line before 8087 lowers BUSY.

NOTES:
1. if mod = 00 then DISP = 0*, disp-low and disp-high are absent
   if mod = 01 then DISP = disp-low sign-extended to 16-bits, disp-high is absent
   if mod = 10 then DISP = disp-high; disp-low
   if mod = 11 then r/m is treated as an ST(i) field
2. if r/m = 000 then EA = (BX) + (SI) + DISP
   if r/m = 001 then EA = (BX) + (DI) + DISP
   if r/m = 010 then EA = (BP) + (SI) + DISP
   if r/m = 011 then EA = (BP) + (DI) + DISP
   if r/m = 100 then EA = (SI) + DISP
   if r/m = 101 then EA = (DI) + DISP
   if r/m = 110 then EA = (BP) + DISP
   if r/m = 111 then EA = (BX) + DISP
   *except if mod = 000 and r/m = 110 then EA = disp-high; disp-low.
3. MF = Memory Format
      00–32-bit Real
      01–32-bit Integer
      10–64-bit Real
      11–16-bit Integer
4. ST(0) = Current stack top
   ST(i) = i^{th} register below stack top
5. d = Destination
      0—Destination is ST(0)
      1—Destination is ST(i)
6. P = Pop
      0—No pop
      1—Pop ST(0)
7. R = Reverse: When d = 1 reverse the sense of R
      0—Destination (op) Source
      1—Source (op) Destination
8. For **FSQRT:** $-0 \le ST(0) \le +\infty$
   For **FSCALE:** $-2^{15} \le ST(1) < +2^{15}$ and ST(1) integer
   For **F2XM1:** $0 \le ST(0) \le 2^{-1}$
   For **FYL2X:** $0 < ST(0) < \infty$
                      $-\infty < ST(1) < +\infty$
   For **FYL2XP1:** $0 \le IST(0)I < (2 - \sqrt{2})/2$
                      $-\infty < ST(1) < \infty$
   For **FPTAN:** $0 \le ST(0) \le \pi/4$
   For **FPATAN:** $0 \le ST(0) < ST(1) < +\infty$

MOTOROLA SEMICONDUCTORS

3501 ED BLUESTEIN BLVD., AUSTIN, TEXAS 78721

MC6845

CRT CONTROLLER (CRTC)

The MC6845 CRT controller performs the interface between an MPU and a raster-scan CRT display. It is intended for use in MPU-based controllers for CRT terminals in stand-alone or cluster configurations.

The CRTC is optimized for the hardware/software balance required for maximum flexibility. All keyboard functions, reads, writes, cursor movements, and editing are under processor control. The CRTC provides video timing and refresh memory addressing.

- Useful in Monochrome or Color CRT Applications
- Applications Include "Glass-Teletype," Smart, Programmable, Intelligent CRT Terminals; Video Games; Information Displays
- Alphanumeric, Semi-Graphic, and Full-Graphic Capability
- Fully Programmable Via Processor Data Bus. Timing May Be Generated for Almost Any Alphanumeric Screen Format, e.g., 80 × 24, 72 × 64, 132 × 20
- Single +5 V Supply
- M6800 Compatible Bus Interface
- TTL-Compatible Inputs and Outputs
- Start Address Register Provides Hardware Scroll (by Page or Character)
- Programmable Cursor Register Allows Control of Cursor Format and Blink Rate
- Light Pen Register
- Refresh (Screen) Memory May be Multiplexed Between the CRTC and the MPU Thus Removing the Requirements for Line Buffers or External DMA Devices
- Programmable Interlace or Non-Interlace Scan Modes
- 14-Bit Refresh Address Allows Up to 16K of Refresh Memory for Use in Character or Semi-Graphic Displays
- 5-Bit Row Address Allows Up to 32 Scan-Line Character Blocks
- By Utilizing Both the Refresh Addresses and the Row Addresses, a 512K Address Space is Available for Use in Graphics Systems
- Refresh Addresses are Provided During Retrace, Allowing the CRTC to Provide Row Addresses to Refresh Dynamic RAMs
- Pin Compatible with the MC6835

MOS
(N-CHANNEL, SILICON-GATE)

CRT CONTROLLER
(CRTC)

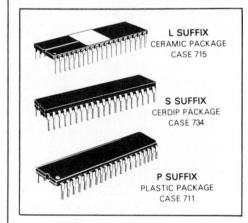

L SUFFIX
CERAMIC PACKAGE
CASE 715

S SUFFIX
CERDIP PACKAGE
CASE 734

P SUFFIX
PLASTIC PACKAGE
CASE 711

PIN ASSIGNMENT

Left	Pin		Pin	Right
GND	1		40	VS
RESET	2		39	HS
LPSTB	3		38	RA0
MA0	4		37	RA1
MA1	5		36	RA2
MA2	6		35	RA3
MA3	7		34	RA4
MA4	8		33	D0
MA5	9		32	D1
MA6	10		31	D2
MA7	11		30	D3
MA8	12		29	D4
MA9	13		28	D5
MA10	14		27	D6
MA11	15		26	D7
MA12	16		25	CS
MA13	17		24	RS
DE	18		23	E
CURSOR	19		22	R/W
VCC	20		21	CLK

ORDERING INFORMATION

Package Type	Frequency (MHz)	Temperature	Order Number
Ceramic L Suffix	1.0	0°C to 70°C	MC6845L
	1.0	−40°C to 85°C	MC6845CL
	1.5	0°C to 70°C	MC68A45L
	1.5	−40°C to 85°C	MC68A45CL
	2.0	0°C to 70°C	MC68B45L
Cerdip S Suffix	1.0	0°C to 70°C	MC6845S
	1.0	−40°C to 85°C	MC6845CS
	1.5	0°C to 70°C	MC68A45S
	1.5	−40°C to 85°C	MC68A45CS
	2.0	0°C to 70°C	MC68B45S
Plastic P Suffix	1.0	0°C to 70°C	MC6845P
	1.0	−40°C to 85°C	MC6845CP
	1.5	0°C to 70°C	MC68A45P
	1.5	−40°C to 85°C	MC68A45CP
	2.0	0°C to 70°C	MC68B45P

DS9838-R1

MC6845

FIGURE 1 — TYPICAL CRT CONTROLLER APPLICATION

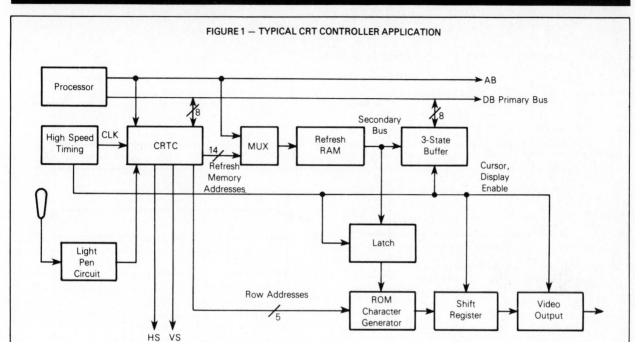

MAXIMUM RATINGS

Rating	Symbol	Value	Unit
Supply Voltage	V_{CC}	-0.3 to $+7.0$	V
Input Voltage	V_{in}	-0.3 to $+7.0$	V

Operating Temperature Range
  MC6845, MC68A45, MC68B45
  MC6845C, MC68A45C
	T_A	T_L to T_H
		0 to 70
		-40 to $+85$
			°C

Storage Temperature Range	T_{stg}	-55 to $+150$	°C

THERMAL CHARACTERISTICS

Characteristic	Symbol	Value	Rating

Thermal Resistance
  Plastic Package
  Cerdip Package
  Ceramic Package
	θ_{JA}	100
		60
		50
			°C/W

The device contains circuitry to protect the inputs against damage due to high static voltages or electric fields; however, it is advised that normal precautions be taken to avoid application of any voltage higher than maximum rated voltages to this high-impedance circuit. For proper operation it is recommended that V_{in} and V_{out} be constrained to the range $V_{SS} \leq (V_{in}$ or $V_{out}) \leq V_{CC}$.

RECOMMENDED OPERATING CONDITIONS

Characteristics	Symbol	Min	Typ	Max	Unit
Supply Voltage	V_{CC}	4.75	5.0	5.25	V
Input Low Voltage	V_{IL}	-0.3	—	0.8	V
Input High Voltage	V_{IH}	2.0	—	V_{CC}	V

Ⓜ MOTOROLA *Semiconductor Products Inc.*

MC6845

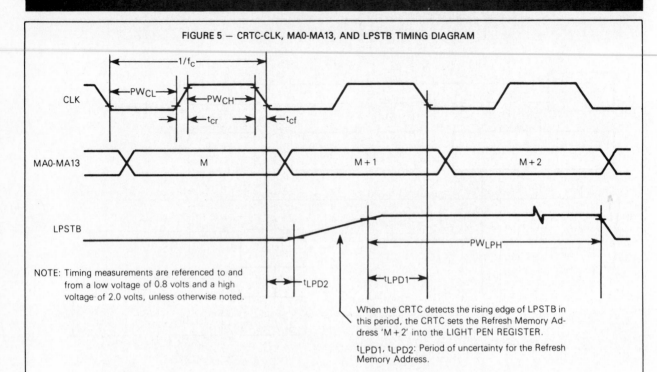

FIGURE 5 — CRTC-CLK, MA0-MA13, AND LPSTB TIMING DIAGRAM

NOTE: Timing measurements are referenced to and from a low voltage of 0.8 volts and a high voltage of 2.0 volts, unless otherwise noted.

When the CRTC detects the rising edge of LPSTB in this period, the CRTC sets the Refresh Memory Address 'M + 2' into the LIGHT PEN REGISTER.

t_{LPD1}, t_{LPD2}: Period of uncertainty for the Refresh Memory Address.

CRTC INTERFACE SYSTEM DESCRIPTION

The CRT controller generates the signals necessary to interface a digital system to a raster scan CRT display. In this type of display, an electron beam starts in the upper left hand corner, moves quickly across the screen and returns. This action is called a horizontal scan. After each horizontal scan the beam is incrementally moved down in the vertical direction until it has reached the bottom. At this point one frame has been displayed, as the beam has made many horizontal scans and one vertical scan.

Two types of raster scanning are used in CRTs, interlace and non-interlace, shown in Figures 6 and 7. Non-interlace scanning consists of one field per frame. The scan lines in Figure 6 are shown as solid lines and the retrace patterns are indicated by the dotted lines. Increasing the number of frames per second will decrease the flicker. Ordinarily, either a 50 or 60 frame per second refresh rate is used to minimize beating between the CRT and the power line frequency. This prevents the displayed data from weaving.

Interlace scanning is used in broadcast TV and on data monitors where high density or high resolution data must be displayed. Two fields, or vertical scans are made down the screen for each single picture or frame. The first field (even field) starts in the upper left hand corner; the second (odd field) in the upper center. Both fields overlap as shown in Figure 7, thus interlacing the two fields into a single frame.

In order to display the characters on the CRT screen the frames must be continually repeated. The data to be displayed is stored in the refresh (screen) memory by the MPU controlling the data processing system. The data is usually written in ASCII code, so it cannot be directly displayed as characters. A character generator ROM is typically used to convert the ASCII codes into the "dot" pattern for every character.

The most common method of generating characters is to create a matrix of dots "x" dots (columns) wide and "y" dots (rows) high. Each character is created by selectively filling in

FIGURE 6 — RASTER SCAN SYSTEM (NON-INTERLACE)

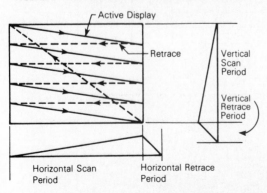

FIGURE 7 — RASTER SCAN SYSTEM (INTERLACE)

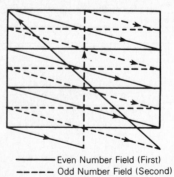

Even Number Field (First)
- - - - - Odd Number Field (Second)

MOTOROLA *Semiconductor Products Inc.*

the dots. As "x" and "y" get larger a more detailed character may be created. Two common dot matrices are 5×7 and 7×9. Many variations of these standards will allow Chinese, Japanese, or Arabic letters instead of English. Since characters require some space between them, a character block larger than the character is typically used, as shown in Figure 8. The figure also shows the corresponding timing and levels for a video signal that would generate the characters.

Referring to Figure 1, the CRT controller generates the refresh addresses (MA0-MA13), row addresses (RA0-RA4), and the video timing (vertical sync — VS, horizontal sync — HS, and display enable — DE). Other functions include an internal cursor register which generates a cursor output when its contents compare to the current refresh address. A light pen strobe input signal allows capture of the refresh address in an internal light pen register.

All timing in the CRTC is derived from the CLK input. In alphanumeric terminals, this signal is the character rate. The video rate or "dot" clock is externally divided by high-speed logic (TTL) to generate the CLK input. The high-speed logic must also generate the timing and control signals necessary for the shift register, latch, and MUX control.

The processor communicates with the CRTC through an 8-bit data bus by reading or writing into the 19 registers.

The refresh memory address is multiplexed between the processor and the CRTC. Data appears on a secondary bus separate from the processor's bus. The secondary data bus concept in no way precludes using the refresh RAM for other purposes. It looks like any other RAM to the processor. A number of approaches are possible for solving contentions for the refresh memory:

1. Processor always gets priority. (Generally, "hash" occurs as MPU and CRTC clocks are not synchronized.)

2. Processor gets priority access anytime, but can be synchronized by an interrupt to perform accesses only during horizontal and vertical retrace times.

3. Synchronize the processor with memory wait cycles (states).

4. Synchronize the processor to the character rate as shown in Figure 9. The M6800 processor family works works very well in this configuration as constant cycle lengths are present. This method provides no overhead for the processor as there is never a contention for a memory access. All accesses are transparent.

FIGURE 8 — CHARACTER DISPLAY ON THE SCREEN AND VIDEO SIGNAL

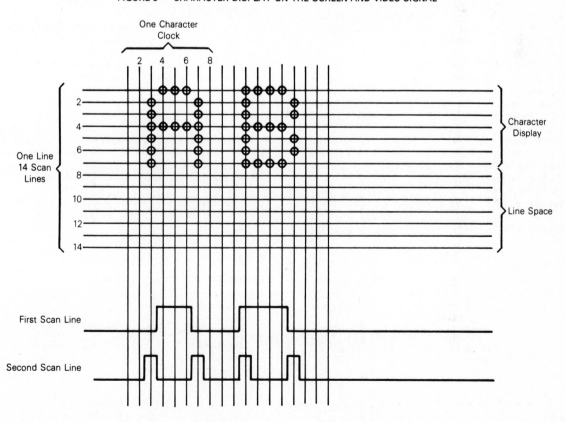

FIGURE 9 — TRANSPARENT REFRESH MEMORY
CONFIGURATION TIMING USING M6800 FAMILY MPU

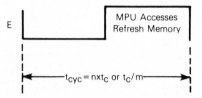

Where: m, n are integers; t_C is character period

PIN DESCRIPTION

PROCESSOR INTERFACE

The CRTC interfaces to a processor bus on the bidirectional data bus (D0-D7) using $\overline{CS}$, RS, E, and R/$\overline{W}$ for control signals.

Data Bus (D0-D7) — The bidirectional data lines (D0-D7) allow data transfers between the internal CRTC register file and the processor. Data bus output drivers are in the high-impedance state until the processor performs a CRTC read operation.

Enable (E) — The enable signal is a high-impedance TTL/MOS compatible input which enables the data bus input/output buffers and clocks data to and from the CRTC. This signal is usually derived from the processor clock. The high-to-low transition is the active edge.

Chip Select ($\overline{CS}$) — The $\overline{CS}$ line is a high-impedance TTL/MOS compatible input which selects the CRTC, when low, to read or write to the internal register file. This signal should only be active when there is a valid stable address being decoded from the processor.

Register Select (RS) — The RS line is a high-impedance TTL/MOS compatible input which selects either the address register (RS = 0) or one of the data register (RS = 1) or the internal register file.

Read/Write (R/$\overline{W}$) — The R/$\overline{W}$ line is a high-impedance TTL/MOS compatible input which determines whether the internal register file gets written or read. A write is defined as a low level.

CRT CONTROL

The CRTC provides horizontal sync (HS), vertical sync (VS), and display enable (DE) signals.

NOTE

Care should be exercised when interfacing to CRT monitors, as many monitors claiming to be "TTL compatible" have transistor input circuits which require the CRTC or TTL devices buffering signals from the CRTC/video circuits to exceed the maximum-rated drive currents.

Vertical Sync (VS) and Horizontal Sync (HS) — These TTL-compatible outputs are active high signals which drive the monitor directly or are fed to the video processing circuitry to generate a composite video signal. The VS signal determines the vertical position of the displayed text while the HS signal determines the horizontal position of the displayed text.

Display Enable (DE) — This TTL-compatible output is an active high signal which indicates the CRTC is providing addressing in the active display area.

REFRESH MEMORY/CHARACTER GENERATOR ADDRESSING

The CRTC provides memory addresses (MA0-MA13) to scan the refresh RAM. Row addresses (RA0-RA4) are also provided for use with character generator ROMs. In a graphics system, both the memory addresses and the row addresses would be used to scan the refresh RAM. Both the memory addresses and the row addresses continue to run during vertical retrace thus allowing the CRTC to provide the refresh addresses required to refresh dynamic RAMs.

Refresh Memory Addresses (MA0-MA13) — These 14 outputs are used to refresh the CRT screen with pages of data located within a 16K block of refresh memory. These outputs are capable of driving one standard TTL load and 30 pF.

Row Addresses (RA0-RA4) — These five outputs from the internal row address counter are used to address the character generator ROM. These outputs are capable of driving one standard TTL load and 30 pF.

OTHER PINS

Cursor — This TTL-compatible output indicates a valid cursor address to external video processing logic. It is an active high signal.

Clock (CLK) — The CLK is a TTL/MOS-compatible input used to synchronize all CRT functions except for the processor interface. An external dot counter is used to derive this signal which is usually the character rate in an alphanumeric CRT. The active transition is high-to-low.

 MOTOROLA *Semiconductor Products Inc.*

Light Pen Strobe (LPSTB) — A low-to-high transition on this high-impedance TTL/MOS-compatible input latches the current Refresh Address in the light pen register. The latching of the refresh address is internally synchronized to the character clock (CLK).

V$_{CC}$ and V$_{SS}$ — These inputs supply +5 Vdc ±5% to the CRTC.

$\overline{RESET}$ — The $\overline{RESET}$ input is used to reset the CRTC. A low level on the $\overline{RESET}$ input forces the CRTC into the following state:

(a) All counters in the CRTC are cleared and the device stops the display operation.

(b) All the outputs are driven low.

NOTE

The horizontal sync output is not defined until after R2 is programmed.

(c) The control registers of the CRTC are not affected and remain unchanged.

Functionality of $\overline{RESET}$ differs from that of other M6800 parts in the following functions:

(a) The $\overline{RESET}$ input and the LPSTB input are encoded as shown in Table 1.

TABLE 1 — CRTC OPERATING MODE

$\overline{RESET}$	LPSTB	Operating Mode
0	0	Reset
0	1	Test Mode
1	0	Normal Mode
1	1	Normal Mode

The test mode configures the memory addresses as two independent 7-bit counters to minimize test time.

(b) After $\overline{RESET}$ has gone low and (LPSTB=0), MA0-MA13 and RA0-RA4 will be driven low on the falling edge of CLK. $\overline{RESET}$ must remain low for at least one cycle of the character clock (CLK).

(c) The CRTC resumes the display operation immediately after the release of $\overline{RESET}$. DE and the CURSOR are not active until after the first frame has been displayed.

CRTC DESCRIPTION

The CRTC consists of programmable horizontal and vertical timing generators, programmable linear address register, programmable cursor logic, light pen capture register, and control circuitry for interface to a processor bus. A block diagram of the CRTC is shown in Figure 10.

All CRTC timing is derived from the CLK, usually the output of an external dot rate counter. Coincidence (CO) circuits continuously compare counter contents to the contents of the programmable register file, R0-R17. For horizontal timing generation, comparisons result in: 1) horizontal sync pulse (HS) of a frequency, position, and width determined by the registers; 2) horizontal display signal of a frequency, position, and duration determined by the registers.

The horizontal counter produces H clock which drives the scan line counter and vertical control. The contents of the raster counter are continuously compared to the maximum scan line address register. A coincidence resets the raster counter and clocks the vertical counter.

Comparisons of vertical counter contents and vertical registers result in: 1) vertical sync pulse (VS) of a frequency and position determined by the registers; 2) vertical display of a frequency and position determined by the registers.

The vertical control logic has other functions.

1. Generate row selects, RA0-RA4, from the raster count for the corresponding interlace or non-interlace modes.

2. Extend the number of scan lines in the vertical total by the amount programmed in the vertical total adjust register.

The linear address generator is driven by the CLK and locates the relative positions of characters in memory with their positions on the screen. Fourteen lines, MA0-MA13, are available for addressing up to four pages of 4K characters, eight pages of 2K characters, etc. Using the start address register, hardware scrolling through 16K characters is possible. The linear address generator repeats the same sequence of addresses for each scan line of a character row.

The cursor logic determines the cursor location, size, and blink rate on the screen. All are programmable.

The light pen strobe going high causes the current contents of the address counter to be latched in the light pen register. The contents of the light pen register are subsequently read by the processor.

Internal CRTC registers are programmed by the processor through the data bus, D0-D7, and the control signals — R/$\overline{W}$, $\overline{CS}$, RS, and E.

REGISTER FILE DESCRIPTIONS

The nineteen registers of the CRTC may be accessed through the data bus. Only two memory locations are required as one location is used as a pointer to address one of the remaining eighteen registers. These eighteen registers control horizontal timing, vertical timing, interlace operation, row address operation, and define the cursor, cursor address, start address, and light pen register. The register addresses and sizes are shown in Table 2.

ADDRESS REGISTER

The address register is a 5-bit write-only register used as an "indirect" or "pointer" register. It contains the address of one of the other eighteen registers. When both RS and $\overline{CS}$ are low, the address register is selected. When $\overline{CS}$ is low and RS is high, the register pointed to by the address register is selected.

TIMING REGISTERS R0-R9

Figure 11 shows the visible display area of a typical CRT monitor giving the point of reference for horizontal registers as the left-most displayed character position. Horizontal registers are programmed in character clock time units with respect to the reference as shown in Figure 12. The point of reference for the vertical registers is the top character position displayed. Vertical registers are programmed in scan line times with respect to the reference as shown in Figure 13.

Horizontal Total Register (R0) — This 8-bit write-only register determines the horizontal sync (HS) frequency by defining the HS period in character times. It is the total of the displayed characters plus the non-displayed character times (retrace) minus one.

 MOTOROLA *Semiconductor Products Inc.*

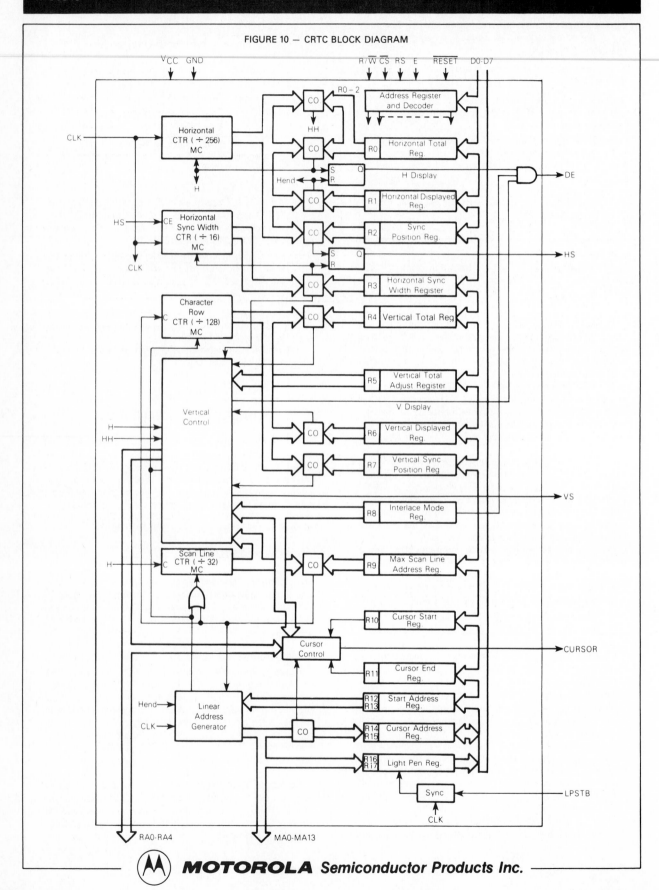

FIGURE 10 — CRTC BLOCK DIAGRAM

MOTOROLA *Semiconductor Products Inc.*

TABLE 2 — CRTC INTERNAL REGISTER ASSIGNMENT

$\overline{CS}$	RS	4	3	2	1	0	Register #	Register File	Program Unit	Read	Write	7	6	5	4	3	2	1	0
		Address Register										Number of Bits							
1	X	X	X	X	X	X	X	—	—	—	—								
0	0	X	X	X	X	X	AR	Address Register	—	No	Yes								
0	1	0	0	0	0	0	R0	Horizontal Total	Char.	No	Yes								
0	1	0	0	0	0	1	R1	Horizontal Displayed	Char.	No	Yes								
0	1	0	0	0	1	0	R2	H. Sync Position	Char.	No	Yes								
0	1	0	0	0	1	1	R3	Sync Width	—	No	Yes					H	H	H	H
0	1	0	0	1	0	0	R4	Vertical Total	Char. Row	No	Yes								
0	1	0	0	1	0	1	R5	V. Total Adjust	Scan Line	No	Yes								
0	1	0	0	1	1	0	R6	Vertical Displayed	Char. Row	No	Yes								
0	1	0	0	1	1	1	R7	V. Sync Position	Char. Row	No	Yes								
0	1	0	1	0	0	0	R8	Interlace Mode and Skew	Note 1	No	Yes							I	I
0	1	0	1	0	0	1	R9	Max Scan Line Address	Scan Line	No	Yes								
0	1	0	1	0	1	0	R10	Cursor Start	Scan Line	No	Yes		B	P		(Note 2)			
0	1	0	1	0	1	1	R11	Cursor End	Scan Line	No	Yes								
0	1	0	1	1	0	0	R12	Start Address (H)	—	No	Yes	0	0						
0	1	0	1	1	0	1	R13	Start Address (L)	—	No	Yes								
0	1	0	1	1	1	0	R14	Cursor (H)	—	Yes	Yes	0	0						
0	1	0	1	1	1	1	R15	Cursor (L)	—	Yes	Yes								
0	1	1	0	0	0	0	R16	Light Pen (H)	—	Yes	No	0	0						
0	1	1	0	0	0	1	R17	Light Pen (L)	—	Yes	No								

NOTES:

1. The interlace is shown in Table 3.
2. Bit 5 of the cursor start raster register is used for blink period control, and bit 6 is used to select blink or no-blink.

FIGURE 11 — ILLUSTRATION OF THE CRT SCREEN FORMAT

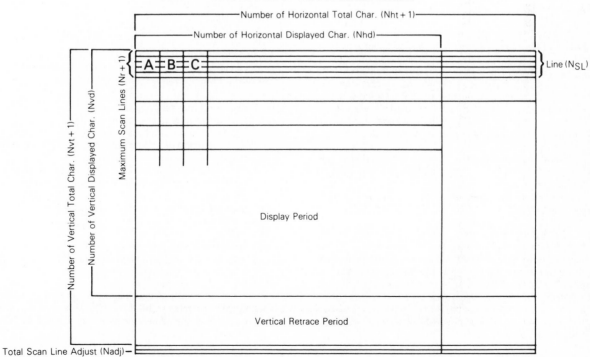

NOTE 1: Timing values are described in Table 5.

 MOTOROLA *Semiconductor Products Inc.*

Horizontal Displayed Register (R1) — This 8-bit write-only register determines the number of displayed characters per line. Any 8-bit number may be programmed as long as the contents of R0 are greater than the contents of R1.

Horizontal Sync Position Register (R2) — This 8-bit write-only register controls the HS position. The horizontal sync position defines the horizontal sync delay (front porch) and the horizontal scan delay (back porch). When the programmed value of this register is increased, the display on the CRT screen is shifted to the left. When the programmed value is decreased the display is shifted to the right. Any 8-bit number may be programmed as long as the sum of the contents of R2 and R3 are less than the contents of R0. R2 must be greater than R1.

Sync Width Register (R3) — This 8-bit write-only register determines the width of the horizontal sync (HS) pulse. The vertical sync pulse width is fixed at 16 scan-line times.

The HS pulse width may be programmed from 1-to-15 character clock periods thus allowing compatibility with the HS pulse width specifications of many different monitors. If zero is written into this register then no HS is provided.

Horizontal Timing Summary (Figure 12) — The difference between R0 and R1 is the horizontal blanking interval. This interval in the horizontal scan period allows the beam to return (retrace) to the left side of the screen. The retrace time is determined by the monitor's horizontal scan components. Retrace time is less than the horizontal blanking interval. A good rule of thumb is to make the horizontal blanking about 20% of the total horizontal scanning period for a CRT. In inexpensive TV receivers, the beam overscans the display screen so that aging of parts does not result in underscanning. Because of this, the retrace time should be about one third the horizontal scanning period. The horizontal sync delay, HS pulse width, and horizontal scan delay are typically programmed with a 1:2:2 ratio.

Vertical Total Register (R4) and Vertical Total Adjust Register (R5) — The frequency of VS is determined by both R4 and R5. The calculated number of character row times is usually an integer plus a fraction to get exactly a 50 or 60 Hz vertical refresh rate. The integer number of character row times minus one is programmed in the 7-bit write-only vertical total register (R4). The fraction of character line times is programmed in the 5-bit write-only vertical total adjust register (R5) as the number of scan lines required.

Vertical Displayed Register (R6) — This 7-bit write-only register specifies the number of displayed character rows on the CRT screen, and is programmed in character row times. Any number smaller than the contents of R4 may be programmed into R6.

Vertical Sync Position (R7) — This 7-bit write-only register controls the position of vertical sync with respect to the reference. It is programmed in character row times. When the programmed value of this register is increased, the display position of the CRT screen is shifted up. When the programmed value is decreased the display position is shifted down. Any number equal to or less than the vertical total (R4) and greater than or equal to the vertical displayed (R6) may be used.

Interlace Mode and Skew Register (R8) — The MC6845 only allows control of the interlace modes as programmed by the low order two bits of this write-only register. Table 3 shows the interlace modes available to the user. These modes are selected using the two low order bits of this 6-bit write-only register.

TABLE 3 — INTERLACE MODE REGISTER

Bit 1	Bit 0	Mode
0	0	Normal Sync Mode (Non-Interlace)
1	0	
0	1	Interlace Sync Mode
1	1	Interlace Sync and Video Mode

In the normal sync mode (non-interlace) only one field is available as shown in Figures 6 and 14a. Each scan line is refreshed at the VS frequency (e.g., 50 or 60 Hz).

Two interlace modes are available as shown in Figures 7, 14b, and 14c. The frame time is divided between even and odd alternating fields. The horizontal and vertical timing relationship (VS delayed by one half scan line time) results in the displacement of scan lines in the odd field with respect to the even field.

In the interlace sync mode the same information is painted in both fields as shown in Figure 14b. This is a useful mode for filling in a character to enhance readability.

In the interlace sync and video mode, shown in Figure 14c, alternating lines of the character are displayed in the even field and the odd field. This effectively doubles the given bandwidth of the CRT monitor.

Care must be taken when using either interlace mode to avoid an apparent flicker effect. This flicker effect is due to the doubling of the refresh time for all scan lines since each field is displayed alternately and may be minimized with proper monitor design (e.g., longer persistence phosphors).

In addition, there are restrictions on the programming of the CRTC registers for interlace operation:

1. The horizontal total register value, R0, must be odd (i.e., an even number of character times).
2. For interlace sync and video mode only, the maximum scan-line address, R9, must be odd (i.e., an even number of scan lines).
3. For interlace sync and video mode only, the number (Nvd) programmed into the vertical display register (R6) must be one half the actual number required. The even numbered scan lines are displayed in the even field and the odd numbered scan lines are displayed in the odd field.
4. For interlace sync and video mode only, the cursor start register (R10) and cursor end register (R11) must both be even or both odd depending on which field the cursor is to be displayed in. A full block cursor will be displayed in both the even and the odd field when the cursor end register (R11) is programmed to a value greater than the value in the maximum scan line address register (R9).

 MOTOROLA *Semiconductor Products Inc.*

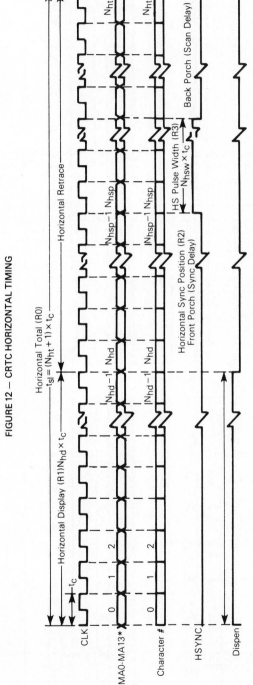

FIGURE 12 — CRTC HORIZONTAL TIMING

* Timing is shown for first displayed scan row only. See chart in Figure 15 for other rows. The initial MA is determined by the contents of start address register, R12/R13. Timing is shown for R12/R13 = 0.

NOTE: Timing values are described in Table 5.

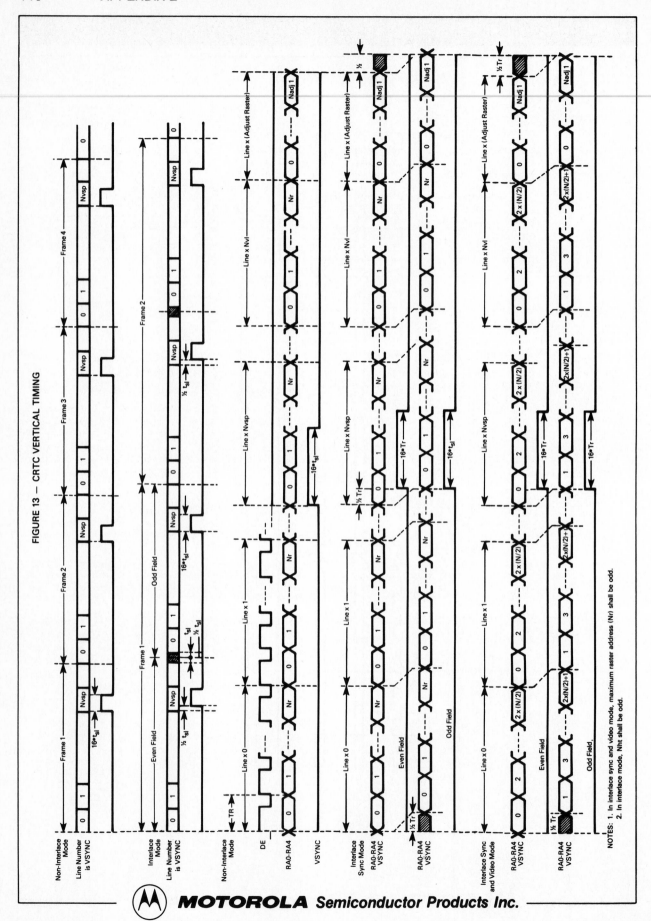

FIGURE 13 — CRTC VERTICAL TIMING

NOTES: 1. In interlace sync and video mode, maximum raster address (Nr) shall be odd.
2. In interlace mode, Nht shall be odd.

MOTOROLA *Semiconductor Products Inc.*

FIGURE 14 — INTERLACE CONTROL

(a) Normal Sync

(b) Interlace Sync

(c) Interlace Sync and Video

Maximum Scan Line Address Register (R9) — This 5-bit write-only register determines the number of scan lines per character row including the spacing; thus, controlling operation of the row address counter. The programmed value is a maximum address and is one less than the number of scan lines.

CURSOR CONTROL

Cursor Start Register (R10) and Cursor End Reigster (R11) — These registers allow a cursor of up to 32 scan lines in height to be placed on any scan line of the character block as shown in Figure 15. R10 is a 7-bit write-only register used to define the start scan line and the cursor blink rate. Bits 5 and 6 of the cursor start address register control the cursor operation as shown in Table 4. Non-display, display, and two blink modes (16 times or 32 times the field period) are available. R11 is a 5-bit write-only register which defines the last scan line of the cursor.

TABLE 4 — CURSOR START REGISTER

Bit 6	Bit 5	Cursor Display Mode
0	0	Non-Blink
0	1	Cursor Non-Display
1	0	Blink, 1/16 Field Rate
1	1	Blink, 1/32 Field Rate

Example of cursor display mode

When an external blink feature on characters is required, it may be necessary to perform cursor blink externally so that both blink rates are synchronized. Note that an invert/non-invert cursor is easily implemented by programming the CRTC for a blinking cursor and externally inverting the video signal with an exclusive-OR gate.

Cursor Register (R14-H, R15-L) — This 14-bit read/write register pair is programmed to position the cursor anywhere in the refresh RAM area; thus, allowing hardware paging and scrolling through memory without loss of the original cursor position. It consists of an 8-bit low order (MA0-MA7) register and a 6-bit high order (MA8-MA13) register.

OTHER REGISTERS

Start Address Register (R12-H, R13-L) — This 14-bit write-only register pair controls the first address output by the CRTC after vertical blanking. It consists of an 8-bit low order (MA0-MA7) register and a 6-bit high order (MA8-MA13) register. The start address register determines which portion of the refresh RAM is displayed on the CRT screen. Hardware scrolling by character or page may be accomplished by modifying the contents of this register.

Light Pen Register (R16-H, R17-L) — This 14-bit read-only register pair captures the refresh address output by the CRTC on the positive edge of a pulse input to the LPSTB pin. It consists of an 8-bit low order (MA0-MA7) register and a 6-bit high order (MA8-MA13) register. Since the light pen pulse is asynchronous with respect to refresh address timing an internal synchronizer is designed into the CRTC. Due to delays (Figure 5) in this circuit, the value of R16 and R17 will need to be corrected in software. Figure 16 shows an interrupt driven approach although a polling routine could be used.

 MOTOROLA *Semiconductor Products Inc.*

FIGURE 15 — CURSOR CONTROL

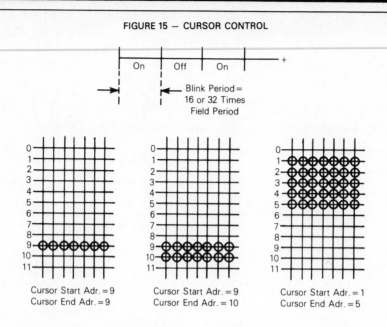

Cursor Start Adr. = 9
Cursor End Adr. = 9

Cursor Start Adr. = 9
Cursor End Adr. = 10

Cursor Start Adr. = 1
Cursor End Adr. = 5

FIGURE 16 — INTERFACING OF LIGHT PEN

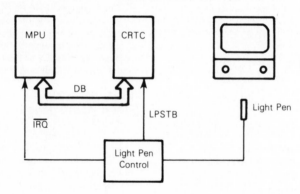

OPERATION OF THE CRTC

TIMING CHART OF THE CRT INTERFACE SIGNALS

Timing charts of CRT interface signals are illustrated in this section. When values listed in Table 5 are programmed into CRTC control registers, the device provides the outputs as shown in the timing diagrams (Figures 12, 13, 17, and 18). The screen format is shown in Figure 11 which illustrates the relation between refresh memory address (MA0-MA13), raster address (RA0-RA4), and the position on the screen. In this example, the start address is assumed to be zero.

TABLE 5 — VALUES PROGRAMMED INTO CRTC REGISTERS

Reg. #	Register Name	Value	Programmed Value
R0	H. Total	$N_{ht} + 1$	N_{ht}
R1	H. Displayed	N_{hd}	N_{hd}
R2	H. Sync Position	N_{hsp}	N_{hsp}
R3	H. Sync Width	N_{hsw}	N_{hsw}
R4	V. Total	$N_{vt} + 1$	N_{vt}
R5	V. Scan Line Adjust	N_{adj}	N_{adj}
R6	V. Displayed	N_{vd}	N_{vd}
R7	V. Sync Position	N_{vsp}	N_{vsp}
R8	Interlace Mode		
R9	Max. Scan Line Address	N_{sl}	N_{sl}

 MOTOROLA *Semiconductor Products Inc.*

July 1990

PC16450C/NS16450, PC8250A/INS8250A
Universal Asynchronous Receiver/Transmitter

General Description

This part functions as a serial data input/output interface in a microcomputer system. The system software determines the functional configuration of the UART via a TRI-STATE® 8-bit bidirectional data bus.

The UART performs serial-to-parallel conversion on data characters received from a peripheral device or a MODEM, and parallel-to-serial conversion on data characters received from the CPU. The CPU can read the complete status of the UART at any time during the functional operation. Status information reported includes the type and condition of the transfer operations being performed by the UART, as well as any error conditions (parity, overrun, framing, or break interrupt).

The UART includes a programmable baud rate generator that is capable of dividing the timing reference clock input by divisors of 1 to ($2^{16}-1$), and producing a 16 × clock for driving the internal transmitter logic. Provisions are also included to use this 16 × clock to drive the receiver logic. The UART includes a complete MODEM-control capability and a processor-interrupt system. Interrupts can be programmed to the user's requirements, minimizing the computing required to handle the communications link.

The PC16450C/NS16450 is an improved specification version of the PC8250C/INS8250-B Universal Asynchronous Receiver/Transmitter (UART). The UART is fabricated using National Semiconductor's advanced 1.25 µ CMOS process.

The PC16450C/NS16450 is functionally equivalent to the original NS16450, INS8250A, NS16C450 and INS82C50A, except that it has improved AC timing specifications and it is CMOS.

Features

■ Easily interfaces to most popular microprocessors.
■ Adds or deletes standard asynchronous communication bits (start, stop, and parity) to or from serial data stream.
■ Holding and shift registers eliminate the need for precise synchronization between the CPU and the serial data.
■ Independently controlled transmit, receive, line status, and data set interrupts.
■ Programmable baud generator allows division of any input clock by 1 to ($2^{16}-1$) and generates the internal 16 × clock.
■ Independent receiver clock input.
■ MODEM control functions (CTS, RTS, DSR, DTR, RI, and DCD).
■ Fully programmable serial-interface characteristics:
— 5-, 6-, 7-, or 8-bit characters
— Even, odd, or no-parity bit generation and detection
— 1-, 1½-, or 2-stop bit generation
— Baud generation (DC to 256 kbaud)
■ False start bit detection.
■ Complete status reporting capabilities.
■ TRI-STATE TTL drive capabilities for bidirectional data bus and control bus.
■ Line break generation and detection.
■ Internal diagnostic capabilities:
— Loopback controls for communications link fault isolation
— Break, parity, overrun, framing error simulation.
■ Fully prioritized interrupt system controls.

Connection Diagram

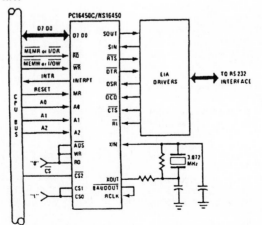

TL/C/8401–1

TRI-STATE® is a registered trademark of National Semiconductor Corporation.

5.0 Block Diagram

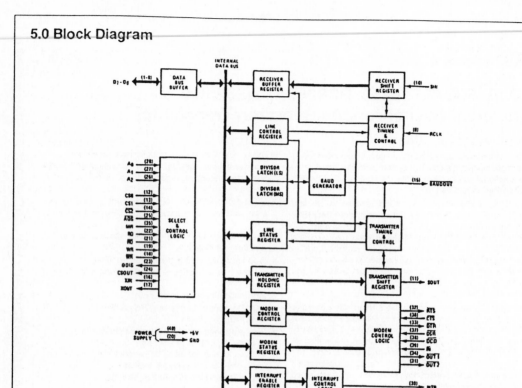

Note: Applicable pinout numbers are included within parenthesis.

TL/C/8401–10

6.0 Pin Descriptions

The following describes the function of all UART pins. Some of these descriptions reference internal circuits.

In the following descriptions, a low represents a logic 0 (0V nominal) and a high represents a logic 1 (+2.4V nominal).

A0, A1, A2: Register Select Pins 26–28: Address signals connected to these 3 inputs select a UART register for the CPU to read from or write to during data transfer. The Register Addresses table associates these address inputs with the register they select. Note that the state of the Divisor Latch Access Bit (DLAB), which is the most significant bit of the Line Control Register, affects the selection of certain UART registers. The DLAB must be set high by the system software to access the Baud Generator Divisor Latches.

ADS: Address Strobe Pin 25: The positive edge of an active Address Strobe (ADS) signal latches the Register Select (A0, A1, A2) and Chip Select (CS0, CS1, CS2) signals.

Note: An active ADS input is required when the Register Select (A0, A1, A2) signals are not stable for the duration of a read or write operation. If not required, tie the ADS input permanently low.

BAUDOUT: Baud Out Pin 15: This is the 16 × clock signal from the transmitter section of the UART. The clock rate is equal to the main reference oscillator frequency divided by the specified divisor in the Baud Generator Divisor Latches. The BAUDOUT may also be used for the receiver section by tying this output to the RCLK input of the chip.

Register Addresses

DLAB	A_2	A_1	A_0	Register
0	0	0	0	Receiver Buffer (read), Transmitter Holding Register (write)
0	0	0	1	Interrupt Enable
X	0	1	0	Interrupt Identification (read only)
X	0	1	1	Line Control
X	1	0	0	MODEM Control
X	1	0	1	Line Status
X	1	1	0	MODEM Status
X	1	1	1	Scratch
1	0	0	0	Divisor Latch (least significant byte)
1	0	0	1	Divisor Latch (most significant byte)

6.0 Pin Descriptions (Continued)

CS0, CS1, $\overline{CS2}$: Chip Select Pins 12–14: When CS0 and CS1 are high and $\overline{CS2}$ is low, the chip is selected. This enables communication between the UART and the CPU. The positive edge of an active Address Strobe signal latches the decoded chip select signals, completing chip selection. If $\overline{ADS}$ is always low, valid chip selects should stabilize according to the t_{CSW} parameter.

CSOUT: Chip Select Out Pin 24: When high, it indicates that the chip has been selected by active, CS0, CS1, and $\overline{CS2}$ inputs. No data transfer can be initiated until the CSOUT signal is a logic 1. CSOUT goes low when the UART is deselected.

$\overline{CTS}$: Clear to Send Pin 36: When low, this indicates that the MODEM or data set is ready to exchange data. The $\overline{CTS}$ signal is a MODEM status input whose conditions can be tested by the CPU reading bit 4 (CTS) of the MODEM Status Register. Bit 4 is the complement of the $\overline{CTS}$ signal. Bit 0 (DCTS) of the MODEM Status Register indicates whether the $\overline{CTS}$ input has changed state since the previous reading of the MODEM Status Register. $\overline{CTS}$ has no effect on the Transmitter.

Note: Whenever the CTS bit of the MODEM Status Register changes state, an interrupt is generated if the MODEM Status Interrupt is enabled.

D_7–D_0: Data Bus, Pins 1–8: This bus is comprised of eight TRI-STATE input/output lines. The bus provides bidirectional communications between the UART and the CPU. Data, control words, and status information are transferred via the D_7–D_0 Data Bus.

$\overline{DCD}$: Data Carrier Detect Pin 38: When low, indicates that the data carrier has been detected by the MODEM or data set. The $\overline{DCD}$ signal is a MODEM status input whose condition can be tested by the CPU reading bit 7 (DCD) of the MODEM Status Register. Bit 7 is the complement of the $\overline{DCD}$ signal. Bit 3 (DDCD) of the MODEM Status Register indicates whether the $\overline{DCD}$ input has changed state since the previous reading of the MODEM Status Register. $\overline{DCD}$ has no effect on the receiver.

Note: Whenever the DCD bit of the MODEM Status Register changes state, an interrupt is generated if the MODEM Status Interrupt is enabled.

DDIS: Driver Disable Pin 23: This goes low whenever the CPU is reading data from the UART. It can disable or control the direction of a data bus transceiver between the CPU and the UART (see Typical Interface for a High Capacity Data Bus).

$\overline{DSR}$: Data Set Ready Pin 37: When low, this indicates that the MODEM or data set is ready to establish the communications link with the UART. The $\overline{DSR}$ signal is a MODEM status input whose condition can be tested by the CPU reading bit 5 (DSR) of the MODEM Status Register. Bit 5 is the complement of the $\overline{DSR}$ signal. Bit 1 (DDSR) of the MODEM Status Register indicates whether the $\overline{DSR}$ input has changed state since the previous reading of the MODEM Status Register.

Note: Whenever the DSR bit of the MODEM Status Register changes state, an interrupt is generated if the MODEM Status Interrupt is enabled.

$\overline{DTR}$: Data Terminal Ready Pin 33: When low, this informs the MODEM or data set that the UART is ready to establish a communications link. The $\overline{DTR}$ output signal can be set to an active low by programming bit 0 (DTR) of the MODEM Control Register to a high level. A Master Reset operation sets this signal to its inactive (high) state. Loop mode operation holds this signal in its inactive state.

INTR: Interrupt Pin 30: This goes high whenever any one of the following interrupt types has an active high condition and is enabled via the IER: Receiver Line Status; Received Data Available; Transmitter Holding Register Empty; and MODEM Status. The INTR signal is reset low upon the appropriate interrupt service or a Master Reset operation.

MR: Master Reset Pin 35: When this input is high, it clears all the registers (except the Receiver Buffer, Transmitter Holding, and Divisor Latches), and the control logic of the UART. The states of various output signals (SOUT, INTR, $\overline{OUT\ 1}$, $\overline{OUT\ 2}$, $\overline{RTS}$, $\overline{DTR}$) are affected by an active MR input. (Refer to Table I.) This input is buffered with a TTL-compatible Schmitt Trigger with 0.5V typical hysteresis.

$\overline{OUT\ 1}$: Output 1 Pin 34: This user-designated output can be set to an active low by programming bit 2 (OUT 1) of the MODEM Control Register to a high level. A Master Reset operation sets this signal to its inactive (high) state. Loop mode operation holds this signal in its inactive state. In the XMOS parts this will achieve TTL levels.

$\overline{OUT\ 2}$: Output 2 Pin 31: This user-designated output can be set to an active low, by programming bit 3 (OUT 2) of the MODEM Control Register to a high level. A Master Reset operation sets this signal to its inactive (high) state. Loop mode operation holds this signal in its inactive state. In the XMOS parts this will achieve TTL levels.

RCLK: Receiver Clock Pin 9: This input is the 16 × baud rate clock for the receiver section of the chip.

RD, $\overline{RD}$, Read Pins 22 and 21: When RD is high or $\overline{RD}$ is low while the chip is selected, the CPU can read status information or data from the selected UART register.

Note: Only an active RD or $\overline{RD}$ input is required to transfer data from the UART during a read operation. Therefore, tie either the RD input permanently low or the $\overline{RD}$ input permanently high, when it is not used.

$\overline{RI}$: Ring Indicator Pin 39: When low, this indicates that a telephone ringing signal has been received by the MODEM or data set. The $\overline{RI}$ signal is a MODEM status input whose condition can be tested by the CPU reading bit 6 (RI) of the MODEM Status Register. Bit 6 is the complement of the $\overline{RI}$ signal. Bit 2 (TERI) of the MODEM Status Register indicates whether the $\overline{RI}$ input signal has changed from a low to a high state since the previous reading of the MODEM Status Register.

Note: Whenever the RI bit of the MODEM Status Register changes from a high to a low state, an interrupt is generated if the MODEM Status interrupt is enabled.

$\overline{RTS}$: Request to Send Pin 32: When low, this informs the MODEM or data set that the UART is ready to exchange data. The $\overline{RTS}$ output signal can be set to an active low by programming bit 1 (RTS) of the MODEM Control Register. A Master Reset operation sets this signal to its inactive (high) state. Loop mode operation holds this signal in its inactive state.

SIN: Serial Input Pin 10: Serial data input from the communications link (peripheral device, MODEM, or data set).

SOUT: Serial Output Pin 11: This is the composite serial data output to the communications link (peripheral, MODEM or data set). The SOUT signal is set to the Marking (logic 1) state upon a Master Reset operation or when the transmitter is idle.

V_{DD}, Pin 40: +5V supply.

V_{SS}, Pin 20: Ground (0V) reference.

6.0 Pin Descriptions (Continued)

WR, $\overline{WR}$: Write Pins 19 and 18: When WR is high or $\overline{WR}$ is low while the chip is selected, the CPU can write control words or data into the selected UART register.

Note: Only an active WR or $\overline{WR}$ input is required to transfer data to the UART during a write operation. Therefore, tie either the WR input permanently low or the $\overline{WR}$ input permanently high, when it is not used.

XIN: (External Crystal Input), Pin 16: This signal input is used in conjunction with XOUT to form a feedback circuit for the baud rate generator's oscillator. If a clock signal will be generated off-chip, then it should drive the baud rate generator through this pin.

XOUT: (External Crystal Output), Pin 17: This signal output is used in conjunction with XIN to form a feedback circuit for the baud rate generator's oscillator. If the clock signal will be generated off-chip, then this pin is unused.

7.0 Connection Diagrams

Dual-In-Line Package

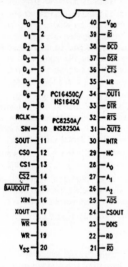

TL/C/8401–11

Top View

Order Number PC16450N/NS16450N
or PC8250AN/INS8250AN
See NS Package Number N40A

PLCC Package

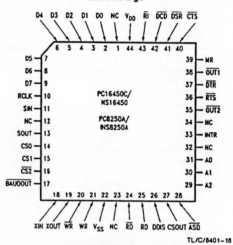

TL/C/8401–18

Top View

Order Number PC16450V/NS16450V
or PC8250AV/INS8250AV
See NS Package Number V44A

TABLE I. UART Reset Functions

Register/Signal	Reset Control	Reset State
Interrupt Enable Register	Master Reset	0000 0000 (Note 1)
Interrupt Identification Register	Master Reset	0000 0001
Line Control Register	Master Reset	0000 0000
MODEM Control Register	Master Reset	0000 0000
Line Status Register	Master Reset	0110 0000
MODEM Status Register	Master Reset	XXXX 0000 (Note 2)
SOUT	Master Reset	High
INTR (RCVR Errs)	Read LSR/MR	Low
INTR (RCVR Data Ready)	Read RBR/MR	Low
INTR (THRE)	Read IIR/Write THR/MR	Low
INTR (Modem Status Changes)	Read MSR/MR	Low
$\overline{OUT\,2}$	Master Reset	High
$\overline{RTS}$	Master Reset	High
$\overline{DTR}$	Master Reset	High
$\overline{OUT\,1}$	Master Reset	High

Note 1: Boldface bits are permanently low.

Note 2: Bits 7–4 are driven by the input signals.

8.0 Registers

The system programmer may access any of the UART registers summarized in Table II via the CPU. These registers control UART operations including transmission and reception of data. Each register bit in Table II has its name and reset state shown.

8.1 LINE CONTROL REGISTER

The system programmer specifies the format of the asynchronous data communications exchange and sets the Divisor Latch Access bit via the Line Control Register (LCR). The programmer can also read the contents of the Line Control Register. The read capability simplifies system programming and eliminates the need for separate storage in system memory of the line characteristics. Table II shows the contents of the LCR. Details on each bit follow:

Bits 0 and 1: These two bits specify the number of bits in each transmitted or received serial character. The encoding of bits 0 and 1 is as follows:

Bit 1	Bit 0	Character Length
0	0	5 Bits
0	1	6 Bits
1	0	7 Bits
1	1	8 Bits

Bit 2: This bit specifies the number of Stop bits transmitted and received in each serial character. If bit 2 is a logic 0, one Stop bit is generated or checked in the transmitted data. If bit 2 is a logic 1 when a 5-bit word length is selected via bits 0 and 1, one and a half Stop bits are generated. If

TABLE II. Summary of Registers

	Register Address										
	0 DLAB = 0	0 DLAB = 0	1 DLAB = 0	2	3	4	5	6	7	0 DLAB = 1	1 DLAB = 1
Bit No.	Receiver Buffer Register (Read Only)	Transmitter Holding Register (Write Only)	Interrupt Enable Register	Interrupt Ident. Register (Read Only)	Line Control Register	MODEM Control Register	Line Status Register	MODEM Status Register	Scratch Register	Divisor Latch (LS)	Divisor Latch (MS)
	RBR	THR	IER	IIR	LCR	MCR	LSR	MSR	SCR	DLL	DLM
0	Data Bit 0 (Note 1)	Data Bit 0	Received Data Available	"0" if Interrupt Pending	Word Length Select Bit 0 (WLS0)	Data Terminal Ready (DTR)	Data Ready (DR)	Delta Clear to Send (DCTS)	Bit 0	Bit 0	Bit 8
1	Data Bit 1	Data Bit 1	Transmitter Holding Register Empty	Interrupt ID Bit (0)	Word Length Select Bit 1 (WLS1)	Request to Send (RTS)	Overrun Error (OE)	Delta Data Set Ready (DDSR)	Bit 1	Bit 1	Bit 9
2	Data Bit 2	Data Bit 2	Receiver Line Status	Interrupt ID Bit (1)	Number of Stop Bits (STB)	Out 1	Parity Error (PE)	Trailing Edge Ring Indicator (TERI)	Bit 2	Bit 2	Bit 10
3	Data Bit 3	Data Bit 3	MODEM Status	0	Parity Enable (PEN)	Out 2	Framing Error (FE)	Delta Data Carrier Detect (DDCD)	Bit 3	Bit 3	Bit 11
4	Data Bit 4	Data Bit 4	0	0	Even Parity Select (EPS)	Loop	Break Interrupt (BI)	Clear to Send (CTS)	Bit 4	Bit 4	Bit 12
5	Data Bit 5	Data Bit 5	0	0	Stick Parity	0	Transmitter Holding Register (THRE)	Data Set Ready (DSR)	Bit 5	Bit 5	Bit 13
6	Data Bit 6	Data Bit 6	0	0	Set Break	0	Transmitter Empty (TEMT)	Ring Indicator (RI)	Bit 6	Bit 6	Bit 14
7	Data Bit 7	Data Bit 7	0	0	Divisor Latch Access Bit (DLAB)	0	0	Data Carrier Detect (DCD)	Bit 7	Bit 7	Bit 15

Note 1: Bit 0 is the least significant bit. It is the first bit serially transmitted or received.

8.0 Registers (Continued)

bit 2 is a logic 1 when either a 6-, 7-, or 8-bit word length is selected, two Stop bits are generated. The Receiver checks the first Stop-bit only, regardless of the number of Stop bits selected.

Bit 3: This bit is the Parity Enable bit. When bit 3 is a logic 1, a Parity bit is generated (transmit data) or checked (receive data) between the last data word bit and Stop bit of the serial data. (The Parity bit is used to produce an even or odd number of 1s when the data word bits and the Parity bit are summed.)

Bit 4: This bit is the Even Parity Select bit. When bit 3 is a logic 1 and bit 4 is a logic 0, an odd number of logic 1s is transmitted or checked in the data word bits and Parity bit. When bit 3 is a logic 1 and bit 4 is a logic 1, an even number of logic 1s is transmitted or checked.

Bit 5: This bit is the Stick Parity bit. When bits 3, 4 and 5 are logic 1 the Parity bit is transmitted and checked as a logic 0. If bits 3 and 5 are 1 and bit 4 is a logic 0 then the Parity bit is transmitted and checked as a logic 1. If bit 5 is a logic 0 Stick Parity is disabled.

Bit 6: This bit is the Break Control bit. It causes a break condition to be transmitted by the UART. When it is set to a logic 1, the serial output (SOUT) is forced to the Spacing (logic 0) state. The break is disabled by clearing bit 6 to a logic 0. The Break Control bit acts only on SOUT and has no effect on the transmitter logic.

Note: This feature enables the CPU to alert a terminal in a computer communications system. If the following sequence is used, no erroneous or extraneous characters will be transmitted because of the break.

1. Load an all 0s, pad character, in response to THRE.

2. Set break after the next THRE.

3. Wait for the transmitter to be idle, (TEMT = 1), and clear break when normal transmission has to be restored.

During the break, the Transmitter can be used as a character timer to accurately establish the break duration.

Bit 7: This bit is the Divisor Latch Access Bit (DLAB). It must be set high (logic 1) to access the Divisor Latches of the Baud Generator during a Read or Write operation. It must be set low (logic 0) to access the Receiver Buffer, the Transmitter Holding Register, or the Interrupt Enable Register.

8.2 TYPICAL CLOCK CIRCUITS

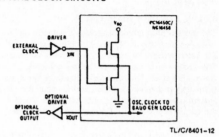

TL/C/8401–12

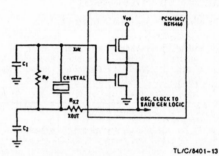

TL/C/8401–13

Typical Oscillator Networks

Crystal	R_P	R_{X2}	C_1	C_2
1.8–8 MHz	1 MΩ	1.5k	10–30 pF	40–60 pF

Note: These R and C values are approximate and may vary 2X depending on the crystal characteristics. All crystal circuits should be designed specifically for the system.

TABLE III. Baud Rates, Divisors and Crystals

Baud Rate	1.8432 MHz Crystal		3.072 MHz Crystal		8.0 MHz Crystal	
	Decimal Divisor for 16 × Clock	Percent Error	Decimal Divisor for 16 × Clock	Percent Error	Decimal Divisor for 16 × Clock	Percent Error
50	2304	—	3840	—	10000	—
75	1536	—	2560	—	6667	0.005
110	1047	0.026	1745	0.026	4545	0.010
134.5	857	0.058	1428	0.034	3717	0.013
150	768	—	1280	—	3333	0.010
300	384	—	640	—	1667	0.020
600	192	—	320	—	833	0.040
1200	96	—	160	—	417	0.080
1800	64	—	107	0.312	277	0.080
2000	58	0.69	96	—	250	—
2400	48	—	80	—	208	0.160
3600	32	—	53	0.628	139	0.080
4800	24	—	40	—	104	0.160
7200	16	—	27	1.23	69	0.644
9600	12	—	20	—	52	0.160
19200	6	—	10	—	26	0.160
38400	3	—	5	—	13	0.160
56000	2	2.86	—	—	9	0.790
128000	—	—	—	—	4	2.344
					2	2.344

8.0 Registers (Continued)

8.3 PROGRAMMABLE BAUD GENERATOR

The UART contains a programmable Baud Generator that is capable of taking any clock input from DC to 8 MHz and dividing it by any divisor from 1 to $2^{16}-1$. The output frequency of the Baud Generator is 16 × the Baud [divisor ≠ = (frequency input) ÷ (baud rate × 16)]. Two 8-bit latches store the divisor in a 16-bit binary format. These Divisor Latches must be loaded during initialization in order to ensure proper operation of the Baud Generator. Upon loading either of the Divisor Latches, a 16-bit Baud counter is immediately loaded.

Table III provides decimal divisors to use with crystal frequencies of 1.8432 MHz, 3.072 MHz and 8 MHz for common baud rates. For baud rates of 38400 and below, the error obtained is minimal. The accuracy of the desired baud rate is dependent on the crystal frequency chosen. Using a division of 0 is not recommended.

8.4 LINE STATUS REGISTER

This 8-bit register provides status information to the CPU concerning the data transfer. Table II shows the contents of the Line Status Register. Details on each bit follow:

Bit 0: This bit is the receiver Data Ready (DR) indicator. Bit 0 is set to a logic 1 whenever a complete incoming character has been received and transferred into the Receiver Buffer Register. Bit 0 is reset to a logic 0 by reading the data in the Receiver Buffer Register.

Bit 1: This bit is the Overrun Error (OE) indicator. Bit 1 indicates that data in the Receiver Buffer Register was not read by the CPU before the next character was transferred into the Receiver Buffer Register, thereby destroying the previous character. The OE indicator is set to a logic 1 upon detection of an overrun condition and reset whenever the CPU reads the contents of the Line Status Register.

Bit 2: This bit is the Parity Error (PE) indicator. Bit 2 indicates that the received data character does not have the correct even or odd parity, as selected by the even-parity-select bit. The PE bit is set to a logic 1 upon detection of a parity error and is reset to a logic 0 whenever the CPU reads the contents of the Line Status Register.

Bit 3: This bit is the Framing Error (FE) indicator. Bit 3 indicates that the received character did not have a valid Stop bit. Bit 3 is set to a logic 1 whenever the Stop bit following the last data bit or parity bit is a logic 0 (Spacing level). The FE indicator is reset whenever the CPU reads the contents of the Line Status Register. The UART will try to resynchronize after a framing error. To do this it assumes that the framing error was due to the next start bit, so it samples this "start" bit twice and then takes in the "data".

Bit 4: This bit is the Break Interrupt (BI) indicator. Bit 4 is set to a logic 1 whenever the received data input is held in the Spacing (logic 0) state for longer than a full word transmission time (that is, the total time of Start bit + data bits + Parity + Stop bits). The BI indicator is reset whenever the CPU reads the contents of the Line Status Register. Restarting after a break is received, requires the SIN pin to be logical 1 for at least ½ bit time.

Note: Bits 1 through 4 are the error conditions that produce a Receiver Line Status interrupt whenever any of the corresponding conditions are detected and the interrupt is enabled.

Bit 5: This bit is the Transmitter Holding Register Empty (THRE) indicator. Bit 5 indicates that the UART is ready to accept a new character for transmission. In addition, this bit causes the UART to issue an interrupt to the CPU when the Transmit Holding Register Empty Interrupt enable is set high. The THRE bit is set to a logic 1 when a character is transferred from the Transmitter Holding Register into the Transmitter Shift Register. The bit is reset to logic 0 whenever the CPU loads the Transmitter Holding Register.

Bit 6: This bit is the Transmitter Empty (TEMT) indicator. Bit 6 is set to a logic 1 whenever the Transmitter Holding Register (THR) and the Transmitter Shift Register (TSR) are both empty. It is reset to a logic 0 whenever either the THR or TSR contains a data character.

Bit 7: This bit is permanently set to logic 0.

Note: The Line Status Register is intended for read operations only. Writing to this register is not recommended as this operation is only used for factory testing.

TABLE IV. Interrupt Control Functions

Interrupt Identification Register				Interrupt Set and Reset Functions		
Bit 2	Bit 1	Bit 0	Priority Level	Interrupt Type	Interrupt Source	Interrupt Reset Control
0	0	1	—	None	None	—
1	1	0	Highest	Receiver Line Status	Overrun Error or Parity Error or Framing Error or Break Interrupt	Reading the Line Status Register
1	0	0	Second	Received Data Available	Receiver Data Available	Reading the Receiver Buffer Register
0	1	0	Third	Transmitter Holding Register Empty	Transmitter Holding Register Empty	Reading the IIR Register (if source of interrupt) or Writing into the Transmitter Holding Register
0	0	0	Fourth	MODEM Status	Clear to Send or Data Set Ready or Ring Indicator or Data Carrier Detect	Reading the MODEM Status Register

8.0 Registers (Continued)

8.5 INTERRUPT IDENTIFICATION REGISTER

In order to provide minimum software overhead during data character transfers, the UART prioritizes interrupts into four levels and records these in the Interrupt Identification Register. The four levels of interrupt conditions in order of priority are Receiver Line Status; Received Data Ready; Transmitter Holding Register Empty; and MODEM Status.

When the CPU accesses the IIR, the UART freezes all interrupts and indicates the highest priority pending interrupt to the CPU. While this CPU access is occurring, the UART records new interrupts, but does not change its current indication until the access is complete. Table II shows the contents of the IIR. Details on each bit follow:

Bit 0: This bit can be used in an interrupt environment to indicate whether an interrupt condition is pending. When bit 0 is a logic 0, an interrupt is pending and the IIR contents may be used as a pointer to the appropriate interrupt service routine. When bit 0 is a logic 1, no interrupt is pending.

Bits 1 and 2: These two bits of the IIR are used to identify the highest priority interrupt pending as indicated in Table IV.

Bits 3 through 7: These five bits of the IIR are always logic 0.

8.6 INTERRUPT ENABLE REGISTER

This register enables the four types of UART interrupts. Each interrupt can individually activate the interrupt (INTR) output signal. It is possible to totally disable the interrupt system by resetting bits 0 through 3 of the Interrupt Enable Register (IER). Similarly, setting bits of this register to a logic 1, enables the selected interrupt(s). Disabling an interrupt prevents it from being indicated as active in the IIR and from activating the INTR output signal. All other system functions operate in their normal manner, including the setting of the Line Status and MODEM Status Registers. Table II shows the contents of the IER. Details on each bit follow.

Bit 0: This bit enables the Received Data Available Interrupt when set to logic 1.

Bit 1: This bit enables the Transmitter Holding Register Empty Interrupt when set to logic 1.

Bit 2: This bit enables the Receiver Line Status Interrupt when set to logic 1.

Bit 3: This bit enables the MODEM Status Interrupt when set to logic 1.

Bits 4 through 7: These four bits are always logic 0.

8.7 MODEM CONTROL REGISTER

This register controls the interface with the MODEM or data set (or a peripheral device emulating a MODEM). The contents of the MODEM Control Register (MCR) are indicated in Table II and are described below. Table II shows the contents of the MCR. Details on each bit follow.

Bit 0: This bit controls the Data Terminal Ready (DTR) output. When bit 0 is set to a logic 1, the DTR output is forced to a logic 0. When bit 0 is reset to a logic 0, the DTR output is forced to a logic 1.

Note: The DTR output of the UART may be applied to an EIA inverting line driver (such as the DS1488) to obtain the proper polarity input at the succeeding MODEM or data set.

Bit 1: This bit controls the Request to Send (RTS) output. Bit 1 affects the RTS output in a manner identical to that described above for bit 0.

Bit 2: This bit controls the Output 1 (OUT 1) signal, which is an auxiliary user-designated output. Bit 2 affects the OUT 1 output in a manner identical to that described above for bit 0.

Bit 3: This bit controls the Output 2 (OUT 2) signal, which is an auxiliary user-designated output. Bit 3 affects the OUT 2 output in a manner identical to that described above for bit 0.

Bit 4: This bit provides a local loopback feature for diagnostic testing of the UART. When bit 4 is set to logic 1, the following occur: the transmitter Serial Output (SOUT) is set to the Marking (logic 1) state; the receiver Serial Input (SIN) is disconnected; the output of the Transmitter Shift Register is "looped back" into the Receiver Shift Register input; the four MODEM Control inputs (DSR, CTS, RI, and DCD) are disconnected; and the four MODEM Control outputs (DTR, RTS, OUT 1, and OUT 2) are internally connected to the four MODEM Control inputs. The MODEM Control output pins are forced to their inactive state (high). In the loopback mode, data that is transmitted is immediately received. This feature allows the processor to verify the transmit-and received-data paths of the UART.

In the loopback mode, the receiver and transmitter interrupts are fully operational. The MODEM Control Interrupts are also operational, but the interrupts' sources are now the lower four bits of the MODEM Control Register instead of the four MODEM Control inputs. The interrupts are still controlled by the Interrupt Enable Register.

Bits 5 through 7: These bits are permanently set to logic 0.

8.8 MODEM STATUS REGISTER

This register provides the current state of the control lines from the MODEM (or peripheral device) to the CPU. In addition to this current-state information, four bits of the MODEM Status Register provide change information. These bits are set to a logic 1 whenever a control input from the MODEM changes state. They are reset to logic 0 whenever the CPU reads the MODEM Status Register.

8.0 Registers (Continued)

Table II shows the contents of the MSR. Details on each bit follow.

Bit 0: This bit is the Delta Clear to Send (DCTS) indicator. Bit 0 indicates that the CTS input to the chip has changed state since the last time it was read by the CPU.

Bit 1: This bit is the Delta Data Set Ready (DDSR) indicator. Bit 1 indicates that the DSR input to the chip has changed state since the last time it was read by the CPU.

Bit 2: This bit is the Trailing Edge of Ring Indicator (TERI) detector. Bit 2 indicates that the RI input to the chip has changed from a low to a high state.

Bit 3: This bit is the Delta Data Carrier Detect (DDCD) indicator. Bit 3 indicates that the DCD input to the chip has changed state.

Note: Whenever bit 0, 1, 2, or 3 is set to logic 1, a MODEM Status Interrupt is generated.

Bit 4: This bit is the complement of the Clear to Send (CTS) input. If bit 4 (loop) of the MCR is set to a 1, this bit is equivalent to RTS in the MCR.

Bit 5: This bit is the complement of the Data Set Ready (DSR) input. If bit 4 of the MCR is set to a 1, this bit is equivalent to DTR in the MCR.

Bit 6: This bit is the complement of the Ring Indicator (RI) input. If bit 4 of the MCR is set to a 1, this bit is equivalent to OUT 1 in the MCR.

Bit 7: This bit is the complement of the Data Carrier Detect (DCD) input. If bit 4 of the MCR is set to a 1, this bit is equivalent to OUT 2 in the MCR.

8.9 SCRATCHPAD REGISTER

This 8-bit Read/Write Register does not control the UART in any way. It is intended as a scratchpad register to be used by the programmer to hold data temporarily.

9.0 Typical Applications

Typical shows the basic connections of an PC16450C/NS16450 to an 8088 CPU

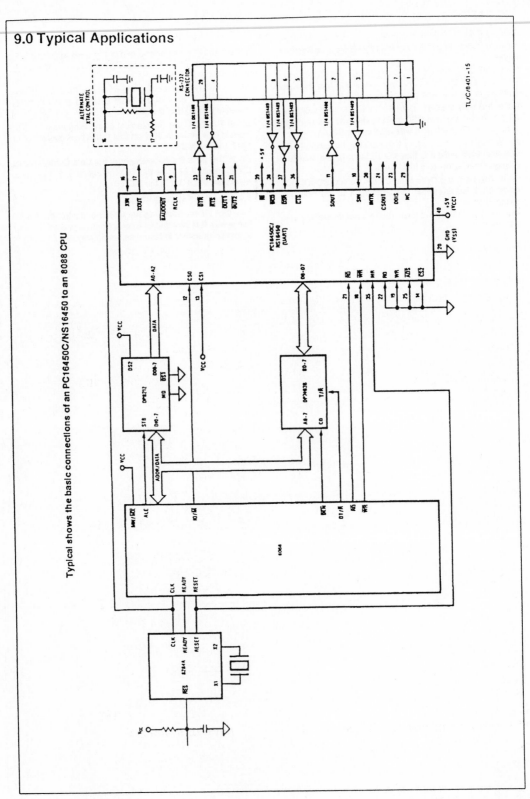

TL/C/8401–15

Index